# 邓嗣禹文集 第三卷

邓嗣禹/著

清代行政管理
中国对西方的反应

彭 靖/主编

华中师范大学出版社

新出图证（鄂）字 10 号
图书在版编目（CIP）数据

邓嗣禹文集. 第 3 卷：英文/（美）邓嗣禹著；彭靖主编. —武汉：华中师范大学出版社，2021.12
ISBN 978-7-5622-9593-8

Ⅰ. ①邓… Ⅱ. ①邓… ②彭… Ⅲ. ①邓嗣禹—文集—英文 ②汉学—研究—美国—文集—英文 Ⅳ. ①K207-53 ②K207.8-53

中国版本图书馆 CIP 数据核字（2022）第 004118 号

### 邓嗣禹文集　第三卷
Ⓒ邓嗣禹著　彭靖主编

| | | | | | |
|---|---|---|---|---|---|
| 责任编辑：董云梅　张　超 | | 责任校对：童　雯 | | 封面设计：罗明波 | |

编辑室：学术出版中心　　　　　　电话：027-67863220
出版发行：华中师范大学出版社有限责任公司　　邮编：430079
社址：湖北省武汉市洪山区珞喻路 152 号
销售电话：027-67861367（发行部）　　传真：027-67863291
网址：http://press.ccnu.edu.cn　　电子信箱：press@mail.ccnu.edu.cn
印刷：湖北恒泰印务有限公司　　督印：刘　敏
开本：710mm×1000mm　1/16　　印张：55.25　　字数：854 千字
版次：2023 年 3 月第 1 版　　印次：2023 年 3 月第 1 次印刷
定价：278.00 元

欢迎上网查询、购书

敬告读者：欢迎举报盗版，请打举报电话 027-67867353

# 文集作者与主编简介

**作者简介：**

邓嗣禹（1905—1988），当代著名历史学家、文献目录学家和汉学家，中国科举制度研究的奠基人。1935年燕京大学硕士毕业后，留校任教。1938年留学哈佛大学，师从著名汉学家费正清，1942年获博士学位。历任芝加哥大学东方研究院院长、印第安纳大学历史系主任、东亚研究中心主任等职，著有《中国考试制度史》《张喜与南京条约》等30余部历史学著作，并将《中国近百年政治史》《颜氏家训》等中国学术名著译成英文版。他的论著曾被翻译成10多种语言。2020年，俄文版《中国考试制度史》获批为"中华学术外译"资助项目，将由俄罗斯圣彼得堡大学出版社出版。

**主编简介：**

彭靖（1962— ），《邓嗣禹文集》主编，"中华学术外译"项目入选者。21岁发表译作，38岁获得教授职称。早年曾师从中国社会科学院近代史研究所所长步平，在《中国考试》《学术界》《教育与考试》等期刊上发表科举与历史学研究论文100余篇，译著有《重访中国》《张喜与南京条约》。历任北京大学、香港国际商学院EMBA总裁班特聘（客座）教授，在美国与中国出版《尘封的历史》等十余部著作。曾获得"鲁迅文学杯"全国文化精英大赛金奖、第十届"丁玲文学奖"提名奖等多种奖项。

# CONTENTS

## CH'ING ADMINISTRATION

FOREWORD ............................................................ 3
AUTHORS' PREFACE ............................................... 4
ON THE TRANSMISSION OF CH'ING DOCUMENTS ......... 8
   1. THE CH'ING POSTAL SYSTEM ........................... 9
   2. THE ACTUAL SPEED OF TRANSMISSION IN THE PERIOD 1842-1860 ............................................. 32
ON THE TYPES AND USES OF CH'ING DOCUMENTS ...... 48
   1. INTRODUCTION .............................................. 48
   2. PROCEDURE IN THE GRAND SECRETARIAT (NEI KO) ............................................................... 50
   3. PROCEDURE IN THE GRAND COUNCIL (CHÜN CHI CH'U) ............................................................. 58
   4. SELECT LIST OF PUBLISHED COLLECTIONS OF CH'ING DOCUMENTS ........................................ 65
   5. CATALOGUE OF TYPES OF DOCUMENTS ............ 69
ON THE CH'ING TRIBUTARY SYSTEM .......................... 128
   1. THE TRADITIONAL ROLE OF TRIBUTE ............... 128
   2. TRIBUTARIES OF THE LATE MING ..................... 140
   3. THE LI FAN YÜAN (COURT OF COLONIAL AFFAIRS) UNDER THE CH'ING ......................................... 149
   4. CH'ING TRIBUTARIES FROM THE SOUTH AND EAST—GENERAL REGULATIONS ......................... 154
   5. EUROPEAN COUNTRIES IN THE CH'ING TRIBUTARY SYSTEM ......................................... 169

| 6. CH'ING TRIBUTE EMBASSIES AND FOREIGN TRADE ………………………………………………………… 183
| 7. A SELECTED LIST OF CH'ING WORKS (1644-1860) ON MARITIME RELATIONS …………… 200
| 8. INDEX OF TRIBUTARIES LISTED IN SIX EDITIONS OF THE *COLLECTED STATUTES* ……………… 214
| APPENDIX 1 ……………………………………… 237
| APPENDIX 2 ……………………………………… 246

## CHINA'S RESPONSE TO THE WEST

PREFACE TO THE 1979 EDITION ……………… 269
ACKNOWLEDGMENTS …………………………… 272
REIGNS OF THE CH'ING DYNASTY …………… 274
1 THE PROBLEM AND ITS BACKGROUND ……… 276
 CHAPTER I INTRODUCTION ……………… 276
 CHAPTER II SOME ELEMENTS IN THE CHINESE INTELLECTUAL TRADITION ……… 286
2 RECOGNITION OF CHINA'S NEED TO KNOW THE WEST, 1839-1860 ……………………………………… 313
 CHAPTER III COMMISSIONER LIN'S PROGRAM FOR MEETING BRITISH AGGRESSION ……… 313
 CHAPTER IV THE POLICY OF CONCILIATION ……… 335
 CHAPTER V THE EMERGENCE OF THE THEORY OF SELF-STRENGTHENING ……… 351
3 THE DESIRE FOR WESTERN TECHNOLOGY, 1861-1870 ……………………………………… 374
 CHAPTER VI TSENG KUO-FAN'S ATTITUDE TOWARD WESTERNERS AND THEIR MACHINERY ……… 374
 CHAPTER VII LI HUNG-CHANG AND THE USE OF WESTERN ARMS ……… 385

  CHAPTER Ⅷ INSTITUTIONS FOR LINGUISTIC AND SCIENTIFIC STUDIES (THE T'UNG-WEN KUAN) ········· 394

  CHAPTER Ⅸ TSO TSUNG-T'ANG AND THE FOOCHOW SHIPYARD ············· 403

4 EFFORTS AT SELF-STRENGTHENING 1871-1896 ············ 411

  CHAPTER Ⅹ THE PROBLEM OF LEADERSHIP: PERSONALITIES AND INSTITUTIONS ············ 411

  CHAPTER Ⅺ TRAINING STUDENTS ABROAD ············ 421

  CHAPTER Ⅻ DIPLOMATIC MISSIONS ABROAD ············ 431

  CHAPTER ⅩⅢ PROBLEMS OF THE INDUSTRIALIZATION EFFORT ············ 449

  CHAPTER ⅩⅣ THE ATTEMPT AT A POSITIVE FOREIGN POLICY ············ 466

5 THE REFORM MOVEMENT THROUGH 1900 ············ 489

  CHAPTER ⅩⅤ PROMOTERS OF INSTITUTIONAL CHANGE ············ 489

  CHAPTER ⅩⅥ K'ANG YU-WEI AND SOME OF HIS ASSOCIATES ············ 512

  CHAPTER ⅩⅦ THE REFORM PROGRAM OF CHANG CHIH-TUNG ············ 541

  CHAPTER ⅩⅧ THE FAILURE OF 1898 ············ 559

  CHAPTER ⅩⅨ THE BOXER UPRISING ············ 579

6 REFORM AND REVOLUTION 1901-1912 ············ 591

  CHAPTER ⅩⅩ THE CONSERVATIVE REFORM MOVEMENT ············ 591

  CHAPTER ⅩⅪ ECONOMIC DEVELOPMENT ············ 617

  CHAPTER ⅩⅫ LIANG CH'I-CH'AO AND NATIONALISM ············ 632

  CHAPTER ⅩⅩⅢ SUN YAT-SEN'S EARLY REVOLUTIONARY PROGRAM ············ 638

7 IDEOLOGICAL FERMENT AND THE MAY FOURTH MOVEMENT
1912-1923 ·············································· 649
 CHAPTER XXIV THE SEARCH FOR NEW PRINCIPLES
 ·················································· 649
 CHAPTER XXV EARLY CONVERTS TO MARXISM ········· 663
 CHAPTER XXVI HU SHIH AND PRAGMATISM IN CHINA
 ·················································· 681
 CHAPTER XXVII SUN YAT-SEN'S REORIENTATION OF THE
 REVOLUTION ·································· 693
 CHAPTER XXVIII LIANG CH'I-CH'AO'S REVIEW OF CHINA'S
 PROGRESS, 1873-1922 ························ 708
POSTFACE A FURTHER APPROACH TO THE PROBLEM
·················································· 719

## RESEARCH GUIDE FOR *CHINA'S RESPONSE TO THE WEST*

NOTES AND SOURCES ································ 728
BIBLIOGRAPHY ······································· 795
GLOSSARY ············································ 868

# CH'ING ADMINISTRATION

# FOREWORD

This volume, the nineteenth of the *Harvard-Yenching Institute Studies*, is financed from the residue of the funds granted during World War II by the Rockefeller Foundation for the publication of Chinese and Japanese dictionaries. This series is distinct from the *Harvard-Yenching Institute Monograph Series* and consists primarily of bibliographical studies, grammars, reference works, translations, and other study and research aids.

# AUTHORS' PREFACE

When we published these three studies of Ch'ing administrative institutions, almost twenty years ago, we regarded them as pioneer steps into virgin territory which many others would soon be exploring and exploiting more thoroughly. We expected our efforts to be quickly superseded. Instead, rather little further work has been done on these subjects. Important researches have been published in ancillary areas—the socio-political structure of late-Ch'ing China, its military history, diplomatic relations, foreign trade, early industrial growth, and domestic rebellions, even its intellectual history and (in Japanese) cultural relations. Yet the day-to-day processes of the bureaucratic machine of the Ch'ing period have commanded little attention, and on their respective subjects these articles have not yet been followed by more definitive work in English. No Chinese-English dictionary of Ch'ing administrative terminology has appeared, although a useful list of terms has been produced in Japanese at Tokyo University.[①] In general, almost no one has studied more fully the flow of official business to and from the emperor; few have explored the details of tribute missions and the trade connected with them.

While this explains why these articles are now reprinted without being reworked, it also raises a critical question about Western studies of

---

[①] See UEDA Toshio 植田捷雄, OGAERI Yoshio 鱼返善雄, BANNO Masataka 坂野正高, ETō Shinkichi 卫藤沈吉, and SOMURA Yasunobu 曾村保信, *Chūgoku gaikō bunsho jiten*: *Shimmatsu-hen* 中国外交文书辞典:晚清 (*Dictionary for Chinese Diplomatic Documents*: *Late Ch'ing*), Tōkyō Gakujutsu Bunken Fukyū Kai 东京学术文献普及会, 1954, pp. 7;139;3.

On the use of late Ch'ing materials in research, and for recent bibliography, see also J. K. FAIRBANK, *Ch'ing Documents*, *An Introductory Syllabus*, 2nd revised edition, Harvard University Press, 1959, 2 vols.

modern China. Are we not trying in this field to go too directly into the big problems raised by contemporary social science—questions of social mobility, of entrepreneurship, of class and power structure and ideology, for example—without having first performed the factual, detailed foundation work which in other, more mature fields has facilitated the eventual asking of such big questions?

Is it not inefficient for Western sinologists either to plunge down into the maelstrom of piecemeal narrations of the events of nineteenth-century Chinese history or to soar up among the cloudbanks of carefully-formulated social-science analyses and conceptual frameworks without first having tied the special terminology of the Chinese documentary record to an established body of equivalent terms in English, traced out in these terms the day-to-day procedures and practices of the major institutions of administration, and so filled in with solid factual detail the now shadowy outlines of the official establishment? In other words, are we not unwisely led by our contemporary modern interests to neglect the study of traditional Chinese governmental processes and institutions?

One argument for such studies, whether of the salt administration, the Li Fan Yüan, the examination system, or the land tax, is that the voluminous records of the late Ch'ing period make possible a comparison of the official system, as formally set up, with its actual operation as seen in day-to-day documents. The latter have been, and remained, available in our libraries. We have no want of Chinese documentation, and in recent years, more and more American researchers have become capable of reading it. What we seem to have lacked is the patience, and indeed the courage, to ask small institutional, operational questions before asking big social ones. The present studies are reissued to assist primarily those who seek detailed and concrete mastery of finite institutional processes under the late Ch'ing government.

We are indebted to the Harvard-Yenching Institute for making these articles available in its *Studies* series, as well as for their original publication in the *Harvard Journal of Asiatic Studies* (*HJAS*). They are here reprinted, in the same order, from *HJAS* 4 (1939: 12-46), *HJAS* 5 (1940: 1-71) and *HJAS* 6 (1941: 135-246).

Attention is called to the forthcoming publication by the Harvard University Press, in the *Harvard East Asian Studies* series, of a volume by E-tu Zen Sun, translator and editor, *Ch'ing Administrative Terms: A Translation of "The Terminology of the Six Boards with Explanatory Notes* (*Liu-pu ch'eng-yü chu-chieh* 六部成语注解). Although not a dictionary, this handbook of the Ch'ing period deals extensively with terms used in the administrative process.

JOHN K. FAIRBANK
SSU-YÜ TÊNG
January 1960

### Note to the Third Printing

The account of the Ch'ing system of correspondence presented on page fifty-one et seq. of this volume should now be modified in the light of recent work by Professor Silas Hsiu-liang Wu, "The Memorial Systems of the Ch'ing Dynasty (1644-1911)" in the *Harvard Journal of Asiatic Studies*, Vol. 27, 1967, pp. 7-75. Mr. Wu has found that *Tsou-pen* and *Tsou-che* are two distinct types of document.

In brief, the Ch'ing inherited from the Ming a system of routine memorials (*Pen-chang*) which were of two kinds, namely *T'i-pen* and *Tsou-pen*. Each had its distinctive uses, more or less as described in our original study; but the emperor in the late seventeenth century began to develop a new system of *Tsou-che* or "palace memorials" as a means of greater speed and secrecy in communication. These documents were sent directly to the emperor by special couriers and so were seen by no one but the sender and the emperor, except as he showed them to his assistants. This new type of document came to be handled largely by the Grand

Council, which began to take shape in 1729 as a new institution to assist the Yung-chêng Emperor. As this development continued during the Ch'ien-lung period, Mr. Wu finds that "the *Tsou-pen* type of routine memorial was abolished as redundant in 1748." Eventually the ancient *T'i-pen* type of routine memorial was also abolished, in 1901.

Thus in the present volume references to *Tsou-pen* after 1748 should generally be revised to read *Tsou-che*; and statements identifying these two types of documents are in error (see below pages 51-52, 58-63, and pages 70ff. under *Che-tsou*, *Tsou-che*, and *Tsou-pen*). In general, Mr. Wu's study is now the most authoritative on this whole subject.

J. K. F.

S. Y. T.

# ON THE TRANSMISSION OF CH'ING DOCUMENTS

## J. K. FAIRBANK and S. Y. TÊNG
## HARVARD UNIVERSITY

Chinese documents relating to foreign affairs in the nineteenth century are now available in large number,[①] but many essential facts concerning them remain obscure. Compared with workers in other fields of diplomatic history, the student of Chinese foreign policy is in a peculiar position. He has a wealth of documents to study but no clear idea of how they came into being. For example, he knows the date on which a memorial was seen by the emperor, but not the date on which it was written. What organs of government drafted, transmitted, recorded, copied, and finally compiled the documents now available—all this has yet to be worked out. The object of this paper is to attack one part of the problem, namely, the manner in which documents relating to foreign affairs were transmitted by postal service between Peking and the provinces—particularly, the amount of time generally required for such transmission.

The postal arrangements here in question are those of the Ch'ing Dynasty before the days of extensive foreign intercourse,[②] and in this early modern period we are concerned only with the transmission of official documents and not with the "letter hongs" or Min Hsin Chü 民信局 (People's Letter Offices) which were developed by private Chinese firms for the use of the general public.[③] Among the many types of official documents current in this period we are concerned primarily with those sent and received by the Chün Chi Ch'u 军机处 (Council of State, or Grand Council, lit. Place of Plans for the Army) which at this time had general charge of relations with the Western barbarians[④]. Nearly all documents on foreign affairs appear to have passed through this body at the capital and to have been carried by horse in the provinces. Consequently we are less concerned with documents carried by foot in the provinces and passing chiefly through the Nei Ko 内阁 (Grand Secretariat, or Imperial Chancery, or Inner Cabinet) at the capital, and these divisions of the general system for the transmission of documents will be mentioned only secondarily.⑤

For ease in analysis, the following discussion relates, first, to certain official regulations, principally those given in the *Ta-ch'ing hui-tien* 大清会典 (Institutes of the Ch'ing Dynasty)⑥, and second, to the actual working of the postal service so far as it can be viewed in the documents themselves.

## 1. THE CH'ING POSTAL SYSTEM

The Chinese official postal service, called by Western writers the I Chan 驿站 (lit. Postal Stages), had a long history, from which most of the Ch'ing arrangements were inherited. It may be noted in passing that for more than a thousand years there had been a distinction between carriage of the post by couriers on foot and by mounted couriers, and that both of these activities had been under the control of the Board of War (Ping Pu 兵部). There are references to a postal service (I 驿) from the Spring and Autumn period; under the Han there had been a distinction between ordinary despatches and express despatches carried by horse.⑦ Under the T'ang the service was already well articulated. According to the *T'ang liu-tien* 唐六典⑧ (The Six Statutes of the T'ang), there were 1639 postal stations, including 1297 on land used by mounted couriers and 260 on waterways. These stations were in charge of postmasters (I Chang 驿长) with postmen (I Fu 驿夫) under them, and are said to have been usually about 30 *li* apart.⑨

Under the Yüan the service was called Chan Ch'ih 站赤 and was administered by the Board of War in the provinces of China; for the vast territory under Mongol control in the northwest there was another organ, the T'ung Chêng Yüan 通政院; a system of express stations (Chi Ti P'u 急递铺) was also developed. The postal system of the Ming included, under the Board of War, a Remount Department (Ch'ê Chia Ch'ing Li Ssǔ 车驾清吏司) and under it a central office in Peking (Hui T'ung Kuan 会同馆) and stations in the provinces for ordinary post carried by horse or by water (Shui Ma I 水马驿), for transporting official baggage (Ti Yün So 递运所) and for express service (Chi Ti P'u). As will appear below, the postal system of the Ming was copied almost as it stood by the Ch'ing, and before describing the special arrangements used for foreign affairs, we may begin with the main elements of the hereditary system, as provided for in the regulations of the early nineteenth century.⑩

The Ch'ing postal service was under the general charge of one of the four sub-departments of the Board of War, which may be called the Remount Department (MAYERS—"Cavalry Remount and Postal Department"). The Remount Department had charge both of the military stud and of the postal service. The regulations for the former make it plain that there was no lack of a supply of horses which could, if necessary, be used for the postal service.⑪

The backbone of the postal service was, of course, the series of stations which extended through the provinces in all directions from the capital. From the central station in Peking, the Huang Hua I 皇华驿, there were four main routes along which these stations were scattered: (1) the northeastern route, from Peking to Mukden and thence to Kirin and Heilungkiang; (2) the eastern route, to Shantung and thence to (a) Anhwei, Kiangsi, and Kwangtung, or (b) Kiangsu, Chekiang, and Fukien; (3) the central route, to Honan and thence to (a) Hupeh, Hunan, and Kwangsi, or (b) Kweichow and Yünnan; (4) the western route, to Shansi and Shensi and thence to (a) Kansu and Sinkiang, or (b) Szechwan and Tibet. There may also be added: (5) the northwestern route, to Kalgan and thence to Uliassutai, and Kobdo or Urga.⑫

Along these various routes there were several different types of stations, each with a different name. The chief distinction was between those called I 驿,⑬ which were usually... and under the control of the local civil authorities, and those called Chan 站, which were usually ... and under the control of the military authorities. The latter (probably derived from Chan Ch'ih of the Yüan) were established for purposes of military intelligence and were to be found chiefly on the two routes to the west and northwest.⑭ At these stations military officers were in charge of the reception and transmission of the post, although the economic support came from the local civil authorities. The name Chan was also used in Kirin and Heilungkiang and for stations along the Great Wall and in Mongolia. T'ang 塘 were military courier stations beyond Chia Yü Kuan on the route to An Hsi and Hami, under military administration but supported by the civil authorities. T'ai 台（or Chün T'ai 军台）were military posts established along the routes to Uliassutai, Kobdo, and Urga. Another type of station was the So 所（standing for Ti Yün So 递运所）which were originally set up for the purpose of transporting baggage and other official property in the provinces; about the end of the eighteenth century, they were annexed to the I, except in Kansu. The relative distribution of these various types of stations is indicated in the subjoined table, from which the predominance of the I, particularly in the coastal provinces, will be obvious.⑮

All the stations mentioned above were designed for the rapid transfer of documents by horse or an equivalent means.⑯ Quite aside from the stations so far mentioned, however, there existed another and subsidiary system of stations for unmounted couriers who transmitted official despatches on foot only. These stations were called P'u 铺 and were to be found in all the provinces, under control of the local authorities. Where the I were some 100 *li* apart, the P'u were usually from 10 to 30 *li* apart.⑰ For purposes of this discussion they are relatively unimportant, and we may confine our attention, for the time being, to the I, through which nearly all documents concerning foreign affairs were sent from the coastal provinces to Peking.

The use of these post stations was regulated by a system of tallies (yu-fu 邮符), which were given to riders going over the route and allowed them to use certain horses or other conveyances and supplies on their way. These tallies were of two kinds: (1) k'an-ho 勘合, which were given to official express riders (kuan ch'ih-i chê 官驰驿者); and (2) huo-p'ai 火牌, which were given to military express riders (ping-i ch'ih-i chê 兵役驰驿者). The latter were also given to candidates for the public examinations coming from Yünnan, Kweichow, and Kansu west of Chia Yü Kuan. Every year the governor-general and governors, provincial commanders-in-chief and brigade generals of the Chinese army, and Tartar generals and lieutenant-generals of the Manchu forces were given huo-p'ai and sometimes also k'an-ho by the Board of War. These tallies could be used whenever mounted couriers needed to be sent.⑱

But these tallies were used also in a much more general way by all officials moving from place to place in their official capacity, and they secured for the holder the service not only of horses but also of attendants, carts, boats, and other facilities. The extent of these facilities depended upon the rank of the official, the route, and the nature of the journey, all of which was minutely specified in the regulations. Thus officials despatched from the capital on a land journey were given tallies for saddle horses, pack horses, and others, in number corresponding to their rank; and on a water journey they were given boatmen. If they did not use horses, they were allowed three men for every horse they would have had. Certain government rations were also allowed them. In addition to government officials, these facilities were extended to tribute bearers from foreign countries. Finally, the I were used for the carriage of public goods. For this purpose again the regulations were most detailed. For example, in the transfer of the land tax silver in Chekiang, for a sum up to Tls. 160,000 a t'ai-p'ing 太平 boat should be used, for a sum between Tls. 160,000 and Tls. 200,000 a sha-fei 沙飞 boat should be used, and so on.⑲ From this it is apparent that the post stations (I) were really used for a good deal more than the transmission of official correspondence, and constituted in effect a service of transport and communication rather than a mere postal service in the Western sense. Its importance was mirrored in the large amounts of revenue set aside for its maintenance.⑳ The transmission of official documents was therefore only one of the activities carried on at the post stations; but for present purposes the other activities may be disregarded.

In transmitting a document by horse post the first necessity was an express warrant (huo-p'iao 火票). The regulations state that "to all public documents for transmission by horse there are to be attached warrants of the Board of War ordering the various post stations along the route to receive and transmit them. On documents coming from the provinces to the capital, or passing back and forth among the provinces, there are pasted way-bills (p'ai-tan 排单). It is the rule that along the route the exact time (shih-k'o 时刻) of arrival at each station shall be noted on the way-bill."㉑ This regulation appears to have applied to all documents sent by horse post, and was elaborated in a number of rules and requirements for the keeping of records and the proper sealing of the documents en route.㉒

In addition it was possible, in the case of important or secret memorials, to send them by a special messenger who would make use of a tally of the type described above (huo-p'ai 火牌).㉓ It was apparently in such cases as this that the provincial officials made use of the tallies given to them each year.

Once a document had been started on its way at express speed, it was expected to travel at the rate of 300 $li$ a day; "but if documents are urgent, then the warrant may state that they are to be transmitted by express at the limit of 400 $li$, 500 $li$, or 600 $li$."㉔ In other words, official intelligence during the period of the Taiping Rebellion and the wars with England was expected, by law, to travel at most only some 200 miles a day. The question as to the rapidity with which documents were actually sent is both interesting and important.

Light is shed on this question by developments in the eighteenth century. In 1708 the maximum speed for urgent despatches was given as 500 *li* a day.㉕ By 1742 this maximum had been raised to 600 *li*; but in 1748-1749 an exception was made for the provinces of Fukien and Kwangtung, where despatches ordered to proceed at the rate of 600 *li* were allowed to travel only 300 *li*. In 1750 it was ordered that the rate of 600 *li* a day should be resorted to only in case of urgent necessity,㉖ and we may conclude that the increase of speed, which may not have been unconnected with the campaigns in Central Asia, had been found expensive, as well as impossible in certain areas. According to the regulations for the Chia-ch'ing and Kuang-hsü periods, at the beginning and end of the nineteenth century, the normal distance per day by horse remained 300 *li*, and the express rate remained limited to 400, 500, or 600 *li*.㉗ In the mountainous areas of Chihli, Honan, Hupeh, Kwangsi, and Kwangtung, where horses could not be used, the maximum of 600 *li* per day was reduced to 400, 300, 240, or even 200 *li*, according to the circumstances.㉘ In short, in the five different editions of the Institutes of the Ch'ing Dynasty there is no mention of a rate of speed higher than 600 *li* a day. By 1842, however, this rate was being occasionally exceeded in practice, and imperial orders were given, and obeyed, for the transmission of documents at the rate of 800 *li* a day, as will be noted below.

The following table 1 is given for purposes of comparison, since it does not refer directly to documents sent by express, as were most of those concerning barbarian affairs. Under A are given the time limits for ordinary documents sent by unmounted courier (p'u-ti); under B are given the time limits for documents sent by horse, such as ordinary memorials (T'i-pên 题本). A third table, for documents sent by express at the rate of 300 *li* or more, can be constructed by inference, from the distances listed, but cannot be regarded as certain because in such calculations numerous allowances must be made for certain areas where, because of the terrain, the distance required per day was reduced by regulation to less than the normal stint. No doubt this qualification would apply with increasing force to the rates of speed higher than 300 *li* a day.㉙

Hours, where given, are calculated at the rate of 2 hours for 1 shih 时.

\* indicates water route, when distinguished from land route.

Distances, in most cases, are given in sources (1), (3), (4), (5), (8), and (9). Except where noted, distances in source (9) agree with those in (3), and distances in (8) agree with those in (4).

Time limits, in most cases, are given in sources (2), (4), (7), (8), and (9)—all of which agree, except where noted, on the number of days given under B for transmission by horse; and in sources (3), (4), (6), (8), and (9), all of which agree, except where noted, on the number of days given under A for transmission "on foot" (p'u-ti).

The variation in the distances recorded in different publications arises from different methods of calculation in each case, measuring sometimes the yamen itself, sometimes the city walls, and sometimes only the border of the province.

This table and the one following (Table 2) include data (1) for all high provincial authorities and (2) for all taotais likely to be in contact with foreigners in the period 1842-1860.

### TABLE 1㉚
### TABLE OF TIME LIMITS FOR TRANSMISSION OF DESPATCHES TO PEKING, TOGETHER WITH DISTANCES, FROM VARIOUS PROVINCIAL YAMEN

Note: This table is arranged alphabetically by cities and is based on the following sources, which are cited by number except in cases of general agreement.

(1) *Ch'ien-lung hui-tien* 66. 5b-6b.

(2) *Ch'ien-lung hui-tien tsê-li* 121. 31-34.

(3) *Tsê-li t'u-yao pien-lan* 则例图要便览,
   original compiler SHIH Chung-yin 石中隐,
   revised edition by WANG You Huai 王又槐 (1794) 10. 5-6.

(4) *Chia-ch'ing hui-tien* 39. 29-30; 54. 14-15.

(5) *Chia-ch'ing ch'ung-hsiu i-t'ung-chih* 嘉庆重修一统志 (1842).

(6) *Ping-pu ch'u-fên tsê-li* 兵部处分则例(1823)4. 32-33b.

(7) *Ping-pu chung-shu chêng-k'ao* (1825) 兵部中枢政考 35. 1-7b.

(8) *Kuang-hsü hui-tien* 51. 12b-13b，69. 13b-15.

(9) *Kuang-hsü hui-tien shih-li* 700. 1-4, 8b-11.

(10) *Kuang-tung t'ung-chih* 广东通志(1864)84-88.

(11) *Chi-fu t'ung-chih* 畿辅通志(1884) 48-55.

(12) *Shan-tung t'ung-chih* 山东通志(1915) 1A.

(13) *Chê-chiang t'ung-chih* 浙江通志(1899) 3.

(14) *Fu-chien t'ung chih* 福建通志(1868) 4.

(15) *T'ung-an hsien-chih* 同安县志(1875) 1. 3.

(16) *Shang-hai hsien-chih* 上海县志(1871) 1. 5.

| Cities (and officials) | Distances to Peking in *li* | Time limits (days) for despatches carried | |
|---|---|---|---|
| | | A, on foot | B, by horse |
| Amoy | 7380 (15) | .. | 30 |
| An-shun (Kweichow) | 7820 (5) | .. | 30 |
| Anking (Anhwei governor) | 2526 (3), 2624 (4), 2615 (1), 2700 (5), *3441 (4), *3430 (1) | 25 | 15 |
| Canton (governor-general, governor, and Tartar general) | 5570 (3), 5604 (4), 5670 (1), 7570 (5) | 56 | 32 |
| Chang-chou (Fukien) | 7525 (5) | .. | 31 |
| Ch'ang-chou (Chekiang) | 2535 (5) | .. | .. |
| Changsha (Hunan governor) | 3757 (3), 3590 (4), 3670 (1), 3585 (5), *5081 (4), *5090 (1) | 37 | 18 days and 18 hours |
| Chang-yeh (see Kan-chou) | | .. | .. |
| Chao-ch'ing (Kwangtung) | 7402 (10) | .. | .. |
| Chao-chou (Chihli) | 720 (11) | .. | .. |
| Ch'ao-chou (Kwangtung) | 9063 (10), (15) | | 38 days and 12 hours |
| Chapu | 3120 (13) | 31 (6) | 16 |

| Cities (and officials) | Distances to Peking in *li* | Time limits (days) for despatches carried ||
|---|---|---|---|
| | | A, on foot | B, by horse |
| Ch'ên-chou (Hunan) | 3650 (5) | | 20 (7) |
| Chengteh | 420 (11) | .. | .. |
| Cheng-ting (Chihli) | 610 (11) | .. | .. |
| Chengtu (Szechwan governor-general) | 4770 (3), 4750 (4), 4675 (1), 5710 (5) | 48 | 24 |
| Chi-ning (Shantung) | 1145 (3), 1200 (5) | 11 (3) | 7 (7) |
| Chia-ying-chou (Kwangtung) | 8763 (3) | .. | .. |
| Chiao-chou (Shantung) | 1600 (12) | .. | .. |
| Chungking | 6670 (5) | .. | 29 |
| Chinkiang | 2300 (3,5) | 23 (6) | 13 (7) |
| Ch'ing-chiang-p'u (Kiangnan conservancy) | 1975 (3) | 20 | 10-12 (7) |
| Ch'ing-chou (Shantung) | 1300 (12) | .. | 8 (8) |
| Ch'iung-chou (Kwangtung) | 9715 (10) | .. | 44 (8) |
| Ch'u-chou (Chekiang) | 4580 (13) | .. | 25 (7) |
| Ch'üan-chou (Fukien) | 7255 (5) | .. | 29 (7) |
| Ch'ung-ming (Kiangsu) | .. | .. | 14 (7) |
| Foochow (governor-general, governor, and Tartar general) | 4775 (3), 4848 (4), 4862 (1), 6130 (5) | 48 | 27 |
| Taiwan, Tai-wan-fu | 7332 (14) | .. | 30 (3) |
| Fu-ming (Fukien) | 7200 (5) | .. | 33 (3) |
| Hai-chou (Kiangsu) | 1700 (5) | .. | .. |
| Hangchow (Chekiang governor) | 3050 (3), 3133 (4), 3117 (1), 3300 (5), *3531 (4), *3486 (1) | 30 | 17 |
| Heilungkiang (Tartar general) | 3983 (3), 3317 (4), 4127 (1), 3300 (5) | 40 | 18 |

| Cities (and officials) | Distances to Peking in *li* | Time limits (days) for despatches carried | |
|---|---|---|---|
| | | A, on foot | B, by horse |
| Ho-chien (Chihli) | 410 (11) | .. | .. |
| Hsing-hua (Fukien) | 6403 (14) | .. | .. |
| Hsü-chou (Kiangsu) | 1165 (5) | | 8 days and 22 hours (7) |
| Hu-chou (Chekiang) | 4300 | .. | 27 (7) |
| Hwaian (director-general of Grain Transport) | 1995 (3), 1975 (5) | 20 | 12 |
| Hui-chou (Kwangtung) Hui-yüan Ch'êng, see Ili | 8485 (5, 10) | .. | 34 (7) |
| Ili | 10044 (4, by I Chan), 10820 (5), 9220 (4, by Chün T'ai), 14549 (9) | 193 (9) | 43 |
| Jehol (Military lieutenant-governor) | 420 (3), 430 (9), 450 (4) | 5 (8) | 4 (7) |
| Kaifeng (Honan governor) | 1545 (3), 1490 (1), 1495 (4), 1540 (5) | 15 | 8 days and 14 hours |
| Kalgan (Military lieutenant-governor of Chahar) | 410 (3), 390 (11) | 4 | 4 (7) |
| Kao-chou (Kwangtung) | 8647 (10, 5) | .. | 37 (8) |
| Kashing | 4020 (13) | .. | .. |
| Kan-chou (or Chang-yeh, Kansu) | 5080 (5) | .. | 28 (8) |
| Kirin | 2882 (3), 2880 (1) 2245 (4), 2300 (5) | 29 (6, 3) | 12 (7) |
| Kiukiang | 4600 (5) | .. | 16 days and 8 hours |
| Kiungchow, see Ch'iung-chou | | | |
| Kobdo | 6280 (9) | 105 (9) | .. |
| Ku-yüan | 3480 (5) | | |

| Cities (and officials) | Distances to Peking in *li* | Time limits (days) for despatches carried | |
|---|---|---|---|
| | | A, on foot | B, by horse |
| Kwei-hua (Shansi) | 1160 (5) | .. | 6 (8) |
| Kweilin (Kwangsi governor) | 5469 (3), 4654 (4), 4909 (1), 7460 (5) | 55 | 24 |
| Kweiyang (Kweichow governor) | 4900 (3), 4755 (4), 4775 (1) | 49 | 28 |
| Lai-chou (Shantung) | 1600 (12) | .. | .. |
| Lanchow (Shên-Kan governor-general) | 4115 (3), 4009 (4), 4040 (5), 4035 (1) | 41 | 17, 18 (4) |
| Lei-chou (Kwangtung) | 9505 (10) | .. | 44 (8) |
| Liu-chou (Kwangsi) | 7830 (5) 1470 (5) | .. | 26 days, 20 hours and a half |
| Lo-ting (Kwangtung) | 7860 (10) | .. | 37 (8) |
| Lung-yen (Fukien) | 7120 (14) | .. | .. |
| Mowming, see Kao-chou | | | |
| Mukden (Shengking) | 1500 (3), 1460 (4), 1470 (5) | 15 | 8 |
| Nanchang (Kiangsi governor) | 3196 (3), 3184 (4), 3225 (1), 4850 (5), *4081 (4), *4090 (1) | 32 | 18 |
| Nanking (governor-general of Liang Kiang) | 2261 (3,7), 2319 (4) | 23 | 13 days and 8 hours |
| Ninghsia (Tartar general) | 4050 (3) | 40 | 23 |
| Ningpo | 4640 (5) | .. | 20 |
| P'an-yü, see Canton | | | |
| Paotingfu (Chihli governor-general) | 360 (3,9), 330 (4) | 4 | 3 |
| Shanghai | 2899 (16) | .. | 17 (7) |
| Shengking (see under Mukden) | | | |
| Shanhaikuan | 670 (3) | 7 | 4 (7,8) |

| Cities (and officials) | Distances to Peking in *li* | Time limits (days) for despatches carried | |
|---|---|---|---|
| | | A, on foot | B, by horse |
| Shaohing (Chekiang) | 4458 | .. | .. |
| Sianfu (Shensi governor, and Tartar general) | 2550 (3), 2540 (4), 2475 (1), 2650 (5) | 25 | 13 |
| Siang Yang (Hupeh) | 2620 (5) | .. | .. |
| Soochow (Kiangsu governor) | 2670 (3), 2743 (4), 2737 (1), *3141 (4), *3091 (1), 2720 (5) | 27 .. | 14 days and 8 hours |
| Suchow, see Hsü-chou | | | |
| Suiyüan (Shansi) | 1125 (3,9), 1145 (4) | 11 | 6 |
| Süanhua | 340 (11) | .. | .. |
| Sungkiang | 2950 (5) | .. | 14 (8) |
| Swatow, see Ch'ao-chou | | | |
| Tatung (Shansi) | 720 (5) | .. | 4 (8) |
| T'ai-an (Shantung) | 1200 (12) | .. | .. |
| T'ai-chou (Chekiang) | 4778 (13) | .. | .. |
| T'ai-ts'ang-chou (Kiangsu) | 2480 (5) | .. | .. |
| Tai-wan-fu, see Taiwan | | | |
| Taiyüan (Shansi governor) | 1250 (3,9), 1200 (5), 1150 (4), 2095 (1) | 12 | 6 |
| Talifu (provincial commander-in-chief) | 11450 (5) | .. | 45 |
| Tarbagatai | 9624 (9) | 161 (9) | .. |
| Têng-chou (Shantung) | 1000 (5) | 22 in 5th, 6th, 7th, 8th mos. 16 (7) all other mos. | (7) |
| Tientsin | 250 (5) | 4 (7) | 3 (7,8,9) |

| Cities (and officials) | Distances to Peking in *li* | Time limits (days) for despatches carried | |
|---|---|---|---|
| | | A, on foot | B, by horse |
| Ti-hua, see Urumtsi | | | |
| T'ing-chou (Fukien) | 5226 | .. | 28 (7) |
| Tinghai | 4960 (13) | .. | 22 |
| To-lun-no-êrh | 700 (11) | .. | .. |
| Tsinan (Shantung governor) | 920 (3), 930 (4), 800 (5) | 9 | 5 |
| Tsitsihar, see Heilungkiang | | | |
| T'ung-chou (Kiangsu) | 3695 (5) | .. | 13 (7) |
| Tushihkow | 420 (11) | .. | .. |
| Uliassutai | 4960 (9) | 83 (9) | .. |
| Urga | 2880 (4, 9) | 48 (9) | .. |
| Urumtsi | 8890 (5) | .. | .. |
| Wenchow (Chekiang) | 4690 (13) | .. | 27 (7) |
| Wuchang (Hukwang governor-general, and Hupeh governor) | 2827 (3), 2690 (4), 2770 (1), *4321 (4), *4330 (1), 3150 (5) | 28 | 14 days and 12 hours |
| Yangchow (Kiangsu) | 2275 (5) | 16 (7) | 13 (7) |
| Yenchow | 1230 (5) | 16 in 5th, 6th, 7th, 8th mos. 12 (7) all other mos. | (7) |
| Yung-ch'un (Fukien) | 7145 (14) | | |
| Yünnanfu (Yün-kwei governor-general, and Yünnan governor) | 6025 (3), 5910 (4), 5930 (1) | 60 | 40 |

The time limits given in this table were used in the following manner. When a document left its point of origin, the day on which it should reach its destination, according to the regulations, was noted "on the face of the cover" 于封面上. When the document was received at its destination, the day of arrival was compared with the day already noted. If the transmission had fallen behind schedule, it was ascertained where the delay had occurred, and the officers in charge at that point were fined.⑨

From the table it will be seen that the distance to be covered by postmen on foot averaged with great regularity 100 *li* a day, say 33 miles, while the distance to be covered at the ordinary horse rate averaged a little less than 200 *li* a day, say 190 *li* or 63 miles. Thus, on foot, despatches would move at the rate of about two and three-quarters miles per hour during a twelve-hour day. By horse they would move at the rate of about five and one-quarter miles an hour during a twelve-hour day. Since documents sent by express were required to be forwarded both day and night, the rate of 300 *li* should not have been difficult of attainment.

Table 2 has been compiled as an aid to the use of Table 1. When provincial officials appear in the *Chou-pan I-wu shih-mo* documents or elsewhere as memorialists, their titles are given but there is usually no other indication as to the place where their memorials were written. We have, therefore, listed by provinces the normal residence of each official likely to have memorialized on foreign affairs, the distance of which from Peking can be found by reference to Table 1. This table 2 is arranged alphabetically by provinces and shows the cities from which the officials listed normally conducted their correspondence. The table is based on *Ch'ing-shih kao* (*chih-kuan chih* 职官志 3-4, *ti-li chih* 地理志 1-27), *Chia-ch'ing hui-tien* 4. 2b-4b, *Kuang-hsü hui-tien* 4. 2b-5, G. M. H. PLAYFAIR, *The Cities and Towns of China* (Shanghai 1910). The officials listed include:

governor-general (or "viceroys," tsung-tu, BRUNNERT no. 820); governors (hsün-fu, BRUNNERT no. 821) [except where noted, the financial commissioners (or "lieutenant-governors," or "treasurers," pu-chêng-shih, BRUNNERT no. 825), and the judicial commissioners (or "provincial judges," an-ch'a-shih, BRUNNERT no. 830), reside at the same places as the governors of their provinces];

taotais (or "intendants," tao-t'ai, of various kinds, BRUNNERT no. 838, usually in charge of one or more prefectures (fu), also listed; those listed below have been selected as most likely to be concerned with foreign affairs);

Tartar generals (or "Manchu generals-in-chief," chiang-chün, BRUNNERT no. 744);

provincial commanders-in-chief (or "generals-in-chief," t'i-tu, BRUNNERT no. 750).

It should be noted, of the two most widely used manuals of official titles, that BRUNNERT pictures the situation after numerous reforms at the end of the Ch'ing period, so that all its details are not accurate for the mid-nineteenth century, while MAYERS' work does not give the details of residence here desired.

**TABLE 2**

**RESIDENCES OF PROVINCIAL OFFICIALS**

| Province | Official | Residence |
| --- | --- | --- |
| Anhwei | governor-general of the Liang Kiang (Anhwei, Kiangsu, and Kiangsi) | Nanking, Kiangsu |
| | governor, with the duties also of provincial commander-in-chief | Anking |
| Chekiang | governor-general of Fukien and Chekiang (Min-Chê), with the duties also of governor of Fukien | Foochow, Fukien |
| | governor | Hangchow |
| | Hang-chia-hu taotai (for Hangchow 杭州, Kashing 嘉兴, and Hu-chou 湖州) | Hangchow |
| | Ning-shao-t'ai taotai (for Ningpo 宁波, Shaohing 绍兴, and T'ai-chou 台州) | Ningpo |
| | Wên-ch'u taotai (for Wenchow 温州 and Ch'u-chou 处州) | Wenchow |
| | Tartar general | Hangchow |
| | provincial commander-in-chief | Ningpo |
| Chihli | governor-general, with the duties also of governor; after 1870 with the duties also of superintendent of trade for the Northern Ports (Pei-yang ta-ch'ên, BRUNNERT no. 820B). | Paoting; after 1870, Tientsin, except in mid-winter. |
| | financial commissioner | Paoting |

| Province | Official | Residence |
|---|---|---|
| Chihli | judicial commissioner | Paoting |
| | superintendent of trade for the Three Ports (Tientsin, Chefoo, and Newchwang, San-k'ou t'ung-shang ta-ch'ên, BRUNNERT no. 820B). | Tientsin, 1861-1870 only |
| | Ch'ing-ho taotai (for Paoting, Ho-chien 河间, Chengting 正定, I-chou 易州, Chao-chou 赵州) | Paoting |
| | Jehol taotai (for Chengteh 承德, Ch'ao-yang 朝阳) | Chengteh |
| | K'ou-pei taotai (for Süanhwa 宣化, Kalgan, Tushihkow 独石口, Tolunor 多伦诺尔厅) | Süanhwa |
| | Tientsin Customs taotai (no territorial jurisdiction) | Tientsin, after 1870 |
| | military lieutenant-governor of Jehol (Jê-ho tu-t'ung, see BRUNNERT no. 897) | Chengteh |
| Fengtien | Shengching (Mukden) Tartar general | Mukden |
| Fukien | governor-general of Fukien and Chekiang (Min-Chê), with the duties also of governor of Fukien | Foochow |
| | governor of Taiwan | Foochow until 1875, then T'ai-pei fu |
| | Fu-ning taotai (for Foochow 福州, Fu-ning 福宁) | Foochow |
| | Hsing-ch'üan-yung taotai (for Hsing-hua 兴化, Ch'üan-chou 泉州, Yung-ch'un 永春) | Ch'üan-chou |
| | T'ing-chang-lung taotai (for T'ing-chou 汀州, Chang-chou 漳州, Lung-yen 龙岩) | Chang-chou |
| | Tartar general, with the duties also of superintendent of maritime customs | Foochow |
| | provincial commander-in-chief | Foochow |

| Province | Official | Residence |
|---|---|---|
| Heilungkiang | Tartar general | Tsitsihar |
| Honan | governor, with the duties also of provincial commander-in-chief | Kaifeng |
| Hu-Kwang | governor-general of the Liang Hu (Hunan and Hupeh) | Wuchang |
| Hunan | governor-general of Hunan and Hupeh, as above | Wuchang, Hupeh |
| Hunan | governor | Changsha |
| Hunan | provincial commander-in-chief | Ch'ên-chou 辰州 |
| Hupeh | governor-general of Hunan and Hupeh as above | Wuchang |
| Hupeh | governor | Wuchang |
| Hupeh | provincial commander-in-chief | Siangyang 襄阳 |
| Jehol | (See under Chihli, of which southern and central Jehol formed a part) | |
| Kansu | governor-general of Shensi and Kansu (Shên-Kan), with the duties also of governor of Kansu | Lanchow |
| Kansu | Tartar general | Ningsia 宁夏 |
| Kansu | provincial commander-in-chief | Chang-yeh 张掖 |
| Kiangnan | (originally one of the Liang Kiang provinces divided in the K'ang-hsi period into Anhwei and Kiangsu, q. v.; the name was preserved thereafter in several official titles: e. g. Kiangnan... | |
| Kiangnan | Tartar general | Nanking |
| Kiangnan | provincial commander-in-chief | Sungkiang |
| Kiangnan | superintendent of maritime customs | Shanghai |
| Kiangnan | These officials are the same as those listed under Kiangsu) | |
| Kiangsi | governor-general of the Liang Kiang (Kiangsi, Anhwei, and Kiangsu) | Nanking, Kiangsu |
| Kiangsi | governor, with the duties also of provincial commander-in-chief | Nanchang |

| Province | Official | Residence |
| --- | --- | --- |
| Kiangsu | governor-general of the Liang Kiang (Kiangsu, Anhwei, and Kiangsi) with the duties also of superintendent of trade for the Southern Ports (Nanyang ta-ch'ên, BRUNNERT no. 820B) after 1866 | Nanking |
| | governor | Soochow |
| | Ch'ang-chên-t'ung-hai taotai (for Changchow 常州, Chinkiang 镇江, T'ung-chou 通州, Hai-mên 海门) | Chinkiang |
| | Hsü-hai taotai (for Suchow 徐州 and Haichow 海州) | Suchow |
| | Huai-yang taotai (for Hwaian and Yangchow) | Hwaian |
| | Su-sung-t'ai taotai (for Soochow 苏州, Sungkiang 松江, and T'ai-ts'ang-chou 太仓州) with the duties of superintendent of maritime customs | Soochow |
| | Chiang-ning taotai (for Kiangning) | Nanking |
| | director-general of grain transport (ts'ao-yün tsung-tu, BRUNNERT no. 834) | Hwaian (Ch'ing-chiang-p'u) |
| | Tartar general, for Kiangnan | Nanking |
| | provincial commander-in-chief, for Kiangnan | Sungkiang |
| Kirin | Tartar general | Kirin |
| Kwangsi | governor-general of the Liang Kwang (Kwangtung and Kwangsi) | Canton, Kwangtung |
| | governor | Kweilin |
| | provincial commander-in-chief | Liu-chow 柳州 |
| Kwangtung | governor-general of the Liang Kwang (Kwangtung and Kwangsi) | Canton |
| | governor | Canton |
| | Hui-ch'ao-chia taotai (for Hui-chou 惠州, Ch'ao-chou 潮州, Chia-ying-chou 嘉应州) | Swatow |

| Province | Official | Residence |
|---|---|---|
| Kwangtung | Kao-lei-yang taotai (for Kao-chou 高州, Lei-chou 雷州, Yeungkong 阳江) | Mowming |
| | Ch'iung-yai taotai (for Kiungchow on Hainan Is. 海南岛 and Yai-chow 崖州) | Kiungchow |
| | Kuang-chao-lo taotai (for Canton, Chao-ch'ing 肇庆, Lo-ting 罗定, Fo-kang 佛冈, Ch'ih-ch'i 赤溪) | P'an-yü |
| | Tartar general | Canton |
| | provincial commander-in-chief | Hu-mên |
| | superintendent of maritime customs (Yüeh hai-kuan chien-tu, the "Hoppo" 粤海关监督, BRUNNERT no. 833A) | Canton |
| | superintendent of maritime customs (Ch'iung hai-kuan chien-tu 琼海关监督) | Kiungchow |
| Kweichow | governor-general of Yünnan and Kweichow (Yün-Kuei) | Yünnan-fu, Yünnan |
| | governor | Kweiyang |
| | provincial commander-in-chief | An-shun |
| Liang Hu | (see Hu-Kwang) | |
| Liang Kiang | governor-general of the Liang Kiang provinces (Kiangsi, Anhwei, and Kiangsu) | Nanking |
| Liang Kwang | governor-general of the Liang Kwang provinces (Kwangtung and Kwangsi) | Canton |
| Min-Chê | governor-general of Fukien and Chekiang (Min-Chê) | Foochow |
| Mongolia | military governor of Uliassutai (wu-li-ya-su-t'ai chiang-chün, BRUNNERT no. 879) | Uliassutai |
| | Imperial Agent at Urga (K'u-lun pan-shih ta-ch'ên, BRUNNERT no. 879A) | Urga |

| Province | Official | Residence |
|---|---|---|
| Shansi | governor, with the duties also of provincial commander-in-chief | Taiyüan |
| Shantung | governor, with the duties also of provincial commander-in-chief | Tsinan |
| | Têng-lai-ch'ing-chiao taotai（for Teng-chow 登州，Lai-chou 莱州，Ch'ing-chou 青州，and Kiaochow 胶州） | Ch'ing-chou |
| Shên-Kan | governor-general of Shensi and Kansu | Lanchow |
| Shensi | governor-general of Shensi and Kansu, as above | Lanchow |
| | governor | Sian |
| | provincial commander-in-chief | Ku-yüan |
| Sinkiang | governor | Lanchow |
| | provincial commander-in-chief | Urumtsi（Ourumtsi, or Ti-hua） |
| | Tartar general and military governor of Ili（I-li chiang-chün, BRUNNERT no. 866） | Hui-yüan ch'êng 惠远城 |
| Szechwan | governor-general | Chengtu |
| | provincial commander-in-chief | Chengtu |
| Tibet | Imperial Resident in Tibet（Chu-tsang ta-ch'ên, BRUNNERT no. 907） | Lhasa |
| Yün-Kwei | governor-general of Yünnan and Kweichow | Yünnan-fu |
| Yünnan | governor-general of Yünnan and Kweichow, as above | Yünnan-fu |
| | governor | Yünnan-fu |
| | provincial commander-in-chief | Tali |

For the administration of the express service, as distinct from the ordinary horse post, there were strict regulations. Ordinary despatches were not to be sent by express.⁽³²⁾

It now remains to note the organs of government which intervened between the postal facilities outlined above and the central authority in Peking. How were edicts started on their journeys over the post routes? How did memorials reach the emperor after their arrival in Peking?

Beginning with the ordinary and routine documents, it may be said in general that the foot-courier service was managed at its Peking end by the Superintendents of Courier Posts (T'i T'ang Kuan 提塘官). There were sixteen of these official residents at Peking representing provincial administrations.⁽³³⁾ Acting as agents of the provincial governments with which they were connected, they were charged with the work of transmitting documents from these governments to the boards or departments in Peking for which they were intended, and of despatching documents from the boards in Peking to the provinces; they also managed the issue of the *T'ang pao* 塘报 for the provinces.⁽³⁴⁾ Similarly, there were sixteen superintendents residing at provincial capitals (Chu Shêng T'i T'ang 驻省提塘) who had charge of the opposite end of the service, transmitting documents to Peking and distributing to provincial authorities the documents and copies of the *T'ang pao* received from Peking.⁽³⁵⁾

Of the sum total of ordinary and routine documents received at the capital by the Superintendents of Courier Posts, only a portion would consist of memorials for imperial consideration. For memorials on ordinary or routine subjects the procedure was that which had been inherited from the Ming period, and since this does not concern us directly, it will be referred to only briefly. Such documents, generally known as T'i-pên 题本,⁽³⁶⁾ were delivered to the Transmission Office (T'ung Chêng Ssǔ 通政司), located on Hsi Ch'ang-an Chieh,⁽³⁷⁾ which since the Ming period had had the duty of receiving all such memorials to the throne, examining them to see whether they were in proper form, deliberating upon punishments in case of irregularities or omissions, or if they were in proper form, delivering them to the Grand Secretariat (Nei Ko 内阁).㊳ Since the Grand Secretariat had been generally eclipsed in importance by the Grand Council (Chün Chi Ch'u) established in 1729, it dealt with few if any of the important documents on foreign affairs, and its manner of dealing with documents need not be gone into.

Documents of importance, transmitted by express and dealt with by the Grand Council, including those on barbarian affairs, were handled at Peking by several different agencies in cooperation. Under the Remount Department of the Board of War there was at the capital a sub-office called Hui T'ung Kuan 会同馆 (Imperial Despatch Office),㊴ which had charge of the central postal station in Peking (Huang Hua I).㊵ Also under the Remount Department of the Board of War was a sub-office called the Couriers Office (Chieh Pao Ch'u), which had the special function of receiving documents sent by express, and transmitting them inward and outward from the court. Memorials received from the provinces by express were sent by it to the Tsou Shih Ch'u 奏事处 (Chancery of Memorials to the emperor). This latter office (also called by MAYERS the Privy Cabinet Office) examined memorials to see if they were in proper form and, if so, handed them over to the Grand Council for presentation to the emperor.㊶

Among these agencies the Couriers Office played the chief part in the process of transmission. "Whenever the Grand Council sends [to the provinces] letters, or memorials which have received the imperial notation (p'i-chê 批折), they are sealed up and handed over [to the Couriers Office] for despatch: the Grand Council hands [them] over [to the Couriers Office] carefully sealed 'We have received an imperial Decree [ordering us] to send a communication'奉旨字寄. By this office they are sealed with nails [in the name of] the Board and covered with boards, and given to the official messengers of the Board of War to be distributed to the stations next in order, for express transmission. All provincial memorials presented by express, after they have received the vermilion notation, are sent back by the Grand Council; whether in despatch boxes or in boards, they also are sealed up by this office [the Couriers Office] and sent for transmission."⁴²

In playing this part, the Couriers Office relied upon the cooperation of the central postal station (Huang Hua I), from which it requisitioned the necessary post horses. The central station "every day sends over horses to be ready for despatch by the Couriers Office of the Remount Department. According to the number of grooms and horses for which tallies have been filled in and issued, it meets the request of the officers and underlings of the express post. According to the number of *li* for which a notation has been made in the warrants it meets the request of the clerks and officers deputed to ride the express post."⁴³

From the résumé of the official regulations given above, we can now attempt to reconstruct the procedure normally followed in the conduct of foreign affairs. As research progresses, this picture will be subject to change without notice, but its main outlines seem certain. Decisions of policy were usually made by the emperor and the Grand Council together. The resulting instructions were put in the form of an Edict from the emperor. This Edict formed the content of a despatch sent by the Grand Council to the provincial officials concerned. This despatch was sent sealed from the Grand Council to the Couriers Office to be put between boards or otherwise prepared for transmission, and further sealed. At about this point an express tally (huo-p'ai) was issued, to be carried by the mounted courier who took the despatch, and an express warrant (huo-p'iao) was also issued, to be attached to the despatch specifying its route and rate of speed.⁴⁴ The central postal station supplied the horses and other facilities named in these two documents; presumably the men sent as couriers came from the Couriers Office. It seems most unlikely that one courier could take an express despatch its entire distance; on this subject we lack information. Transmission of documents in the opposite direction, from the provinces to Peking, must have followed a procedure roughly similar to this, except that memorials went from the Couriers

Office to the Chancery of Memorials (Tsou Shih Ch'u) for examination, before reaching the Grand Council and the emperor.

## 2. THE ACTUAL SPEED OF TRANSMISSION IN THE PERIOD 1842-1860

The data presented above have been drawn from the official regulations, and it remains to be seen whether actual practice corresponded to these rules. To what extent were documents related to foreign affairs transmitted more rapidly than the regulations required? How fast could they be sent in time of crisis?

To answer these questions, at least two bodies of material can be drawn upon. The first is the collection of documents published by the Palace Museum authorities in Peiping in 1930, cited above, and known as *Ch'ou-pan i-wu shih-mo* 筹办夷务始末. Unfortunately, these published documents on barbarian affairs, having been compiled in the latter half of the 19th century for imperial use, omit the date of writing of each memorial. The entire series is dated and arranged according to the day on which the documents either were seen by the emperor (in the case of memorials) or emanated from him (in the case of Edicts). Consequently it is only possible to infer the date on which a given memorial was written from internal evidence, if such there be. From such evidence it is possible to calculate, in some cases, the time required for the transmission of a memorial to the capital, or of an Edict to the provinces. Evidence so gleaned is presented in Table 4.

Another body of material exists in the archives, where, fortunately, the originals of the memorials received from the provinces bear upon them notations of the dates on which they were despatched and received. After the publication of the *Ch'ou-pan I-wu shih-mo* documents, Prof. T. F. TSIANG 蒋廷黻 of the Tsing Hua University, Peiping, had copies taken of unpublished documents on barbarian affairs supplementary to the

*Ch'ou-pan I-wu shih-mo* selection. The following table 3 has been constructed on the basis of these documents. It should be noted that relatively few of these unpublished documents were considered of importance requiring the highest degree of express transmission, so that, as a class, the published documents appear to have been transmitted more rapidly.

Table 3 shows the time consumed in transmission of memorials to the Grand Council (Chün Chi Ch'u) 1842-1861 inclusive. It is abstracted from data given in *Documents Supplementary to the I-wu shih-mo*, based on the *Chün Chi Ch'u Archives* (Library of the Tsing Hua University), used by kind permission of Prof. T. F. TSIANG, sometime head of the Department of History. These unpublished copies from the archives in most cases contain two dates, one written in the summary heading of the memorial, and also in the conclusion of it, indicating the day on which the memorial was presented to the emperor, and a second date written in a separate column after the conclusion of the memorial, indicating the day on which it was despatched by the sender. In the case of published memorials, only the former of these dates is reproduced; these supplementary documents therefore provide data otherwise inaccessible outside the archives. Provinces for which this collection contains less than five examples are omitted. It will be obvious that the total number of examples analyzed in this table is too small to permit exact statistical analysis. Figures under "Average time taken" and "Time most frequently taken" are therefore presented only to convey a rough impression; with that qualification, they are not without value. Under the latter category, figures in parentheses indicate the number of times that the preceding figure (for number of days consumed) appears in our list compiled from the documents. All other figures, except those in the last column, represent days. The distinction between "foreign trade" and "foreign affairs" represents a marked difference observed in the time taken for the transmission of documents relating to trade and to diplomacy respectively; customs reports consistently took more time to reach the capital and receive consideration. Place names represent all the documents sent by officials who normally were stationed at those places; the documents themselves do not indicate the place from which they were despatched, and since some officials were driven from their official residences during the period of the Taiping Rebellion, it is obvious that the table contains an irremediable degree of error as a result of that fact. Such officials, however, were seldom driven far from their normal residences in the provinces here concerned; and our data in general do not indicate any appreciable lengthening of the time taken for transmission of documents during the years of the Rebellion.

TABLE 3

| Provinces Cities | Subject | Total no. of examples | Fastest time recorded | Slowest time recorded | Average time taken | Time most frequently taken |
|---|---|---|---|---|---|---|
| Kwangtung | | | | | | |
| Canton | for. aff. | 30 | 18 | 41 | 20.5 | 20 (9) |
| | for. tr. | 40 | 19 | 81 | 43.3 | 37 (5) |
| Fukien | | | | | | |
| Foochow | for. aff. | 19 | 15 | 47 | 27.5 | 15 (3) 30 (2) |
| | for. tr. | 40 | 29 | 128 | 58.1 | 30,33,34, 43(2) |
| Chekiang | | | | | | |
| Hangchow | for. aff. | 15 | 6 | 22 | 9.5 | 7 (5) |
| | for. tr. | 17 | 17 | 81 | 29.8 | 22 (3) |
| Kiangsu | | | | | | |
| Nanking | for. aff. | 20 | 10 | 25 | 12.4 | 10 (4) |
| | for. tr. | 7 | 13 | 38 | 23.2 | ... |
| Shanghai | for. aff. | 5 | 7 | 14 | 10 | 9 (2) |
| | for. tr. | 3 | 18 | 38 | 25 | ... |
| Soochow | for. tr. only | 17 | 13 | 25 | 17.7 | 15,19(3) |

| Provinces Cities | Subject | Total no. of examples | Fastest time recorded | Slowest time recorded | Average time taken | Time most frequently taken |
|---|---|---|---|---|---|---|
| Chihli | | | | | | |
| Tientsin | for. aff. | 13 | 1 | 3 | 1.3 | 1(10) |
| | for. tr. | 32 | 2 | 10 | 3.2 | 3(23) |
| Shanhaikuan | for. aff. | 4 | 4 | 8 | 5.5 | 4(2) |
| | for. tr. | 2 | 10 | 29 | .. | .. |
| Heilungkiang | | | | | | |
| Aigun | for. aff. only | 10 | 6 | 26 | 9.3 | 7(6) |
| Sinkiang | | | | | | |
| Ili | for. aff. | 4 | 32 | 37 | 34.7 | .. |
| | for. tr. | 2 | 40 | 47 | .. | .. |
| Grand total | | 280 | | | | |

Table 4 shows the time consumed in correspondence between Peking and provincial officials 1842-1860 inclusive. It is based upon the memorials and Edicts published in *Ch'ou-pan i-wu shih-mo* and covers all documents in that collection between the dates indicated. Three types of data have been abstracted by comparing the dates on which memorials were presented to the emperor and Edicts were issued by him, as published at the head of those documents, with other dates found in the body of some of the documents: (1) number of days elapsed between the issue of an Edict to the Grand Council and the date of its receipt by the addressee in the provinces, i. e., time from Peking to the province; (2) number of days elapsed between the receipt of an Edict in the provinces and the presentation to the emperor of a memorial in reply to that Edict, i. e., time for an answer from the province to Peking; (3) number of days elapsed between the issue of an Edict at Peking and the presentation to the emperor, again at Peking, of an answering memorial from the provinces, i. e., time for a round trip, Peking to Peking. As in the preceding table, the number of examples is too few to allow exact statistical analysis. It is obvious, also, that under 2 and 3 allowance must be made, to an indeterminate degree, for time consumed in the preparation of an answer to the imperial Edict; the figures given undoubtedly are greater than the number of days consumed in transmission of the memorial in reply—we do not know how much greater. Perhaps there is compensation in the fact that these figures do indicate the speed with which official business could sometimes be transacted. To students of the documents it seems unnecessary to explain the types of internal evidence, found in the body of some documents, which have here been used; to others it may be said in brief that one of the niceties of documentary style lies in the punctilious reference to the date of issue or receipt by the emperor of all documents discussed. This alone makes possible the roundabout analysis summarized below. Names of provinces represent the high officials of those provinces, in nearly every case the governor-general and/or governor.

TABLE 4

| Province | Type of data | Total no. of examples | Fastest time recorded | Slowest time recorded | Average time taken | Time most often recorded |
| --- | --- | --- | --- | --- | --- | --- |
| Kwangtung | 1) | 7 | 15 | 49 | 24 | 15 (3) |
|  | 2) | 9 | 26 | 77 | 45.2 | 37,50 (2) |
|  | 3) | 21 | 29 | 188 | 80.1 | — |
| Fukien | 1) | 4 | 15 | 20 | 16.5 | 15 (2) |
|  | 2) | 9 | 14 | 55 | 37 | 49 (2) |
|  | 3) | 9 | 29 | 159 | 62.7 | 29,36 (2) |
| Chekiang | 1) | 20 | 6 | 23 | 8.3 | 7 (11) |
|  | 2) | 24 | 7 | 40 | 18 | 11 (3) |
|  | 3) | 24 | 13 | 51 | 25.7 | 17 (3) |
| Kiangsu | 1) | 21 | 3 | 58 | 13,6 | 5,6,7 (3) |
|  | 2) | 28 | 6 | 42 | 20.4 | 7 (4) |
|  | 3) | 55 | 10 | 97 | 35.4 | 11 (4) |

| Province | Type of data | Total no. of examples | Fastest time recorded | Slowest time recorded | Average time taken | Time most often recorded |
|---|---|---|---|---|---|---|
| Anhwei | 1) | 3 | 6 | 11 | 8 | — |
|  | 2) | 5 | 7 | 26 | 12.4 | — |
|  | 3) | 6 | 12 | 26 | 16.6 | — |
| Chihli | 1) | 32 | 1 | 15 | 2.6 | 2 (16), 1 (7) |
|  | 2) | 39 | 2 | 20 | 6.7 | 3 (8) |
|  | 3) | 42 | 3 | 95 | 10.5 | 3 (9), 4 (7) |
| Shantung | 1) | 2 | 5 | 4 | 4.5 | — |
|  | 2) | 5 | 6 | 14 | 8.4 | 7 (2) |
|  | 3) | 8 | 8 | 158 | 14.7 | 11 (3) |
| Fengtien | 1) | 11 | 4 | 10 | 6.6 | 5 (4) |
|  | 2) | 15 | 10 | 29 | 14.6 | 15 (3) |
|  | 3) | 12 | 8 | 65 | 20.5 | 8, 15, 17 (2) |
| Kirin | 3) | only 5 | 11 | 42 | 26.4 | — |
| Chahar | 1) | 5 | 2 | 3 | 2.4 | 2 (3) |
|  | 2) | 5 | 3 | 12 | 7.2 | — |
|  | 3) | 5 | 4 | 14 | 8.6 | 8 (2) |
| Grand total |  | 431 | | | | |

From these tables we may deduce that documents could regularly be transmitted between Canton and Peking in 15 days, and between Nanking and Peking in 5 days. The record time of 3 days between Nanking and Peking was made in 1842 and is an isolated example. It may be assumed that communication between other points and Peking could be established, when necessary, in periods of time proportionate to the different distances involved—except that transmission was slower over the difficult terrain of Kwangtung and Fukien and other regions noted in the regulations. Thus if we calculate the rates of speed achieved, without allowance for time required in handling at either end, we find the highest rate recorded is about 375 *li* a day from Canton, and from Nanking about 730 *li* a day (for the record time of 3 days) or about 440 *li* a day (for 5 days).㊺

References in the documents show that express rates above 300 *li* were used infrequently, their use being indicated by the insertion at the end of the document of such phrases as "memorialized by express post"由驿驰奏, which apparently required merely the 300 *li* rate, "memorialized at the express rate of 400 *li*," or again "memorialized at the express rate of 500 *li*," or "memorialized secretly at the rate of 600 *li*" 由六百里密奏. Finally, orders were also given for the use of a rate of 800 *li* a day, although such a rate is nowhere mentioned in the official regulations. Examples are infrequent, but are scattered widely enough to indicate that the 800 *li* rate was an established mode of procedure.㊻ In nearly every instance the express rates, including 800 *li*, are referred to in connection with a memorial rather than an Edict; this reflects the fact that express rates were not to be used by the provincial authorities without authorization, and does not necessarily indicate that they were less used by the Grand Council in conveying Edicts to the provinces.

We have found no reference to an express rate of 700 *li* per day, nor any indication when the 800 *li* rate may first have been used. Correlation between the various express rates and the number of days required for transmission by each has not been possible in any regular manner because of the paucity of data.㊼

By way of generalization it can only be remarked that the performance of the postal service in the period 1842-1860 measures up, to a surprising degree, to the standards set in the regulations in force during the whole of the nineteenth century. Documents were transmitted faster than we might have supposed, in many cases, and faster than foreign observers at the time always realized. Since the data are offered primarily to assist students working upon specific problems presented in the documents, further comment seems unnecessary.

**NOTES:**

①The chief published collection is *ch'ou-pan i-wu shih-mo* 筹办夷务始末, Peiping 1930; photolithograph of the original compilations made by imperial command and presented, 80 *chüan* for the period 1836-1850, in 1856; 80 *chüan* for the period 1851-1861, in 1867; and 100 *chüan* for the period 1862-1874, in 1880.

②The modern Chinese postal service was not developed until the creation after 1858 of modern organs of administration, particularly the Imperial Maritime Customs Service and the Tsungli Yamen, followed by the establishment in 1876 of the Wên Pao Chü 文报局 (Despatch Office) for the transmission of Chinese diplomatic documents abroad, the institution of the Shu Hsin Kuan 书信馆 (Letter Office) by the Customs after 1878, and the final establishment of the national postal service under Sir Robert Hart in 1896. The latter was separated from the Customs in 1911, and China joined the International Postal Union in 1914. Cf. H. B. MORSE, *The International Relations of the Chinese Empire*, vol. 3, London, 1918.

③This popular service is said to have been inaugurated in the fifteenth century and to have spread chiefly from Ningpo among the coastal provinces, eventually extending even into the northwest. It included the sending of ordinary and of registered letters, transmission of parcels and of money orders, and even the transportation of baggage. In the nineteenth century before their supersession by the modern postal service, firms of this type commanded a wide network of several thousand offices in China with branches among the Chinese communities overseas. Cf. CHANG Liang-jên, Chung-kuo li-tai yu-chih kai-yao 张梁任, 中国历代邮制概要 (A General Survey of the Postal System of Successive Dynasties), *Tung-fang tsa-chih* (*The Eastern Miscellany*) 32 no. 1, research section, 10b-12b.

④barbarian 一词含有贬义，在本书中多次出现，但因英语中对汉语"蛮夷"等词未有对应词，同时也为了尊重作者，故保留原单词。

⑤ Translations of official titles follow H. S. BRUNNERT and V. V. HAGELSTROM, *Present Day Political Organization of China*, Shanghai 1912, trans. by A. BELTCHENKO and E. E. MORAN, cited below as BRUNNERT. W. F. MAYERS, *The Chinese Government*, Shanghai 1897, revised by G. M. H. PLAYFAIR, cited below as MAYERS, although less comprehensive is often more accurate for this early period. Place names follow the Chinese Postal Atlas when feasible, or G. M. H. PLAYFAIR, *The Cities and Towns of China*, Shanghai 1910 (Wade System).

⑥The various editions of the *Ta-ch'ing hui-tien* are referred to below by the reigns in which they appeared, as: *K'ang-hsi hui-tien* (imperial preface dated 1690), *Yung-chêng hui-tien* (imperial preface dated 1732), *Ch'ien-lung hui-tien* and *Ch'ien-lung hui-tien tsê-li* (both compiled under imperial auspices in 1748), *Chia-ch'ing hui-tien* and *Chia-ch'ing hui-tien shih-li* (both completed in 1818), *Kuang-hsü hui-tien* and *Kuang-hsü hui-tien shih-li* (both published in 1899).

⑦PAI Shou-i, *Chung kuo chiao-t'ung shih* 白寿彝, 中国交通史 (History of Chinese Communications), Shanghai 1937, gives a brief summary on pp. 145-148, 179-190.

⑧Kuang-ya shu-chü edition 1895, 5. 12.

⑨Cf. CH'ÊN Yüan-yüan, *T'ang-tai i-chih k'ao* 陈沅远, 唐代驿制考 (A Study of the Postal System in the Tang Dynasty), *SHNP* 1, no. 5 (Aug. 1933) 61-92; a detailed analysis with maps and bibliography.

⑩Unless otherwise noted, the account in this paper is drawn from *Chia-ch'ing hui-tien* 39, especially 17-34.

⑪For the military stud the bannermen at Peking were required to feed in stables a total of 2400 official horses (Kuan Ma 官马). In addition there were to be 2000 kept horses (Shuan Ma 拴马) maintained among the troops and various sections of government, 3188 horses maintained by bannermen in Chihli, and other similar arrangements of supply. At provincial cities and points of importance fixed numbers of horses were also to be kept, often by the thousand; at Nanking, for example, there were to be 359 maintained by the civil authorities and 5726 by the military, while nearby at Ching K'ou 京口 were to be another 143 and 2274 respectively.

⑫Cf. *Yung-chêng hui-tien* 142.7; PAI Shou-i, *op. cit.* (see note 7) 188.

⑬The stations (I 驿) of each province are controlled by the sub-prefecture (t'ing 厅), department (chou 州), and district (hsien 县) [officials]. Occasionally there are specially established postal inspectors (I Ch'êng 驿丞) in charge of postal matters. The expenses and provisions, postmen, and horses [for these stations] come within the administration of the seal-holding officials [yin-kuan 印官]. All are subject to the direct investigation of the intendants and prefects, and also to the general superintendence of the financial commissioner of the province who is concurrently in charge of mounted courier affairs (*Chia-ch'ing hui-tien* 39. 17a). Although the station at Mukden was called I 驿, it was really a military station under the control of the Mukden Board of War 盛京兵部.

⑭ Of these two routes, "one passes through Kalgan and along the Altai Military Post Road to transmit despatches to the North Road 北路. One skirts the Outer Wall and crosses over Shansi, Shensi, and Kansu, emerges through Chia Yü Kuan and connects with the military courier stations to transmit despatches to the West Road 西路." *Ibid.*

⑮ Totals of post stations in the provinces, omitting stations in Mongolia and the northwest, from *Chia-ch'ing hui-tien* 39.18:

| Province | I | I and Chan | Chan |
|---|---|---|---|
| Chihli | ... | 185 | ... |
| Shengching | 29 | ... | ... |
| Kirin | ... | ... | 38 |
| Heilungkiang | ... | ... | 36 |
| Shantung | 139 | ... | ... |
| Shansi | ... | 125 | ... |
| Honan | 120 | ... | ... |
| Kiangsu | 40 | ... | ... |
| Anhwei | 81 | ... | ... |
| Kiangsi | 47 | ... | ... |
| Fukien | 68 | ... | ... |
| Chekiang | 59 | ... | ... |
| Hupeh | 71 | ... | ... |
| Hunan | 62 | ... | ... |
| Shensi | ... | 129 | ... |
| Kansu | total of I, Chan, T'ang, and So 331 | | |
| Szechwan | 65 | ... | ... |
| Kwangtung | 10 | ... | ... |
| Kwangsi | 19 | ... | ... |
| Yünnan | 81 | ... | ... |
| Kweichow | 23 | ... | ... |
| Totals | 914 | 439    331 | 74 |
| Grand total of above | | | 1758 |
| Grand total in *Chia-ch'ing hui-tien*, including 273 stations in Mongolia and the northwest | | | 2031 |

(The So appear to have been abolished, except in Kansu, sometime between the compilation of the *Ch'ien-lung hui-tien* and the *Chia-ch'ing hui-tien*, i. e. before 1818.) It should be noted that among the various editions of the *hui-tien*, the total number of stations listed was greatest in the Chia-ch'ing edition.

| Period | Total stations listed |
| --- | --- |
| K'ang-hsi (1662-1722) | 842 |
| Yung-cheng (1723-1735) | 899 |
| Ch'ien-lung (1736-1795) | 792 |
| Chia-ch'ing (1796-1820) | 2031 |
| Kuang-hsü (1875-1908) | 1777 |

Cf. *K'ang-hsi hui-tien* 100. 2b, 101. 26b; *Yung-chêng hui-tien* 141. 4b, 142. 7; *Ch'ien-lung hui-tien tsê-li* 120. 1-9b; *Chia-ch'ing hui-tien* 39. 18; *Kuang-hsü hui-tien* 51. 2.

⑯It is stated that horses, or donkeys, were used in all the provinces except Fukien, Kwangtung, and Kwangsi; oxen and camels were used in Manchuria and Mongolia, respectively; and carts and boats were used in appropriate places, the latter particularly in the south. *Chia-ch'ing hui-tien* 39. 18b-21b; *Kuang-hsü hui-tien* 51. 2b-4.

⑰"Within every province the sub-prefectures, departments, and districts all establish station masters (P'u-ssǔ 铺司). Those from the capital to the various provinces are also called Ching T'ang 京塘. Each uses postmen and post-soldiers on foot to transmit public documents. Their rations are accounted for from the land tax reported to the Board of Revenue." *Chia-ch'ing hui-tien* 39. 18a; *Kuang-hsü hui-tien* 51. 1-2. Cf. list of the P'u in *Chia-ch'ing hui-tien shih-li* 523-557.

⑱The number of post tallies, of both types, distributed for annual use was as follows:

| Officials | huo-p'ai | k'an-ho |
| --- | --- | --- |
| governor-general of Liang Kiang, Hu-Kwang, Yün-Kwei, Shên-Kan, Liang Kwang, Min-Chê, Szechwan, and director-general of grain transport, each | 20 | ... |
| governor-general of Chihli, directors-general of the Yellow River and Grand Canal Conservancy (one in Kiangnan, one in Shantung), governors of Kiangsu, Anhwei, Chekiang, Hupeh, Hunan, each | 18 | ... |
| governors of Shantung, Shansi, Honan, Kiangsi, Fukien, Kwangtung, Kwangsi, Yünnan, Kweichow | 16 | ... |
| provincial commander-in-chief of Kansu | 4 | 10 |

| Officials | huo-p'ai | k'an-ho |
|---|---|---|
| All other provincial commanders-in-chief, each | 4 | ... |
| All brigade generals, all salt comptrollers, each | 2 | ... |
| Mukden Prefect, all literary chancellors, each | 4 | ... |
| Mukden Board of War | 20 | 20 |
| Tartar generals of Kirin and Heilungkiang | 10 | 10 |
| All other Tartar generals, each | 4 | 4 |

Provincial financial commissioners in charge of posts, number not fixed.

The officials last named were to estimate their annual needs and request tallies from the Board of War. Cf. *Chia-ch'ing hui-tien* 39. 22b. They were not given a fixed number of tallies because they were themselves in general charge of the provincial postal service. All tallies actually used were to be reported to the Board of War at the end of each year.

⑲*Chia-ch'ing hui-tien* 39. 23a-27a. These extensive regulations provide also for annual reports, punishment for misuse of postal facilities, and the general upkeep and use of the service.

⑳With certain exceptions, the stations were maintained from the land tax. Their total cost, although said to have been reduced, was estimated at Tls. 3,000,000 in the middle of the nineteenth century. CHANG Shou-yang, *Huang-ch'ao chang-ku hui-pien* 张寿镛, 皇朝掌故汇编 (A Compilation on Governmental Affairs of the Reigning Dynasty), 1902, *nei-pien* 51. 7b. With this may be compared the amounts authorized for the upkeep of the service in *Chia-ch'ing hui-tien* 39. 21, which totalled in the neighborhood of Tls. 2,000,000 in silver alone, not counting allowances of rice, beans, and fodder (totals given *op. cit.* 12. 6a-7a and *Chia-ch'ing hui-tien shih-li* 558. 18b differ, but do not fall below this round figure). At this period (about 1818) the estimated annual yield of the land tax totalled Tls. 32,845,474. Cf. *Chia-ch'ing hui-tien* 11. 16b. The regulations show an obvious desire to limit expenditure, specifying the rates at which the populace might be paid when their services were enlisted, requiring that only a certain proportion of the post horses, usually thirty or forty per cent, could "fall down and die" 倒毙 in one year, and fixing the prices payable for new horses. These prices varied between Tls. 6 in Heilungkiang and Tls. 18 in Kweichow. *Chia-ch'ing hui-tien* 39. 19b.

㉑*Chia-ch'ing hui-tien* 39. 27a.

㉒As to all important public documents from the provinces—on the one hand they are to he transmitted by horse at express speed 飞递, and on the other hand, there is to be prepared a report to the provincial government for their records. Each yamen which receives documents for express transmission and each departmental and district postal station which forwards them along the route is to inform the said yamen in charge of the post stations, for its examination and information, as to the year, day, and month of receiving and transmitting [the documents] and as to the yamen concerned in the matter." Trimonthly reports to the provincial authorities and annual reports to the Board of War were then to be made. Documents were to be sent sealed in despatch boxes 报匣, or sealed in boards 夹版, or sealed in cloth or paper. *Ibid.* 27b-28a.

㉓"As to all memorials 题奏 on important matters, such as impeachments of officials... sent forward by a special messenger, it is permitted to use one huo-p'ai filled in for two horses. If there are documents being sent on the same day by officials stationed at the same place, they may be put together under one tally but it may only be filled in for two horses." *Ibid.* The categories of documents to be regularly transmitted by horse are given by another source as follows: a. documents despatched by the Grand Council, b. important documents sent from the boards and other offices at the capital to the provinces, c. important documents in the opposite direction, d. memorials and tablets of congratulation to the emperor from civil and military officials in the provinces, sent on the occasion of imperial birthdays, big festivals, and the like, e. memorials of an urgent nature from the director-general of the Yellow River Conservancy. *Ping-pu chung-shu chêng-k'ao* 兵部中枢政考 (A Study of the Central Administration of the Board of War), compiled under imperial auspices, preface dated 1825, 33. 25-27.

㉔*Ibid.* 27a.

㉕*Ch'ien-lung hui-tien tsê-li* 121. 30.

㉖*Ibid.* 37-38.

㉗*Chia-ch'ing hui-tien* 39. 27a; *Kuang-hsü hui-tien* 51. 10b, 12.

㉘*Chia-ch'ing hui-tien* 39. 28b-39b; *Kuang-hsü hui-tien* 51. 12; *Kuang-hsü hui-tien shih-li* 700. 11-13b.

㉙Cf. list of exceptions in *Chia-ch'ing hui-tien* 39. 28b and *Kuang-hsü hui-tien* 51. 12. The more important may be summarized as follows, all distances being substitutions for the rate of 600 *li*: in the region of Luan P'ing, Chengteh, and Süanhwa in Chihli, 300 *li*; in the region of Tê Hua on the border of Kiangsi, Fukien, and Chekiang, 400 *li*; from Tung Hu to Siangyang in Hupeh, 400 *li*; in the mountainous area of Kwangsi, 300 *li*; in the mountainous area of Kweichow, 240 *li*; from Canton along the West River or to Hunan and Kiangsi, 200 *li*; from Canton to Fukien, 240 *li*; in Szechwan generally, 400 *li*; in Fukien generally, 300 *li*; from Hengchow in Hunan to the Kwangtung border, 240 *li*. It may be noted that there are no exceptions on the route between Kiangsu and the capital.

㉚ For explanatory remarks see the preceding paragraphs in the text.

㉛ *Ping-pu ch'u-fên tsê-li* 4.33, which also states that the penalty for each case of delay was one year's salary.

㉜ Violations of this rule were punishable by degradation of three ranks in the Ch'ien-lung period or two ranks in the later Chia-ch'ing period. Cf. *Ch'ien-lung hui-tien tsê-li* 121.35b; *Ping-pu ch'u-fên tsê-li* 24.11. "Ordinary despatches of the governor-general and governors of the various provinces are all to be sent by the soldiers of the foot-courier stations; it is not permitted to use the horse post without authority. For all documents issued by the Grand Council (Chün Chi Ch'u), which are all to be forwarded by horse at express speed, the limit fixed per day is 300 *li*. If there is a matter of extra emergency, then the formula may be added 'daily to go 400 *li*, 500 *li*, or 600 *li*.' As to memorials of provincial governor-general and governors 奏折 which ought to be transmitted by special messenger, they ought not unauthorizedly to use the horse post." The regulations enjoined care in keeping the use of the express to a minimum, e. g. an Edict sent out at the 600 *li* rate need not necessarily be replied to at that same rate. *Chia-ch'ing hui-tien* 39.31a.

㉝ Namely, Chihli, Shantung, Shansi, Honan, Kiangnan, Kiangsi, Fukien, Chekiang, Hupeh, Hunan, Shensi and Kansu, Szechwan, Kwangtung, Kwangsi, Yünnan and Kweichow, Director-general of Grain Transport and Director-general of Yellow River Conservancy (one for the last two). These men were metropolitan military graduates (wu chin-shih) or officers of similar grade, nominated by the high provincial authorities of the areas which they represented, and under the general control of the Board of War. *Chia-ch'ing hui-tien* 39.33b.

㉞ In greater detail, their duties included the following: a. transmission of official documents from the Heads of Departments (Pu-yüan i. e. Presidents of the Six Boards and of the Superior Courts) to the provincial governments, and from the provincial governments to the Heads of Departments; b. the sending of imperial Decrees and of seals 敕印 to the provincial authorities with whom each superintendent was particularly connected; c. the publication of all documents of which copies were to be distributed—this included imperial Edicts and orders, and memorials on ordinary subjects. The superintendents were by regulation to go in person to the Liu K'o or Imperial Supervisorate (Office of Scrutiny, MAYERS no. 188), and have copies of the documents made, printed, and distributed. This publication was known as the *T'ang pao* (Courier News) and was the fundamental form of the famous *Peking Gazette* (*Ching pao* 京报). Manuscript copies were sent to the high provincial authorities. Printed copies were also made, and reprints were made in the provinces. *Chia-ch'ing hui-tien* 39. 33-34; cf. also S. COULING, *Encyc. Sinica* 429.

㉟BRUNNERT no. 435B; Ko Kung-chên, *Chung-kuo pao-hsüeh shih* 戈公振, 中国报学史 (A History of Chinese Journalism), Shanghai 1927, 41.

㊱ The subject of the various forms of documents used in the imperial correspondence is an intricate one, with which we propose to deal in a later article.

㊲ *Shun-t'ien fu-chih* 顺天府志 (1884), 7.8.

㊳ *Li-tai chih-kuan piao* 历代职官表 (1783), *Ssŭ-pu pei-yao* ed., 21.3a.

㊴To be distinguished of course from the *Hui T'ung Ssŭ I Kuan* 会同四译馆 under the control of the Board of Rites and in charge of barbarian tribute missions.

㊵Here were maintained 500 post horses, 250 grooms, 150 carts, 150 cart horses, and 150 drivers. The annual upkeep devolved upon the Board of Revenue. *Chia-ch'ing hui-tien* 39. 32-33; *K'ang-hsi hui-tien* 100. 1; *Yung-chêng hui-tien* 141. 1.

㊶ *Chia-ch'ing hui-tien* 39. 32-33. It also took charge of communications between the emperor and the Grand Council when the latter was not in personal attendance, according to MAYERS.

㊷ *Chia-ch'ing hui-tien* 39. 32.

㊸ *Ibid*. This text is over-concise. The relationship of these various agencies can be diagrammed as follows:

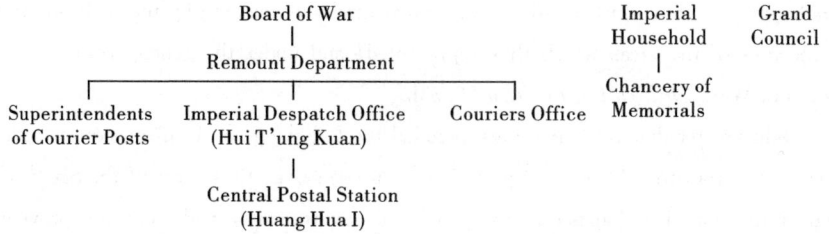

There is no indication that the Superintendents of Courier Posts were concerned in the transmission of documents sent by express and dealt with by the Grand Council.

㊹Cf. *Chia-ch'ing hui-tien* 39.23b: 凡差给驿者，皆验以邮符：曰勘合，曰火牌; *ibid*. 27a: 凡驿递，验以火票。

㊺The maximum observed rates of speed may be calculated as follows. In several cases, as between Tsinan and Peking, they show merely that no documents were sent with great urgency. We know that documents passed between Peking and Canton in 15 days, i. e. at a rate of *ca*. 375 *li* a day, by reference to Table 1. Between Peking and some other cities the rates were as follows:

| | | | |
|---|---|---|---|
| Foochow in 15 days | at a rate of *ca*. | 320 *li* | a day |
| Hangchow in 6 days | " | 510 | " |
| Shanghai in 7 days | " | 400 | " |
| Nanking in 3 days | " | 730 | " |
| Anking in 6 days | " | 430 | " |
| Tsinan in 5 days | " | 180 | " |
| Tientsin in 1 day | " | 250 | " |
| Mukden in 4 days | " | 375 | " |
| Aigun in 6 days | " | 550 | " |
| Ili in 32 days | " | 310 | " |

㊻ For random examples see *Ch'ou-pan I-wu shih-mo*, Tao-kuang period, 48. 5a ("at 600 *li* or 800 *li* with extra urgency memorialize by express"), Edict May 25, 1842; *ibid*. 55. 3b (regarding an intra-provincial despatch sent at 800 *li*) memorial received July 23, 1843; *Wên-tsung-hsien huang-ti shêng-hsün* 文宗显皇帝圣训 (sacred Instructions of the Emperor Wên-tsung-hsien) 16. 1a (in 1853), 17. 6a (1856).

㊼Many references to the performance of the imperial post may, of course, be found among writings of contemporary Western observers. In 1794 a memorial from Canton sent at 500 *li* a day secured an answer from Peking sent at 600 *li* a day within 30 days (J. J. L. DUYVENDAK, The Last Dutch Embassy to the Chinese Court 1794-1795, *TP* 34. 19). MACARTNEY was told in 1793 that despatches could go 1500 miles in 10 or 12 days (H. ROBBINS, *Our First Ambassador to China*, London 1908, 350). Although such references can be multiplied from Western literature on the period 1842-1860, their accuracy cannot often be controlled.

# ON THE TYPES AND USES OF CH'ING DOCUMENTS

J. K. FAIRBANK and S. Y. TÊNG[①]

HARVARD UNIVERSITY

## 1. INTRODUCTION

This article, like its predecessor "On the Transmission of Ch'ing Documents,"[②] is designed to aid American students of modern Chinese history. As every such student realizes to his discomfort, the available Chinese documents[③] present several problems that are not presented to an equal degree by Western documents. The problem of dating memorials has been attacked in the article mentioned above. Many more difficult questions await the coming generation. In general we lack knowledge of the administrative institutions of the Ch'ing Dynasty which produced the documents now available. Like observers for centuries past, we are obliged to accept the utterances of the emperor without clearly knowing who drafted them or how they were approved. It is obvious that our appraisal of imperial policy must wait upon our understanding of how it was made. As one step in this direction, the present study attacks the problem of the procedure followed by the central administration in dealing with the documents presented to it.

It need hardly be remarked that we are here concerned with a very complex administrative system, the accumulation of centuries, parts of which were certainly in decay before 1900 but all of which continued formally in existence until after that time. The structure of this administrative system is on the whole faithfully portrayed in the *Institutes* or *Collected Statutes of the Ch'ing* (*Ta-ch'ing hui-tien* 大清会典)

(hereafter referred as *Collected Statutes*),④ from which we know the composition and duties of the central administrative organs—the Grand Secretariat (Nei Ko 内阁) and Grand Council (Chün Chi Ch'u 军机处)⑤—and of the other offices at the capital. On the other hand, the actual functioning of these bodies, in close relation one to another, has been relatively little studied,⑥ attention having been devoted thus far chiefly to the identification of the voluminous archives⑦ which they left behind.

When taken together, the *Collected Statutes* and the archives give us an opportunity to study the progress of memorials and other documents as they passed through a succession of offices at the capital on their way to and from the imperial presence. On these routine journeys their progress was marked by the creation of other records in the form of duplicate copies, summaries, or entries in official registers, each of which was called by a special name. Moreover, the various original and duplicate memorials, depending on their nature and the emperor's action in regard to them, became differentiated and deposited accordingly, under different classifications. When other types of correspondence and accounts are added, it is not surprising to find that the archives of an important body like the Grand Council are classified under one hundred and fifty-five different headings. A similar situation might be created if the British documents in the Public Record Office were sub-divided and classified according to whether they had been seen by the sovereign or not, whether they had been taken to a cabinet meeting or not, and so on, each category bearing a different name.

Thus the categories of classification in the archives mirror quite closely the steps in procedure followed in the actual conduct of administration. In short, to understand how decisions were taken one must understand the types of documents made in the process; and the two problems cannot be divided. Therefore we present below in section 5 a catalogue of the chief types of documents; while in the pages that precede an attempt is made to summarize the administrative procedure in the

Grand Secretariat and Grand Council. The activities of the Hanlin Academy (Han Lin Yüan 翰林院, also called the National Academy, or College of Literature), and of some other bodies which dealt with ceremonial rather than political matters, are touched upon only indirectly.

For the reader's guidance it may be noted that in form the administrative initiative usually rested with the emperor's ministers rather than with the emperor. Business of all kinds, great or small, was first brought up in a memorial to the emperor; imperial action then followed. There were memorials of different types, and various forms that the imperial action might take regarding them. The most common of the latter were (1) a simple Endorsement (p'i 批), (2) a Rescript (chih 旨), usually somewhat more lengthy—both of which were written on the original memorial—and (3) an Edict (yü 谕), which was an independent document. (Our choice of English equivalents for these and other terms is explained in section 5 below, term by term.) These imperial declarations were considered important not only because they set in motion the wheels of state but also, and to a greater degree, because they partook of the sanctity of the imperial person. Just as all references to the emperor or to things associated with him must be elevated (t'ai-t'ou 抬头) from one to three characters above the ordinary text of a document, so all statements emanating from him received extraordinary and reverent attention. This attitude, combined with the fact that the emperor usually ruled as well as reigned, provides a chief point of contrast with Western administrative procedure. Thus a Chinese Edict often corresponds roughly to Western Instructions, but it would hardly be correct to say that it was a mere equivalent.

## 2. PROCEDURE IN THE GRAND SECRETARIAT (NEI KO)

In brief, the Grand Secretariat was an institution inherited from the

Ming and was the highest administrative body of the empire until the creation of the Grand Council in 1729.⑧ After that date and throughout the nineteenth century the Grand Secretariat continued to function, but only as a body of secondary importance dealing with routine matters.⑨ It became unimportant as a policy-making body but it still formed the apex of the routine administration. Details of its procedure are therefore recorded with some care in the various editions of the *Collected Statutes* and form a convenient starting point. For present purposes the multifarious ceremonial and ritualistic duties of the Grand Secretariat will be disregarded, except as they may be subsumed in the catalogue below, section 5, with reference to certain types of documents.

For the inauguration of administrative business there were two fundamental types of memorial, the T'i-pên 題本 and the Tsou-pên 奏本 (also called Tsou-chê 奏折). As to the historical difference between them, which was not always very distinct, we quote below the evidence selected by a leading student of the subject.⑩

From this it will be seen that T'i-pên concerned chiefly routine local civil affairs and bore the seal of the memorialist; Tsou-pên concerned chiefly important matters of state or the personal affairs of the memorialist and did not bear the seal of the memorialist. (The published memorials on foreign affairs in the nineteenth century are usually Tsou-pên.) In practice the memorials on routine administration which came to the Grand Secretariat were, ordinarily, T'i-pên; and the memorials on important matters which came to the Grand Council were, ordinarily, Tsou-pên. We have found no statutory connection between the T'i-pên form of memorial and the Grand Secretariat, such that memorials of that type were required to go to that body. But since both came to be concerned chiefly with routine business, seasonal reports, accounts, and the like, the memorials coming to the Grand Secretariat were usually T'i-pên, and they are therefore the first thing to consider.

The chief key to what follows lies in the marked dichotomy⑪ between the treatment of routine and of important affairs, which may be roughly diagrammed for the reader's future reference as follows:

|  | ROUTINE AFFAIRS | IMPORTANT AFFAIRS |
| --- | --- | --- |
| Memorialized in the form of | T'i-pên | Tsou-pên |
| Submitted first to | Transmission Office or Grand Secretariat | Chancery of Memorials |
| First considered by | Grand Secretariat | the Emperor |
| Action proposed by | " " | Grand Council |
| Action taken in the form of | Rescript or Endorsement, | Edict or Rescript or Endorsement |

T'i-pên for eventual presentation to the emperor came to the Grand Secretariat from two sources: (a) offices at the capital and (b) offices in the provinces. The offices at the capital included the Six Boards (Liu Pu 六部) and the various subordinate Courts, Departments, and Superintendencies; T'i-pên from these sources were called Pu-pên 部本. The offices in the provinces included those of governor-general (Viceroys), governors, generals-in-chief (Tartar generals), and the like; T'i-pên from these sources came through the postal service⑫ and the Transmission Office (T'ung Chêng Ssǔ 通政司) and were called T'ung-pên 通本. An analysis of procedure must begin with the arrival of T'ung-pên from the provinces.

(1) Routine memorials from the provinces (T'ung-pên) were delivered by the official posted to the Transmission Office (T'ung Chêng Ssǔ), where they were first examined as to form and then, ordinarily, transmitted to the Grand Secretariat.

In form the memorial must comply with the regulations as to the number of lines and characters per page and as to the honorary elevation of certain characters; it must bear the writer's title and name at the beginning and the date of its despatch at the end; it should be stamped with the writer's seal of office, and a summary of its contents on a separate slip of paper (T'ieh-huang 贴黄) should be attached at the end.⑬ If such a summary were missing, it should be supplied by the Transmission Office.⑭ If the memorials were in improper form, in any one of several respects, it might either be rejected and sent back to the sender or sent to the Grand Secretariat to secure an imperial decision regarding it.

Thus the power of the Transmission Office, although much less extensive than under the Ming[15], was still considerable. As the first office at the capital to read T'i-pên from the provinces, it held a strategic position, with power to return a memorial unaccepted, to impeach the memorialist, and at times even to interpret the content of a memorial in making a summary of it. Only the secret memorials of officials in office were exempt from this scrutiny, and since the memorials here in question concerned routine business it is unlikely that many of them were secret. On the other hand, various measures were taken during the course of the Ch'ing period further to restrict the power of the Transmission Office.[16] As will be noted below, the Grand Council was set up in 1729 partly for this purpose.

Here it should be noted that when a T'i-pên was first presented one or more duplicate copies were presented with it. Other copies might subsequently be made. Since these duplicates do not concern the main steps in procedure, they are discussed chiefly in section 5 below; see under Chieh-t'ieh, Fu-pên.

(2) Routine memorials from offices at the capital (Pu-pên) were sent directly to the Grand Secretariat.

At first glance this statement might be challenged on the grounds of ancient tradition[17] and of various references in the literature, where it is sometimes declared that all memorials were presented for the emperor's inspection before they were sent to the Grand Secretariat.[18] All memorials were of course presented to the emperor at some point; the question here is whether T'i-pên from the capital (i. e. Pu-pên), as distinct from Tsou-pên, were presented to the emperor first of all, rather than later in the procedure. The *Collected Statutes* seem to leave little doubt that Pu-pên were sent first to the Grand Secretariat instead of to the emperor.[19] In view of the immense number of these documents and of the fact that they concerned routine business, this would seem to have been the only practical procedure. (As will be noted below in section 3, important memorials, i. e. Tsou-pên, went first to the emperor.)

(3) On arrival at the Grand Secretariat, routine memorials (T'i-pên) of both types (T'ung-pên and Pu-pên) were again examined for irregularities of form and were prepared for reading.

Thus if T'ung-pên arrived from the provinces written in Chinese only, as was no doubt usually the case, a copy of the summary was required to be prepared in Manchu.⑳ A duplicate copy of the entire memorial (Fu-pên) was also made.㉑

(4) At the Grand Secretariat the T'i-pên were read first by the minor officers of the Secretariat, who proposed what action should be taken upon them.

These minor officers of the Secretariat totalled in the nineteenth century nearly 250 men, of whom a good deal more than half were Manchus, as may be seen by reference to the subjoined table.㉒ It was one of their functions to suggest in the first instance what the imperial decision should eventually be. For each memorial they wrote on a slip of paper a draft㉓ of an imperial Endorsement or Rescript. A draft Endorsement, for example, might order the matter in question to be referred to a Board for further deliberation, or it might be no more than the laconic and recurrent "Noted" (Chih-tao-liao 知道了). For all routine decisions there was of course an established phraseology.㉔ In appropriate cases two, three, or even four such phrases might be suggested, each one drafted on a separate slip according to certain regulations, and both or all presented at the same time as alternatives for the imperial choice.㉕ In such cases, or even when a single draft was presented, a special note might be added to explain the basis on which the proposals had been made.㉖ All drafts were written in both Chinese and Manchu and the two writers of the draft signed it on the back. The slip of paper bearing the draft, about four by seven inches in size, was then attached to the original memorial.⑳ The readers also dealt with the maps, lists, accounts, bound volumes, and other enclosures that might accompany a memorial (see below, sec. 5: Huang-ts'ê), determining whether according to the regulations they should be submitted to the emperor along with the memorial.㉘

It is evident that this drafting by the minor officers of the Secretariat was conventional in nature and involved questions of mere procedure rather than of policy. In any case the decisions of these men were reviewed by their superiors.

(5) The drafts of Endorsements and Rescripts, together with the original memorials concerned, were then seen and passed upon by the Grand Secretaries (Ta Hsüeh Shih 大学士).

There were usually four of these officials, two Manchus and two Chinese, plus two Assistant Grand Secretaries, one Manchu and one Chinese. We lack evidence as to whether, the institution of prime minister having been abolished, one of these half dozen high officials might make important decisions representing them all; no doubt the pressure of business would sometimes require it, in which case the ya-pan 押班 or head secretary on duty may perhaps have taken the decision.㉙

Every draft was approved, rejected, or changed by the Grand Secretaries.㉚ It was then sent to the Manchu and Chinese Registries (P'iao Ch'ien Ch'u 票签处) of the Grand Secretariat, where it was copied out in Manchu and Chinese on a formal double slip.㉛ It was then ready to be presented to the emperor along with the memorial concerned.

(6) On the following day at dawn the memorial (T'i-pên) was presented to the emperor by the Grand Secretaries in audience, and the draft of the Endorsement or Rescript was subsequently approved, or changed, or if there were more than one, selected; or a separate Edict was issued to deal with the matter.㉜

(7) The imperial decision having thus been made, the memorial was endorsed (see below, sec. 5: p'i) accordingly.

In the case of T'i-pên this was seldom done by the emperor's own hand. Rather, the memorial and the approved form of Endorsement were sent to the Endorsements Copying Office (P'i-pên Ch'u 批本处), where a staff of Manchu secretaries copied the Endorsement in Manchu onto the memorial in red ink. The Endorsement in Chinese was copied on in red ink by the minor officers of the Grand Secretariat after the memorial had been returned to that body.㉝ Both these Endorsements in red ink were called P'i-hung 批红 (endorsed in red) to distinguish them from Chu-p'i 朱批 (Vermilion Endorsement) or Yü-p'i 御批 (imperial Endorsements), which were sometimes written on documents by the emperor's own hand. Memorials endorsed in red ink (P'i-hung) were given the name Hung-pên 红本 (red memorials) and also called P'i-pên (endorsed memorials).㉞ The imperial Endorsements were also copied onto the duplicates (Fu-pên) of the original memorials, already mentioned; but in this case the Endorsement was copied on in plain black ink. The duplicates were supposed to be stored in the Office of Imperial Historiography (Huang Shih Ch'êng 皇史宬).㉟

(8) Within two days after its presentation, a memorial was required to be sent down from the imperial presence and action taken accordingly.㊱

The original memorial (T'i-pên) was archived. Now endorsed in red, it was handed over to the Receiving and Forwarding Office (Shou Fa Hung-pên Ch'u 收发红本处), through which it was placed in the safekeeping of the Six Sections (Liu K'o 六科) of the Office for Scrutiny of Metropolitan Officials (Chi Shih Chung Ya Mên 给事中衙门), a part of the Censorate. At the end of every year all original memorials were required to be returned from this division of the Censorate and were stored by the Office for... Red Memorials.㊲ Cf. *op. cit.* 2-21b line 8.

After notice had been given them by the Six Sections, copies of the original memorial were made by the offices of government concerned. Thus the imperial will was made known.㊳

(9) If an Edict, instead of an Endorsement or a Rescript, were issued as a result of the presentation of a T'i-pên through the Grand Secretariat, then the Grand Council would usually be involved in the drafting. It is of course unlikely that many T'i-pên would call for an Edict in reply. In any case, since the activity of the Grand Secretariat in connection with the drafting of Edicts appears to have been in practice subordinate to that of the Grand Council, it will be considered below, section 3.

Under normal conditions, if we may trust the *Collected Statutes*, the procedure summarized above would have occupied about four days, from the time when the T'i-pên was first read until the time when the imperial Endorsement or Rescript had been formally copied onto it and further action could be taken accordingly. If necessary, the emperor's decision could be returned to the Grand Secretariat on the same day that a memorial was presented.

By way of comment it may be pointed out that there was an ample arrangement in this procedure for checks and balances. Each draft Endorsement or Rescript was written out in both Manchu and Chinese, by secretaries who signed their names, and was then copied by another secretariat after the Grand Secretaries had approved it. Similarly, following the imperial approval, the Manchu and Chinese versions of the Endorsement or Rescript were written onto the memorial in red ink by two separate offices. The likelihood of ill-considered drafting or of incorrect recording of decisions was thereby reduced. The announcement of the imperial will was hedged about with equal precautions. The imperial decision in each case could be copied by the other organs of government only after it had been received by the Censorate (the Six Sections, to be exact), although the decision had been originally suggested by the Grand Secretariat. The original document was then retained for the rest of the year by the officers of the Censorate while the Grand Secretariat itself retained only a copy. Certainly there was little opportunity for changes in the text of an imperial decision once it had been made. This ensured accuracy. But it must also have put a premium on the use of time-worn phraseology and the purely automatic treatment of official business. Minor secretaries were not likely to attempt innovations, and yet the initiative rested largely with them. From the point of view of an archivist, on the other hand, no more admirable system has ever been devised, and historians may well be grateful, even when they become lost in the profusion of records and copies.

## 3. PROCEDURE IN THE GRAND COUNCIL (CHÜN CHI CH'U)

The Grand Council (lit. Military Plans Office, also called Privy Council or Council of State) was a smaller, more informal, and much more powerful body than the Grand Secretariat. In its first form the Council was established during the Yung-chêng reign in 1729⑲ to deal secretly with imperial military strategy, the most obvious cause of its creation being the contemporary campaigns in the northwest. Further research is likely to show, however, that the Council filled a need long felt, for it is apparent that the early Ch'ing emperors had come to require the help of a compact, carefully selected, and rather unceremonious body to assist in their personal rule. The Grand Secretariat, having been the apex of the bureaucratic pyramid for generations past, could not serve this purpose. Accordingly the K'ang-hsi Emperor had made use of Fu Chêng Ta Ch'ên 辅政大臣 (assistant administrators) and later of the officials in the Nan Shu-fang 南书房 (south library) to assist him in dealing with important business. Similarly the Yung-chêng Emperor had set up the Grand Council, which thus appears to have been the final solution of a long-standing problem.⑳

We have already noted that the creation of the Council roughly coincided with the establishment of certain regulations concerning the use of T'i-pên (memorials on routine public affairs bearing the memorialist's seal of office) and Tsou-pên (memorials on important or personal affairs and not bearing the memorialist's seal of office, see note 10). The latter form of memorial, as officials themselves testified, was simpler and more expeditious; it came to be used generally for communications to the emperor passing through the Grand Council. It is evident that important political factors must have underlain these administrative changes—both the Council and the Tsou-pên were tools making for greater efficiency, greater secrecy, and more freedom from bureaucratic impedimenta.

The power of the Council derived partly from its very informality. It was not given a separate section in the *Collected Statutes* until the Chia-ch'ing edition of 1818. The number of Grand Councillors was never fixed. Usually there were five or six, but the number ranged between extremes of three and twelve.[41] They could be selected from among the Grand Secretaries and the Presidents and Vice-presidents of Boards, as well as from among the Secretaries of the Grand Council itself (Chün Chi Chang-ching 军机章京, also called Hsiao Chün Chi 小军机). This arrangement was most important, for it made it possible to select carefully the really influential, or otherwise desirable, ministers, sidestepping the thorny problem of promotions from the bureaucratic hierarchy. Thus one or more of the Councillors (until after 1862) was always a Grand Secretary as well, and so formed a direct link between the two bodies. Statistics indicating the degree to which the Council and the Secretariat were merged, through their common personnel, are given below.[42] In a similar manner, during the existence of the Tsungli Ya-mên (for the management of foreign affairs) from 1861 to 1901 there were eighteen men who held office in both that body and the Council.[43]

A natural characteristic of this central organ of administration was the secrecy which surrounded its activities. Minor clerks were dispensed with and the clerical drudgery required for the handling of all important documents was borne by the Secretaries themselves, documents of less importance being sent to the Military Archives Office and elsewhere for routine treatment. At the beginning of the nineteenth century the number of Secretaries was fixed at 32, half Manchu and half Chinese, to be selected from the staffs of such bodies as the Grand Secretariat, the Six Boards, and the Court of Colonial Affairs; they had to be recommended by their superiors and were granted an audience with the emperor. After 1860 four Manchu and four Chinese Secretaries were assigned to work in the Tsung Li Ya-mên. Thus the relatively small number of the Council's Secretaries, carefully selected and guaranteed as they were, made the Council staff a very compact body, quite closed to the uninitiated. Officials entering its service at first had to be instructed in the office routine.㊹

This secrecy and compactness accorded with the fact that the volume of important business was relatively small, seldom amounting to more than fifty or sixty memorials a day.㊺ In short, the Grand Council was in many respects a sort of imperial private secretariat, as exemplified in the fact that the Councillors followed the emperor wherever he might go and had special apartments at Jehol or Yüan Ming Yüan.㊻ As a result, the procedure of the Council is much less fully described in the *Collected Statutes* than that of the Grand Secretariat, and can be summarized only approximately.

(1) Tsou-pên (important memorials) from the provinces were delivered at the capital to an office at the Palace called the Chancery of Memorials (Tsou Shih Ch'u 奏事处).

This Chancery of Memorials thus occupied in relation to Tsou-pên a position comparable to that of the Transmission Office (T'ung Chêng Ssǔ) in relation to T'i-pên; but there is no evidence that it ever exercised comparable power. It had a small staff headed by an Imperial Bodyguard, a high official specially selected from the Guards within the Palace, who was assisted by six Secretaries (chang-ching 章京) selected and guaranteed from other offices; there were also two Clerks.㊼ Tsou-pên from the provinces, delivered by courier,㊽ were marked on the outside "official despatch (kung-wên 公文) to the Chancery of Memorials," and were received by the clerks of the Chancery at whatever time they arrived. They were then handed to the Secretaries, who in turn handed them to the Chancery eunuchs for presentation, the latter being of course in a position to convey them to the emperor's private apartments. Officials below a certain rank were not normally allowed to present Tsou-pên.[49] Other than this regulation, there is no indication in the *Collected Statutes* that the Chancery officials could emulate those of the Transmission Office in the manipulation of red tape for ulterior ends.

(2) Tsou-pên from officials at the capital were likewise delivered to the Chancery of Memorials to the emperor.

Every morning at dawn the Secretaries of the Chancery were required to receive memorials at the Palace gate. Memorialists who were presenting personal memorials were required to present them in person; this applied to Presidents of Boards and all others at the capital except princes and men over sixty (sui). The memorials so received were then handed to the Chancery eunuchs for presentation to the emperor.[50]

(3) Tsou-pên were presented from the Chancery of Memorials directly to the emperor.

It need hardly be added that this would have significance only in proportion as the emperor really desired to rule as well as reign; but the evidence indicates that the Ch'ing emperors invariably desired to do so.[51] Their early morning examination of memorials was no mere formality. On the contrary, the Chia-ch'ing Emperor forbade the practice of sending duplicates of Tsou-pên to the Grand Council.[52] There is a good deal of evidence to show that the emperor usually saw important memorials before they were seen by his chief ministers.[53]

(4) The emperor inspected the memorials and made his decisions and comments regarding them.

At this first inspection he might make a simple Endorsement (p'i) settling the matter in question; in such case the imperial decision could be transmitted through the Council without further discussion or delay. On the other hand, matters which he wished to discuss with his Councillors, or regarding which he wished them to prepare the draft of an Edict or the like, would be so indicated. Thus his turning down one corner of a memorial would mark it for further consideration (see sec. 5, Chê-pên).

(5) The memorials were then sent down to the Grand Council to be dealt with as indicated by the emperor.

On their arrival at the Council, the Secretaries of that body classified and distributed them. Those on which an imperial decision had already been reached were dealt with in the routine manner described below. But usually some memorials were still a live issue—those which bore no Endorsement or were endorsed "There is a separate Rescript" (ling yu chih 另有旨) or which were otherwise indicated for discussion, as by the turning down of a corner. Regarding these documents the Secretaries under the Councillors' direction, or perhaps the Councillors themselves, prepared drafts of an imperial decision, whether Edict, Rescript, or Endorsement, in preparation for the audience of the following morning. Such memorials were called "audience memorials" (chien-mien chê 见面折). Usually there were only a few each day.㉝

(6) On the following day at dawn the documents held over in this manner from the previous day were dealt with by the emperor and the Grand Councillors in audience.㉟

Here again there are few regulations, except as to where the ministers should sit in the imperial presence. There was evidently no bar to thorough and informal discussion. The Councillors would present both the memorials in question and also their own drafts and memoranda or minutes (P'ien, see sec. 5).

(7) When the imperial decision regarding a Tsou-pên had been made, either by the emperor alone when he first saw the document or subsequently in concert with his Councillors, the documents concerned were then returned to the Grand Council and copies were made.㊱

Ordinary Tsou-pên were sent to be copied by the Military Archives

Office. But those which had been presented as secret, or bore Vermilion Endorsements which should be kept secret, or which were originals that were to be transmitted in Letters or Edicts, were all copied by the Secretaries of the Grand Council in person.[57]

(8) The imperial will was then made known.

Copies might be sent to the Grand Secretariat or to the Board of War for transmission by horse post to the provinces or to various Boards at the capital for them to act upon. Edicts, which were drafted by the Grand Councillors as one of their chief functions, might be addressed to the Councillors themselves (see sec. 5, Yü) or to the Grand Secretariat. In any ease, they would not be addressed to the high officials in the provinces; the latter would receive the imperial will in the form of a Court Letter (T'ing-chi, see sec. 5) sent to them by the Council and embodying in it the imperial Edict. On the other hand, Edicts of less importance or addressed to no particular officials would be publicly issued by the Grand Secretariat, in which case they might subsequently reach the provinces through the medium of the Peking Gazette in one or another of its forms (see sec. 5, T'ang-pao). The fullest description of the procedure just described is that given by Prince Kung, which we quote in part below.[58]

It is an interesting question how long this process usually required. From the *Collected Statutes* we know that memorials from the capital were to be handed in at dawn, those from the provinces might arrive at any time. The emperor read memorials at dawn. He also saw the Grand Councillors at that time, and they remained on call to be seen at any other time it might be necessary. Memorials seen by the emperor were sent down to the Council in the morning, providing their "morning work" (tsao-shih 早事). Finally, it is stated that memorials were usually seen by the emperor one day before they were considered by the Council. From this and similar evidence we may conclude that, ordinarily, a memorial might be presented at dawn or during the course of one day and be seen by the emperor on that day or at dawn of the following day; in either case it would ordinarily be sent down to the Council on the second day; if it was to be discussed further, it would then be brought back by the Councillors on the morning of the third day for a final decision. This may have been the routine with business which was not pressing. On the other hand, there was every opportunity to speed up the process ad libitum, and an urgent memorial might be received, presented, and discussed by the emperor and his Councillors all within the space of a few hours.⁵⁹

(9) Finally, the memorials were returned through the Chancery of Memorials to the original memorialist, whether in the provinces or at the capital. This afforded a form of direct contact between the emperor and his officials, at least in the case of memorials bearing an imperial notation.⁶⁰

A brief conclusion may be suggested. First, it is plain that this paper is no more than a preliminary survey. We have touched upon a score or more of institutions and steps in procedure, on each of which a monograph should be written. For such work the various editions of the Cases Supplementary to the *Collected Statutes* (*hui-tien tsê-li*, or *shih-li*), cited above, provide an inexhaustible storehouse of material, which may be supplemented by the documentary collections and writings of Chinese officials. American students of government and political science have so far left it untouched.

Secondly, this survey confirms the view that the Grand Council was all-important and the Grand Secretariat almost negligible in the making of important decisions of policy during the nineteenth century, particularly before 1860. In the investigation of the origins of Ch'ing policy, either in internal or in foreign affairs, the Grand Councillors and the Secretaries to the Grand Council must be the foci of attention; the latter had more influence in the drafting of Edicts and such documents than did the high dignitaries of the Grand Secretariat who were not in the Council, yet we have at present few studies regarding them.

Finally, for an understanding of Ch'ing policy attention must be centered upon the personality of the emperor and the influences affecting him. Our survey indicates that the emperor was required to play a part, passive though it might be, in the making of every important decision. This fact of personal rule has been commented upon for generations past, yet its implications, from an administrative point of view, have seldom been explored. From the summary of procedure given above, it is patent that the emperor was obliged to act as a sort of clearing-house for all important matters. We may well inquire whether this did not produce a bottle-neck in the flow of administrative business. Under an emperor of only ordinary vigor it is a pertinent question whether the press of routine work did not stifle both his initiative and his adaptability. In other words, the central administration of the Ch'ing, and indeed the whole Chinese tradition of the personal rule of the Son of Heaven, demanded a superman at the head of affairs. The lack of a superman, and the rapid multiplication of state affairs, must be an important factor in the collapse of the Ch'ing administration during the nineteenth century. Considerations such as the above challenge the attention of the political scientist, while for the diplomatic historian they are all-important.

## 4. SELECT LIST OF PUBLISHED COLLECTIONS OF CH'ING DOCUMENTS

This list is presented partly to facilitate references in section 5 below and partly to call this material to the attention of students who have not been specializing in bibliography. The list is in no sense exhaustive, and new collections of documents are continually appearing. It is meant to include the chief examples of the material now available, which would not be out of place in every Chinese library. Several collections of documents obviously based on collections here noticed have been omitted. There is a large and rapidly growing critical bibliography relating to these various collections, the description of which is beyond the scope of this paper; but attention should be called to an early comprehensive study of Ch'ing historical literature in general by Erich HAENISCH (Das Ts'ing-shi-kao und die sonstige chinesische Literatur zur Geschichte der letzten 300 Jahre, *AM* 6. 403-444 [1930]) and to the recent study by K. N. BIGGERSTAFF, some Notes on the Tung-hua lu and the Shih-lu (*HJAS* 4. 101-115), in which further references may be found. There is an obvious need for further studies similar to Prof. BIGGERSTAFF'S dealing with single collections. For a more complete list of Palace Museum publications of documents than that here presented, cf. KOESTER.

Chang-ku ts'ung-pien 掌故丛编 (Collected historical documents) pub. monthly by the Department of Historical Records (Wên Hsien Kuan 文献馆), Palace Museum, Peiping; first issue Jan. 1928, beginning with the eleventh issue the title was changed to *Wên-hsien ts'ung-pien* 文献丛编, see below.

Chin-tai Chung-kuo wai-chiao-shih tzu-liao chi-yao 近代中国外交史资料辑要 (A Source Book of Important Documents Relating to the Modern Diplomatic History of China), compiled with prefaces by CHIANG T'ing-fu 蒋廷黻 (T. F. TSIANG), 2 vols. Shanghai 1931-1934.

Ch'ing-chi wai-chiao shih-liao 清季外交史料 (Historical Materials Concerning Foreign Relations in the Late Ch'ing Period 1875-1911), 218 chüan, 卷首 1 chüan, and for the Hsüan-t'ung Period (1909-1911) 24 chüan, compiled by WANG Yen-wei 王彦威 and WANG Liang 王亮 Peiping 1932-1935.

Ch'ing Hsüan-t'ung ch'ao Chung-Jih chiao-shê shih-liao 清宣统朝中日交涉史料 (Historical Materials Concerning Sino-Japanese Relations in the Hsüan-t'ung Period 1909-1911), 6 chüau, Palace Museum, Peiping 1932.

Ch'ing Kuang-hsü ch'ao Chung-Fa chiao-shê shih-liao 清光绪朝中法交涉史料 (Historical Materials Relating to Sino-French Relations in the Kuang-hsü Period 1875-1908), 22 chüan, Palace Museum, Peiping 1933.

Ch'ing Kuang-hsü ch'ao Chung-Jih chiao-shê shih-liao 清光绪朝中日

交涉史料 (Historical Materials Concerning Sino-Japanese Relations in the Kuang-hsü Period 1875-1908), 88 chüan, Palace Museum, Peiping 1932.

Ch'ing san-fan shih-liao 清三藩史料 (Historical Materials Concerning the Three Feudatories of the Early Ch'ing Period, i. e. Wu San-kuei et al.), 5 vols., Palace Museum, Peiping 1932.

Ch'ing-tai wai-chiao shih-liao 清代外交史料 (Historical Materials Concerning Foreign Relations in the Ch'ing Period), 6 vols. for the Chia-ch'ing period 1796-1820 and 4 vols. for the Tao-kuang period 1821-1850, Palace Museum, Peiping 1932-1933.

Ch'ing-tai wên-tzu-yü tang 清代文字狱档 (Archives on the Ch'ing Literary Inquisition), 12 vols., Palace Museum, Peiping 1931 et seq.

Ch'ou-pan i-wu shih-mo 筹办夷务始末 (The Complete Account of Our Management of Barbarian Affairs), photolithograph of the original compilation, 80 chüan for the later Tao-kuang period 1836-1850, presented to the emperor 1856; 80 chüan for the Hsien-fêng period 1851-1861, presented 1867; 100 chüan for the T'ung-chih period 1862-1874, presented 1880, Palace Museum, Peiping 1930.

Chu-p'i shang-yü 朱批上谕, same as *Chu-p'i yü-chih*, q. v.

Chu-p'i yü-chih 朱批谕旨 (Vermilion Endorsements and Edicts [of the Yung-chêng Period 1723-1735, including the Memorials Concerned]), preface of the Ch'ien-lung Emperor dated 1738, 112 vols.

I-wu shih-mo, see Ch'ou-pan i-wu shih-mo.

Ku-kung o-wên shih-liao 故宫俄文史料 ("Documents in Russian Preserved in the National Palace of Peiping," K'ang-hsi and Ch'ien-lung periods, 1662-1722 and 1736-1795), compiled by LIU Tsê-jung 刘泽荣, with Chinese translation by WANG Chih-hsiang 王之相, p. 312, Peiping 1936.

Liu-shih-nien lai Chung-kuo yü Jih-pên 六十年来中国与日本 (China and Japan in the Last Sixty Years), 7 vols., compiled by WANG Yün-shêng 王芸生, Tientsin 1932-1934.

Ming-ch'ing shih-liao 明清史料 (Historical Materials of the Ming and

Ch'ing Periods), 4 vols., edited by the Institute of History and Philology, Academia Sinica, 1930-1931.

Ming-ch'ing shih-liao i-pien 明清史料乙编 (second series), 10 vols., Commercial Press, Shanghai 1936.

Shêng-hsün, see Shih-ch'ao shêng-hsün.

Shih-ch'ao shêng-hsün 十朝圣训 (Sacred Instructions or Exhortations of Ten Reigns, 1616-1874), 922 chüan, 286 vols., last preface Jan. 6, 1880.

Shih-liao hsün-k'an 史料旬刊 (Historical Materials Published Every Ten Days), 40 vols., Palace Museum, Peiping 1930-1931.

Shih-liao ts'ung-k'an ch'u-pien 史料丛刊初编 (Miscellaneous Historical Materials, First Series), 10 vols., compiled by Lo Chên-yü 罗振玉, Tung-fang hsüeh-hui, 1924.

Shih-liao ts'ung-pien 史料丛编 (Miscellaneous Historical Materials), 12 vols., compiled by Lo Chên-yü 罗振玉, 1933.

Shih-lu, see Ta-ch'ing li-ch'ao shih-lu.

Ta-ch'ing li-ch'ao shih-lu 大清历朝实录 (Veritable Records of Successive Reigns of the Ch'ing Dynasty), 4485 chüan, Ōkura Shuppan Kabushiki Kaisha 大藏出版株式会社, Tōkyō 1937-1938; cf. W. FUCHS, Beiträge zur mandjurischen Bibliographie und Literatur, Tōkyō 1936, 58-71.

T'ai-p'ing t'ien-kuo chao-yü 太平天国诏谕 (Proclamations and Edicts of the T'ai-p'ing t'ien-kuo Era), compiled by HSLAO I-shun, 1 vol., National Academy of Peiping 1935. Also T'ai-p'ing t'ien-kuo ts'ung-shu 太平天国丛书 (Collected Writings of the T'ai-p'ing t'ien-kuo) compiled by the same, 10 vols., Shanghai 1936.

T'ai-p'ing t'ien-kuo wên-shu 太平天国文书 (Documents on the T'ai-p'ing t'ien-kuo), 1 vol., Palace Museum, Peiping 1933.

Tung-hua lu 东华录, various editions; cf. K. N. BIGGERSTAFF in HJAS 4. 101-115.

Wên-hsien ts'ung-pien 文献丛编 (Collectanea from the Historical

Records Office), 19 vols., Palace Museum, Peiping 1930-1937.

Yung-chêng shang-yü 雍正上谕 (Edicts of the Yung-chêng Emperor, 1723-1735), 24 vols., compiled by CHANG T'ing-yü 张廷玉 and others, 1741.

## 5. CATALOGUE OF TYPES OF DOCUMENTS

One type of document is distinguished from another chiefly by the character or characters that introduce the main body of the text. Thus an Edict normally begins simply with the character *yü*, meaning in effect that the emperor issued the Edict which then follows. Memorials usually begin with the memorialist's official title and name, followed by a character which indicates the type of the memorial. But in the case of less important documents, such as correspondence between minor local officials, classification by this method becomes less trenchant, and the highly technical documentary phraseology gradually evaporates into the dull words of every day. We have tried to draw the line at the point where this unhappy process becomes noticeable (cf. e. g. GILES 9816).

This catalogue is arranged alphabetically by WADE-GILES romanization and is meant to serve two purposes. In the first place, we wish to suggest English designations for the commoner types of documents in order to facilitate the establishment of a generally accepted usage among Western translators. An accepted usage is particularly desirable because much research on modern China will probably be published without benefit of Chinese characters. The old custom, on account of the fact that each translator has his own terminology, is likely to produce a confusion of Edicts, Decrees, mandates, commands, and other referents that will tax our mental agility. Fortunately, Western research on the Ch'ing period is so little advanced that the opportunity still exists to agree upon a common vocabulary, with the efficiency and economy which it would provide, providing a miraculous coöperation to that end can be achieved. We hope therefore that the suggestions of other workers, which will be offered in modification of our own, will be given publicity. It is not the object of the present compilation to put forward a revised terminology; we have tried, like the sage, merely to codify that which is already established. As with a system of romanization, English translations of Chinese terms are often mere conventions. It is important first that the translation should be reasonably accurate in meaning, and then that it should follow the tradition to be found in the literature of the field.

All translators of Ch'ing documents will be familiar with three text-books, in which the traditional usage is chiefly recorded:

①T. F. WADE, 文件自迩集 *Wên-chien tzŭ-erh chi*, A series of papers selected as specimens of Documentary Chinese, designed to assist students of the language as written by the officials of China; in sixteen parts with key, London 1867, 2 vols;

②F. HIRTH,新关文件录 *Hsin-kuan wên-chien lu*, Text Book of Documentary Chinese, with a vocabulary, for the special use of the Chinese Customs Service, Shanghai 1885, 2 vols, cited as HIRTH;

③The second edition of no. 2, rearranged, enlarged, and edited by C. H. BREWITT-TAYLOR, Shanghai 1909-1910, 2 vols., is cited as BREWITT-TAYLOR.

To these volumes should be added W. F. MAYERS, *The Chinese Government*, Shanghai 1897, revised by G. M. H. PLAYFAIR, Appendix sec. 3, "Forms of Official Correspondence;" and H. A. GILES, *A Chinese-English Dictionary*, Shanghai 1912. All these works were compiled by men who had spent long years in official service in China, often in daily correspondence with the authorities. The translations of Chinese terms which they adopted, especially those in GILES' dictionary, which we cite frequently below, represent the considered usage of a generation or more of consular and customs officials. They have entered so largely into the literature on nineteenth century China that little can be gained by a wanton revision of terms, except where clarity makes it necessary. On the other hand, it must be remembered that these observers were not versed in the inner workings of the metropolitan administration, knew little of its procedure, and were not personally acquainted with many types of documents which have been published from the archives in the last decade. What follows is intended to supplement rather than to include the notes and suggestions available in BREWITT-TAYLOR.

In the second place, this catalogue is intended to indicate how a given type of document was used, again for the convenience of Western students. To this end, references have been given where possible to published examples of each type. We omit from the list minor variations of a given type and also a multitude of names of various kinds of archives and records which are referred to by modern Chinese archivists (see note 7) but the exact nature of which is not always clear, and which are in any case not available to students outside the archives. It has not seemed worthwhile to record the formal phraseology with which each type of document normally begins and ends; many follow the form exemplified in the Chao-hui, beginning... *wei chao-hui shih* 为照会事(in the matter of a communication) and ending ... *hsü-chih chao-hui chê* 须至照会者（a necessary communication）, cf. BREWITT-TAYLOR 2.10 "Col. 12."

A division of the catalogue into sub-categories would not be easy, for there is no sharp and useful dividing line between documents exchanged between government offices and documents submitted to the emperor, nor between the latter and documents issued by the emperor. To facilitate the study of related types we offer the following incomplete analytical summary.

- **DOCUMENTS EXCHANGED BETWEEN GOVERNMENT OFFICES.**

In the Chinese scheme of things the typological names of these documents often serve to indicate the relative rank of the correspondents. This relationship can be indicated in translation only by a convention, since documents of this sort in the West would nearly all be called despatches. To indicate the three general forms of relationship between the correspondents, we suggest Order or Orders (from a superior), Communication (from an equal), and Report (from a subordinate or inferior); these might also be rendered "a despatch ordering," or "a despatch communicating," and so on. A despatch from an inferior in rank who is not a direct subordinate presents a nice problem, which we have not tried to solve.

Communications: Chao-hui, Chao-fu, Chih-hui, I-hui, I-tzǔ, I-wên, Kung-han, Tzǔ, Tzǔ-ch'êng, Tzǔ-hsing, Tzǔ-hui, Tzǔ-pao, Tzǔ-wên.

Despatches from ministers of state, in most cases the Grand Council, conveying imperial Edicts or the like: Chi-hsin, Chiao-chih, Chiao-p'ien, Ch'üan-yü, Han, T'ing-chi, Tzǔ-chi.

Orders: Cha, Cha-fu, Ku-tieh, Kuan-wên, Ling, P'ai, P'ai-p'iao, Tieh.

Petitions: several of the entries below under Reports are translated as Petition in certain contexts, e. g. when presented to an official by a commoner.

Reports: Ch'êng, Ch'êng-wên, Hsiang-wên, Ping, Shên, Shên-wên, Tieh-ch'êng, Tzǔ-ch'êng.

- **DOCUMENTS SUBMITTED TO THE EMPEROR.**

Copies of memorials: Chieh-t'ieh, Fu-pên, Shih-shu, Lu-shu.

Endorsed memorials: Hung-pên, see also P'i-hung.

Memorials: Chê-tsou, Ch'i-pên, Liu-ts'ao chang-tsou, Pên-chang, Piao-chang, Piao-pên, Po-pên, Pu-pên, T'i-pên, T'i-tsou, Tsou-chê, Tsou-pên, T'ung-pên.

Summaries of memorials: Lu-shu, Shih-shu, T'ieh-huang.

Supplementary memorials: Chia-p'ien, Fu-p'ien, Fu-tsou, P'ien, P'ien-tsou, Tsou-p'ien.

Tributary memorials: Kung-piao, Wai-fan piao-chang.

- **DOCUMENTS ISSUED FROM THE EMPEROR.**

Commands: Ch'ih, Ch'ih-yü, Ch'üan-ch'ih, Tso-ming-ch'ih.

Decrees: Chih, Chih-shu, Chih-tz'ŭ, Ling-chih.
Edicts: Chu-yü, Shang-yü, Yü, Yü-chih.
Endorsements: Chu-pi, Chu-p'i, P'i-hung, Yü-p'i.
Instructions: Hsün-yü, Shêng-hsün.
Ordinance: Kao.
Patents: Ch'ih-ming, Kao-ming, Ts'ê.
Proclamations: Chao, Chao-huang, Chao-kao.
Rescript: Chih.
Utterances in general: Ssŭ-lun, copies: T'a-huang and T'êng-huang.

- **DOCUMENTS ENCLOSED IN OTHER DOCUMENTS.**

Chia-p'ien, Ch'ing-tan, Ch'ing-ts'ê, Huang-ts'ê, Pao-hsiao-ts'ê, P'ien, Tsou-hsiao-ts'ê.

### CHA 扎 or 剳 ORDER.

A document sent from a superior to a subordinate, GILES 127, 142; an order from a superior to a subordinate under his jurisdiction, *Tz'ŭ-hai* 辞海 (no better authority found).

Ex.: *Shih-liao hsün-k'an* 7.221, from the Grand Council to provincial officials. For 剳 cf. *Chang-ku ts'ung-pien* 2. section 2. 15a, from the Grand Council to the Ch'ang Lu salt administrator.

### CHA-FU 剳付 ORDER.

Used from provincial treasurers to prefects and magistrates, MAYERS 139; from provincial commanders-in-chief to Prefects and lower local officials, and from provincial governors to Colonels and lower military officials, *Tz'ŭ-hai* citing *Ch'ing-hui-tien* (exact reference not found).

Ex.: photographs of originals issued by WU San-kuei, *Ch'ing san-fan shih-liao* 2 and 3.

### CHA-HSING 剳行 DECLARATION.

By the *Treaty of Nanking* 1842 art. xi, Chinese high officers in the provinces were to address subordinate British officers under the term "Declaration" (Cha-hsing), but the term did not become well established and was superseded by Chao-hui; cf. also French *Treaty of Whampoa* 1844 art. XXXⅲ.

Ex.: HIRTH no. 48, Tsungli Yamên to Inspector general of Customs 1870; no. 66, same to same 1882.

**CHAO 诏 Imperial PROCLAMATION, MANDATE.**

One of the Ssǔ-lun, q. v., uttered by the emperor; see also under Kao; to announce to the people as has been the custom for emperors since the time of the Han Dynasty, GILES 470.

Ex.: *Ho-pei ti-i po-wu-yüan pan-yüeh-k'an* 河北第一博物院半月刊 (Semi-monthly Publication of the First Museum of Hopei) no. 17, May 25, 1932, a circular order of the Shun-chih period for the seizure of CHÊNG Ch'êng-kung (Koxinga); *Yung-chêng shang-yü*, K'ang-hsi 61st year, eleventh month.

**CHAO-FU 照覆[or 复] COMMUNICATION IN REPLY.**

A reply to a Chao-hui, q. v.

Ex.: *Wên-hsien ts'ung-pien* 23. sec. 2. 1b, from Lord Elgin to Prince Kung 1860.

**CHAO-HUANG 诏黄 Yellow bill bearing a PROCLAMATION.**

A copy of an imperial utterance (Ssǔ-lun) written in black on yellow paper; another name for T'êng-huang, q. v.

**CHAO-HUI 照会 COMMUNICATION.**

Addressed to an official slightly inferior in rank; MAYERS 139 gives eight situations in which it was used; the *Treaty of Nanking* 1842 art. xi declares that "Her Britannic Majesty's Chief High Officer in China shall correspond with the Chinese High Officers, both at the Capital and in the Provinces, under the term 'Communication' 照会" (Chao-hui). By degrees the term became accepted for correspondence between Chinese and foreign officials generally, irrespective of rank. The American *Treaty of Wanghsia* 1844 art. XXX provided that Chao-hui should be used by the superior authorities, the consuls, and the local officers, civil and military, of both countries. The French *Treaty of Whampoa* 1844 art.

xxxiii followed the British definition. Cf. *Ch'ing-chi ko-kuo chao-hui mu-lu* 清季各国照会目录 (Index of Communications with the Various Countries in the Late Ch'ing Period), Palace Museum, Peiping 1935.

Ex.: *Shih-liao hsün-k'an* 4. 108b, reference to a Chao-hui to the ruler of Annam in the Yung-chêng period; *Wên-hsien ts'ung-pien* 17, photograph of a Chao-hui of 1884.

### CHAO-KAO 诏诰 Imperial PROCLAMATIONS AND ORDINANCES.

Used as a general term for imperial pronouncements of several kinds, equivalents to the Ssǔ-lun, q. v. Cf. P'ÊNG Wên-chang 彭蕴章, preface to the *Nei-ko han-p'iao-ch'ien chung-shu shê-jên t'i-ming* 内阁汉票签中书舍人题名 (Names of the Secretaries of the Chinese Registry of the Grand Secretariat), edition 1861, 2. 4-5: "Proclamations and ordinances are the chief writings of the Grand Secretariat" (also quoted by HSÜ [1] 183).

### CHÊ-PÊN 折本 MEMORIAL.

Lit. folded memorial, i. e. with the corner of one sheet turned down; done by the emperor when reading it, to mark it for further treatment. Cf. *Nei-ko hsiao-chih* (A Brief Sketch of the Grand Secretariat) 3 line 9; "When the emperor looked at the memorials, if there were some on which he wished to change the draft proposal (ch'ien 签), then he would turn down one corner and send it out … " The memorials so marked were then brought in for discussion when the ministers had audience with the emperor, cf. *Chia-ch'ing hui-tien* 2. 17a line 10; 8a line 8: "After Pu-pên have been submitted, those which have not yet received an Edict or a Rescript in reply and have been folded (Chê-pên) and sent down are collected and stored according to the day."

### CHÊ-TSOU 折奏 MEMORIAL.

Same as Tsou-pên, q. v.; the terms Chê-tsou and Tsou-chê occur more often than Tsou-pên; the latter has been used in the text above for convenience, to contrast with T'i-pên.

Ex.: *Shih-liao hsün-k'an* 1 gives examples beginning with title, date, and chin-tsou 谨奏 (reverently memorializes), and ending with chin-tsou and date; *Wên-hsien ts'ung-pien* 6, third section. 1.

### CH'ÊNG 呈 REPORT, Petition.

Addressed by subordinate to superior officials; used by minor district officials to Prefects, MAYERS 140; when addressed to an official by a commoner, Petition, cf. *Fa-lü ta-tz'ŭ-shu* 法律大辞书 (Dictionary of Legal Terms), Shanghai 1936, 534; also used of presentation of documents to the emperor.

Ex.: *Ch'ing san-fan shih-liao* 2. 111 et passim; *Shih-liao hsün-k'an* 13. 445a.

### CH'ÊNG-WÊN 呈文 REPORT, Petition.

Addressed by subordinates to superiors, same as Ch'êng; cf. MAYERS 140.

Ex.: *Chang-ku ts'ung-pien* 10. 3.

### CH'I-CHÜ-CHU 起居注 CHRONICLES.

Lit. Notes of the emperor's activity—a brief day-by-day record of the emperor's actions, chiefly those of a ceremonial and routine administrative nature, nominally including both his statements and his movements, recorded by a staff of officials in a separate department (Ch'i Chü Chu Kuan 起居注馆, BRUNNERT 204: Office for Keeping a Diary of the Emperor's Movements; we prefer to follow the translation suggested by Dr. FERGUSON, *Wên-hsien lun-ts'ung* 33). These notes were sent to the Grand Secretariat at the end of each year and kept in the storehouse. They were based partly on the duplicate copies of memorials which were sent to the Grand Secretariat; see under Chieh-t'ieh. For the regulations regarding types of material to be included in the Chronicles cf. *Chia-ch'ing hui-tien shih-li* 792. 8b.

Ex.: *Shih-liao ts'ung-k'an ch'u-pien* 4 et passim; *Shih-liao hsün-k'an* 1. 16a; *Shih-liao ts'ung-pien* passim.

### CH'I-PÊN 启本 MEMORIAL.

Practically the same as T'i-pên: memorials presented to the regent of

1644-1646, after which the form was no longer used; cf. HSÜ (1) 187-188; *Tung-hua lu* June 5, 1646 (Shun-chih 6.5b, 1911 edition).

Ex.: *Ming-ch'ing shih-liao* 2.102 et passim; *Ch'ing san-fan shih-liao* 1.2.

### CHIA-P'IEN 夹片 SUPPLEMENTARY MEMORIAL.

Lit. inserted slip; submitted with a memorial for the purpose of adding to it after it had been formally concluded; but see under P'ien.

Ex.: *Shih-liao hsün-k'an* 10.350b.

### CHIAO-CHIH 交旨 DESPATCH.

Lit. to transfer a Rescript: from ministers of state to subordinate departments, ordering that certain action be taken in accordance with an imperial decision; cf. *Kuo-hsüeh lun-wên so-yin* 国学论文索引 (Index to Sinological Articles) 3.113: "... after the ministers have received the imperial will, they transmit it to their subordinates to be carried out accordingly—this is called Chiao-chih."

Ex.: *Tung-fang tsa-chih* 东方杂志 (The Eastern Miscellany), sixth year (1909) no. 3, 13.

### CHIAO-P'IEN 交片 SHORT DESPATCH.

From ministers of state (Grand Councillors) to other departments; see also under P'ien; cf. TÊNG Chih-ch'êng 196.

Ex.: *Wên-hsien ts'ung-pien* 14. section 2.2.

### CHIEH-T'IEH 揭帖 a. placard, b. duplicate COPY.

a. In common parlance, a placard—usually of a libellous or seditious character; also an accusation, a plaint (GILES 1455).

Ex.: *Shih-liao hsün-k'an* 5.143b, copy of a seditious placard. This meaning appears to have been used also technically in the procedure, cf. *Chia-ch'ing hui-tien* 2.6: "To T'ung-pên... on which there is writing in improper form or a seal which is not clear or a date which is erased and rewritten, the Transmission Office should attach a placard 加揭帖."

b. Duplicate copy of a memorial of any kind; according to the

*Collected Statutes* three such copies were to be made, at least of T'ung-pên; cf. *Chia-ch'ing hui-tien* 54. 13b: "Three copies accompany a memorial 随本之揭帖三; one is kept at the (Transmission) Office, one is sent to the Board (in question), one is sent to the Section (of the Office of Scrutiny of the Censorate, i. e. the particular Section concerned with the Board in question). Five days after a T'i-pên has been sealed and sent to the Grand Secretariat (from the Transmission Office), the duplicate copies for the Board and the Section are handed to the Superintendents of Military Posts for distribution." The existence of these duplicate copies necessitated repeated efforts at secrecy; and it was ordered that the copies should on no account be distributed until five days after the original T'i-pên had been sent to the Grand Secretariat; cf. *Chia-ch'ing hui-tien shih-li* 781. 7b, memorial sanctioned in 1734. In addition to the copies already mentioned, in 1729 it was decided that "for all T'i-pên and Tsou-pên of the various provinces one additional copy (Chieh-t'ieh) shall be written and sent to the Chronicles Office (Ch'i Chü Chu Kuan, BRUNNERT 204: Office for Keeping a Diary of the Emperor's Movements). After it has been used in compiling the records, the copy shall then be sent to the Grand Secretariat for preservation"; cf. *Kuang-hsü hui-tien shih-li* 14. 35b (by count; next to last page of the chüan); HSÜ (1) 188.

Ex.: *Wên-hsien ts'ung-pien* 13 passim; *Ming-ch'ing shih-liao* 1, 2 passim. Chieh-t'ieh end with the formula "In addition to preparing a T'i-pên (Tsou-pên, Ch'i-pên), there is a dutifully prepared copy; a required copy" 除具题外 (or 除具奏外, or 启外), 理合具揭, 须至揭帖者. Apparently as a development of the above, we find that reports of legal cases were called Hsing-pu 刑部 chieh-t'ieh; cf. *Fa-lü ta-tz'ŭ-shu* 1426. There were also Ping-pu 兵部 Chieh-t'ieh; cf. *Wên-hsien ts'ung-pien* 13. 3.

**CHIEN 柬 LETTER.**

Lit. a slip of paper; chien-shu 柬书 a note, a letter—written on a card, GILES 1668.

Ex.: *Shih-liao hsün-k'an* 2. 61b, 63b, from the ruler of Annam to

Chinese governor-general regarding a boundary settlement.

### CHIH 旨 Imperial RESCRIPT, imperial DECREE.

Fundamentally, the imperial will; hence, the imperial decision on a memorial, recorded in red ink on the original. In practice it appears usually to be translated as Rescript when found attached to the memorial, Decree when there is no reference to the original memorial. It differs from an Edict (yü) in that the latter is throughout a separate document; differs from an Endorsement (p'i) usually by giving specific rather than routine orders regarding the subject matter of the memorial. In length a Rescript is usually shorter than an Edict, longer than an Endorsement. Rescripts were drafted by the Grand Secretariat, Edicts by the Grand Council; cf. *Shu-yüan chi-lüeh* 22. 2b.

Ex.: Decrees (chih) published separately: *Ch'ing-tai wên-tzu-yü tang* 2. section 4. 3, section 5. 4; 4. section 3. 4, section 7. 4.

### CHIH 制 Imperial DECREE.

One of the imperial utterances (Ssŭ-lun), q. v.; examination lists, patents, and the like began with the phrase "Having received from Heaven the imperial succession, the Emperor Decrees as follows…" 奉天承运皇帝制曰.

Ex.: *Wên-hsien ts'ung-pien* 14. photographic reproduction.

### CHIH-HUI 知会 COMMUNICATION.

Lit. to notify, to inform; used in correspondence between government offices; similar to I-hui, q. v., except that the latter appears usually to send documents as well as to inform about a subject, whereas Chih-hui merely informs.

Ex.: *Ming-ch'ing shih-liao* 7. 699, from the Board of Ceremony to the Inspectorate of the Grand Secretariat (Chi Ch'a Fang); *Wên-hsien ts'ung-pien* 21. section 2. 1 from the Imperial Household to the Board of Ceremony.

### CHIH-SHU 制书 Imperial DECREE.

An imperial command, GILES 1910; lettre du souverain,

COUVREUR 859; Ta-ch'ing lü-li an-yü 大清律例按语 (Commentary on the *Ta-ch'ing lü-li*) 1847 edition, preface by HUANG Ên-t'ung 黄恩彤 3.4 chih-shu section: "The words of the Son of Heaven are called Chih; Shu is then the recording of his words, as in Chao 诏, Ch'ih 敕, Yü 谕, Cha; matters which have been memorialized, sanctioned, and put into practice are not in this category."

**CHIH-TZ'U 制辞 Imperial DECREE.**

Appears to be practically the same as Chih alone, q. v.

**CH'IH 敕, 勅, or 勑 IMPERIAL COMMAND.**

One of the imperial utterances, see Ssǔ-lun.

**CH'IH-MING 敕命 PATENT BY COMMAND.**

Used to confer titles of honor on officials below the fifth rank, and others; cf. *Chia-ch'ing hui-tien* 2.4b: "The conferring of titles by imperial command on the dependencies of the empire (wai-fan, i. e. in Mongolia, Tibet, etc.), the extending of favor and conferring of titles of honor on officials of the sixth rank and below, and hereditary nobility not in perpetuity (i. e. gradually diminished), is (done by) a patent by command." It must follow a fixed form, according to the rank involved.

Ex.: *Wên-hsien ts'ung-pien* 14, photographic reproduction.

**CH'IH-SHU 敕书 Letters PATENT.**

Similar to Kao-ch'ih, q. v.

**CH'IH-YÜ 敕谕 COMMAND-EDICT (?).**

Used to depute officials and to issue special Edicts; there are many different forms, among which are two sub-types: a. a Nominative Command (Tso-ming ch'ih), and b. a Transmitted Command (Ch'üan-ch'ih); cf. *Chia-ch'ing hui-tien* 2.4b: "Instructions and announcements to the dependencies of the empire (wai-fan) and officials in the provinces by means of Nominative Commands and Transmitted Commands are called Command Edicts"; *Ch'ien-lung hui-tien* 2.5: "(In appointing) officials to posts outside the capital—to governor-general, governors, literary chancellors, salt controllers, superintendents of the Imperial manufactories, provincial commanders-in-chief, brigade-generals, et al., a Nominative Command is composed and issued; to provincial financial commissioners, judicial commissioners, intendants, grain intendants, and colonels, lieutenant, colonels, and majors, a transmitted command only is given."

Ex.: *Shih-liao ts'ung-k'an ch'u-pien* 9.1.

## CHING-PAO 京报 PEKING GAZETTE.

See under T'ang-pao.

## CH'ING-TAN 清单 LIST, INVENTORY, etc.

A list of items; a general term—the list may deal with any subject and may be used in any way, sometimes appended to other documents and submitted to the emperor.

Ex.: *Wên-hsien ts'ung-pien* 14. last section; *Shih-liao hsün-k'an* 5.159b, introduced by the phrase chi-k'ai 计开 (as follows).

## CH'ING-TS'Ê 清册 or 青册 GREEN BOOK.

Accounts, lists, reports, and such documents appended to memorials and submitted in yellow binding to the emperor (i.e. Huang-ts'ê, q.v.) were copied and submitted to the metropolitan office concerned in a blue-green binding, whence the name Ch'ing-ts'ê. Thus Green Books were usually copies of Yellow Books, cf. HSÜ(1). 190. Their origin (?) is explained as follows: in 1651 a Metropolitan Censor memorialized that "the ministers of the central government control the expenditure of the national revenue, and the ministers of the provinces control its income. When the amount of income is not clear, then the amount of expenditure is obscure. It is requested that beginning in 1651 the office of the financial commissioner of each province should calculate the revenue of the entire province, dividing it into various items, and make a bound volume for submission to the governor-general, governor, and judicial commissioner of the province for their examination and comparison; this should respectfully be copied into a Yellow Book and the governor should join (with the governor-general) in memorializing the total amount submitting (the Yellow Book) along with the memorial for the emperor's inspection. There should also be made a Green Book, which should be sent in a despatch to the various offices concerned at the capital, for examination and checking. Then it may be possible to put a stop to the provincial authorities' deceitful concealment, and it may also be possible to examine into the incongruities of the metropolitan authorities' (accounts)." Cf. *Tung-hua lu*, 1911 edition Shun-chih 16. 17 line 4 (August 1, 1651).

Ex.: *Shih-liao ts'ung-k'an ch'u-pien* 7. sec. 2, sec. 3.

**CHU-PI 朱笔 THE VERMILION PEN, or ENDORSEMENT.**

Same as Chu-p'i, q. v.

**CHU-P'I 朱批 VERMILION ENDORSEMENT.**

A conventional term for an Endorsement or comment (see under p'i) written on a memorial by the emperor's own hand, as distinct from P'i-hung (q. v.) made by the officials of the Grand Secretariat—both being in red ink.

Ex. *Shih-liao hsün-k'an* 1. 20b (in text), 21a (at end).

**CHU-YÜ 朱谕 VERMILION EDICTS.**

Copies of imperial utterances, written in red on yellow paper, see under T'êng-huang.

**CH'ÜAN-CH'IH 傳敕 TRANSMITTED COMMAND.**

From the emperor to lower provincial officials and the dependencies of the empire, see under Ch'ih-yü.

**CH'ÜAN-YÜ 傳谕 TRANSMITTED EDICT.**

Sent from the Grand Council to lower provincial officials and embodying in its text important imperial commands, a form of T'ing-chi, q. v.

Ex.: *Chang-ku ts'ung-pien* 7. 43b; *Shih-liao hsün-k'an* 6. 192.

**FU 覆 interchangeable with 复 IN REPLY.**

Combined with the names of various kinds of documents to indicate a reply to the document received, as Chao-fu, q. v., Tzŭ-fu (cf, *Shih-liao hsün-k'an* 2.64a), etc.

**FU-PÊN 副本 COPY, duplicate of a T'i-pên.**

A copy made at the Grand Secretariat for preservation at the Office of Imperial Historiography (Huang Shih Ch'êng) after the imperial Endorsement (copied onto the original T'i-pên in red ink) had been copied onto it in black ink; cf. HSÜ (1) 188; *Chia-ch'ing hui-tien* 2.6a: "For all memorials a duplicate is prepared: in addition to the original copy (chêng-pên 正本) of T'ung-pên and Pu-pên, a duplicate (Fu-pên) is copied out. After the original memorial has obtained a Rescript, it is sent to the Section (k'o, i.e. one of the Six Sections of the Censorate). The duplicate is stored for reference."

**FU-P'IEN 附片 SUPPLEMENTARY MEMORIAL.**

A memorial (Tsou-pên) sent under the same cover with another, usually on a different although related subject; but see under P'ien.

Ex.: those printed in *Shih-liao hsün-k'an* 4.130 et passim, are often headed p'ien, begin with the character tsai 再 (further), and are referred to in the conclusion as Fu-p'ien; *op. cit.* 10.363b is headed Fu-p'ien and concluded 謹附片具奏.

**FU-TSOU 附奏 SUPPLEMENTARY MEMORIAL.**

Same as Fu-p'ien, q.v.

**HAN 函 LETTER.**

An example of the breakdown of the traditional terminology; in general, a letter of any kind; GILES 3809 gives a dozen uses. In the later nineteenth century used by the Tsung-li ya-mên in its correspondence with other offices, often combined as mi-han 密函 (secret letter), hsin-han 信函 (letter), or tzǔ-han 咨函 (despatch-letter).

Ex.: *Ch'ou-pan I-wu shih-mo*, T'ung-chih section 50.28b line 7, mi-han from the Ya-mên to high provincial authorities; id. line 10, the text of the letter referred to is headed hsin-han; id. 52.24a, tzǔ-han; *Chang-ku ts'ung-pien* 7, sec. 1.42a gives a document sent from the Grand Council in 1793 and designated han by the compiler.

**HSIANG-WÊN 详文 Detailed REPORT.**

Addressed by a subordinate to a superior, MAYERS 141 gives situations for its use.

Ex.: *Wên-hsien ts'ung-pien* 22, sec. 5.32b, a report of the British consul at Tientsin to LI Hung-chang; FAN Tsêng-hsiang 樊增祥, *Fan-shan chêng-shu* 樊山政书 (My Writings on Administration), Nanking 1910, 2.24.

**HSÜN-YÜ 训谕 INSTRUCTIONS AND EDICTS.**

Not a type of document; used to refer to Edicts in general.

Ex.: *Chang-ku ts'ung-pien* 1, sec. 4.1; *Shih-liao hsün-k'an* 39.408a line 4.

**HUANG-TS'Ê 黄册 YELLOW BOOK.**

Also called Pao-hsiao-ts'ê and sometimes Tsou-hsiao-ts'ê, q. v. Tax accounts, construction reports, examination results, and such documents submitted to the emperor along with memorials, i. e. in a manner similar to Western "enclosures," were normally bound in yellow paper or silk, whence the name; see under Ch'ing-ts'ê. Yellow Books were thus key documents in routine administration; they dealt with a wide variety of subjects and were of several different kinds; SHAN Shih-yüan (2) 272-275 lists some 60 different categories, classified by content, among those preserved in the Palace archives. WANG Chêng-kung 王正功, *Chung-shu tien-ku hui-chi* 中书典故汇纪 (Collected Notes on the History and Regulations of the Grand Secretariat) 1916 edition, 3.36b line 8, states that "the Yellow Books which are submitted along with the memorials of the various metropolitan officials and provincial governor-general and governors are given to the Records Office to be preserved in the Great Storehouse (of the Grand Secretariat)." Most of them were submitted annually, some monthly and others triennially, and it has been estimated that the offices at the capital must have received every year well over 2,000 volumes. Unfortunately these volumes appear to have been less valuable than memorials, from the point of view of the official historian, and only some 13,000 are now said to survive in the Palace archives; see HSÜ (1) 190-194.

Ex.: *Shih-liao ts'ung-pien*, 二集, 3.

**HUNG-PÊN 红本 ENDORSED MEMORIAL.**

Lit. red memorial, so called because it bore an imperial Endorsement written on it in red ink by the officials of the Grand Secretariat after imperial approval of the form of Endorsement; see text, section 2. Two kinds of Hung-pên are distinguished, those submitted through the Grand Secretariat and those submitted through the Imperial Household Department (Nei Wu Fu). SHAN Shih-yüan (1) 150-151 quotes the passage in the *Collected Statutes* cited in note 33, which defines Hung-pên as T'i-pên endorsed in red, and then adds his own observation that Hung-pên is another name for T'i-pên because they bear the memorialist's seal, which would be in red, while Po-pên, q. v., is another name for Tsou-pên because the latter do not bear the memorialist's seal. This explanation seems possible but improbable because it gives the term Hung-pên two meanings, one of which includes the other (i. e. T'i-pên as a class include all T'i-pên endorsed in red). SHAN himself adheres in a previous article (2) 271 to the definition we prefer, given in the *Collected Statutes*. The subject deserves clarification.

**I-HUI 移会 COMMUNICATION.**

Used in correspondence between government offices; similar to Chih-hui, except that it appears to imply the sending of documents as well as information.

Ex.: *Ming-ch'ing shih-liao* 7. 685-698, from the Board of War to the Archives Office, and also to the Inspectorate, of the Grand Secretariat.

**I-TZU 移咨 COMMUNICATION.**

Between officials of equal or approximately equal rank; cf. GILES 12, 342.

Ex.: *Shih-liao hsün-k'an* 1. 19a line 4; *Chia-ch'ing hui-tien shih-li*

12. 22a, from Hanlin Academy to Grand Secretariat.

### I-WÊN 移文 COMMUNICATION.

Between officials of equal or approximately equal rank, cf. MAYERS 138.

### KAO 稿 ROUGH DRAFT.

Not a technical term but used to designate some published items.

Ex.: *Chang-ku ts'ung-pien* 1. sec. 1, drafts of Edicts of the K'ang-hsi period; *Shih-liao hsün-k'an* 4. 108b, draft of a communication to Annam.

### KAO 诰 ORDINANCE.

One of the imperial utterances, see Ssǔ-lun; not greatly different from Chao (proclamation); cf. *Ch'ien-lung hui-tien* 2. 2: "to announce to the empire is called Chao, to make manifest instructions is called Kao." Judging by the documents remaining in the archives, however, HSÜ (1) 184 concludes that, in general, proclamations emanating from the emperor were called Chao, while those from the father of the emperor, the Great Empress Dowager, and the Empress Dowager, of which there are very few remaining, were called Kao. Three of the twenty-five imperial seals were used for issuing ordinances: to ministers and officials, for foreign countries, and the whole empire, respectively; cf. *Chiao-t'ai-tien pao-p'u* 交泰殿宝谱 (Imperial Seals in the Chiao-t'ai Hall), Peiping 1929.

### KAO-CH'IH 诰敕 PATENT.

A collective term for Kao and Ch'ih considered together; credentials, letters patent (entitles the holder to use Ch'ih-ming, by imperial command), GILES 1943; see under Ch'ih-shu; cf. *Chia-ch'ing hui-tien* 2. 21b: "the Patent Office (Kao Ch'ih Fang 诰敕房) has charge of the receiving and issuing of patents; it investigates into their selection and drafting and the form in which it would be best to write them out." An imperial seal for conferring patents by command was used to seal Kao-ch'ih; cf. *Chiao-t'ai-tien pao-p'u*, cited above under Kao.

**KAO-MING** 诰命 **PATENT BY ORDINANCE.**

Used to confer titles of honor on officials of the fifth rank and above, and others; cf. *Chia-ch'ing hui-tien* 2. 4b: "to extend favor and confer titles of honor on officials of the fifth rank and above, and hereditary nobility which may be handed down in perpetuity (i. e. without diminution) is (done by) a patent by ordinance."It must follow a fixed form, according to the rank involved. See Ch'ih-ming.

**K'OU-KUNG** 口供 **VERBAL DEPOSITION.**

Not a technical term, but used to designate material of the type indicated; viva voce evidence, GILES 6572.

Ex.: *Shih-liao hsün-k'an* 8. 281.

**KU-TIEH** 故牒 **ORDER.**

From superior to subordinate officials; cf. MAYERS 139 for typical situations.

**KUAN-WÊN** 关文 **ORDER.**

From superiors to subordinates; cf. MAYERS 140 for typical situations; GILES 6368, a passport; no published examples found.

**KUNG-HAN** 公函 **COMMUNICATION.**

Lit. official letters; a very general term, for despatches between independent departments of government; see Han; cf. *Fa-lü ta-tz'ǔ-shu* 法律大辞书 158: "Public documents used in communication between administrative organs which are not subordinate one to another, are called Kung-han."

**KUNG-PIAO** 贡表 **TRIBUTARY MEMORIAL.**

The memorials submitted to the emperor together with tribute objects from the rulers of the seven tributary states adjoining China, viz. Korea, Liu Ch'iu, Annam, Nan-chang 南掌 (or Lao-huo 老挝 on the southern border of Yünnan), Siam, Sulu, Burma, as listed in *Kuang-hsü hui-tien* 39. 2.

Ex.: *Ku-kung yüeh-k'an* 故宫月刊 (*The Palace Monthly*) no. 5, Jan. 1930, photograph of a list of tribute from Annam.

**KUNG-TAN 供单 DEPOSITION.**

Same as Kung-tz'u, q. v.

Ex.: *Shih-liao hsün-k'an* 34. 246, 250.

**KUNG-TZ'U 供词 DEPOSITION.**

Not a type of document; similar to K'ou-kung; the evidence in a case; GILES 6572.

Ex.: *Shih-liao hsün-k'an* 34. 232b, recording both questions and answers in evidence; *I-wu shih-mo*, Tao-kuang section 68. 37a, deposition of an official.

**KUO-SHU 国书 National letter, CREDENTIALS.**

A document given to (the ruler of) a foreign country; in the nineteenth century and later, diplomatic credentials.

Ex.: *Shih-liao ts'ung-k'an*, ch'u-pien 1. sec. 2 a letter from the Emperor T'ai-tsung (1627-1643) to the king of Korea; *Wên-hsien ts'ung-pien* 8. 12b; *Chung-ying-fa wai-chiao tz'ŭ-tien* 中英法外交辞典 (Dictionary of Words and Phrases of International Law and Diplomacy in English and French with Chinese Translations), Ministry of Foreign Affairs 1925, 152-159.

**LING 令 ORDER.**

A general term, not important as a type of Ch'ing document; a modern name for official documents used in proclaiming laws, appointing and dismissing officials, and generally for commands to subordinates, cf. *Fa-lü ta-tz'ŭ-shu* 253.

**LING-CHIH 令旨 DECREE.**

Issued from the emperor during the early years of the dynasty, apparently similar to ordinary chih 旨.

Ex.: *Shih-liao ts'ung-pien* 4, of date 1644 and later.

**LIU-TS'AO CHANG-TSOU 六曹章奏 MEMORIALS.**

Lit. memorials of the six (i. e. Boards) officials; another name for the Shih-shu, q. v.

Ex.: *Shih-liao ts'ung-pien* 4; *Shih-liao ts'ung-k'an*, ch'u-pien 6, summaries of the various memorials of the Six Boards.

**LU-SHU 录书 COPIED MATERIALS.**

Summaries of Hung-pên kept at the Six Sections of the Censorate; see under Shih-shu.

**LUN-YIN 纶音 IMPERIAL UTTERANCES.**

Lit. silken sounds, i. e. the emperor's words, see under Ssŭ-lun.

**P'AI 牌 ORDER.**

From superior to subordinate officials; MAYERS 140.

Ex.: *Ch'ing san-fan shih-liao* 5, photograph of a ling-p'ai.

**P'AI-P'IAO 牌票 ORDER.**

From superior to subordinate officials, same as P'ai; cf. MAYERS 140.

**PAO-HSIAO-TS'Ê 报销册 REPORT, etc.**

A common type of Huang-ts'ê, q. v.

**PÊN-CHANG 本章 MEMORIAL.**

general term for T'i-pên and Tsou-chang 奏章 considered together.

**P'I 批 ENDORSEMENT, COMMENT.**

A word of broad meaning used technically with reference to the notations made by an official on a memorial presented to him. In general such notations might be either comment or instructions, the latter probably couched in administrative jargon. Notations of the latter type, when made by or on behalf of the emperor, correspond in a general way to the notations made by Western rulers, cabinet ministers, and others, on the back or on the docket of a diplomatic document. In China the term was also used of the reply made by an official to a subordinate; GILES 9048 gives half a dozen such compounds. But the typical imperial notations, such as the set phrase Chih-tao-liao (Noted) or Kai-pu chih-tao (Let the Board in question be informed), are mere signals for administrative action, not comments or replies, and we have therefore suggested the translation Endorsement.

**P'I-HUNG 批红 RED ENDORSEMENT (lit. endorsed in red).**

The act of writing onto a memorial in red ink the Endorsement which has been approved by the emperor; unlike Vermilion Endorsements (Chu-p'i), a Red Endorsement was not added by the emperor's own hand; see text section 2.

### PIAO-CHANG 表章 TRIBUTARY MEMORIAL.

A memorial to the emperor; under the Ch'ing often a memorial from the ruler of a tributary state; see Kung-piao.

Ex.: *Ming-ch'ing shih-liao* 7. 641-664, from the king of Korea to the emperor on a variety of subjects; *Ho-pei ti-i po-wu-yüan pan-yüeh-k'an* (Semi-monthly Publication of the First Museum of Hopei) 2. 1 (Oct. 10, 1931), photograph of Korean Piao-chang of the Ch'ien-lung period.

### P'IEN 片 SHORT SUPPLEMENTARY.

Lit. a single sheet or slip of paper, which may be contrasted with chê 折 as in Tsou-chê meaning a folded paper, i. e. a longer document. We are in doubt as to the exact implication of this term. In the phrases Chia-p'ien, Fu-p'ien, and Tsou-p'ien (q. v.) it sometimes appears to indicate an additional statement submitted to the emperor along with a memorial; but it also denotes a brief memorial, or "minute," in answer to a Rescript or on a simple topic (so also with Ch'êng-p'ien, a supplementary or brief report). The problem is complicated by the fact that items headed P'ien are published without any indication as to whether they did or did not originally accompany another document.

Ex.: P'ien submitted in response to a Rescript, *Chang-ku ts'ung-pien* 1. 12b, 2. 17a, 7. 28b, 8. 49a-b, et passim. P'ien which appear as short informal memorials, *op. cit.* 7. 42b, 44a, 8. 58b, 59b, 62a, et passim; *Shih-liao hsün-k'an* 8. 277a et passim prints P'ien of the Grand Council (Chün-chi-ch'u p'ien) which seem similar to Western minutes; id. 13. 471 gives both a memorial and the P'ien which accompanied it. The problem deserves further attention.

### PING 稟 REPORT, PETITION.

A general term, used technically of a document to a superior from a minor official or a common citizen.

Ex.: *Ch'ing san-fan shih-liao* 3. 272 et passim; *Shih-liao hsün-k'an* 39. 424b.

### PING-CH'ÊNG 禀呈 REPRESENTATION.

The French *Treaty of Whampoa* 1844 art. xxxiii provided that French and Chinese merchants or other non-official persons should use the form Representation in addressing officials of the other country. We have found no examples of its use.

### PING-MING 禀明 REPRESENTATION.

By the *Treaty of Nanking* 1842 art. xi, merchants and others not in official positions, either Chinese or British, were to address the British and Chinese officials, respectively, under the term Representation. The American *Treaty of Wanghsia* 1844 art. xxx made a similar provision.

### PO-PÊN 白本 UNENDORSED MEMORIAL.

Lit. white memorial, as distinct from Hung-pên (red memorial) on which an imperial endorsement had been written in red ink; hence Po-pên are memorials (T'i-pên) which have not been seen by the emperor, cf. HSÜ (1) 186, SHAN Shih-yüan (1) 150-151. For further discussion, see under Hung-pên.

### PU-PÊN 部本 MEMORIAL.

Memorials of the T'i-pên type from the offices of government at the capital (pu-yüan); see text sec. 2; cf. *Chia-ch'ing hui-tien* 2. 6a: "Memorials from the Six Boards and memorials from the offices of the various departments, palaces, courts, and superintendencies (in Peking), after they have been submitted to the Six Boards, are in general called Pu-pên." According to HSÜ (1)186, they were submitted in both Chinese and Manchu versions.

### SHANG-YÜ 上谕 IMPERIAL EDICT.

A rather general term, used to refer to Edicts (yü), and sometimes also to Rescripts (chih).

Ex.: *Shih-liao hsün-k'an* 6. 178b-185. six examples beginning with date and "the Grand Secretariat has received an Imperial Edict" (Nei-ko fêng shang-yü); *op. cit.* 7. 237, two examples headed Shang-yü and beginning with date and "a Rescript has been received" (fêng chih).

### SHÊN 申 REPORT.

Addressed by subordinates to superior officials; GILES 9816 gives half a dozen compounds, the more important of which are given below.

Ex.: *Ch'ing san-fan shih-liao* 3. 253 et passim.

### SHÊN-CH'ÊN 申陈 STATEMENT.

By the *Treaty of Nanking* 1842 art. Xi, subordinate British officers were to address Chinese high officers in the provinces under the term Statement (Shên-ch'êng); but the term did not become firmly established, and was superseded by Chao-hui. The American *Treaty of Wanghsia* 1844 art. xxx provided that Shên-ch'êng should be used by inferior officers of either government in addressing superior officers of the other. The French *Treaty of Whampoa* 1844 art. xxxiii followed the British definition and called it "exposé."

### SHÊN-CH'ÊNG 申称 TO REPORT.

See under Shên.

Ex.: HIRTH no. 48, Inspector general of Customs to Tsungli Yamên 1870.

### SHÊN-WÊN 申文 REPORT.

See under Shên; cf. MAYERS 140 for uses.

### SHIH-SHU 史书 HISTORICAL MATERIALS.

Copies of the summaries (T'ieh-huang) of endorsed memorials. Cf. *Kuang-hsü hui-tien* 69. 3b: "All memorials that are received back (by the Six Sections of the Censorate) are added to the Shih-shu and Lu-shu (q. v.) ... After Hung-pên have been sent for copying, two other copies are taken by the Section (k'o). Those presented to the official historians to be recorded are called Shih-shu; those stored at the Section for compilation are called Lu-shu. Both are proofread and stamped with a seal; the Shih-shu are sent to the Grand Secretariat, and the Lu-shu are kept at the Section." According to SHAN Shih-yüan (1) 151, the Shih-shu now preserved in the storehouse of the Grand Secretariat are all copies of the T'ieh-huang (Summaries) of Hung-pên, not of the Hung-pên themselves in full. HSÜ (1) 188 agrees that Shih-shu are summaries of Hung-pên and so form a detailed index to the latter; in the Ming period, he adds, Shih-shu were called Liu-ts'ao chang-tsou (q. v.) and Lu-shu were called Lu-su 录疏.

### SSǓ-LUN 丝纶 IMPERIAL UTTERANCES.

Lit. silken cords; cf. the *Li-chi* 礼记 (Book of Rites) 30, Tzǔ-i 缁衣 (COUVREUR 2. 517): "the prince's words are like silk threads, they issue forth like cords" (GILES, s. v). A general term for Decrees, proclamations, ordinances, and commands emanating from the emperor; cf. *Chia-ch'ing hui-tien* 2. 4a: "The emperor's words (Lun-yin) which are transmitted to the people are called decree (chih), proclamation or mandate (Chao), ordinance (Kao), or command (Ch'ih); all are drafted in proper form and submitted to the emperor. Whenever there is a great ceremonial observance to be promulgated to all the officials, then the form Decree (chih-tz'ǔ) is used; whenever there is a great political matter to be announced to the ministers and the people and to be handed down as a rule of law, then the proclamation or ordinance is used... All are drafted ahead of time and submitted to the emperor, to reverently await the imperial decision..."

### T'A-HUANG 拓黄 YELLOW PRINTS.

Printed copies of imperial utterances (Ssǔ-lun), see also under T'êng-huang; according to HSÜ (1) 185, imperial utterances "which were printed on yellow paper from wood-cut blocks were called Yellow Prints, such as the Command-Edicts (Ch'ih-yü) which were issued to the officials who had audience with the emperor in the early Ch'ing period."

### TANG 档 ARCHIVE.

Also Tang-an 档案 and Tang-tzǔ 档子, used extensively in compounds designating various archival collections. The ramifications of the Ch'ing archives are indicated in the literature cited in note 7; no attempt is made to comprehend the subject in this paper.

**T'ANG-PAO 塘报 PEKING GAZETTE.**

Lit. courier news, also called Ching-pao, Ti-ch'ao, Ti-pao, etc. Not a type of document but one of the chief means of dissemination of important documents into the provinces, consisting of copies of documents sent from the capital to the high provincial officials for their information; sometimes printed, and sometimes reprinted in the provinces for further circulation; also made up and distributed by private firms. The term Peking Gazette thus is a generic term, including many forms, both official and non-official. On T'ang-pao see our article "On the Transmission of Ch'ing Documents," *HJAS* 4, 35-36. The most thorough account of the subject in general is R. S. BRITTON, *The Chinese Periodical Press* 1800-1912, Shanghai 1933, 7-17, which also reproduces facsimiles. The Peking Gazette is an ideal subject for an extensive monograph.

Ex.: BRITTON, *op. cit.*; *Ch'ing san-fan shih-liao* 3. 259 et passim; *Ming-ch'ing shih-liao* 2. 116 et passim. We take this occasion to present a document not otherwise available:

A memorial of August 5, 1842, presented by the governor of Chekiang, LIU Yün-k'o 刘韵珂 and the acting governor, PIEN Shih-yün 卞士云 describes the private distribution of the Peking Gazette. It had been complained that copies were obtained and examined regularly by the British, who consequently knew the plans of the empire. "We would humbly observe that the *Capital News* (Ching-pao 京报) respectfully copies the Edicts and Rescripts which are publicly issued from the emperor every day, and it also inserts memorials (Tsou-chê) from the ministers at the capital and in the provinces. Its original purpose was to acquaint the provincial authorities in detail with the affairs of the empire. All matters with which it is concerned can be dealt with forthwith; for this reason it has not been forbidden. But all councils of state are

uniformly inserted in it in detail; it is essential that it be kept secret...
(Measures would therefore be taken to apprehend the traitors who conveyed it to the English) ... As to the *Capital News* which your servants read every day, it is copied and sent out by the superintendent of Courier Posts stationed at the capital, and relayed by the superintendent stationed at the provincial capital. But we have heard that aside from this there are also a *Liang-hsiang News* (良乡报 i. e. from Liang-hsiang Hsien in Shun-t'ien Fu, Chihli) and a *Cho-chou News* 涿州报 i. e. from Cho-chou, also in Shun-t'ien Fu, Chihli). The matters which they publish are comparatively more detailed than the superintendent of the Posts' News; and their transmission is also relatively faster. We hear that at Liang-hsiang and Cho-chou there are men who manage this business; and many of the officials and gentry at great expense buy and read these Gazettes. Consequently in the affairs of each province there are things of which the officials have not yet been informed and which others know ahead of them, and there are also things which the officials do not know and others do know. We would humbly observe that the transmission of the *Capital News* to the rebellious barbarians surely is the deed of traitorous natives in the other provinces, and it is to be feared that the men who copy and send it for them also are not limited to one place...
(Measures should therefore be taken first at the capital itself)."
*Documents Supplementary to the I-wu shih-mo, Based on the Chün Chi Ch'u Archives*, Tsing Hua University Library, no. 1504-1505 [a ms.], courtesy of Dr. T. F. TSIANG.

**T'ÊNG-HUANG 誊黄 YELLOW COPIES.**

Copies of imperial utterances (Ssŭ-lun); GILES 10,884 gives the colloquial definition "yellow notices, in Chinese and Manchu, placarded in the street to announce some joyful event such as a general pardon, remission of the land-tax, etc."; HSÜ (1) 185 gives the technical explanation—"proclamations and ordinances, command-edicts (Ch'ih-yü), and palace examination lists [and other types of imperial utterances] were all written in black characters on yellow paper and were called Yellow Copies or Yellow Proclamations (chao-huang). Those which used yellow paper and vermilion characters were called Vermilion Edicts (Chu-yü)." See T'a-huang.

**TI-CH'AO 邸抄 PEKING GAZETTE.**

See under T'ang-pao.

**TI-PAO 邸报 PEKING GAZETTE.**

See under T'ang-pao.

**T'I-PÊN 题本 MEMORIAL.**

Memorials to the emperor usually on routine public business and submitted through the Grand Secretariat, as contrasted with Tsou-pên, and Ch'i-pên, q. v. T'i-pên as a general type were further differentiated, according to their origin or the treatment they received, as T'ung-pên or Pu-pên, Hung-pên or Po-pên, and the like. The evolution of the T'i-pên is summarized in the text of section 2 note 10. We summarize below SHAN Shih-k'uei's description of the regulations regarding the size and format of the T'i-pên (page references to his sources are inserted where possible):

The T'i-pên of the Ming and Ch'ing periods were not the same size. The Ming T'i-pên were generally smaller than the Tsou-pên, but in the Ch'ing period they were generally larger.

Since the Ming Tsou-pên were said to be one foot three inches from top to bottom (Chinese measurement), and the T'i-pên were said to be smaller, the latter must have measured about one foot (i. e. 14 English inches). T'i-pên of the Ch'ing period measured 7.9 inches (Chinese) vertically and 3.6 inches horizontally. Tsou-pên of the Ch'ing period measured 7 inches vertically and 3.4 inches horizontally. Thus both types of documents appear to have been smaller in the Ch'ing than in the Ming period. On the Ch'ing T'i-pên, the T'ang-k'ou (i. e. the space available for writing, exclusive of margins at top and bottom) was 5.3 inches. An Edict of Aug. 17, 1652 (printed in *Tung-hua lu*), ordered that all memorials conform to the proper size.

The regulations for writing T'i-pên were on the whole the same in the Ming and Ch'ing periods. "In both cases, each page had six columns, and each column twenty characters. But in the Ming form there were twenty spaces (in each column); the ordinary text was written in (the lower) eighteen spaces, with the upper two spaces for honorary elevation of characters. The Ch'ing form also had twenty spaces, with ordinary text in (the lower) eighteen spaces and three spaces for honorary elevation (i. e. one space above the column)—this was a point of difference." It was settled in 1651 (*Ta-ch'ing hui-tien shih-li* 1042. 1) that references within a memorial to the imperial palaces should be elevated one space; to his majesty the emperor, an imperial Edict, a Rescript, or anything imperial—two spaces; to heaven and earth, the ancestral temples, the imperial tombs, temple names of emperors, and Edicts and Rescripts of imperial ancestors—three spaces, hence protruding one space into the upper margin.

In 1528 it had been settled that the chief offices, brevet titles, surnames and given names of officials should all be written in one column, with no limit as to the number of characters; and the Ch'ing followed this rule. In both cases the official title and personal name of the memorialist were followed by the phrase "reverently presents a T'i-pên regarding" a certain subject 謹題为某事.

At the end came the phrase "reverently presented, requesting the imperial will"謹題请旨.

The number of characters which might be written in a T'i-pên was not limited in the Ming period, although the total was required to be noted. In 1645, however, the Ch'ing established the regulation that no T'i-pên should exceed three hundred characters in length (*Chia-ch'ing hui-tien shih-li* 10. 2b line 7). "Although for memorials on criminal cases and on revenue matters it will be difficult to adhere to that number of characters, yet it is not permitted that they be repetitious and prolix.

Take the main ideas of the memorial and gather them together in a summary (T'ieh-huang) in order to facilitate its being looked over; it should not exceed one hundred characters. If the number of characters surpasses the limit, and a great many clauses are inserted, or if the summary in comparison with the original memorial is confused and different in meaning, the office in question must not seal it up for presentation but take it to be an offense against the regulations and conduct an examination and impeachment."

However, this regulation of 1645 was not meticulously followed in practice, and by 1724 it had become a dead letter. (Although Mr. SHAN does not suggest it, one cannot help wondering if the Transmission Office was not taking advantage of the technicality; see note 15). *Chia-ch'ing hui-tien shih-li* 10. 4a quotes an imperial decision of 1724 which states, "T'i-pên and Tsou-pên according to the old regulations, except for criminal cases and revenue matters, were not to exceed three hundred characters and the summaries were not to exceed one hundred characters; and if the number of characters overflowed the limit, the Transmission Office was authorized to refuse the memorial and send it back. But important memorials, such as those dealing with how to promote prosperity, do away with abuses, encourage the doing of good, or punish evil—properly ought to be quite detailed, which will be of advantage to government; if there is a fixed limit to the number of characters and it is not allowed to raise many topics, the result must be to omit too much or be too brief. Hereafter, as regards T'i-pên and Tsou-pên, except those in which there are mistakes regarding the proper form or honorary elevation (of certain characters), the Transmission Office should not act on its own authority and refuse and return them because the number of characters or of items dealt with is excessive and offends against the regulations."

Ex.: *Wên-hsien ts'ung-pien* 24 passim; *Ming-ch'ing shih-liao* 2. 119, 138, 171; 4. 311; 7. 671; *Ho-pei ti-i bo-wu-yüan pan-yüeh-k'an* (Semi-monthly Publication of the First Museum of Hopei) no. 23 (Aug.

25, 1932) gives a photograph of a T'i-pên of 1655.

### T'I-TSOU 题奏 MEMORIALS.

T'i-pên and Tsou-pên considered together as a class.

### TIEH 牒 ORDER.

Addressed by superior to subordinate officials, MAYERS 140; no examples found.

### TIEH-CH'ÊNG 牒呈 REPORT.

Addressed by subordinate to superior officials, MAYERS 140; no examples found.

### T'IEH-HUANG 贴黄 SUMMARY.

Lit. yellow sticker, a slip of paper attached to a memorial (T'i-pên) at the end, bearing a summary of the contents to facilitate reference; not allowed to exceed one hundred characters, cf. SHAN Shih-k'uei (1) 185 quoted under T'i-pên above. Cf. *Kuang-hsü hui-tien* 69. 13: "On a separate sheet of paper there is copied a selection of the important statements in the memorial, which is pasted on at the end of the memorial and is called a T'ieh-huang"; also *Ch'ien-lung hui-tien* 81. 14. SHAN Shih-yüan (1) 151 states that the term was not confined to summaries made for T'i-pên but applied to all ordinary public documents written on yellow silk or paper and presented for imperial inspection. A form of T'ieh-huang was also used by the Board of War; and by usage the term was applied to summaries not written on yellow paper. T'ieh-huang were eventually bound up to form the Shih-shu, q. v.

### T'ING-CHI 廷寄 COURT LETTER.

In general, a secret document sent from the Grand Council to provincial officials embodying in its text imperial commands; used only on important business. Included two sub-types: a. Tzŭ-chi, sent to provincial officials of higher rank, and b. Ch'üan-yü, sent to provincial officials of lower rank, s. v.

Cf. *Chia-ch'ing hui-tien* 3. 2b: "Either an urgent Edict or a secret Edict, which is not handed down publicly through the Grand Secretariat, is called a Court Letter. [It is sealed by the Grand Council and given to the Courier's Office for transmission at a certain rate of speed]. As to its form, if it goes to a Generalissimo, an Imperial commissioner, a general-in-chief, an Amban, a lieutenant-general, a deputy lieutenant-general, an Imperial Agent and commandant of the forces, a governor-general, a governor, or a literary chancellor—it is called a 'Despatch (Tzǔ-chi) sent by the Grand Council.' If it goes to a salt-controller, a superintendent of customs, or a provincial judicial or financial commissioner—it is called a 'Transmitted Edict (Ch'üan-yǔ) from the Grand Council.' Both bear the year, month, and day on which the imperial will was received." Cf. also *Shu-yüan chi-lüeh* 27. 3a-b. The statement in GILES 11, 284 defining T'ing-chi as "a confidential letter sent directly from the Palace to the highest provincial officials, with instructions for their guidance in important matters," thus refers really to the sub-form Tzǔ-chi.

Ex.: *Wên-hsien ts'ung-pien* 14, sec. 2. 9b; *Shih-liao hsün-k'an* 3. 101a, 102a, headed T'ing-chi and reading Chün-chi ta-ch'ên tzǔ-chi 军机大臣字寄. All those printed in id. appear to be Tzǔ-chi rather than Ch'üan-yü; they conclude with the phrase Tsün-chih chi-hsin ch'ien-lai 遵旨寄信前来 (in obedience to the imperial will a letter is sent forward), cf. id. 5. 153b. Thus it is apparent that the form of T'ing-chi addressed to the higher provincial officials (i. e. Tzǔ-chi) came to stand for T'ing-chi as a whole.

**TS'Ê 册 PATENT.**

Used for establishing the titles of an Empress, imperial concubine, and the like, of various types; cf. *Chia-ch'ing hui-tien* 2. 2a.

Ex.: Boston Museum of Fine Arts, loaned from coll. of M. KAROLIK, 230. 38: "Jade book" of 1723.

**TSO-MING-CH'IH 坐名敕 NOMINATIVE COMMAND.**

From the emperor to higher provincial officials and the dependencies of the empire; see under Ch'ih-yü.

**TSOU-CHÊ 奏折 MEMORIAL.**

Same as Tsou-pên, q. v.

**TSOU-HSIAO-TS'Ê** 奏销册 ACCOUNTS, REPORTS.

See under Huang-ts'ê.

**TSOU-PÊN** 奏本 MEMORIAL.

Also called Tsou-chê and Chê-tsou; memorials submitted usually through the Chancery of Memorials (Tsou Shih Ch'u) on important public business or the private business of the memorialist and not bearing his seal of office—as contrasted with T'i-pên, q. v. For the long battle between the two chief forms of memorial, see text section 2 note 10. In general the Tsou-pên was a more direct, simple, and expeditious type of memorial, usually more valuable historically but unfortunately less highly differentiated than T'i-pên into subcategories susceptible of study. For the procedure followed in presenting Tsou-pên, see text section 3.

Ex.: the memorials printed in *Ch'ou-pan I-wu shih-mo* throughout consist almost entirely of Tsou-pên; *Shih-liao ts'ung-k'an ch'u-pien* 2 publishes Tsou-pên dated from 1632 on; *Shih-liao hsün-k'an* passim prints several Tsou-pên originating from the Grand Council (Chün-chi-ch'u tsou).

**TSOU-P'IEN** 奏片 SHORT MEMORIAL, MINUTE?

P'ien-tsou also appears; see under P'ien. Evidently a short memorial or "minute," usually in response to a Rescript; cf. TÊNG Chih-ch'êng 195.

Ex.: *Shih-liao hsün-k'an* 3. 99a et seq. ; *Chang-ku ts'ung-pien* 7. sec. 1. 42b.

**T'UNG-PÊN** 通本 MEMORIAL.

Memorials of the T'i-pên type from the higher provincial authorities submitted through the Transmission Office (T'ung Chêng Ssǔ) and the Grand Secretariat. Usually submitted only in Chinese, a Manchu translation being made at the Grand Secretariat; cf. HSÜ (1) 186. Cf. *Chia-ch'ing hui-tien* 2. 6a: "Memorials from the generals-in-chief, governor-general, governors, provincial commanders-in-chief, brigade generals, literary chancellors, and salt controllers of the various provinces, from the prefects of the metropolitan prefecture and of Mukden, and from the Five Boards at Mukden, all of which are sent to the Transmission Office and from the Transmission Office to the Grand Secretariat—are Tung-pên."

### TZǓ 咨 COMMUNICATION.

Used between officials of equal or approximately equal rank: MAYERS 138, GILES 12,344; sent to the Grand Council in particular from other offices at the capital and in the provinces. Used in many compounds, see below.

Ex.: *Ch'ou-pan I-wu shih-mo*, Tao-kuang section 67. 48b, from general-in-chief to governor-general; id. 68. 34a, from Board of Revenue to governor-general.

### TZǓ-CH'ENG 咨呈 COMMUNICATION.

Addressed from one official or office to another slightly superior in rank, MAYERS 139; from an official or office not directly subordinate, *Fa-lü ta-tz'ŭ-shu* 875; GILES 12, 344 states, "to submit to the consideration of—used (e. g.) by an officer while temporarily holding a higher appointment than his own, to a high official, provided that his personal rank allows of the use of a Tzǔ in correspondence."

Ex.: *Shih-liao hsün-k'an* 13. 472a, from the substantive Shantung governor to the Grand Council in 1832; *Ming-ch'ing shih-liao* 7. 679, from the Board of Ceremony to the Grand Secretariat.

### TZǓ-CHI 字寄 DESPATCH.

Sent from the Grand Council to higher provincial authorities and embodying important imperial commands, a form of T'ing-chi, q. v.

Ex.: *Chang-ku ts'ung-pien* 2, sec. 2, an example sent under the name of a Grand Secretary (i. e. concurrently a Grand Councillor); *Shih-liao hsün-k'an* 5. 153.

### TZǓ-HUI 咨会 COMMUNICATION.

An official despatch between equals, GILES 12, 344.

Ex.: *Shih-liao hsün-k'an* 4. 110a, draft copy of a communication to

Annam, Yung-chêng period (this seems inconsistent with GILES); *Ch'ou-pan I-wu shih-mo*, Tao-kuang section 67. 46b, from one governor-general to another; id., Hsien-feng period 42. 24a line 7, from an Imperial commissioner to the American chieftain.

### TZŬ-HSING 咨行 COMMUNICATION.

An official despatch between equals, GILES 12, 344.

EX.: *Ch'ou-pan I-wu shih-mo*, Tao-kuang section 67. 7b, from governor-general to superintendent of customs.

### TZŬ-PAO 咨报 COMMUNICATION.

A report, as from a Minister to the Foreign Office, GILES 12, 344.

Ex.: *Shih-liao hsün-k'an* 13. 474b, reference to a Tzŭ-pao to the Shantung governor from the Têngchow brigade general.

### TZŬ-WÊN 咨文 COMMUNICATION.

An official despatch between equals, GILES 12, 344.

Ex.: *Ming-ch'ing shih-liao* 8. 701, from the Board of War to the Board of Revenue.

### TZŬ-YÜ 字谕 ORDER.

To inferiors, especially from officials to commoners, a general term for letters.

Ex.: *Shih-liao hsün-k'an* 5. 168-169, three examples from the Chinese authorities to British merchants in 1822, *Wên-hsien ts'ung-pien* 1, photograph of a Tzŭ-yü from the Yung-chêng Emperor.

### YU-TSOU 又奏 ADDITIONAL MEMORIAL.

Not a separate type of document; when one memorialist submits more than one memorial at a time, those after the first bear this heading, sometimes followed by tsai 再 (further) as in the case of Fu-p'ien, q. v. Edicts are similarly treated.

Ex.: *Ch'ou-pan I-wu shih-mo* passim.

### YÜ 谕 Imperial EDICT.

A strong case could be made for translating this term as instruction, by analogy to Western procedure; but since it is the best known and most important of all documents issuing from the emperor, it seems particularly desirable to follow the traditional usage. The early British officials like T. F. WADE usually translated it as Decree; but Dr. H. B. MORSE and others since then have generally used Edict. Being a separate document, an Edict usually opens with a summary of a memorial or of previous business; it may be addressed to the Grand Council, or the Grand Secretariat, or others, or to no one at all. Discussed in text above, section 3.

**YÜ-CHIH 谕旨 Imperial EDICT.**

A general term used to refer to Edicts (yü) or Rescripts (chih) which have been received.

Ex.: *Shih-liao hsün-k'an* 3. 99b, headed Yü-chih, the text reading Nei-ko fêng shang-yü (the Grand Secretariat has received an imperial Edict); id. 103b, headed Yü-chih, the text reading fêng chih (a Rescript has been received).

**YÜ-PAO 御宝 IMPERIAL SEAL.**

Twenty-five imperial seals are listed in the *Collected Statutes*, each with a different name and form; cf. *Chia-ch'ing hui-tien* 2. 9a-2. 10b: "Whenever the emperor's words (lun-yin) are made known, an imperial seal is requested and used." The officers of the Grand Secretariat have charge of their use, together with the palace eunuchs, who have charge of their safe-keeping. For each occasion when a seal is to be used a memorial must be presented, except for the conferring of patents (Kao-ming, Ch'ih-ming, and Ch'ih-shu). *Ch'ien-lung hui-tien* 2. 5b states that requests for a seal are merely presented to the Imperial Household Department. The subject merits further study; cf. W. FUCHS, Beiträge zur mandjurischen Bibliographie und Literatur, Tōkyō 1936, 108-111. Ex.: *Chiao-t'ai-tien pao-p'u* (Imperial Seals in the Chiao-t'ai Hall), gives photographic reproductions of the twenty-five seals.

**YÜ-P'I 御批 IMPERIAL ENDORSEMENT.**

Same as Chu-p'i, q. v.

Ex.: *Shih-liao hsün-k'an* 7. 236b.

**YÜ-TIEH** 玉牒 **IMPERIAL GENEALOGY.**

Lit. jade record; the genealogical record of the imperial family, GILES 11,122; cf. *Ch'ien-lung hui-tien* 1 (the Imperial Clan Court) 1b.

Ex.: *Wên-hsien ts'ung-pien* 20. 22 gives a photographic illustration.

**WAI-FAN PIAO-CHANG** 外藩表章 **TRIBUTARY MEMORIAL.**

See under Kung-piao and Piao-chang: memorials submitted to the emperor by the political or religious dignitaries of Mongolia, Sinkiang, Tibet, etc. (wai-fan) and of tribes and feudatories such as Turfan, etc. ; cf. HSÜ (1) 194-195.


**NOTES:**

①We are indebted to Prof. K. N. BIGGERSTAFF of Cornell University for assistance in the preparation of section 5 of this paper.

②*HJAS* 4. 12-46.

③The chief published collections of Ch'ing documents, which should be available in all Chinese libraries, are listed alphabetically by romanization in section 4 of this article, including abbreviated titles by which reference hereafter is made.

④Editions of the *Ta-ch'ing hui-tien* are cited below by the reigns in which they appeared, viz. *K'ang-hsi hui-tien* (pub. 1690), *Yung-chêng hui-tien* (preface 1732), *Ch'ien-lung hui-tien* and *Ch'ien-lung hui-tien tsê-li* (both completed 1764), *Chia-ch'ing hui-tien* and *Chia-ch'ing hui-tien shih-li* (both completed 1818), *Kuang-hsü hui-tien* and *Kuang-hsü hui-tien shih-li* (both published 1899).

These editions differ markedly in their treatment of some subjects. In general the K'ang-hsi and Yung-chêng editions are similar in content, the Ch'ien-lung edition differs greatly from its predecessors, and the Chia-ch'ing and Kuang-hsü editions are largely the same. Thus the various editions provide extensive material for the study of the evolution of the Ch'ing administration. We have taken the Chia-ch'ing edition (1818) as a basis; that of 1899 is modelled upon it.

⑤Translations of official titles follow H. S. BRUNNERT and V. V. HAGELSTROM, *Present Day Political Organization of China*, Shanghai 1912, cited as BRUNNERT. It is unfortunate that this comprehensive manual includes so many ephemeral titles created during the reforms that preceded the revolution of 1911-1912. W. F. MAYERS,

*The Chinese Government*, Shanghai 1897, revised by G. M. H. PLAYFAIR, cited as MAYERS, is briefer but often more accurate for the nineteenth century.

⑥HSIEH Pao-chao 谢保樵, *The Government of China* 1644-1911, Balt. 1925, 68-87, summarizes parts of the *Kuang-hsü hui-tien* pertinent to this paper and contains much valuable data. Its usefulness as a reference work is seriously marred by the lack of an index; romanizations and footnote references are often imperfect in form. To Dr. HSIEH'S credit it should be remembered that this was a pioneer work compiled before the publication of the *Ch'ing-shih kao* and most of the documentary collections.

⑦Much has been written during the last decade on Ch'ing archives, but often without reference to the subject of procedure. The more valuable articles include the following, cited below by author:

CHANG Tê-tsê 张德泽, *Chün-chi-ch'u chi ch'i tang-an* 军机处及其档案(The Grand Council and its Documents), *Wên-hsien lun-ts'ung* 文献论丛 (Collected Articles from the Historical Records Office), Palace Museum, Peiping, Oct. 1936, Part 2, 57-84. CHAO Ch'üan-ch'êng 赵泉澄, *Pei-ching ta-hsüeh so-tsang tang-an ti fên-hsi* 北京大学所藏档案的分析 (Archives in the Peking University), *Chung-kuo chin-tai ching-chi-shih yen-chiu chi-k'an* 中国近代经济史研究集刊(Studies in Modern Economic History of China) 2 no. 2, May 1934 (Special Issue on Archives of Ming and Tsing Governments, cited in this article as *Ching-chi-shih yen-chiu*) 222-254.

FANG Keng-shêng 方甦生, *Ch'ing-tai tang-an fên-lei wên-t'i* 清代档案分类问题 (Problems in the Classification of Documents of the Ch'ing Dynasty), *Wên-hsien lun-ts'ung* 27-48.

HSÜ (1) HSÜ Chung-shu 徐中舒, *Chung-yang yen-chiu-yüan li-shih yü-yen yen-chiu-so so-tsang tang-an ti fên-hsi* 中央研究院历史语言研究所所藏档案的分析 (Archives in the Institute of Philology and History, Academia Sinica), *Ching-chi-shih yen-chiu*, 169-221.

HSÜ (2), HSÜ Chung-shu 徐中舒, *Nei-ko tang-an chih yu-lai chi ch'i chêng-li* 内阁档案之由来及其整理(The Origin and Reconditioning of the Archives of the Grand Secretariat), *Ming-ch'ing shih-liao* 1, 1-14.

HSÜ (3), HSÜ Chung-shu 徐中舒, *Tsai-shu nei-ko ta-k'u tang-an chih yu-lai chi ch'i chêng-li* 再述内阁大库档案之由来及其整理 (Further Remarks on the Origin and Reconditioning of the Archives of the Great Storehouse of the Grand Secretariat), *CYYY* 3.537-576, Peiping, 1934.

KOESTER, Hermann KÖSTER (sic), The Palace Museum of Peking, *Monumenta serica* 2. 167-190 (1936-1937).

SHAN Shih-k'uei 单士魁, *Ch'ing-tai T'i-pên chih-tu k'ao* 清代题本制度考 (The System of T'i-pên of the Ch'ing Dynasty), *Wên-hsien lun-ts'ung*, Part 2, 177-189.

SHAN Shih-yüan (1) 单士元, *Ch'ing-tai tang-an shih -ming fa-fan* 清代档案释名发凡 (An Introduction to the Terminology of Documents of the Ch'ing Dynasty), *Wên-hsien lun-ts'ung*, Part 2, 147-154.

SHAN Shih-yüan (2) 单士元, *Ku-kung po-wu-yüan wên-hsien-kuan so-tsang tang-an ti fên-hsi* 故宫博物院文献馆所藏档案的分析 (Archives in the Library of the Palace Museum), *Ching-chi-shih yen-chiu*, 270-280.

TÊNG Chih-ch'êng 邓之诚, *T'an chün-chi-ch'u* 谈军机处 (A Lecture on the Chün Chi Ch'u), *SHNP* 2, no. 4, 193-198.

⑧ For the date 1729, see note 39 below.

⑨ YEH Fêng-mao 叶凤毛, *Nei-ko hsiao-chih* 内阁小志 (A Brief Sketch of the Grand Secretariat), published 1765, describes the various sub-offices of the Secretariat, which were housed in a group of buildings inside the front gate of the Palace in the south-eastern section. His list omits two of the sub-offices listed in *Chia-ch'ing*° and *Kuang-hsü hui-tien* and includes six others not listed in the °*hui-tien*, among the latter being the Grand Council, a body that technically was an offshoot of the Secretariat in origin. The twelve sub-offices listed in the °*hui-tien* and in Hsü (1) 199 are as follows:

• Archives Offices (Tien Chi T'ing 典籍厅), divided into a northern and a southern section, the northern section in general dealing with matters concerning the emperor and the southern section in general dealing with matters concerning other offices of government and so having charge of the seals used in all correspondence of the Grand Secretariat.

• Manchu Copying Office (Man Pên Fang 满本房).

• Chinese Copying Office (Han Pên Fang 汉本房).

• Mongolian Copying Office (Mêng-ku Fang 蒙古房).

• Manchu Registry (Man P'iao Ch'ien Ch'u 满票签处).

• Chinese Registry (Han P'iao Ch'ien Ch'u 汉票签处).

• Honorary Titles Office (Kao Ch'ih Fang 诰敕房).

• Inspectorate (Chi Ch'a Fang 稽察房).

• Receiving and Forwarding Office (Shou Fa Hung-pên Ch'u 收发红本处), i. e. for Hung-pên.

- Mess Allowance Storehouse (Fan Yin K'u 饭银库).
- Duplicate Memorial Storehouse (Fu-pên K'u 副本库); BRUNNERT calls this Archives Office (no. 138) and contains no translation for Tien Chi T'ing.
- Endorsement Copying Office (P'i-pên Ch'u 批本处).

The function of most of these offices will appear from the text and notes below.

⑩ SHAN Shih-k'uei's quotations and comments may be summarized as follows, beginning with the Ming period (quotations are from the next source indicated; we have inserted page references, in some cases to earlier editions):

Regulations for the Ch'i-pên 启本, Tsou-pên, and T'i-pên were fixed in 1382, the system being that memorials from ministers or subjects to the emperor were Tsou-pên, those to the heir apparent were Ch'i-pên. Later, because Tsou-pên from officers at the capital were inconvenient, T'i-pên were used for all public business…

According to the Ming regulations, "all offices at the capital and in the provinces on all public matters use T'i-pên; but for all matters which, although of public concern, are routine reports or memorials of congratulation, such as requests for clemency, confessions of guilt, the return of imperial credentials, thanks for favors, petitions from soldiers and civilians, proposals and complaints—they use Tsou-pên" (*Ming hui-tien* 212). Thus the Ming appears to have used Tsou-pên more than T'i-pên.

The Ch'ing followed the Ming tradition, but by 1725 began to make changes. "In 1725 imperial approval was given to systematize the usage of T'i-pên and Tsou-pên. The order was given to the various provincial governor-general, governors, commanders-in-chief, and Brigade generals that thereafter all matters concerning taxes and provisions, judicial cases, troops, (military) horses, and other matters large or small concerning local civil affairs, should all be presented in the form of T'i-pên, stamped with the seal (of the office of origin) and a subject-title written on the memorial (chü-t'i 具题). Private affairs concerning the official personally should all use the Tsou-pên form, and even though he was an official with a seal of office, he was not to be allowed to use the seal. If there was an offense against the fixed regulations for T'i-pên and Tsou-pên, it was to be referred to the Board (of Punishments) for discussion and sentence" (*Kuang-hsü hui-tien shih-li* 13. 4b line 6).

Further and more detailed regulations were established in 1729. "Hereafter for matters concerning the recommendation and impeachment of subordinate officials, taxes and provisions, troops and horses, law cases involving life or robbery, punishments, and all other public matters, according to the regulations T'i-pên should be used. Congratulatory expressions; reports of an official concerning his arrival at a new post, taking over the seals of office, leaving his post, or handing over (to a successor); acknowledgments of the receipt of imperial commands (chih) or Edicts (yü) or of books distributed to all provincial offices, whether reporting dates of receipt or expressing gratitude; the sending of congratulations or statements of thanks on behalf of all the officials and people of a province; cases the reports of which are not originally clear and concerning which a Rescript was received ordering a further memorial—all these matters belong to the category of public affairs; T'i-pên ought to be used. As to (matters concerning) the arrival of any official at a new post, his promotion or transfer, his receipt of honorary distinctions, his being honorably recorded (for good service), or pardoned, or degraded and punished, or degraded and deprived of rank but left at his post; or matters concerning expressions of gratitude for special grants or rewards, or words of thanks on behalf of subordinate officials—Tsou-pên ought to be used; none should be stamped with the seal of office" (*Kuang-hsü hui-tien shih-li* 1412. 4 line 9).

Thus the chief point of difference in the regulations is that Tsou-pên were not to be stamped with the memorialist's seal of office, while T'i-pên were to be stamped with the seal and were to have a subject-title written on them. Up to 1748 also, T'i-pên were used for public affairs and Tsou-pên for private affairs.

In 1748 a thorough-going change was attempted. An Edict of that year declared that the forms of T'i-pên and Tsou-pên had been taken over from the Ming "because at that time the rules and regulations had been abandoned or relaxed and the Transmission Office and the Grand Secretariat utilized the names of public (affairs) and private (affairs) in order to facilitate the extension of its grasp (of government business). In reality all are statements presented to the throne. Why is it necessary to divide them into different kinds? Let T'i-pên be used in all cases where Tsou-pên have been used, with a view to showing administrative simplicity" (*Ch'ien-lung hui-tien tsê-li* 2. 3b line 7).

This reform did not succeed, however, and Tsou-pên continued to be used. In 1750 an Edict specified that the action of provincial officials "in impeaching undutiful subordinate officers, whether requesting that they be deprived of rank, or requesting that they resign from office, or requesting that they be degraded pending reform—all are local public affairs and are not at all matters which ought to be managed with secrecy, and it is right and proper to write a memorial and add a title to it—which will then accord with the regulations. Recently there have been cases where the governor-general and governors have first prepared a memorial reporting to the emperor in the form of a

Tsou-pên and have expressed themselves separately in a T'i-pên impeaching (an official); this may still be considered permissible. But there are also cases constantly arising in which Tsou-Chê (i. e. Tsou-pên) are used in place of T'i-pên; this really is not consistent with the regulations. Let circular instructions be issued to the governor-general and governors of the various provinces that whenever there arises an occasion for this sort of Tsou-pên of impeachment, they should use T'i-pên, in order to display great circumspection" (*Kuang-hsü hui-tien shih-li* 13. 7a line 9).

In 1795, because the usage regarding T'i-pên and Tsou-pên was still not uniform, it was decided that for ordinary routine matters Tsou-pên should be abolished and T'i-pên should be used instead. A memorial of Aug. 9, 1795, stated that "in the management of local affairs by the provincial governor-general and governors, all matters which concern the receipt of a Rescript, or important cases involving life or robbery, heterodox religions, or changes in the old regulations, and all important matters which concern the sufferings or distress of the people, ought of course to be memorialized at the time in Tsou-pên. If there are ordinary routine affairs for all of which there are recorded decisions or archives which can be consulted, there is no need to present special Tsou-pên and stir up trouble. But the administration of the various provinces is not yet systematized. There are cases where T'i-pên are presented according to regulation but again a Tsou-pên is also presented to report (the same thing). There are cases where the various provinces memorialize the emperor by the T'i-pên form, and yet one or two provinces alone use Tsou-pên. There are also instances where legal cases involving life or robbery have already been concluded and there are supplementary impeachments to be made in the case, which can be made uniformly through T'i-pên; and yet memorials of impeachment are nevertheless presented in Tsou-pên form. Again, in the case of T'i-pên (recommending) the promotion, transfer, or appointment of Sub-prefects and Magistrates to fill a vacancy—if there are really important vacancies, it was originally permitted that a special memorial (Tsou-pên) be presented making the request; for other, ordinary vacancies of course one should follow the regulations and present T'i-pên. There are times when a certain man is required at a certain place, but the man's term of service is not yet complete; (in such cases) there is no bar to making a clear statement in a memorial. But governor-general and governors, because of the rule regarding special recommendations, abruptly go ahead and present a confusion of memorials and entreaties; this should also be ordered to stop" (*Kao-tsung shih-lu*, Aug. 9, 1795).

In this way Tsou-pên appear to have survived every attempt to abolish them. Meanwhile T'i-pên continued to be used, but, up to the later Ch'ien-lung period at least, no uniformity in their use had yet been achieved.

A second attempt at reform was made in 1901 when LIU K'un-i 刘坤一 and CHANG Chih-tung 张之洞 memorialized proposing the abolition of T'i-pên. "T'i-pên originally were the old system of the Ming. Since there were copies (Fu-pên) and summaries (T'ieh-huang) which had to be all copied in Sung characters, there were complications and delays. Our dynasty in the Yung-chêng period issued an Edict ordering that the ministers and officials should make a change and put important affairs in Tsou-Chê (i. e. Tsou-pên), which in simplicity, speed, and ease of reading far surpass T'i-pên. For fifty years past there have been many cases in which the various provinces have already changed to Tsou-pên. In the winter of the present year the ministers of state accompanying the emperor have already memorialized requesting a temporary cessation of the use of T'i-pên. Hereafter it is proposed to request a careful investigation and discussion, that the T'i-pên may be forever dispensed with, and change made to Tsou-pên and despatches (tzǔ 咨), respectively" (*Tung-hua lu*, Oct. 2, 1901).

SHAN Shih-k'uei concludes, "the above-quoted memorial of CHANG Chih-tung and others requesting the abolition of the T'i-pên does not appear to have been carried out. Today the great storehouse of the Grand Secretariat still retains T'i-pên of the year 1903, which is sufficient proof of the fact." On the other hand, the *Ch'ing-shih kao* (*chih-kuan chih* 2. 6b line 12) states that the Transmission Office was abolished in 1902 because the transformation of T'i-pên into Tsou-pên had deprived it of its special function.

The reader who has read thus far will perhaps agree that the subject of T'i-pên and Tsou-pên is a thorny one.

⑪Cf. KUNG Tzǔ-chên 龚自珍, *Shang ta-hsüeh-shih shu* 上大学士书 (A Letter to the Grand Secretaries), in *Ting-an wên-chi pu-pien* 定庵文集补编 3. 5 line 7, *Ssŭ pu ts'ung-k'an* edition: "The Grand Council handles Edicts, the Grand Secretariat handles Rescripts; the Grand Council handles Tsou-pên memorials, the Grand Secretariat handles T'i-pên memorials. The difference between these two bodies was clearly distinguished."

⑫Regarding the postal service for the transmission of documents to the capital, see our article cited in note 2 above.

⑬Summarized from *Chia-ch'ing hui-tien* 54. 13a.

⑭Decreed in 1644; cf. *K'ang-hsi hui-tien* 148. 1b last line; *Chia-ch'ing hui-tien shih-li* 781. 2.

⑮The Transmission Office in the Ming period attained great power because all memorials intended for the emperor had first to be opened and passed by it. Indeed, memorials on important matters had to be stamped and recorded by the Office before presentation to the throne, so that it became the chief means of communication (the "throat and tongue") of the emperor. This led to malpractices and eventual reform. Under the Ch'ing the power of the Transmission Office was cut down and it was arranged that secret memorials (fêng-shih 封事) presented at the palace gate should be transmitted to the throne directly by the Chancery of Memorials (Tsou Shih Ch'u 奏事处) to the emperor; T'i-pên from offices at the capital should be sent directly to the Grand Secretariat; and only T'i-pên from officials in the provinces should be sent first to the Transmission Office (*Li-tai chih-kuan piao* 历代职官表 [Table of Offices and Officials of Successive Dynasties], *Ssŭ-pu pei-yao* 四部备要 edition 21. 17b; cf. also *Huang-ch'ao wên-hsien t'ung-k'ao* 皇朝文献通考 [Chekiang shu-chü edition 1882] 82. 11b-13). The regulations were of course by no means as simple as this summary would indicate. Thus an Edict of 1645 provided that all Tsou-pên from offices at the capital should be presented through the Transmission Office (*Kuang-hsü hui-tien* 148. 1b; *Ch'ien-lung hui-tien tsê-li* 151. 1a), an inconsistency explainable on the ground of its early date.

⑯The manifold regulations on this subject deserve summarization in a separate article. Thus in 1682 an Edict was issued that, "except for the secret memorials of officials in office, which should be sealed and presented to the emperor as usual, the secret memorials of discarded and unemployed officials and of irresponsible shysters should first be examined by the Transmission Office; those that ought to be sealed, will be sealed up for presentation to the emperor, and those that ought not to be sealed will strictly rebuked and returned unaccepted" (*Yung-chêng hui-tien* 225. 3b line 4). But an Edict of 1708 provided that, because the Transmission Office refused to accept so many memorials on account of improper form, thus delaying the conduct of business, it should therefore be ordered to report at the end of each month how many memorials had been rejected and their subjects (*op. cit.* 225. 2b line 6). In 1724 it was ordered that memorials should no longer be rejected and returned (*Chia-ch'ing hui-tien shih-li* 781. 2). In 1738, however, there was a return to the system preceding 1724 (*ibid.*).

⑰The traditional practice had begun to decay in the late Ming period; cf. SUN

Ch'êng-tsê 孙承泽, *Ch'un-ming mêng-yü lu* 春明梦余录, Ku-hsiang chai 古香斋 pocket edition, 23. 28a: "The old regulation of our ancestors... was that the eunuchs first set up the imperial table, then presented the official documents, and then retired outside the door; they waited until the imperial inspection was finished and then sent (the documents) to the Grand Secretariat for drafting (i-p'iao 拟票)—this was the usual practice. But in the early years of the Lung-ch'ing period (1567-1572), I do not know why, the Emperor... merely took the memorials in his hands and glanced over one or two lines in a cursory fashion, and there were some that he did not look at at all..."

⑱E. g. *Chia-ch'ing hui-tien shih-li* 10. 3a last line; *Kuang-hsü hui-tien shih-li* 13. 3a last line: "1660 Edict: as to the memorials (Pên-chang) which are presented (Tsou) by the various metropolitan offices, if they are sent down on the same day for the proposal (i. e. drafting) of a Rescript, since the memorials (Pên-chang) are numerous and extremely important, it is to be feared that it will be difficult to deal with them carefully in a short time. Hereafter the memorials of the various offices and of the censors are all to be presented (Tsou) to the emperor every day at noon, to await the emperor's opening and inspection. On the following day they are to be sent down for the drafting of Rescripts, in order to facilitate careful Examination, Endorsement, and sending down. Memorials (Pên-chang) of all sorts which are sealed up by the Transmission Office have first been sent to the Grand Secretariat to be read and presented. Hereafter let the said office itself proceed to seal them up and present them to the emperor. After the emperor has seen them, they will be sent down and read. If there are secret memorials (Mi-pên), again let the said office seal them up and present them, no matter what the time may be. The various Boards should be informed in a transmitted Edict, so that each may act accordingly."

It will be seen that the references to types of memorials here are ambiguous and confusing, Pên-chang being generally a generic term for memorials of all kinds. In the following passage, however, the all-important distinction between T'i-pên and Tsou-pên is more clearly brought out (*Chia-ch'ing hui-tien shih-li* 10. 3a line 5): "1656 Edict: heretofore the memorials (Tsou-chê) of the Censors and of the various Manchu and Chinese officials at the capital all have first been sent to the Grand Secretariat; hereafter all should follow the example of the Boards and go direct to the palace for presentation. The T'i-pên which are sent from the provinces to the Transmission Office and the memorials (Pên-chang) of the various officials at the capital should still, as heretofore, be sent to the Transmission Office for it to send in turn to the Grand Secretariat." This was, of course, before the creation of the Grand Council.

⑲See, e. g., the passage just quoted, note 18.

⑳*Chia-ch'ing hui-tien* 2. 6a:"(Pu-pên and T'ung-pên) first arrive at the Grand Secretariat; when T'ung-pên arrive at the Secretariat, if they are not written in both Manchu and Chinese, the Chinese Copying Office translates the attached summary (T'ieh-huang) and the Manchu Copying Office copies it in Manchu characters and it is sent to the Registry (P'iao Ch'ien Ch'u)." Cf. *op. cit.* 2. 17b: in the Manchu Copying Office there were 39 Manchu Secretaries and 24 Manchu copyists (T'ieh-hsieh chung-shu 贴写中书); *op. cit.* 2. 18b: the Chinese Copying Office had charge of the receiving and forwarding of T'ung-pên and its chief officers—two Manchu and two Chinese Readers, with assistants—decided whether the time limit for this operation should be long or short; thus for all matters concerning promotion, demotion, departure from a post, or dismissal, the Office set a time limit beyond which the work of translating and forwarding must not be delayed. The Secretaries of the Office—31 Manchus, 8 Chinese bannermen, and 16 Manchu copyists—had charge of the translation of memorials into Manchu.

㉑See section 5, Fu-pên.

㉒The personnel listed in the *Collected Statutes* may be summarized as follows:

| | Manchus | Chinese | Chin. bannermen | Mongols |
|---|---|---|---|---|
| *K'ang-hsi hui-tien* 2. 1b total 184 | 98 | 40 | 23 | 23 |
| *Yung-chêng hui-tien* 2. 1b | id. | | | |
| *Ch'ien-lung hui-tien* 1. 1 total 170 | 95 | 43 | 12 | 20 |
| *Chia-ch'ing hui-tien* 2 passim total 252 | 164 | 46 | 14 | 28 |
| *Kuang-hsü hui-tien* 2 passim | id. | | | |

The offices listed included Grand Secretaries (usually 4), Assistant Grand Secretaries (2 or 4), these two categories not being listed before the Ch'ien-lung period; Sub-Chancellors (usually 10), Readers (usually 8), Assistant Readers (usually 15), Archivists (usually 6), Secretaries (143, then 124, then 204). It will be seen that the personnel was increased in the nineteenth century chiefly by the addition of Manchu Secretaries. Secretaries, of course, merely assisted in drafting proposals.

㉓ The phrases i-ch'ien 拟签 and p'ian-i 票拟 may be translated "to write a proposal," in Western parlance "to draft"; the regulations do not use the term kao 稿, the usual word for a rough draft or preliminary copy.

㉔*Chia-ch'ing hui-tien* 2. 6b: "As to the form of the draft label, whenever the contents of T'ung-pên ought to be discussed and replied, then they are given to the various Boards and Departments at the capital, which are to 'deliberate and memorialize,' or 'investigate and deliberate,' or 'examine judicially and deliberate,' or 'deliberate and decide punishment,' or 'deliberate with great care,' or 'deliberate with haste.' When there is no need of deliberation and reply, then they are given to the various Boards for their information." Cf. SHAN Shih-k'uei 185: "For the phraseology of the draft proposals there were established forms. Thus in the case of T'ung-pên it would be, 'Let the said Board be informed' (kai-pu chih-tao 该部知道), 'Let the Board of Civil Office be informed,' 'Let the Board of War be informed,' 'Let the Three High Courts of Judicature (San Fa Ssǔ) be informed,' and so on. If when a memorial was presented to the throne it was accompanied by a volume of documents or the like (Ts'ê), then the draft proposal would be 'Let the said Board be informed and also send the volume,' or 'Let the volume be retained for inspection,' and so on. If it were a Pu-pên, then it would be 'Let it be as recommended' (i-i 依议), 'Noted', 'According to the proposal that he ought to be strangled, let him be held in prison until the autumn assizes are concluded and then be sentenced; for the rest, let it be as recommended,' and so on. Of the several hundred thousand T'i-pên with red Endorsements preserved today from the Ch'ing period, the great part are of this sort." Other expressions commonly used by the emperor in making Endorsements included "Seen" (lan 览), "Let the Nine Chief Ministries of State speedily deliberate and memorialize" (Chiu-ch'ing su-i chü-tsou 九卿速议具奏), "The content of the memorial is thoroughly comprehended" (So-tsou chü-hsi 所奏俱悉). Any of these notations might of course be followed by remarks ad hoc.

㉕ *Chia-ch'ing hui-tien* 2. 7a: "When there are two proposals, a pair of slips is written out: as to the form of a pair of slips, whenever the various Boards present T'i-pên requesting certain things, there are cases where (the officers of the Secretariat) do not dare to suit their own convenience as to whether permission ought to be given or refused; or where there is deliberation as to merit or guilt or rewards or honors, and the decision may be light or severe; or where punishments (of officials for administrative errors) ought to be deliberated upon or ought to be remitted; or where alternative requests are made in the memorial to await an imperial decision… in all such cases a pair of slips is written out according to the draft." Cases of three slips or four slips were treated similarly.

㉖ Cf. *Chia-ch'ing hui-tien* 2 8a.

㉗SHAN Shih-k'uei describes a proposal slip as being smaller than the page of a T'i-pên, a bit over seven inches from top to bottom and a bit over four inches wide, the Manchu writing on the left and the Chinese on the right. The Assistant Readers and Secretaries who wrote the proposal slips signed their names on the reverse, the Manchu and the Chinese in the right and left corners, respectively. Slips of this kind are still preserved in the Palace, including some volumes of model forms to be used on T'ung-pên and Pu-pên, e. g. "For T'ung-pên with a single slip: We have read the minister's memorial of thanks; Seen; Let the said Board be informed. For Pu-pên with a single slip: Let the Palace examination be held on—day; Let it be as recommended."

㉘*Chia-ch'ing hui-tien* 2. 6b: "If there are maps or volumes: reports on river works and all sorts of official construction regularly ought to be written up with both maps and bound volumes (of reports), to accompany the memorial when it is submitted to the emperor. Reports on the taxes and crops of any place, and memorials from the court assize and the autumn assize, all are written in volumes [similarly for the examination records]. If there is a list: if the memorial contains a list which regularly ought to be presented to the emperor, such as lists of names, lists of vacancies, records of officials' careers, or lists of sacrifices—having been examined as to whether they ought to be retained or ought to be sent on, all are differentiated and proposals made regarding them in the proposal slip. Those which are not covered in the regulations, as to whether they ought to be retained or sent, are not mentioned in the proposal slip."

㉙Cf. WU Ao 吴鳌, *Nei-ko chih* 内阁志 (An Account of the Grand Secretariat) 2b line 7, in *Chieh-yüeh-shan-fang hui-ch'ao* 借月山房汇钞 3: "According to the state statutes there is a ya-pan, (the post) is assigned to a Manchu Grand Secretary; the order of precedence of the others (is decided by) asking the imperial will to settle it…" A good deal of the office routine of the Secretariat is described in this work.

㉚This system had begun in the Ming period. According to *Li-tai chih-kuan piao* 4. 12b-13a, the Grand Secretaries were first commanded in the Hsüan-tê period (1426-1435) to prepare drafts of Rescripts and attach them to memorials that were to be presented. An Edict of 1659 stated that the Secretariat had originally been established to save the emperor's time and the Grand Secretaries had therefore been ordered to draft Rescripts for the emperor's final decision (*Chia-ch'ing hui-tien shih-li* 11. 7a line 6). For the Ch'ing regulations cf. *K'ang-hsi hui-tien* 2. 7, *Ch'ien-lung hui-tien* 2. 2b, *Ch'ien-lung hui-tien tsê-li* 2. 8.

㉛*Chia-ch'ing hui-tien* 2. 6b line 6: "Drafts are made and then copied on slips:

every day the T'ung-pên and Pu-pên that ought to be submitted to the emperor are carefully looked over and checked by the Assistant Readers and others, who write out draft proposal slips. After the Grand Secretaries have seen and decided upon these slips, they order the Secretaries of the Registries to copy them out in Manchu and Chinese on a formal double slip (ho-pi chêng-ch'ien 合璧正签). On the following day at dawn they are respectfully transmitted to the emperor" (We have taken ch'ien 签 in its most literal meaning as a slip of paper, which fits the context of the *Collected statutes*). *Op. cit* 2. 19b line 7: "Every day, for the T'ung-pên and Pu-pên, slips are rough-drafted by the Chinese Assistant Readers and their colleagues and sent to the Manchu Registry. The Assistant Readers and others (of the Registry) carefully compare the Manchu text and examine the slip to see whether it is in proper form. They rough-draft a slip in Manchu. They submit the duplicate copy (of the memorial) to the Grand Secretaries at the Grand Council 以副本呈军机处大学士 and they submit the original copy to the Grand Secretaries at the Secretariat, who examine it and decide upon the draft. Thereupon the formal slip is copied out... All memorials presented to the emperor are differentiated as to whether they are urgent or not urgent, important or not important. They are reverently stored in a box," which is labelled accordingly. Cf. also *op. cit.* 2. 20a for the duties of the Chinese Registry.

㉜Cf. *Chia-ch'ing hui-tien* 2. 8a. The emperor might reserve some memorials (chê-pen, see under sec. 5) for further consideration; this step in procedure is discussed in, sec. 3.

㉝*Op. cit.* 2. 23a line 7: "After memorials have been presented to the emperor and sent back down again, the Endorsements Copying Office, copying the slip of Manchu writing decided upon by the emperor, and using red ink, writes the Endorsement on the face of the memorial." *Op. cit.* 2. 17b line 3: "After the memorials have been handed down and received, the Chinese Sub-Chancellors (of the Grand Secretariat), copying the slip of Chinese writing decided upon by the emperor, and using red ink, write the Endorsement on the face of the memorial."

㉞Cf, SHAN Shih-k'uei 185.

㉟Cf. *id.* 188. SHAN quotes several sources to show that the duplicates were required to be stored in the Huang Shih Ch'êng, including an eyewitness of the Ch'ien-lung period who saw them there piled as high as a mountain; SHAN adduces evidence that most of them must have been burned in 1899, to be gotten rid of—at least very few have been found.

㊱*Chia-ch'ing hui-tien* 2. 8b line 9: "All memorials that have been presented (to the emperor) are sent down at the end of two days; those that ought to be sent down immediately are not to take more than one day: after a memorial which has been submitted has received a Rescript, it is sent down to the Endorsement Copying Office. On the following day the Office writes on the Endorsements, and on the day after that, (the memorial) is handed down to the Grand Secretariat. In case it is an important matter and the Rescript is received and handed down with haste, it is immediately handed down to the Grand Secretariat on the same day that the memorial is (first) presented."

㊲Cf. *op. cit.* 2. 21b line 8.

㊳*Op. cit.* 2. 8a line 6: "After the Endorsement has been written on in Manchu and Chinese, (a memorial) is a Hung-pên. Junior Metropolitan Censors from the Six Sections go to the Grand Secretariat and respectfully receive it, and subsequently give notice that it may be copied to the various yamen concerned."

㊴Various dates have been assigned for the creation of the Grand Council, probably because that body went through several reorganizations in its early years (e. g. MAYERS 13-1730; *Ch'ing-shih kao*, *chih-kuan chih* 1. 4a-1732; *Kuang-hsü hui-tien shih-li* 1051. 10, in memorial of 1683-1730; HSIEH Pan-chao 77-1730). However, the *Shih-lu* (cf. CHANG Tê-tsê 57 quoting *Shih-tsung shih-lu* 世宗实录 82. 6a) and *Ch'ing-shih kao* (56, *Chün-chi ta-ch'ên nien-piao* 军机大臣年表 [Chronological Table of Grand Councillors] 1) agree on the sixth month of 1729 as the date for the establishment of the Chün Chi Fang 军机房. From this event the early evolution of the Grand Council may be traced as follows (*op. cit.* 1-8):

1729 July 5—appointment of the Imperial Prince of I, Yün-hsiang 怡亲王允祥, together with CHANG T'ing-yü 张廷玉 and CHIANG T'ing-hsi 蒋廷锡 as a board of three for the secret management of necessary military affairs.

1732 third month—the title of Chün Chi Fang was changed to Pan Li Chün Chi Ch'u 办理军机处.

1735—the duties of the latter office were taken over by the Tsung Li Shih Wu Ch'u 总理事务处.

1738 Jan. 17—the Pan Li Chün Chi Ch'u was restored.

1741—it began to be referred to simply as the Chün Chi Ch'u.

㊵The most informative modern studies of the Grand Council are those by TÊNG Chih-ch'êng and CHANG Tê-tsê (see note 7 above). The origin of the Council is also attributed to the fact that the offices of the Grand Secretariat were inconveniently located at some distance from the emperor's apartments. The Secretariat was just inside the front gate of the Palace on the east; thus it was outside the first inner gate (T'ai-ho Mên 太和门) on the axis leading back through the main halls of the Palace complex. On the other hand, the Nan Shu-fang was just west of the Ch'ien-ch'ing Mên 乾清门, more than halfway along the main axis; and the Lung-tsung Mên 隆宗门 where the Grand Council had its offices, was on the western side of the same great court which led to the Ch'ien-ch'ing Mên on the north—i.e. the Grand Council was located in the very heart of the Forbidden City, close to the emperor. Cf. CHAO I 赵翼, *Yen-pao tsa-chi* 檐曝杂记 (Miscellaneous Notes) 1. la, in his *Ou-pei ch'üan-chi* 瓯北全集 (Complete Works of Ou-pei [= CHAO I]), 1877.

㊶Between 1729 and 1911 there were 47 years in which the number of Councillors was five, 48 years in which it was six, and 31 years in which it was 7; cf. *Ch'ing-shih kao*, *Chün-chi ta-ch'ên nien-piao*.

㊷ The tables just mentioned and *Ch'ing-shih kao*, *Ta-hsüeh-shih nien-piao* (Chronological Table of Grand Secretaries) give the names of the members of each body in each year. A simple addition of these lists of names, counting each name once each time it appears, gives a total of approximately 1140 names of Grand Councillors listed in the period 1729-1911, and approximately 1310 names of Grand Secretaries in the same period; a comparison of the two lists year by year gives the following results: years in which only one official was concurrently a Grand Councillor and a Grand Secretary—22,

years in which 2 officials were in both bodies—78,

years in which 3 officials were in both bodies—41,

average number of officials in both bodies each year (1729-1911)—2.35.

In other words a little less than half of the personnel of the Council were, on the average, Grand Secretaries. It is noteworthy that during the T'ung-chih period (1862-1874) there were only three years in which one official was in both bodies; in the other years of that period the two bodies had no personnel in common.

㊸CHANG Tê-tsê 61 lists them as follows: Prince Kung 恭 (I-hsin 奕䜣), Wên-hsiang 文祥, Kuei-liang 桂良, Pao-yün 宝鋆, SHÊN Kuei-fên 沈桂芬, LI Hung-tsao 李鸿藻, Ching-lien 景廉, WANG Wên-shao 王文韶, Tso Tsung-t'ang 左宗棠, YEN Ching-ming 阎敬铭, HSÜ Kêng-shên 许庚身, SUN Yü-wên 孙毓文, HSÜ Yung-i 徐用仪, WÊNG T'ung-ho 翁同龢, LIAO Shou-hêng 廖寿恒, Yü-lu 裕禄, CHAO Shu-ch'iao 赵舒翘, Ch'i-hsiu 启秀. It will be seen that these men represented loyalty as much as ability. The Manchu methods of preserving control in the central government are beyond the scope of this paper; HSIEH Pao-chao, *op. cit.* 81, gives some very interesting figures on the proportion of Manchus (a majority on the average) in the Grand Council.

㊹Cf. LIANG Chang-chü 梁章钜, *Shu-yüan chi-lüeh* 枢垣记略 (Brief Notes on the Central Administration), author's preface dated 1823, revised by Prince Kung, I-hsin, who extended it to the Kuang-hsü period, adding 12 chüan to make a total of 28; chüan 22. 4a line 9: "(the Council) for the purpose of secrecy has only (high) officials (kuan 官) and no minor officers (li 吏). Aside from the memorials which are issued for copying every day and handed over to the writers of the Military Archives Office to be transcribed—all documents received or to be issued, archives to be registered, and items regarding which a Rescript has been received and which are ordered to be sealed and deposited, are taken care of by the Secretaries (chang-ching) in person. The regulations and names (of documents) are handed down from the senior officials. Even for capable officials of other departments and bureaus, when they first enter the Council, there are things that they do not understand." Id. ch. 15-19 lists 109 Councillors and some 750 Secretaries up to 1875. For the regulations regarding the Secretaries, cf. *Chia-ch'ing hui-tien* 3. 11b.

㊺Cf. TÊNG Chih-ch'êng 197. Even this figure is probably high for the earlier part of the nineteenth century, if we consider that within the eighteen provinces there were only 18 governors, 10 governor-general, and 8 generals-in-chief; two important memorials a week from each such official, not a low average perhaps, would produce only ten memorials a day for the consideration of the emperor and the Council. The diary of the Grand Councillor WÊNG T'ung-ho (*Wêng wên-chung kung chi-jih* 翁文忠公日记, 40 vols., Shanghai 1928, 21. 84b-101 et passim) in the busy years 1882-1883 records some days on which the diarist drafted none or only one document, others on which he dealt with half a dozen Edicts publicly issued (ming-fa 明发) and one or two court letters (tzǔ-chi 字寄, see sec. 5), other days on which he (and his colleagues?) dealt with 15 documents in audience with the emperor. A total of more than 50 endorsements to handle in one day is especially remarked upon, so also a total of 70 memorials received from the provinces (wai chê 外折) in one day.

㊻Cf. *Chia-ch'ing hui-tien* 3. 1b. The sub-offices of the Council, listed in id. 3. 12a-16b, included: a. the Military Archives Office (Fang Lüeh Kuan 方略馆); b. the Manchu-Chinese Translation Office (Nei Fan Shu Fang 内翻书房); c. the Chancery for the Inspection of Imperial Edicts (Chi Ch'a Ch'in Fêng Shang Yü Shih Chien Ch'u 稽察钦奉上谕事件处, BRUNNERT 105a, "Publication" cannot be justified); d. the Imperial Patent Office (Chung Shu K'o 中书科). BRUNNERT assigns all but the third of these to the Grand Secretariat; it is true that their staffs partly derived from the Secretariat, but they are listed in the *Collected Statutes* under the Grand Council, with which their work was closely associated, as noted below.

㊼There were also Chancery eunuchs (Tsou-shih t'ai-chien 奏事太监) not described in detail in the *Collected Statutes*; and in addition to the staff which handled memorials (Tsou-pên) in Chinese and Manchu, there was another smaller one for Mongolian correspondence. There were of course detailed regulations regarding the handling of Tsou-pên from the capital, in yellow boxes; those that were secret were specially sealed between boards; cf. *Chia-ch'ing hui-tien* 65. 9b-12b.

㊽Cf. our article in *HJAS* 4. 37.

㊾Cf. regulations in *Chia-ch'ing hui-tien* 65. 10a, b.

㊿*Ibid*. The *Collected Statutes* do not support BRUNNERT 105 in the statement that "Metropolitan establishments present their memorials to the Grand Council directly."

㉑Cf. CHAO I's account (*op. cit*. 1. 7a line 1) of the Ch'ien-lung Emperor's activity: "Ten or more of my comrades (in the Council) would take turns every five or six days on early morning duty and even so would feel fatigued. How did the emperor do it day after day? Yet this was even in ordinary times when there was no (important) business. When there was fighting on the western border and military reports arrived, even at midnight he most still see them in person and would be inclined to summon the Grand Councillors and give instructions as to the proper strategy, using a hundred to a thousand words. I would draw up the draft at the time; from the first rough draft to the presentation of the formal version it might take one to two hours, and the emperor, having thrown on some clothes, would still be waiting."

㉒One of the charges against Ho-shên, who usurped great power in the later years of the Ch'ien-lung period, was that he had improperly instructed the provincial authorities to make an extra copy of their memorials and send it to the Grand Council at the same time that the original was sent in for the emperor. By the Chia-ch'ing Emperor the practice was vigorously denounced and prohibited for all time; an Edict of Feb. 12, 1799, declared that all persons entitled to present Tsou-pên thereafter ought to present them "directly to the Throne, and it is not to be permitted that they send duplicates in addition to the Grand Council; the high civil and military officials of the various offices at the capital also shall not previously inform the Grand Councillors of the matters which they are presenting in Tsou-pên; after the various offices at the capital have transmitted their Tsou-pên, the emperor can immediately see (the officials concerned) in audience so as to hold discussions and instruct the offices in question how to manage matters without the Grand Councillors' being involved in giving instructions" (LIANG Chang-chü, *Shu-yüan chi-lüeh* 1. 9b).

Pao-chao HSIEH, *op. cit.* 86, gives a very loose translation of this passage and interprets it without ascertainable justification as an imperial effort to break the power of the Grand Council; this interpretation appears to overlook the historical context, particularly the recent Ho-shên case. We have found no evidence to support HSIEH'S implied statement, *loc. cit.*, that before 1799 memorials were read by the Councillors before the emperor saw them.

㊃Cf. CHÜ Hung-chi 瞿鸿機, *Pao-chih chi-lüeh* 僿直纪略 (Brief Notes of an Official on Duty), postface 1920, 8a-9b; we are indebted to Mr. Chaoying FANG of the Library of Congress for this reference and other assistance: "Memorials from the provinces are all transmitted (to the emperor) a day ahead. When the emperor and Empress Dowager have finished inspecting them, there are some which the emperor has endorsed at the time, there are some which are set aside and not yet endorsed. Both types are sent down to the Councillors to be examined by them, which is called the "morning work" (tsao-shih 早事). (In the same way,) when the Councillors have finished inspecting the memorials, they first take the memorials which have Endorsements and hand the memorials over to the Secretaries to be sorted out and recorded for the archives. For those which have been set aside and not yet endorsed, the Councillors may discuss the draft of an Endorsement or Rescript. They put the memorials in a box and insert a memorandum listing how many there are, and respectfully requesting that Vermilion Endorsements be sent down."

㊄Cf. TÊNG Chih-ch'êng 195; also under note 59 below.

㊅*Chia-ch'ing hui-tien* 3. la: "On ordinary days (the Grand Councillors) are on duty in the Forbidden City in order to await a summons to audience; the hall of the Grand Council is inside the Lung-tsung Mên. Every day in the period from three to five a. m. the Grand Councillors attend at this place. As soon as the management of affairs is finished, the eunuchs of the Chancery of Memorials transmit a Rescript ordering them to disperse, whereupon they go off duty. They are summoned to audience at no fixed time, either once or several times (a day). When the Grand Councillors have come before the emperor, mats are spread upon the floor and they are graciously allowed to sit down. All Tsou-pên which are sent down to various departments of government and which have received the Vermilion Endorsement 'There is a separate Rescript,' or on which there is a Rescript but not yet a Vermilion Endorsement—all are offered up to await an imperial decision. When a Rescript has been received, they go out."

(56)*Chia-ch'ing hui-tien* 3. 2a: "All Edicts and Rescripts which have been publicly issued, after they have been handed down, are sent down to the Grand Secretariat.

"Those which are handed down for a special purpose are called Edicts; those which are handed down in answer to a request presented in a memorial are called Rescripts; or if they are in answer to a request presented in a memorial and are to be proclaimed at the capital and in the provinces, they also are called Edicts. In form, an Edict reads 'the Grand Secretariat has received an imperial Edict'; a Rescript reads 'a Rescript has been received.' On each is recorded the year, month, and day on which it was received. After the drafts above mentioned have been presented to the emperor and the imperial decision has been sent down, those handed down for a special purpose (i. e. Edicts) are immediately sent to be copied; those handed down in answer to a memorial (i. e. Rescripts) are sent to be copied together with the original memorial. Other memorials, such as those which have received the Vermilion Endorsements 'Let the Board in question deliberate and memorialize,' 'Let the Board in question be informed,' are also immediately sent to be copied. All those which have received the Vermilion Endorsement 'Seen', or the Vermilion Endorsement 'Noted' or a Vermilion Endorsement approving or not approving the matter memorialized, or a Vermilion Endorsement which teaches and admonishes, or which praises and encourages, all are examined to see whether they are matters which ought to be dealt with by the Boards and Departments (pu-yüan 部院) at the capital, in which case they are sent to be copied; while those that do not concern the Boards and Departments are not sent to be copied.

"Those which are sent to be copied are given to the Secretaries of the Grand Secretariat, who receive and distribute them for copying (by clerks). Of Memorials which have not received a Vermilion Endorsement, a copy is made from the original memorial. Of Memorials which have received a Vermilion Endorsement, whether or not they are sent to be copied, a duplicate is made. An original memorial bearing a Vermilion Endorsement, if it was a memorial from an office at the capital, is deposited in the Grand Council; if it was a memorial from a province or city (government), then it is returned (to the memorialist).

"Memorials which have been presented by a special messenger are given of memorials to the emperor in the Palace to be sealed up and sent back. Memorials which have been sent in by horse post are sealed up by the Grand Council and given to the Couriers Office of the Board of War for transmission. If a memorial was originally sent in by horse post but there is no need of haste in returning, it is sealed up and retained until a convenient opportunity for sending.

"When the distribution and copying of the memorials at the Grand Secretariat is finished, then the memorials which have been received there are taken back, and together with the memorials which have not been sent to be copied, are placed in the archives.

"Edicts ordering the Grand Councillors to take action, after they have been handed down, are then sealed up and sent off.

"Either an urgent Edict, or a secret Edict, which is not handed down publicly through the Grand Secretariat is called a Court Letter (T'ing-chi 廷寄). It is sealed up by the Grand Council and given to the Couriers Office of the Board of War for transmission."

(57)See under note 58 below.

(58)Cf. LIANG Chang-chü, *op. cit.* 22.4b-6: "Every day between four and eight a.m. memorials (Tsou-pên) must be sent down from the emperor to the Grand Council; the Secretaries divide them up and send them to the various Grand Councillors in succession to read and examine. This is called Receiving the Memorials (chieh-chê 接折). All memorials which have received a Vermilion Endorsement 'There is a separate Rescript,' or for which there is a Rescript but no Vermilion Endorsement as yet received, are collected separately in a yellow box and given to the Grand Councillors, who offer them up respectfully in audience and ask for a Rescript. This is called Having an Interview (chien-mien 见面).

"The Secretaries on duty for a certain day take the Tsou-pên which have been received on that day, the Memoranda (p'ien-tan 片单) which have been transmitted, and the Edicts and Rescripts which have been received from the emperor and carefully classify and record them. Vermilion Endorsements are respectfully recorded in toto, while the particulars of Edicts, Rescripts, and memorials are epitomized. On those which should be sent to the Grand Secretariat the Secretaries mark the character 'Transfer' (chiao 交); on those which should be sent to the Board of War the

Secretaries mark 'For Transmission by Horse' (ma-ti 马递) and the number of *li* to be covered per day. (All these documents) are bound up in thick volumes, one for the spring and summer seasons, one for the autumn and winter seasons. This is called Keeping up with the Work on Hand (sui-shou 随手; cf. remarks of SHAN Shih-yüan 149 on Sui-shou teng-chi tang 随手登记档).

"In copying Edicts and Rescripts that are publicly issued and all types of Memoranda, paper with six ruled lines is used; in copying letters (chi-hsin 寄信) and Edicts to be transmitted (ch'üan-yü 传谕), paper with five ruled lines is used, each line having twenty characters. This is called Having on hand for Transmission (hsien-ti 现递).

"If there are some that have too great a number of characters and must be copied and transmitted in haste, then one man is ordered to cut the draft up into sections, which are divided and quickly copied. This is called Marking off Sections (tien-k'ou 点扣). When the parts have been copied out, they are pasted together again. This is called Joining up Sections (chieh-k'ou 接扣).

"After the documents have been handed to the Ta-la-mi (head of a section of eight Secretaries) to be proofread, they are collected in a yellow box and sent to the Grand Councillors who carefully examine them to see that there are no errors and then give them to the palace eunuchs for presentation to the emperor. This is called Reporting of Rescripts (shu-chih 述旨).

"Documents which have been revised by the Vermilion Pen (Chu-pi 朱笔) are said to have Passed the Vermilion (kuo-chu 过朱). (KUAN Shih-ming 管世铭, *Yün-shan-t'ang shih-chi* 韫山堂诗集 [Collected Poems of Yün-shan-t'ang] ed. 1894, 15. 2 line 2 explains this as To Transfer the Vermilion, i. e. onto a copy of the original document.)

"When a proposed Edict or Rescript has been prepared ahead of time, and after copying has been kept in a box with a view to its being submitted at the proper time, it is called a Document Prostrate on the Ground (fu-ti k'ou 伏地扣).

"When the emperor happens to go on a journey and a document is submitted at the first post station, it is called Transmitted at Dismounting (hsia-ma ti 下马递).

"Whenever an Edict or a Rescript accompanying a memorial is given to the Chinese Registry of the Grand Secretariat, or whenever an Edict or a Rescript not called for by a memorial but handed down specially is given to the Manchu Registry of the Grand Secretariat, or whenever letters and Edicts to be transmitted by horse post are given to the Board of War, or if they are to be given to the various Boards to be discussed in haste or dealt with in haste and so are given specially to the Boards—in all these cases the recipient is made to sign his name and mark in a notebook. This is called to Transfer for Issue (chiao-fa 交发).

"All copying of memorials is the business of the Military Archives Office; in the case of memorials which have been secretly presented or which are the originals used in letters or in Edicts to be transmitted with care, or which have Vermilion Endorsements and ought to be kept secret—in all such cases the Secretaries of the Grand Council themselves make the copies. As each copy of a memorial is finished, the Secretary in question takes the original and the copy and compares them, and then records on the face of the copy what was memorialized by a certain man on a certain subject, the month and day, and whether or not it is to be transferred (chiao 交). This is called Filling in the Face (k'ai-mien 开面).

"The Secretaries on duty for the day take the original memorials from the provinces which have been received on that day, putting each in its original envelope, and deliver them to the Chancery of Memorials. This is called Transferring the Memorials (chiao-chê 交折).

"The Edicts and Rescripts received on that day and the Memoranda transmitted are copied and bound into a volume; day by day this is added to, and it is changed for a new volume every month. This is called Cleaning the Archives (ch'ing-tang 清档).

"Memorials and Memoranda despatched from the Grand Council, or returned from the Grand Secretariat or elsewhere, and preserved in this office form one bundle every day and a package every half-month. This is called the Monthly Memorials (yüeh-chê 月折)."

(59)Prof. TÊNG Chih-ch'êng 197 states that it was a rule that the issuing of all imperial Edicts must be completed by the Council officers on the same day that the decisions concerned were handed down from the emperor.

(60)Cf. *Chia-ch'ing hui-tien* 3. 2a, espec. last line; also 65. 11b and *Kuang-hsü hui-tien* 82. 12a: "Every day the various memorials which are transmitted (excepting those memorials transmitted by express post, all of which are handed by the Chancery eunuchs directly to the Grand Council for sealing and returning [fa 发], and which are not returned [fa-hsia 发下] by the Chancery)—all other memorials from the provinces, no matter whether they have received a Rescript or not, are securely sealed by the Chancery eunuchs; on the following day they are handed to the Chancery to be returned (in each case) to the man originally transmitting the memorial, to be reverently received by him. As to the various memorials transmitted at the capital (excepting those which are retained by the emperor and are returned by the Grand Council, or which are ordered to be handed to the ministers of state having audience on that day, to be returned by them)—regarding all other memorials which are returned by the Chancery, whether they have received the Rescript 'Let it be as recommended' or have received the Rescript 'Noted,' straightway the Chancery transmits the imperial will that (the memorial) may be received (by the memorialist)." The later fate of returned memorials is a puzzling question. HSÜ (1) 186 describes the vast number of Tsou-pên, over 100,000 for the Ch'ien-lung period, preserved in the Palace archives. The question whether and in what manner returned memorials would have found their way into the archives demands further attention.

# ON THE CH'ING TRIBUTARY SYSTEM

J. K. FAIRBANK AND S. Y. TÊNG
HARVARD UNIVERSITY

## 1. THE TRADITIONAL ROLE OF TRIBUTE

Chinese foreign policy in the nineteenth century can be understood only against its traditional Chinese background, the tributary system. This system for the conduct of foreign relations had been directly inherited from the Ming Dynasty (1368-1644) and modified to suit the needs of the Ch'ing government. As a Confucian world-order in the Far East, it continued formally in existence until the very end of the nineteenth century, and was superseded in practice only gradually, after 1842, by the British treaty system which has until recently governed the foreign relations of Siam, Japan, and other states, as well as China. The Chinese diplomatic documents of a century ago are therefore really unintelligible unless they are studied in the light of the imperial tributary system which produced them. [1]

The ramifications of this vast subject, in political theory, in international trade, and in diplomacy, have been explored by a few pioneer scholars, [2] some of whom have traced the development of the administration of foreign trade from the Sung up to the late Ming, while others have painstakingly established translations of texts concerning the seven great Ming expeditions of the early fifteenth century. These expeditions under the eunuch CHÊNG Ho 郑和 and others in the period 1405-1433 took Chinese fleets of as many as 60 vessels and 27,000 men into the Indian Ocean and in some cases as far as Arabia and Africa, and the period has rightly attracted attention as the high point of Chinese tributary relations. Studies of the tributary system in the Ch'ing period, however, are less numerous; relatively little effort has been made to link the sorry Chinese foreign policy of the nineteenth century with the great tradition which lay behind it. To do so will require the efforts of many workers over a long period.

The present article attempts a preliminary survey of the tributary system as it developed under the Ch'ing Dynasty. In order to reach useful conclusions on a subject of such magnitude, we have based this study chiefly upon the various editions of the *Collected Statutes*,[③] which not only are the fundamental official source for the general structure of the system, but also reflect its history, as mirrored in successive changes and revised editions, over a period of more than two hundred years. The *Collected Statutes*, moreover, were issued both as a record of administrative practice and as a guide to the bureaucracy in its day by day activities. In this they excel for our purposes the official compilations of a later date, such as the *Draft History of the Ch'ing Dynasty (Ch'ing-shih kao)*, which are at one remove from the scene and compiled by, if not for, posterity. Before proceeding to the presentation and analysis of this material, we offer below a brief explanatory discussion of the function of tribute in the Chinese state, which may serve to pose further problems for research.

For purpose of analysis it may be pointed out (1) that the tributary system was a natural outgrowth of the cultural preeminence of the early Chinese, (2) that it came to be used by the rulers of China for political ends of self-defense, (3) that in practice it had a very fundamental and important commercial basis, and (4) that it served as the medium for Chinese international relations and diplomacy. It was, in short, a scheme of entire things, and deserves attention as one historical solution to problems of world-organization.

Behind the tributary system as it became institutionalized in the Ming and Ch'ing periods lay the age-old tradition of Chinese cultural superiority over the barbarians.④ Continuously from the bronze age, when Shang civilization first appears as a culture-island in north China, this has been a striking element in Chinese thought, perpetuated by the eternal conflict between the settled agrarian society of the Yellow River basin and the pastoral nomads of the steppe beyond the Great Wall, as well as by the persistent expansion of the Chinese to the south among the tribes whose remnants are now being absorbed in Yunnan and Kweichow. From this contact with the nomads of the north and west and with the aborigines of the south, the Chinese appear to have derived certain basic assumptions which may be stated as follows: first, that Chinese superiority over the barbarians had a cultural rather than a mere political basis; it rested less upon force than upon the Chinese way of life embodied in such things as the Confucian code of conduct and the use of the Chinese written language; the sign of the barbarian was not race or origin so much as non-adherence to this way of life. From this it followed, secondly, that those barbarians who wished to "come and be transformed" (lai-hua), and so participate in the benefits of (Chinese) civilization, must recognize the supreme position of the emperor; for the Son of Heaven represented all mankind, both Chinese and barbarian, in his ritual sacrifices before the forces of nature. Adherence to the Chinese way of life automatically entailed the recognition of the emperor's mandate to rule all men. This supremacy of the emperor as mediator between Heaven and Earth was most obviously acknowledged in the performance of the kotow, the three kneelings and nine prostrations to which European envoys later objected.⑤ It was also acknowledged by the bringing of a tribute of local produce, by the formal bestowal of a seal, comparable to the investiture of a vassal in medieval Europe, and in other ways. Thus the tributary system, as the sum total of these formalities, was the mechanism by which barbarous non-Chinese regions were given their place in the all-embracing Chinese political, and therefore ethical, scheme of things.⑥

　　This general theory is of course familiar to the most casual student of

Chinese history, and yet the realities of the situation are still a matter of dispute. In the intercourse between the Chinese state and the barbarians, commercial relations became inseparably bound up with tributary. Trade was conducted by barbarian merchants who accompanied the tributary envoy to the frontier or even to the capital; sometimes it was conducted by the members of the mission itself. That tribute was a cloak for trade has been a commonplace ever since merchants from the Roman orient arrived in China in 166 A. D. claiming to be envoys of Marcus Aurelius. Thus Benedict DE GOEZ, crossing Central Asia in the year 1604, describes the "sham embassies" of merchants from the Western kingdoms who "forge public letters in the names of the kings whom they profess to represent" and "under pretence of being ambassadors go and offer tribute to the emperor."⑦ Innumerable other examples could be cited wherein tribute, in the minds of the tribute bearers, was merely a formality connected with trade; at Macao and Canton, indeed, the Europeans in their concentration upon the substance of commerce eventually forgot all about the formality which theoretically still went with it.

This economic interpretation, however, is made from the point of view of the barbarians. The motivation of the Court is a different matter.

The argument that the tributary system was developed by the Court chiefly for political defense has been succinctly stated by Dr. T. F. TSIANG: "Out of this period of intense struggle and bitter humiliation [the eleventh and twelfth centuries], the neo-Confucian philosophy, which began then to dominate China, worked out a dogma in regard to international relations, to hold sway in China right to the middle of the nineteenth century ... That dogma asserts that national security could only be found in isolation and stipulates that whoever wished to enter into relations with China must do so as China's vassal, acknowledging the supremacy of the Chinese emperor and obeying his commands, thus ruling out all possibility of international intercourse on terms of equality. It must not be construed to be a dogma of conquest or universal dominion, for it imposed nothing on foreign peoples who chose to remain outside the Chinese world. It sought peace and security, with both of which international relations were held incompatible. If relations there had to be, they must be of the suzerain-vassal type, acceptance of which meant to the Chinese acceptance of the Chinese ethic on the part of the barbarian...

"It must not be assumed that the Chinese Court made a profit out of... tribute. The imperial gifts bestowed in return were usually more valuable than the tribute... Chinese statesmen before the latter part of the nineteenth century would have ridiculed the notion that national finance and wealth should be or could be promoted by means of international trade. On China's part the permission to trade was intended to be a mark of imperial bounty and a means of keeping the barbarians in the proper state of submissiveness..."⑧

Thus we might conclude that trade and tribute were cognate aspects of a single system of foreign relations, the moral value of tribute being the more important in the minds of the rulers of China, and the material value of trade in the minds of the barbarians; this balance of interests would allow mutual satisfaction and the system would continue to function. From this it might be concluded further that the tributary system really worked in reverse, the submission of the barbarians being actually bought and paid for by the trade conceded to them by China. But this is an over-simplification which runs counter to the whole set of ideas behind the system, and it also overlooks the interesting possibility, which deserves exploration, of an imperial economic interest—for instance, in the silk export trade. In short, it seems impossible at present to make more than one generalization: that the tributary system was a framework within which all sorts of interests, personal and imperial, economic and social, found their expression. Further study should reveal an interplay between greed and statecraft, dynastic policy and vested interest, similar to that in other great political institutions.

One untouched aspect of the system is its functioning as a diplomatic medium. Since all foreign relations in the Chinese view were ipso facto tributary relations, it followed that all types of international intercourse, if they occurred at all in the experience of China, had to be fitted into the tributary system. Thus Chinese envoys were sometimes sent abroad to spy out the enemy or to seek allies, and foreign envoys came and conducted negotiations at the capital, all within this framework. As an introduction to this aspect of the subject, we quote below from the prefaces to the sections on tributary ritual in the *Ta-Ming chi-li* 大明集礼 (Collected Ceremonies of the Ming Dynasty), an official work of the Ming period.⑨ Naturally, these prefaces recount what the Court hoped everyone would believe had generally occurred during the course of Chinese history, but this merely enhances their value for our purpose. (We omit passages recounting details concerning various tribes and rulers.)

"CEREMONIAL FOR VISITORS: (1) FOREIGN KINGS PRESENTING TRIBUTE AT COURT (Fan-wang ch'ao-kung 蕃王朝贡).

"The kings of former times cultivated their own refinement and virtue in order to subdue persons at a distance, whereupon the barbarians (of the east and north) came to Court to have audience. This comes down as a long tradition 其来尚矣.

"In the time of King T'ang of Yin (trad. dates B. C. 1766-1754), the Ti-ch'iang [an ancient Tibetan tribe in E. Kansu and Kokonor], distant barbarians, came to offer gifts and to visit the king. In the time of (King) T'ai Mou (trad. dates B. C. 1637-1563) the remote tribes [ch'ung-i 重译 i. e. those so far off as to require repeated interpretations] which came to Court (consisted of) 76 countries.

"When King Wu of the Chou (trad. dates 1122-1116) overcame the Shang, (there was) a great meeting of the feudal lords and the barbarians on the four quarters (Ssǔ-i), and there was written (the chapter on) the meeting of the princes.⑩ In the autumn officials (section) of the *Chou li*,⑪ (it is stated that) the interpreting officer had charge of the envoys of the countries of the wild tribes of the south and east (man-i), of Min (Fukien?), of the north (mai), and of the west (jung-ti), and gave them instructions and explanations.

"The Han Dynasty established (an officer) in charge of guests and official interpreters, a chief and assistants, to guide the barbarians (Ssŭ-i) who came to Court to present tribute. Also they established (an office) in charge of dependent states, and a chief interpreter of the nine [languages; i. e. one capable of speaking the tongues of foreign nations]. Under the Emperor Wu in 111 B. C. the Yeh-lang [chieftain, from the Yunnan-Szechwan frontier] came to Court. Thereafter the outer barbarians sent tribute to Court without interruption. In 53 B. C. the chieftain of the Hsiung-nu came to the Court. In 51 B. C. the Hsiung-nu chieftain, Chi-chü-shan⑫ 稽居㹚 came to Court. Both had audience at the Sweet Spring Palace.⑬ In 28 B. C. the barbarians from all sides (Ssŭ-i) came to the Court and received direction from the grand master of ceremonial for ambassadors.⑭ Under the Emperor Shun in 136 A. D. the king of the Wo-nu (Japan?) came to Court. For all of these there were regulations for entertainment at banquets and the bestowal of gifts.

"Under the T'ang there established the Chu K'o Lang Chung 主客郎中 (Secretary in Charge of Guests), in charge of all the barbarians (fan) who came to Court. His activities in receiving and entertaining (them) were four in number: Going out to meet and greet them (lao 劳); preparing them for audience (i. e. warning them); foreign kings receiving an audience; banqueting the rulers of foreign states. The ceremonies for these (activities) were detailed…

"In the Sung period there were more than forty states which presented tribute at Court, all of them merely sending envoys to present the tribute. Although foreign kings did not regularly themselves come to the Court for audience, still the ceremonies for reception and audience which appear in the books of ceremony are about the same as for the T'ang.

"Yüan Dynasty: in 1210 the king of the Uigurs, I-tu-hu 亦都护, came to Court. Under Shih-tsu (Kublai Khan) in 1264, an imperial command was given to the King of Korea (Kao-li), Chih 植, ordering him to cultivate the ceremony of shih-chien.⑮ In the sixth month Chih came to the Court at Shang-tu ["Xanadu," near modern Dolonor]. Thereafter when the (rulers of) foreign countries came to Court, they waited for the day of a great Court assembly on the first day of the first month or on an imperial birthday, and then performed the ceremony.

"Now it is proposed, as to the reigning dynasty, that when foreign kings come to Court, there shall first be despatched an official of the city of Nanking (Ying-t'ien fu) to go out to meet them and greet them. When they have arrived at the Residence⑯ there shall be sent further (an official of) the Board (of Ceremony) at the capital to prepare a feast. Thereupon they shall practice the ceremonies. They are to have imperial audience in the Fêng-t'ien Hall 奉天殿 and to have audience with the Heir-apparent in the Eastern Palace. When the imperial audiences are finished, a banquet is offered to them. The officers and departments (of government) at the capital all are to prepare banquets to entertain them. When they return, officers are to be sent to escort them out of the boundaries. Now all their ceremonial is drawn up to form the section on "Foreign kings presenting tribute at court..."⑰

"(2) FOREIGN ENVOYS PRESENTING TRIBUTE AT COURT (Fan-shih ch'ao-kung 蕃使朝贡).

"According to the *Chou li*, 'when the envoys from the four quarters arrive, if they are great guests then they are received ceremoniously; if they are small guests then their presents are accepted and their statements are listened to.'⑱ By small guests is meant the official envoys sent by foreign countries. The envoys of foreign countries all are barbarians, and do not practice these ceremonies. Therefore one only listens to their statements, and that is all. When King Wu overcame the Shang, he opened communications with the nine I (eastern barbarians) and the eight

Man (southern barbarians)... States at a great distance came to offer up presents; in all cases their offerings were accepted and their statements were listened to.

"Under the Han... (a total of) thirty-six states were all dependents of the Middle (Kingdom) and offered tribute... (when) they came to present offerings, they all received rewards so as to send them away with gifts.

"In the T'ang when foreign envoys offered tribute, the ceremonies for their banqueting and audience had four parts: going out to meet and greet them; preparing them for audience; receiving the foreign envoys' congratulatory memorials and presents; and the emperor's banquet for the envoys of foreign countries...

"Under the Sung when the envoys of foreign countries arrived, they were feasted and given audience in the hall of the palace (tzǔ-ch'ên tien 紫宸殿) and in the Ch'ung-chêng Hall 崇政殿. The ceremonies for going out to meet and greet (the envoys), preparing them for audience, and entertaining them at banquets, all were the same as for the T'ang...

"In the Yüan period from the time of the Emperor T'ai-tsu (Jenghis Khan, 1206-1227) the Uigurs (wei-wu-êrh 畏吾儿), the Moslems (hui-hu 回鹘), the Tanguts (Hsi Hsia), the Western Regions, and Koryǒ all sent envoys to present tribute. After the time of the Emperor Shih-tsu (Kublai Khan 1260-1294), Annam, Champa, Yunnan, Laos,⑲ Northern Burma (Mien kuo 缅国), Tali (in Yunnan), and Fu-lang,⑳ all sent envoys to offer up tribute.

"Under the reigning dynasty in 1369, the country of Champa sent a minister (named) Hu-tu-man 虎都蛮 to come with tribute; Koryǒ sent a minister, the President of the Board of Ceremonies, HUNG Shang-tsai 洪尚载; Annam sent a minister, T'UNG Shih-min 同时敏, and others. All presented tribute of local produce. When they had arrived (at the borders of China), an officer memorialized for the emperor's information and went out of the capital (ch'u kuo mên 出国门) to meet and greet them. On an appointed day after they had presented a tributary memorial and presents of local produce at the Fêng-t'ien Hall, they presented their memorials and local produce at the central palace (i. e. to the empress) and at the eastern palace (to the heir-apparent). After the emperor sent officials to the Residence (hui-t'ung-kuan) to give them banquets, the heir-apparent again sent officials to treat them ceremoniously. The departments and offices at the capital all held banquets. When they were about to return, a legate was sent to console them and escort them out of the boundaries. If it was an ordinary Court, then the clerks in the Grand Secretariat (chung-shu) took receipt of the tributary memorials and the local produce. On the following day the envoys followed the ushers into an imperial audience, and their banquet was conferred upon them. The emperor and the heir-apparent composed rescripts (to the tributary memorials) and treated (the envoys) ceremoniously. We now arrange these ceremonies to form the section on 'Foreign envoys presenting tribute at court...'"④

"(3)SENDING (CHINESE) ENVOYS (ABROAD) (Ch'ien-shih 遣使).

"In ancient times the Son of Heaven, toward the feudal princes who had submitted to him, occasionally would observe the ceremony of inquiring about charities, congratulations, or mourning sacrifices. Envoys were not yet sent to pay visits outside the Nine Chou (i. e. the empire).

"In the Han period the Emperor Kao (B. C. 206-195) sent LU Chia 陆贾 on a mission to Nan-yüeh (Kwangtung-Kwangsi), conferring upon him a seal of office. In the time of the filial (Emperor) Wên (B. C. 179-157) LU Chia again was sent, receiving an imperial mandate (chao) to go to Nan-yüeh. When the filial (Emperor) Wu (B. C. 140-87) had dealings with the barbarians (Ssŭ-i) he sent CHANG Ch'ien 张骞 on a mission to the Western Regions (in the capacity of) an imperial guard (lang 郎), and Su Wu 苏武 on a mission to the Hsiung-nu as a lieutenant-general (chung lang chiang 中郎将). Thereafter whenever a foreign kingdom had a bereavement, condoling inquiries were made; when they came with inquiries and presents, they were answered and rewarded; when they tendered their allegiance, an imperial seal was bestowed upon them. The Emperor Kuang-wu in 50 A. D. sent the lieutenant-general TUAN Ch'ên 段郴 and the assistant governor WANG Yü 王郁, on a mission to the southern chieftain (of the Hsiung-nu). The chieftain prostrated himself to receive the imperial mandate. In 55 A. D. the chieftain died and (the emperor) sent the lieutenant-general, TUAN Ch'ên, in command of an army to go and offer condolences…

"In the T'ang period when an envoy was sent to a foreign country he was called 'an envoy to foreign countries' (ju-fan shih 入蕃使)…

"In the Sung period when an envoy was sent to a foreign country he was called 'an envoy with a state message' (kuo-hsin shih 国信使). The Emperor T'ai-tsu in 975 sent the Hsi shang ko mên shih (西上阁门使 Usher of the Upper Western Hall), HAO Ch'ung-hsin 郝崇信, on a mission to the Khitan, with the secretary of the Court of Sacrificial Worship as his assistant. From this time on, messengers were sent without interruption…

"Under the Yüan in 1211 (the emperor) sent an envoy to the kingdom of the Uigurs. Their ruler, I-tu-hu, was greatly pleased, and treated (the envoy) with very extensive ceremony. For this reason he sent an envoy to pay tribute. In 1260 (the Emperor, i. e. Kublai Khan) sent the Director of the Board of Ceremonies, MÊNG Chia 孟甲, and the Assistant Department Director LI Chün 李俊, as envoys to Annam and Tali. In 1266 he sent the Vice-President of the Board of War, Hei-ti 黑的, as envoy to Japan. In 1291 he sent the President of the Board of Ceremonies, CHANG Li-tao 张立道, as envoy to Annam; in 1293 he also sent LIANG Tsêng 梁曾 and CH'ÊN Fu 陈孚 as envoys to Annam, to summon envoys to come to the Court; he also gave an imperial command that the son (of the ruler of Annam) should come for an audience.

"The reigning dynasty has united the whole empire into one. Various envoys have been sent out in order to show compassion to those at a distance. To such countries as Korea (Kao-li), Annam, and Champa imperial proclamations have been promulgated and the imperial commands have been sent to them. Furthermore by imperial command envoys have gone and conferred the imperial seal. The dynasty has also sent down fragrant presents in order to make sacrifices to the mountains and streams of these countries. Its purpose in soothing and subduing the barbarians of the four quarters is most complete. We now in detail set forth the ceremonies connected with the issue of imperial proclamations, the conferring of a seal, and the bestowals and gifts to form the section on 'Sending Envoys…'"[2]

From the official résumé just quoted, several things stand out. Relations between the Son of Heaven and his tributaries were on an ethical basis, and hence reciprocal. The tributaries were submissive and reverent, the emperor was compassionate and condescending. These reciprocal relationships required formal expression. Presentation of tribute was a ritual performance, balanced by the forms of imperial hospitality and bestowal of imperial gifts. Hence the great importance of ceremonies, so complicated that they must be practiced under guidance beforehand. The detailed regulations given at length in official Chinese works[3] might fruitfully be compared with the feudal and ecclesiastical ceremonies of medieval Europe.

But, as in European experience, very practical results were achieved within this cloak of ritual. Mourning for the dead being a major ceremony in the Confucian life, the emperor could properly send his envoys abroad on the death of a foreign ruler, at just the time when it was desirable to have information as to the new ruler and perhaps exert pressure upon affairs in the foreign state. TUAN Ch'ên, in going to offer condolences to the Hsiung-nu, incidentally took an army with him. Bestowal of an imperial seal upon a new ruler has obvious analogies to the recognition of new governments practiced in the West. Diplomatic courtesies of a sort were extended to tributary envoys, who traveled by government post and received state burial if they died in China. Other comparisons can be made to show that the tributary system functioned, among other things, as a diplomatic medium. The fact that the normal needs of foreign intercourse could be met in this egocentric manner tended to perpetuate it, and made any other system seem impossible, hence the fatal tenacity with which, the Ch'ing Court in the modern period tried to solve its foreign problems through the ancient tributary mechanism.

## 2. TRIBUTARIES OF THE LATE MING

The foregoing essay has attempted to suggest certain lines of approach to this subject, any one of which might be made a topic in itself. The nature of the sources, however, seems to prescribe a certain order of investigation: studies of political theory and national psychology connected with tribute must wait upon a more complete understanding of the basic facts of the system, in particular upon an understanding of its economic basis—what were the conditions of trade between the tributaries and China? This important commercial aspect, in turn, can be approached perhaps most easily through a study of the so-called tribute embassies themselves—whence did they come and how often? This brings us to the immediate question: what places outside of China were actively tributary, and what fluctuations can be observed in their sending of embassies?

Students of the Ch'ing period are fortunate not only in their opportunities in a virgin field but also in the fact that a number of eminent scholars have established, by their studies of the Ming period, certain *points d'appui* from which Ch'ing studies may take their start. Researches on the maritime expeditions under CHÊNG Ho are a case in point, to say nothing of those concerning medieval travellers in Central Asia. Since, moreover, the Ch'ing took over the Ming administration almost as it stood and altered it only by degrees, and the Ch'ing system of government can really be understood only against its Ming background. We therefore begin with a glance at the tributary system of the late Ming period.

With the exception of certain aboriginal border tribes under the supervision of the Board of War, all Ming tributary relations were under the management of the Reception Department (Chu K'o Ssŭ 主客司) of the Board of Ceremonies.[24] We present below (table 1) the tributaries listed under the Reception Department in the last Ming edition of the *Collected Statutes* (1587).[25] It will at once be observed that this list includes those distant places visited by the fleets under CHÊNG Ho some two centuries earlier, with most of which formal relations had ceased as soon as the Chinese expeditions failed to reappear after 1433. It therefore gives a totally incorrect impression of the number of countries actively tributary in 1587; it is, rather, a list of all countries with which the Ming Dynasty had ever had nominal tributary relations.[26] For the reader's guidance it may be totaled as follows, under the categories given in the *Collected Statutes*:

COURT TRIBUTE:

[1] Barbarians of the east and south, part one: 18 (Korea through Tan-pa);

[2] Barbarians of the east and south, part two: 45 (Sulu through Cananore);

[3] Northern barbarians:

    Small princes toward the north: 3 entries (Mongol princes, et al.)
    Barbarians of the northeast: 2 entries (Jurchen, et al.)
    Western barbarians; part one: 4 entries (Hami etc.)
        38 countries of the Western Regions
        13 other western places.

[4] Western barbarians, part two: (Tibet, and aboriginal or border tribes, some 20 entries, not listed in this article.)

(Total entries listed below in this article: 123.)

The Chinese version of these place names and the mechanics of their identification we have confined to an index, part 8 below.

In anticipation of our second problem, how often these tributaries were recorded as sending tribute (which may indicate the frequency of trade), we note after each place the dates② mentioned by the compilers of the *Collected Statutes* in connection with each place as they listed it. These may be presumed to be important milestones at least in the opinion of the compilers. (The first seven states, Korea through Champa, sent tribute with comparative regularity, and the compilers of the *Collected Statutes* gave certain additional facts which we indicate regarding the periodicity and route of their tribute embassies.)

### TABLE 1  MING TRIBUTARIES AS OF 1587

| COUNTRY | TRIBUTE EMBASSIES | PERIODICITY | ROUTE VIA |
|---|---|---|---|
| Korea (Chao-hsien) | 1369 ff. | 1372, every 3 yrs. or 1 yr.; after 1403, annual | Yalu R., Liao-yang, Shanhaikuan |
| Japan | 1374 refused, accepted 1381, 1403-1551 occasional | 10 yrs. | Ningpo |
| Liu-ch'iu | 1368 ff. | 2 yrs. | Foochow |
| Annam | 1369 ff. | 3 yrs. | P'ing-yang chou, Kwangsi |
| Cambodia (Chên-la) | 1371 ff. | Court tribute indefinite | Kwangtung |
| Siam | 1371 ff. | 3 yrs. | Kwangtung |
| Champa | 1369 ff. | 3 yrs. | Kwangtung |
| Java (Chao-wa) | 1372, 1381, 1404, 1407 | 1443 every 3 yrs., later indefinite | |

| COUNTRY | TRIBUTE EMBASSIES | COUNTRY | TRIBUTE EMBASSIES |
|---|---|---|---|
| Pahang | 1378, 1414 | Samudra (Hsü-wên-ta-na) | 1383 |
| Pai-hua | 1378 | | |
| Palembang (San-fo-ch'i) | 1368, 1371, 1373, 1375, 1377 | Samudra (Su-mên-ta-la) | 1405, 1407, 1431, 1435 |
| Brunei (P'o-ni) | 1371, 1405, 1408, 1414, 1425 | Chola (Hsi-yang So-li) | 1370, 1403 |

| COUNTRY | TRIBUTE EMBASSIES |
|---|---|
| Chola (So-li) | 1372 |
| Lan-pang | 1376 (in periods 1403-1424, 1426-1435 joined a neighboring country in sending tribute) |
| Tan-pa | 1377 |
| Sulu | 1417, 1421 |
| Ku-ma-la | 1420 |
| Calicut | 1405, 1407, 1409 |
| Malacca | (via Kwangtung) 1405, 1411, 1412, 1414, 1424, 1434, frequently 1445 ff., 1459 |
| Borneo (? So-lo) | 1406 |
| Aru | 1407 with Calicut et al. |
| Quilon | 1407 with Samudra et al. |
| Bengal | 1408, 1414, 1438 |
| Ceylon | 1411, 1412, 1445, 1459 |
| Jaunpur | 1420 |
| Syria (Fu-lin) | 1371 |
| Cochin | 1404, 1412 |
| Melinde | 1414 |
| The Philippines (Lü-sung) | 1372, 1405, 1576 (via Fukien) |
| Tieh-li | |
| Jih-lo-hsia-chih | sent tribute with |
| Marinduque | Java in 1405 |
| (Ho-mao-li) | |
| Ku-li-pan-tsu (Pansur?) | 1405 |
| Ta-hui | 1405 |
| Hormuz | 1405 |

| COUNTRY | TRIBUTE EMBASSIES |
|---|---|
| Coyampadi (Kan-pa-li) | 1414 |
| Cail | Yung-lo period (1403-1424) |
| Djofar | " |
| Maldive Is. | " |
| Burma (A-wa) | " |
| Lambri (Nan-wu-li) | " |
| Kelantan | " |
| Ch'i-la-ni | " |
| Hsia-la-pi (Arabia?) | " |
| K'u-ch'a-ni | " |
| Wu-shê-la-t'ang | " |
| Aden | " |
| Rum, Asia Minor | " |
| Bengal (P'êng-chia-na) | " |
| Shê-la-ch'i | " |
| Pa-k'o-i | " |
| Coyampadi (K'an-pa-i-t'i) | " |
| Hei-ka-ta (also Pai-ka-ta in 1432) | " |
| La-sa | " |
| Barawa, Africa | " |
| Mogadisho | " |
| Lambri (Nan-p'o-li) | " |
| Ch'ien-li-ta | " |
| Cananore (Jurfattan) | |

The list of tributaries in the *Wan-li hui-tien* then continues with the northern barbarians, chiefly the Wa-la (Oirats), as quoted below.⑱ It then continues: "Western barbarians, first section: from Lanchow in Shensi one crosses the (Yellow) River and goes 1500 *li* to reach Su-chou. From Su-chou west 70 *li* is the Jade Gate (Chia Yü Kuan). Everything outside the Jade Gate is called the western regions. But to the south of Shensi everything beyond the frontier from Szechwan to Yunnan is called the western tribes (Hsi-Fan). In the western regions are seven districts: Hami, Anting, A-tuan (Khotan?), Ch'ih-chin Mongolia, Ch'ü-hsien, Han-tung, and Han-tung the Left, all west of the Gate, Hami being the farthest west 皆在关西而哈密又最西…"

| | | | |
|---|---|---|---|
| Hami | tribute begun 1404, annual from 1465, every 5 yrs. from 1475 | district of Han-tung | |
| | | Ch'ih-chin Mongolia | 1404, every 5 yrs. from 1563 |
| district of Anting | begun 1374 | district of Ch'ü-hsien | 1437 |

"The tribute sent to the Court by the thirty-eight countries of the western regions all passes through Hami. As to their periods for tribute, it may be sent off perhaps once in 3 or once in 5 years. The (number of) men may not exceed 35." (The 38 countries are as follows:)

| | | | |
|---|---|---|---|
| | | Ilibalik (and Bashibalik) | sent tribute 1391, 1406,1413,1418(?), 1437, continuous from 1457 |
| Herat | sent an envoy in (1402), 1409, 1437 | | |
| Ha-san | | Nieh-k'o-li (or Mieh-k'o-li) | |
| Ha-lieh-erh | | | |
| Sha-ti-man | | Badakshan (Pa-tan-sha) | |
| Kashgar | | | |
| Ha-ti-lan (Khotelan?) | | Balkh | |
| Sairam (Sai-lan) | | Almalik? | |
| Sao-lan (Sairam?) | | Togmak | |

| | |
|---|---|
| Chalish | Ya-hsi |
| Kan-shih | Yarkand |
| Bukhara? | Jung (Western barbarians?) |
| P'a-la | |
| Shiraz | Pai |
| Nishapur | Wu-lun |
| Kashmir | Alani |
| Tabriz | Khotan? (A-tuan) |
| Kuo-sa-ssǔ | Yeh-ssǔ-ch'êng |
| Khodjend? (Huo-t'an) | K'un-ch'êng (Kunduz?) |
| Khodjend (Huo-chan) | Shê-hei |
| Kucha (K'u-hsien) | Pai-yin |
| Khodjend (Sha-liu-hai-ya) | K'o-chieh |

(The list continues with further countries in the west as follows:)

| | | | |
|---|---|---|---|
| Turfan including after 1430: | 1430, 1497, 1509, 1510, after 1523 once in 5 yrs. | Medina | Hsüan-tê period (1426-1435) |
| Karakhodjo (Huo-chou); | 1409, 1430 | Khotan (Yü-t'ien) | 1408 |
| Liu-ch'ên city | 1430 | Jih-lo | Yung-lo period (1403-1424) |
| Samarkand | 1387, 1389, 1391, etc.; after 1523 once in 5 yrs. | Badakshan (Pa-ta-hei-shang) | " |
| Kingdom of Rum (Asia Minor) | after 1524 once in 5 yrs., via Kansu | Andkhui | " |
| | | Isfahan | " |
| Arabia (Tien-fang, Mecca?) | Hsüan-tê period (1426-1435), 1517, in Chia-ching period (1522-1566) fixed to be once in 5 yrs. | Khorassan | 1432 |
| | | Ê-chi-chieh | Chia-ching period (1522-1566) |
| | | Ha-hsin | " |

(The list concludes with Tibet (chüan 108), followed by a score of temples and tribes of the Tibetan border or the southwest.)

When compared with the lists recorded in other Ming sources, this one appears to be relatively complete,㉒ enabling us to make the following tentative analysis:

Eliminating the first seven adjacent states and those entries which appear to be duplicates, there are some 50 tributaries communicating by sea (of which about 15 remain unidentified so far as we know). A dozen of these states are recorded as sending tribute *before* the period of the great Ming expeditions under CHÊNG HO (c. 1405-1433). But only half a dozen are recorded as doing so *after* 1433 (Java 1463 ff., Samudra 1435, Malacca 1459, Bengal 1438, Ceylon 1459, Philippines 1576—an exception, concerned with a reward for the seizure of pirates). Moreover, with the exception noted, not one of these maritime tributaries is recorded as arriving *after* 1460.

Turning to the tributaries communicating by land, if we pass over the Mongols and others on the north, and the western frontier districts such as Hami, we find a list of 38 tributaries of the western region which are said to communicate via Hami. These are listed without comment and are almost the same list, item for item, as that given in the *Ming History* (Cf. BRETSCHNEIDER 2. 314-315), also without comment. Almost half of these places are of doubtful identity, so far as we are aware, and the entire list, so closely and yet not exactly copied later in the *Ming History*, seems like a hand-me-down—a traditional roll-call without validity for our purposes; perhaps its origin can be found in some work of an earlier period. By contrast, the dozen western places which conclude the list, and concerning which details are given, are plainly of historical importance, particularly Turfan, Samarkand, Rum, and Arabia. These four places, plus Ilibalik and the two obscure items at the end, appear to be the chief "tributaries" which functioned independently via Central Asia, all the others being grouped under Hami. They seem well suited to serve as the alleged or actual sources of merchants in caravan trade. It is significant that their tributary activity appears regularly established at the beginning of the Chia-ching period after 1522.

These observations warrant the hypothesis that the chief activity in the sending of tribute embassies under the Ming shifted from the southern sea-routes to the northwestern land-routes after the middle of the fifteenth century, just as the capital had been shifted from Nanking to Peking in 1421.

This general hypothesis is supported by reference to the lists of tribute embassies recorded at the end of each annual section in the annals of the *Ming History* (*Ming-shih pên-chi*). For analytical purposes we have constructed a chart of these embassies as recorded for the period 1369-1643. Publication of so voluminous a document does not seem feasible, particularly when there are so many problems of identification and the like still unsolved; but certain observations may be based upon it. Judging by the completeness with which the embassies from the Southern Sea and the Indian Ocean were recorded during the period of the great maritime expeditions,㉚ this record given in the annals may be considered complete enough for survey purposes. ㉛

(1) First it is worth noting again that embassies from Southeast Asia began to come to the Ming capital from the very beginning of the dynasty, years before the first of the maritime expeditions under CHÊNG Ho were sent out. This is not surprising in view of the long growth of Chinese trade with this region and the Mongol expeditions which had already sailed through it. Thus in the period from 1369 to 1404 (CHÊNG Ho's first expedition occupied the years 1405-1407) tribute is recorded from Java (Chao-wa) in 11 different years, from Java (Shê-p'o) in 1378, from Brunei (P'o-ni) in 1371, from Pahang (P'êng-hêng) in 1378, from Samudra (Hsü-wên-ta-na) in 1383, from Palembang (San-fo-ch'i) in Sumatra 6 times, and from Chola (So-li) on the Coromandel coast of India in 1372. This agrees with the dates given in the *Collected Statutes* and

noted above.

In this period embassies from states adjacent to China—Korea (Kao-li, Koryŏ), Liu-ch'iu, Annam, Champa, Cambodia, Siam—are comparatively regular and frequent. It is noteworthy, however, that relatively few are recorded from Central Asia: Samarkand 3 times, Bashibalik once, and but few others.

(2) During the much-studied period of the maritime expeditions up to 1433, when tribute embassies from the Indian Ocean graced the court frequently, the activity of embassies from Central Asia steadily increased. Beginning in 1421 the Wa-la (Oirats) are recorded in almost every year up to 1453. Meanwhile Badakshan, Shiraz, and Ispahan are recorded for 1419, Herat in 1415 and later, Ilibalik from 1426; and, most important, Hami, the funnel for Central Asian trade, begins to be regularly recorded in 1415, as does Turfan also.

(3) During the remainder of the fifteenth century after the end of the maritime expeditions in 1433, some countries adjacent to China are recorded with a good deal of regularity with the exception of Korea (Chao-hsien) which appears in the record only a few times after 1397 (perhaps because it could be taken for granted), while Japan is recorded half a dozen times. Of the many countries from the Indian Ocean and the South Sea, only Java and Malacca (recorded 10 times between 1439 and 1481) continue with much regularity, Ceylon (Hsi-lan-shan) being recorded along with Malacca in 1445 and 1459. Meanwhile tribute embassies from Hami are noted in more than half the years of the period (1434-1500), Turfan and Samarkand less frequently, about one year in four, and Ilibalik half a dozen times. Thus there is a marked shift of tributary activity from the maritime south to the continental west.

(4) During the sixteenth century there is a thinning out of the number of embassies noted in the annals. Liu-ch'iu appears 50 times, every other year on the average. Annam, however, appears, only 19 times; Siam,

only 9; Champa, 4 (to 1543); and Japan, 7. By way of contrast, the embassies recorded from Central Asia remain relatively numerous: ... Hami, 19; Turfan, 24; Samarkand, 16; Arabia (T'ien-fang), 13; and Rum (Lu-mi, in Asia Minor), 6.

(5) In the last years of the dynasty, 1600-1643, the embassies from Central Asia wither away like those from elsewhere: Liu-ch'iu, 15; Annam, 7; Siam, 9 ... Turfan, 3; Hami, 3; Samarkand, Arabia, and Rum, each once (in 1618, with Hami and Turfan).

Certain implications of these data are discussed below in section 6.

## 3. THE LI FAN YÜAN (COURT OF COLONIAL AFFAIRS) UNDER THE CH'ING

The inauguration of the Ch'ing Dynasty led to a thorough reshuffling of the relations between China and Central Asia. The Ch'ing therefore divided their inheritance of tributaries from the Ming into two categories, those from the east and south, who continued to be under the Reception Department (Chu K'o Ssǔ) of the Board of Ceremonies, and those from the north and west, who were put under a new agency, the Li Fan Yüan 理藩院. Since this article is concerned primarily with the former, among whom were included the maritime nations of Europe, we shall take only brief note of the Ch'ing tributaries to the north and west.

The tributaries of the north and west were primarily the Mongols. So important were Mongol relations that a special department of the Ch'ing administration, a Mongolian Office (Mêng-ku Ya-mên), was set up, some years before the entrance into China. In 1638 this Mongolian Office was changed into the Li Fan Yüan,[32] the so-called Court of Colonial Affairs or Mongolian Superintendency,[33] which continued as an important part of the government of China under the Ch'ing Dynasty.

It is worth noting first of all that the Li Fan Yüan managed Manchu-Mongol relations through the forms of the ancient tributary system.[34]

The K'ang-hsi edition of the *Hui-tien* introduced this new department in these rapturous terms: ③

"When our Dynasty first arose, its awe-inspiring virtue (tê) gradually spread and became established. Wherever its name and influence reached, there were none who did not come to Court. As to the leaders of the Mongolian tribes, those who first tendered their allegiance all submitted to our jurisdiction and are regarded as of one body (with the Manchus). Those who came later were a vast host; and all of them coming with their whole countries or with their entire tribes happily tendered their allegiance. Since the land was extensive, the people were numerous. Thereupon they were ordered each to preserve his own territory, and in the years for audience to present a regular tribute. The abundant population and the vast area—from ancient times down to the present there had been nothing like them! Therefore, outside the Six Boards, there was established the Court of Colonial Affairs (Li Fan Yüan)..."

Thus the origin of tribute is affirmed to lie, as usual, in the all-pervading virtue of the Son of Heaven, while the cognate principles of imperial compassion and reverent barbarian submission are expressed in another introductory passage, on Court assemblies:⑧ "Among the 49 banners, from the princes on down, annually or seasonally there must be some who come to the capital. They are made to divide the years (of their attendance) to represent each other, in order to save them labor and weariness, and hay and grain are given to them, in order to relieve their exhaustion and fatigue. Thus the system of visiting (the Court) for audience and the benevolence (of the emperor) in soothing and guiding them are both accomplished."

The general nature of the administration exercised by this new agency will appear from a recital of the main divisions of the K'ang-hsi *Statutes* concerning it. Successive sections dealt with the Ranks of Nobility among the Mongolian princes; the Assemblies, held triennially and concerned with judicial matters, fines being exacted for non-attendance; the

Registers of Males, including all between 18 and 60, with penalties for false report; the Postal Transmission system, with regulations for the use of post-station horses and facilities; the system of Guard Houses, with prohibitions of unannounced movements, unauthorized trips to Kuei-hua to sell horses, overstepping of tribal boundaries, or use of others' pasture, and the like; a set of Strict Prohibitions regarding Persons Absconding, with penalties; the Soothing and Reuniting of Persons who Absconded, with penalties for noncoöperation.[37] As Mr. Lattimore points out,[38] these regulations were in general designed to check the reuniting of the Mongol tribes under another Jenghis Khan, a process which could occur only when relationships in Mongolia were so fluid as to allow the concentration of many personal loyalties under one tribal leader. Further regulations then dealt with assemblies at Court, presentation of tribute, banquets, Court tribute, and bestowal of rewards—all in the traditional forms of the tributary relationship.[39]

The later Ch'ing rulers appear to have covered the tributary relationship with a sugar coating heavy enough to make it decidedly palatable. On the one hand it was decreed that "the various ranks of princes among the Mongols at the New Year festival all in Court dress are to look toward the throne and perform the ceremony of the three kneeling and nine knockings of the head";[40] and there were further regulations for the presentation of tribute and the bestowal of gifts and banquets in return. Yet within the limits of these formalities the system was developed to allow a maximum of Manchu supervision and control with a minimum of irritation on the part of the Mongols. The nobility among the Inner Mongols, for example, were divided into three classes (pan), of which one came to Court each year in rotation, just before New Years. Limits were put on the number of retainers that each might bring to the capital and on the length of time they might stay, and they were required to practice the ceremonies on their arrival; but beneath all these details the fact stands out that considerable payments were made to and for them.

The seven ranks of Mongol nobility each received annually from the imperial coffers an emolument (禄 lu) corresponding to his rank. In the case of a first class prince, this stipend might come to Tls. 2000 in silver (fêng yin 俸银) and 25 rolls of silks (fêng pi 俸币) or satin (fêng tuan 俸缎). "Chieftains (Dzassak), hereditary nobles (Daidji), and Tabu-nang, have a stipend of Tls. 100 in silver and 4 rolls of satin."⑪ Further, the expenses of the noble's suits were taken care of in Peking, provisions being due to them for as much as 40 days. Thus a chieftain, the lowest of the seven ranks, was allowed to have ten retainers and receive provisions while in Peking in the following amounts: every day, in silver Tls. 1.61, in rice 6.5 pints; for three riding horses and ten lead horses, every day for fodder Tls. 0.875511.⑫ There were also the customary banquets and presents, and even a gift of travel expenses on departure. In contrast to all these imperial donations, the *statutory* tribute presented at Court, as recorded for the late nineteenth century, was purely nominal. "The annual tribute of Inner (Mongol) chieftains is not to exceed… one sheep and one bottle of milk-wine (koumiss).⑬ (This use of the velvet glove does not imply that the Mongols did not contribute heavily elsewhere.) In the nineteenth century the regulations for Outer Mongolia, including the lamaseries, and for East Turkestan (the moslems of the Hami and Turfan areas) were along the same lines.⑭ The Dalai Lama and others in Tibet were likewise now included in the system.⑮

Enough has been said to indicate that the traditional system of tribute was applied to northern and western Asia, though in a form adapted to new circumstances. This success in using old bottles for new wine must have given strength to the continuing Ch'ing effort to keep the European traders bottled up at Macao and Canton.

As a second point it is noteworthy that the jurisdiction of the Li Fan Yüan was extended to Central Asia only gradually. Relations with Turfan were not under its control until sometime after 1732 (see Table 2 in section 4 below). It appears that the Manchu conquests which built up a great continental empire including Mongolia, Tibet, etc.—ending with the conquest of Kashgar by 1760—led to a reorganization of the Li Fan Yüan and an extension of its activities.[46] This meant in turn that tributary relations and tributary trade with the continent to the north and west of China were put in a special category, removed from the inherited tributary administration under the Board of Ceremonies. Central Asian trade in the later Ch'ing period thus becomes a special study, connected with the administration of the Li Fan Yüan, and until extensive research is done upon the working of this new agency, Ch'ing relations with Central Asia cannot easily be fitted into our picture of the tributary commercial system as a whole. In particular, a correlation between tribute and trade, such as it may have been for the Ming period, becomes impossible for this area under the Ch'ing because tributary embassies ceased to be even a chief form of economic intercourse.

For this reason an examination of the tributary embassies from the north and west recorded at the end of each annual section in the *Draft History of the Ch'ing* (*Ch'ing-shih kao*, *pên-chi*, see Table 5 below) cannot yield results as significant as those gained in this way for the Ming period. The chart which we have constructed of these recorded embassies shows a vast profusion of Mongol tribes and dignitaries presenting tribute at various times up to the beginning of the K'ang-hsi period (1662). From that time on, however, places in the north and west practically disappear from the record; during the remainder of the dynasty the embassies listed are almost entirely from the south and east. The classification of Turfan as a tributary until after 1732 might be taken to indicate that up to that time it was serving as a funnel for caravan trade with regions to the west, as Hami had done under the Ming; but the tribute embassies recorded in the *Ch'ing-shih kao* as from Turfan are so very few as to leave the whole question in obscurity.

## 4. CH'ING TRIBUTARIES FROM THE SOUTH AND EAST—GENERAL REGULATIONS

Before touching upon the status formally accorded to Europeans in the Ch'ing tributary system, we must look at the general scheme into which they were fitted. The Ch'ing regulations for the Reception Department of the Board of Ceremonies were modelled upon those which have been described, by Professors CHANG Tê-ch'ang, YANO Jinichi, T. C. LIN, UCHIDA Naosaku, and others, for the Ming period.⑰ Needless to say, an understanding of these rules will explain many of the points of friction that arose when Sino-European diplomatic relations became intensified. We therefore quote at length the statement of administrative principles made in the 1690 (K'ang-hsi) edition of the *Collected Statutes*.⑱ (We have ourselves numbered the sections of the text, to facilitate reference.)

"GENERAL REGULATIONS FOR THE PRESENTATION OF TRIBUTE AT COURT:

"The prosperity of the united country exceeds that of all previous ages. East, west, north, and south, those who declare themselves submissive feudatories and present tribute at Court are beyond counting. As to the Mongolian tribes, the Court of Colonial Affairs (Li Fan Yüan) has been especially established to control them. Likewise the various aboriginal tribes are under the control of the Board of War. As for those which are under the Reception Department and the Residence for Tributary Envoys—the years when they present tribute come at certain intervals, the persons who come to Court are of a certain number, the local products (presented as tribute) are of a certain amount, and the rewards bestowed are of certain categories. Here we put the general regulations first of all, and then the various countries in order according to their priority in presenting tribute:

(1) "In the Ch'ung-tê period (1636-1643) it was settled that on (the rulers of) all foreign countries which tendered their submission there should be bestowed an imperial patent of appointment (ts'ê-kao), and there should be conferred a noble rank, and thereafter whenever memorials and official despatches ought to be presented, they should all be dated by the Ta Ch'ing dynastic reign-title. On the occasion of imperial birthdays, New Years days, and winter solstices, they should present a memorial in the imperial presence and offer a tribute of local products, and present a (congratulatory) tablet to the empress and the heir-apparent and offer a tribute of local products, sending an official delegate to the Court for congratulations.

(2)"In the Shun-chih period (1644-1661) it was settled that whenever foreign countries presented tribute to the Court with a memorial and local products as proof of the fact, the governor-general and governor concerned should examine their authenticity and then permit them to present a memorial and send the tribute to Court.

(3)"Whenever foreign countries, in presenting tribute to the Court, send back the imperial seal granted them in the Ming period, the local authorities may be allowed to present a memorial (on their behalf).

(4)"The officers and servants who bring tribute on any one occasion must not exceed a hundred men; only twenty officers and servants may enter the capital, all the rest remaining at the border to await their reward. The ships which bring tribute must not be more than three; each ship must not exceed a hundred men.

(5)"Whenever a tribute envoy reaches the capital, the local products which he is presenting as tribute are reported by the Residence for Tributary Envoys to the Board of Ceremonies. The Superintendent in charge of the said Residence goes to the Residence, examines the things, and sends officers and underlings to control them. The said Board memorializes for the emperor's information. The tribute objects are handed in to the Imperial Household Department. Elephants are transferred to the Imperial Equipage Department; horses are transferred to the Palace Stud. Daggers, deer's skin, blue squirrel skin [ch'ing-shu p'i 青黍皮 for ch'ing-shu p'i 青鼠皮] and such things are handed over to the Imperial Armory. All sulphur brought in is kept and given to the governor-general and governor concerned, to be stored.

(6) "For foreigners to send presents to the governor-general and governor concerned (in their case) is forbidden in perpetuity.

(7) "Whenever a foreign ship comes privately to trade without reason and not in a year when tribute is presented, the governor-general and governor concerned shall forthwith stop it and drive it away.

(8) "Whenever a foreign country sends tribute, all those ships which take charge of tribute and ships which keep watch on tribute, and the like, aside from the ships specified by the regulations, are to be stopped and sent back. They must not be allowed to enter.

(9) "Whenever the principal tribute ship has not arrived, the ships which protect tribute or keep watch on the tribute are not allowed to trade.

(10) "Whenever a foreign tribute envoy happens to die en route, the Board of Ceremonies shall memorialize to order the Inner Secretariat[49] to compose a funeral essay (to be recited and burned at the grave) and the financial commissioner on the spot to prepare the sacrificial offerings. A High Official (T'ang Kuan 堂官, B 304) shall be sent to offer the sacrifices on one occasion, and also arrange for a cemetery, set up a stone, and confer an (imperial) inscription. If an envoy who came with (the deceased) volunteers to take back the corpse, he may do so. If (an envoy) reaches the capital and dies, a wooden coffin and red satin shall be supplied and an official of the Department of Sacrifices shall be sent to issue the imperial orders for the sacrifices. The carts and men which were to be supplied by the Board of War and the clothing and satins and such things which were to be presented (to the deceased) shall still be handed over to the envoy who came with him, for him to take back and bestow.

If an attendant of the tribute mission dies at the capital, a coffin and red silk shall be supplied; if he dies en route, (the mission) may proceed to bury him of its own accord.

(11) "When a tribute envoy returns to his country, by regulation there is deputed a Ceremonial Usher of the Court of Colonial Affairs (Ssǔ Pin Hsü Pan 司宾序班, B 940) and there is issued to him an official express rider's tally (k'an-ho). He is sent along with the official post and on the way is watched over and urged on, and not allowed to loiter and cause trouble, nor to trade in goods forbidden by the regulations. (When the envoy) has been clearly handed over to the governor concerned, (the Ceremonial Usher) at once returns (to the capital). The governor-general and governor concerned, according to the regulations, send (the tribute envoy) out of the frontier.

(12) "In 1664 it was settled that whenever foreign countries admire (Chinese) civilization (mu-hua) and come with a tribute of local produce, it should be examined and accepted as they present it, without adhering too closely to the old regulations.

(13) "In 1666 it was memorialized and sanctioned that when foreign countries present a memorial to the throne they need not give it to an envoy, sent to bring it along with him. They should be ordered to depute a special officer to give it to the governor-general and governor concerned, who will in turn memorialize on their behalf.

(14) "In 1667 it was settled that whenever a foreign country tenders a document to the governor-general and governor (concerned in its case), the said officers should straightway open and examine the original document, deliberate, and memorialize the throne.

(15) "No governor-general, governors, provincial commanders-in-chief, or other such officials may unauthorizedly and of their own accord send a communication (i-wên) to a foreign country.

(16) "In 1669 it was memorialized and sanctioned that whenever the principal and assistant tribute envoys of a foreign country and the fixed

number of their attendants come to the capital, their provisions en route and the men, horses, boats, and carts of the postal service are to be supplied, in accordance with the regulations, by the governor-general and governor concerned. They are to depute officials to accompany (the tribute mission), and troops to escort it to the capital. When the tribute envoy returns to his country, for the provisions en route and the men and boats of the post service, the Board of War is to provide them with postal tallies. As to the men (of the mission) who have remained at the frontier, the local authorities concerned according to the regulations give them provisions and carefully guard them. Later when the tribute envoy returns to his country, they are sent along with him out of the frontier."[50]

Since foreign trade was technically tributary trade, we quote further the regulations of 1690 on foreign trade,[51] omitting an initial passage on commerce with Korea, and numbering the sections.

"THE TRADE OF FOREIGN COUNTRIES:

(1) "... In the Shun-chih period (1644-1661) it was fixed that after foreign countries bringing tribute to Court have come to the capital and their rewards have been distributed to them, a market may be opened in the Residence for Tributary Envoys, either for three days or for five days. But Korea and Liu Ch'iu need not adhere to this time limit. The Board of Ceremonies shall communicate with the Board of Revenue, which shall ahead of time detach Wu-lin men[52] to do the receiving and buying. When the despatch in reply has passed through the Board (of Ceremonies) then they shall issue a notice (of the opening of the market) and despatch officials to superintend it. They shall give orders for just and fair trade. It is altogether prohibited to collect or buy works of history. As to black, yellow, purple-black, large flowered, Tibetan, or lotus satins; together with all forbidden implements of war, saltpetre, ox-horn, and such things—all shopmen and hongists shall bring their goods to the Residence (for sale) and exchange them justly and fairly.

(2) "Dying-cloth, thin silk, and such goods shall be handed back

within fixed limits. If there are any who buy on credit and intentionally delay (payment), cheating or seeking 'squeeze', with the result that the foreigners wait a long time, they, together with those who trade with them in private, will be condemned; and will be put in the cangue for one month in front of their shops. If there are foreigners who purposely violate the prohibitory regulations and secretly enter people's houses to trade, the goods dealt in privately will be confiscated. In the case of those who have not yet been given their (imperial) rewards (i. e. gifts), there will be consideration of a proportional diminution.

(3) "All soldiers and commoners inside or outside the Residence or neighboring on any side, who deal in prohibited goods on behalf of foreigners, will be condemned to the cangue for a month, and banished to the border for military service for life. If there are those who take contraband implements of war, copper or iron, or such things, and sell them to foreigners to get profit, according to the law for taking military implements out of the border in secret and thereby revealing affairs (of military importance), the ringleaders' heads will be cut off and exposed as a warning to the multitude. At the time of trade, the Board of Ceremonies will issue a notice giving such official information.

(4) "Whenever a foreign tributary envoy returns to his country, the officers and men who escort him on his way are not permitted to trade privately in contraband goods.

(5) "In 1664 it was fixed that when a foreign country presents tribute, as to goods brought along at this opportunity, if the tributary envoy wishes himself to provide the porters and transportation in order to bring the goods to the capital for trade, he may do so. If he wishes to trade there (at the port or place of entrance) the governor-general and governor concerned shall select capable officers and depute them to superintend (the trade), so that no trouble may arise.

(6) "In 1685 it was proposed and imperially sanctioned that, as to

the goods brought in foreign tribute vessels, if there is a stoppage in the collection of their customs duties, the other (goods) brought privately for trade may be traded; and it is permitted that the officials of the Board (of Revenue) who have been deputed (to superintend), collect customs duties according to the regulations.

(7) "It is also proposed and imperially sanctioned that when a foreign merchant's vessel returns to its country, in addition to contraband goods, it shall not be allowed to take people of the interior (i. e. Chinese passengers), nor to export secretly such things as big beams, iron nails, oil, or hemp for making ships. Of rice and grain it may only take (enough for) provisions; it is not allowed to carry more. When trade is finished and it is time to return to their country, the governor-general and governor concerned shall select and depute virtuous and able officers who shall make a strict examination and put a stop to smuggling.

(8) "Whenever people of the interior (i. e. Chinese) have strayed to foreign countries and wish to return by ship to their native place, they may be permitted to come back to their former territory; they shall report in detail to the local authorities concerned, who shall make an investigation and allow them to return to their native place.

(9) "On the day when a foreign vessel completes its trade, the officers and men of the foreign country are all to be sent hack; they must not linger at length within (China).

(10) "Whenever a tribute vessel returns to its own country, the goods which it takes along are exempt from the collection of customs duties. It was also proposed and imperial agreement was given that 'heretofore implements of war have been prohibited and not allowed to be taken away for sale to foreign countries; but when merchants come and go on the high seas, if they have no military weapons with which to protect themselves, it is to be feared that they may be plundered; hereafter for merchants of the interior (China) engaged in trade, such things as the

cannon and military implements which they carry with them, ought to be in proportion to the size of the ship and the number of men. The governor-general and governor concerned should deliberate and fix the number, and at the time when a voyage is begun, they should order the officers who collect customs duties on the seacoast and the officers who are defending the seaports, to examine clearly the numbers (of arms) and permit them to be taken along. When they return they shall make a further examination in comparison with the original numbers.'"⑬

The foregoing principles of administration were made more numerous and detailed in the Ch'ien-lung edition of the *Statutes*, which were thoroughly revised and expanded and set the standard for the last century and a half of the dynasty's existence. These Ch'ien-lung regulations of 1764 were in effect, for instance, at the time of the MACARTNEY and AMHERST embassies of the British and during the Dutch embassy of VAN BRAAM and TITSINGH in 1794-1795. They help to explain the demands, such as that for the practice of the kotow, which annoyed the European representatives so much. (For the reader's convenience we have italicized the topic headings, and given serial numbers to each section in the original text, some sections of which are omitted.)⑭

"CEREMONIAL FOR VISITORS (PIN-LI 宾礼), COURT TRIBUTE:

(1)"*As to the countries of the barbarians on all sides (ssŭ-i) that send tribute to Court*, on the east is Korea; on the southeast, Liu-ch'iu and Sulu; on the south, Annam and Siam; on the southwest, Western Ocean (hsi-yang), Burma, and Laos. (For the barbarian tribes of the northwest, see under Court of Colonial Affairs.) All send officers as envoys to come to Court and present tributary memorials and pay tribute.

(2)"*As to the imperial appointment of kings of (tributary) countries*, whenever the countries which send tribute to Court have a succession to the throne, they first send an envoy to request an imperial mandate at the Court. In the cases of Korea, Annam, and Liu-ch'iu, by imperial command the principal envoy and secondary envoy (s) receive the imperial patent (of appointment) and go (to their country) to confer it 奉敕往封. As for the other countries, the patent (of appointment) is bestowed upon the envoy who has come (from his country) to take it back, whereupon an envoy is sent (from that country) to pay tribute and offer thanks for the imperial favor.

(3)"*As to the king of Korea*, (the patent) is bestowed upon his wife (fei 妃) the same as upon the king. When the son grows up, then he requests that it be bestowed upon him as the heir-apparent. In all cases officials of the third rank or higher act as principal and secondary envoys. Their clothing and appearance, and ceremonial and retinue (i-ts'ung) in each case are according to rank. In the cases of Annam and Liu-ch'iu, officials of the Hanlin Academy, the Censorate, or the Board of Ceremonies, of the fifth rank or below, act as principal and secondary envoys; (the emperor) specially confers upon them 'unicorn' (ch'i-lin) clothing of the first rank, in order to lend weight to their journey. In ceremonial and retinue (i-ts'ung) they are all regarded as being of the first rank. When the envoys return, they hand back their clothing to the office in charge of it.

[(4)Periodicity of tribute, (5)Route of tribute envoys, see Table 3 below.]

(6)"*As to tribute objects*, in each case they should send the products of the soil of the country. Things that are not locally produced are not to be presented. Korea, Annam, Liu-ch'iu, Burma, Sulu, and Laos all have tribute of their customary objects. Western Ocean and Siam do not have a customary tribute…

(7)"*As to the retainers* (who accompany an envoy), in the case of the Korean tribute envoy there are one attendant secretary, three chief interpreters, 24 tribute guards, 30 minor retainers who receive rewards, and a variable number of minor retainers who do not receive rewards. For Liu-ch'iu, Western Ocean, Siam, and Sulu, the tribute vessels are not to exceed three, with no more than 100 men per vessel; those going to the capital are not to exceed 20. When Annam, Burma, and Laos send tribute, the men are not to exceed 100, and those going to the capital are not to exceed 20. Those that do not go to the capital are to be retained at the frontier. The frontier officials give them a stipend from the government granary, until the envoy returns to the frontier, when he takes them back to their country.

[(8) Presentation of tributary memorials, after arrival at Peking.]

(9) "*As to the Court ceremony*, when a tribute envoy arrives at the capital at the time of a Great Audience or of an Ordinary Audience, His Majesty the Emperor goes to the T'ai Ho 太和 palace and, after the princes, dukes, and officials have audience and present their congratulations, the ushers lead in the tributary envoys and their attendant officers, each of them wearing his country's court dress. They stand in the palace courtyard on the west in the last place. When they hear (the command of) the ceremonial ushers they perform the ceremony of three kneelings and nine knockings of the head [the full kotow]. They are graciously allowed to sit. Tea is imperially bestowed upon them. All this is according to etiquette (for details see under the Department of Ceremonies). If (a tribute envoy) does not come at the time of an Audience, he presents a memorial through the Board (of Ceremonies) asking for an imperial summons to Court. His Majesty the Emperor goes to a side hall of the palace (pien-tien)... etc.⁵⁵

[(10)-(13). There follow details concerning further ceremonies, with performances of the kotow; banquets; and imperial escorts, including those provided for Westerners because of their services as imperial astronomers.]

(14) "*As to trade*—when the tribute envoys of the various countries

enter the frontier, the goods brought along in their boats or carts may be exchanged in trade with merchants of the interior (China); either they may be sold at the merchants' hongs in the frontier province or they may be brought to the capital and marketed at the lodging house (i. e. the Residence for Tributary Envoys). At the customs stations (lit. passes and fords) which they pass en route, they are all exempted from duty. As to barbarian merchants who themselves bring their goods into the country for trade—for Korea on the border of Shêng-ching [Fengtien province], and at Chung-chiang 中江 [northeast of Chengtu, Szechwan], there are spring and autumn markets, twice a year; at Hui-ning [southeast of Lanchow, Kansu], one market a year; at Ch'ing-yüan [in Chihli, now Chao-hsien], one market every other year—(each) with two interpreters of the Board of Ceremonies, one Ninguta (Kirin) clerk, and one Lieutenant to superintend it. After twenty days the market is closed. For the countries beyond the seas, (the market) is at the provincial capital of Kwangtung. Every summer they take advantage of the tide and come to the provincial capital (Canton). When winter comes they wait for a wind and return to their countries. All pay duties to the (local) officers in charge, the same as the merchants of the interior (China).

(15) "*As to the prohibitions*—when a foreign country has something to state or to request, it should specially depute an officer to bring a document to the Board (of Ceremonies), or in the provinces it may be memorialized on behalf (of the country) by the governor-general and governor concerned. Direct communication to the Court is forbidden. For a tribute envoy's entrance of the frontier and the tribute route which he follows, in each case there are fixed places. Not to follow the regular route, or to go over into other provinces, is forbidden. It is forbidden secretly (ssŭ 私, i. e. without permission) to buy official costumes which violate the regulations, or books of history, weapons, copper, iron, oil, hemp, or combustible saltpetre; or to take people of the interior or rice

and grain out of the frontiers. There are boundaries separating the rivers and seas; to catch fish beyond the boundaries is forbidden. The land frontiers are places of defensive entrenchments where Chinese and foreign soldiers or civilians have established military colonies or signal-fire mounds, or cultivated rice-fields and set up huts; to abscond and take shelter (on either side) is forbidden. It is forbidden for civil or military officials on the frontier to communicate in writing with foreign countries on public business. When commissioned to go abroad, to receive too many gifts, or when welcomed in coming and going, privately to demand the products of the locality (i. e. as "squeeze") is forbidden. Offenses against the prohibitions will be considered according to law.

[(16) Charity and sympathy to be shown regarding foreign rulers' deaths, calamities, etc.]

(17) "*As to the rescue* (of distressed mariners)—when ships of foreign merchants are tossed by the wind into the inner waters (of China), the local authorities should rescue them, report in a memorial the names and number of distressed barbarians, move the public treasury to give them clothing and food, take charge of the boat and oars, and wait for a wind to send them back. If a Chinese merchant vessel is blown by the wind into the outer ocean, the country there can rescue it and give it aid, put a boat in order and send them (the merchants) back, or it may bring them along on a tribute vessel so as to return them. In all such cases an imperial patent is to be issued, praising the king of the country concerned; imperial rewards are to be given to the officers (of the tributary country) in different degrees."

These regulations conclude with a section on the Residence for Tributary Envoys (Hui T'ung Ssǔ I Kuan), which was organized much as in the Ming period.⁶⁰

The two following synoptic tables present essential data showing the vicissitudes of the Ch'ing tributary system.

## TABLE 2  REGULAR CH'ING TRIBUTARIES

Table of regular tributaries as listed in the various Ch'ing editions of the *Collected Statutes*, in the order of listing. For data regarding each country, see the index at the end of this article and Table 3 below.

| K'ang-hsi 72.4-19b (1690) | Yung-chêng 104.4-38b (1732) | Ch'ien-lung 56.1 (1764) | Chia-ch'ing 31.2-4 (1818) | Kuang-hsü 39.2-3 (1899) |
|---|---|---|---|---|
| Korea | Korea | Korea | Korea | Korea |
| Turfan | Liu-ch'iu | Liu-ch'iu | Liu-ch'iu | Liu-ch'iu |
| Liu-ch'iu | Holland | Sulu | Annam | Annam |
| Holland | Annam | Annam | Laos | Laos |
| Annam | Siam | Siam | Siam | Siam |
| Siam<br><br>Western Ocean country (73.1a-12a) | The countries of the Western Ocean (viz. Portugal, the Papacy)[b] | The countries of the Western Ocean<br>Burma<br>Laos | Sulu<br><br>Holland[a]<br>Burma | Sulu<br>Burma |
| The various monasteries of the Western Tribesmen (i.e. Eastern Tibet)<br><br>The Manchurian tribes (lit. the tribes of the eastern sea) | Sulu<br>Turfan<br>Monasteries of the Western Tribesmen (as in K'ang-hsi)<br>Barbarian Monasteries of the border region of Szechwan province | | Western Ocean (Portugal, I-ta-li-ya, Portugal, England)[c]<br><br>Countries having commercial relations[d] | |

(a) Holland was omitted in 1764, having been inactive since 1686, but reappears in 1818.

(b) Specific European countries were not listed by name, though easily identifiable.

(c) Portugal appears as two different countries with very similar names. I-ta-li-ya was the Papacy.

(d) For the list of countries having commercial relations with China in the Chia-ch'ing (1818) edition of the Hui-tien (ch. 31.3-4) see part 6 below. The list included Portugal (Kan-ssǔ-la), France (Fa-lan-hsi, or Fo-lang-hsi; stated to be the same as Fu-lang-chi, Portugal), Sweden, and Denmark.

**TABLE 3  FREQUENCY AND ROUTES OF EMBASSIES**

Table of the statutory frequency, and the routes of regular tribute embassies, as listed in the various Ch'ing editions of the *Collected Statutes*.

Note: the phraseology is chiefly translated from the *Collected Statutes*; the order of the countries varies in the different editions, see Table 2.

| K'ang-hsi 72. 3b-19b | Yung-chêng 104. 4-38b | Ch'ien-lung 56. 1 | Chia-ch'ing 31. 4 | Kuang-hsü 39. 3 |
|---|---|---|---|---|
| KOREA | | | | |
| Has annual tribute and festival tribute, an annual custom; tribute route via Fêng-huang-ch'êng 凤凰城 | Same as K'ang-hsi | Comes annually, crossing the Yalu R. to enter the boundaries; via the land route from Fêng-huang-ch'êng, goes to Mukden, enters Shanhaikuan and proceeds to the capital | Tribute four times a year, presented all together at the end of the year, tribute route from Fêng-huang-ch'êng to Mukden, entering Shanhaikuan | Same as Chia-ch'ing |
| LIU-CH'IU | | | | |
| Fixed tribute period once in two years; tribute route via Min-hsien, Fukien 闽县 | " " " | Comes every other year via Min-an-chên 闽安镇, Fukien[a] | Tribute once every other year via Min-an-chên, Fukien | " " " |
| ANNAM | | | | |
| Tribute period at first fixed at once in three years; later changed to twice in six years; tribute route via P'ing-yang-chou, Kwangsi 凭祥州 | " " " | Comes again after six years, via T'ai-p'ing-fu 太平府[b], Kwangsi | Tribute once in two years, sending an envoy to Court once in four years to present two tributes together, via P'ing-yang-chou in Kwangsi entering Chên-nan-kuan 镇南关 | " " " |
| SIAM | | | | |
| Tribute period once in three years, tribute route via Kwangtung | " " " | Three years, via Hu-mên 虎门 (i. e. Bocca Tigris, Canton)[a] | Tribute once in three years, via Hu-mên, Kwangtung | " " " |

| | K'ang-hsi 72. 3b-19b | Yung-chêng 104. 4-38b | Ch'ien-lung 56. 1 | Chia-ch'ing 31. 4 | Kuang-hsü 39. 3 |
|---|---|---|---|---|---|
| **HOLLAND** | | | | | |
| | Tribute period at first fixed at once in eight years, later changed to once in five years; tribute route via Kwangtung, recently changed to Fukien | " " " | Omitted | Tribute at no fixed period; the old regulations were for tribute once in five years; via Hu-mên, Kwantung | omitted |
| **WESTERN OCEAN** | | | | | |
| | Because this place is distant, a tribute period was not fixed; tribute route via Kwangtung. Recently some of these people have remained to dwell at Macao | The countries are distant and it is difficult to fix tribute periods; tribute objects also are not fixed in quantity; tribute route via Kwangtung | A long route; tribute at no fixed period, via Macao, Kwangtung[a] | Tribute at no fixed periods, via Macao, Kwangtung | omitted |
| **TURFAN** | | | | | |
| | Tribute period once in five years; tribute route via Shensi-Kansu | Same as K'ang-hsi | omitted | omitted | omitted |
| **LAOS (Nan-chang)** | | | | | |
| | omitted | omitted | Comes once in ten years, via P'u-erh-fu 普洱府[b] in Yunnan | Tribute once in ten years, via P'u-erh-fu in Yunnan | Same as Chia-ch'ing. |
| **SULU** | | | | | |
| | omitted | (tribute began 1726), tribute route via Fukien | Five years, via Amoy[a] | Tribute once in five years or more, via Amoy | Tribute once in five years, via Amoy, Fukien |
| **BURMA** | | | | | |
| | omitted | omitted | A long route; tribute at no fixed periods, via Yung-ch'ang-fu 永昌府[b] in Yunnan | Tribute once in ten years, via T'êng-yüeh-chou 腾越州 in Yunnan | Same as Chia-ch'ing |

(a) Regarding Liu-ch'iu, Sulu, Western Ocean, and Siam, the text reads "they all float their ships on the sea and pass through the ocean to enter the boundaries (of China)."

(b) Regarding Annam, Burma, and Laos, the text reads, "all travel by land and knock at the door (*k'uan-kuan* 款关) to enter the boundaries."

In comment on the foregoing tables it may be noted that until after 1732 relations with Turfan and certain places in E. Tibet were not yet under the jurisdiction of the Li Fan Yüan, while Russia was under it until 1858[57] and so does not appear here. Spain and America (the United States) are not listed as countries. The Western Ocean (Hsi-yang) grows from one country in 1690 to several countries in 1732, and in the latter case is treated at some length, tribute objects being listed for each of the three countries incorrectly distinguished. Western Ocean is retained as a sort of catch-all for the Europeans until after 1818. Meanwhile Holland is in high favor in the first two editions, after its naval assistance to the imperial forces in the 1660s, but is dropped in the Ch'ien-lung period and reappears in 1818 presumably because of the embassy of 1794-1795. The total of countries listed[58] is markedly less than for the Ming period, even deducting for the transfer of northern and western continental places to the Li Fan Yüan.

## 5. EUROPEAN COUNTRIES IN THE CH'ING TRIBUTARY SYSTEM

Just as the ancient forms of tribute were adapted to provide a vehicle for Manchu-Mongol relations under the Li Fan Yüan, so a similar adaptation of the traditional system was achieved in the case of the Europeans who came by sea after 1500.[59] This modification was worked out during a period of two generations of conflict between the Ming and the Portuguese, and resulted in the middle of the sixteenth century in the Macao system whereby the Portuguese barbarians, already tributary in form, were made innocuous in fact by a sort of quarantine. They lived on the walled-off peninsula at Macao, paying a land rent to the local Chinese authorities and going to Canton only periodically to trade. Into this system the English East India Company fitted itself at the beginning of the eighteenth century, although by the end of that period Canton was becoming the real center of foreign activity. Until the third decade of the nineteenth century the effort at quarantine continued. Foreigners were restricted to the Canton factories, outside the city walls, until 1858; even the first treaties after 1842 had restricted them to the five treaty ports or a day's journey therefrom. This bare recital should suggest that the Ch'ing administration was by no means incapable of adaptation in the face of danger. Ch'ing foreign policy was blindly stubborn in support of the ancient system but not lacking in defensive makeshifts.

In the seventeenth century the Portuguese had been safely confined to Macao and the other Western countries had not yet grown to be a menace. The K'ang-hsi edition of the *Statutes* expatiates upon their tributary activity, particularly that of Holland, with evident satisfaction. The record of European embassies is as follows; note the high degree of confusion which obtained in the case of Western Ocean country (Hsi-yang kuo 西洋国).[60]

"THE COUNTRY OF HOLLAND: Holland is in the southeastern sea. In 1653 it asked (the privilege of) sending tribute. In 1656 it sent tribute... [for periodicity and route, see Table 3].

"In 1653 the country of Holland sent an envoy sailing across the sea requesting permission to cultivate (friendly relations) by sending tribute to Court. In 1655 the governor of Kwangtung memorialized stating that the country of Holland had sent an envoy to offer a tributary memorial and local produce, and to ask (the privilege of) presenting tribute (at Court). The Board of Ceremonies replied giving permission that the governor-general and governor concerned should consider deputing officials and troops to escort him to the capital; the number of men coming to the capital should not exceed twenty. It was also ordered that the governor-general and governor concerned should select three or four men well versed in the language of Holland, to come along with them. In 1656 the envoys of Holland, Pieter VAN GOYER (and) Jacob VAN KEYSER (Pi-li-wo-yüeh-yeh-ha (or k'a)-kuei-jo 哔呖哦悦嘢哈哇嗃,⑩ and others reached the capital. They lodged at the Residence for Tributary Envoys and presented one memorial. The Board of Ceremonies replied, giving permission that tribute be presented once in five years, the route to be through Kwangtung; each time tribute was presented, the officers and subordinates should not exceed one hundred men, and those officers and subordinates entering the capital should be only twenty men; the rest should all wait and dwell in Kwangtung; the taotai of that region should guard them with great care; when the men who had gone to the capital returned, they should all together be sent back to their native country; they must not dwell permanently on the seacoast. An imperial Rescript was received (reading): 'The country of Holland reveres righteousness and pays its allegiance by sailing across the sea to cultivate tributary (relations). We are mindful that the route is dangerous and long. Let them come once in eight years to Court, thus manifesting our compassionate sympathy for men from afar.'

"In 1663 the country of Holland sent an admiral [Balthasar BORT?; ch'u hai wang 出海王] in command of warships to Min-an-chên [near Foochow], where they helped exterminate the sea rebels, and also asked permission to trade. An imperial Rescript was received: 'Let them come to trade once in two years.' In 1664 the country of Holland sent the admiral to assist the (imperial) troops in exterminating pirates; they recovered Amoy and Chin-mên 金门 [in Fukien]. Two command-edicts (ch'ih-yü) were promulgated and officials and clerks of the Board of Ceremonies were sent to go there and offer them a reward, presenting them with silver and satin. Together with the governor-general concerned they gave (these things) to the Hollanders to take back with them.

"In 1666 Holland [Pieter VAN HOORN?][62] presented tribute and traded. An imperial Rescript was received: 'Since Holland sends tribute once in eight years, let its biennial trade be permanently suspended.' In 1667 it was memorialized and imperial agreement was received 'Holland has broken the regulations and come via Fukien to present tribute. Aside from the present occasion, which will not be discussed, hereafter in a year when they send tribute they must enter via Kwangtung; they must not be allowed to enter by other routes.'

"In 1686 it was agreed and imperially sanctioned that 'the time for Holland's presentation of tribute originally was fixed at once in eight years. Now the king of that country, having been moved by the receipt of the imperial benevolence, again asks a fixed time (for tribute). He should be permitted (to send tribute) once in five years. The places of trade may only be in the two provinces of Kwangtung and Fukien. On the day when (trade) is completed, straightway order them to return to their own country.' It was further ordered that the tribute route of Holland be changed to come via Fukien. Further, it was agreed and imperially sanctioned that 'the route from Holland is dangerous and long. To navigate the seas and present tribute is grievous toil. Hereafter, as to the local produce presented as tribute, let the (fixed) amount be considered and reduced.'

"WESTERN OCEAN COUNTRY (Hsi-yang kuo): Western Ocean is in the southeastern sea... [for tribute period and route, see Table 3].

"In 1667 the governor of Kwangtung memorialized stating that Western Ocean country [i.e. Portugal] had sent an official to present tribute, with one principal tribute vessel and three escorting vessels. In 1668 it was memorialized and imperially sanctioned that when Western Ocean sent tribute thereafter the ships must not exceed three, and each ship must not exceed one hundred men. In 1669 it was memorialized and imperially sanctioned to order the principal and secondary envoys and their retinue, twenty-two persons, to come to the capital. The subordinates detained at the border were to be given provisions by the local authorities concerned, and also to be carefully guarded. In 1670 the tributary envoy of Western Ocean country, Manoel DE SALDANHA (Ma-no-wu-sa-la-ta-jo 吗诺吻萨喇哒嚄) arrived at the capital, presented a tributary memorial, and offered tribute. After he had been rewarded with gifts and a banquet, an Usher of the Court of Colonial Affairs (Li Fan Yüan) was deputed to escort him back to Kwangtung and hand him over to the governor-general there, who should depute an officer to escort him out of the frontier. The tributary envoy of Western Ocean country, Manoel DE SALDANHA (Ma-no-sa-erh-ta-nieh 玛讷撒尔达聂)⁶³ traveled as far as the region of Shan-yang in Kiangnan [i. e. Huai-an, Kiangsu] and died of illness.⁶⁴ The Board of Ceremonies memorialized and it was imperially sanctioned that the Inner Secretariat [of the Nei San Yüan] should compose a funeral address and the local financial commissioner prepare the sacrificial offerings; a high official of the Board should be sent to offer sacrifices one time and also arrange a place for burial, erect a stone tablet and confer an (imperial) inscription; if the tributary envoy accompanying (the deceased) wished to take the remains back with him, he should be allowed to suit his own convenience.

"In 1678 the king of Western Ocean country, Alfonso [A-fêng-su 阿丰肃, i. e. Alfonso VI of Portugal] sent an envoy [Bento Pereyra DE FARIA] who presented a tributary memorial, offered a lion (as tribute), and came to the capital. The Board of War supplied him en route with provisions and with the men and boats of the postal stations. The Board of Ceremonies again sent an official to escort him back to Kwangtung, to hand him over to the governor-general and governor there, who deputed an official to escort him out of the frontier."⁶⁵

In these accounts the manner in which the European envoys are assimilated to the traditional system, even to Confucian sacrifices for the dead Portuguese envoy, are so striking as hardly to require comment. Whatever the facts, the official record is preserved perfectly intact.

The Chien-lung edition of the *Hui-tien* (1764), regulations from which were quoted in the preceding section, made no detailed reference to European countries in its section on tribute,⑥ although the voluminous *Tsê-li* published simultaneously of course contain much material, into which we have gone not gone.⑥⑦

The Chia-ching edition completed in 1818 is for our purposes by far the most interesting version of the *Statutes*. This formed the last real revision—the Kuang-hsü edition of 1899 being modeled closely upon it—and in it there is preserved the same agreement with traditional tributary forms as in the earlier editions. Here the countries of Europe which are about to beat down the gates are complacently listed alongside Sungora, Kelantan, Trengganu, Ligor, and similar small places of the Malay peninsula. European geography and peoples are still in shadowy confusion and relegated to obscurity. Perhaps we must assume that the official compilers by 1818 really knew the situation more fully but disdained to give the European invaders their due prominence. In that case we have at least an indication of stubborn prejudice and wishful thinking. At all events, these descriptions remained official, and were no doubt for a time consulted by the bureaucracy, until the publication of the last edition of the *Collected Statutes* in 1899. In the 1899 edition all reference to these Western countries was omitted, although the other passages on Korea, Annam, etc., already out of date, were reprinted verbatim. We give these official summaries at length below so that the references to Europeans may be seen *in situ*.⑥⑧

"THE COUNTRIES OF THE BARBARIANS THAT SEND TRIBUTE TO COURT ARE (AS FOLLOWS):

"KOREA (Chao-hsien): Korea is the same as ancient Kao-li (Koryŏ). During the period of Ming Hung-wu (1368-1398) LI Ch'êng-kuei 李成桂 (Kor. I. Sŏnggye) established himself as king and changed the name of the country to Korea (Chao-hsien). In 1637 King LI Tsung 李倧 (Kor. I. Chong) put his whole country forward to offer its allegiance and was appointed by imperial command⁶⁹ King of Korea. This country's border on the north is the Ch'ang-pai mountains, on the northwest it is the Yalu river, on the northeast it is the Tumen river, on the east, south, and west it is the seacoast.

"LIU-CH'IU: Liu-ch'iu at the beginning of the Ming consisted of Chung-shan 中山, Shan-nan 山南, and Shan-pei 山北 (lit. the central mountains, south of the mountains, and north of the mountains), each having a king. Subsequently Shan-nan and Shan-pei were absorbed by Chung-shan. In 1654 the eldest son of the King of Liu-ch'iu, SHANG Chih 尚质, handed in the patent and seal of the late Ming period, whereupon an imperial command appointed him King of Chung-shan. This country is in the great southeastern sea to the east of Fukien.

"ANNAM (Yüeh-nan): Yüeh-nan is the ancient Chiao-chih. Its old name was Annam. In 1666 the eldest son of (the king of) Annam, LI Wei-hsi 黎维禧, handed in the patent and seal of the Ming period, whereupon he was appointed by imperial command King of Annam. In 1789 the LI family lost the throne. The country chose JUAN Kuang-p'ing 阮光平 to be head of the country (kuo-chang). He came (lit. knocked at the gate) to offer allegiance and also asked that he might come to Court. Thereupon JUAN Kuang-p'ing was appointed by imperial command King of Annam. In 1802 JUAN Kuang-tsuan 阮光纘 again lost the throne. The head of the state of Nung-nai 农耐 [Nung was in Tongking-Kwangsi], JUAN Fu-ying 阮福映, sent an envoy to present (at Court) a memorial and tribute. He also tied up and sent escaped pirates from the seas of Fukien and Kwangtung and presented the patent and seal formerly received by Annam. The Emperor Jên-tsung (Chia-ch'ing period) approved his respectful submissiveness and issued a proclamation changing the name of the country to Yüeh-nan, whereupon by imperial command he appointed JUAN Fu-ying King of Yüeh-nan. This country's northern border is Kwangsi, its western, Yunnan; on the east and south, the coast of the great sea (ta-hai). Over the sea to the south is the ancient territory of Jih-nan 日南 [southern part of Annam]; it also was absorbed in Yüeh-nan.

LAOS (Nan-chang): Nan-chang is the same as Lao-chua. In 1730 the king of the country, Su-ma-la-sa 素马喇萨, first sent an officer to present a memorial and bring tribute. By imperial proclamation a command-edict (ch'ih-yü) was bestowed on the king of the said country. In 1795 an imperial command first appointed him King of Nan-chang. This country is beyond the frontier of the southernmost part of Yunnan.

SIAM (Hsien-lo): Siam in ancient times was two countries, Dvaravati (Lopburi, Lo-hu 罗斛) and Haripunjaya (Hsien 暹). Later Haripunjaya was absorbed by Dvaravati and thereupon they made the country of Siam. In 1653 it first sent an envoy requesting (the privilege of tribute). In 1673 an imperial command first appointed Sên-lieh-p'o-la-chao-ku-lung-p'o-la-ma-hu-lu-k'un-ssǔ-yu-t'i-ya-p'u-ai 森列拍腊照古龙拍腊马呼陆坤司由堤雅普埃 King of Siam.⑪ In 1766 (the country) was crushed by Burma. In 1781 a native of the country, CHÊNG Chao 郑昭, recovered the territory and took revenge. The king of the country had no progeny and chose CHÊNG Chao to be head of the country. He sent an envoy to present tribute. In 1786 an imperial command appointed CHÊNG Hua 郑华 king of the country. This country is south of Burma, cut off from China. Its southern coast is on the great sea, and all intercourse with it is by the sea-route.

SULU: Sulu in 1726 first sent an envoy to present tribute. In 1727 by imperial proclamation a command-edict⑫ was conferred on the king of that country. It is in the southeastern sea.

HOLLAND:⑫ Holland, also called the red-haired barbarians (hung-mao fan) in 1653 first communicated a tribute.⑬ In 1664 they assisted the imperial troops in attacking and capturing Chin-mên [outside Amoy]. An Edict was imperially proclaimed to praise them. This country is in the southwestern sea. Later they seized Java (Ka-la-pa) and thereupon divided their people and inhabited it, but still governed at a distance through Holland.

BURMA: Burma (Mien-tien) is the same as Ava (A-wa). In 1750 the king, Mang-ta-la 蟒达喇, first sent an officer to present a memorial and offer tribute. In 1790 an imperial command appointed Mêng-yün 孟陨 King of Ava and Burma (A-wa mien-tien). This country is beyond the frontier barriers of T'ien-ma 天马 and Hu-chü 虎踞 in the department of T'êng-yüeh, Yunnan.

WESTERN OCEAN: (Hsi-yang):⑭ the countries of the Western Ocean consist of:

PORTUGAL (po-êrh-tu-chia-li-ya): In 1670 the king Alfonso [A-, fêng-su, Alfonso VI] first sent an officer [Manoel DE SALDANHA] to present a memorial and bring tribute.

I-TA-LI-YA: In 1725 the king, Benedict [Po-na-ti-to 伯纳第多, Pope Benedict XIII at Rome] first sent officers [GOTHARD and ILDEPHONSE] to present tribute.

PORTUGAL (po-êrh-tu-ka-êrh): In 1727 the king, John [Jo-wang 若望, John V] first sent an officer [A. M. DE SOUZA Y MENEZAS] to present tribute.

ENGLAND: In 1793 sent an officer [Lord MACARTNEY] to present tribute. In each case an imperial proclamation was conferred on the kings of the said countries. These countries all are in the southwestern sea.

"The remaining countries have commercial intercourse (with China):⑮ The trading countries are as follows: JAPAN, that is, the dwarfs (wo-tzǔ). It is in the eastern sea and trades with China at the island of Nagasaki in that country; it and P'u-t'o [i. e. Puto shan, the sacred Buddhist site in the Chusan Archipelago] are opposite peaks on east and west. From here (Puto) to there the water route is forty watches. From Amoy to Nagasaki, with a north wind one enters via the Goto Archipelago (wu-tao), with a south wind one enters T'ien-t'ang.⑯ The water route is seventy-two watches.

CHIANG-K'OU KUO (Siam?) is in the southwestern sea. It has

traded since 1729. From that country one traverses the Paracel Islands (and the ocean?)⑰ to arrive at Lu-wan-shan,⑱ and entering port via the Bocca Tigris one reaches the border of Kwangtung. The route is estimated at 7200 $li$; from Amoy the sea route is 160 watches. CAMBODIA, the ancient Chên-la, is in the southwestern sea between Annam and Siam. The route from the Bocca Tigris into port is the same as for the country of Chiang-k'ou. The water route from Amoy is 170 watches. Adjoining (Cambodia) is the country of YIN-TAI-MA (Chantebun?). The water route to it from Amoy is 140 watches. The country of SUNGORA is in the southwestern sea. It is a dependency of Siam and has traded (with China) continuously since 1729.⑲ The water route to this country from Amoy is 180 watches. Adjoining Sungora are the three countries of JAYA (Ch'ih-tzǔ), LIGOR, and PATANI. Jaya borders upon Sungora on the northeast. The water route from Amoy to this country is the same as to Sungora. Ligor on the east borders upon Jaya. The water route from Amoy is 150 watches. Patani (Ta-ni) is also called Ta-nien. On the northeast it borders upon Ligor. The water route from Amoy is the same as for Ligor. These three countries have all traded (with China) continuously since 1729. JOHORE is in the southwestern sea. It has traded continuously since 1729. Across the ocean it is 9,000 $li$ to the border of Kwangtung; they enter port through the Bocca Tigris. From Amoy the water route is 180 watches. Dependencies of Johore are the three countries of TRENGGANU, TAN-TAN, and PAHANG. From Trengganu to the border of Kwangtung the route is estimated at 9,000 $li$. From Amoy to Tan-tan by sea is 130 watches. Pahang and Johore adjoin one another. ACHIN is in the southwestern sea. It is traditionally said to be the old country of Samudra. The country of LÜ-SUNG 吕宋 (lit. Luzon, i. e. the Philippines) is situated in the southern sea, southeast of Fêng-shan sha-ma-chi,⑳ Taiwan. The water route to Amoy is 72 watches. In the Ming period it was taken by the Fo-lang-chi [Spanish or Portuguese]. The name of the country was retained (by them). In 1717 an Edict was handed down putting a stop to trade with the southern (? text blurred) ocean. After 1727 there was trade as before. The country of MANG-CHÜN-TA-LAO (Mindanao?) is in the southeastern sea. It has traded continuously since 1729. The water route from Amoy is 150 watches. The country of KA-LA-PA originally was the old land (? text blurred) of Java. It was taken over by Holland; the name of the country was retained. It is in the southern sea, and has traded continuously since 1727. The water route from Amoy is 280 watches. PORTUGAL (Kan-ssŭ-la) is in the northwestern sea near England. FRANCE (Fa-lan-hsi 法兰西), also called Fu-lang-hsi 弗郎西 is the same as the Portugal (Fo-lang-chi 佛郎机) of the Ming period, in the southwestern sea; after absorbing the Philippines (Lü-sung), they divided their people and lived there, still governing it at a distance from France (Fa-lan-hsi). Also the people of this country from the late Ming period have come in and lived at Macao in Heung-shan. The present dynasty continued the previous arrangement and every year orders them to pay a land-rent in silver. But their people are forbidden to enter the provincial capital (Canton). The sea route from this country to China is more than 50,000 *li*. SWEDEN (Jui-kuo) is in the northwestern sea; the sea-route is calculated to be over 60,000 *li* to Kwangtung. They have traded since 1732. DENMARK (Lien-kuo) is in the northwestern sea. The route to Kwangtung is the same as for Sweden. After they came to Kwangtung for trade in the Yung-chêng period (1723-1735), it became an annual affair."⁸⁰

The amazing confusion exhibited in these entries was nothing new and had come down from the eighteenth century or earlier, when the Franks, the Portuguese, the French, Italy, the Spanish, the Philippines, and even Holland in the course of time had all become pretty thoroughly mixed up together in Chinese geographical writings. The important thing is not that such errors had arisen but that they persisted so long in the Ch'ing period. The degree of confusion existing in the middle of the eighteenth century is well illustrated in the *Illustrations of the Regular*

## TABLE 4  EARLY EUROPEAN EMBASSIES TO THE COURT OF PEKING

Note: dates refer to Western calendar years in which an embassy was in Peking. Unless otherwise noted, all these embassies appear actually to have arrived at the capital and to have had audience of the emperor. For each embassy we have tried to note the chief research recently published with reference to it. Lists of embassies, none completely accurate, are given by PAUTHIER, L. PFISTER (*Notices biographiques et bibliographiques sur les Jesuits* … p. 506, also p. 610, completed by Havret), and S. COULING (*The Encyclopaedia Sinica*, p. 160, from PFISTER).

| PORTUGAL | HOLLAND | RUSSIA[8] | PAPACY[9]/BRITAIN |
|---|---|---|---|
| 1520-1521 Thomé Pires sent by Emmanuel[1] | 1656 Pieter van Goyer and Jacob van Keyser | 1656 Féodor Isakovitch Baikov by Alexis I Mikhailovitch | |
| 1670 Manoel de Saldanha by Alfonso VI[2] | 1665? Pieter van Hoorn[5] | 1676 Nicolas G. Spathar Milescu by Alexis I | |
| 1678 Bento Pereyra de Faria[3] | 1686[6] | 1689 Féodor Alexiévitch Golovin by regent Sophia (to Nerchinsk, not to Peking) | |
| | | 1693-1694 Isbrand Ides by Peter I | 1705 Patr. T. Maillard de Tournon by Clement XI |
| 1727 A. Metello de Souza y Menezes by John V[4] | | 1720-1721 Leon Vassiliévitch Izmailov by Peter I (1721-1725 Laurent Lange trading agent) | 1720 Patriarch Mezzabarba by Clement XI |
| | | 1726-1727 Sava Vladislavitch ("Raguzinski") by Catherine I | 1725 PP. Gothard and Ildephonse by Benedict XIII |
| 1753 F.-X. Assis Pacheco y Sampayo by Joseph I | | 1767 Capt. I. Kropotov by Catherine II | |
| | 1795 Isaac Tithsing[7] | 1805-1806 Count Golovkin by Alexander I (turned back at Urga) | 1793 Lord Macartney by George III[10] |
| | | 1808-1820 (no audiences) | 1816 Lord Amherst by George III |

①CHANG T'ien-tsê 43-44 states that the King left the choice of an ambassador to the Governor of India, who chose PIRES; see also CHANG Wei-hua 张维华, *P'u-t'ao-ya ti-i-tz'ǔ lai-hua shih-ch'ên shih-chi k'ao* 葡萄牙第一次来华使臣事迹考 "The First Portuguese Embassy to China," *SHNP* 1 no. 5 (Aug. 1933). 103-112; YANO (2).

②PELLIOT (4).

③*K'ang-hsi hui-tien* 72. 18b cites this embassy as sent by Alfonso (A-fêng-su). (Although Alfonso VI had been exiled in 1667, his brother Pedro ruled in his name until 1683.)

④PFISTER 610 gives data concerning the arrival of this embassy.

⑤DUYVENDAK (5) 337 n. 4, 338 n. 1 states that this embassy was in 1665 and that references to 1666 in a Chün Chi Ch'u memorandum of 1794 and to 1667 in the *Kuang-hsü hui-tien shih-li*, are incorrect. Similarly the *Ch'ing-shih kao, pên-chi*, records the embassy under 1667, the *K'ang-hsi hui-tien* under 1666 (see text above), and COULING p. 150 as of 1668. Prof. DUYVENDAK'S masterly treatment of the last Dutch embassy naturally arouses the hope that he will deal similarly with these early ones.

⑥*K'ang-hsi hui-tien* 72. 13b (see text above after note 62), and DUYVENDAK (5). 337-338 refer to this embassy, but we have not noticed much material concerning it. *Ch'ing-shih kao* also lists it, as from William of Orange.

⑦DUYVENDAK (3), (4), and (5).

⑧A number of minor Russian emissaries reached Peking whom we have not listed, some of them, like BAIKOV, being merely "agents." COULING 160, following PFISTER, lists 11 Russian embassies; but on pp. 491-492 for the same period COULING lists a total of 18 "Russian representatives and envoys to China." The latter list, obviously from a different (though unnamed) source, includes a mission "received by the Chinese emperor" (MILOVANOV and KOBIAKOV 1670) which is *not* in PFISTER'S list; and at the same time it omits embassies of 1808 and 1820 which *are* listed by PFISTER. Meanwhile both lists omit a certain BRATISHCHEV, cited by STANTON, who was sent to seek a treaty in 1754, and actually received a letter from the Li Fan Yüan. Much further work along the lines laid down by Dr. STANTON is plainly required. On the whole subject see J. F. BADDELEY, *Russia, Mongolia, China* …, London 1919; G. CAHEN, *Histoire des relations de la Russie avec la Chine* … *(1689-1730),* Paris 1911; J. W. STANTON, "Russian Embassies to Peking during the Eighteenth Century," *University of Michigan Historical Essays* (1937), pp. 97-112; and LIU Hsüanmin, "Russo-Chinese Relations up to the *Treaty of Nerchinsk*," *Chinese Social and Political Science Review* 23 (1940). 391-440.

⑨Papal relations are referred to by PFISTER, passim, among others.

⑩E. H. PRITCHARD, *The Crucial Years of Early Anglo-Chinese Relations, 1750-1800*, Pullman 1986, ch. 5-10 gives an invaluable treatment from the British records.

*Tributaries of the Imperial Ch'ing (Dynasty)*, a compilation of drawings of barbarians of all countries, with explanatory text, illustrating the costume of the sexes and of various social classes in each case.⑫ The material for this imperial work was collected by the high provincial authorities and sent to the Grand Council for presentation to the emperor. Yet in the explanatory text the following statements occur: 1.23, I-ta-li-ya presented tribute in 1667 (actually Holland) and the Pope came to do so in 1725; 1.47, England is a dependency of Holland; 1.49, France is the same as Portugal; 1.51, Sweden is a dependency of Holland; 1.61, Sweden (Jui) and England (Ying-chi-li) are shortened names for Holland; 1.71, the Spanish in the Philippines (Lü-sung) are the Portuguese (Fo-lang-chi) who took Malacca and Macao. (This exaggerated impression of Holland evidently stems from the seventeenth century.)

As the most striking commentary on this persistent confusion it may be noted finally that in November 1844 the Imperial Commissioner Ch'i-ying 耆英, who had just finished the negotiation of treaties with the Great Britain, the United States, and France and was presumably the highest authority in China on the subject of Western countries, reported to the emperor that France (Fo-lan-hsi 佛兰西) was the Fo-lang-chi (Portugal) of the Ming period, whence derived the French interest in Christianity; after the arrival of Matteo RICCI, he explained, "the Frenchmen suddenly yielded Macao to Portugal, themselves returning to their own country; that those barbarians should be ten times as powerful as Portugal and yet willingly give up the place was (due to) their submission to the teaching of Matteo RICCI."⑬ Plainly the ideology of the tributary system with all its implications survived in the nineteenth century in large part because of pure ignorance—an ignorance so profound that the growth of a conscious Chinese foreign policy was seriously inhibited.

The above table of European embassies to Peking, in compiling which we are much indebted to the assistance of Prof. C. S. GARDNER, is offered here as an aid to further study. These embassies illustrate all the problems of the tributary system in its decline—the growth of trade unconnected with formal tribute, the European dislike of the kotow and demand for equal status, the tragic Chinese ignorance of the west. It is amazing that a larger number of systematic studies have not been made of these successive experiments in Sino-Western relations.

## 6. CH'ING TRIBUTE EMBASSIES AND FOREIGN TRADE

The successive editions of the *Collected Statutes* reflect a changing situation but do not reveal its realities in any detail. As a first step toward the study of the real activity of individual tributaries we submit the following table of embassies recorded in the period 1662-1911. The years 1644-1661 are omitted because in that period are recorded well over a hundred Mongol tribes and others, many of which we have been unable to identify, and almost none of which are recorded after the beginning of the K'ang-hsi period in 1662—evidently because their activity under the Li Fan Yüan by that time was considered as in a different category from that of the traditional tributaries remaining under the Board of Ceremonies.

No one source, unless it be the 1200 odd unindexed volumes of the *Ch'ing shih-lu* 清实录,[84] gives a complete list of tribute embassies to the Court of Peking under the Ch'ing. The following table has been compiled from the annals of the *Draft History of the Ch'ing* (*Ch'ing-shih kao*, *pên-chi*) and the *Tung-hua lu* 东华录.[85] Both these sources at the end of each annual section usually give a list of tribute embassies, and usually they agree, particularly in the first half of the nineteenth century (Chia-ch'ing and Tao-kuang periods, excepting 1829-1831). But sometimes one records embassies which the other does not, and sometimes embassies are recorded in the text of an annual section in either work but not in the summary list at the end of the section. Thus embassies from Nepal and the Dzungars are often recorded only in the text, not at the end. We have distinguished among these sources within sources by numerals:

1 = recorded at the end of the annual section of the *Ch'ing-shih kao*, *pên-chi*.

2 = at the end of *Tung-hua lu*.

3 = in the text of the *Ch'ing-shih kao*.

4 = in text of *Tung-hua lu*.

We have searched 3 (the text of the *Ch'ing-shih kao*) during most of the period covered, particularly for the Ch'ien-lung era when summaries at the end were usually omitted in both sources. The more extensive text of the *Tung-hua lu* (4) has been searched only for the first decade after 1662 and elsewhere spasmodically. Each item represents a reference to actual tribute (kung 贡) and has been checked, although not double-checked; further references can doubtless be found in these sources but not, we believe, in numbers sufficient to change the general picture here presented.

On the other hand, the more complete record available in the mountain of documents compiled to form the *Ch'ing shih-lu* upsets to some degree calculations based upon the *Ch'ing-shih kao*; for the *Ch'ing Shih-lu* contains numerous annual references to the presentation of tribute (from Mongol tribes, Tibet, and such places) not mentioned in the *Ch'ing-shih kao*. This appears from an examination of the *Ch'ing Shih-lu* for 1644, 1654, 1664, and so on at ten year intervals through 1834. This discrepancy might be explained on the theory that reference to ordinary tribute from places under the jurisdiction of the Li Fan Yüan came to be regularly excluded from the *Ch'ing-shih kao*. But it appears that the exclusion went even further, and sometimes applied to embassies from the south and east. Thus the *Ch'ing Shih-lu* for 1664 (3rd year of K'ang-hsi, ch. 11. 3b, 12. 24b) records tribute from Annam and Liu-ch'iu, while the *Ch'ing-shih kao*, *pên-chi*, for the same year, does not. The *Ch'ing Shih-lu* for 1674 (13th year of K'ang-hsi, ch. 45. 10b) records tribute from Annam, while the *Ch'ing-shih kao*, *pên-chi*, for the same year, does not. Other examples could be cited to indicate that the annals of the *Ch'ing-shih kao* present an incomplete record of tribute embassies.⁸⁶ It is hardly surprising that the compilers of the Ch'ing history, working in the twentieth century, should give an imperfect record of the functioning of an institution which really perished long before the dynasty itself. As a result it would appear that a relatively complete record of Ch'ing tribute embassies can be secured only through a page by page examination of the twelve hundred odd volumes of the *Ch'ing shih-lu*. This we have not attempted, but we hope someone else will do so. Until this happy event, the data given below appear to be the best available.

TABLE 5   TRIBUTE EMBASSIES 1662-1911

| Reign Title | Reign Year | Calendar Year | KOREA 朝鮮 | LIU-CH'IU 琉球 | ANNAM 安南 | SIAM 暹羅 | BURMA 缅甸 | LAOS 南掌 | SULU 苏禄 | NEPAL 廓尔喀 | DZUNGARS 准噶尔 | RUSSIA 俄罗斯 | (EUROPEAN) | (MISC.) |
|---|---|---|---|---|---|---|---|---|---|---|---|---|---|---|
| K'ang-hsi | 1 | 1662 | *12 | ... | ... | ... | ... | ... | ... | ... | ... | ... | ... | ... |
| | 2 | 1663 | *1 | ... | ... | ... | ... | ... | ... | ... | ... | ... | *34ᵃ HOLL. | ... |
| | 3 | 1664 | *12 | *2 | *4 | ... | ... | ... | ... | ... | ... | ... | ... | ... |
| | 4 | 1665 | *12 | *12 | ... | *12 | ... | ... | ... | ... | ... | ... | ... | ... |
| | 5 | 1666 | *12 | *12 | ... | ... | ... | ... | ... | ... | ... | ... | ... | ... |
| | 6 | 1667 | *12 | ... | ... | ... | ... | ... | ... | ... | ... | ... | *12 HOLL. | ... |
| | 7 | 1668 | *12 | ... | *12 | *12 | ... | ... | ... | ... | ... | ... | ... | ... |
| | 8 | 1669 | *12 | *12 | ... | ... | ... | ... | ... | ... | ... | ... | ... | ... |
| | 9 | 1670 | *12 | ... | ... | ... | ... | ... | ... | ... | ... | ... | *24 PORT. | ... |
| | 10 | 1671 | *12 | *12 | ... | ... | ... | ... | ... | ... | ... | ... | ... | ... |
| | 11 | 1672 | *12 | ... | ... | *4 | ... | ... | ... | ... | ... | ... | ... | ... |
| | 12 | 1673 | *12 | ... | *1 | *2 | ... | ... | ... | ... | ... | ... | ... | *4ᵇ |
| | 13 | 1674 | *12 | *12 | ... | ... | ... | ... | ... | ... | ... | ... | ... | ... |
| | 14 | 1675 | *12 | ... | ... | ... | ... | ... | ... | ... | ... | ... | ... | ... |
| | 15 | 1676 | *12 | ... | ... | ... | ... | ... | ... | ... | *34 | ... | ... | ... |
| | 16 | 1677 | *12 | ... | ... | ... | ... | ... | ... | ... | ... | ... | ... | ... |
| | 17 | 1678 | *12 | ... | ... | ... | ... | ... | ... | ... | ... | ... | *12 PORT. | ... |
| | 18 | 1679 | *12 | *12 | *12 | ... | ... | ... | ... | ... | ... | ... | ... | ... |
| | 19 | 1680 | *12 | *12 | ... | ... | ... | ... | ... | ... | ... | ... | ... | ... |
| | 20 | 1681 | *12 | *2 | ... | ... | ... | ... | ... | *13ᶜ | ... | ... | ... | ... |

| Reign Title | Reign Year | Calendar Year | KOREA 朝鲜 | LIU-CH'IU 琉球 | ANNAM 安南 | SIAM 暹罗 | BURMA 缅甸 | LAOS 南掌 | SULU 苏禄 | NEPAL 廓尔喀 | DZUNGARS 准噶尔 | RUSSIA 俄罗斯 | (EUROPEAN) | (MISC.) |
|---|---|---|---|---|---|---|---|---|---|---|---|---|---|---|
| K'ang-hsi | 21 | 1682 | *12 | … | *12 | … | … | … | … | … | … | … | … | … |
| | 22 | 1683 | *12 | *12 | … | … | … | … | … | … | … | … | … | … |
| | 23 | 1684 | *12 | *2 | … | *12 | … | … | … | … | … | … | … | … |
| | 24 | 1685 | *12 | *12 | … | … | … | … | … | … | *1c | … | … | … |
| | 25 | 1686 | *12 | … | *12 | … | … | … | … | … | … | … | *12 HOLL. | *12b |
| | 26 | 1687 | *12 | … | … | … | … | … | … | … | … | … | … | … |
| | 27 | 1688 | *12 | *12 | … | … | … | … | … | … | … | … | … | … |
| | 28 | 1689 | *12 | *2 | … | … | … | … | … | … | … | … | … | … |
| | 29 | 1690 | *12 | … | … | … | … | … | … | … | … | … | … | … |
| | 30 | 1691 | *12 | *12 | *1 | … | … | … | … | … | … | … | … | … |
| | 31 | 1692 | *12 | … | … | … | … | … | … | … | … | … | … | … |
| | 32 | 1693 | *12 | *12 | … | … | … | … | … | … | … | … | … | … |
| | 33 | 1694 | *12 | … | … | … | … | … | … | … | … | … | … | … |
| | 34 | 1695 | *12 | *12 | … | … | … | … | … | … | … | … | … | … |
| | 35 | 1696 | *12 | … | … | … | … | … | … | … | … | … | … | … |
| | 36 | 1697 | *12 | *12 | *12 | … | … | … | … | … | … | … | … | … |
| | 37 | 1698 | *12 | … | … | … | … | … | … | … | … | … | … | … |
| | 38 | 1699 | *12 | *12 | … | … | … | … | … | … | … | … | … | … |
| | 39 | 1700 | *12 | … | … | … | … | … | … | … | … | … | … | … |
| | 40 | 1701 | *12 | *12 | … | … | … | … | … | … | … | … | … | … |
| | 41 | 1702 | *12 | *1 | … | … | … | … | … | … | … | … | … | … |
| | 42 | 1703 | *12 | *12 | *12 | … | … | … | … | … | … | … | … | … |
| | 43 | 1704 | *12 | … | … | … | … | … | … | … | … | … | … | … |
| | 44 | 1705 | *12 | *12 | … | … | … | … | … | … | … | … | … | … |
| | 45 | 1706 | *12 | … | … | … | … | … | … | … | … | … | … | … |
| | 46 | 1707 | *12 | *12 | … | … | … | … | … | … | … | … | … | … |
| | 47 | 1708 | *12 | … | … | *2 | … | … | … | … | … | … | … | … |
| | 48 | 1709 | *12 | *12 | … | … | … | … | … | … | … | … | … | … |
| | 49 | 1710 | *12 | … | *12 | … | … | … | … | … | … | … | … | … |
| | 50 | 1711 | *12 | *12 | … | … | … | … | … | … | … | … | … | … |
| | 51 | 1712 | *12 | … | … | … | … | … | … | … | … | … | … | … |
| | 52 | 1713 | *12 | *12 | … | … | … | … | … | … | … | … | … | … |
| | 53 | 1714 | *12 | … | … | … | … | … | … | … | … | … | … | … |
| | 54 | 1715 | *12 | *12 | … | … | … | … | … | … | … | … | … | … |
| | 55 | 1716 | *12 | … | *12 | … | … | … | … | … | … | … | … | … |
| | 56 | 1717 | *12 | … | … | … | … | … | … | … | … | … | … | … |

| Reign Title | Reign Year | Calendar Year | KOREA 朝鲜 | LIU-CH'IU 琉球 | ANNAM 安南 | SIAM 暹罗 | BURMA 缅甸 | LAOS 南掌 | SULU 苏禄 | NEPAL 廓尔喀 | DZUNGARS 准噶尔 | RUSSIA 俄罗斯 | (EUROPEAN) | (MISC.) |
|---|---|---|---|---|---|---|---|---|---|---|---|---|---|---|
| K'ang-hsi | 57 | 1718 | *12 | *12 | *12 | ... | ... | ... | ... | ... | ... | ... | ... | ... |
| | 58 | 1719 | *12 | *12 | ... | ... | ... | ... | ... | ... | ... | ... | ... | ... |
| | 59 | 1720 | *12 | *12 | ... | ... | ... | ... | ... | ... | ... | ... | ... | ... |
| | 60 | 1721 | *12 | *12 | *12 | ... | ... | ... | ... | ... | ... | ... | ... | ... |
| | 61 | 1722 | ... | ... | ... | ... | ... | ... | ... | ... | ... | ... | ... | ... |
| Yung-chêng | 1 | 1723 | *12 | *12 | ... | ... | ... | ... | ... | ... | ... | ... | ... | ... |
| | 2 | 1724 | *1 | ... | *1 | *1 | ... | ... | ... | ... | ... | ... | ... | ... |
| | 3 | 1725 | *1 | *12 | ... | ... | ... | ... | ... | ... | ... | ... | *12 POPE | ... |
| | 4 | 1726 | *1 | *1 | ... | ... | ... | *12 | ... | ... | ... | ... | ... | ... |
| | 5 | 1727 | *1 | ... | ... | ... | ... | ... | ... | ... | ... | *1 | ... | ... |
| | 6 | 1728 | *1 | ... | ... | ... | ... | ... | ... | ... | ... | ... | ... | ... |
| | 7 | 1729 | *12 | *12 | ... | ... | ... | ... | ... | ... | ... | ... | ... | ... |
| | 8 | 1730 | *1 | ... | *12 | ... | ... | *1 | ... | ... | ... | ... | ... | ... |
| | 9 | 1731 | *1 | *12 | ... | ... | ... | ... | ... | ... | ... | ... | ... | ... |
| | 10 | 1732 | *1 | ... | ... | ... | ... | ... | ... | ... | ... | ... | ... | *1[d] |
| | 11 | 1733 | *1 | ... | *1 | ... | ... | *1 | ... | ... | ... | ... | ... | ... |
| | 12 | 1734 | *1 | *12 | ... | ... | ... | ... | ... | ... | ... | ... | ... | ... |
| | 13 | 1735 | *2 | ... | ... | ... | ... | ... | ... | ... | *3 | ... | ... | ... |
| Ch'ien-lung | 1 | 1736 | *12 | ... | *12 | *12 | ... | *12 | ... | ... | ... | ... | ... | ... |
| | 2 | 1737 | *12 | *12 | *23 | ... | ... | *23 | ... | ... | ... | ... | ... | ... |
| | 3 | 1738 | *23 | *23 | *23 | ... | ... | ... | ... | ... | *3 | ... | ... | ... |
| | 4 | 1739 | *23 | ... | ... | ... | ... | ... | ... | ... | ... | ... | ... | *3[g] |
| | 5 | 1740 | *23 | *23 | ... | ... | ... | ... | ... | ... | ... | ... | ... | ... |
| | 6 | 1741 | *2 | *23 | ... | ... | ... | *23 | ... | ... | ... | ... | ... | ... |
| | 7 | 1742 | *23 | *3 | ... | ... | ... | ... | ... | ... | *3 | ... | ... | ... |
| | 8 | 1743 | *23 | *23 | *23 | ... | ... | *23 | ... | ... | *3 | ... | ... | ... |
| | 9 | 1744 | *23 | *2 | ... | ... | ... | ... | ... | ... | ... | ... | ... | ... |
| | 10 | 1745 | *23 | ... | ... | ... | ... | ... | ... | ... | *3 | ... | ... | ... |
| | 11 | 1746 | *23 | ... | ... | ... | ... | ... | ... | ... | *3 | ... | ... | ... |
| | 12 | 1747 | *2 | ... | ... | ... | ... | *3[e] | ... | ... | ... | ... | ... | ... |
| | 13 | 1748 | *23 | *23 | ... | ... | ... | ... | ... | ... | ... | ... | ... | ... |
| | 14 | 1749 | *2 | ... | ... | *2 | ... | *3 | ... | ... | ... | ... | ... | ... |
| | 15 | 1750 | *23 | *2 | ... | ... | *23 | ... | ... | ... | ... | ... | ... | ... |
| | 16 | 1751 | *2 | *2 | ... | ... | *3 | ... | ... | ... | ... | ... | ... | ... |
| | 17 | 1752 | ... | ... | ... | ... | ... | *3 | ... | *3 | ... | ... | *3 PORT. | *3[g] |
| | 18 | 1753 | *2 | ... | ... | ... | ... | *3 | ... | *3[f] | ... | ... | *3 PORT. | ... |

| Reign Title | Reign Year | Calendar Year | KOREA 朝鲜 | LIU-CH'IU 琉球 | ANNAM 安南 | SIAM 暹罗 | BURMA 缅甸 | LAOS 南掌 | SULU 苏禄 | NEPAL 廓尔喀 | DZUNGARS 准噶尔 | RUSSIA 俄罗斯 | (EUROPEAN) | (MISC.) |
|---|---|---|---|---|---|---|---|---|---|---|---|---|---|---|
| Ch'ien-lung | 19 | 1754 | *2 | *23 | *23 | ... | ... | ... | *23 | ... | ... | ... | ... | ... |
|  | 20 | 1755 | *23 | *23 | ... | ... | ... | ... | ... | ... | ... | ... | ... | ... |
|  | 21 | 1756 | *2 | *2 | ... | *23 | ... | ... | ... | ... | ... | ... | ... | ... |
|  | 22 | 1757 | *123 | *123 | ... | *123 | ... | ... | ... | ... | ... | ... | ... | *3ʰ |
|  | 23 | 1758 | *23 | ... | ... | ... | ... | ... | ... | ... | ... | ... | ... | *3ʰ |
|  | 24 | 1759 | *2 | ... | ... | ... | ... | ... | ... | ... | ... | ... | ... | ... |
|  | 25 | 1760 | *12 | ... | ... | ... | ... | *12 | ... | ... | ... | ... | ... | ... |
|  | 26 | 1761 | *2 | ... | ... | ... | ... | *3 | ... | ... | ... | ... | ... | ... |
|  | 27 | 1762 | *23 | ... | ... | ... | ... | ... | ... | ... | ... | ... | ... | *13ⁱ |
|  | 28 | 1763 | *2 | ... | ... | ... | ... | ... | ... | ... | ... | ... | ... | ... |
|  | 29 | 1764 | *23 | ... | ... | ... | ... | ... | ... | ... | ... | ... | ... | ... |
|  | 30 | 1765 | *23 | ... | ... | ... | ... | ... | ... | ... | ... | ... | ... | ... |
|  | 31 | 1766 | *12 | *12 | ... | ... | ... | ... | ... | ... | ... | ... | ... | ... |
|  | 32 | 1767 | *2 | ... | *2 | ... | ... | ... | ... | ... | ... | ... | ... | ... |
|  | 33 | 1768 | *2 | *2 | ... | ... | ... | ... | ... | ... | ... | ... | ... | ... |
|  | 34 | 1769 | *2 | ... | ... | ... | ... | ... | ... | ... | ... | ... | ... | ... |
|  | 35 | 1770 | *2 | *2 | ... | ... | ... | ... | ... | ... | ... | ... | ... | ... |
|  | 36 | 1771 | *2 | ... | ... | ... | ... | *2 | ... | ... | ... | ... | ... | ... |
|  | 37 | 1772 | *2 | *2 | ... | ... | ... | ... | ... | ... | ... | ... | ... | ... |
|  | 38 | 1773 | *12 | ... | *12 | ... | ... | ... | ... | ... | ... | ... | ... | ... |
|  | 39 | 1774 | *12 | *12 | ... | ... | ... | ... | ... | ... | ... | ... | ... | ... |
|  | 40 | 1775 | *2 | *2 | ... | ... | ... | ... | ... | ... | ... | ... | ... | ... |
|  | 41 | 1776 | *2 | ... | ... | ... | *3 | ... | ... | ... | ... | ... | ... | ... |
|  | 42 | 1777 | *2 | ... | ... | *3 | ... | ... | ... | ... | ... | ... | ... | ... |
|  | 43 | 1778 | *23 | *23 | ... | ... | ... | ... | ... | ... | ... | ... | ... | ... |
|  | 44 | 1779 | *2 | ... | ... | ... | ... | ... | ... | ... | ... | ... | ... | ... |
|  | 45 | 1780 | *23 | *2 | ... | ... | ... | ... | ... | ... | ... | ... | ... | ... |
|  | 46 | 1781 | *23 | ... | *2 | *23 | ... | *23 | ... | ... | ... | ... | ... | ... |
|  | 47 | 1782 | *2 | *2 | ... | *2 | ... | ... | ... | ... | ... | ... | ... | ... |
|  | 48 | 1783 | *23 | ... | ... | ... | ... | ... | ... | ... | ... | ... | ... | ... |
|  | 49 | 1784 | *12 | *12 | *12 | *12 | ... | ... | ... | ... | ... | ... | ... | ... |
|  | 50 | 1785 | *12 | ... | ... | ... | ... | ... | ... | ... | ... | ... | ... | ... |
|  | 51 | 1786 | *12 | *12 | ... | *12 | ... | ... | ... | ... | ... | ... | ... | ... |
|  | 52 | 1787 | *2 | ... | ... | ... | ... | ... | ... | ... | ... | ... | ... | ... |
|  | 53 | 1788 | *2 | *2 | ... | ... | *3 | ... | ... | ... | ... | ... | ... | ... |
|  | 54 | 1789 | *2 | ... | *23 | ... | ... | ... | ... | ... | ... | ... | ... | ... |

| Reign Title | Reign Year | Calendar Year | KOREA 朝鲜 | LIU-CH'IU 琉球 | ANNAM 安南 | SIAM 暹罗 | BURMA 缅甸 | LAOS 南掌 | SULU 苏禄 | NEPAL 廓尔喀 | DZUNGARS 准噶尔 | RUSSIA 俄罗斯 | (EUROPEAN) | (MISC.) |
|---|---|---|---|---|---|---|---|---|---|---|---|---|---|---|
| Ch'ien-lung | 55 | 1790 | *23 | *23 | *23 | *3 | *23 | *23 | ... | ... | ... | ... | ... | ... |
| | 56 | 1791 | *23 | ... | *2 | *2 | *23 | ... | ... | ... | ... | ... | ... | ... |
| | 57 | 1792 | *2 | ... | *23 | *2 | ... | ... | ... | *23 | ... | ... | ... | *3[k] |
| | 58 | 1793 | *2 | *2 | *23 | ... | *2 | ... | ... | ... | ... | ... | *23 ENG.[j] | ... |
| | 59 | 1794 | *2 | ... | ... | ... | ... | ... | ... | *3 | ... | ... | *23 HOLL. | ... |
| | 60 | 1795 | *2 | *12 | *12 | *12 | *12 | *12 | ... | *1 | ... | ... | *12 ENG.[j] | ... |
| Ch'ia-ch'ing | 1 | 1796 | *12 | ... | ... | ... | ... | ... | ... | ... | ... | ... | ... | ... |
| | 2 | 1797 | *12 | *12 | ... | *12 | ... | ... | ... | ... | ... | ... | ... | ... |
| | 3 | 1798 | *12 | ... | ... | *12 | ... | ... | ... | ... | ... | ... | ... | ... |
| | 4 | 1799 | *12 | ... | ... | *12 | ... | ... | ... | ... | ... | ... | ... | ... |
| | 5 | 1800 | *12 | *12 | ... | ... | ... | ... | ... | ... | ... | ... | ... | ... |
| | 6 | 1801 | *12 | ... | ... | *12 | ... | ... | ... | ... | ... | ... | ... | ... |
| | 7 | 1802 | *12 | ... | ... | ... | ... | ... | ... | ... | ... | ... | ... | ... |
| | 8 | 1803 | *12 | ... | *12[l] | ... | ... | ... | ... | ... | ... | ... | ... | ... |
| | 9 | 1804 | *12 | ... | ... | *12 | ... | ... | ... | ... | ... | ... | ... | ... |
| | 10 | 1805 | *12 | ... | ... | ... | ... | ... | ... | ... | ... | ... | *123 ENG. | ... |
| | 11 | 1806 | *12 | *12 | ... | ... | ... | ... | ... | ... | ... | ... | ... | ... |
| | 12 | 1807 | *12 | *12 | ... | ... | *12 | ... | ... | ... | ... | ... | ... | ... |
| | 13 | 1808 | *12 | *12 | ... | ... | ... | ... | ... | ... | ... | ... | ... | ... |
| | 14 | 1809 | *12 | *12 | *12 | ... | *12 | ... | ... | ... | ... | ... | ... | ... |
| | 15 | 1810 | *12 | ... | ... | *12 | ... | ... | ... | ... | ... | ... | ... | ... |
| | 16 | 1811 | *12 | *12 | ... | *12 | *12 | ... | ... | ... | ... | ... | ... | ... |
| | 17 | 1812 | *12 | ... | ... | *12 | ... | ... | ... | ... | ... | ... | ... | ... |
| | 18 | 1813 | *12 | *12 | *12 | *12 | ... | ... | ... | ... | ... | ... | ... | ... |
| | 19 | 1814 | *12 | *12 | ... | ... | ... | ... | ... | ... | ... | ... | ... | ... |
| | 20 | 1815 | *12 | *12 | ... | *12 | ... | ... | ... | ... | ... | ... | ... | ... |
| | 21 | 1816 | *12 | ... | ... | ... | ... | ... | ... | ... | ... | ... | *123 ENG. | ... |
| | 22 | 1817 | *12 | *12 | *12 | ... | ... | ... | ... | ... | ... | ... | ... | ... |
| | 23 | 1818 | *12 | *12 | ... | ... | ... | ... | ... | ... | ... | ... | ... | ... |
| | 24 | 1819 | *12 | *12 | *12 | *12 | ... | *12 | ... | ... | ... | ... | ... | ... |
| | 25 | 1820 | *12 | ... | ... | *12 | ... | ... | ... | ... | ... | ... | ... | ... |
| Tao-kuang | 1 | 1821 | *12 | *12 | *12 | ... | ... | ... | ... | ... | ... | ... | ... | ... |
| | 2 | 1822 | *12 | *12 | ... | *123 | ... | ... | ... | ... | ... | ... | ... | ... |
| | 3 | 1823 | *12 | *12 | ... | *12 | *12 | ... | ... | *3[q] | ... | ... | ... | ... |
| | 4 | 1824 | *12 | *12 | ... | ... | ... | ... | ... | ... | ... | ... | ... | ... |
| | 5 | 1825 | *12 | *12 | ... | *12 | *12 | ... | ... | ... | ... | ... | ... | ... |

| Reign Title | Reign Year | Calendar Year | KOREA 朝鲜 | LIU-CH'IU 琉球 | ANNAM 安南 | SIAM 暹罗 | BURMA 缅甸 | LAOS 南掌 | SULU 苏禄 | NEPAL 廓尔喀 | DZUNGARS 准噶尔 | RUSSIA 俄罗斯 | (EUROPEAN) | (MISC.) |
|---|---|---|---|---|---|---|---|---|---|---|---|---|---|---|
| Tao-kuang | 6 | 1826 | *12 | *12 | … | … | … | … | … | … | … | … | … | … |
| | 7 | 1827 | *12 | *12 | … | *12 | … | … | … | … | … | … | … | … |
| | 8 | 1828 | *12 | *12 | … | … | … | … | … | … | … | … | … | … |
| | 9 | 1829 | *23 | *2 | *2 | *2 | *23 | … | … | … | … | … | … | … |
| | 10 | 1830 | *2 | *2 | … | *23 | … | … | … | … | … | … | … | … |
| | 11 | 1831 | *23 | *2 | *2 | *23 | … | … | … | … | … | … | … | … |
| | 12 | 1832 | *12 | *12 | … | *12 | … | *12 | … | … | … | … | … | … |
| | 13 | 1833 | *12 | *12 | *12 | … | *12 | … | … | … | … | … | … | … |
| | 14 | 1834 | *12 | *12 | … | *12 | … | … | … | … | … | … | … | … |
| | 15 | 1835 | *12 | *12 | … | … | … | … | … | … | … | … | … | … |
| | 16 | 1836 | *12 | … | … | *12 | … | … | … | … | … | … | … | … |
| | 17 | 1837 | *12 | *12 | *12 | *12 | … | … | … | … | … | … | … | … |
| | 18 | 1838 | *12 | *12 | … | *12 | … | … | … | … | … | … | … | … |
| | 19 | 1839 | *12 | *12 | … | … | … | … | … | … | … | … | … | … |
| | 20 | 1840 | *12 | … | … | … | … | … | … | … | … | … | … | … |
| | 21 | 1841 | *12 | *12 | … | … | … | *12 | … | … | … | … | … | … |
| | 22 | 1842 | *12 | *12 | … | … | … | … | … | *1 | … | … | … | … |
| | 23 | 1843 | *12 | … | … | *12 | *12 | … | … | … | … | … | … | … |
| | 24 | 1844 | *12 | … | … | *12 | … | … | … | … | … | … | … | … |
| | 25 | 1845 | *12 | … | *12 | … | … | … | … | … | … | … | … | … |
| | 26 | 1846 | *12 | *12 | … | … | … | … | … | … | … | … | … | … |
| | 27 | 1847 | *12 | *12 | … | … | … | … | … | … | … | … | … | … |
| | 28 | 1848 | *12 | *12 | *12 | *12 | … | … | … | … | … | … | … | … |
| | 29 | 1849 | *12 | *12 | *12 | … | … | … | … | … | … | … | … | … |
| | 30 | 1850 | *14 | *14 | … | … | … | … | … | … | … | … | … | … |
| Hsien-fêng | 1 | 1851 | *1 | *1 | … | … | … | … | … | … | … | … | … | … |
| | 2 | 1852 | *1 | … | … | *1 | … | … | … | … | … | … | … | … |
| | 3 | 1853 | *1 | *1 | *1 | *1 | *1 | *1 | … | … | … | … | … | … |
| | 4 | 1854 | *14 | *1 | … | … | … | … | … | … | … | … | … | … |
| | 5 | 1855 | *1 | *1 | … | … | … | … | … | … | … | … | … | … |
| | 6 | 1856 | *1 | … | … | … | … | … | … | … | … | … | … | … |
| | 7 | 1857 | *1 | *1 | … | … | … | … | … | … | … | … | … | … |
| | 8 | 1858 | *14 | *1 | … | … | … | … | … | … | … | … | … | … |
| | 9 | 1859 | *1 | *1 | … | … | … | … | … | … | … | … | … | … |
| | 10 | 1860 | *1 | … | … | … | … | … | … | … | … | … | … | … |
| | 11 | 1861 | *3 | … | … | … | … | … | … | … | … | … | … | … |

| Reign Title | Reign Year | Calendar Year | KOREA 朝鮮 | LIU-CH'IU 琉球 | ANNAM 安南 | SIAM 暹羅 | BURMA 緬甸 | LAOS 南掌 | SULU 蘇祿 | NEPAL 廓爾喀 | DZUNGARS 准噶爾 | RUSSIA 俄羅斯 | (EUROPEAN) | (MISC.) |
|---|---|---|---|---|---|---|---|---|---|---|---|---|---|---|
| T'ung-chih | 1 | 1862 | *12 | *12 | ... | ... | ... | ... | ... | ... | ... | ... | ... | ... |
| | 2 | 1863 | *12 | ... | ... | ... | ... | ... | ... | ... | ... | ... | ... | ... |
| | 3 | 1864 | *12 | *12 | ... | ... | ... | ... | ... | ... | ... | ... | ... | ... |
| | 4 | 1865 | ... | ... | ... | ... | ... | ... | ... | *3 | ... | ... | ... | ... |
| | 5 | 1866 | *12 | *12 | ... | ... | ... | ... | ... | ... | ... | ... | ... | ... |
| | 6 | 1867 | *12 | *12 | ... | ... | ... | ... | ... | ... | ... | ... | ... | ... |
| | 7 | 1868 | *12 | ... | ... | ... | ... | ... | ... | ... | ... | ... | ... | ... |
| | 8 | 1869 | *12 | *12 | *12 | ... | ... | ... | ... | ... | ... | ... | ... | ... |
| | 9 | 1870 | *12 | ... | ... | ... | ... | ... | ... | ... | ... | ... | ... | ... |
| | 10 | 1871 | *12 | *12 | *12 | ... | ... | ... | ... | ... | ... | ... | ... | *2[m] |
| | 11 | 1872 | *12 | ... | ... | ... | ... | ... | ... | ... | ... | ... | ... | ... |
| | 12 | 1873 | *1 | ... | ... | ... | ... | ... | ... | ... | ... | ... | ... | ... |
| | 13 | 1874 | ... | ... | ... | ... | ... | ... | ... | ... | ... | ... | ... | ... |
| Kuang-hsü | 1 | 1875[p] | *1 | *1 | ... | ... | *1 | ... | ... | ... | ... | ... | ... | ... |
| | 2 | 1876 | ... | ... | ... | ... | ... | ... | ... | ... | ... | ... | ... | ... |
| | 3 | 1877 | ... | *3[n] | *3 | ... | ... | ... | ... | ... | ... | ... | ... | ... |
| | 4 | 1878 | *1 | ... | ... | ... | ... | ... | ... | *1 | ... | ... | ... | ... |
| | 5 | 1879 | *1 | ... | ... | ... | ... | ... | ... | *1 | ... | ... | ... | ... |
| | 6 | 1880 | *1 | ... | ... | ... | ... | ... | ... | *1 | ... | ... | ... | *3[o] |
| | 7 | 1881 | *1 | ... | *1 | ... | ... | ... | ... | ... | ... | ... | ... | ... |
| | 8 | 1882 | *1 | ... | ... | ... | ... | ... | ... | ... | ... | ... | ... | ... |
| | 9 | 1883 | *1 | ... | *1 | ... | ... | ... | ... | ... | ... | ... | ... | ... |
| | 10 | 1884 | *1 | ... | ... | ... | ... | ... | ... | ... | ... | ... | ... | ... |
| | 11 | 1885 | ... | ... | ... | ... | ... | ... | ... | ... | ... | ... | ... | ... |
| | 12 | 1886 | *1 | ... | ... | ... | ... | ... | ... | ... | ... | ... | ... | ... |
| | 13 | 1887 | *1 | ... | ... | ... | ... | ... | ... | ... | ... | ... | ... | ... |
| | 14 | 1888 | ... | ... | ... | ... | ... | ... | ... | ... | ... | ... | ... | ... |
| | 15 | 1889 | *13 | ... | ... | ... | ... | ... | ... | ... | ... | ... | ... | ... |
| | 16 | 1890 | ... | ... | ... | ... | ... | ... | ... | ... | ... | ... | ... | ... |
| | 17 | 1891 | ... | ... | ... | ... | ... | ... | ... | ... | ... | ... | ... | ... |
| | 18 | 1892 | *1 | ... | ... | ... | ... | ... | ... | ... | ... | ... | ... | ... |
| | 19 | 1893 | ... | ... | ... | ... | ... | ... | ... | ... | ... | ... | ... | ... |
| | 20 | 1894 | *1 | ... | ... | ... | ... | ... | ... | ... | ... | ... | ... | ... |
| | 21 | 1895[r] | ... | ... | ... | ... | ... | ... | ... | ... | ... | ... | ... | ... |
| | 34 | 1908 | ... | ... | ... | ... | ... | ... | ... | *3 | ... | ... | ... | ... |
| Hsüan-t'ung | 1 | 1909 | ... | ... | ... | ... | ... | ... | ... | ... | ... | ... | ... | ... |

a. "The country of Holland sent an envoy who presented tribute and requested permission to assist the imperial army in carrying on the war against Taiwan; an exceptional reward was bestowed upon him." Presumably refers either to BORT or to VAN KAMPEN and NOBEL, none of whom reached Peking?

b. Turfan.

c. O-lu-t'ê 厄鲁特, i. e. Oëlot (Western Mongols), later followed by the Dzungars. M. COURANT, *L'Asie Centrale aux XVII$^e$ et XVIII$^e$ siècles*, Paris 1912, summarizes Manchu-Mongol relations in this period as recorded in the *Tung-hua lu*.

d. Pa-pu-êrh kuo 巴布尔国. Cf. 巴布 Parbuttiya, i. e. Nepal, BRUNNERT 907.

e. Presentation of tribute not specifically mentioned.

f. Tribute ordered permanently stopped; in the following year the Dzungars surrendered.

g. 布鲁克巴之额尔德尼第巴 The Erdeni Regent of the Sakya, or Brugba, i. e. Tibet. Cf. BRUNNERT 906.

h. Kirghiz (Ha-sa-k'o).

i. 库尔勒伯克 K'u-êrh-lê Beg; and also Afghanistan (Ai-wu-han).

j. 1792: permission for tribute embassy (MACARTNEY) given; 1793: embassy; 1795: tribute not presented at Court.

k. 霍罕额尔德尼伯克那尔巴图 The Ho-han Erdeni Beg, Na-êrh-pa-t'u?

l. Annam (An-nan) became Yüeh-nan.

m. Japan.

n. Liu-ch'iu tribute to China stopped by Japan; tribute envoy to China sent back.

o. 察木多帕克巴拉胡土克图. The Po-k'o-pa-la Living Buddha of Chamdo, Tibet.

p. Only sources 1 and 3 are used after 1874.

q. Three khans from Tibet 西藏巴勒布部库库木颜布叶楞三汗.

r. Nothing recorded from here through 1907.

The picture presented above in Table 5 may be summarized as follows for the two centuries from 1662 to 1860:

Korea—tribute embassies every year with only one or two exceptions;

Liu-ch'iu—embassies every other year on the average, actually in some 115 years out of the two centuries mentioned, and annually in the period 1813-1835—this has significance for the trade between China and Japan;

Annam—some 45 years in the two centuries mentioned, of which 24 were in the second century—a slight (recorded) increase in the latter part of the period;

Siam—some 48 years during the two centuries mentioned, of which 11 were in the first century and 37 in the period from 1780 to 1860—a marked (recorded) increase in the latter part of the period;

Burma—some 16 years between 1750 and 1853, of which 12 were after 1789—i. e. chiefly in the nineteenth century;

Laos—some 17 years between 1730 and 1853, rather evenly scattered about ten years apart;

Sulu—some 7 years between 1726 and 1754.

The remaining tributaries listed after 1662 are either European, or from the north or west; the latter total a dozen miscellaneous items, including Nepal (the Gurkas) on ten occasions between 1792 and 1908, the Western Mongols (Oëlots, Dzungars) on at least ten occasions, and Tibet, Turfan, and certain tribes, all very occasionally. Nepal sent tribute before the 1818 edition of the *Collected Statutes* but was not regularly enrolled in it.

From these indications, such as they are, it would appear that, in the latter of the two centuries between 1662 and 1860, embassies from Korea continued regularly, those from Liu-ch'iu and from Annam increased in frequency, and those from Siam and Burma showed a marked increase. According to this table, recorded embassies totalled 216 in the first century and 254 in the second (1762-1860 inclusive). Leaving Korea out of account, as a constant factor, the average number of embassies per year during 1662-1761 was 1.16, whereas in the years 1801-1860 it was 1.68. It therefore appears that embassies increased as the dynasty grew older—that the height of Ch'ing power in the eighteenth century saw less tributary activity than the period of decline in the first half of the nineteenth century.

There is as yet no way of passing final judgment upon the completeness of the references recorded in the sources upon which this conclusion is based. It is conceivable that as the dynasty grew weaker an effort was made to maintain prestige by recording tributary embassies more completely. Judging by the regularity of the bureaucratic scribal activity under the Ch'ing, so far as we know, this seems unlikely. In any case this evidence, even if it be a mere selection of data, must be reckoned with as it stands until an index has been made for the *Ch'ing Shih-lu*, and it or other sources have yielded further references. What are we, then, to make of this evidence?

The most obvious suggestion is that this increase in the sending of embassies was prompted by commercial motives. The alternative explanation would seem to lie in the realm of international politics. Under the latter heading, if it can genuinely be separated from economic interests, might lie the increase of Burmese and Nepalese activity, following the Chinese campaigns against these countries in 1765-1769 and 1792, respectively. The activity of Sulu and of Laos do not seem to fit any particular pattern of explanation. That of Siam and of Liu-ch'iu, however, particularly the latter, might be tentatively ascribed to an increased interest in commerce. Whether the embassies were themselves commercial or merely auxiliarily to trade remains to be investigated. But at least in the case of Liu-ch'iu a strong argument may be advanced for the commercial explanation, since Liu-ch'iu was the entrepôt for Sino-Japanese trade; and as a matter of fact a good deal (almost a third) of the recorded increase in the total of embassies is due to Liu-ch'iu. By statute this kingdom should have sent tribute every second year, but it was recorded in 55 years between 1806 and 1860. We summarize below a rather interesting report written by the British Vice-consul at Foochow in 1851 describing at first hand the process of tributary trade.⑦

The suggestion that embassies, at least in some cases, increased in number to provide a vehicle for an expanding commerce naturally raises the whole question of the relation between trade and tribute in the modern period. Having already raised a good many more problems than have been solved, we venture to put forward a brief interpretation of tributary trade in general.

(1) It is a truism that in the modern period Chinese exclusiveness was broken down by maritime trade with the West, which increased to a point where it could not be confined within tributary channels. This process was most spectacular in the case of the opium trade in the nineteenth century which provided the lubrication for the entire Anglo-American commercial penetration, and which rapidly increased the flow of Sino-Western commerce built up by the eighteenth century tea trade under the East India Company. It was this continued growth of trade that brought on the fatal trial of strength between the tributary system and the Great Britain, from which stemmed the débacle of the later nineteenth century. The subject has already been much studied.

(2) By contrast, the expansion of Chinese native trade in the Ch'ing period has been relatively neglected. The junk trade from Amoy and Canton to the East indies and Malaya⑧ has been tacitly accepted as the logical background of the spectacular Ming expeditions under CHÊNG Ho, but scholarly studies of that period of Chinese imperial expansion have been largely devoted to unavoidable textual problems rather than to its economic history. After the expeditions ceased in 1433 Chinese commerce with Southeastern Asia remains obscure until after the arrival of the Portuguese at Malacca in 1511, when the story of European penetration begins as noted in the preceding paragraph.

It is generally accepted that the Portuguese at Malacca, in the Moluccas, and elsewhere entered into an east-west trade which had previously been flourishing under Arab domination. It is an obvious next step to posit that the Portuguese and their successors the Dutch and English also entered into a north-south trade, which was already flourishing between China and Southeastern Asia and was conducted largely by the Chinese. This may be taken as a truism. A recent student of the Spanish in the Philippines,[88] for example, points out that Manila prospered chiefly as an entrepôt between China and America, the China-Manila trade being conducted by the Chinese. In other words, early European trade with eastern Asia was grafted onto the Chinese junk trade which already flourished there. Native Chinese commercial expansion stemming from the Mongol period, or probably much earlier, paved the way for the European invasion of China by sea. Should we not assume that it also for a time kept pace with the growth of Western Commerce?[89]

(3) The vitality of the Chinese junk trade with Malaya in the early nineteenth century is dearly reflected in the list of countries recorded in the 1818 edition of the *Collected Statutes* as having commercial rather than tributary intercourse with China. From the account of these countries, translated in section 4 above, the following table may be constructed:

**TABLE 6　NON-TRIBUTARY TRADING COUNTRIES 1818**

| Place | No. of "watches" (ching 更)[90] distant from Amoy | No. of *li* distant from Canton; remarks |
|---|---|---|
| Siam? (Chiang-k'ou) | 160 to Amoy | 7200 to Canton |
| Cambodia (Tung-pu-chai) | 170 " " | same route to Canton as Chiang-k'ou |
| Yin-tai-ma (Chantebun?) (Malay Peninsula begins here?) | 140 " " …… | (adjoins Cambodia) …… |
| Ligor | 150 " " | (adjoins Jaya) |
| Jaya (Ch'ih-tzŭ) | same as Sungora (180) | (adjoins Sungora) |
| Sungora | 180 to Amoy | …… |
| Patani | same as Ligor (150) | (adjoins Ligor?) |

| Place | No. of "watches" (ching 更)⁹⁰ distant from Amoy | No. of *li* distant from Canton; remarks |
|---|---|---|
| (Siamese-Malayan border comes here?) | ...... | ...... |
| Trengganu | ...... | 9,000 to Kwangtung border |
| Tan-tan | 130 to Amoy | ...... |
| Pahang | ...... | (adjoins Johore) |
| Johore | 180 to Amoy | 9,000 *li* to Kwangtung border |
| (end of Malay peninsula) | ...... | ...... |
| (revert to eastern route) | ...... | ...... |
| Lü-sung (P. I.) | 72 to Amoy | ...... |
| Mang-chün-ta-lao (Mindanao?) | 150 to Amoy | ...... |
| Java (Batavia?) | 280 to Amoy | ...... |

A glance at the *Atlas van Tropisch Nederland*, Blad. 10b, or any good map of the region⁹² will show how plainly these places form a chain of ports of call on the coastal trade route from Amoy to the Straits. That this list is an accurate contemporary record is confirmed in a pleasantly unexpected manner by the report of a British empire-builder, Captain Francis LIGHT, the chief founder of Penang, who sent home about the year 1788 a list of places in Malaya entitled "A Brief Account of the Several Countries Surrounding Prince of Wales' Island with Their Production."⁹³ The places of trade listed by Capt. LIGHT are as follows; note the nearly perfect correspondence with the Chinese list published 30 years later: Siam, Chantebon, Chia, Sangora, Pattany, Ligore, Tringano, Pahang, Jahore, Rheo... (5 items)... Acheen...

Considering the wealth of place names and points of trade recorded in Malaya at earlier periods, the relatively close correspondence of these two sources would indicate that they mirrored the same situation, i. e. that the Chinese list of 1818 was based on fact. Confirmation may be found in other Chinese works.⁹⁴

(4) The most important thing about this list is the fact that it was

frankly labelled "trading countries" 互市诸国, not "tributaries." In the Ming period Kelantan, Pahang, and Johore had been officially enrolled as tributaries. Now they were not. Evidently this was a tardy acknowledgment of the situation created in the fifteenth century when tribute embassies from Southeastern Asia, with the chief exception of Malacca, ceased to arrive at Peking just as soon as CHÊNG Ho stopped coming to get them—although trade with Southeast Asia continued.

In this context the voyages of CHÊNG Ho may be regarded as an effort to bring the sources of Chinese maritime trade into the formal structure of the tributary system. Foreign places communicating by land were by official tradition regarded as tributary and were so enrolled, as were those foreigners who came by sea. But the effort to extend this system to keep up with the expansion of Chinese maritime trade was too costly and after 1433 it was given up. The tributary system no longer worked by sea, and the compilers of 1818 finally acknowledged the fact.

(5) It is not difficult to see why this should be so. Like the Chinese state as a whole, the tributary system had developed upon the land without experience of the sea; and in accord with the position of the Middle Kingdom as the center of eastern Asiatic civilization, it had functioned passively. The barbarians came to China, the Chinese had no reason to go abroad. During the first two millennia of Chinese history the tributary system had continued to be based upon land frontiers, and whenever the government was even moderately strong the trade which crossed these territorial boundaries could be controlled. The Jade Gate was merely the most notable of many points of control. On the land frontiers there appears to be ample evidence that the traditional system functioned, in its own peculiar way, down to the end of the Ming period and even later. The "tributary envoys" who came to China from the defunct Kingdom of Rum in 1618 may have been great liars but they did no more violence to the system than their ancestors from "Constantinople" had done.

Moreover, the ancient caravan trade across Central Asia had been necessarily limited in volume and inclined to concentrate upon luxury goods of little weight and high value. Such goods could find their best market at the capital. Merchants bound for the metropolis found it easy to come in the train or in the guise of a tribute embassy. Even if they stopped at the frontier, they could still be enrolled as part of an embassy. Similarly trade and tribute from a state like Korea, coming by land over a fixed route to the market and the throne at Peking, retained a natural connection—particularly when the foreign ruler himself monopolized the trade.

(6) It was far different with sea trade, which presented new problems of regulation. Staple cargoes reaching a southern Chinese port could not possibly be transported to Peking and only a token or luxury trade accompanied the envoy to the capital. The development of a staple trade, made possible by the use of ships, obliged foreign merchants to reside in the seaports of South China, and resulted in the Arab communities at Zayton and Canton. This called forth an adaptation of the tributary system which has already been noted. The foreign community was quarantined in its own quarter under its own headman. The adaptation was successful and was applied after 1500 to Macao and the Thirteen Factories, the theoretical connection between trade and tribute being kept alive spasmodically by embassies from some of the new maritime trading countries. Like the Russians in the north, the Europeans and their trade who came to the south were kept under control at certain places on the frontier for the cognate purposes of safety and profit.

The real problem was presented by the expansion of maritime trade in Chinese hands to which we have already referred. The junk fleets of Amoy and Canton conducted a foreign trade not only outside the capital but even outside the frontiers of China, quite beyond control through tributary forms. Countries which remained passively abroad while the Chinese went to them could no longer be enrolled as tributaries attracted irresistibly by the civilization of the Middle Kingdom. Finally the connection of foreign trade and tribute, always an idea but not always a fact, was dealt another blow when countries like the United States, Sweden, and Denmark began to trade prosperously at Canton without ever sending to Peking anything that could be called a tribute embassy. Tribute had at last been eclipsed by trade.

(7) If in these circumstances our suggestion is correct, that embassies grew more frequent in the early nineteenth century in order to facilitate a generally expanding trade in Eastern Asia, then the tributary system had indeed fallen upon evil days and was being prostituted by the tributaries and no doubt by Chinese merchants as well. This had happened before, but now it served most inopportunely to increase the inadaptibility of the Chinese state and preserve a useless official myth. For insofar as the traditional system seemed to be confirmed by these embassies, the Chinese were left to face the Western maritime invasion with an outmoded foreign policy suited only to the land and the far past.

This interpretation points to two lines of study, in the history of trade and of ideas, as most pressingly needed to explain the dichotomy in China's reaction to the West a century ago—on the one hand, the intellectual inadaptability of the Chinese scholar-bureaucracy; on the other, the activity of Chinese merchants as abettors of the Western invasion. Source materials for these lines of study are suggested below.

# 7. A SELECTED LIST OF CH'ING WORKS (1644-1860) ON MARITIME RELATIONS

This selection is arranged in a roughly chronological order and includes official compilations, gazetteers, and private works and essays, all of which provide source material for one or both of two main types of investigation: for students of economic history, information as to maritime trade routes, ports, ships, goods, and trading places; for students of intellectual history, examples of Chinese thought and knowledge concerning the maritime countries and their trade in the period covered. Within the limits of this period—that is, the Ch'ing Dynasty before the Westerners had penetrated inland to dwell at Peking and in the Yangtze valley and so become known at first hand—we have tried to indicate certain works of primary and certain others of typical value. We have excluded works on Japan, Liu-ch'iu, and land-frontier countries; works written by foreigners in Chinese, including primarily those of Western missionaries; works referring nominally to an earlier period, like the *Ming History* or the *Hsü wên-hsien t'ung-k'ao*;⑮ and works containing material drawn from the period but compiled later, such as the *Kuo-ch'ao jou-yüan chi* 国朝柔远记 of WANG Chih-ch'un 王之春 (1896). It need hardly be remarked that no study of Chinese knowledge of the West can be conducted without reference to Matteo RICCI and his successors among the Jesuits at Peking. The declining influence of RICCI'S world-map has been studied in a very interesting article by Mr. Kenneth CH'ÊN,⑯ following the lead of Prof. HUNG.⑰ Several items by Jesuits or showing such influence may be found in the huge and fundamental collection of Ch'ing works on geography compiled by WANG Hsi-ch'i in 84 volumes.⑱ Aside from one or two illustrative items, we have excluded materials to be found in this collection, which fortunately has been indexed in the new classified catalogue of the Chinese-Japanese Library of the Harvard-Yenching Institute (Cambridge 1938-    ).⑲

In the Ch'ing period three works on the maritime nations and their trade, judging by the quotations of other scholars, appear to have had more than usual influence. They were compiled at intervals of a little over a century. The first was the *Tung-hsi-yang k'ao* 东西洋考 of CHANG Hsieh 张燮 completed in 1617,⑳ sections from which are translated by GROENEVELDT and which has more recently been studied by WADA. The other two, which fall within the period here considered, were the *Hai-kuo wên-chien lu* 海国闻见录 completed in 1730 (no. 8 below) and the *Hai-kuo t'u-chih* 海国国志 completed in 1842-1852 (no. 32 below). Both these works deserve monographic attention.

For the study of Chinese maritime trade the materials appear to become unusually rich in the early nineteenth century just before the crisis over foreign trade at Canton. The brief first-hand account of a blind linguist entitled simply *Hai-lu* (no. 20), was taken down in 1820; the enlargement of the gazetteer of Kwangtung province, edited by the great scholar JUAN Yüan, was completed about the same time (no. 21); a nautical guidebook, *Hai-wai chi-yao*, was completed in 1828 (no. 23); Prof. HSÜ Ti-shan has unearthed at Oxford a manuscript describing the Chinese side of Western trade up to 1832 (no. 24); the gazetteer of Amoy (no. 25), home port of Chinese junk trade with the Straits, was completed in the 1830's followed by the valuable gazetteer of the Canton maritime customs (no. 26). All of this was done before the hectic awakening precipitated by the first war with England and these works must in some sense be regarded as forebears of the famous geographies of the world compiled in the 1840's by WEI Yüan (no. 32) and HSÜ Chi-yü (no. 33). If to such sources as these there could be applied the same high scholarship which has been bestowed upon earlier and more fashionable periods, one main door to the understanding of modern Chinese economic history could be unlocked. Though recent, these materials do not lack for textual conundrums and problems of identification. These geographical works in turn are no more than background material for the study of Chinese policy as reflected in the collected writings of officials (see, e. g., no. 29).

(1) Ku Yen-wu 顾炎武, *T'ien-hsia chün-kuo li-ping shu* 天下郡国利病书 (A Critical Account of the Divisions and States of the Empire), 120 chüan, author's preface dated 1662, republished 1816, later editions 1831, 1879.

A critical geographical work by an outstanding Ch'ing scholar. Ch. 119 is devoted to the various barbarians beyond the seas (Hai-wai chu-fan 海外诸藩) and discusses Japan, Liu-ch'iu, and countries of the southeast including Fo-lang-chi. Ch. 120 discusses the tribute and trade of these maritime countries (Ju-kung hu-shih), including reference to trade routes and to the history of the administration of foreign trade, down through the Ming and in some cases into the Ch'ing period.

(2) CHANG Yü-shu 张玉书 (1642-1711), *Wai-kuo chi* 外国纪 (A Record of Foreign Countries), pp. 13, in *Chao-tai ts'ung-shu*, ts'ê 104; and *Chang Wên-chên Kung chi* 张文贞公集 (Block-print edition of 1792) 8. 19-29. (Reference to 1675 in text).

By a famous scholar, editor-in-chief of the *K'ang-hsi Dictionary* and the *P'ei-wên yün-fu* and one of the editors of the *Ming History*. Deals with various tributary tribes in Manchuria and Mongolia, plus Korea, Russia, Siam, Holland, Liu-ch'iu, Annam, and Hsi-yang, with references to Christianity.

(3) Yu-t'ung 尤侗 (1618-1704), *Wai-kuo chu-chih tz'u* 外国竹枝词 1 chüan (29 pp.), n. d., in *Chao-tai ts'ung-shu*, ts'ê 3, and *T'an-chi ts'ung-shu*, ts'ê 11.

This is a verse narration, with notes in prose, of the usual Ming list of countries and places; about one page or less to an item, rather miscellaneously arranged, e. g. Europe succeeds Hami. Does not appear important, except to indicate the knowledge possessed by a famous essayist concerning foreign countries.

(4) LU Tz'ŭ-yün 陆次云, *Pa-hung i-shih* 八纮译史 4 chüan, 2 ts'ê, author's preface dated 1683. Published separately, as well as in the *Lung-wei mi-shu* 龙威秘书, ts'ê 75, and *Shuo-k'u* 说库, ts'ê 44.

Deals with more than a hundred tributary or trading countries or places, grouped (often incorrectly) by the four points of the compass. Ch. 2 includes references to several European countries. In several cases includes transliterations of native languages.

Note also by the same author: *I-shih chi-y*ü 译史纪余 4 chüan, n. d. Usually published together with the preceding.

Supplementary to the *Pa-hung i-shih*, including descriptions of seas and their products, poems of Chinese envoys, illustrations of foreign coins, and copies with translations of the credentials (kuo-shu) of Korean and Mohammedan envoys.

(5) Lu Ying-yang 陆应旸 (original author), *Kuang-yü chi* 广舆记 (A Record of the Broad World), revised edition by Ts'AI Fang-ping 蔡方炳, 24 chüan, 7 ts'ê, preface by Ts'AI dated 1686, block-print edition 1707.

A systematic survey of the provinces, which in chüan 24 takes up the conventional Ming list of tributaries but appears to add little if anything from the Ch'ing period.

(6) LAN Ting-yüan 蓝鼎元 (1680-1733), *Lun Nan-yang shih-i shu* 论南洋事宜书 (A Discussion of a Proper Policy Regarding the Southern Ocean), in his *Lu-chou ch'u-chi* 鹿洲初集 3.1-6 (first published 1732, republished 1880), also in CHU K'o-ching 朱克敬, *Jou-yüan hsin-shu* 柔远新书 3.14-17, and in *Hsiao-fang-hu-chai*, ts'ê 54. Arranged by the compiler as of 1724.

A brief note by a well-known scholar urging abolition of the ban on maritime trade. He argues that trade with the Southern Ocean would benefit China, ridicules the ignorance of his contemporaries, and gives a brief survey of foreign countries.

(7) *Ch'in-ting ku-chin t'u-shu chi-ch'êng* 钦定古今图书集成 10,000 chüan, presented to the emperor in 1725.

The great Ch'ing encyclopaedia in the geography section on border barbarians, *Fang-yü hui-pien*, *Pien-i tien* 方舆汇编,边裔典, chüan 83-106 in particular, contains material on southern and western places. Thus chüan 85, 97-101, 103-106 include tributaries of the Ming period, maritime and continental mixed together. Ch. 87 under "unidentified countries" (wei-hsiang 未详) includes Spain, America, and others like Damascus (?), while ch. 108 lists also as "unidentified countries" I-ta-li-ya, Sicily, Mexico, and Banjermassin among others—all of which raises the question of the influence of RICCI.

(8) CH'ÊN Lun-ch'iung 陈伦炯, *Hai-kuo wên-chien lu* 海国闻见录 (A Record of Things Seen and Heard among the Maritime Nations), 1 chüan, maps 1 chüan, author's preface 1730, other prefaces 1743, 1744, wood-block reprint 1793; also in *I-hai chu-chên* 艺海珠尘, ts'ê 10, and *Chao-tai ts'ung-shu*, ts'ê 55.

A well-known and systematic treatment of the maritime nations. The author's father had had experience in the Southern Ocean on missions in search of KOXINGA'S remnants after the subjugation of Taiwan, and finally became Manchu Brigade general at Canton in 1718. The author himself became a Brigade general in Taiwan after 1721, traveled in Japan, and made extensive inquiries. The maps, old style, are of value, and the book appears to have remained a standard work down into the nineteenth century.

(9) YIN Kuang-jên 印光任 and CHANG Ju-lin 张汝霖, *Ao-mên chi-lüeh* 澳门纪略 (A Brief Record of Macao), 2 chüan, preface dated 1751, reprinted 1800.

The authors were successively officials in the Macao area. In ch. 2 they first describe the maritime trading countries of the southeast for some 15 pages, including the rivalry of the Portuguese and the Dutch, and then concentrate upon the Portuguese at Macao, their way of life in much detail, concluding with accounts of the Western calendar and language.

(10) *Huaug-Ch'ing chih-kung t'u* 皇清职贡图, 9 chüan, (Illustrations of the Regular Tributaries of the Imperial Ch'ing) compiled by TUNG Kao 董诰 and others under imperial auspices: ordered 1751, completed 1760, Palace edition 1761.

Illustrations of some 300 aboriginal or border tribes or countries, with explanatory text; ch. 1 refers to several European countries. See note 82.

(11) *Ta-ch'ing i-t'ung chih* 大清一统志 (Gazetteer of the Ch'ing Empire), compiled by CHIANG T'ing-hsi 蒋廷锡 and others under imperial auspices, imperial preface dated 1744, slightly revised in 1764,

reprinted in 1849.

Chüan 353-356 at the end deal with tributary states. See appendix 2.

(12) *T'ai-wan-fu chih* 台湾府志 (Gazetteer of T'ai-wan-fu, Taiwan), 26 chüan, first compiled 1694, revised 1741 and 1774. Harvard has a block-print edition of 1888 reprinted from the 1872 edition.

Ch. 19. 37-49 on foreign islands (wai-tao) refers to Liu-ch'iu, Japan, Java (Ka-la-pa), Western Ocean, Holland, Siam, etc., and searoutes and trade regulations.

(13) *Ch'ing t'ung-tien*: *Huang-ch'ao t'ung-tien* 皇朝通典, 100 chüan, ordered compiled under imperial auspices in 1767. Covers the period 1644-1785.

Chüan 97-99 on border defense, Pien-fang 边防, discuss the tributaries in general plus Japan and Liu-ch'iu, the maritime nations of the south, and those of the west, respectively. Several identifications of countries (e. g. Chêng-ch'ien, Ching-hai, and Hu-lu, 98. 18b-20b) are recorded.

(14) *Ch'ing t'ung-k'ao*: *Huang-ch'ao wên-hsien t'ung-k'ao* 皇朝文献通考 compilation ordered 1747, completed 1786 or 1787, covering material to 1785, Chekiang Shu-chü edition 1882.

Ch. 293-300 describe the barbarians at length. See appendix 2.

(15) WANG Ta-hai 王大海, *Hai-tao i-chih* 海岛逸志 (A Treatise on the Islands of the Sea), 6 chüan, pub. 1791, in *Hsiao-fang-hu-chai*, ts'ê 54, chih 10, pp. 479-489.

Describes a score or more of the islands in the Southern Ocean, Chinese immigration, products, etc. The author had made a voyage to some of the islands he describes.

(16) *Fu-chien t'ung-chih chêng-shih-lüeh* 福建通志政事略 (A Survey of Administrative Affairs, for the Gazetteer of Fukien Province), bound MSS., 15 chüan in 17 ts'ê, n. d., worm-eaten and with some marginal corrections; the text refers to the year 1794, if not later.

Ch. 14 gives a brief survey of the regulation of foreign trade since the

Sung and the countries concerned. Ch. 15 consists of 8 pages on barbarian trade, referring to Liu-ch'iu, Sulu, and Holland, i. e. those tributary via Foochow.

(17) HUNG Liang-chi 洪亮吉 (1746-1809), *Ch'ien-lung fu-t'ing-chou-hsien t'u-chih* 乾隆府厅州县图志 (Gazetteer of Administrative Areas, Ch'ien-lung Period) 50 chüan, completed 1803.

A private compilation similar to the *Ta-ch'ing i-t'ung chih* but more condensed. Tributary and trading countries are described in the last chüan, classified by location. The author was well known as a historian. See appendix 2.

(18) YEH Ch'iang-yung 叶羌镛, *Lü-sung chi-lüeh* 吕宋纪略 (A Brief Description of the Philippines), 3½ pp., in *Hsiao-fang-hu-chai*, ts'ê 76, chih 10, chüan 8, item 5 from end.

Notes on the customs, products, language, and commerce of the Philippines. One date in the text refers to 1812.

(19) *Chia-ch'ing ch'ung-hsiu i-t'ung chih* 嘉庆重修一统志 (Gazetteer of the Empire, Revision of the Chia-ch'ing Period), 560 chüan, a revision under imperial auspices of the *Ta-ch'ing i-t'ung chih* of the Ch'ien-lung period, (q. v.), the material extending to 1820; lithophotographic edition from the Palace manuscript, published by the Commercial Press, Shanghai, 1934.

The last few chüan deal with 43 foreign countries from Korea to France, touching upon their location, history, products, and relations with China.

(20) HSIEH Ch'ing-kao 谢清高 (1765-1821), *Hai-lu* 海录 (A Maritime Record), 2 chüan.

① Wood-block edition, preface by YANG Ping-nan 杨炳南, T. Ch'iu-hêng 秋衡, of Chia-ying 嘉应 (Kwangtung), as author, describing how he obtained the information in 1820 from HSIEH, who had traveled abroad for 14 years, learned the languages and customs of the Southern Sea, and finally lost his eyesight and became an interpreter at Macao—an unusual repository of first-hand information. (WYLIE 53 makes no reference to HSIEH by name and gives the publication date as 1842).

② Another edition in the Chinese-Japanese Library at Harvard, revised and with notes by LÜ T'iao-yang 吕调阳, preface by him dated 1870, is assigned to HSIEH as author without reference to YANG Ping-nan. This later edition appears to be the better known, e. g. CHANG Wei-hua 109. It differs from the former in having Western style maps and extensive notes, largely condensed from the original edition.

This work merits extensive attention as a first-hand source on Chinese southern trade in the early nineteenth century. It gives sailing directions for and brief descriptions of more than 60 countries or places, from the Malay peninsula around to the coasts of India, and through the East Indies, including references to Europe. Its eye-witness quality is indicated, for example, when the writer, YANG, states that Japan is omitted because the narrator, HSIEH, had not gone there on his travels. A work entitled *Hai-lu chu* 海录注 by FÊNG Ch'êng-chün has been advertised. Note also Prof. FÊNG's discussion of this work in *Yü-kung* 6 (no. 8-9). 113-114.

(21) *Kuang-tung t'ung-chih* 广东通志 (Gazetteer of Kwangtung Province), WYLIE 36 refers to a first edition of 1683;

①Yung-chêng edition: 64 chüan, preface dated 1731.

Ch. 58 on the outer barbarians (wai-fan) gives an historical survey and an orthodox Ming list of 31 countries with comments.

②JUAN Yüan 阮元 edition: 334 chüan, compiled in 1818, JUAN being editor-in-chief as well as then governor-general at Canton, published 1822, reprinted 1864, the blocks having been burned in 1857.

Ch. 170. 36-42 lists Siam, Holland, Western Ocean, England, etc. as tributaries, the account being based partly on the archives (tang-ts'ê). Ch. 180 gives an historical summary of maritime trade and customs administration. Ch. 330. 32-62 discusses some 90 maritime countries or places, including the Europeans, using both standard accounts and local records, e. g. 61b the country of Pi-li-shih 比利时 (Britain?) is recorded simply as having "entered port" (chin-k'ou) in 1752. (A common source can no doubt be established for parts of this work and of the *Yüeh hai-kuan chih*.) Ch. 100. 52b has a passage on Macao. The high scholarship of the chief editor, as well as its extensive detail, make this a work of importance.

(22) Ho Ch'ang-ling 贺长龄, compiler, *Huang-ch'ao ching-shih-wên pien* 皇朝经世文编 (A Collection of Essays of the Reigning Dynasty, of Practical Value), 120 chüan, compiler's preface 1826.

Ch. 83. 37-39 contains LAN Ting-yüan's essay on southern maritime trade (noted above, no. 6), followed by a similar item, and others on coastal defense, Taiwan, suppression of piracy, and the like.

These essays have value as reflecting the thought of the times. Unfortunately a supplementary collection (*Huang-ch'ao ching-shih-wên hsü-pien*) compiled by Ko Shih-chün 葛士浚 and published in 1888 contains material chiefly post-1860.

(23) LI Tsêng-chieh 李增阶, *Hai-wai chi-yao* 外海纪要 (A Record of Essentials Concerning the Outer Seas), postface 1828, in CH'ÊN K'un 陈坤, compiler, *Ts'ung-chêng hsü-yü-lu* 从政绪余录, 7 chüan, preface 1881, forming ts'ê 19-22 in *Ju-pu-chi chai hui-ch'ao* 如不及斋汇钞. A handbook of information and advice for sailing captains, divided into 23 sections on sheltered harbors (23 places listed); on the armament of ships, choice of pilots, and sea-fighting; on the itineraries for sailing vessels from Canton up the coast to Shanghai, from Amoy to Taiwan and the Philippines, and from Amoy to the Straits and beyond, with times required (e. g. 12-13 days to Palembang); plus extensive tables for use in navigations, calculation of tides, and the like. Careful study of this work should yield invaluable conclusions regarding Chinese maritime (junk) trade in the early nineteenth century.

(24) HSÜ Ti-shan 许地山 ed., *Ta-chung-chi* 达衷集, Commercial Press, Peiping, 1931, pp. 237.

A valuable collection of documents transcribed by Prof. HSÜ from a MSS. found in the Bodleian Library, dealing ① with the voyage of the East India Company ship *Lord Amherst* up the China coast in 1832 under H. H. LINDSAY to test out the market (petitions to the local authorities and proclamations and replies from them); and ② correspondence at Canton between the Chinese authorities, the Hong merchants (HOWQUA and others), and the English, dating from the late XVIII and early XIX centuries. This material is of first rate value as illuminating the Chinese side of the correspondence summarized in Dr. H. B. MORSE'S *Chronicles of the East India Company*.

(25) *Hsia-mên chih* 厦门志 (Gazetteer of Amoy), compiled by CHOU K'ai 周凯 and others, 16 chüan, completed 1832, last preface 1839.

Ch. 5 contains interesting details regarding shipping, including Chinese vessels in oceanic trade (yang-ch'uan, p. 27) and barbarian vessels of various types (31-35). Ch. 6-7 on Taiwan imports and customs administration are followed in ch. 8 by a systematic discussion of 31 maritime trading nations, their location, harbors, products, etc. evidently based in part on original data in addition to such works as the *Tung-hsi-yang k'ao* and *Hai-kuo wên-chien lu*; Amoy being a chief port in southern trade, the use of this material should yield unusually valuable results.

(26) LIANG T'ing-nan 梁廷枬, *Yüeh-hai-kuan chih* 粤海关志 (Gazetteer of the Maritime Customs of Kwangtung), 30 chüan, reference to 1839 in text; Ch. 1-4, 21-25, and 26-30 (ts'ê 1, 7, and 8) reprinted Peiping 1935 et seq. in the *Kuo-hsüeh wên-k'u* 国学文库 series.

Of the three volumes of this rare work so far published, the second and third deal with tributary trade and the barbarian merchants at Canton, ch. 21-24 in particular describing tributary relations with Siam, Liu-ch'iu and European states, and trade relations with 24 maritime countries including America and certain obscure places recorded as having "entered port" at one time. A valuable primary source based partly on archives.

(27) LIN Tsê-hsü 林则徐, trans., *Hua-shih i-yen* 华事夷言 (Barbarian Statements Concerning Chinese Affairs), 1 chüan, 3 pp., *Hsiao-fang-hu-chai* ts'ê 77, chih 11, ch. 9, item 3.

Evidently a fragment of the work done by Commissioner LIN'S corps of Chinese translators at Canton, probably in 1839 (cf. Gideon CH'ÊN, *Lin Tsê-hsü*, Peiping 1934, pp. 7-10). Miscellaneous content including references to the Thirteen Factories, Hong Merchants, interpreters, Russia, Chinese population, opium, currency, etc. The Western originals should not be hard to find, perhaps in the *Chinese Repository*.

(28) Ho Ta-kêng 何大庚, *Ying-i shuo* 英夷说 (A Treatise on the English Barbarians), in *Hsiao-fang-hu-chai*, ts'ê 77, chih 11, chüan 9, item 4. Follows LIN Tsê-hsü's *Hua-shih i-yen* and consists of five lines expatiating on the danger of British expansion in Malaya. N. d., post 1819 by reference to Singapore in text.

(29) CHANG Shu-shêng 张树声, *Yang-wu ts'ung-ch'ao* 洋务丛钞 (A Miscellaneous Collection on Foreign Affairs) pub. 1884.

Contains 11 works on military and foreign affairs, chiefly post-1860 but including LIN Tsê-hsü on Russia, and YAO Ying 姚莹 (1785-1853) on Anglo-Russian relations. The papers of YAO Ying (*Chung-fu-t'ang ch'üan-chi* 中复堂全集 pub. 1867) contain a work reflecting his experience as an official in Taiwan during 1838-1843 and his views on foreign policy (ts'ê 5-9, entitled *Tung-ming wên hou-chi* 东溟文后集, 14 chüan). This is of course but one of many such collections.

(30) WANG Ch'ing-yün 王庆云 (1798-1862), *Shih-ch'ü yü-chi* 石渠余纪 also entitled *Hsi-ch'ao chi-chêng* 熙朝纪政, 6 chüan, 6 ts'ê, n. d., 1890 wood-block edition.

Useful notes on various aspects of administration by an official who rose to be President of the Board of Works. Ch. 6 contains material on maritime trade (shih-po), plus Edicts on the MACARTNEY and AMHERST embassies.

(31) *Fu-chien t'ung-chih* 福建通志 (Gazetteer of Fukien Province), 278 chüan, first compiled 1737, revised several times, particularly in 1835 (date of preface); published with some further revision (material dated 1842) in 1871.

Ch. 269 discusses the barbarians tributary through Foochow—Liuch'iu, Holland, Sulu—with Japan also. Ch. 270 surveys the official regulation of maritime trade, quoting Edicts, from the Sung down to 1842, followed by a list of foreign trading countries (pp. 18-19).

(32) WEI Yüan 魏源, *Hai-kuo t'u-chih* 海国图志 (An Illustrated Gazetteer of the Maritime Countries), 100 chüan; the preface to the 1876 edition states that it was completed in 1842 in 60 chüan, 40 more being completed in 1852 to make 100 chüan; reprinted in 100 chüan in 1876 (Harvard has only the 1852 and 1876 editions, each 100 chüan). Gideon CH'ÊN (*Lin Tsê-hsü* ... 24) names three editions: 50 chüan in 1844, 60 chüan in 1847, and 100 chüan in 1852, and gives a valuable appraisal of changes in later editions of the work and LIN Tsê-hsü's probable connection as author of part of it.

A monumental and historically important survey of foreign countries and the barbarian menace compiled at the time of the first war with England. (WYLIE 53 condemns the author as not impartial). Ch. 5-18 deal with countries of southeast Asia, followed by India at some length; ch. 37-58 deal with Europe; ch. 71 begins a description of the Western religions, calendar, customs, armament, astronomy, and the like. The work had widespread influences, and justice cannot be done it here.

Note also by the same author: Shêng-wu chi 圣武记 (A Record of Imperial Military Activities), 14 chüan, preface to first edition 1842, 3rd and revised edition 1846, in *Ssŭ-pu pei-yao* edition of the Chung Hua Book Co.

A famous work narrating the military campaigns of the Ch'ing, including those into Mongolia, Sinkiang, Tibet, Nepal; against Russia, Korea, Burma, Annam and the border tribes of the southeast; and concerning Taiwan, the suppression of coastal pirates, and of internal rebels in the early nineteenth century—only in small part on maritime relations. A valuable supplementary section deals with military organization and history. A section was translated by E. H. PARKER as *A Chinese Account of the Opium War*, Shanghai 1888; Gideon CH'ÊN (*Lin Tsê-hsü*... 28) points out that the account of this war is omitted in several editions of the work.

*Hsiao-fang-hu-chai* contains a number of brief items by WEI Yüan, e. g. *Ying-chi-li hsiao-chi* 英吉利小记 (A Brief Account of England), pp. 1½, (ts'ê 77, chih 11, chüan 9, item 8). A brief survey touching on finances, the non-use of opium, religion, quaint customs, etc.

(33) HSÜ Chi-yü 徐继畬, *Ying-huan chih-lüeh* 瀛环志略 (A Brief Description of the Oceans Roundabout), 10 chüan, title page and prefaces dated 1848. Another edition, somewhat revised and dated 1873, contains prefaces dated 1849.

A universal geography, by the barbarian-relations expert of Fukien who had been directly connected with the opening of the treaty ports in that province and became governor of it in 1847 (cf. *IWSM-TK* 78). Other high officials lent their names to the title page, the plates were preserved at the (governor's) Ya-men 本署藏板 and the work is plainly an invaluable reflection of the knowledge possessed by the Chinese authorities appointed after the first treaties to stem the Western invasion. Chüan 1-3 concern Asia, 4-7 Europe, and 8-10 Africa and America. HSÜ confesses in the directions to the reader (fan-li) that "place names of foreign countries are very difficult to distinguish; if ten persons make translations, all ten will be different." Hsü made careful use both of Chinese works, such as the *Hai-kuo wên-chien lu* of a century before, and of Western maps, noting many differences in transliteration between the two. His text is punctuated, place names are marked, and sources cited.

*Hsiao-fang-hu-chai* contains several brief items by HSÜ Chi-yü 徐

继畲, e. g. ①*Wu-yin-tu lun* 五印度论 (ts'ê 54, chih 10, p. 413). Deals briefly with the British in India.

②*Ti-ch'iu chih-lüeh* 地球志略 (A General Description of the Earth), two pages (ts'ê 1, chih 1, p. 7-8). Largely geographical, concerning the poles, equator, continents, etc; references to Antarctic explorations conducted two years previously by France, England, Spain, and the United States—evidently those of D'URVILLE (1837-1840), WILKES (1839-1840), and Ross (1841-1843)—date this fragment as probably just previous to HSÜ'S universal geography of 1848.

(34) HSIA Hsieh 夏燮, pseud. Chiang-shang-chien-sou 江上蹇叟 (lit. "the lame old man on the river"), *Chung-hsi chi-shih* 中西纪事 (A Record of Sino-Western Affairs), 24 chüan in 8 ts'ê, first preface 1851 (Tao-kuang 30th year, 12th month), second preface to revised edition 1859, last preface 1865; extra title-page bears date Oct. 1868.

An important survey of Chinese relations with the West, throughout the modern period down to the 1860's (in the later editions); apparently well based on documents, contemporary sources, and even some Western books, with chapters divided according to periods, concentrating on the post-treaty era.

Material of probable value, which we have not been able to examine: *Hai-wai fan-i lu* 海外番夷录, compiled by WANG Yün-hsiang 王蕴香 and published in a wood-block edition in 1844 by the Ching-tu shu-liu-hsüan 京都漱六轩, Peking, 4 ts'ê.

This collection contains an item by WANG Wên-t'ai 汪文泰, *Hung-mao-fan Ying-chi-li k'ao-lüeh* 红毛番英吉利考略 (A Study of the Red-haired English Barbarians?), listed by WYLIE 53 as published in 1841.

# 8. INDEX OF TRIBUTARIES LISTED IN SIX EDITIONS OF THE *COLLECTED STATUTES*

The identification of places mentioned above is concentrated here in order to disencumber the text and to provide a minimum reference list of places important in Ch'ing economic relations, also to indicate certain places still requiring identification. A number of items from the Ming period are obscure and probably unimportant, and others have been recognized and discussed at length by scholars of several generations. Ming names of course frequently persist in the Ch'ing literature, such as that noted in the preceding section, at the same time that new forms are recorded. It is much to be hoped that expert attention will be devoted to the place names appearing in texts of the modern period down to 1860. No doubt many items not traced by us can be elucidated by workers better versed in this difficult specialty.

Note: This list includes all places listed as tributary in the following: *Wan-li hui-tien* 105. 80-107. 88b (Li-Pu, chüan 63-65); *K'ang-hsi hui-tien* 72. 4-19b; *Yung-chêng hui-tien* 104. 4-38b; *Ch'ien-lung hui-tien* 56. 1; *Chia-ch'ing hui-tien* 31. 2-4; *Kuang-hsü hui-tien* 39, 2-3; a few items are added. Nearly all these tributaries are listed as countries (kuo) in the sources. Variants are noted but not indexed unless they appear in the above sources; cross references are suppressed when they would form an adjoining item. Authorities are cited by abbreviations, as in appendix 1 below. Note that the Mongol tribes and others under the Court of Colonial Affairs (Li Fan Yüan) in the Ch'ing period, and a few Tibetan monasteries in *Wan-li hui-tien* 108 are omitted. Abbreviations: B = BRUNNERT (see appendix 1 below), H = HERMANN, P = PLAYFAIR. Ctry. =country, Tn. = Town, Tr. = Tribe. * * = listed as tributary in one or more editions of the *Ta-Ch'ing hui-tien*. * = listed as having commercial relations in the 1818 edition.

Arrangement: place-name, location, *Hui-tien* reference, identification.

* ACHIN (Acheen, Acheh, Atjeh): Ya-chi 亚齐. No. tip of Sumatra. *Wan-li* 106. 84b; *Chia-ch'ing* 31. 3b.

GROENEVELDT 92 gives Atjeh, corrupted by Europeans to Achin or Acheen. *Ch'ing t'ung-k'ao* 297. 17b follows the *Ming History* in stating that this was the name given in the Wan-li period to what was formerly called Su-mên-ta-la; but the latter is now identified by

PELLIOT (3) 214, also MILLS 11, as "Samudra harbour, near Pasai on the north coast of Sumatra; this port (says MILLS) was also the starting point of the voyage to the Nicobar Islands and Ceylon." See under Lambri below, also Samudra.

ADEN: A-tan 阿丹. Arabia. *Wan-li* 106.84b.

    ROCKHILL (1) 76.

AFGHANISTAN: Ai-wu-han 爱乌罕 (Mod. A-fu-han 阿富汗). *Kuang-hsü* 68.8.

ALANI (Aas, Aorsi): A-su 阿速 Tr., in the Caucasus. *Wan-li* 107.87b.

    BRETSCHNEIDER 2.84-90; H: 50D2.

ALMALIK?: An-li-ma 俺力麻. Tn., in No. Sinkiang. *Wan-li* 107.87b.

    Cf. BRETSCHNEIDER 2.33-89; FÊNG (2) 2: A-li-ma-li 阿力麻里.

A-LU KUO see Aru.

ANDIJAN (Andedjan): An-chi-yen 安集延. Anc. Ferghana. *Ch'ing t'ung-k'ao* 299.7b.

    FÊNG (2) 2; H: 17 II C½.

ANDKHUI (Andkhoi): An-tu-huai 俺都淮. Tn., W. of Balkh, Bukhara. *Wan-li* 107.88b.

    BRETSCHNEIDER (2) 275; P: 119.

AN-LI-MA see Almalik?

AN-CHI-YEN see Andijan.

* * ANNAM (Yüeh-nan): An-nan 安南. Ctry. *Wan-li* 105.81b; *K'ang-hsi* 72.14; *Yung-chêng* 104.24; *Ch'ien-lung* 56.1; *Chia-ch'ing* 31.2a; *Kuang-hsü* 39.2a. Name changed officially to Yüeh-nan in 1803.

AN-TING 安定. District in Kansu. *Wan-li* 107.87.

    TS'ÊN 166: modern Harashar (Ha-la-sha-erh); BRETSCHNEIDER 2. 205-208.

AN-TU-HUAI see Andkhui.

ARABIA (1): T'ien-fang 天方. *Wan-li* 107.88a.

    DUYVENDAK (1) 9; Mecca; H: 54D3; Arabia; PELLIOT (2) 296; Arabie, La Mecque.

? (2): Hsia-la-pi 夏剌比. *Wan-li* 106.84b.

 (?) TING 28: same as Arabia.

ARU: A-lu 阿鲁 also 亚鲁. Ctry., N. E. coast of Sumatra. *Wan-li* 106.84.

 H: 54F4; ROCKHILL(1) 75.

A-SU see Alani.

A-TAN see Aden.

A-TUAN see Khotan?

A-WA see Burma.

BADAKSHAN (Badakashan): (1) Pa-ta-hei-shang 八答黑商. Ctry. and Tn., No. of Kabul, C. Asia. *Wan-li* 107.88b.

 BRETSCHNEIDER 2.276-278; Fêng (2) 4.

(2) Pa-tan-sha 把丹沙. *Wan-li* 107.87b.

 BRETSCHNEIDER 2.272.

BALKH: Pa-li-hei 把力黑. Tn., So. C. Asia. *Wan-li* 107.87b.

 BRETSCHNEIDER 100; Fêng (2) 4.

BANJERMASSIN: Ma-ch'ên 马辰. So. coast Borneo. *Ch'ing t'ung-k'ao* 293.1b.

 Cf. HSÜ Chi-yü 2.2 (map): Ma-shên 马神; *Huang-Ch'ing chih-kung t'u* 1.55: same as Wên-lang-ma-shên in the southeastern sea 文郎马神—a scribal error for Wên-chi-ma-shên.

BARAWA: Pu-la-wa 不剌哇. Tn., So. of Mogadisho, Africa. *Wan-li* 106.84b.

 H: 54D4; FÊNG (2) 6.

BASHIBALIK: Pieh-shih-pa-li 别失八里. Tn., ancient Urumtsi (Tihwa), Sinkiang; anc. country of Moghulistan. *Wan-li* 107.87b.

 BRETSCHNEIDER 2.225-244.

BENGAL: (1) Pang-ko-la 榜葛剌. Ctry. *Wan-li* 106.84.

 ROCKHILL (1) 436; FÊNG (1) 12.

(2) P'êng-chia-na 彭加那. *Wan-li* 106.84b.

 ROCKHILL (1) 68, 435: P'êng-chia-la 彭加剌; FÊNG (2) 5.

BILLITON: Ma-yeh-wêng 麻叶瓮. Island E. of Sumatra. *Ch'ing i-t'ung chih*, Ch'ien-lung ed., 356.36.

WU Han 174; FÊNG (1) 15.

BOLOR: Po-lo-êrh 博罗尔. Tn. and Ctry., E. of Badakshan in the Hindu Kush. HUNG Liang-chi 50.18b.

FÊNG (2) 6. 洛.

BORNEO: So-lo 娑罗, presumably a scribal error for P'o-lo 婆罗, mod. form 婆罗洲 P'o-lo-chou. (P'o-lo does not appear in the *Hui-tien* text). *Wan-li* 107.84: "In 1406 the eastern king and the western king each sent an envoy to present tribute at Court."

GROENEVELDT 101: Borneo.

BRUNEI (Bornui): (1) P'o-ni (Sung-Yüan form) 淳泥 Ctry., N. W. Borneo. *Wan-li* 105.82b.

ROCKHILL, (1) 66. Also written 渤.

(2) Wên-lai 文莱 (Ming form)

Wu Han 137; *Huang-Ch'ing chih-kung t'u* 1.57 identifies Wên-lai with P'o-lo (Borneo), erroneously, as do CHANG Hsieh and the *Ming Shih*; WADA 127-128 suggests that P'o-ni was recorded from the western (hsi-yang) trade route while Wên-lai (or P'o-lo) came through the eastern (tung-yang) route.

BUKHARA?: Pu-ha-la 卜哈剌. *Wan-li* 107.87b.

FÊNG (2). 6 from the *Yüan* History quotes 卜哈儿 and 不花剌.

\*\*BURMA: (1) A-wa 阿哇. Ctry. *Wan-li* 106.84b. (2) A-wa 阿瓦; *Kuang-hsü* 39.2b: same as Mien-tien. (3) Mien-tien 缅甸; *Ch'ien-lung* 56.1; *Chia-ch'ing* 31.3; *Kuang-hsü* 39.2b.

BURUT (Black Kirghiz, Kara-Kirghiz): Pu-lu-t'ê 布鲁特. Tr, No. C. Asia. HUNG Liang-chi 50.17.

MAYERS no. 532; H: 66CD2/3; *Ch'ing t'ung-k'ao* 299.3, 5: moslem tribe S. W. of the Dzungars, with Eastern (Tung) and Western (Hsi) divisions.

CAIL: Chia-i-lê 加异勒. So. India, opposite Ceylon. *Wan-li* 106.84b.

DUYVENDAK (2) 386.

CALICUT: Ku-li 古里. Ctry., S. W. coast of India. *Wan-li* 106. 83b.
　GROENEVELDT 44; H: 54E4; Ku-li-fo.

\* CAMBODIA: (1) Chên-la 真腊; *Wan-li* 105. 81b. (2) Chien-pu-chai(sai) 柬埔寨; *Chia-ch'ing* 31. 3. (3) Tung-pu-chai 东埔寨, common error for Chien-pu-chai; e. g. *Ch'ing t'ung-k'ao* 293. 1. This variant is discussed by PELLIOT (Memoires sur les coutumes de Cambodge), BEFEO 2. 127.

CANANORE (Jurfattan): Sha-li-wan-ni 沙里湾泥. S. E. Coast India, No. of Calicut. *Wan-li* 106. 84b.
　FÊNG (1) 12, 16; Wu Han 168: Jurfattan; *ibid*. 174: Sha-li-pa-tan 沙里八丹 Jarfattan, mod. Cananore. PELLIOT (2) 287: Jurfattan?

CEYLON: Hsi-lan-shan 锡 (or 细) 兰山. *Wan-li* 106. 84. H: no. 927-928.

CHALISH: Ch'a-li-shih 察力失. Tn., near Ilibalik, Sinkiang. *Wan-li* 107. 87b.
　H. 55F2.

CHAMPA: Chan-ch'êng 占城 (Variants: Chan-pu-lao 占不劳, Chan-po 占波, Chan-la 占腊). *Wan-li* 105. 82.
　PELLIOT (3) 216: Chinese name for native Chan 占.

CHAO-HSIEN see Korea.

CHAO-NA-P'U-ERH see Jaunpur.

CHAO-WA see Java.

CHÊNG-CH'IEN 整欠. (?). HUNG Liang-chi 59. 9. *Ch'ing t'ung-tien* 98. 18b: located 1000 *li* outside P'u-êrh fu (Yunnan), sent tribute in 1775.

CHÊN-LA see Cambodia.

CHIA-I-LÊ see Cail.

\* CHIANG-K'OU see Siam.

CHIEN-CHOU 建州. District in E. Manchuria. *Wan-li* 107. 86b.
　H: 55H2; T. C. LIN (2) 867: a center of the Jurchen.

CH'IEN-LI-TA 千里达. *Wan-li* 106. 84b.

Cf. ROCKHILL (1) 67: Ch'ien-li-ma 千里马. Unidentified; possibly near northern Maldive Is.

CHIEN-PU-CHAI see Cambodia.

CH'IH-CHIN-MÊNG-KU 赤斤蒙古. Milit. district in Kansu (Yü-mên hsien 玉门县). Wan-li 107.87b.

BRETSCHNEIDER 2.211-215; P: 995

*CH'IH-TZŬ see Jaya.

CH'I-LA-NI 奇剌泥. Unidentified. Wan-li 106.84b.

CHI-LAN-TAN see Kelantan.

CHING-HAI 景海. (?). HUNG Liang-chi 50.9b.

Ch'ing t'ung-tien 98.19: sent tribute 1775 with Chêng-ch'ien, q. v.

CHIU-CHIANG see Palembang.

CHOLA: (1) So-li 琐里. Ctry., on the Coromandel coast, S. E. India. Wan-li 105.83.

PELLIOT (1) 328-329: same as (2).

(2) Hsi-yang so-li 西洋琐里. Wan-li 105.83: a country on the seacoast near So-li.

GROENEVELDT 44 gave W. Soli; CHANG Wei-hua 175-176 shows the two to be identical.

CH'Ü-HSIEN 曲先. District in Kansu. Wan-li 107.87b.

H: 55F3; BRETSCHNEIDER 2.210.

COCHIN: K'o (Ko)-chih 柯枝. Ctry. on the Malabar coast, S. W. India. Wan-li 106.84b.

COIMBATORE see Coyampadi

COYAMPADI (Coimbatore): (1) K'an-pa-i-t'i 坎巴夷替. S. E. India, No. of Cochin. Wan-li 106.84b.

FÊNG (1) text 42.

(2) Kan-pa-li 甘把 (or 巴) 里.

DUYVENDAK (2) 386 suggests "Coyampadi?"; PELLIOT (2) 290, 296: probably "Koyampadi (Coimbatore)"; FÊNG (1) 11.

*DENMARK: Lien-kuo 嗹国. Chia-ch'ing 31.4.

DJOFAR (Dufar, Zufar): Tsu-fa-êrh 祖法儿. Tn., So. Arabia or Tso-fa-êrh 左法儿. *Wan-li* 106.84b.

    ROCKHILL (1) 611n.

Ê-CHI-CHIEH 额即乩. Unidentified. *Wan-li* 107.88b.

\* \* ENGLAND: Ying-chi-li 英吉利. *Chia-ch'ing* 31.3.

Ê-LO-SSŬ see Russia.

EUROPE: Not formally listed, see Western Ocean.

FA-LAN-HSI (France) 法兰西 see under Portugal.

\* FRANCE: Fa-lan-hsi, confused with Portugal, q. v.

FU-LIN see Syria.

FU-LO-CHÜ 芙洛居, presumably an error for Mei-lo-chü, see Molucca.

FU-YÜ see To-yen.

HA-HSIN 哈辛. Unidentified. *Wan-li* 107.88b.

    TING Chien 2.30: in W. Persia.

HA-LIEH see Herat.

HA-LIEH-ERH: 哈烈儿. Unidentified. *Wan-li* 107.87b.

    TING Chien 2.28b: same as Ha-lieh (Herat).

HAMI: Ha-mi 哈密. Tn., Sinkiang. *Wan-li* 107.87.

    P: 1907.

HA-SAN 哈三. Unidentified. *Wan-li* 107.87b.

    TING Chien 2.28b.

HAN-TUNG 罕东. District in Kansu (Tun-huang hsien). *Wan-li* 107.87b.

    P: 1980; BRETSCHNEIDER 2.218.

HA-SHIH-HA-ERH see Kashgar.

HA-TI-LAN 哈的兰. (?). *Wan-li* 107.87b.

    BRETSCHNEIDER 2.315: probably Khotelan.

HEI-KA-TA 黑葛达. Unidentified. *Wan-li* 106.84b.

HEI-LOU see Khorassan.

HERAT: Ha-lieh 哈烈. Tn., Afghanistan. *Wan-li* 106.87b.

    P: 1906; BRETSCHNEIDER 2.278-290; FÊNG (2) 13.

\* \* HOLLAND: Ho-lan 荷兰. *K'ang-hsi* 72.12a; *Yung-chêng* 104.22;

*Chia-ch'ing* 31.3.

    Popularly known as the "Red-haired foreigners (barbarians)," Hung-mao fan 红毛蕃, a term also used for the English, cf. CHANG Wei-hua 107-108. In the Ming period written 和兰, cf. DUYVENDAK (3). 30n. 4.

HO-MAO-LI or HO-MAO-WU, see Marinduque.

HORMUZ (Ormuz): Hu-lu-mo-ssǔ 忽鲁谟斯 or Hu-lu mu-ssǔ 忽鲁母思 Tn., Persian Gulf. *Wan-li* 106. 84b.

    GROENEVELDT 44.

HSIA-LA-PI see Arabia?

HSIAO-KO-LAN see Quilon.

HSIEN-LO see Siam.

HSI-LAN-SHAN see Ceylon.

HSI-PAN-YA see Spain.

HSI-PU-LU-T'Ê see Burut.

HSI-YANG see Western Ocean.

HSI-YANG SO-LI see Chola.

HSÜ-WÊN-TA-NA see Samudra.

HU-LU: 胡卢 or 葫芦. HUNG Liang-chi 50. 8b.

    Lit. "bottle-gourd country"? Cf. ROCKHILL (1) 91 under Chan-ch'êng; *Ch'ing t'ung-tien* 98. 20b: located 18 stages outside Yung-ch'ang fu, Yunnan—sent tribute in 1746.

HU-LU-MO-SSǓ see Hormuz.

HUNG-MAO FAN see Holland.

HUO-CHAN see Khodjend.

HUO-CHOU see Karakhodjo.

HUO-T'AN see Khodjend.

ILIBALIK: I-li-pa-li 亦力把力. Sinkiang near mod. Kuldja. *Wan-li* 107. 87b. H; 55F2; BRETSCHNEIDER 2. 225: later name for Bashibalik.

ISFAHAN (Ispahan): I-ssǔ-fu-han 亦思弗罕. Tn., Persia. *Wan-li* 107. 88b.

    \* \* I-TA-LI-YA see under Portugal.

\*JAPAN： Jih-pên 日本 or Wo-nu 倭奴. *Wan-li* 105. 80b； *Chia-ch'ing* 31. 3.

JAUNPUR： Chao-na-p'u-êrh 沼纳扑儿. Mid-India near Benares. *Wan-li* 106. 84b.

FÊNG (1) 17-18. Same as old Fo-kuo 佛国.

\*JAVA： (1) Shê-p'o 阇婆, Chinese pre-Mongol transcription； (2)Chao-wa 爪哇, post-Mongol （Fukien） transcription， GROENEVELDT 45. *Wan-li* 105. 82.

ROCKHILL (1) 66： Majapahit.

(3)Ka-la-pa 噶喇吧 or 葛剌. *Chia-ch'ing* 31. 3b.

WANG Kuo-wei 54； CHANG Wei-hua 110： old Chinese name for Batavia, hence for Java as a whole.

\*JAYA (Chaya, Jaiya)： Ch'ih-tzǔ 赤仔. W. Siam. *Chia-ch'ing* 31. 3b. *Hai-kuo wên-chien lu* 1. 25b gives 斜 Hsieh (hsia) -tzǔ, translated by SCHLEGEL 298 as Chaya. Captain Francis LIGHT, quoted above part 6, between Chantebon and Sangora (sic) listed "Chia—Province West of Siam—produces Cotton, Dyes, Birdsnest, Salt Fish, Dryed Shrimps—Manufactures Silk and Cotton Clothes—Plundered and destroyed by the Burmers 1787" [C. E. WURTZBURG "A Brief Account of the Several Countries Surrounding Prince of Wales' Island…", *J. Mal. Br. R. A. S.*, vol. 16 part 1 (July 1938). 123-126]. W. LINEHAN, "A History of Pahang," *J. Mal. Br. R. A. S.* 14 part 2 (June 1936). 9 refers to Jaiya or Chaiya as near Ligor.

JIH-LO-HSIA-CHIH 日罗夏治. Unidentified. *Wan-li* 106. 84b.

JIH-LO 日落. Unidentified. *Wan-li* 107. 88b.

BRETSCHNEIDER 2. 314.

JIH-PÊN-KUO see Japan.

\*JOHORE： Jou-fo 柔佛. Ctry., So. Malay penin. *Chia-ch'ing* 31. 3b.

GROENEVELDT 135.

JUI KUO see Sweden.

JUNG 戎. "Western barbarians." Unidentified. *Wan-li* 107.87b.

 *Tao-i chih-lüeh* (Wang 30) has a Jung on the Malay Peninsula.

JURFATTAN see Cananore.

KA-LA-PA see Java.

K'AN-PA-I-T'I see Coyampadi.

KAN-PA-LI see Coyampadi.

KAN-SHIH 干失. Unidentified. *Wan-li* 107.87b.

 TING Chien 2.29 line 4.

KAN-SSŬ-LA see Portugal.

KARAKHODJO: Huo-chou 火州. Tn., E. of Turfan, Sinkiang, *Wan-li* 107.88.

 P: 1900; ancient Kao-ch'ang; BRETSCHNEIDER 2.186-188.

KASHGAR: Ha-shih-ha-êrh 哈失哈儿. Tn., Sinkiang. *Wan-li* 107.87b.

 P: 3224.

KASHMIR: K'o-shih-mi-êrh 克失迷儿. *Wan-li* 107.87b.

 FÊNG (2) 18.

KELANTAN: Chi-lan-tan 急兰丹. Ctry., E. coast Malay penin. No. of Trengganu. *Wan-li* 106.84b.

 ROCKHILL (1) 65, 121; CHANG Wei-hua 109; KUWABARA 7.86: same as Ki-lan-i-tai 急阑亦带 of the Yüan period.

KHODJEND: (1) Huo-chan 火占. Tn., in Kokand, C. Asia. *Wan-li* 107.87b.

 P: 2414.

(2) Sha-liu-hai-ya 沙六海牙. *Wan-li* 107.87b.

 TING Chien 2.29b: Sha-lu-hai-ya 沙鹿海牙, ancient name for above; confirmed by BRETSCHNEIDER 2.253, who calls it Shahrokia.

? (3) Huo-t'an 火坛. *Wan-li* 107.87b.

 TING Chien 2.29b; no confirmation found.

KHORASSAN: Hei-lou 黑娄. Afghanistan. *Wan-li* 107.88b.

 BRETSCHNEIDER 2.272-273; FÊNG (2) 13; same as Herat.

KHOTAN: (1) Yü-t'ien 于阗. Tn., in Sinkiang. *Wan-li* 107.88b.

Ancient name of Khotan, mod. Ho-t'ien 和闐; cf. P: 2058.

? (2) A-tuan 阿端. *Wan-li* 107. 87b.

KIRGHIZ (Cossacks): Ha-sa-k'o 哈萨克. Tr., No. C. Asia.

   B863a. Divided into Eastern (Tso 左) and Western (Yu 右).

K'O-CHIEH 克乩. Unidentified. *Wan-li* 107. 87b.

   Cf. TING Chien 2. 29b.

KO-CHIH see Cochin.

\*\*KOREA: (1) Kao-li 高丽. (Koryŏ) pre-Ming; (2) Chao-hsien 朝鲜 *Wan-li* 105. 80; *K'ang-hsi* 72. 3b; *Yung-chêng* 104. 4; *Ch'ien-lung* 56. 1; *Chia-ch'ing* 32. 2; *Kuang-hsü* 39. 2.

K'O-SHIH-MI-ÊRH see Kashmir.

KOYAMPADI see Coyampadi.

KUANG-NAN see Quang-nam.

KUCHA: K'u-hsien 苦先. Tn., Aksu district, Sinkiang. *Wan-li* 107. 87.

   TS'ÊN Chung-mien 152-153; H: 55F3.

K'U-CH'A-NI 窟察尼. Unidentified. *Wan-li* 106. 84b.

K'U-HSIEN see Kucha.

KU-LI see Calicut.

KU-LI-PAN-TSU see Pansur.

KU-MA-LA 古麻剌. Ctry. Unidentified. *Wan-li* 106. 83b.

K'UN-CH'ÊNG see Kunduz?

K'UNG-KA-ERH 控噶尔. Unidentified. HUNG Liang-chi 50. 21.

KUO-SA-SSŬ 果撒思. Unidentified. *Wan-li* 107. 87b.

KUNDUZ?: K'un-ch'êng 坤城. Possibly the Tn. and Ctry. in N. E. Afghanistan? *Wan-li* 107. 87b.

   TING Chien 2. 28b; cf. H: 60B3.

LACON see Ligor.

LAMBRI: (1) *Nan-p'o-li* 南渤利. Ctry., No. tip of Sumatra, mod. Achin. *Wan-li* 106. 84b.

   GROENEVELDT 44, 89; ROCKHILL (1) 67.

(2) Nan-wu-li 南巫里 same place; cited as different country in Ming

History [PELLIOT (1) 327; (2) 288].

LAN-PANG 览邦. Unidentified. *Wan-li* 105. 83.

TING Chien 15: island group east of Singapore.

LAO-CHUA see Laos.

* * LAOS (Lao-chua): Nan-chang 南掌. Ctry., No. Indo-Chinese penin. *Ch'ien-lung* 56. 1; *Chia-ch'ing* 31. 2b; *Kuang-hsü* 39. 2b.

*Ch'ing t'ung-k'ao* 296. 28: Nan-chang. is the name first used in the Chia-ching period (1522-1566) for the Lao-chua 老挝 tribes, situated between the borders of Annam, Siam, and Yunnan; cf. H: 56B4: Laotien. MAYERS no. 329 states that Lao-chua is the designation attributed in Chinese literature to the Shan tribes, q. v.; CHANG Ch'êng-sun 69: Lao-chua is the popular name, Nan-chang the official one (kuo-hao). Cf. SOULIÉ and TCHANG, "Les barbares soumis du Yunnan," *BEFEO* 8. 155-156.

LA-SA 剌撒. Tn., Arabia or Africa. *Wan-li* 106. 84b.

ROCKHILL (1) 616: probably on Somali coast of Africa; WU Han 168: the *Wu-pei-chih-t'u* 武备志图 puts La-sa in Arabia N. W. of Aden. Cf. PELLIOT (2) 287 n. 3.

LIEN-KUO see Denmark.

* LIGOR (Lacon): Liu-k'un 六昆 (or 坤). Ctry., on E. coast Malay penin. No. of Sungora (now in Siam). *Chia-ch'ing* 31. 3b.

KUWABARA (1) 280; CHANG Wei-hua 109. ROCKHILL (1) 109 identifies Lo-wei 罗卫 as "Ligor (?)."

LIU-CH'ÊN 柳陈. Tn., E. of Karakhodjo, Sinkiang. *Wan-li* 107. 88.

BRETSCHNEIDER 2. 31: Lukchak; FÊNG (2) 24: Lukchun.

* * LIU-CH'IU 琉球. Ctry., E. China sea. *Wan-li* 105. 81; *K'ang-hsi* 72. 10; *Yung-chêng* 104. 16b; *Ch'ien-lung* 56. 1; *Chia-ch'ing* 31. 2; *Kuang-hsü* 39. 2.

ROCKHILL (1) 64: N. W. Formosa; PELLIOT (1) 332 n. 7: much debated by Japanese scholars as to whether this is mod. Ryukyu Is. or Formosa. Ming sources distinguish Greater (Ta) and Lesser (Hsiao)

Liu-ch'iu, e. g. WU Han 149. Presumably Liu-ch'iu throughout the Ch'ing period is the modern Ryukyu Is., although earlier the name referred to Formosa, cf. WADA 131.

LIU-K'UN see Ligor.

LIU-SHAN see Maldive Is.

LU-MI see Rum.

LÜ-SUNG see Philippines.

MA-CH'ÊN see Banjermassin.

MALACCA: Man-la-chia 满剌加. Ctry., S. W. coast Malay penin. *Wan-li* 106. 83b.

Many variants: Ma-la-chia 马剌加, Ma-liu-chia 马六甲.

MALDIVE ISLANDS: Liu-shan 溜山. S. W. of Indian penin. *Wan-li* 106. 84b.

ROCKHILL (1) 82, 387.

MA-LIN see Melinde.

\* MANG-CHÜN-TA-LAO 莽 (GILES 7667) 均达老. ? *Chia-ch'ing* 31. 3b. Possibly for Magindanao i, e., Mindanao? (cf. WADA 135, 157, 160-161 where various forms are given; none are the same as this).

MAN-LA-CHIA see Malacca.

MARINDUQUE?: Ho-mao-li 合貓里 or Ho-mao-wu 合猫物 or 务. P. I., So. of Luzon. *Wan-li* 106. 84b.

WADA 156 quoting CHANG Hsieh, *Tung-hsi-yang k'ao*: same as Mao-li-wu (Marinduque); probably in fact indicating the adjacent island of Camarine, according to WADA 157.

MA-YEH-WÊNG see Billiton.

MECCA see Arabia (T'ien-fang).

MEDINA: Mo-tê-na 默德那. Tn., Arabian coast of Red Sea. *Wan-li* 107. 88b.

MEI-(MI)-LO-CHÜ see Molucca.

MELINDE: Ma-lin 麻林. Tn., E. coast of Africa, No. of Mombasa. *Wan-li* 106. 84b.

ROCKHILL (1) 83.

MIEH-K'O-LI see Nieh-k'o-li.

MIEN-TIEN see Burma.

MINDANAO see Mang-chün-ta-lao?

MOGADISHO (Mogedoxu, etc.): Mu-ku-tu-tz'ǔ 木骨都束. Tn., E. coast Africa. *Wan-li* 106.84b.

 GROENEVELDT 44.

MOLUCCA: Mei-lo-chü 美洛居.

 Correct form for Fu-lo-chü 芙洛居.

  HUNG Liang-chi 50.5:芙洛居; Cf. *Ch'ing i-t'ung chih* 356.7 美洛居.

  WADA 161; Wu Han 183.

MO-TÊ-NA see Medina.

MU-KU-TU-TZ'Ǔ see Mogadisho.

NAN-CHANG see Laos.

NAN-P'O-LI see Lambri.

NAN-WU-LI see Lambri.

NIEH-K'O-LI 乜克力. Tr., E. of Hami, Sinkiang? *Wan-li* 107.87b.

 TING Chien 2.2b; cf. BRETSCHNEIDER 2.178.

NISHAPUR: Ni-sha-wu-erh 你沙兀儿. Tn., in Persia, province Khorassan. *Wan-li* 107.87b.

 P: 4555, 4665.

OIRAT: Wa-la 瓦剌. Tr., Mongols. *Wan-li* 107.85.

 BRETSCHNEIDER 2.159-173 confuses Oirat with the later Oëlot.

\*PAHANG: P'êng-hêng 彭亨. Ctry., E. coast Malay penin. *Wan-li* 105.82b.

 ROCKHILL (1) 65: P'êng-k'êng; Wu Han 149: another Ming name P'ên-hêng 湓亨.

PAI 白. Unidentified. *Wan-li* 107.87b.

 BRETSCHNEIDER 2.315: probably the city of this name in E. Turkestan. Cf. also under Shan below.

PAI (PO)-HUA 百花. Unidentified. *Wan-li* 105.82b. Cf. Lu Tz'ǔ-yün

(*Pa-hung i-shih* 2.26): same as ancient Chu-nien 注辇, mod. Coromandel.

PAI-I see Shan tribes.

PAI-KA-TA:白葛达. Unidentified. *Wan-li* 106.84b.

    TING 1.28b, 2.19 suggests that this maritime tributary is Bukhara.

PAI-YIN 摆音. Tr., unidentified. *Wan-li* 107.87b.

    Listed as in the Western Regions. Cf. also under Shan.

PA-K'O-I 八可意. Unidentified. *Wan-li* 106.84b.

P'A-LA 怕剌. Unidentified. *Wan-li* 107.87b.

    Cf. old kingdom of Pala, N. E. India, H: 39F2?

PA-LA-HSI 巴剌西. Unidentified. *Hsü wên-hsien t'ung-k'ao* 239.24b.

PALEMBANG: (1) San-fo-ch'i 三佛齐. E. Sumatra, anc. Srivijaya. *Wan-li* 105.82b.

    GROENEVELDT 62, 73. KUWABARA 7.17 and FÊNG(4) 228 agree in identifying it with Palembang.

(2) Chiu-chiang 旧港, later name (for a smaller area?)

    ROCKHILL (1) 66; FÊNG (1) 11.

PA-LI-HEI see Balkh.

PANG-KO-LA see Bengal.

PANSUR: Ku-li-pan-tsu 古里班卒. W. coast of Sumatra near Bārūs (Baroes). *Wan-li* 106.84b.

    FUJITA (WANG 60): identifies Pan-tsu as given in *Tao-i chih-lüeh* with Pin-su 宾窣, and the "Pansur, Fansur" of the Arabs, ku-li meaning "island" (cf. *ibid*. 63b quoting GERINI).

PA-TA-HEI-SHANG see Badakshan.

*PATANI: Ta-ni 大泥 (also Ta-nien 大年). Ctry., So. of Sungora, E. coast Malay penin. (now in Siam). *Chia-ch'ing* 31.3b.

    CHANG Wei-hua 109; WANG Kuo-wei 43b: also by error identified by Ming writers with Brunei (P'o-ni). WADA 128 n. 3 suggests this was because the name P'o-ni came through the Western (hsi-yang) trade route. KUWABARA 7.83 suggests the identity of Patani (Ta-ni) with the Ta-li 大力 country of the Yüan period.

PA-TAN-SHA see Badakshan.

P'ÊNG-CHIA-NA see Bengal.

P'ÊNG-HÊNG see Pahang.

\* PHILIPPINES (Luzon): Lü-sung 吕宋. Ctry. *Wan-li* 106. 84b; *Chia-ch'ing* 31. 3b.

> CHANG Wei-hua 73-74: Lü-sung was the pre-Spanish name, later applied to Spain as "Great Luzon" Ta-lü-sung 大吕宋. For example see *IWSM-TK* 76. 16 (July 1846); by contrast Hsiao-lü-sung 小吕宋 came to be used for the Philippines (Manila), e. g. *ibid*. 71. 23b (May 1844). The Fukien authorities in Feb. 1847 identified Hsi-pan-ya (Spain) as Ta-lü-sung (*ibid*. 77. 14b).

PIEH-SHIH-PA-LI see Bashibalik.

P'O-LO see Borneo.

PO-LO-ERH see Bolor.

P'O-NI see Brunei.

\* \* PORTUGAL: Portugal, Spain, Italy, and France were constantly confused for one another, or not distinguished.

(1) Fo-lang-chi 佛朗机 i. e. Franks, originally derived by the Chinese from the Arabs as a term for the West in the period of the Crusades; revived for the Portuguese after 1500. Also used for the Spanish and later confused with France, see (2). Cf. CHANG Wei-hua 5-6. *Ch'ing t'ung-k'ao* 298. 31b: same as Ho-lan-hsi 和兰西, capital Pa-li-shih 巴离士 (Paris); occupied and traded at Macao (sic).

(2) Fa-lan-hsi (France) 法兰西 or Fu-lang-hsi 弗郎西. *Chia-ch'ing* 31. 4: same as the Fo-lang-chi of the Ming period; occupied the Philippines (Lü-sung), lived at Macao (sic). CHANG Wei-hua 5 gives half a dozen variants of Fa-lan-hsi; Ho-lan-hsi, noted above, tends to confuse it with Holland.

(3) I-ta-li-ya (Rome or Italy, also Portugal) 意达里亚. *Chia-ch'ing* 31. 3: the king, Po-na-ti-to (Pope Benedict XIII) sent tribute in 1725. Cf.

*Ch'ing t'ung-k'ao* 298. 6-8: a peninsula in the Mediterranean, capital Rome, etc., in 1670 and 1678 the king, A-fêng-su (Alfonso VI of Portugal), sent tribute, etc. CHANG Wei-hua 155-156: early used for Europe (Rome) and in the Ming History for Catholic missionaries. In early nineteenth century documents the Portuguese at Macao were referred to as I-ta-li-ya kuo (lit. the country of Italy), e. g. *IWSM-TK* 71. 1 (Mar. 1844); but it was explained that while this name had been given the Jesuit missionaries and so applied to Macao, the country really involved at Macao was Ta-hsi-yang, see below. Meanwhile when an Italian missionary was seized it was stated in June 1848 that Italy (I-ta-li kuo) on its part had no headman in Kwangtung 查意大理国并无夷目在粤 (*ibid*. 79. 17), i. e. it was an entirely new country. (4) Ta-hsi-yang 大西洋. A general term for Europe as opposed to the Indian Ocean (Hsiao-hsi-yang), see under Western Ocean; but also used for Portugal as a single country, e. g. *IWSM-TK* 70. 1b (Dec. 1843), 72. 3 (July 1844).

(5) Po-êrh-tu-chia-li-ya (Portugal) 博尔都嘉利亚 *Chia-ch'ing* 31. 3: the king, A-fêng-su (Alfonso VI) first sent tribute in 1670.

(6) Po-êrh-tu-ka-êrh (Portugal) 博尔都噶尔. *Chia-ch'ing* 31. 3: first sent tribute in 1727.

(7) Kan-ssŭ-la 干丝腊. *Chia-ch'ing* 31. 4: near England in the northwestern sea. CHANG Wei-hua 69: used for the Portuguese by error, being derived from "Castilla," the Spanish in the Philippines; this accords with the suggestion of PELLIOT (5) 69 n. 3 where other transcriptions for Portugal are also mentioned.

PU-HA-LA see Bukhara.

PU-LA-WA see Barawa.

QUANG-NAM: Kuang-nan 广南. E. coast of Indo-China. *Wan-li* 107. 87b.

*Ch'ing t'ung-k'ao* 196. 30: anc. Nan-chiao 南交, bounded by Annam, Champa, Burma, and Siam; MASPERO ("Royaume de Champa," *TP* 11. 195): an old capital of Champa; cf. KUWABARA 7. 19; and L.

AUROUSSEAU in *BEFEO* 22. 158-160. *Hai-kuo wên-chien lu* 19b: the same as Annam.

QUILON (Kulam): Hsiao-ko-lan 小葛兰. S. W. tip of India. *Wan-li* 106. 84.

> ROCKHILL(1) 67: Hsiao-chü-nan 小具喃, Kain Colam; cf. *ibid*. 76, 83, 425.

RUM: Lu-mi 鲁迷 or 密. Ctry., E. Asia Minor. *Wan-li* 107. 88.

> H: 54C3; BRETSCHNEIDER 2. 306-308.

RUSSIA: Ê-lo-ssǔ 俄罗斯.

> Not listed in the sources here covered; in the Ch'ing under the Li Fan Yüan (see part 3 above). BRETSCHNEIDER 2. 73-81 summarizes *Yüan History* references.

SAIRAM: Sai-lan 赛兰. Tn., N. E. of Tashkent, C. Asia. *Wan-li* 107. 87b.

> P: 5347; FÊNG (2) 31.

SAMARKAND: Sa-ma-êrh-han 撒马儿罕. Tn., C. Asia. *Wan-li* 107. 88.

> P: 5342.

SAMUDRA: (1) Hsü-wên-ta-na 须文达那. E. coast Sumatra. *Wan-li* 105. 83: "it is said to be the same as" (2). (2) Su-mên-ta-la 苏门答剌, *Wan-li* 105. 83; *Chia-ch'ing* 31. 3b.

> Translated by earlier writers as Sumatra and identified with Achin (q. v.) following Chinese sources. PELLIOT (3) 214 now concludes that it corresponds to the present village of Samudra on the Pasai River, and MILLS 6n. works out the probable location from a Chinese sailing chart as "near Meraksa about 5 miles west of the Pasai River."

SAN-FO-CH'I see Palembang.

SAO-LAN: 扫兰. ? *Wan-li* 107. 87b.

> Variant for Sairam? This is another guess by Mr. TING.

SHA-LI-WAN-NI see Cananore.

SHA-LIU-HAI-YA (Shahrokia) see Khodjend.

SHAN TRIBES: Pai-i 摆夷. No. Indo-China penin.

MAYERS no. 329: "The Shans of the border-land between Yunnan and Burmah term themselves, and are commonly known as, Pai I 百夷. Chinese official writers, however, describe them as Lao Chua (Laos), and the designation Pai I is applied in the description of the tribes of Yunnan (*Nan Man Chih* 南蛮志. Book III ... ) to the aborigines of the Kuangsi frontier..." SOULIÉ and TCHANG, in *BEFEO* 8. 352 quoting *Nan tchao ye che*, identify the 白人 Po-jen with the 百夷 "Pai-yi" and 摆夷 "Pa-yi," all being of Thai race. J. SIGURET, *Territoires et populations des confins du Yunnan* (Peiping 1937) 137 classes the Pai-i 摆夷 as a Shan tribe in Yunnan.

SHA-TI-MAN: 沙的蛮. ? *Wan-li* 107. 87b.

Lit. "Barbarians of the desert." Cf. BRETSCHNEIDER 2. 315.

SHÊ-HEI 舍黑. Tn. , So. coast Arabia? *Wan-li* 107. 87b.

TING Chien 2. 29b: in Arabia, same as Sha-ha 沙哈; cf. H: 50D4 Escier, (No. 2113) 施曷 Shih-ho, Shihr.

SHÊ-LA-CH'I 舍剌齐. Shulistan? *Wan-li* 106. 84b.

BRETSCHNEIDER 2. 127-128.

SHÊ-P'O see Java.

SHIRAZ: Shih-la-ssŭ 失剌思. Tn. , Persia. *Wan-li* 107. 87b.

P: 5677; BRETSCHNEIDER 2. 292-294, 128.

\* \* SIAM: (1) Hsien-lo 暹罗. Ctry. *Wan-li* 105. 81b; *K'ang-hsi* 72. 16; *Yung-chêng* 104. 27; *Ch'ien-lung* 56. 1; *Chia-ch'ing* 31. 2b; *Kuang-hsü* 39. 2b. ? (2) Chiang-k'ou 港口. *Chia-ch'ing* 31. 3: a country, 160 watches from Amoy.

*Hai-kuo wên-chien lu* (a work completed in 1730, see under part 7 above) 1. 25, in describing the sailing route from Amoy to Siam, gives its destination as Hsien-lo chiang-k'ou, translated by Schlegel 197 as "the estuary of Siam," 188 watches from Amoy; to enter port (ju-chiang) it is 40 watches more. *Hai-lu* (a work completed about 1820) 1. 2 likewise refers to Hsien-lo chiang-k'ou as the end of the sea route to Siam. In the list quoted above (part 5) from the 1818 edition of the

*Hui-tien*, Chiang-k'ou kuo occupies the place where one would necessarily expect to find Siam, which on its part is not listed; the identification of Chiang-k'ou kuo as identical or connected with Siam should be easily proved by further research. For example, the *Ch'ing t'ung-tien* 98.13 states that the king is named Chêng 郑. The contemporary king of Siam had this same surname.

SO-LI see Chola.

SO-LO see Borneo.

SPAIN: Hsi-pan-ya 西班牙. Not formally listed in the *Hui-tien*, confused with Portugal, q. v.; see Philippines.

* * SULU: Su-lu 苏禄. Sulu Archipelago. *Wan-li* 106.83b; *Yung-chêng* 104.36; *Ch'ien-lung* 56.1; *Chia-ch'ing* 31.2b; *Kuang-hsü* 39.2b. ROCKHILL (1) 66; UCHIDA 32 gives variants.

SUMATRA see Samudra.

* SUNGORA (Sunkla): Sung-chü-lao 宋腒朥. Ctry., on E. coast Malay penin., No. of Patani (now in Siam, mod. Sunkla). *Chia-ch'ing* 31.3b. CHANG Wei-hua 109: same as Sung-ch'ia 宋卡 or Sung-chiao 宋脚, Sawng Kia or Sungora; KUWABARA (1) 280.

SYRIA: Fu-lin 拂菻. E. coast of Mediterranean, incl. Palestine. (originally the Byzantine empire). *Wan-li* 106.84b. HERRMANN 38 distinguishes between Greater Fu-lin as the E. Roman Empire, and Sham, Smaller Fu-lin 扶临, in Syria.

* SWEDEN: Jui-kuo 瑞国. *Chia-ch'ing* 31.4.

TABRIZ: T'ieh-pi-li-ssŭ 帖必力思. Tn., Persia. *Wan-li* 107.87b. FÊNG (2) 35.

TA-HUI 打回. Unidentified. *Wan-li* 106.84b.

T'AI-NING, district of, see To-yen.

TA-NI see Patani.

TA-NIEN see Patani.

TAN-PA 淡巴. ? *Wan-li* 105.83. Lu Tz'ŭ-yün (*Pa-hung i-shih* 2.26b): same as ancient Lang-ya-hsiu 狼牙修; cf. FÊNG (4) 226: Lankāsuka, on the northern Malay peninsula.

*TAN-TAN 单呾. *Chia-ch'ing* 31. 3b (text indistinct): dependency of Johore, listed between Trengganu and Pahang. Cf. FÊNG (4) 221:丹丹, 单单, and 旦旦 (241 n. 1) all appear to refer to the same place on the Malay peninsula. This seems more probable than the early suggestion of FERRAND 13. 299-300 that Tan-tan might be "dans la partie orientale de la mer de Java."

TASHKENT: T'a-shih-kan 塔什干. C. Asia. *Ch'ing t'ung-k'ao* 299. 12b.

P: 154.

TIBET: Wu-ssŭ-tsang 乌思藏. *Wan-li* 108. 88b; *K'ang-hsi* 73. 1; *Yung-chêng* 105. 1.

Also T'u-fan, Hsi-tsang, etc., cf. B: 906; and P: 2502 for variants.

TIEH-LI 碟里. Unidentified. *Wan-li* 106. 84b.

T'IEH-PI-LI-SSŬ see Tabriz.

T'IEN-FANG see Arabia (Mecca).

TING-CHI-NÜ see Trengganu.

TOGMAK: T'o-hu-ma 脱忽麻. C. Asia. *Wan-li* 107. 87b.

BRETSCHNEIDER 2. 161; cf. H: 69C2 Tokmak.

TO-YEN: the districts of To-yen 朵颜, Fu-yü 福余, and T'ai-ning 泰宁 in So. Manchuria. *Wan-li* 107. 86b.

H: 55GF2.

*TRENGGANU: Ting-chi-nü 丁机奴. Ctry., E. coast Malay penin. No. of Pahang. *Chia-ch'ing* 31. 3b.

ROCKHILL (1) 65, 118; CHANG Hsieh 4. 11b gives Ting-chi-i 丁机宜 as a dependency of Java, adjacent to Johore; WANG Kuo-wei 29b gives Ting-chia-lu 丁家庐 as Tringganu; *Ch'ing t'ung-k'ao* 297. 16-17: a dependency of Johore. KUWABARA 7. 85 identifies it as Ting-ko-êrh 丁呵儿 of the Yüan period.

TSO-FA-ÊRH see Djofar.

TSO-HA-SA-K'O see Kirghiz.

TSU-FA-ÊRH see Djofar.

T'U-LU-FAN see Turfan.

TUNG-PU-LU-T'E see Burut.

TUNG-YANG see under Western Ocean.

\* \* TURFAN (anc. Kao-ch'ang): T'u-lu-fan 土鲁番. Tn., Sinkiang. *Wan-li* 107. 88; *K'ang-hsi* 72. 8b; *Yung-chêng* 104. 37b.

P: 6670.

TURGUT: T'u-êrh-ku-t'ê 土尔古特. Tr. C. Asia. *Ta-Ch'ing i-t'ung chih* 355. 34.

Cf. B: 864, 903.

URIANGHAI: Wu-liang-hai 乌梁海. District in E. Inner Mongolia and So. Manchuria. *Wan-li* 107. 85.

P: 7182; T. C. LIN (2) 867.

WA-LA see Oirat.

WÊN-LAI see Brunei

WÊN-TU-SSǓ-T'AN 温都斯坦. Unidentified. HUNG Liang-chi 50. 21.

\* \* WESTERN OCEAN COUNTRY(IES): Hsi-yang(chu)-kuo 西洋(诸)国. *K'ang-hsi* 72. 18; *Yung-chêng* 104. 30; *Ch'ien-lung* 56. 1; *Chia-ch'ing* 31. 3: at first (1690) singular, later a generic term for European countries. Cf. CHANG Wei-hua 155-156: Ta-hsi-yang for Europe; Hsi-yang in the early Ming meant the So. Sea and Indian Ocean west of Borneo, as opposed to Tung-yang from Borneo east (quoting CHANG Hsieh, *Tung-hsi-yang k'ao*); see also the more full (and earlier) discussion in WADA 123-125: Hsi- and Tung-yang originally referred to the trade routes along (Hsi) the Indo-Chinese-Malayan coast and (Tung) to the Philippines, Molucca, etc., respectively. Ta-hsi-yang was also used for Portugal (q. v.) in particular.

WO-NU see Japan

WU-LUN 兀伦. Unidentified. *Wan-li* 107. 87b.

Cf. ROCKHILL (1) 238: Wu-lun 巫仑, a dependency of Java.

WU-SHÊ-LA-T'ANG 乌涉剌踢. Unidentified. *Wan-li* 106. 84b.

WU-SSŬ-TSANG see Tibet.

YA-CHI see Achin.

YA-ÊRH-KAN see Yarkand.

YA-HSI: 牙昔. Unidentified. *Wan-li* 107. 87b.

  TING Chien 2. 29b gives Aksu.

YARKAND: (1) Ya-êrh-kan 牙儿干. Tn., Sinkiang. *Wan-li* 107. 87b.
(2) Yeh-êrh-ch'in (Hui-hui kuo) 叶尔钦. *Ta-Ch'ing i-t'ung chih* 355. 36

  Cf. FÊNG (2) 41: Yeh-êrh-ch'iang 牙儿羌, Ch'ing name for Yarkand.

YEH-SSŬ-CH'ÊNG 耶思成. Unidentified. *Wan-li* 107. 87b.

YING-CHI-LI see England.

\* YIN-TAI-MA 尹代吗. Unidentified, near Cambodia; possibly Chantebun? *Chia-ch'ing* 31. 3b: listed between Cambodia and Ligor. Cf. *Hai-kuo wên-chien lu* 196: K'un-ta-ma 昆大吗 between Cambodia and Siam.

YÜEH-NAN see Annam.

YU-HA-SA-K'O see Kirghiz.

YÜ-T'IEN see Khotan.

# APPENDIX 1

  Bibliographical note: Research on various aspects of this enormous and ramified subject has accumulated to a point where general surveys should be of value. At the same time, most of the work done has been on the Ming period, leaving a gap between it and the nineteenth century. The following modern writings relating to maritime relations and/or the tributary system, although largely concerned with the Ming or earlier periods, are selected as essential background materials for the study of the Ch'ing period. They are arranged alphabetically by author and are so cited in the article, particularly in the index of place names, section 8. For analytical purposes they may be classified under five heads:

  (1) On administration: KUWABARA'S masterly study of Sung and

Yüan foreign trade has not been equalled for a later period; CHANG Tê-ch'ang, T. C. LIN, YANO, and UCHIDA, among others, describe the Ming organs of administration dealing with foreigners.

(2) On sea-routes and the Ming expeditions: WADA discusses the route via the Philippines and MILLS that via Malaya; GROENEVELDT, HIRTH and ROCKHILL, among others, translate valuable texts while the expeditions under CHÊNG Ho first studied by ROCKHILL and his predecessors are dealt with in an important series of monographs by PELLIOT, DUYVENDAK, and FÊNG, which revise previous work while not supplanting it.

(3) On relations via Central Asia: BRETSCHNEIDER is still a chief work for the Ming period; the immense volume of Ch'ing materials concerning the Li Fan Yüan appear hardly to have been touched.

(4) On the Europeans: CHANG Wei-hua has done a valuable study of the sections on European countries in the *Ming History*, and CHANG T'ien-tsê a study of Macao (note PELLIOT'S review)...; this article does not attempt to refer to the work done on the Jesuit missions.

(5) On Ch'ing relations with neighboring states: ROCKHILL (on Korea and Tibet), CHANG Ch'êng-sun and YANO (1) (on Burma), and DEVERIA (on Annam, inadequate) barely enter upon this vast subject.

This cursory survey reveals many lacunae in our knowledge of Ch'ing foreign relations: Ch'ing administration in Central Asia; Sino-Dutch relations in the seventeenth century; tributary relations with Siam, Laos, and Liu-ch'iu; the Chinese side of foreign trade in general. Studies such as those of Prof. DUYVENDAK on the last Dutch embassy are much needed. In section 7 above we attempted to list some of the Ch'ing sources which await critical use. In the list which follows, some items are included as worthy of avoidance.

Abbreviations:

B = H. S. BRUNNERT and V. V. HAGELSTROM, *Present Day*

Political Organization of China, trans, from Russian by A. BELTCHENKO and E. E. MORAN, Shanghai, 1912.

H = A. HERRMANN, Historical and Commercial Atlas of China, Cambridge, 1935.

P = G. M. H. PLAYFAIR, The Cities and Towns of China, A Geographical Dictionary, Shanghai, 1910 (1879).

IWSM-TK is used below for Ch'ou-pan i-wu shih-mo 籌辦夷务始末 Tao-kuang 道光 section, 80 chüan, Peiping 1930.

Atlas van Tropisch Nederland, Batavia 1938 (cf. Blad. 10b, Earlier History). BRETSCHNEIDER, E., Mediaeval Researches from Eastern Asiatic Sources ... London 1910 (1888), reprint 1937. Note that the section based on Ming-shih and Ta-Ming i-t'ung chih appeared with characters in China Review 5 (1876-1877).

CHANG Ch'êng-sun 张诚孙, Chung-Ying Tien-Mien chiang-chieh wên-t'i 中英滇缅疆界问题 (Sino-Burmese Frontier Problems), YCHP Monograph Series no. 15, Peiping 1937; espec, pp. 85-91.

CHANG Hsi-lun 张锡纶, Shih-wu-liu-ch'i shih-chi chien Chung-kuo tsai Yin-tu-chih-na chi Nan-yang-Ch'ün-tao ti mao-i 十五六七世纪间中国在印度支那及南洋群岛的贸易 (Chinese Trade in Indo-China and the Southern Sea Archipelago in the 15th, 16th, and 17th Centuries) Shih-huo 食货 2 no. 7 (Sept. 1935). 22-30. A brief survey based on the Ming History; interesting suggestions and bibliography.

CHANG Tê-ch'ang 张德昌, Ming-tai Kuang-chou chih hai-po mao-i 明代广州之海舶贸易 (Maritime Trade of Canton in the Ming Period), CHHP 7 no. (June 1932). 1-18. English version: "Maritime Trade at Canton during the Ming Dynasty," The Chinese Social and Political Science Review 17 (1933). 264-282. See also note 90 below.

CHANG T'ien-tsê 张天泽, Sino-Portuguese Trade from 1514 to 1644, a Synthesis of Portuguese and Chinese Sources, Leyden 1934. Equally important review by PELLIOT (5).

CHANG Wei-hua 张维华,"Ming-shih Fo-lang-chi Lü-sung Ho-lan I-ta-li-ya ssŭ-chuan chu-shih"明史佛朗机吕宋和兰意大里亚四传注释(A Commentary of [sic] the Four Chapters on Portugal, Spain, Holland and Italy in the History of the Ming Dynasty), *YCHP monograph series no. 7*, Peiping 1934. A valuable study which makes good use of the findings of PELLIOT and others.

DEVERIA, G., *Histoire des relations de la Chine avec l'Annam-Vietnam du XVI<sup>e</sup> au XIX siècle, d'après des documents chinois*, Paris 1880. Not of much use.

DUYVENDAK, J. J. L., (1) *Ma Huan re-examined*, Amsterdam 1933.

—— (2) The true dates of the Chinese maritime expeditions in the early fifteenth century, *TP* 34 (1939). 341-412.

—— (3) The last Dutch Embassy to the Chinese Court (1794-1795), *TP* 34 (1938). 1-137.

—— (4) The last Dutch Embassy in the "Veritable Records," *TP* 34 (1938). 223-227.

DUYVENDAK, J. J. L., (5) "Supplementary Documents on the last Dutch Embassy to the Chinese Court," *TP* 35 (1940). 329-353.

"Embassies to the court of Peking ... ," *The Chinese Repository* 14 (1845). 153-156. Extracts from *Chia-ch'ing hui-tien* 31, which reproduce, with some inaccuracies, part of the data presented in tables 2 and 3.

FÊNG Ch'êng-chün 冯承钧, (1) *Ying-yai shêng-lan chiao-chu* 瀛涯胜览校注 [Critical Notes on the Ying-yai shêng-lan (1451)] Shanghai 1935. Reviewed by PELLIOT (3); our citations are from introduction.

—— (2) *Hsi-yü ti-ming* 西域地名 (Place names in the Western Regions), pub. by Hsi-pei k'o-hsüeh k'ao-ch'a-t'uan 西北科学考察团, n. p. 1930. A useful list but gives only general source references.

—— (3) *Hsi-yü nan-hai shih-ti k'ao-chêng i-ts'ung* 西域南海史地考证

译丛(Collected Translations of Critical Studies of Historical Places in the Western Regions and the Southern Sea); and *ibid...hsü-pien* (supplement), both Commercial Press 1934. Translates 25 articles, 17 of them by Prof. PELLIOT; a useful collection, even though translated.

—— (4) *Chung-kuo nan-yang chiao-t'ung shih* 中国南洋交通史 (History of Chinese Intercourse with the Southern Sea), Shanghai 1937. An annotated collection of sources, up into the Ming period. Perhaps the most useful single work so far available.

FERRAND, G., "Le K'ouen-louen et les anciennes navigations interocéaniques dans les mers du sud," *JA* ser. 11, tome 13 (1919). 239-333, 431-492, tome 14. 5-68, 201-241. Based on pre-Ch'ing bibliography, like most items here listed; strikingly illustrates the phonetic problems presented by Asiatic place names.

FUJITA Toyohachi 藤田丰八, *Tōsei kōshō shi no kenkyū* 东西交涉史の研究(A Study of the History of Relations between East and West), 2 vols. Tōkyō 1932-1933. Vol. 2 contains a useful index of plane names. See also under WANG Kuo-wei.

GROENEVELDT, W. P., *Notes on the Malay Archipelago and Malacca, compiled from Chinese sources*, n. p. 1876. Includes translated extracts from the *Ming History, Tung-hsi-yang k'ao*. etc.

HIRTH, F., and ROCKHILL, W. W., trans., *Chau Ju-kua: His Work on the Chinese and Arab Trade in the Twelfth and Thirteenth Centuries, Entitled Chu-fan-chi*, St. Petersburg 1911. Like the preceding item, must of course be used in conjunction with the more recent work of PELLIOT, DUYVENDAK et al.

HOU Hou-p'ei 侯厚培"*Wu-k'ou t'ung-shang i-ch'ien wo-kuo kuo-chi mao-i chih kai-k'uang*"五口通商以前我国国际贸易之概况(General Condition of our Country's International Trade before the Opening of the Treaty Ports, i. e. before 1843), *CHHP* 4 no. 1 (June 1927). An early study, now quite superseded by other work.

JAMIESON, G., "The Tributary Nations of China," *China Review* 12 (1883). 94-109. Translates extracts from *Chia-ch'ing hui-tien* 31 and *Chia-ch'ing hui-tien shih-li* 392-393 which require careful and extensive checking. Used as the basis for the chapter "China and her tributaries" (reprinted from the *National Review*, June 1884) in R. S. GUNDRY, *China and Her Neighbors*, London 1893.

K. (pseudonym), "Audiences Granted by the Emperors of China to Western envoys," *China Review* 3 (1874). 67-83. A pot-pourri quoting chiefly Western sources; no longer of value.

KUO Yu-i 郭有义, trans., MOMOSE Hiromu 百濑弘, "Ming-tai Chung-kuo chih wai-kuo mao-i" 明代中国之外国贸易 (China's Foreign Trade in the Ming Period), *Shih-huo* 4 no. 1 (June 10, 1936). 42-51. Japanese original in *Tōa* 东亚 8 no. 7 (1935). 95-110.

KUWABARA Jitsuzō 桑原隲藏, On P'u Shou-kêng, a man of the Western Regions..., *Memoirs of the Research Department of the Tōyō Bunko*, no. 2 (Tōkyō 1928). 1-79; 7 (1935). 1-104.

LIN, T. C., (1) "Manchuria in the Ming Empire," *Nankai Social and Economic Quarterly*, 8 no. 1 (April 1935). 1-43.

—— (2) "Manchurian Trade and Tribute in the Ming Dynasty: A study of Chinese Theories and Methods of Control over Border Peoples," *ibid.* 9 no. 4 (Jan. 1937). 855-892.

MAYERS, W. F., *The Chinese Government*..., 3d edition, revised by G. M. H. PLAYFAIR, Shanghai 1897 (1878).

MILLS, J. V., "Malaya in the Wu-Pei-Chih Charts," *J. of the Malayan Branch of the R. A. S.*, 15 part 3 (Dec. 1937). 1-48. A work of great value, on a subject first developed by PHILLIPS. Conclusions given in part in DUYVENDAK, "Sailing Directions of Chinese Voyages," *TP* 34 (1938). 230-237.

MOMOSE Hiromu see Kuo Yu-i, trans.

MORRISON, Rev. R., *A View of China for Philological Purposes*..., Macao 1817, 80-86, gives a rather miscellaneous list of 30 tributaries "as they stand on the records of the Board of Rites and Ceremonies"; exact source not stated. An interesting compilation rather than a translation, including the principal maritime tributaries of the early Ming.

PAUTHIER, G., *Histoire des relations politiques de la Chine avec les puissances occidentales* ..., Paris 1859. Translates, not impeccably, the section on tributary ritual in the 1824 edition of the *Ta-Ch'ing t'ung-li*, noting certain differences with the edition of 1756 previously translated by PAUTHIER as "Documents officiels chinois sur les ambassades étrangères, envoyés près de l'empéreur de la Chine," *Revue de l'Orient* 2 (1846). 1-22.

PELLIOT, P., (1) "Les Grands Voyages Maritimes Chinois au Debut du XV Siècle," *TP* 30 (1933). 237-452.

—— (2) "Notes Additionelles sur Tcheng Houo et sur sea voyages," *TP* 31 (1935). 274-314.

—— (3) "Encore à propos des voyages de Tcheng Houo," *TP* 32 (1936). 210-222.

—— (4) "L'Ambassade de Manoel de Saldanha à Pékin," *TP* 27 (1930). 421-424. Gives evidence for 1670 as the date rather than 1667.

—— (5) "Un ouvrage sur les premiers temps de Macao," *TP* 31 (1934). 58-94. A review of CHANG T'ien-tsê, giving new material as well as corrections.

PRITCHARD, Earl H., *The Crucial Years of Early Anglo-Chinese Relations, 1750-1800*, Pullman 1936; pp. 403-430 give a useful bibliography of Western materials on early modern relations and includes a list of Chinese materials.

For other items relating to European embassies, Russian relations, and the like, see under table 4 above.

ROCKHILL, W. W., (1) "Notes on the Relations and Trade of China with the Eastern Archipelago and the Coasts of the Indian Ocean during the Fourteenth Century," *TP* 14-16 (1913-1915). passim; sep. pub. Leiden 1915.

ROCKHILL, W. W., (2) *China's Intercourse with Korea from the XVth Century to 1895*, London 1905.

——(3) *The Dalai Lamas of Lhasa and Their Relations with the Manchu Emperors of China*, 1644-1908, Leyden 1910; from *TP* 11 (1910) 1-104.

——(4) "Diplomatic Missions to the Court of China: The Kotow Question," *American Historical Review* 2 (1897). 427-442, 627-643. Revised and extended as *Diplomatic Audiences at the Court of China*, London, 1905.

SCHLEGEL, G., "Geographical Notes," *TP* 9 (1898). 177-200, 273-298. Not reliable but has a few useful references.

TING Ch'ien 丁谦, "Ming-shih ko wai-kuo chüan ti-li k'ao-chêng" 明史各外国传地理考证 (A Critical Study of the Geography of the *Ming History* Chapters on Foreign Counties), in the *Chê-chiang t'u-shu-kuan ts'ung-shu* 浙江图书馆丛书 (Collectanea of the Chekiang Library), ts'ê 8 (1915). Certain of Mr. TING'S errors are indicated in CHANG Wei-hua 102-103 and in WADA 157. His work contains a plethora of unsupported guesses.

TS'ÊN Chung-mien 岑仲勉, "Ming-ch'u Ch'ü-hsien A-tuan An-ting Han-tung ssǔ-wei k'ao" 明初曲先阿端安定罕东四卫考 (A Study of the Four Districts of Ch'ü-hsien... at the Beginning of the Ming Period), *Chin-ling hsüeh-pao* 金陵学报 6 no. 2 (Nov. 1936). 151-172.

UCHIDA Naosaku, see WANG Huai-chung trans.

WADA Sei (和田清), "The Philippine Islands as known to the Chinese before the Ming Period," *Memoirs of ... the Tōyō Bunko* (*The Oriental Library*) no. 4 (Tōkyō 1929). 121-166. Makes extensive critical use of CHANG Hsieh, *Tung-hsi-yang k'ao*.

WANG Huai-chung 王怀中, trans., UCHIDA Naosaku 内田直作 "Ming-tai ti ch'ao-kung mao-i chih-tu"明代的朝贡贸易制度（The System of Court Tribute and Trade in the Ming Period）, *Shih-huo* 3 no. 1 （Dec. 10, 1935）. 32-37. Published originally in *Shina kenkyū* 支那研究 37 （1935）. 91-101.

WANG Kuo-wei 王国维 trans., FUJITA Toyohachi author, *Tao-i chih-lüeh chiao-chu* 岛夷志略校注［Critical Notes on the *Tao-i chih-lüeh* （Brief Gazetteer of the Island Barbarians, by Wang Ta-yüan 汪大渊 1349］ in *Hsüeh-t'ang ts'ung-k'o* 雪堂丛刻 ts'ê 10. Synthesizes modern critical work on an important Yüan text.

WU Han 吴晗, "Shih-liu shih-chi ch'ien chih Chung-kuo yü Nan-yang" 十六世纪前之中国与南洋 "China and South Sea Islands ［sic］ before 16th Century," *CHHP* 11 no. 1 （Jan. 1936）. 137-186.

YANAI Watari 箭内亘. *Tōyō tokushi chizu* 东洋读史地图 （Far Eastern Historical Atlas）, revised edition Tōkyō 1926.

YANO Jinichi 矢野仁一, （1） Biruma no Shina ni taisuru chōkō kankei ni tsuite 缅甸の支那に对する朝贡关系に就いて （On Burmese Tributary Relations with China）, *Tōyō Gakuhō* 东洋学报 17 （1928）. 1-39.

——（2） *Shina kindai gaikoku-kankei kenkyū* 支那近代外国关系研究 （A Study of Modern Chinese Foreign Relations）, Kyōto 1928. This volume is centered upon Ming and Ch'ing relations with the Portuguese and discusses each of their embassies.

*Yü-kung pan-yüeh k'an* 禹贡半月刊"The Chinese Historical Geography, Semimonthly Magazine" （Peiping 1934-1937）. A chief repository of recent Chinese research on its subject, containing articles too numerous to list here. Cf. in particular vol. 6 no. 8-9 （Jan. 1, 1937）, a special research number on the South Sea area 南洋研究专号.

For Chinese works not in this list see above under section 7.

# APPENDIX 2

A note to page 194.

With the lists of tributaries from the Ch'ing editions of the *Hui-tien* may be compared certain others:

(1) a list of 57 tribes or states given by HUNG Liang-chi in his *Ch'ien-lung fu-t'ing-chou-hsien t'u-chih* (see under section 7 above), ch. 50;

(2) a list of 31 tributaries in the Ch'ien-lung edition of the *Ta-ch'ing i-t'ung chih* (completed 1764), 353-356;

(3) a list of 43 such places in the revised edition of this gazetteer, *Chia-ch'ing ch'ung-hsiu i-t'ung chih* (covering material to 1820), 550-560; and

(4) a list of 32 tributaries in the *Ch'ing t'ung-k'ao* (covering the period from the beginning of the Ch'ing to 1785), 293-300. We take HUNG Liang-chi's list as a framework because it is both analytically arranged and the most extensive.

Key: O＝not listed, ＋＝listed, * ＝not in the lists of six editions of the *Hui-tien* given above.

| 1. HUNG Liang-chi | 2. I-t'ung chih (1764) | 3. I-t'ung chih (Chia-ch'ing) | 4. Ch'ing t'ung-k'ao |
|---|---|---|---|
| **EASTERN BORDER:** | | | |
| Korea (Chao-hsien) | ＋ | ＋ | ＋ |
| Liu-ch'iu | ＋ | ＋ | ＋ |
| Japan | ＋ | ＋ | ＋ |
| Sulu | ＋ | ＋ | 0 |
| Marinduque? (Ho-mao-wu) | (Ho-mao-li) | ＋ | 0 |
| * Molucca | ＋ | ＋ | 0 |
| Brunei (P'o-li, Wên-lai) | ＋ | ＋ | 0 |

| | 1. HUNG Liang-chi | 2. I-t'ung chih (1764) | 3. I-t'ung chih (Chia-ch'ing) | 4. Ch'ing t'ung-k'ao |
|---|---|---|---|---|
| SOUTHERN AND SOUTHEASTERN BORDER: | | | | |
| Annam (An-nam) | | + | (Yüeh-nan) | (An-nan) |
| Laos (Nan-chang) | | + | + | + |
| * Kuang-nan | | 0 | + | + |
| Burma (Mien-tien) | | 0 | + | + |
| * Hu-lu | | 0 | + | + |
| * Chêng-ch'ien | | 0 | + | 0 |
| * Ching-hai | | 0 | 0 | 0 |
| Siam | | + | + | + |
| Chiang-k'ou (Siam?) | | 0 | + | + |
| Cambodia (Tung-pu-chai) | | 0 | (Chien-pu-chai) | + |
| Sungora | | 0 | + | 0 |
| Johore | | 0 | + | + |
| Achin | | 0 | + | 0 |
| Philippines (Lü-sung) | | + | + | + |
| Mang-chün-ta-lao | | 0 | 0 | 0 |
| Java (Ka-la-pa) | | (Chao-wa) | (Ka-la-pa) | + |
| I-ta-li-ya | | 0 | 0 | + |
| Portugal (Po-erh-tu-ka-erh-ya) | | 0 | 0 | + |
| Portugal (Fo-lang-chi) | | + | 0 | + |
| Western Ocean | | + | + | 0 |
| Lambri | | + | + | 0 |
| Champa | | + | + | 0 |
| Cambodia (Chên-la) | | + | 0 | 0? |
| Brunei (P'o-ni) | | + | + | 0 |
| * Billiton | | + | + | 0 |
| Palembang (San-fo-ch'i) | | + | 0 | 0 |
| WESTERN AND NORTHWESTERN BORDER: | | | | |
| * Eastern Burut | | 0 | 0 | + |
| * Western Burut | | 0 | 0 | + |
| * Andijan | | 0 | 0 | + |
| Badakshan | | 0 | 0 | + |
| * Bolor | | 0 | 0 | + |

| 1. HUNG Liang-chi | 2. I-t'ung chih (1764) | 3. I-t'ung chih (Chia-ch'ing) | 4. Ch'ing t'ung-k'ao |
|---|---|---|---|
| **WESTERN AND NORTHWESTERN BORDER:** | | | |
| * Afghanistan | 0 | 0 | + |
| Bengal (Pang-ka-la) | + | + | 0 |
| Syria (Fu-lin) | + | + | 0 |
| Calicut | + | + | 0 |
| Cochin | + | + | 0 |
| Ceylon | + | + | 0 |
| Chola (Hsi-yang-so-li) | + | + | 0 |
| * Wên-tu-ssŭ-t'an | 0 | 0 | 0 |
| * K'ung-ka-erh | 0 | 0 | 0 |
| England | 0 | + | + |
| Portugal (Kan-ssŭ-la) | 0 | 0 | + |
| Holland | + | + | + |
| Sweden | 0 | + | + |
| Denmark | 0 | + | + |
| * Tashkent (following Badakshan) | 0 | 0 | + |
| **NORTHERN BORDER:** | | | |
| * Russia | + | + | + |
| * Turgut | + | 0 | 0 |
| "Eastern Kirghiz | 0 | 0 | + |
| * Western Kirghiz | 0 | 0 | + |
| 0 | Yarkand (Yeh-êrh-ch'in, Moslems) | 0 | 0 |
| 0 | Samudra (Su-mên-ta-la) | 0 | 0 |
| 0 | 0 | Pahang | + |
| 0 | 0 | * Banjermassin (Ma-ch'ên) | 0 |
| 0 | 0 | Trengganu | 0 |
| 0 | 0 | Malacca (Ma-liu-chia) | 0 |
| 0 | 0 | Palembang | 0 |
| 0 | 0 | France | 0 |

It is apparent that even officially published lists of tributaries had no fixed membership. Since countries that made contact by trade almost necessarily attained a nominal tributary status, such lists are of greater value for economic than for political history. Yet even for this purpose they hark back so plainly to the bygone glories of the Ming (e. g. Ceylon, Chola, Calicut) that their value is dubious.

**NOTES**:

①We are indebted to Prof. C. S. GARDNER for assistance on several points, particularly regarding the table of Western embassies in part 5. This article, like its predecessors, is intended to deal with administrative problems of importance for the study of Chinese foreign relations in the nineteenth century. Cf. J. K. FAIRBANK and S. Y. TÊNG, *On the Transmission of Ch'ing Documents*, HJAS 4. 12-46; On the Types and Uses of Ch'ing Documents, *ibid*., 5. 1-71.

②For this long bibliographical note, including the abbreviations used in notes, see appendix 1 of this article.

③*Ta-ming hui-tien* 大明会典 or *Ta-ch'ing hui-tien* 大清会典; the various editions are cited hereafter by the reigns in which they were issued, chronologically as follows:

*Wan-li hui-tien* (*Ta-ming hui-tien*, preface dated 1587),

*K'ang-hsi hui-tien* (*Ta-ch'ing hui-tien*, published 1690),

*Yung-chêng hui-tien* (preface 1732),

*Ch'ien-lung hui-tien*, and *Ch'ien-lung hui-tien tsê-li* (both completed 1764),

*Chia-ch'ing hui-tien*, and *Chia-ch'ing hui-tien shih-li* (both completed 1818),

*Kuang-hsü hui-tien*, and *Kuang-hsü hui-tien shih-li* (both pub. 1899).

④Satisfactory equivalents of certain key terms are not easily established. Fan 藩 (fence, boundary, frontier) as used with reference to countries outside China has a connotation somewhere in between "foreign" and "barbarian"; we have usually used the gentler term.

Man, I, Jung, and Ti 蛮夷戎狄 in conjunction refer to the barbarians of the south, east, west, and north, respectively; but I serves also as a generic term for all barbarians together (Cf. *Wên-hsien t'ung-k'ao* 324. 4). The term Ssŭ-i 四夷 (lit. "Four barbarians") is a collective term for the various barbarians dwelling in the four quarters of the compass on the periphery of the civilized world of which China was the center. It therefore indicates the barbarians in general—all the barbarians, not those of any particular places. BRUNNERT 392 is in error in translating Hui T'ung Ssǔ I Kuan 会同四译(for 夷)馆 as "Residence for Envoys of the Four Tributary States; here were domiciled Envoys from Korea, Siam, Tonkin, and Burma..."

Under the Ming the Ssǔ I Kuan had had charge of relations both with the barbarians of the north and west and with those of the east and south, there being no Li Fan Yüan (see sec. 3). Thus the *Ssǔ-i-kuan k'ao* 四夷馆考 (Lo Chên-yü ed., 1924) records relations with the Mongols, Samarkand, Turfan, Tibet, Hami, etc., and also with Champa, Japan, Java, Burma, and the like.

⑤YANO (2) 151-180 summarizes numerous Chinese and Western references to the subject.

It should be emphasized that the relationship to the Son of Heaven expressed by the kotow was shared by all mankind, Chinese and barbarian alike. The highest dignitaries of the empire performed this ceremony on appropriate occasion—as did the emperor himself when paying reverence to Heaven (pai-t'ien 拜天). The kotow performed unilaterally, on the other hand, expressed an inferiority of status in the universal order, without which there could be no order. It was therefore appropriate, honorable, and indeed good manners when performed in the right context. Other contexts might require less elaborate ceremonies, such as one kneeling and three prostrations. Strictly speaking, this was also a "knocking of the head," k'o-t'ou 磕头. For clarity we suggest the term "full kotow" for three kneelings and nine prostrations, (theoretically) knocking the head upon the ground, san-kuei chiu-k'ou li 三跪九叩礼; "modified kotow" for three kneelings and nine reverences bowing the head over the hands upon the ground, san-kuei chiu-pai li; and "single kotow" or "double kotow" for one-third or two-thirds, respectively, of the full kotow—i-kuei san-k'ou li, êrh-kuei liu-k'ou li.

This universal order of ceremony which expressed the order of all mankind may be illustrated by the following random references to the *Ta-Ch'ing t'ung-li* (chüan 42 chün-li, military ceremonial): in the ceremony of announcing the sacrifices, the emperor performed the modified kotow (4b). On receiving a seal indirectly from the emperor, a generalissimo (Ta Chiang Chün; cf. B 658: Field Marshal) and his staff performed the full kotow (12b). In another ceremony, they and the princes and high ministers of state followed the emperor in the modified kotow (21). The princes and ministers later performed one kneeling and one prostration (i-kuei i-k'ou li), and again one head-knocking from their seats 各于坐次行一叩礼 (21b). When a Mongolian prince met a prince of the imperial Manchu clan, they both performed a double kotow (Ch. 46 pin-li, ceremonial for guests. 1). Officials at the capital and in the provinces saluted each other with three formal bows (5, 11, 15 san-i 三揖; cf. GILES 5394 tso-i 作揖 "to make a salute by bending the body until the hands touch a little below the knees, and then rising and raising the hands to the level of the eyebrows"). To a superior official, a single kotow might also be used, perhaps followed by three bows (14b, 16b, 17). Bows and similar formalities were also prescribed for apprentices, friends, and relatives (20-21). In all these, the prescriptions regarding precedence in entering doors and directions faced in sitting were equally detailed.

It should be noted a. that all ceremonies between individuals were reciprocal in the sense that both parties took part; b. that the ceremonial for barbarian visitors (chüan 45, pin-li) was an integral part of the whole body of ceremonial just referred to. Egalitarian Westerners were ill-prepared to maintain their proper status, or any other, in this system of rites.

⑥Various aspects of the rationale of tribute have been eloquently set forth by T. C. LIN (2), and its general background by Owen LATTIMORE, *Inner Asian Frontiers of China*, New York, 1940.

⑦Sir Henry YULE, revised by H. CORDIER, *Cathay and the Way Thither*... (4 vols. London 1913-1916) 4. 235, 242, 243 n. For other examples cf. GROENEVELDT 4-5, DUYVENDAK (1) 74 n., (2) 378-379. CHANG Hsing-lang 张星烺 [*Chung-hsi chiao-t'ung shih-liao hui-p'ien* 中西交通史料汇编 (Miscellaneous Historical Materials on Sino-Western Relations), vol. 5, p. 534] states that the Kansu governor reported in 1502 that there were more than 150 self-styled rulers (wang) trading from the Western Regions; cf. *Ming-shih* 332. 6 (T'ung-wên shu-chü ed. 1894).

⑧T. F. TSIANG (CHIANG T'ing-fu 蒋廷黻), "China and European Expansion" (*Politica* 2 no. 5, Mar. 1936, pp. 1-18), pp. 3-4. A lecture delivered at the London School of Economics.

⑨*Ta-Ming chi-li* (Palace edition, 1530). We quote from the first two or three pages, respectively, forming general introductions (tsung-hsü 总序) to ch. 30-32 (pin-li 宾礼 Ceremonial for Visitors 1-3).

⑩Wang-hui 王会, forming chüan 7 in the *I chou shu* 逸周书; cf. Kuang han-wei ts'ung-shu 广汉魏丛书, 1592 edition, ts'ê 34-36.

⑪Cf. *Chou Li* 周礼, Hsiang-hsi 象胥 38. 14b (in Shih-san-ching chu-su 十三经注疏, Kiangsi edition, 1815) (BIOT 2. Kiu 34. fol. 26-27).

⑫Cf. *Ch'ien Han shu*（Palace edition，1739）94 sec. B. 3b. Established as chieftain 58 B. C.，*ibid*. sec. A. 37. The name is given here as Chi-hou-shan；likewise in *K'ang-hsi tzǔ-tien* 康熙字典 under 狲.

⑬Kan-ch'üan kung 甘泉宫，a summer palace in Shensi，N W. of Ch'ang-an，dating from the time of the First Emperor，cf. GILES（*A Chinese-English Dictionary*，1912）5823.

⑭Ta hung lu 大鸿胪，cf. Hung Lu Ssǔ 鸿胪寺，Court of State Ceremonial in T'ang and Ch'ing，B 935；KUWABARA 7. 14 refers to it as "the office of foreign affairs."

⑮世见 Cf. *Chou li* 大行人 Ta hsing jên 37. 20：世壹见（BIOT 2. 406：En un siècle ou dans un age d'homme，ils doivent une visite a l'empéreur）.

⑯Kuan 馆，standing for Hui T'ung Kuan 会同馆. This refers of course to the Hui T'ung Ssǔ I Kuan 会同四译（or 夷）馆 under the Board of Ceremonies，rather than to the Hui T'ung Kuan（Imperial Despatch Office，MAYERS 182 Ⅹⅳ）under the Board of War；but it presents a typical problem of translation—the reference being known to all，what English words shall be generally used for it? BRUNNERT 392 gives Residence for Envoys of the Four Tributary States，an erroneous interpretation as noted above（note 4）. CHANG Tê-ch'ang 273 uses the romanization Hui-tung-kwan，without attempting a translation，but this otherwise sound procedure involves in this case ambiguity with the office above mentioned under the Board of War. T. C. LIN（2）879 offers Cosmopolitan Palaces，which is sound in meaning but perhaps a bit flamboyant. CHANG T'ien-tsê 50 sidesteps the problem of translating Hui T'ung Kuan by using Ssǔ-i-kuan；this is no solution for the non-sinological reader. In order to conform as closely as possible to the chief manual now available（BRUNNERT）we suggest Residence for Tributary Envoys.

DUYVENDAK（3）45-49 uses "lodginghouse" but not as an official title，and agrees that LIN has "rather overtranslated." Prof. DUYVENDAK also describes（from the *Chia-ch'ing hui-tien shih-li*）some seven locations of establishments used to house embassies at various dates，all nominally under or part of the Hui T'ung Kuan，a title which therefore cannot easily be associated with one particular place.

⑰*Ta-Ming chi-li* 30. 1-2b.

⑱Cf. *Chou Li*，Hsiao hsing jên 37. 24（BIOT 2.411）.

⑲金齿 chin-ch'ih，lit. gold teeth，Laos or Shan tribes who gilded their teeth.

⑳拂郎 GILES 3659 identifies this with Fu-lin 拂菻，now recognized as the Eastern

Roman Empire or Syria.

㉑ *Ta-Ming chi-li* 31. 1-3.

㉒ *Ibid*. 32. 1-3.

㉓ Cf. *Wan-li hui-tien* 58, 8b line 9: "Reception by a foreign country of a seal and goods... the foreign king and his officials in a body all kneel. The envoy proclaims the imperial Decree, reading, 'His Majesty the Emperor commands his envoy—(to be filled in by name) to take a seal and confer it on your country's king—and also confer— goods.' When this proclamation is finished, the envoy holds up in both hands the seal which is conferred and the—goods, and facing the west gives them to the foreign king. The foreign king kneels and receives them, and gives them to his attendants. When this is finished, the ceremonial conductor (yin-li 引礼) calls out, 'Fall prostrate; rise (to a kneeling position); get up.' The official usher calls out the same (commands). The foreign king and his officials in a body all fall prostrate, rise (to a kneeling position), and get up..." etc. PAUTHIER 14-22 gives a not impeccable but useful translation of *Ta-ch'ing t'ung-li* 大清通礼 (edition 1756) ch. 43 on tributary ceremony in general.

㉔ The *Collected Statutes* open as follows (*Wan-li hui-tien* 105. 80, in ts'ê 7): "Reception Department: the Directors, Assistant Directors, and Second Class Secretaries share the charge of matters connected with the various barbarians' presentation of tribute at Court, and their entertainment and the bestowal of gifts upon them. They select their interpreters and attendants, and make known to them the prohibitory regulations. They also have control over gifts made, by imperial grace to the various officials (of the empire) and the tribute of local produce from the various provinces. "Court tribute (ch'ao-kung): at the beginning of the dynasty the Court tribute (i. e. presented at Court) of the various foreign countries and of the tribal officials among the barbarians was clearly recorded in the *Administrative Duties* [chih-chang 职掌 for *Chu-ssŭ chih-chang* 诸司职掌 (Administrative duties of the various offices), the first work listed in the bibliography given in *Wan-li hui-tien*, ts'ê 1, preceding chüan 1]. Thereafter those who longed to be transformed (i. e. civilized, mu-hua chê 慕化者) multiplied, the cases and precedents daily increased, and the Tribal Officials Office (t'u-kuan ya-mên) was set up. For this, see under the Board of War; matters concerning Court tribute are appended here.

"Barbarians of the east and south, part one: see the *Ancestral Instructions* [tsu-hsün 祖训, for *Huang-Ming tsu-hsün* 皇明祖训, another work listed in the bibliography just noted] and the *Administrative Duties*; there are altogether twenty countries. The *Ancestral Instructions* enumerate the unconquered barbarians as follows: Korea (Kao-li), Japan, Great and Small Liu-ch'iu, Annam, Cambodia, Siam, Champa, Samudra, Western Ocean (Hsi-yang), Java, Pahang, Pai-hua (Po-hua?), Palembang, Brunei—altogether fifteen countries. In the *Administrative Duties* there are also recorded the countries of Chola, Western Ocean Chola, Lan-pang, Tan-pa, Samudra—which is a bit different from the *Ancestral Instructions*." The *Statute* continues from here as quoted in note 26.

㉕*Wan-li hui-tien* 105-108. For comparative purposes we take this list from the *Ming hui-tien* as the most exact available description of the situation in 1587, a century before the first edition of the *Ta-Ch'ing hui-tien* in 1690. It may be compared with the quite similar list given in the *Ming History*, ch. 320-332, a survey of which was published by BRETSCHNEIDER in 1876 et seq. (see appendix 1).

㉖ This fact is indicated by indirection in the opening passages of the *Collected Statutes*: "At the beginning of the Hung-wu period (1368-1398) various envoys were sent with imperial proclamations to go and announce them to the various barbarians, with a view to establishing peace over the four seas (i. e. all the world). Frequently there were accompanying envoys (with the imperial envoys, on their return) who came to Court to present tribute. In 1375 it was imperially ordered that Annam, Korea, and Champa should send tribute to Court every three years, and when a king in those countries succeeded to the throne then the heir-apparent should appear (at Court). During the Yung-lo period (1403-1424) on several occasions there were troubles in the Western Ocean and (the emperor) sent palace (i. e. eunuch) envoys with 30,000 seamen, taking gold and silks to bestow them as imperial gifts. There were sixteen envoys who accompanied (the Chinese, on their return) to present tribute at Court."

Nothing further is said concerning tribute presented during the century and a half which had preceded the publication of the *Wan-li hui-tien*.

㉗ In the *Collected Statutes* most events are dated by year only. The lunar Chinese year overlaps the Gregorian by about 34 days, say 10%. It follows that on the average one in ten of the year dates given in the *Collected Statutes* will represent a time (in the Western month of January) which is really in the succeeding year.

㉘ "Court Tribute, part three: Northern barbarians. Of the northern barbarians, the Tatars (ta-ta, Tartars) are the largest. Since the Mongolian Yüan (Dynasty) retired into the Gobi, the remaining troublemakers for generations have called (themselves) Khans (k'o-han, kagan). On the east is Urianghai, on the west Hami, on the north Wa-la. The Wa-la (Oirats) became strong and several times defeated the Tatars. Thereafter Urianghai and Hami both tendered their allegiance. But Urianghai was then divided to form the three (military) districts of To-yen, etc. (i. e. To-yen, Fu-yü, and T'ai-ning). The chief of the Wa-la, Ma-ho-mu 马哈木, was invested as Prince of Shun-ning 顺宁. The Tatar chief of the Altai offered his allegiance and was invested as Prince of Ho-ning 和宁. Both sent envoys to present tribute. Thereafter they were rebellious and submissive in an uncertain manner. In the Ch'êng-hua period (1465-1487) the small princes also sent tribute. The tribute was without a fixed period. In the Lung-ch'ing period (1567-1572) Anda 俺达 was invested as Prince of Shun-i 顺义. Every year he sends a tribute of horses and has traded (with China) to the present time uninterruptedly. The small princes extending toward the north (are as follows): The three princes of the Wa-la, [tribute begun 1403; annual, with interruptions, from 1458], the Prince of Shun-i [tribute annual from 1570], the districts of To-yen, Fu-yü, and T'ai-ning [1388, tribute twice a year from 1403]. The northeastern barbarians are as follows: [Jurchen et al., tribute irregular because of distance]. On the west of the sea (is) Chien-chou [annual tribute]."

BRETSCHNEIDER 2. 159-173 gives an extensive critical account of the same subject-matter drawn from the *Ming History*, and a similar account appears in *JA* ser. 9, vol. 7 (1896). 173-179.

㉙With this list from the *Hui-tien* of 1587 may be compared that given in the (pre-Ming) *Wên-hsien t'ung-k'ao* 文献通考 ch. 324-332, which includes a total of 97 barbarian places or peoples. The Ch'ing supplement to this work (*Ch'ing-ting hsü wên-hsien t'ung-k'ao*), ch. 239-250, the compilation of which was ordered in 1747, in a corresponding section lists some 125 places or peoples; this is chiefly for the Ming period and a great number of the entries are for aboriginal or border tribes or places really within the confines of nineteenth century China.

Another work, the *Ta-ming i-t'ung chih* 大明一统志 ch. 89-90—used by BRETSCHNEIDER—gives a list of 56 tributaries, all of which are included in the list given above. BRETSCHNEIDER 2. 176-315 chiefly from the *Ming History* sections on foreign countries (*Ming-shih wai-kuo chüan*, ch. 329-332), lists 43 tributaries plus 38 smaller places (29 via Hami) all of which had intercourse with China from the west by land; a score of these are not in the list above, half of them being very obscure items.

㉚PELLIOT (1) 317 n. states that all the South Sea embassies in the period of the Ming expeditions were recorded in the *Ming-shih pên-chi*. In the case of Central Asian embassies the *Hui-tien* seems to refer to some not recorded in the *Pên-chi*. This is not unexpected, judged by the example of the Ch'ing records analyzed in part 6. On the other hand nearly all the references to 15th century embassies from Java and Champa collected by FERRAND 14. 5-11 are included in the *Ming History*.

㉛The annals (Chung-hua shu-chü edition) list some 36 tributaries arriving in the period 1369-1404, some 55 in the period 1405-1433, some 16 in 1434-1500, and some 14 in the long period 1500-1643.

㉜In the sixth month of 1638; cf. *Li-tai chih-kuan piao* 历代职官表 (Table of Offices and Officials of Successive Dynasties), compiled by CHI Chün 纪昀 et al., Kuang-ya shu-chü 广雅书局 edition, 17.5.

㉝Although the term "Colonial" seems unfortunate, we favor the translation of BRUNNERT (a) because some sort of translation is necessary for non-sinologists and (b) for the sake of conformity to a manual of titles. MAYERS 183 gives a descriptive translation, "The Mongolian Superintendency... which has sometimes been called the Colonial Office." P. HOANG, *Mélanges sur l'administration* (*Variétés sinologiques* no. 21, Chang-hai 1902) 135 gives a more literal version, "Cour suprême de l'administration des Vassaux." Dr. H. B. MORSE and many others have followed MAYERS. HSIEH Pao-chao (*The Government of China 1644-1911*, Balt. 1925) 322, under American influence, uses "Department of Territories."

㉞Here as everywhere the reader must remember that tribute was a *substitute* for more forceful domination, rather than an expression of such domination. In actual fact, as Owen LATTIMORE puts it, "control was by manipulation rather than by Decree" (*The Mongols of Manchuria*, N. Y. C. 1934, 50).

HSIEH Pao-chao, *op. cit.*, not only thoroughly misrepresents the nature of the tributary system (pp. 235-237) but also fails to indicate its use in the government of Mongolia and Tibet (pp. 321-341).

㉟*K'ang-hsi hui-tien* 142.

㊱*Ibid*., 143.1.

㊲*Ibid*., 142 *passim*.

㊳Owen LATTIMORE, *Inner Asian Frontiers of China* 90. The Li Fan Yüan kept a record of boundaries, with maps, of ranks and titles, and of genealogies, revised every decade; it conferred patents of nobility, enforced regulations of the sort mentioned above, and had a hand in marriages. Among other things it is provided that Mongols who have had smallpox are to be received in audience at Peking while those who have not had it, and therefore might carry it, are to be received in audience at Jehol. Cf. *Kuang-hsü hui-tien* 64. 10a. The *Huang-ch'ao fan-pu yao-lüeh* 皇朝藩部要略 (A General Survey of the Feudatory Tribes under the Reigning Dynasty) (18 chüan, piao 4 chüan, preface 1839, colophon 1845) gives a chronological summary of Edicts on these matters of administration.

㊴ *K'ang-hsi hui-tien* 143-144.

㊵ *Kuang-hsü hui-tien* 65. 4.

㊶ *Ibid.*, 65. 1.

㊷ *Ibid.*, 5b.

㊸ *Ibid.*, 4.

㊹ *Ibid.*, chüan 68.

㊺ Cf. *Kuang-hsü hui-tien* 67. 12b-13b: "Tribute from Tibet arrives at fixed intervals: Tibet (Hsi Tsang, i. e. central Tibet, Lhasa) once every year sends an envoy to present tribute. Anterior Tibet (Ch'ien Tsang, i. e. eastern Tibet) and Ulterior Tibet (Hou Tsang, i. e. western Tibet) each sends tribute once every third year... The Po-k'o-pa-la Living Buddha of Chamdo (eastern Tibet) sends an envoy to present tribute once every five years ... The Gurkha Erdeni King (King of Nepal) sends an envoy to present tribute once in five years ..." Officers are deputed to escort these tributary envoys, who are often abbots; their suites are limited in size but they are allowed to use the postal stations, for which purpose the Board of War issues tallies, and so on.

㊻ In the first two editions of the *Statutes* the Li Fan Yüan was divided into four departments, as follows: a. Department of Records of Merit (Lu Hsün Ch'ing Li Ssǔ 录勋清吏司), b. Department of Guests (Pin K'o 宾客), c. Department for Receiving Princes of Outer Mongolia (Jou Yüan 柔远, BRUNNERT. 495. 4; lit. "for gracious treatment of persons from afar"), d. Judicial Department (Li Hsing 理刑). In the third and later editions, that is, from 1764 on, there were six departments; these are named as follows in BRUNNERT 495. 1-6, where further details may be found: a. Department of the Inner Mongols, b. of the Outer Mongols, c. for Receiving Princes of Inner Mongolia, d. for Receiving Princes of Outer Mongolia, e. Department of Eastern Turkestan, f. Judicial Department. There were in addition a Treasury, a Mongol Translation Office, a Tangut Studies Office, Inspectors, Secretaries, a Chancery, and so on. For the nineteenth century the Mongol tribes and banners may be tabulated as follows (for details see BRUNNERT pp. 442-464, which, however, omits a simple synoptic table such as this):

| AREA | TRIBES | BANNERS |
|---|---|---|
| Inner Mongolia (So. of the Gobi) ································ | 24 | 49 |
| Outer Mongolia (across the Gobi) ································ | 6 | 86 |
| Kokonor (Ch'ing Hai Mongolia) (Kukunor) ···················· | 5 | 28 |
| Kobdo (between the Altai and the T'ien Shan, Oelots, Durbets, etc.) ················································ | 11 | 34 |
| Hami-Turfan (Moslems) ············································ | ... | 2 |

Cf. *Kuang-hsü hui-tien* 63-68 or, for details, *Ch'in-ting Li-Fan-Yüan tsê-li* 钦定理藩院则例 (1908 movable type edition, 64 chüan).

㊼See appendix 1.

㊽*K'ang-hsi hui-tien* 72 (Board of Ceremonies 33). 1-3b: "Reception Department: The Senior Secretaries, Second-class Secretaries, and Second-class Assistant Secretaries divide the charge of the barbarians that send tribute to the Court, the receiving and entertainment of them, and the bestowal of presents upon them. They examine their translated documents; they explain the prohibitory regulations, together with the Superintendent of the Residence for Tributary Envoys. All rewards bestowed upon officials and the local tribute of the various provinces are also under their control." (The general regulations then follow.)

㊾Nei Yüan 内院, presumably the Nei Mi Shu Yüan 内秘书院, one of the Nei San Yüan 内三院, in charge of correspondence with foreign countries.

㊿*Ibid*. *Yung-chêng hui-tien* 104. 1-3b, aside from minor textual changes, is practically identical in connect with *K'ang-hsi hui-tien* 72. 1-3b, only one or two items having been added; the chief difference is that the earlier edition presents the material chronologically, the later edition under topic headings.

(51)*K'ang-hsi hui-tien* 73. 12-14b.

(52)乌林人, a transliteration of the Manchu title for K'u Shih 库使 Treasury Overseers. For this information we are indebted to Mr. S. POLEVOY.

(53)*K'ang-hsi hui-tien* 73. 12-14b.

(54)*Ch'ien-lung hui-tien* 56. 1-8b.

(55)The practice of the ceremonies is charmingly described in Prof. DUYVENDAK'S long article. (3) "The Last Dutch Embassy to the Chinese Court (1794-1795)."

(56)*Ch'ien-lung hui-tien* 56. 8b-11. Cf. *Wan-li hui-tien* 109. 99b; *K'ang-hsi hui-tien*73. 14b; YANO (2) 133-150.

⑤⑦Cf. *Chia-ch'ing hui-tien* 52 (Li Fan Yüan). 23. The Imperial Agent at Urga was in charge of frontier affairs concerning Russia and correspondence with the Russian "Senate" (sa-na-t'ê ya-mên 萨那特衙门).

⑤⑧See appendix 2: Additional lists of Ch'ing tributaries.

⑤⑨On the treatment of Europeans as tributaries in the Ming period see the study of the *Ming History* by CHANG Wei-hua.

⑥⓪*K'ang-hsi hui-tien* 72. 12-14.

⑥①For a list of western envoys to China, see table 4. Cf. ROCKHILL (4)437-442, for a brief account of the Dutch Embassy of 1656.

⑥②See table 4, for this and later names inserted in text.

⑥③Plainly the same person as above, but here given entirely different characters, which are different again in the Yung-chêng edition 104. 30b line 6.

⑥④This is in conflict with Prof. PELLIOT'S statement (4) 424 that SALDANHA "mourut en revenant à Macao, à la fin de 1670 ou dans le courant de 1671." Note that this case was treated according to the regulation translated above, following note 49.

⑥⑤*K'ang-hsi hui-tien* 72. 12-14.

⑥⑥*Ch'ien-lung hui-tien* 56.

⑥⑦A great mass of material, on the subjects touched upon in the regulations translated above, is included in the *Hui-tien tsê (shih)-li*; cf. *Kuang-hsü hui-tien shih-li* 502-514, 219, 251, 307. DUYVENDAK (3) illustrates the great possibilities of this material (also JAMIESON 99-109, but quite unreliably).

⑥⑧*Chia-ch'ing hui-tien* 31. 2-4; except where otherwise noted, this text reads the same as *Kuang-hsü hui-tien* 39. 2-3.

PAUTHIER (*Histoire* 178-182) published various extracts from this chüan in 1859. JAMIESON in 1883 in the *China Review*, 12. 96-98, published a very rough translation of this passage, which was made without benefit of PAUTHIER'S work, omitted or confused a number of passages, and failed in many identifications. DUYVENDAK (3)52 translates the main headings given in *Kuang-hsü hui-tien* 39, but not this passage.

⑥⑨Ch'ih-fêng 敕封 which we translate as "appoint by imperial command," and ch'ih-yü 敕谕, "command-edict," used for Laos and Sulu, both appear to correspond in a general way to the conferring of "letters patent" in the west. We avoid the Western term because it would over-simplify the Chinese situation.

⑦⓪Unidentified.

(71)Note that appointment is conferred on the rulers of Laos and of Sulu by a less exalted form of document (ch'ih-yü).

(72)This section was omitted from the Kuang-hsü edition.

(73)Evidently refers to preliminary correspondence regarding the embassy of 1656, cf. the K'ang-hsi account translated above.

(74) Omitted from Kuang-hsü edition. Paragraphing inserted by us under this heading.

(75)All this section was omitted from the Kuang-hsü edition.

(76)天堂. HSÜ Chi-yü's atlas of 1848, *Ying-huan chih-lüeh* 1. 15b (map), in a highly abstract manner shows Nagasaki behind an island, evidently the Goto Archipelago; the southern entrance so formed is labelled Wu-tao mên, "Goto Archipelago entrance," and the northern is labelled T'ien-t'ang mên.

(77)七洲大洋. FUJITA (WANG 66) identifies Ch'i-chou as the Paracel Is. off the east coast of Indo-China. *Hai-kuo wên-chien lu* 41b (map) shows 七洲洋 off the southeast tip of the Indo-Chinese peninsula. Perhaps this phrase should be taken as the "great ocean of the Paracels."

(78)鲁万山. Lu Wan Shan, according to the *Hai-lu* 1. 1, is the same as Wan Shan, a mountainous island in the sea outside Canton which served as the navigator's final landmark on the voyage home. *Hai-kuo wên-chien lu* 2. 55 (map) shows Lao Wan Shan 老万山 in the sea south of Lintin Is. between the present Hongkong and Macao.

(79)The reference to the official resumption of trade with southeast Asia about 1729 adds one more question to the many that already present themselves concerning administrative reforms in the Yung-chêng period. The era 1723-1735 stands out as one of reorganization along many lines, and deserves intensive study.

(80)在台湾风山沙马崎东南. *Hai-kuo wên-chien lu* 1. 60 (map of T'ai-wan) shows Fêng-shan on the west coast near the south tip and Sha-ma-ch'i-t'ou 沙马崎头 at the south tip; WADA 153-154 (quoting *T'ai-wan-fu chih*) gives Sha-ma-chi-t'ou shan 沙马矶头山 as equivalent to the present Mao-pi-t'ou Cape.

(81)*Chia-ch'ing hui-tien* 31. 3-4.

(82)*Huang-Ch'ing chih-kung t'u* compilation imperially ordered 1751, Palace edition 1761, 9 chüan.

(83)*IWSM-TK* 73. 3b.

(84)*Ta-Ch'ing li-ch'ao shih-lu* 大清历朝实录, Tokyo (1937), 1220 vols. Cf. K. BIGGERSTAFF, Some Notes on the *Tung-Hua Lu* and the *Shih-Lu*, *HJAS* 4. 101-

115. Prof. BIGGERSTAFF 112 points out that even this collection is by no means complete in its coverage of Edicts.

⑧⑤ *Shih-i-ch'ao tung-hua lu* 十一朝东华录, compiled by WANG Hsien-ch'ien and P'AN I-fu (cf. BIGGERSTAFF *loc. cit.*), Kuang-pai-sung-chai 广百宋斋 edition, Shanghai 1891. Our copy of the *Ch'ing-shih kao* contains prefaces by CHAO Êrh-hsün dated 1927 and by CHIN Liang dated 1928, making it of the first or Peking edition [cf. C. H. PEAKE, A Comparison of the Various Editions of the *Ch'ing Shih Kao*, TP 35 (1940). 354-363].

⑧⑥ For example, CH'I Kun 齐鲲 and FEI Hsi-chang 费锡章, *Hsü Liu-ch'iu kuo chih-lüeh* 续琉球国志略 (Supplement to the Brief Gazetteer of Liu-ch'iu), latest date in text 1809, dated in Harvard catalogue 1808, in ch. 2 for the period 1757-1809 record tribute sent from Liu-ch'iu for ten years not recorded in our table; the latter, on the other hand, records tribute from Liu-ch'iu in six years not recorded in this work. Again, the *Yüeh-hai-kuan chih* 21.17-45 during the period 1665-1839 refers to the tributary activity of Siam in a score of years in which Siamese tribute is not recorded in our table, while the latter records tribute in a dozen years when this work does not. Some of these discrepancies may of course be explained by the difference in place of the variant observers; tribute recorded at Canton or Liu-ch'iu may have reached Peking in a different year or not at all.

⑧⑦ For the conduct of the Liu-ch'iu trade at Foochow, ten Chinese brokers were named for life, being collectively responsible for each other like the old Cohong at Canton. These monopolists similarly had a semi-official status, which was practically hereditary; they reported to the government on the trade and through their monopoly were able to profit extensively from it.

The procedure was described as follows: the tributary envoy from Liu-ch'iu on his arrival called on the taotai and financial commissioner of the province and was in turn given an entertainment, which the financial commissioner did *not* attend, the Marine Magistrate (Hai-fang?) usually doing the honors. He then handed in a list of the tribute presents and of the import cargo and the armament of his two vessels—which being approved, he started on his journey to Peking under official escort and his ships were allowed to break bulk. After examining the list of imports, the official brokers, each undertaking to dispose of a certain share of the total, would state to the Liu-ch'iu traders the prices they were prepared to give for imports and to demand for exports. The Liu-ch'iu traders on their part brought specie to cover the extra cost of their exports; this was in the form of small Japanese gold coins containing a good deal of alloy, which the Chinese brokers could easily transport to Canton or Soochow for sale if it could not be converted into sycee locally. The Liu-ch'iu traders' sole compensation while in the hands of the monopolists was the fact that they were freed from all official customs duties, although not from the unavoidable presents to Chinese officials.

The Liu-ch'iu trade flourished because at least one half of it was for re-export to Japan on the occasion of the annual Liu-ch'iuan tribute missions there, and goods were brought to Foochow from Liu-ch'iu on credit repayable in two to five months, after transfer of goods to the Japanese trade could be completed. Even though freed from customs duties, the Liu-ch'iu cargoes were not accurately reported to the Foochow customs; following "old custom" the same imports would be reported year after year with but slight variation, so that less than half the cargo was really reported, most of it being smuggled by the brokers with the knowledge of the authorities. The Consul suspected that this was done to obviate some statutory limit placed upon the size of the trade.

When the tributary envoy returned from Peking, all accounts were closed. The envoy again called on the financial commissioner and received another entertainment under the heading, says the Consul, of "tender mercies and hospitality to strangers from afar" which the Chinese were so fond of quoting. The envoy also received Tls. 500 from the financial commissioner to defray the expenses of his late journey to Peking. Finally as a parting ceremony, dressed in full Liu-ch'iu costume, he performed a grand kotow to the emperor on an elevated platform at the custom house, in gratitude for the exemption of his ships from duty.

The Liu-ch'iuans like all foreigners were classed as I, barbarians. At Foochow they were restricted to the suburbs, where the Residence for the Tributary Envoy was situated, and they were not allowed without authorization to enter the city walls or the interior. In 1851 the new King of Liu-ch'iu was still a minor, aged 17, his father having died two or three years before, and was due to be installed in his kingship in the following year (1852), when an imperial commissioner would be sent to Liu-ch'iu with an imperial document and presents of silks and satins. Customarily this high official was selected from Fukien and departed from Foochow with 500 picked troops in two large war junks. "It is calculated, what with presents to the Ambassador and his escort, their maintenance, and the cargo which the Loochooans are forced to purchase at heavy prices from the members of the Embassy, that it will cost Loochoo no less than thirty thousand Taels of silver."(Vice-consul SINCLAIR, Foochow, no. 26 to Sir George BONHAM, June 18, 1851, *British Consular Archives*, Foochow.)

(88)The existence of this great southern trade of Chinese junks from Canton and Amoy was recognized in the following passage in *Chia-ch'ing hui-tien* 31. 15 (omitted in Kuang-hsü edition), in a section listing native products of trading countries: "As to the various countries which are near the northwest, such as Portugal (Kan-ssŭ-la), Sweden, and Denmark, in all cases the barbarian merchants of those countries come to China (nei-ti) to trade. They come in summer and go back in winter. As to the various countries in the southeastern sea—Cambodia, Sungora, Johore, Trengganu, Achin, and so on—and the countries in the South Sea—the Philippines (Luzon) and others—in all cases the merchants of our own harbors of Kwangtung and the merchants of Chekiang and Fukien in the winter and spring go to these various countries to trade, and in summer and autumn then come back..."

(89)W. L. SCHURZ, *The Manila Galleon*, New York, 1939.

(90)This early Sino-Western commercial competition in Malaya is touched upon in an article by Prof. CHANG Tê-ch'ang 张德昌, Ch'ing-tai ya-p'ien chan-chêng ch'ien chih Chung-hsi yen-hai t'ung-shang 清代鸦片战争前之中西沿海通商 (Sino-Western Coastal Trade in the Ch'ing period before the Opium War), *CHHP* 10 (1935), 97-145.

(91)The length of one sea watch (kêng, Pek. ching) appears to be as uncertain as the length of one *li* on land. WANG Ta-hai (*Hai-tao i-chih*, see under section 7) 479 gives one watch as 50 *li* 每更五十里, while a nineteenth century source, YEH Ch'iang-yung (*Lü-sung chi-lüeh*) 3, states flatly that one ching is 100 *li* 凡海中记里，以一百里为一更. At this rate he figures 124 ching as 12,400 *li* and estimates the distances Shanghai-Ningpo as 12 ching, Ningpo-Amoy as 40, Amoy-Lü-sung as 72. For the Ming period 300 to 400 years earlier, however, MILLS 7 describes a "Kêng" (ching) or watch as 2. 4 hours in Chinese navigation; and WADA 152 states that one ching equalled 60 *li*, say 20 miles, 10 ching being covered in 24 hours with a favorable wind. These statements demand careful investigation of nineteenth century practice. MILLS' calculations are of course borne out by the facts.

MILLS 43 calculates that Chinese junks of the Ming period according to the sailing directions used by them appear to have traveled 2. 93 miles an hour in shore waters, and to have averaged 6. 25 miles an hour in open waters; whereas a modern junk might go at most 8. 5 miles an hour.

⑨²HSÜ Chi-yü's geography of 1848, 1. 23b, 2. 1b (maps of S. E. Asia), gives nearly all this list of places.

⑨³Communicated by C. E. WURTZBURG (originally enclosed in CORNWALLIS to DUNDAS, Jan. 7, 1789), *J. of the Malayan Branch of the R. A. S.*, vol. 16 part 1 (July 1938). 123-126.

⑨⁴Cf. the following passage from the *Hai-kuo wên-chien lu* (block print ed., preface 1730, 1. 25b; we quote SCHLEGEL'S translation in *TP* [1898]. 298): " South from Siam are Chaya, Lakon (Ligor) and Sungora which are all tributary states of Siam. Patani,Kelantan, Tringano, and Pahang all follow each other in succession along the (central) mountain ridge."

⑨⁵For a bibliography of Ming works on barbarian relations, cf. CHU Shih-chia 朱士嘉, Ming-tai ssŭ-i shu-mu 明代四裔书目, *Yü-kung* 5 no. 3-4 (April 11, 1936). 137-158.

⑨⁶Kenneth CH'ÊN, "Matteo Ricci's contribution to, and influence on, geographical knowledge in China," *JAOS* 59 (1939). 325-359; refers to a number of early Ch'ing works, several of which are included in the present list. For the original Chinese version of this article see CH'ÊN Kuan-shêng 陈观胜 in *Yü-kung* 5 no. 3-4. 51-72.

⑨⁷HUNG Wei-lien 洪煨莲 (William HUNG), K'ao Li-ma-tou ti shih-chieh ti-t'u 考利玛窦的世界地图 (A Study of the World-map of Matteo RICCI), *Yü-kung* 5. no. 3-4 (April 11, 1936). 1-50.

⑨⁸WANG Hsi-ch'i 王锡祺 *Hsiao-fang-hu-chai yü-ti ts'ung-ch'ao* 小方壶斋舆地丛钞 (Collected Copies of Works on Geography, from the Hsiao-fang-hu Study), preface dated 1877, type print, Shanghai; second supplement preface dated 1897. Contains a total of 1438 titles, including the two supplements, in 84 volumes (ts'ê), some 6000 pages. Cited later as *Hsiao-fang-hu-chai* with number of chih 帙, ts'ê, and page where possible.

⑨⁹Another important collection from which we cite several works is the *Chao-tai ts'ung-shu* 昭代丛书 originally compiled by CHANG Ch'ao 张潮, enlarged by YANG Fu-chi 杨复吉 and revised by SHÊN Mou-tê 沈楙德, first pub. 1697, revised ed,1833, reprinted 1876.

Several items in this list are also noted in A. WYLIE, *Notes on Chinese Literature* ... London 1867, with which our findings sometimes differ.

Since completing this article, we have seen the valuable contribution of Mr. Fêng-t'ien CHAO, "An Annotated Bibliography of Chinese Works on the First Anglo-Chinese War," *Yenching Journal of Social Studies*, 3 no. 1 (October 1940). 61-103, which gives further data concerning half a dozen of the items listed below.

⑩ (A study of the eastern and western ocean [routes]), 12 chüan, in the *Hsi-yin-hsien ts'ung-shu*, ts'ê 18-21.

# CHINA'S RESPONSE TO THE WEST
a documentary survey
1839-1923

# PREFACE TO THE 1979 EDITION

Since a quarter of a century ago when *China's Response to the West* was first published, the historical literature concerning its subject matter has increased several times over. To the extensive publication of documentary collections and monographs in Peking, Shanghai, and Taipei, including a notable series of studies from the Modern History Institute of Academia Sinica, there has been added a flood of scholarly work in Japanese and an equally large flow of publication in Western languages, especially in English. The bibliography of this subject has been completely transformed.

Yet the subject itself, including China's need to acquire Western technology in order to meet urgent problems, has not passed into the dustbin of history but has taken on a new vitality. Once again we need historical perspective, for today's programs for modernization in China echo in many ways the movement for self-strengthening of a hundred years ago. For such a comparison this volume is still the most representative collection of documents and commentary on the seminal era from 1839 to 1923. The persons and documents here dealt with are still of major significance.

This partly is because China's great social revolution of recent decades came to center stage only after 1923. In more skeptical terms, these documents have not yet become outdated by the establishment of a wholly new canon of documentation based on a radically new view of the period up to 1923. For example, the history of folk religious cults, of peasant protest, of the emancipation of women, of modern vernacular literature, of Chinese law, or of the Chinese experience overseas is just beginning to be exhumed from the record and newly appraised by pioneer researches. One could put together another entire volume dealing with this new growth of historical subject matter. But such additions, while bringing the broad picture of modern China more up to date in its overall proportions, would not make the present materials invalid or irrelevant.

As astute critics have pointed out, the concept of China's response to the West implies a theoretical acceptance of the sociobiological idea of stimulus (or challenge) and response popularized by Arnold Toynbee among others in his twelve-volume *A Study of History* (1934-1961); and such an approach seems to undervalue China's indigenous tradition and creativity—as if the Chinese people were passive recipients of a foreign impact and became active in revolutionary changes only because of it. We would agree that the stimulus/response concept has its limitations, not least because stimulus and challenge are vague and ambivalent terms which may mean either a stimulus subjectively felt or a consciously perceived challenge or even changed circumstances which historians in retrospect view as having been stimulating or challenging.

Those who read beyond the title of *China's Response to the West* will note, however, that we concluded at the beginning that "the terms 'stimulus' (or 'impact') and 'response' are not very precise. We are in danger of assuming that there was a previous 'Western impact' merely because there was later activity which we call a 'Chinese response.' This 'Chinese response' or activity is the thing we want to study, but it obviously was part of Chinese conduct as a whole. In other words, the Western impact was only one of many factors in the Chinese scene. The response to it can only be unscrambled with difficulty from Chinese history in general" (p. 283). In constructing the book, we therefore began with "Some elements in the Chinese intellectual tradition" as its first topic.

This volume ends with the preliminary acceptance of Marxism-Leninism as of 1923. But foreign influences—Soviet, Japanese, American, and others—have continued to affect Chinese history. The historian's task of unscrambling has grown with time. Chinese perceptions of the outer world and what to do about it must still be studied, but they are still only one strand in the great Chinese revolution of modern times.

Researchers among the Chinese sources in this field need a considerable apparatus of scholarly reference notes, guidance on sources, bibliographical listings of publications and a glossary of Chinese characters for names and terms used in the text. All these apparatuses were supplied in a companion volume entitled *Research Guide for "China's Response to the West"* (Harvard University Press, 1954, 84 pages).

If this book is of use today, it is because it was put together by a wide-ranging collaborative effort not only between the two principal authors but also between them and Chao-ying Fang, E-tu Zen Sun, and some thirty others mentioned in the Acknowledgments, who altogether represented most of the sinological scholarship available at the time in a rather small and still homogeneous field. At first, very bulky draft was circulated in 1950, representing the support of the Institute of Pacific Relations, which had not yet been destroyed in the McCarthyite furor of the early 1950s, and of the Humanities Division of the Rockefeller Foundation, which had already pioneered for twenty years in the promotion of Chinese studies in America. This reprinting of the 1961 edition may be taken therefore as a tribute to the foresight of William L. Holland of the Institute of Pacific Relations, David H. Stevens of the Foundation, and Mortimer Graves of the American Council of Learned Societies. The one of us born nearer at hand may also point out that this book is evidence of the broad indebtedness of American sinology to scholars of Chinese origin.

S. Y. T.<br>
J. K. F.<br>
March 1979

# ACKNOWLEDGMENTS

William L. Holland, Secretary general of the Institute of Pacific Relations, originally inspired this volume. Its completion has been aided by grants from the Institute and from the Humanities Division, Rockefeller Foundation. From its inception this has been a joint enterprise among a number of specialists in Chinese studies, whose contributions in varying degree have been so numerous and pervasive that detailed acknowledgment would require a statement more complex than a holding company's income tax return. We have been aided most tangibly in the process of production by Chao-ying Fang and E-tu Zen Sun, whose contributions have principally concerned the nineteenth and twentieth centuries, respectively. They are co-authors, though not to be held responsible for the final product. Knight Biggerstaff, E. R. Hughes, K. C. Liu, Earl Swisher, C. Martin Wilbur, and Mary C. Wright have contributed either manuscript materials or copious comments on the first draft, which was circulated in September 1950. For less extensive though similarly appreciated criticism and suggestions we are indebted among others to Banno Masataka, Theodore de Bary, Frank L. Benns, Eugene P. Boardman, Derk Bodde, Conrad Brandt, Ch'en Shou-yi, Kaiming Chiu, Martha Davidson, Immanuel C. Y. Hsu, William Hung, Marius Jansen, Joseph R. Levenson, Ralph Powell, Benjamin Schwartz, Kuan-wai So, Stanley Spector, T. H. Tsien, Hellmut Wilhelm, Karl A. Wittfogel, Arthur F. Wright, Lien-sheng Yang, and Zunvair Yue. In particular we wish to thank Dr. Hu Shih for helpful criticism of Chapter XXVI. We are immensely indebted to Ai-li Chin for expert help on the Bibliography and Glossary, to Rosamond Chapman for editorial assistance, and to Margaret Teng for preparing the index. For the mechanics of this work, see the companion volume.

*Note:* The companion volume, entitled *Research Guide for "China's Response to the West,"* has been published separately so that this main volume may be more easily available to interested readers. The *Research Guide for* "China's Response to the West" contains the brief reference notes corresponding to the numbers in the text, together with extensive discussions of sources, a full bibliography of Western, Chinese, and Japanese works, and a glossary of Chinese terms. All of these data, however, are prepared only for sinological specialists. Though such specialists are in our view an important national asset, they are unfortunately rather few in number, and the materials which we have compiled especially to assist their research are therefore published separately.

S. Y. T.
J. K. F.
September 1953

# REIGNS OF THE CH'ING DYNASTY

| | |
|---|---|
| Shun-chih | 1644-1661 |
| K'ang-hsi | 1662-1722 |
| Yung-chêng | 1723-1735 |
| Ch'ien-lung | 1736-1795 |
| Chia-ch'ing | 1796-1820 |
| Tao-kuang | 1821-1850 |
| Hsien-feng | 1851-1861 |
| T'ung-chih | 1862-1874 |
| Kuang-hsü | 1875-1908 |
| Hsuan-t'ung | 1909-1911 |

*A Note on Style of Translation.* Our first draft of September 1950 reproduced Chinese names literally, as given in the original sources—thus Ku Yen-wu was at times referred to by his other name, Ku T'ing-lin; Prince Kung by his personal name, I-hsin; or Tseng Kuo-fan by his posthumous name, Tseng Wen-cheng-kung. Similarly, Shanhaikuan, where the Great Wall meets the sea, when referred to by the single character *kuan* was translated as "the Pass (i. e. , Shanhaikuan)"; and we generally inserted parentheses around phrases implied by but not literally expressed in the Chinese original. This scholarly exactitude, while reassuring to other scholars for whom it was unnecessary, could only distract and bewilder the uninitiated general reader. To avoid perpetuating that sterile esotericism which has bedevilled the Chinese people and their Western students throughout history, we have now simplified the text. One man is cited by one name, not several. An emperor is known by his reign title, e. g. , K'ang-hsi. Our translations try to give the full meaning of the original, even if part of it was only implied by the context. *Square brackets* enclose material added by way of editorial explanation, including page numbers from the original text. *Capitalization* in translations is used to indicate the Chinese elevation (to the top of the next line) of characters referring to the emperor, the dynasty, and the like. *Dates* given for memorials are normally those on which they were seen by the emperor, i. e., later than the actual date of composition.

# 1 THE PROBLEM AND ITS BACKGROUND

## CHAPTER I  INTRODUCTION

This is a survey of one of the most interesting, but neglected, aspects of modern history—the way in which the scholar-official class of China, faced with the aggressive expansion of the modern West, tried to understand an alien civilization and take action to preserve their own culture and their political and social institutions.

Since China is the largest unitary mass of humanity, with the oldest continuous history, its overrunning by the West in the past century was bound to create a continuing and violent intellectual revolution, the end of which we have not yet seen. The traditional system of tribute relations between the ancient Chinese empire and the "outside barbarians," who had formed the rest of China's known world, came to an end with the Anglo-Chinese *Treaty of Nanking* in 1842. For a full century after 1842, China remained subject to a system of international relations characterized by the "unequal treaties" established by the Western powers, beginning with the *Treaty of Nanking*, and not formally abolished until 1943.

Throughout this century of the "unequal treaties," the ancient society of China was brought into closer and closer contact with the then dominant and expanding society of Western Europe and America. This Western contact, lent impetus by the industrial revolution, had the most disastrous effect upon the old Chinese society: In every sphere of social activity the old order was challenged, attacked, undermined, or overwhelmed by a complex series of processes—political, economic, social, ideological, cultural—which were set in motion within China as a result of this penetration of an alien and more powerful society.

The massive structure of traditional China was torn apart much as the earth's crust would be disrupted by a comet passing too near. In the end, the remnants of the old China—its dress and manners, its classical written language and intricate system of imperial government, its reliance upon the extended family, the Confucian ethic, and all the other institutional achievements and cultural ornaments of a glorious past—had to be thrown into the melting pot and refashioned. The old order was changed within the space of three generations.

The ancient Chinese society, which had grown and developed through four millennia as the world's most populous and in many ways most highly cultured state, has been remade within a few score years. Rapid change is nothing new to Westerners, but the rate of social change in modern China has exceeded anything we can imagine for it has included the collapse of old ways and the growth of new ways on a scale and at a tempo unprecedented in history.

### Modern China, a Problem in Understanding

The West may well be disconcerted to note that this strenuous century of modern Chinese contact has now finally resulted in the rise to power of Chinese Communism. Since this event is certainly the most portentous in the whole history of American foreign policy in Asia, every intelligent American must strive to understand its significance. Does the Chinese communist victory constitute, as it seems to some, a rejection of the West? Or is it, in a sense, a final step in accepting certain aspects of the West? Or again, is it merely the latest phase of a continuing process within the body of Chinese society? Final answers to such oversimplified questions cannot be expected. Evidence may be cited to support all three of these suggested interpretations and several more besides: the new order at Peking is nationalistically committed to rejecting all forms of inferiority to the West, such as the "unequal treaties"; it is a genuine and thus far

(1953) quite orthodox branch of the international communist movement, although few may wish to call that movement a proper form of "Western" influence; and it is at the same time obviously the climax of a revolutionary process long endemic in the Chinese body politic.

Underlying this book is the belief that modern China, including the communist rise to power there, can be understood only against the background of its contact with the West. A knowledge of China's growth as a traditional society is, of course, prerequisite. But the contemporary scene within the Middle Kingdom cannot be understood merely by reference to classical worthies like the Duke of Chou (*ca.* eleventh century B. C. ) or the philosophical maxims of Confucius (551-479? B. C. )and Mencius (390? - 305 B. C.) or the thought of a medieval scholar like Chu Hsi (A. D. 1130-1200). New forces are at work, induced by the modern experience of the Chinese people. The origin and growth of these forces can be studied only within the context of the century of Western influence. Nationalism, party dictatorship, the cult of the masses, the worship of technology, the leadership of youth, and the emancipation of women—all these are new elements inspired mainly by Western contact...

In spite of all the furor of change in recent decades, the hold of the past is still curiously strong in present-day China. Not far below the surface lies the ancient civilization of the Middle Kingdom, a subsoil which limits and conditions the new growth. Our efforts at analysis inevitably differentiate between the ancient Chinese heritage and modern Western influences. We assume that they each contributed, in varying degree, to the modern society which we knew up to 1949...Exactly how the heritage from the past and the influences from abroad have interacted within Chinese society during the last century is, of course, the nub of our problem. In many instances the conflict between traditional China and the West no doubt produced a stalemate. In the realm of law, for example, it might be argued (until such time as legal scholars apply themselves more fully to Chinese studies) that the impact of Western law served to undermine the Confucian ethic as a basis for administration and the achievement of social justice, without being able to take its place. It may be that the weakening of the ethical basis of the Confucian state was not compensated by a firm establishment of Western legal institutions, and that China has been left somewhere in between.

In this volume we study the period from 1839 to 1923 because it spans the century from the first arrival of the Western powers in force to the first acceptance of Marxism-Leninism. In 1839 Commissioner Lin Tse-hsü (1785-1850) strove to settle the opium problem by destroying the opium stocks of foreign merchants, thereby precipitating the showdown between China's ancient tributary system and the expanding power of Britain. In 1923 Sun Yat-sen (1866-1925), having already led a republican revolution which ended the ancient imperial system in 1911, finally adopted some of the methods (although not the creed) of the Russian Communists. Between these two leaders of their generations who appear at the opening and close of our period lies an enormous gulf, so vast that they would have had great difficulty in understanding each other's conversation. Commissioner Lin had been trained in the Confucian classics, Dr. Sun in Western medicine. Lin represented an imperial potentate whose dynasty was the twenty-ninth in succession to have its history recorded as ruling all or part of the Chinese empire since its first unification in 221 B. C. Sun had worked most of his life to destroy that empire. In the end, he accepted communist help only in order to create a regime adequate to take the empire's place.

Paradoxically, however, these two men exemplify the unity which underlies the amazing diversity of modern China's history. Both Lin, the old-style mandarin, and Sun, the modern revolutionist, were concerned with the government of the Chinese state. Both felt the Western stimulus and reacted strongly to it. Both were patriots. Like all other Chinese officials, scholars, and revolutionists who will be quoted in this book, they were vitally concerned with the fate of China, its civilization, and way of life. Behind all the variety of viewpoints, assumptions, analyses, and proposals put forward for China's salvation during this century of change and collapse there has been a cultural bond, a strong consciousness of China as an entity and of the Chinese people as a unit in history. "All-under-Heaven" (*T'ien-hsia*, the empire) and the "Middle Kingdom" (*Chung-kuo*, China) have remained primary concepts, starting points of the reformer's thinking. Thus the leadership of modern China in the period 1839-1923 remained ethnocentric and China-centered…

Any study of the acculturation of one society by another involves a number of independent variables. One must appraise and characterize the value systems or ideals of both societies, and this requires one to generalize upon a scale so broad as to be sometimes almost meaningless. The "American way of life" must be compared with the "Chinese way of life." Not only must the student of cultural miscegenation turn from one culture to the other, ambivalently, but he must also live in the past as well as the present, and appreciate the Confucianism of old China as well as the utilitarianism of Victorian England. This is a well-nigh impossible task at a time when we know so little of the actual content of life and thought in premodern China. But the attempt must be made, sooner or later, as best we can. The documents and commentaries in this volume are presented as a first step in this direction.

### Some Preliminary Definitions

Let us begin by clarifying certain concepts. First of all, it would be quite unrealistic to think of premodern or "traditional" China (or the "Confucian state") as archaic and static, backward and unchanging. Chinese society has always been in a process of change, older values and institutions giving way gradually to newer ideals and forms. Through this evolutionary development, China's ancient ways have undergone continuous modification as century followed century. The China of 1839 was vastly different from that of Confucius or Mencius, and also very different from the medieval China of Neo-Confucian philosophers like Chu Hsi. When we call the Chinese society of the early nineteenth century "traditional," we are only stressing its close continuity with its own China-centered heritage from the past.

Secondly, we face the problem: what was the general nature of this traditional Chinese society? It was most unlike that of Western Europe and America; but how? Among several answers that could be given, one of the most illuminating (for those who seek to put societies in categories) is the concept of old China as an example of "Oriental Society." Even before Karl Marx used the term "Asiatic mode of production," Western scholars like J. S. Mill had noted certain general characteristics which seemed to make the ancient empires of the Near East and Asia quite different in kind from the society of Europe. Social historians today are developing this concept; while we can hardly try to summarize it here, we can note certain features. Traditional China, like other ancient empires, came to be organized under a centralized monolithic government in which the official bureaucracy dominated most aspects of large-scale activity—administrative, military, religious, economic, political. This agrarian bureaucratic state got its revenue largely from the agricultural production of the illiterate peasantry, who also provided the manpower for the conscript armies and for the corvée labor which was used to control the water supply through diking and ditching. Large-scale public works, like the Great Wall or the Grand Canal, comparable to roads and airfields today, have been built by this mass-labor force, mobilized and superintended by the officials. The latter were of course drawn from the small literate element of the Chinese population, the literati who could transact public business using the intricate Chinese writing system. Since only the well-to-do could normally afford the years of study required for literacy in the classics, officials came more from the landlord-gentry class than from the peasant masses. Thus the landlords produced scholars, and the scholars became officials, forming a complex upper stratum so closely interrelated and interdependent that the ideal men of distinction were landlord-scholar-officials, rather than generals or merchants.

In this society, the individual was generally subordinated to his family group. The scholars and administrators, like the emperor above them, were expected to follow an ethical rather than a purely legal code of conduct. A Western-type individualism and the supremacy of law never became established, nor the personal freedom under law represented by our civil liberties and institution of private property. (The legal safeguards of personal liberty are, to be sure, a rather recent and not yet perfect achievement in the West.) At any rate, the old China was based on the farming family and ruled by the bureaucrat. It was politically centralized while economically decentralized, and strong in the customary ethical sanctions which preserved the patriarch and the ruler at the top of the social hierarchy, while weak in the institutions of property and enterprise. All this has affected the capacity of the Chinese state to follow the Western pattern of capital investment and industrialization. As we shall note below, China's modern industrial enterprises had to be under official patronage if not control, yet the tradition was to invest one's personal savings in land rather than in productive industry. This undoubtedly impeded China's industrialization.

Perhaps enough has been said to indicate how the institutional patterns of old China influenced her response to the West in every sphere—economic and political as well as military, social, and intellectual. We forego at this point any further effort to define the general nature of the old Chinese society. Although we are about to look at bits of the record, we cannot expect to see the whole picture in detail ahead of time; for the detailed picture has still to be put together.

Our explanation of terms may conclude with two further points. First, to say as some do that nineteenth-century China was "feudal" or "semi-feudal" seems to us not very meaningful, if we judge these terms by their use in European or Japanese history. China does not fit into the proper institutional pattern. Second, the terms "stimulus" (or "impact") and "response" are not very precise. We are in danger of assuming that there was a previous "Western impact" merely because there was later activity which we call a "Chinese response." This "Chinese response" or activity is the thing we want to study, but it obviously was part of Chinese conduct as a whole. In other words, the Western impact was only one of many factors in the Chinese scene. The response to it can only be unscrambled with difficulty from Chinese history in general. Until we can work out a more precise analytic framework, the title of this study will remain more metaphorical than scientific.

### The Scope of this Volume

These considerations give us a limited objective—to mark some of the broad outlines and trace some of the main patterns in the intellectual history of modern China's attempt to comprehend the West and adjust to it. We proceed on the assumption that Western influence did indeed precipitate the remaking of Chinese life and values. Every patriot and statesman since the time of Lin Tse-hsü has had to consider China's relationship to the West as one of the primary problems confronting the Chinese state and its people. Beginning with the movement for coastal defense, there has been a succession of formulations and reformulations of the ancient "barbarian problem." The imitation of Western arms, the program of "Self-strengthening" through Western studies, later through industrialization and eventually through institutional reform, the movement for revolution and republicanism, the cult of "Science and Democracy," the literary "Renaissance," the adoption of party tutelage and "democratic centralism"—all these and many other programs have had their day and contributed to the long struggle for the remaking of Chinese life. All of them have been related, in greater or less degree, to the Western influence on China, even down to the alleged "American imperialism"...

Within this single volume we make no formal effort to describe or define the Western impact. The inequalities of the treaties are well enough known: the foreign consuls' legal jurisdiction over their nationals known as extraterritoriality; the conventional treaty tariff and the commercial exploitation that went hand in hand with it; the treaty ports which, as Chiang Kai-shek so fervently declared in *China's Destiny*, became centers of infection whence the old social order was contaminated and broken down. Less has been written to evaluate the social influence of the great Protestant, and also the revived Catholic, missionary movements of the nineteenth century. Similarly the influence of Western studies in China and of Chinese students who had studied in the West has been only imperfectly evaluated. The monographic work essential to scholarship has not yet been done. Scholarly conclusions can hardly yet be formed.

Our main effort, therefore, is to stimulate and assist the kind of monographic study necessary to any intellectual progress in this field. It will not be enough for Western social scientists to apply new interpretations to the meager record of modern Chinese history thus far available. Not enough facts are known. We cannot rely on propagandist "scholarship," with its dogmatic disregard for the truth—or rather, its Procrustean regard for the truth as a relative matter—to give us the real story. It is necessary for trained and competent Asian and Western scholars alone and in collaboration to spend long periods of time in translation and research, else we shall never know what has really happened in China since its opening to the West.

The memorials, essays, and diaries of Chinese statesmen and reformers form perhaps the most convenient and practicable avenue of approach to this immensely difficult subject. Texts are artifacts. Their original meaning can be wrung out with patience. In the process, reflections and interpretations will occur to the translator. The corpus of Chinese literature is well organized, within its own universe of discourse.

Statements of fact and idea can often be cross-checked and verified. Every author whose writings are quoted below could profitably become the subject of monographic research. To this end, we have given bibliographical suggestions, in our *Research Guide* (see Notes and Sources), which are intended to supplement the aid to be found in Dr. A. W. Hummel's invaluable *Eminent Chinese of the Ch'ing Period 1644-1912*, 2 vols., (Washington, D. C., 1943-1944). We have tried in our own commentaries to avoid duplicating the material presented by Fang Chao-ying, Tu Lien-che and the various other contributors to that biographical dictionary. It is assumed that the user of this volume will have it at hand.

Since so many of these items are memorials addressed to the emperor, it should be explained to non-specialists that official business in the Chinese empire was formally transacted and decisions made by the process of proposal from the high officials and decision by the ruler and his advisers. It was almost literally a case of "Man proposes, God (or the Son of Heaven) disposes." Consequently, for a policy to get any official result, it had to be embodied in a proper document or report ("memorial") from one of the emperor's officials, whereupon an imperial edict or Decree could be issued to summarize, comment upon, or confirm it. Whether or not an edict was to follow, the emperor was expected to append at the end of a memorial, after he had read it, a brief comment, even so brief as "Noted" or "I am informed" (equivalent to "OK"), just to show that he was on the job. This comment is usually called a "vermilion endorsement," since the emperor used red ink. The recorded date of a memorial was normally the day when the emperor saw it, not the actual date of writing.

The bold new program of translation and comment which this volume represents will in the course of time seem to have been overbold, if not foolhardy, and no longer new. But it is our thesis that the field of modern Chinese intellectual history has lain fallow far too long. Our selections of material have had to be arbitrary and without benefit of prolonged research on all the persons and movements dealt with, but this is a pump-priming operation, conducted on the assumption that Western students of China will increase in number and productivity, and that they will not fail to meet the intellectual challenge of modern China's metamorphosis.

## CHAPTER Ⅱ   SOME ELEMENTS IN THE CHINESE INTELLECTUAL TRADITION

In nineteenth-century China, more than in most times and places, the problems of the day were met in terms of the past. During China's long history, orthodoxy of thought had been stressed by one ruler after another, ever since the first emperor of the Ch'in in 213 B. C. burned the books hostile to his regime. A great continuity of intellectual tradition had thus been established, constantly preserved by the official historians and by the literati who mastered the ancient classics. The orthodoxy of ideas inculcated in this way was used by the imperial government to ensure the loyalty and obedience of its subjects. Consequently, both unorthodox ideas and foreign ideas were potentially dangerous to the regime in power.

Here we see one channel of Western influence—Western ideas could become weapons in the struggle for power within China. Both the institutional reformers of 1898 and the republican revolutionists of 1911 eventually demonstrated this. Even the Taiping rebels of 1851-1864 invoked the Christian *Bible* to support their cause. More recent and successful rebels have used Marx and Lenin. Yet the process of ideological change in modern China had to begin with the reinterpretation of the Chinese heritage, rather than with its denial and rejection.

In this chapter, therefore, we must take note of three major elements in the intellectual background of nineteenth-century Chinese thinkers: one was the ethnocentric, even "nationalistic," ideology of certain scholars who had opposed the alien rule of the Manchus; the second was the influence left by the early Catholic missionaries; the third was the traditional attitude of the Ch'ing court toward the West.

## a. Some Early Ch'ing "Nationalist" Thinkers

These independent-minded Chinese scholars of the early Ch'ing period (1644-1911) courageously challenged the orthodoxy which the new Manchu rulers were fostering. While remaining within the bounds of the Chinese classical tradition, they boldly questioned some of the doctrines of the day, especially the philosophy of Wang Yang-ming (1472-1529). Beginning in the last years of the Ming Dynasty (1368-1644), they argued against certain traditional interpretations of Confucianism and demanded drastic re-examination of the classics, thus setting a precedent and providing a stimulus for the scholars of the late nineteenth century. The precedent that they set, however, should not be exaggerated—the methods and interpretations of these seventeenth-century scholars did not come down in an unbroken tradition out of which the late Ch'ing reformers emerged. On the contrary, some of them were all but forgotten and were rediscovered only after Western contact had obliged Chinese reformers to look in their own past for precedents which would justify their new interpretations of Chinese tradition. It was in this way, as convenient predecessors in the exposition of ideas they now found necessary, that the reformers of 1898 used seventeenth-century scholars like Ku Yen-wu and Huang Tsung-hsi. Among other things, these men had opposed alien rule, by the Manchus or any other non-Chinese. Two centuries later their writings naturally became of value to patriotic scholars who sought an ideological basis for modern Chinese nationalism.

One major form of China's response to Western contact has thus been the reappraisal of Chinese tradition, in the effort to use it for modern purposes. The next few pages illustrate the type of writings available for this endeavor.

*Huang Tsung-hsi* (1610-1695) was a famous scholar of the late Ming, whose political treatise, written in 1663, was called *Ming-i tai-*

*fang lu*. (For data on this and other works, see our separate *Research Guide*.) The tenets of this work were derived from two sources: a) Mencius' thesis, that the people are the most important members of any state, while the ruler is less significant; b) a chapter of the *Book of Rites* (*Li-chi*) which presents the idea that "the empire is for the public," *T'ien-hsia wei-kung*, i. e., it is not for one person. (This was a slogan later used by Sun Yat-sen. For these Chinese characters, see list in the *Research Guide*.) The main points of Huang's political philosophy were that the institution of ruler is for the benefit of the people and the ruler and his ministers are public servants of the people. A good ruler should be loved by the people as their parent, but a bad ruler should be killed. Huang approved tyrannicide. After the legendary golden age, he argued, political disorder in China had resulted from the neglect of duty by rulers who considered the empire their private property. Huang still believed in enlightened monarchy, although he disapproved the practice of "patterning after the ancestors" or ancestral law (*fa-tsu*), according to which all emperors of a dynasty should obey the regulations laid down by the dynastic founder. He also argued that a good legal system is of primary importance, while able administrators are secondary. One of the reformers of 1898, T'an Ssu-t'ung (see Ch. XVI below), is said to have printed several hundred thousand copies of excerpts from Huang's *Ming-i tai-fang lu* for secret distribution, to promote his own ideas of reform. These excerpts strongly influenced the thinking of the late Ch'ing period.

Writing "On the ruler," Huang says:①

At the beginning of creation, every man was selfish and every man was self-seeking. There was public good in the empire but probably no one cared to promote it; there was public evil in the empire, but probably no one cared to get rid of it. Then there appeared a man who did not consider his personal interest as the object of benefit but made it possible

---

① The reader's attention is called to the Note on pages 268-269.

for the people of the empire to share the benefit... The assiduous toil of this man must have been a thousand or a myriad times more than that of the people of the empire. Well, after spending himself a thousand or a myriadfold in assiduous toil, he still did not enjoy the benefit... Rulers of later ages were different. They considered that the authority to bestow benefit and harm was entirely concentrated in their own hands; the benefit of the empire was entirely received by them, while the harm of the empire was entirely given to others [p. 2]... They considered the empire as their chief item of personal property... In ancient times the people of the empire were the primary interest, the ruler was secondary, and what the ruler planned and did was for the empire. Now the ruler has the primary interest, the people of the empire are secondary... and the one who does great harm to the empire is the ruler... In ancient times the people of the empire loved their ruler, comparing him to their parents, respecting him as Heaven; that was indeed not too much. Now the people of the empire hate their ruler, looking on him as an enemy, calling him a dictator (*tu-fu*); this is certainly the position he occupies.

On the subject of the minister, Huang says [p. 3], "When I enter government service, I work for the empire, not for the ruler; for the myriads of the populace, not for one family." In his chapter "On the law," he writes [p. 5]:

What is called law is for the protection of the one imperial personage and is not the law for the sake of society as a whole... Some critics say that each dynasty should have its own laws, and that to obey ancestral law is filial piety... These are plagiarized statements of vulgar scholars [p. 6]... Some commentators even say, there is government by man, no government by law; I should say, government by law should come before government by man.

*Ku Yen-wu* (1613-1682), also known as Ku T'ing-lin, was a very learned scholar who with Huang Tsung-hsi and others tried to restore the Ming Dynasty. He traveled extensively in North China, carrying on a kind of geographic, topographic, and economic survey. Stressing agriculture, irrigation, and rural economics, he encouraged the use of labor-saving machinery and the opening of mines. As a reaction against the philosophy of Wang Yang-ming, Ku advocated the pursuit of knowledge "of practical use to society," *ching-shih chih-yung*. Among his famous works are the *Jih-chih lu* (Notes of daily accumulation of knowledge), dealing with a large variety of subjects; and the *T'ien-hsia chün-kuo li-ping shu* (A book on the strategic and economic advantages and disadvantages of the counties and states of the empire), author's preface dated 1662. He was also a pioneer scholar in Chinese philology and he emphasized the inductive method of research in classics and history.

Living in the same environment, Huang and Ku both reacted against the political oppression of the early Ch'ing period. Their thinking was largely similar, but in attacking despotism Huang took the people as the fundamental element of the state, while Ku did not consider them of such cardinal importance. Ku attacked the overconcentration of authority in the hands of the emperor. Although he eulogized ancient feudalism as a means of sharing the empire among the public, he still did not think that it should be restored. Instead, he favored the division of state authority among local magistrates who should have full power in developing education, agriculture, and military affairs. The power of each magistrate should be again divided among the heads of small political divisions, where the people should have considerable right of self-government. He hated the way in which the scholar-literati acted as a law unto themselves in rural communities and objected to the legal restriction of the people's freedom.

Ku Yen-wu was in favor of reform: "If the laws or institutions are not reformed, it will be impossible to meet the present crisis. We are already in a situation where we must reform, yet we still try to avoid actually doing it... This will certainly cause great corruption."[②]

Ku favored thorough reform, not a patchwork; reform based on present conditions and not restricted by ancestral law:

When our predecessors initiated legislation, they could not thoroughly study the facts and circumstances and prepare in advance for future revision. Their successors followed what was already a corrupt practice, and were restricted by the established statutes which they could not change, or had to make by-laws, to amend them. Thereupon, the more numerous the laws, the more they were abused. All the affairs of the empire became more vexatious. The result was that the laws were not understood and not enforced. The upper and the lower classes tried to fool each other, the only consideration being that they should not neglect the system laid down by their ancestors. This state of affairs was most prevalent in the Ming Dynasty.③

But Ku Yen-wu searched for a golden age in the past. His political purpose was "to make use of Chinese institutions and to transform the barbarians" (*yung-hsia pien-i*). He tried to restore the self-confidence of the Chinese people, to develop the Chinese traditional ethics and wisdom. In a letter to a friend he says that his purpose in writing the *Jih-chih lu* was "to disperse rebellion and to cleanse away the dirt of politics, to model after our antiquity and to use the political and social systems of the Hsia [ancient China], to supply more information to future students and to wait for a good time of administration by future emperors."④

Fortunately Ku Yen-wu was not bigoted nor bound by Chinese traditionalism. He recognized the good points of the barbarians also: "There are some Chinese customs which are inferior to those of foreign countries." He admired the frugal, assiduous, and military spirit of the Khitans. He praised the honest customs of the Uigurs, who made only slight differences of rank between the ruler and his ministers. He thought the system of encouraging the cultivation of arable land and its equal distribution under the Toba Wei Dynasty (A. D. 386-534) in northwest China might serve as a model for later ages.⑤

*Wang Fu-chih* (1619-1692), also called Wang Ch'uan-shan, was a renowned historical critic and a voluminous writer. After the Ming Dynasty was overthrown he retired to a small boat-shaped island in Hengyang, Hunan, where he lived the life of a hermit, writing books for some forty years. Because he had little association with other scholars, he became an independent thinker.⑥ From his historical and inductive approach to political problems, he built up his theory of evolution—that the legal system should be changed from time to time and in each dynasty be a single unit. Accordingly Wang objected to all conservative attempts at restoration of the past; it is futile, he thought, to imitate antiquity. The society of ancient times was rightly governed by ancient law; the political system of today cannot rightly be enforced in the society of the future. The administration of each dynasty should fit the needs of its time and be adjusted to contemporary conditions. For instance, in the old days, it was a good system for soldiers to become farmers and vice versa, but in modern times when warfare has become far more complicated, it is necessary to have well-trained, specialized soldiers; untrained farmers cannot at the same time serve as soldiers.⑦

Wang Fu-chih discovered another theory—that every species and race, all the way from insects to human beings, aims at its own preservation and organization. Self-preservation is a natural law. Even the ants know how to protect themselves; human beings are certainly not to be excepted. Since the forming of groups is inherent in human nature and the establishment of a ruler is for the purpose of protecting the group, it is logical and necessary for the group to govern itself. Each race should be controlled by its own ruler, and should never allow any encroachment by an alien race. In other words, all states should be national states and self-governing. He would rather have even a usurper on the throne than a foreign race dominating China.⑧

Still another of Wang's new ideas was that differences of culture are produced among various races which live in different geographical zones. Since the barbarians and the Chinese were bred in different places, their spirit, actions, and customs also differed. China should not allow barbarians to invade her territory and her culture. Wang considered that culture fluctuates and civilization does not stay in one place. He observed that in many cases culture has progressed from barbarism to civilization, while in other cases it has remained stagnant. He thought there was a possibility of China being reduced to a barbarous or savage condition. Wang's method for forestalling a barbarian invasion was to make good use of the time element. "He who would succeed in controlling barbarians should have a good knowledge of the times and seasons. When the combination of circumstances favors attack, he attacks; when it favors defense, he defends."⑨

*Chu Chih-yü* (1600-1682), also called Chu Shun-shui, was another ethnocentric thinker who had great influence in both China and Japan. Born in the same district as Huang Tsung-hsi, he fled to Annam and Japan to request aid against the invading Manchus. Having failed in repeated attempts to overthrow the Manchu rule, he remained in Japan after 1659. His scholarship attracted the attention of Japanese savants who not only studied under him but recommended him to be a teacher of Prince Tokugawa Mitsukuni, grandson of the great Ieyasu. Under Mitsukuni's auspices he prepared a detailed description of the Chinese state worship of Confucius and gave advice on the compilation of the colossal *Dai Nihon shi* or "History of Great Japan," a work which later influenced the leaders of the Meiji Restoration of 1868.

Chu was a man of great integrity and an advocate of pragmatism. His anti-Manchu writings, entitled *Yang-chiu shu-lueh*, were to be a great stimulus to rebellious Chinese youth near the end of the Ch'ing Dynasty. Before his death Chu requested that his body should "not be returned to China so long as the Manchus rule."⑩

### The Literary Inquisition

The growth of Chinese "national" feeling against the Manchu regime, stimulated by writers like Huang Tsung-hsi, Ku Yen-wu, Wang Fu-chih, and Chu Chih-yü, was suppressed by the literary inquisition. This reached its height under Emperor Ch'ien-lung (1736-1795), when more than two thousand selected Chinese works were wholly or partly destroyed. The partisans of the Ming had given the Emperor K'ang-hsi (1662-1722) much trouble and, even after their political suppression, had left many writings which expressed dissatisfaction or resentment against the Manchus. A purge of such works had actually begun after 1644.⑪

As an example of the inquisition, we may note the case of Lü Liu-liang (1629-1683) and Tseng Ching (1679-1736). Lü was a classicist as well as a pamphleteer. He refused to take the civil service examinations but instead wrote commentaries on Sung philosophy in which he openly deplored the plight into which China had fallen and the inability of the Chinese people to check the disaster of the Manchu invasion. His expression of anti-Manchu sentiment was quite influential and during the Yung-chêng period (1723-1735) led a certain Tseng Ching, a *chü-jen* (provincial graduate) of Hunan, and his disciples to attempt to overthrow the Manchu government. Tseng was so much interested in Lü Liu-liang's writings that he sent one of his loyal students to read them all at the latter's home in Chekiang, and to get acquainted with Lü's disciples. In 1728 Tseng Ching sent the same student to persuade the governor-general of Szechwan and Shensi to rebel against the Manchus. This was reported to the court and ruthless punishment was dealt to the partisans, descendants, relatives and disciples of all the persons involved. Most of the writings of Lü and Tseng were destroyed. But from the *Ta-i chueh-mi lu*, a work which consists of all the arguments of Emperor Yung-chêng in defense of himself and his throne, as well as from the testimony of Tseng Ching, one can still trace a little of the nationalist spirit behind this abortive rebellion.⑫

Ideas and events of this sort were known to the Chinese scholars of the nineteenth century as part of their native tradition. In their response to the West they were necessarily more under the influence of this tradition than of any other. Just as the China of today can be more thoroughly understood by reference to the nineteenth century, so the record of Chinese thought must be pursued farther back, in order to gain that overall perspective which the historian seeks. Is it not possible, for example, that the effectiveness with which the Ch'ing government suppressed the growth of creative and ethnocentric anti-Manchu thought in the eighteenth century contributed directly to China's inability to respond more vigorously to the Western stimulus a century later?

After the literary inquisition had reached its height in the late eighteenth century, the "nationalist" movement was represented chiefly by secret societies of various names and forms which sought to overthrow the Manchus. Some of these societies contributed, in some degree, to the Taiping Rebellion and subsequently to Dr. Sun Yat-sen's revolutionary movement. The study of the secret societies deserves separate monographic treatment, beyond the scope of this volume. [13]

## b. *The Early Jesuit Influence in China*

The first extensive cultural contact between China and Europe began near the end of the sixteenth century, when the Jesuit missionaries, in the wake of the Portuguese, reached China by sea. Their dual function is well known: they not only diffused Western ideas in China, including elements of mathematics, astronomy, geography, hydraulics, the calendar, and the manufacture of cannon, but they also introduced Chinese (particularly Confucian) ideas into Europe. [14] The Jesuits found it easier to influence China's science than her religion. Perceiving this, they used their scientific knowledge as a means of approach to Chinese scholars. Although a small number of their Chinese converts took part in the translation and compilation of religious and scientific books, the majority of the native scholars, entrenched in their ethnocentric cultural tradition, were not seriously affected by the new elements of Western thought.

The great Jesuit pioneer, Matteo Ricci (1552-1610), tried to fit Catholicism into Chinese thought. In general he accepted Confucianism in its most ancient phase but rejected the Confucian development after Han and T'ang, especially the Neo-Confucianism of the Sung. He accepted the term *Shang-ti*, the highest deity in the Confucian classics, but not the *T'ai-chi* or "Supreme Ultimate" of the Neo-Confucians. Ricci and his followers likewise accepted the *hsien-ju*, the early Confucianists, but not the *hou-ju*, the Confucianists of later ages.⑮

The cosmological ideas of the Roman Catholic Church and of Neo-Confucianism differed in several important respects: a) the Neo-Confucians did not recognize a creator or almighty God in the universe; instead, they believed that the growth of creatures is by *li* or "natural law"; b) they recognized the existence of *hsin* (mind or conscience), which is somewhat comparable to the soul of Christianity, but they did not believe that this mind or conscience is bestowed by God; c) they acknowledged that every human being has the power and free will to reach his best state of development, to be free from sin or crime, and without God's help to go to Heaven. While both the Catholics and the Neo-Confucianists sought to understand the universe, to distinguish truth, to cultivate virtue and to teach people how to be good, their purposes appear to have been just sufficiently similar to bring them into rivalry and conflict.⑯

### The Various Forms of Chinese Interest

Those Chinese scholars who accepted both Christianity and Western science, like Hsü Kuang-ch'i (1562-1633) believed that Western learning overcame the shortcomings of Confucianism and replaced Buddhism; and that Confucianism and Christianity could be developed in China in parallel fashion. Their acceptance of what Ricci had to offer was based first of all on a rational appreciation of the Jesuits as philosopher-gentlemen. One late Ming writer says:⑰

The *T'ien-chu kuo* [the Lord-of-Heaven country, i. e., the Catholic state, presumably Italy], lies further to the west from the Buddhist state [India]. Their people understand literature and are as scholarly and elegant as the Chinese. There is a certain Li-ma-tou [Matteo Ricci] who came from the said state, and after four years reached the boundary of Kwangtung by way of India. Their religion worships *T'ien-chu* ["the Lord of Heaven," the Catholic term for God], just as the Confucianists worship Confucius and the Buddhists, Buddha. Among his books there is one entitled *T'ien-chu shih-i* (The true meaning of Christianity) which frequently explains the truth by comparison with Confucianism but sharply criticizes the theories of nothingness (*hsü-wu*) and emptiness of Buddhism and Taoism... I am very much delighted with his ideas, which are close to Confucianism but more earnest in exhorting society not to resemble the Buddhists, who always like to use obscure, incoherent words to fool and frighten the populace... He is very polite when he talks to people and his arguments, if challenged, can be inexhaustible. Thus in foreign countries there are also real gentlemen.

Firearms and applied science further commended the Jesuits to the court of Peking, as they already had to the daimyo of Japan. Long before Ricci finally received a court stipend in Peking in 1601, European weapons had been introduced into South China. But apparently they were not widely welcomed until Japan invaded Korea in 1592. The Japanese, benefiting by the early Portuguese importation of firearms after 1542, won victories in Korea, and the Chinese recognized the necessity of improving their weapons. In 1622 the Ming emperor, already threatened by the new Manchu power beyond the Wall, sent an envoy to Macao seeking Jesuit help in casting cannon. In the following year Westerners were summoned to the capital for this purpose. Ch'ü Shih-ssu (Thomas Ch'ü, 1590-1651) memorialized the throne in 1628 requesting the study of Western cannon and other weapons; he declared that in 1619 an imperial Decree had ordered Hsü Kuang-ch'i to search for Western weapons and that he had obtained four cannon. Li Chih-tsao (1565-1630) had secured twenty-three more from Canton in 1621. Thus the Ming sought Western cannon for defense against the Manchus much as the Manchu government two centuries later was to seek Western cannon and the help of the "Ever Victorious Army" at Shanghai to suppress the Taiping Rebellion. The Ming Dynasty attempted to acquire Portuguese artillery and three or four hundred men from Macao to repel a Manchu invasion; but apprehension over having Western soldiers in China led to the cancellation of the mission at Nanchang. Only the commander, Gonzales Tedeira, and a few others continued to Peking.[18]

Thereafter in the waning years of the Ming not only Jesuits but also other foreigners from Macao went to Peking, both to make weapons and to serve in the Chinese forces. In 1639 Franciscus Sambiaso presented to the emperor many gifts, including a clock, binoculars, maps, an organ, a mirror, and a parrot. He submitted a memorial to the throne calling attention to the need for a good calendar, the selection of ores, the promotion of international trade and the purchase of Western guns. This actually constituted a modernization program for China; but the Ming Dynasty was busily engaged in warfare against the Manchus and among these recommendations the Chinese emperor took an interest only in the calendar and the guns.[19]

While the conversion to the Roman Catholic faith of such Chinese scholar-officials as Hsü Kuang-ch'i and Li Chih-tsao is well known, it nevertheless poses several questions. First, what element in Christianity was responsible for its friendly reception by certain scholars and members of the imperial family, several score of whom are said to have been converted by 1640?[20] Did their baptism mean acceptance of basic Christian tenets, or were these converts won over by rationalism (as opposed to faith), because they believed Christianity to be less unworldly than Buddhism and Taoism? Both Hsü and Li were also interested in Western guns and cannon, and on his part Matteo Ricci accepted some Chinese phraseology (e. g., *Shang-ti*), and admitted the validity of ancient Confucian teachings. Do these signs indicate that, rather than a fundamental conversion to a new faith, the Chinese acceptance of the Christian religion was only a manifestation of tolerance?

Secondly, it is noteworthy that the immediate Jesuit influence in China was through items of practical significance, such as cannon, the calendar, or Ricci's map of the world. Why is so little trace of Christian doctrine to be found in the writings of Chinese scholars in the subsequent century? If this is to be explained by the fact that government suppression cut off contact and the relatively few professed converts had few successors, we still face the question why the minds of the non-Christian scholars were not more permanently influenced by Western knowledge or ideas.

Such questions raise the knotty problem of the Chinese religious consciousness. The long and complex religious experience of the Chinese people had included, among many other faiths, the great flowering of Buddhism in the seventh and eighth centuries, a religion characterized by belief in an incarnate yet divine savior. We know that Chinese Buddhism had a profound influence upon the subsequent Neo-Confucian philosophy, although the extent of this influence is still being appraised. It is plain that China's early experience of Buddhism lay behind her later reaction to Christianity, in ways that remain to be studied. [21]

If we turn the other way and look at the centuries after the Jesuit contact, we may assume that the use of Western cannon in the seventeenth century served as a useful precedent in the minds of officials in the nineteenth century. The authentic record of the use of Western cannon two-centuries before must also have helped the nineteenth-century officials to admit the superiority of Western arms.

## The Conservative Antagonists of Western Christianity and Science

Opposition to the Jesuits and other Western missionaries was motivated partly by the xenophobic suspicion that foreigners were spies; partly by ethical scruples against Christian religious ceremonies which seemed contrary to Chinese customs such as the veneration of Heaven, ancestors and Confucius; and partly by professional jealousy, on the assumption that if Catholicism were to become prevalent in China, the decline of the doctrines of Confucius, Buddha, and Lao-tzu would damage the position of their protagonists. Soon after Ricci's death in 1610, troubles had begun.

The Chinese Buddhist leadership appears to have been vehemently anti-Catholic. Meanwhile most Chinese scholars remained dogmatically opposed to the Westerners' religion. Lacking enthusiasm for their religion, they also disliked their science. From 1659 on, the scholar Yang Kuang-hsien (1597-1669) wrote a number of treatises denouncing the Christian religion and criticizing the calendar made by Adam Schall von Bell. In 1664 he charged Schall with errors in astronomical calculation, and accused the missionaries, with their "million followers" scattered throughout the land, of plotting against the state and indoctrinating the people with false ideas. [22]

The calendar controversy in particular was caused by the opposition of traditionalists. In a sense, it represented a first symptom of unrest in the Chinese academic world caused by Westerners, just as the Opium War of 1840-1842 was to be the first such disturbance in China's modern political history. The conservatives objected to Western scientific instruments, arguing that clocks were expensive but useless, that cannon could not annihilate enemies but usually burned the gunners first, and that on Ricci's map of the globe China was not in the very center and was not large enough. They also objected to Western painting because it lacked forceful strokes. [23]

Since such objections were not conclusive, the conservative scholars adopted another tactic, quoting irrelevant Confucian classics to refute the newly introduced Western knowledge. Yang Kuang-hsien says that the calendar of the legendary Emperors Yao and Shun should be used, even though its predictions may be inaccurate. Juan Yuan (1764-1849), a nineteenth-century representative of the anti-Western-science school, says that it is unbelievable that the earth is rotating and he who believes it rebels against the Confucian classics.㉔ A more powerful line of attack was to make a forced interpretation of Western discoveries, cite some vague references from the Chinese classics, and claim a Chinese origin of Western science. In this way it was claimed that the Western calendars were derived from the chapter "Yao-tien" in the *Book of History*; the essential ideas of Western discussions of the earth were derived from the commentary on the tenth chapter of *Tseng-tzu*;㉕ and the formula for computing the circumference of a circle had been figured out and handed down by Tsu Ch'ung-chih (429-500).㉖ As for algebra, it was said to have been the method of Li Yeh of the Yuan Dynasty, while other elements of Western mathematics were derived from the ancient mathematical classic, *Chou-pi suan-ching*.㉗

Behind all this condemnation of Western learning lay the basic political fact that the Manchu rulers of China could not tolerate the propagation of a foreign religion which asserted the spiritual supremacy of Rome over Peking. By 1640 Japan, under the Tokugawa, had proscribed Christianity and foreign contact (except for the Dutch in Nagasaki) as politically dangerous. In China by the end of the seventeenth century there were Catholic congregations in all but two of the provinces; the Roman Catholic faith was banned in the Yung-chêng period (1723-1735), though less drastically than in Japan (Chinese Christians were compelled to follow the example of those in Japan and trample on the cross).㉘ Even before 1773, when the Jesuit order was dissolved by the Pope, the missionaries at the Chinese court had been limited to serving as technical personnel—painters, musicians and architects—rather than as persons of intellectual importance. They had lost influence as a link between Western and Chinese culture.

## The Jesuits and Chinese Science and Technology

It remains an interesting question what influence the Catholic missionaries had on the native Chinese tradition in mathematics, medicine, and similar fields. We know that Western military superiority, which forced China into closer contact with Europe and America, was a product of technology. Like the tank-and-airplane team today, British gunboats in the 1840's proved decisive in battle. The inadequacy of China's military techniques—her musketeers, mounted archers, and banner-decked war junks—was a symptom of scientific backwardness. Yet it would be quite wrong to conclude that Chinese society had always lagged behind the West in her material culture. On the contrary, medieval China's earlier use of printing, the compass, and gunpowder had indicated her comparative advancement over medieval Europe. The native roots of science and technology in China have not yet been thoroughly examined, although the modern world has already gained useful drugs (like ephedrine) from the old Chinese pharmacopoeia, and the products of many Chinese craftsmen and artists have long been recognized as without peer abroad. How far Chinese technology was influenced by the West before the nineteenth century is still uncertain.

The superiority of the Jesuit knowledge of mathematics was soon recognized by Chinese scholars. Since the thirteenth century, when the abacus had begun to replace the old Chinese calculating rods,[29] the Chinese mathematics based on the latter method of calculation had fallen gradually into neglect. By the late sixteenth century even the foremost scholars knew practically nothing about higher mathematics. Hence the publication of the Chinese translation of Euclid's *Elements of Geometry* in 1607, and certain Jesuit works on mathematics and calendric calculation in subsequent years, created a new interest among the scholars in mathematical studies.[30] The Western method of calculation, writing down the progress and results of reasoning step by step, probably had more appeal for Chinese scholars than the use of the abacus. Under the first four Ch'ing emperors, the Imperial Board of Astronomy was almost continuously entrusted to one or more Catholic missionaries in Peking. Emperor K'ang-hsi himself studied mathematics under several Jesuits and so did certain selected officials in a special school.㉛ Thus, for more than a century, Chinese mathematicians learned only from Western teachers or translated texts. It was not until the 1770's that rare ancient Chinese textbooks on mathematics began to be reprinted and studied.㉜ As more and more masterpieces of Chinese mathematics reappeared, the history of its development before the fourteenth century became better known. Yet the Western methods of calculation remained prevalent and, because they were sufficient as a means for understanding and solving the problems posed in ancient Chinese texts, few scholars bothered to learn again how to manipulate the cumbersome calculating rods. Thus an interest in ancient Chinese mathematics was revived in the late eighteenth century, while Western mathematics as introduced in the preceding century continued to be fully accepted and studied. More modern Western texts were translated after 1850.㉝

The Chinese level of mechanical technology, as summarized in the work, *T'ien-kung k'ai-wu* (Natural resources utilized for manufacturing) of 1637, was probably as high as the material resources and sciences of the day permitted. The early Jesuits introduced some ideas about labor-saving machines but they failed to rouse any general interest. Among the Western manufactured articles that were admired most in China were clocks, organs, telescopes, and eyeglasses, but only the last of these was imitated by Chinese artisans.㉞

Similarly, in medicine, a Jesuit work on anatomy printed in 1635 did not arouse much interest among Chinese physicians. Certain new drugs such as quinine were imported but in quantities too small to have any lasting influence. The real beginning of Western medicine in China was Dr. Alexander Pearson's introduction of vaccination against smallpox in

1805. Although limited at first to Canton, this technique soon spread to other parts of China and was also adopted by Chinese physicians. In the 1830's the Protestant missionaries began to establish free clinics and hospitals as the best means to promote Christianity, having found that the Chinese officials and gentry usually would permit and occasionally even sponsor such philanthropic institutions. Thereafter modern medicine and medical education had a steady growth in China. Yet at the same time the old Chinese medicine, except in the field of surgery, has widely persisted.㉟

Surveying and map-making were other kinds of Western technology that the Jesuits brought to China. A general cartographic survey of the empire in the period 1707-1717 was conducted by teams of Jesuit fathers with trained Chinese students, one of whom later took an active part in the surveying of the newly conquered area in Turkestan and Ili (1755-1759). All this produced a number of the most accurate maps of Eastern Asia which had yet been made; but in China some of them were not even printed and those that were published did not have much circulation. Only in Europe were these maps put to good use. After the middle of the eighteenth century the technique of surveying and map-making was lost among the Chinese. It had to be learned as a new subject more than one hundred years later.㊱

All in all, the residual influence of the Western technology made available to China through the early missionaries seems to have been rather slight. Even when present, it was seldom acknowledged. Meanwhile an anti-Western political tradition had become well established.

### c. The Attitude of the Ch'ing Court toward the Westerners

The Chinese monarchy under Ch'ing continued to be a powerful and centralized institution. The emperor was expected to carry a heavy administrative burden day by day, to rule as well as reign. All official business of any importance was supposed to pass before him. The Son of

Heaven at the top of the Chinese social pyramid was indeed expected to perform a superhuman function, supervising the major personnel, the use of funds and military forces, public works and ceremonies, on a vast and intricate scale.

Two results flowed from this emphasis on the monarchy: one was that a ramified and conservative administrative mechanism had to be maintained at Peking to carry on the various imperial functions under the emperor's aegis. The other was that the emperor himself, as a single man, had all he could do to keep up with his daily duties and meet the dynasty's problems, without seeking further fields of activity outside the court. He was not easily susceptible to new influences coming from abroad, yet his response to them was an essential act of leadership if the Chinese state was to make any response at all. The attitude of the emperor, or the court which surrounded and assisted him, was therefore of prime importance in China's relations with the West—a circumstance which the Jesuits had clearly perceived.

Since the court's attitude was to play a great part in the nineteenth-century acceptance of the West, let us note briefly the precedents which the early Ch'ing emperors bequeathed to their less fortunate successors of a later day.

When the Manchu conquerors first came to Peking in 1644, they found the Jesuit Adam Schall there, in charge of a bureau compiling a set of monographs on Western methods of calculation for making the calendar. Schall was permitted to continue his work, and when he had the new calendar for 1645 prepared in time for publication, his position as head of the Imperial Bureau of Astronomy was confirmed. During the following two hundred years, except for a short interruption, some Catholic missionary was always in charge of that Bureau. The first Manchu emperor in China, Shun-chih (1644-1661), was very friendly towards Schall and sometimes sought the aged missionary's advice. His successor, K'ang-hsi (reigned 1662-1722) was even more conciliatory towards the Jesuits and made use of their services to a considerable extent. During a controversy in 1669, when their predictions concerning astronomical phenomena were proved correct, he became interested in Western mathematics. Thereafter, the emperor studied Western mathematics and scientific subjects and kept several of the Jesuits near at hand to provide information or translations. In 1689 he sent two of them with the embassy from China which went to negotiate a treaty with the Russians at Nerchinsk—a treaty demarcating the Sino-Russian boundary in the northeast which remained in force down to the 1840's. For more than a century after 1689, Western missionaries at Peking served as interpreters whenever Russian or other European diplomatic missions came there. K'ang-hsi also employed them to teach selected young students mathematics and art, and to supervise the repairing of clocks and music boxes. In the last decade of his reign, as we have noted, he sent them out in teams to conduct a cartographic survey of the whole empire. He also tried his best to arbitrate rationally in the so-called rites controversy between the Jesuit and other Catholic orders. The tolerance of this illustrious ruler, however, did not always stretch to the point of permitting missionary work in the entire empire. Evidently fearing that political repercussions would follow provincial proselytizing, K'ang-hsi introduced a system of passports in order to allow only certain missionaries in Peking and Macao. This policy was followed by his successors.⑦

Yung-chêng (1723-1735) developed a dislike for Western missionaries because some of them had taken the side of his opponents on the issue of his succession to the throne. He tolerated those who had official posts in Peking, but he deported many others who were working in the provinces.⑧ Under Ch'ien-lung (1736-1795), European mechanics were still employed to assemble and repair the clockworks and other devices brought from Europe, and several Jesuit missionaries served as architects of the buildings and landscape garden in Italian style which formed a part of the Old Summer Palace. About 1747 a fountain in the Western style was constructed by Michel Benoist, and this became the nucleus of a group of buildings in the Italian style designed by Castiglione.[39] By the last years of Ch'ien-lung, however, when the Macartney embassy of 1793 visited Peking from England, the Europeans had ceased to play much part at the Ch'ing court. Their long-continued activities there, perhaps because more technical than ideological, had evidently not given the Ch'ing rulers any real understanding of the West. The center of contact shifted to Canton.

Until this time, the missionaries at Peking had usually been referred to as "men of the Western Ocean" (*Hsi-yang jen*), meaning Europeans. But as Sino-Western contact and conflict increased in the early nineteenth century, the generic term "barbarians" (*i*), long applied to the Europeans at Canton, came into more general use. In the traditional Chinese society, every person had his place and designation; and since the early Portuguese adventurers who reached China by sea after 1514 were non-Chinese in culture, and also inclined to piracy and rapine, this appellation had been fitting both in the old Greek sense of "barbarian" as "outlandish" and in the later sense of the term as "barbarous." The non-Chinese of Inner Asia had provided an inexhaustible reservoir of "barbarians" since the beginning of Chinese history. There was nothing novel in the idea of bellicose foreigners turning up on the Chinese frontier. The Portuguese and their successors had been assimilated into the Confucian scheme of things by being allowed to dwell on the southeast coast at Macao or Canton under a careful, if polite, quarantine. The success of the Jesuits at Peking had been an inside job, quite distinct from the trade of Western merchants on the South China coast. By the end of the eighteenth century, the Western world was represented there chiefly by the British East India Company trading at Canton, where a complex of Sino-Western problems was gradually accumulating over such questions as diplomatic equality, taxation of trade, and legal procedures. It was most unfortunate for the Ch'ing Dynasty at Peking and the Chinese and Manchu-officials who represented it at Canton that the Chinese concept of the West had been so little developed.

Knowing little of the West in fact, China's ruling class applied to it the ancient theory of tributary relations—the grand and ancient concept that the Middle Kingdom was indeed, the center of civilization, that the Son of Heaven actually represented all mankind in his functions as a moral and ceremonial intermediary between human society and the unseen forces of Nature, and that all the surrounding tribes and peoples should naturally recognize this central fact. The Chinese theory of state, in short, was that of a universal empire. Foreign rulers who wished contact or trade with the empire should first enroll as tributaries, accept investiture, send envoys to perform the kotow (three kneelings and nine prostrations) before the Son of Heaven, and otherwise obey the regulations for tributary intercourse. As European contact increased, the Ch'ing court persisted in the effort to fit Western nations into this traditional and outmoded tributary framework.[40] Perhaps the most famous example of this attitude is the lofty and condescending edict of Ch'ien-lung to King George Ⅲ in 1793, which read in part:[41]

AN IMPERIAL EDICT TO THE KING OF ENGLAND: You, O King, are so inclined toward our civilization that you have sent a special envoy across the seas to bring to our Court your memorial of congratulations on the occasion of my birthday and to present your native products as an expression of your thoughtfulness. On perusing your memorial, so simply worded and sincerely conceived, I am impressed by your genuine respectfulness and friendliness and greatly pleased.

As to the request made in your memorial, O King, to send one of your nationals to stay at the Celestial Court to take care of your country's trade with China, this is not in harmony with the state system of our dynasty and will definitely not be permitted. Traditionally people of the European nations who wished to render some service under the Celestial

Court have been permitted to come to the capital. But after their arrival they are obliged to wear Chinese court costumes, are placed in a certain residence, and are never allowed to return to their own countries. This is the established rule of the Celestial Dynasty with which presumably you, O King, are familiar. Now you, O King, wish to send one of your nationals to live in the capital, but he is not like the Europeans, who come to Peking as Chinese employees, live there and never return home again, nor can he be allowed to go and come and maintain any correspondence. This is indeed a useless undertaking.

Moreover the territory under the control of the Celestial Court is very large and wide. There are well-established regulations governing tributary envoys from the outer states to Peking, giving them provisions (of food and traveling expenses) by our post-houses and limiting their going and coming. There has never been a precedent for letting them do whatever they like. Now if you, O King, wish to have a representative in Peking, his language will be unintelligible and his dress different from the regulations; there is no place to accommodate him...

[p. 14] The Celestial Court has pacified and possessed the territory within the four seas. Its sole aim is to do its utmost to achieve good government and to manage political affairs, attaching no value to strange jewels and precious objects. The various articles presented by you, O King, this time are accepted by my special order to the office in charge of such functions in consideration of the offerings having come from a long distance with sincere good wishes. As a matter of fact, the virtue and prestige of the Celestial Dynasty having spread far and wide, the kings of the myriad nations come by land and sea with all sorts of precious things. Consequently there is nothing we lack, as your principal envoy and others have themselves observed. We have never set much store on strange or ingenious objects, nor do we need any more of your country's manufactures...

In such terms the Englishmen and Scotsmen who were about to

batter down the gates and destroy the Middle Kingdom's ancient superiority over all other peoples were still categorized as uncultured barbarians outside the pale of civilization. Chinese and Manchu officials, making systematic reports in their memorials to the emperor, regularly applied to the British and Americans at Canton the same terms that were traditionally used with reference to the Burut and other tribes of Central Asia or to the Lo-lo and Miao-tzu aborigines of southwest China. Curiosity about Europe and America appears to have been very slight among the ruling class of China. The confusion based on ignorance was confounded by the difficulties of translation between the Chinese and European languages. The Portuguese had been called *Fo-lang-chi* ("Franks") because they came from the same region as the Franks who had fought the Saracens at the time of the Crusades. When the French arrived, France (*Fo-lang-hsi*) was confused with Portugal. The union of Spain and Portugal in the late sixteenth century confused those two countries in the Chinese mind. The presence at Portuguese Macao of Italian Jesuits identified Portugal with *I-ta-li*. Meanwhile the Dutch from Holland (*Ho-lan*) were confused with the French, and when a Dutch king took the British throne, Holland became confused with England.㊷

If the names of the European barbarians were topsy-turvy, their habitat was even more so. Since they all arrived by ship from the "Southern Ocean" (*Nan-yang*), through which Chinese merchants plied their trade by junk with Southeast Asia, it was often assumed that these European barbarians dwelt somewhere to the southwest, beyond the minuscule sultanates and ports-of-call like Sungora, Patani, and Johore which were strung along the Malay peninsula. When Europe was assigned to its proper place in the "Western Ocean" (*Hsi-yang*), confusion still resulted from the fact that this had been the very logical name anciently assigned to the Indian Ocean west of Malaya. Europe had to be called "Great Western Ocean" (*Ta-hsi-yang*) to distinguish it.

The personal characteristics of the strange people who came to China from Europe were well known to the Chinese linguists, hong merchants, and compradores who specialized in the foreign trade. But to most of the empire, Europeans were known only through rumor and folklore. Some of the latter has been enshrined in books of the period, which comment on the barbarians' "dazzling white" flesh, high noses, and "red hair" (*Hung-mao*, the name of the Dutch in particular). "Their custom is to esteem women and think lightly of men. Marriages are left to mutual arrangement," says one imperial compilation of the 1750's,[43] thereby indicating the curious and chaotic state of Western mores. But this Chinese observation of the West hardly went beyond the superficialities of manners—"they wear short coats and tip their black felt hats as a sign of politeness. The Swedes take snuff, which they carry in little containers made of golden thread." This appears to have been about the level of understanding of the West which prevailed in China in the period when the Industrial Revolution was beginning to remake the world. The diplomatic effort of Lord Amherst at Peking in 1816, like that of Macartney in 1793, was labeled a "tribute mission from the King of England" and did little to educate the Chinese upper class. After all, between 1655 and 1795, there had been some seventeen missions from Western countries, including Russia, which got as far as audience with the emperor, and all but the British had performed the kotow. The record contained nothing to show that Europeans were not tributary to China like other countries, whenever they wanted relations with China at all. Indeed, the Chinese records available to Commissioner Lin Tse-hsü in 1839 also state *pro forma* that Macartney performed the kotow, although we know he did not.[44]

As the export trade in teas and silks at Canton grew in volume and value, a few accounts of it and of the foreign trading nations were drawn up by Chinese chroniclers. One of these accounts, the "Maritime record" (*Hai-lu*), was taken down by a scholar from the lips of an old blind interpreter who in his youth had sailed the seas.[45] He describes the many-storied houses of England, the three bridges of London and its plethora of prostitutes, how the soldiers wear red and the women wear narrow-waisted dresses, tight above and full below—all exotic enough, but hardly enlightening. This and other works of its kind do state, however, that England lives by overseas trade and by seizing profitable posts like Bombay, Bengal, and Singapore. At the beginning of our story in 1839, the British position in India was well-known and the strength of England's naval guns had already been exhibited on the coast of China. Yet the Chinese officials of the 1840's seem to have been profoundly ignorant of what they faced. One of their first efforts, aside from self-defense, had to be the study of Western geography, to learn the name, location, products, and size of each country—almost like children in school.

# 2  RECOGNITION OF CHINA'S NEED TO KNOW THE WEST, 1839-1860

## CHAPTER III  COMMISSIONER LIN'S PROGRAM FOR MEETING BRITISH AGGRESSION

Unlike the Japanese, the Chinese of a century ago did not look back on a tradition of borrowing from abroad. The empire was vast and its institutions were slow to change. It took the rulers of China two decades, after the first defeat by British arms in 1840, to acknowledge the necessity of studying the West—a necessity which many Japanese students of the "Dutch learning" had recognized even before the arrival of Commodore Perry in 1853. Japanese scholars, though secluded from foreign contact, were evidently more curious about the Western world than their contemporaries in China, who knew of the Western merchants at Canton but made little effort to seek them out. ①

Since the Chinese officials in Ch'ing Dynasty were supremely ignorant of the West but well-versed in human nature and in Chinese tradition, they at once applied to the British those concepts and practices which had become traditional in China's dealings with barbarians—particularly the joint methods of coercion and persuasion... This was the approach of the famous Commissioner Lin Tse-hsü when he precipitated the Opium War in 1839 by blockading the British merchants at Canton and destroying their opium. His letter to Queen Victoria which forms our first document below was an appeal to conscience, just as his drastic action at Canton was a resort to force. Unfortunately for Lin, this combined approach failed in both its aspects; for British gunboats soon retaliated with superior power, while the British refused to acknowledge that the opium trade was the main and only point in dispute ... Chinese opinion saw the evil of the opium trade, which poisoned an increasing number of Chinese smokers and drained China's vital silver supply out of the country. But this was too simple a view of the problem which China faced.

We present below two brief items by Lin Tse-hsü. One was written when he tried to chastise the British, and one afterward. There follows a longer selection from the first famous geography of the 1840's, a book which tried to describe the West, almost for the first time in Chinese history. Finally, we note the early growth of nationalistic anti-foreignism at Canton, a sentiment which was eventually to motivate great changes.

In the first document, the righteous moral tone of Commissioner Lin's appeal to Queen Victoria in 1839 is certainly striking. It indicates that the opium question in the minds of Chinese officials was not entirely, as some have alleged, a matter of economics; the responsibility of the Confucian monarch for the welfare of the common people was also involved. Lin Tse-hsü had reached Canton as imperial commissioner on March 10, 1839, and soon coerced the British merchants into surrendering their opium stocks, which were publicly destroyed. But by August it had become apparent to him that the opium trade could be finally checked only at its source. This famous letter to "the ruler of England" (*Ying-kuo wang*, i. e., without distinction of sex) was therefore a further and unprecedented effort to solve an insoluble problem.

Lin's phraseology toward the British ruler is courteous within the limits of traditional tributary language. His theory that the barbarians must perish without the rhubarb,② tea, and other exports from China is a manifestation of Chinese egocentricity ... Lin's use of rewards and punishments to make merchants calculate their advantage and disadvantage is in the Chinese tradition of administrative law. It is plain that the imperial commissioner expected human nature to be the same in Britain as in China. More importantly, he expected it to respond equally to the dictates of moral conscience.

## DOC. 1  LIN TSE-HSü's MORAL ADVICE TO QUEEN VICTORIA, 1839③

A communication: magnificently our great Emperor soothes and pacifies China and the foreign countries, regarding all with the same kindness. If there is profit, then he shares it with the peoples of the world; if there is harm, then he removes it on behalf of the world. This is because he takes the mind of heaven and earth as his mind.

The kings of your honorable country by a tradition handed down from generation to generation have always been noted for their politeness and submissiveness. We have read your successive tributary memorials saying, "In general our countrymen who go to trade in China have always received His Majesty the Emperor's gracious treatment and equal justice," and so on. Privately we are delighted with the way in which the honorable rulers of your country deeply understand the grand principles and are grateful for the Celestial grace. For this reason the Celestial Court in soothing those from afar has redoubled its polite and kind treatment. The profit from trade has been enjoyed by them continuously for two hundred years. This is the source from which your country has become known for its wealth.

But after a long period of commercial intercourse, there appear among the crowd of barbarians both good persons and bad, unevenly. Consequently there are those who smuggle opium to seduce the Chinese people and so cause the spread of the poison to all provinces. Such persons who only care to profit themselves, and disregard their harm to others, are not tolerated by the laws of heaven and are unanimously hated by human beings. His Majesty the Emperor, upon hearing of this, is in a towering rage [p. 34]. He has especially sent me, his commissioner, to come to Kwangtung, and together with the governor-general and governor jointly to investigate and settle this matter.

All those people in China who sell opium or smoke opium should receive the death penalty. If we trace the crime of those barbarians who through the years have been selling opium, then the deep harm they have wrought and the great profit they have usurped should fundamentally justify their execution according to law. We take into consideration, however, the fact that the various barbarians have still known how to repent their crimes and return to their allegiance to us by taking the 20,183 chests④ of opium from their storeships and petitioning us, through their consular officer [superintendent of trade], Elliot, to receive it. It has been entirely destroyed and this has been faithfully reported to the Throne in several memorials by this commissioner and his colleagues.

Fortunately we have received a specially extended favor from His Majesty the Emperor, who considers that for those who voluntarily surrender there are still some circumstances to palliate their crime, and so for the time being he has magnanimously excused them from punishment. But as for those who again violate the opium prohibition, it is difficult for the law to pardon them repeatedly. Having established new regulations, we presume that the ruler of your honorable country, who takes delight in our culture and whose disposition is inclined towards us, must be able to instruct the various barbarians to observe the law with care. It is only necessary to explain to them the advantages and disadvantages and then they will know that the legal code of the Celestial Court must be absolutely obeyed with awe.

We find that your country is sixty or seventy thousand *li* [three *li* make one mile, ordinarily] from China. Yet there are barbarian ships that strive to come here for trade for the purpose of making a great profit. The wealth of China is used to profit the barbarians. That is to say, the great profit made by barbarians is all taken from the rightful share of China. By what right do they then in return use the poisonous drug to injure the Chinese people? Even though the barbarians may not necessarily intend to do us harm, yet in coveting profit to an extreme, they have no regard for injuring others. Let us ask, where is your conscience? I have heard that the smoking of opium is very strictly forbidden by your country; that is because the harm caused by opium is clearly understood. Since it is not permitted to do harm to your own country, then even less should you let it be passed on to the harm of other countries—how much less to China! Of all that China exports to foreign countries, there is not a single thing which is not beneficial to people: they are of benefit when eaten, or of benefit when used, or of benefit when resold: all are beneficial. Is there a single article from China "which has done any harm to foreign countries?" Take tea and rhubarb, for example; the foreign countries cannot get along for a single day without them. If China cuts off these benefits with no sympathy for those who are to suffer, then what can the barbarians rely upon to keep themselves alive? Moreover the woolens, camlets, and longells [i. e., textiles] of foreign countries cannot be woven unless they obtain Chinese silk. If China, again, cuts off this beneficial export, what profit can the barbarians expect to make? As for other foodstuffs, beginning with candy, ginger, cinnamon, and so forth, and articles for use, beginning with silk, satin, chinaware, and so on, all the things that must be had by foreign countries are innumerable. On the other hand, articles coming from the outside to China can only be used as toys. We can take them or get along without them. Since they are not needed by China, what difficulty would there be if we closed the frontier and stopped the trade? Nevertheless our Celestial Court lets tea, silk, and other goods be shipped without limit and circulated everywhere without begrudging it in the slightest. This is for no other reason but to share the benefit with the people of the whole world.

The goods from China carried away by your country not only supply your own consumption and use, but also can be divided up and sold to other countries, producing a triple profit. Even if you do not sell opium, you still have this threefold profit. How can you bear to go further, selling products injurious to others in order to fulfill your insatiable desire?

Suppose there were people from another country who carried opium for sale to England and seduced your people into buying and smoking it; certainly your honorable ruler would deeply hate it and be bitterly aroused. We have heard heretofore that your honorable ruler is kind and benevolent. Naturally you would not wish to give unto others what you yourself do not want. We have also heard that the ships coming to Canton have all had regulations promulgated and given to them in which it is stated that it is not permitted to carry contraband goods. This indicates that the administrative orders of your honorable rule have been originally strict and clear. Only because the trading ships are numerous, heretofore perhaps they have not been examined with care. Now after this communication has been dispatched and you have clearly understood the strictness of the prohibitory laws of the Celestial Court, certainly you will not let your subjects dare again to violate the law.

We have further learned that in London, the capital of your honorable rule, and in Scotland (Su-ko-lan), Ireland (Ai-lun), and other places, originally no opium has been produced. Only in several places of India under your control such as Bengal, Madras, Bombay, Patna, Benares, and Malwa has opium been planted from hill to hill, and ponds⑤ have been opened for its manufacture. For months and years work is continued in order to accumulate the poison. The obnoxious odor ascends, irritating heaven and frightening the spirits. Indeed you, O King, can eradicate the opium plant in these places, hoe over the fields entirely, and sow in its stead the five grains [i. e., millet, barley, wheat, etc.]. Anyone who dares again attempt to plant and manufacture opium should be severely punished. This will really be a great, benevolent government policy that will increase the common weal and get rid of evil. For this, Heaven must support you and the spirits must bring you good fortune, prolonging your old age and extending your descendants. All will depend on this act.

As for the barbarian merchants who come to China, their food and drink and habitation are all received by the gracious favor of our Celestial

Court. Their accumulated wealth is all benefit given with pleasure by our Celestial Court. They spend rather few days in their own country but more time in Canton. [p. 35] To digest clearly the legal penalties as an aid to instruction has been a valid principle in all ages. Suppose a man of another country comes to England to trade, he still has to obey the English laws; how much more should he obey in China the laws of the Celestial Dynasty?

Now we have set up regulations governing the Chinese people. He who sells opium shall receive the death penalty and he who smokes it also the death penalty. Now consider this: if the barbarians do not bring opium, then how can the Chinese people resell it, and how can they smoke it? The fact is that the wicked barbarians beguile the Chinese people into a death trap. How then can we grant life only to these barbarians? He who takes the life of even one person still has to atone for it with his own life; yet is the harm done by opium limited to the taking of one life only? Therefore in the new regulations, in regard to those barbarians who bring opium to China, the penalty is fixed at decapitation or strangulation. This is what is called getting rid of a harmful thing on behalf of mankind.

Moreover we have found that in the middle of the second month of this year [April 9] Consul [Superintendent] Elliot of your nation, because the opium prohibition law was very stern and severe, petitioned for an extension of the time limit. He requested a limit of five months for India and its adjacent harbors and related territories, and ten months for England proper, after which they would act in conformity with the new regulations. Now we, the commissioner and others, have memorialized and have received the extraordinary Celestial grace of His Majesty the Emperor, who has redoubled his consideration and compassion. All those who within the period of the coming one year (from England) or six months (from India) bring opium to China by mistake, but who voluntarily confess and completely surrender their opium, shall be exempt from their punishment. After this limit of time, if there are still those who bring opium to China then they will plainly have committed a wilful violation and shall at once be executed according to law, with absolutely no clemency or pardon. This may be called the height of kindness and the perfection of justice.

Our Celestial Dynasty rules over and supervises the myriad states, and surely possesses unfathomable spiritual dignity. Yet the Emperor cannot bear to execute people without having first tried to reform them by instruction. Therefore he especially promulgates these fixed regulations. The barbarian merchants of your country, if they wish to do business for a prolonged period, are required to obey our statutes respectfully and to cut off permanently the source of opium. They must by no means try to test the effectiveness of the law with their lives. May you, O King, check your wicked and sift your vicious people before they come to China, in order to guarantee the peace of your nation, to show further the sincerity of your politeness and submissiveness, and to let the two countries enjoy together the blessings of peace. How fortunate, how fortunate indeed! After receiving this dispatch will you immediately give us a prompt reply regarding the details and circumstances of your cutting off the opium traffic. Be sure not to put this off. The above is what has to be communicated. [Vermilion Endorsement:] This is appropriately worded and quite comprehensive (*Te-t'i chou-tao*).

In retrospect it is plain that the Manchu-Chinese defiance of Britain never had the slightest chance of military success. Confident of their power, the British soon opened hostilities, and in 1840 Commissioner Lin was recalled from Canton in disgrace for having produced a war instead of a settlement. As punishment he was ordered to start on his way into exile in Ili.⑥ On the basis of his recent experience with the British at Canton, he wrote letters in 1842 to various friends frankly admitting China's military inferiority to the West and favoring her purchase and manufacture of ships and guns patterned after the Western model. This confession is in sharp contrast with his former intransigent action in Canton. Had his plans for making modern weapons been carried out, China's modernization movement might have been advanced twenty years. Unfortunately, with the Court opposed to it, he dared not make an overt advocacy of Westernization but told only his friends and asked them to keep it confidential. One of these letters, translated below, was addressed to Wu Tzu-hsü,⑦ a compiler of the Hanlin Academy and a good friend of Wo-jen and Tseng Kuo-fan (on these men, see Chapter VI and Doc. 18).

## DOC. 2  A LETTER OF LIN TSE-HSü RECOGNIZING WESTERN MILITARY SUPERIORITY, 1842⑧

[Lin describes to his friend how impossible it proved to control the barbarians, p. 19.] The rebels' ships on the open sea came and went as they pleased, now in the south and now suddenly in the north, changing successively between morning and evening. If we tried to put up a defense everywhere, not only would we toil and expend ourselves without limit, but also how could we recruit and transport so many troops, militia, artillery, and ammunition, and come to their support quickly? ...

When I was in office in Kwangtung and Kwangsi, I had made plans regarding the problems of ships and cannon and a water force. Afraid that there was not enough time to build ships, I at first rented them. Afraid that there was not enough time to cast cannon and that it would not be done according to the regulations, I at first bought foreign ones. The most painful thing was that when the Hu-men [the Bogue or "Tiger's mouth," the entrance to the Canton River] was broken into, a large number of good cannon fell into the hands of the rebellious barbarians. I recall that after I had been punished two years ago, I still took the risk of calling the Emperor's attention to two things: ships and guns. At that time, if these things could have been made and prepared, they still could have been used with effect to fight against the enemy in Chekiang last fall [1841]. Now it is even more difficult to check the wildfire. After all, ships, guns, and a water force are absolutely indispensable. Even if the rebellious barbarians had fled and returned beyond the seas, these things would still have to be urgently planned for, in order to work out the permanent defense of our sea frontiers. Moreover, unless we have weapons, what other help can we get now to drive away the crocodile and to get rid of the whales? ...

But at this time I must strictly observe the advice to seal my lips as one corks the mouth of a bottle. However, toward those with identical aims and interests, I suddenly spit out the truth and am unable to control myself. I extremely regret my foolishness and carelessness. Nevertheless, when I turn my thoughts to the depth of your attention to me, then I cannot conceal these things from myself. I only beg you to keep them confidential. By all means, please do not tell other persons.

Lin Tse-hsü's concern over the British problem had led him while at Canton to compile information on the West and to suggest strategic principles for holding Britain at bay. As the British governor of Hongkong wrote later, "When Lin... got involved with Europeans, he availed himself of the aid of interpreters, and of every work he could procure, either native or foreign, to obtain a knowledge of... every country of the world beyond China... the missionary tracts, the Chinese monthly magazine, a treatise on commerce, a description of the United States and of England, a work on geography, etc., which were all, more or less, abridged or abstracted. Translations were also made of all such articles in the newspapers as contained anything concerning China, and especially opium."[9] The result was a famous geography book on the "maritime countries" (*Hai-kuo t'u-chih*) which was compiled by the well-known scholar Wei Yuan (1794-1857), making use of Lin's materials. Some sections of the work name Lin as the compiler. Wei Yuan's first acknowledgment at the beginning of his preface is to the "Gazetteer of the four continents" (*Ssu-chou chih*), which was probably a compilation of translations from Murray's *Cyclopaedia of Geography* and was published by Lin in 1841.⑩ After Lin was dismissed in disgrace, Wei Yuan completed the compilation and revised it several times. The first edition, 50 *chüan*, was published in 1844, the second in 60 *chüan* in 1849, and the third in 100 *chüan* in 1852.⑪

Wei Yuan had published in 1842 his famous "Record of imperial military exploits" (*Sheng-wu chi*) in which he surveyed the campaigns of the Ch'ing Dynasty since its founding. He was a good scholar of military history and economic geography and a critical student of the classics. Indeed, his academic position in the mid-nineteenth century was almost comparable to that of Ku Yen-wu in the seventeenth and Tai Chen (1724-1777) in the eighteenth. During the Opium War, however, Wei Yuan was a minor civilian official at Yangchow and he did not receive the *chin-shih* degree until 1844. While he was familiar with the British military campaigns, his views on strategy and high policy undoubtedly derive from those of Lin Tse-hsü.

In the following section on military strategy against the British, there crops up the doctrinaire fallacy into which so much Chinese scholarly thinking was inclined to fall—a tendency to settle strategic questions on the basis of theories, closely reasoned but inadequately based on fact. Even so, his advocacy of land defense rather than sea battles is sensible and he at least explodes the theories so widely expounded in memorials of the period that British vessels could be sunk by divers boring holes in their bottoms, or burned by fireships floating against them.

In the field of diplomacy, Lin and Wei Yuan enunciate principles which were time-tested in their day and have been used effectively since. "Using barbarians to control barbarians," the Chinese counterpart of the balance-of-power concept in Western Europe, is not a foolproof stratagem (any more than is the balance of power). But like that similar device of empires, "divide and rule," it is often inexpensive and requires only a modest investment of force. "Learning the superior skills of the barbarians" strikes a more novel note, although it was soon to become the spirit of an entire epoch in nearby Japan and the slogan of many Chinese reformers.

In applying the principle of using barbarians, Lin at once hit upon the possibility of getting the Russians to invade India, which would indeed have put a stop to the British foray in China. The idea of using France and the United States against England was a similar shot in the dark, but wider of the mark. Exactly how far the Americans and French actually sought to mediate in the Opium War is not yet known.⑫

Lin's practical proposals to translate Western books, to build shipyards and arsenals, ships and guns, to hire foreign technical instructors and train selected Chinese personnel, and to alter the military examinations, all forecast the main line of China's development. The great question is, why was all this delayed for almost exactly twenty years?

## DOC. 3   WEI YUAN'S STATEMENT OF
## A POLICY FOR MARITIME DEFENSE, 1842⑬

*Plans for Maritime Defense.* Section a, discussion of defensive strategy, first part

Ever since the barbarian incident, the strategy which has been contrived in the generals' tents and which has been carried out in the field has been, if not war, then peace; if not peace, then war. No one has yet devoted himself to the discussion of defensive measures…

There are two policies for self-defense. First, to defend the open ocean is not as good as to defend the seaports, and to defend the seaports is not as good as to defend the inland rivers. Second, the transferring of distant troops from other provinces is inferior to the training of local troops, and the transferring of water forces is inferior to the training of local marines. There are two methods of attacking the barbarians, namely, to stimulate countries unfriendly to the barbarians to make an attack on them, and to learn the superior skills of the barbarians in order to control them. There are two methods of making peace with the barbarians, namely, to let the various trading nations conduct their trade so as to maintain peace with the barbarians, and to support the first treaty of the Opium War so as to maintain international trade. Now let us first speak of defense...

He who intends to control the enemy must cause the enemy to lose his basis of superiority. Does the superiority of barbarian ships lie in warfare in the open sea or in the inland rivers? There are only two measures we can use to resist the enemy: one is to attack them with cannon and the other is to attack them with fire... If our cannon merely hit the side of a ship, a ship in the open ocean, easily maneuvered on deep water, it simply shudders and withdraws; it will neither be broken [p. 2] nor sunk. We must hit the mast and the bridge before it is rendered unnavigable, yet immediately a steamboat will tow it to another harbor to repair it overnight. Only when we hit the ammunition hold will there be an explosion causing it to turn over or sink. There is no such thing as to have someone swim to the bottom of the ship to bore a hole and make it sink. This is the first difficulty. If we have fire ships put out to sea to burn the barbarian warship, the hull material is so solid and thick that even if it is burned it will not catch fire. It is necessary to use fire arrows or rockets to burn the sails, ropes, oil, fuel and munitions, and attack the rudder and bridge of the ship. Yet, on the top of the mast of a barbarian ship there is always a barbarian soldier with a telescope looking into the distance. Before our fire ships reach them, they will long since have cut their anchors and escaped. This is the second difficulty.

[The author goes on to say that it is better to attack foreign ships in inland rivers where Chinese guns can hit them and where they will be unable to maneuver in the more shallow and narrow waters; where iron chains and sunken boats can hinder their movement and fire ships can be sent from all directions to burn them. In this situation, it is argued, the guns of the foreign ships cannot hit the Chinese soldiers, who will lie behind thick walls.]

[P. 3b] The phrase "enticing the enemy to enter the inland rivers" means that soldiers, guns and mines are sown on land and in the water as if making a pit to wait for tigers, or setting a net to wait for fish. We must make sure that we have control over their fate before we let them enter our strategic area. It does not mean that we should open the door and invite the bandits in as guests...

[P. 13] The Japanese barbarians [who raided China in the sixteenth century] were strong in land fighting and weak in water warfare, because the pirates who came were all desperadoes from poor islands, who had no means to build large ships and big guns, but relied upon sheer courage to cross the ocean, and depended upon their swords and spears to invade China. Therefore, whenever they went ashore it was impossible to resist them. But when the Japanese ships met the junks of Fukien and Kwangtung, then they were like rice on a grindstone. If the Japanese ships met big cannons and firearms, they would be like goats chased by wolves... In general, the strength of the Japanese was on the land. To attack them on the open ocean was to assail their weak point. The strength of the British barbarians is on the ocean. Wait for them in the inland rivers. Wait for them on the shore and they will lose their strength. Unfortunately, the Ming people, in warding off the Japanese, did not know how to oppose them on the ocean, and nowadays those who are guarding against the British do not lay ambushes in the interior. Thus, the really effective ideas in the world must necessarily be contrary to the opinion of the multitude of mediocre minds...

*Plans for Maritime Defense.* Section c, discussion of offensive strategy

[P. 36] The inland defense having been consolidated, let us now discuss the external offensive. Yo Fei [1103-1142] says that to use a government force to attack pirates is difficult; to use pirates to attack pirates is easy... What is the method for using sea barbarians to fight against sea barbarians?

To plan barbarian affairs it is necessary to know first the barbarians' conditions. To understand the barbarians' conditions it is necessary first to know the barbarians' geographical situations. Now let us first explain their circumstances.

The enemy countries of which the British barbarians are afraid are three: Russia, France, and America. The vassal states of our country of which the British are afraid are four: the Gurkhas [i. e., Nepal], Burma, Siam, and Annam. The methods for attacking England are, first, from the land; and second, from the ocean. The method of attacking her from the land lies in India. The countries which are close to India are Russia and the Gurkhas. The Russian capital and the English capital are separated by a few countries and not connected by land routes. But by water, one route is by the Mediterranean sea and the other one by the Baltic sea, where a force that sails from Russia in the morning could reach England in the evening. In 1691 the King of England [sic] used warships to attack Russia by the Mediterranean sea but failed and returned home. Thereafter, the two countries had no intercourse and their military struggle was concentrated in India.

India is on the southwest of the Onion Range, and adjacent to our further Tibet, the Gurkhas, and Burma. From the homeland of the British barbarians, India is several myriad *li*. The British barbarians used warships and occupied the three parts of India, in the east, the south, and center. The Russian troops then, from the space between the Yellow Sea and the Caspian Sea, attacked and subdued the various nomadic tribes and made connection with the two western and central parts of India. They were only separated by the Himalayas. Each side was guarded by heavy garrisons of troops. From Bengal to Malwa in East India and from Bombay to Madras in South India opium is prevalent. The British barbarians annually collect from opium taxes more than ten million (taels) silver, and the Russians are jealous. When the British barbarians mobilized Indian [p. 37] troops and warships to invade China, they were greatly afraid that Russia might take advantage of their weakness to invade Hindustan (Author's note: in central India). There was also a rumor that Russian messengers had started a trip from Petersburg to China (Author's note: Petersburg is her eastern capital), and the British were scared of the two ox horns [i. e., pincers]... Therefore, the British barbarians' fear of Russia lies not in her national capital but in India. This is one opportunity which might be used.

The Gurkhas are in the western part of further Tibet and are close to eastern India. When in the middle of the Ch'ien-lung period our troops invaded the Gurkha barbarians, the British barbarians' warships in India also took that opportunity to attack their eastern boundary. So after the stoppage of commerce with the British barbarians last year, the Gurkha barbarians immediately informed our Imperial Resident in Tibet that they were willing to send troops to attack India. At that time, if the Gurkhas had been permitted to cause trouble on their east and Russia to invade on the west, then India might have been collapsed and the enemy vessels would have had anxiety over their internal garrisons. This is a second opportunity which might have been used. Thus, when there were opportunities which might have been taken, they were not utilized; this is not because the outer barbarians cannot be used, but because we need personnel who are capable of making arrangements with them.

There is no better method of attacking England by sea than to use France and America. France is very close to the English barbarians, being separated only by an arm of the sea. America and the English barbarians, on the other hand, are separated by a great ocean. Beginning from the period at the end of the Ming and the beginning of this dynasty, France colonized the northeast territory of America. Cities and towns were built, markets and ports were opened. The British barbarians suddenly attacked and seized them. Thereupon the French barbarians and the English barbarians became bitter enemies. Later on the British barbarians levied numerous and heavy taxes which caused the thirteen parts of America to start a righteous revolt to drive them out. At the same time the Americans asked France to help them. Several hundred warships of the three countries, and several hundreds of thousands of soldiers and seamen were kept on duty for several years. The Americans cut the British supply lines. The British soldiers were in hunger and distress, and the British ceded territory and asked for peace. The Americans then entirely recovered the twenty-seven parts of their original land [p. 38], and the British barbarians only retained the four parts in the northeast corner [i. e., Canada]. They did not dare invade the United States any more.

Even the land of India was also opened by Holland and France, but was taken over by the British barbarians... This is the condition of the various countries.

As for commerce at Canton, the British barbarians are the most fierce and arrogant while France and America are the most amicable and obedient. After the stopping of trade, the British barbarians even used warships to prevent other countries trading with us. The various countries were all resentful and said that if the British barbarians did not withdraw their troops for a lengthy period, they would each be obliged to go home and send ships of war to dispute the issue with them. Last year [1840] after the general for Rebellion Pacification⑩ had mobilized his troops, the barbarian headman among the Americans at Canton at once came to mediate. Thereupon, Elliot submitted a document saying that he was only asking that he might carry on trade as usual. He dared not make demands even regarding the cost of the burned opium and the status of Hongkong. This is the third opportunity which might have been used.

Unfortunately, when the peace negotiations had not yet been settled, our troops suddenly attacked the barbarian factories and unexpectedly injured several Americans by mistake. Thereupon, the American headman no longer made any effort to mediate. But France, after the British barbarians for the second time had broken the truce, in the winter sent a military officer with a ship of war to Canton... [The author then describes how, through suspicion and bureaucratic delay, China failed to take advantage of an alleged French offer to mediate with the British.]

The situation today is this: if there is a discussion about getting and using Western warships, then someone is sure to say that he fears borrowing aid from the outer barbarians would show our weakness. Yet when suddenly our weakness has been several times more fully exposed than this would have involved, they have been glad to do it without shrinking. If there is a discussion about building ships, making weapons, and learning the superior techniques of the barbarians, they say it is too expensive. But when suddenly the cost is ten times more than this, they again say it is a matter of exigency to meet an emergency and is not regrettable. If there is a discussion about the translation of barbarian books and prying into barbarian affairs, they are sure to say it would cause trouble. (Note: during the reign of Chia-ch'ing there was someone in Kwangtung who intended to publish a book giving transliterations of Chinese and barbarian characters, which would be very convenient for Chinese translating their characters. Yet it was forbidden by the Kwangtung authorities.) When suddenly something has happened, then they ask, "What is the distance between the English capital and the Russian capital?" Or, "Via what route can the English barbarians communicate with the Mohammedan tribes? ..."

Regarding these countries, with which we have had trade relations for two hundred years, we indeed know neither their locations nor their interrelations of friendship or enmity. Can it even yet be said that we are paying attention to frontier affairs? In the Han Dynasty, the Western Regions were utilized to attack the Hsiung-hu [Huns]. In the T'ang Dynasty, Turfan was utilized to attack India and the Uighurs were utilized to attack Turfan. Emperor K'ang-hsi used the sailing ships of Holland to attack Taiwan and he also allied with the Russians to exert pressure on Djungaria. From ancient times those who tried to control the outer barbarians only prevented their alliance with our enemies to plan against us, but did not prevent their alliance with us to attack our enemies; they only prevented the leaking of Chinese intelligence to the outside, but we have not heard that they prohibited the conditions of foreign countries being revealed to China. Thus, he who wishes to control the outer barbarians must [p. 40] begin by understanding their circumstances, and he who wishes to understand their circumstances must begin by establishing a bureau for the translation of barbarian books. He who wishes to train men of ability in frontier affairs must begin by using the governor-general and governors who pay attention to frontier affairs...

Before the peace settlement, it behooves us to use barbarians against barbarians. After the peace, it is proper for us to learn their superior techniques in order to control them. The superior techniques of the barbarians are three: (1) warships, (2) firearms, and (3) methods of maintaining and training soldiers. Let us give an account of the past events of this dynasty.

At the beginning of the K'ang-hsi period, the sailing ships of Holland were sent to suppress Taiwan. The European Nan-huai-jen [Ferdinand Verbiest] was ordered to make cannon to suppress the rebellion of the three feudatories;⑮ and Europeans were selected and appointed to the Imperial Board of Astronomy to be officers in charge of the calendar. Today the British barbarians not only have occupied Hongkong and accumulated a great deal of wealth as well as a proud face among the other barbarians, but also have opened the ports and cut down the various charges so as to grant favor to other barbarians. Rather than let the British barbarians be good to them, in order to enlarge their following, would it not be better for us ourselves to be good to them, in order to get them under our control like fingers on the arm? ... [This was the reasoning behind China's acceptance of the most-favored-nation clause and her extension to the other Western nations of the treaty privileges given the British in 1842-1843.]

[Wei Yuan then describes Western shipbuilding.] The materials in their shipyards are piled up like hills and craftsmen congregate there like a cloud. [p. 41] Within twenty or thirty days a large warship can be completed. They can instantly spread the sails and adjust the tiller with a few shouted orders. Their craftsmen compete with each other in their talents and abilities. In construction they compete for speed and in navigation also. Construction goes on all year long, the fire illuminates the sky, and the noise shakes the earth. Thus, while the British ships and guns are regarded in China as due to extraordinary skill, in the various countries of Europe they are considered as quite ordinary. In Canton international trade has been carried on for two hundred years. At first the products of their strange skills and clever craftsmanship were received, and then their heterodox religions and poisonous opium. But in regard to their conduct of war and the effectiveness of their weapons, we are learning not a single one of their superior skills. That is, we are only willing to receive the harm and not... the benefit of foreign intercourse.

Let us establish a shipyard and an arsenal at two spots, Chuenpi and Taikoktow⑯ outside of the Bogue in Kwangtung, and select one or two persons from among the foreign headmen who have come from France and America, respectively, to bring Western craftsmen to Canton to take charge of building ships and making arms. In addition, we should invite Western helmsmen to take charge of teaching the methods of navigating ships and of using cannon, following the precedent of the barbarian officials in the Imperial Board of Astronomy. We should select clever artisans and good soldiers from Fukien and Kwangtung to learn from them, the craftsmen to learn the casting of cannon and building of ships, and the good soldiers to learn their methods of navigation and attack... In Kwangtung there should be ten thousand soldiers; in Fukien, ten thousand; in Chekiang, six thousand; and in Kiangsu, four thousand. In assigning soldiers to the ships we must rely on selection and training. [p. 42] Eight out of ten should be taken from among the fishermen and smugglers along the sea coast. Two out of ten should be taken from the old encampments of the water forces. All the padded rations and extra rations of the water force should be ... used for the recruiting and maintenance of good soldiers. We must make the water forces of China able to navigate large (lit., "storied") ships overseas, and able to fight against foreign barbarians on the high seas...

While Chinese officials like Lin and Wei Yuan were reacting to the British invasion by formulating theories of statecraft, another type of reaction became manifest among the Cantonese populace. In 1841, after British forces had fought their way up the river to the great walled metropolis, exacted a "ransom,"① and then withdrawn, there began an anti-foreign movement which seems to have been one of the first stirrings of modern Chinese nationalism. From this time on, in a succession of "incidents" recorded in British blue-books, hostile placards were posted denouncing the presence and activities of foreigners, and those who ventured too far into the countryside were occasionally stoned or beaten and in some cases even killed. The background of this anti-Western feeling around Canton has not yet been thoroughly studied. It is plain, however, that members of the scholar-gentry class, with official backing from the imperial government, gave the popular movement leadership and encouragement if not actual inspiration, much as was later to be the case in north China in 1900. The resulting "Canton city question" (focused on the issue of admitting Westerners within the city walls, as distinct from the Thirteen Factories outside the walls) remained a diplomatic storm center until the Anglo-French occupation of Canton in the second war of 1856-1860. To indicate the violent spirit of this Cantonese protonationalism, we quote part of the famous denunciation posted by the villagers of San-yuan-li after the British had withdrawn their forces in 1841. The villagers, who had suffered economically from the war, maintained an armed resistance and claimed to have repulsed the British. This "Placard of the patriotic people of Kwangtung denouncing the

English barbarians" was in vigorous and often vulgar terms, though obviously not the composition of a mere peasant.

### DOC. 4  CANTONESE DENUNCIATION OF THE BRITISH, 1841⑱

The thoroughly loyal and patriotic people of the whole province of Kwangtung instruct the rebellious barbarian dogs and sheep for their information. We note that you English barbarians have formed the habits and developed the nature of wolves, plundering and seizing things by force [p. 16] ... In trade relations, you come to our country merely to covet profit. What knowledge do you have? Your seeking profit resembles the animal's greed for food. You are ignorant of our laws and institutions, ignorant of right principles... You have no gratitude for the great favor of our Celestial Court; on the contrary you treat us like enemies and do us harm. You use opium to injure our common people, cheating us of our silver and cash [p. 17]... Although you have penetrated our inland rivers and enticed fellows who renounce their fathers and their ruler to become Chinese traitors and stir up trouble among us, you are only using money to buy up their services—what good points have you? ... Except for your ships being solid, your gunfire fierce, and your rockets powerful, what other abilities have you? ...

[p. 19] We patriots have received the favor of the Celestial Dynasty in nourishing us for two centuries. Today, if we do not exterminate you English barbarians, we will not be human beings. You have killed and injured our common people in many villages, and seriously hurt the universal harmony. You also completely destroyed the coffins in several places, and you disastrously damaged the Buddhist statues in several monasteries. This is properly a time when Heaven is angered and mankind is resentful; even the ghosts and spirits will not tolerate you beasts...

[p. 20b] Our hatred is already at white heat. If we do not completely exterminate you pigs and dogs, we will not be manly Chinese able to support the sky on our heads and stand firmly on the earth. Once we have said this, we will never go back on it, even if frustrated ten thousand times. We are definitely going to kill you, cut your heads off and burn you to death! Even though you ask people to admonish us, we will not obey. We must strip off your skins and eat your flesh, and then you will know how tough (*li-hai*) we are ... We ought really to use refined expressions. But since you beasts do not understand written characters, therefore we use rough, vulgar words to instruct you in simple terms...

This type of inflammatory anti-foreignism remained endemic at Canton until after 1858 and embarrassed the officials on both sides who sought to develop peaceful Sino-Western relations.

## CHAPTER IV  THE POLICY OF CONCILIATION

The alternative to Commissioner Lin's policy of coercing the barbarians was to conciliate them. This required the use of negotiation instead of force, but it was still within the Chinese traditional pattern of relations with the barbarians. It did not involve any borrowing from the West or reform of Chinese ways. The militant defiance of the Opium War period gave way to the conciliatory policy under which the first treaties were signed: with Britain at Nanking in 1842, and with the Americans and French in 1844. On the basis of the treaties the first treaty ports were opened for foreign residence and trade under the protection of foreign consuls and gunboats—at Shanghai as well as Canton, Amoy, Foochow, and Ningpo. Yet this new order of Sino-Western relations, having been obtained by force, was grudgingly conceded. The treaties represented a defeat of the Ch'ing regime, even though they were euphemistically referred to as means of "pacifying" the barbarians or "bringing them under control" through the imperial "compassion for strangers coming from afar."

As has long been noted, the policy of conciliation or appeasement was carried out mainly by Manchus—notably by Ch'i-shan in 1840-1841 and by the imperial clansman Ch'i-ying from 1842 to 1848—whereas the policy of non-appeasement was represented mainly by Chinese such as Lin Tse-hsü in 1839-1840 and Yeh Ming-ch'en at Canton from 1848 to 1858. The Manchu element in the Ch'ing government of China appears at this time to have been concerned for the welfare of the dynasty more than for that of China as a whole. At least they were more willing than the Chinese officials to buy off the barbarians by concessions which would preserve the dynasty even though sacrificing a certain amount of Chinese cultural pride and economic interest. Whether or not this generalization can stand, it seems evident that the negotiators of the first treaties, under the pressure of *force majeure*, were relatively heedless of the long-term economic repercussions of the treaty settlement. They confined their attention mainly to the immediate problem of mollifying the invaders and keeping them from further warlike acts. For this purpose, Ch'i-ying in particular exerted himself over a period of several years to establish and maintain an intimate personal relationship with the foreign envoys: Sir Henry Pottinger (1789-1856) who negotiated for the British, the American Caleb Cushing (1800-1879), and the Frenchman Th. de Lagrené.① Ch'i-ying's obvious intent was to achieve a sort of personal ascendancy by which to influence the course of the barbarians' policies and actions in China. He also tried to use the United States and France against England.

Since this personal contact with the invaders put any Ch'ing official in mortal danger of denunciation as a traitor or dupe of the foreigners (on a theory of "guilt by association") Ch'i-ying was obliged constantly to excuse and defend himself on this score in his memorials to the throne. His two-faced position between the emperor and the barbarians is well illustrated in the following document—the famous memorial which he wrote after he had negotiated the early British, American, and French treaties. It was later found by the British among the archives of the Canton governor-general, Yeh Ming-ch'en, at the time when that obstinate xenophobe was captured in 1858 during the Anglo-French war with China. Thomas Wade translated it and took it to Tientsin, where the aged Ch'i-ying, then in his seventy-second year, had suddenly appeared as a treaty negotiator. His appointment, however, incurred the jealousy of the imperial negotiators already on the spot and was rejected by the British and French envoys. Confronted in 1858 with this memorial of fourteen years before, Ch'i-ying lost countenance, withdrew from the negotiations, and was graciously permitted by the emperor to strangle himself with a silken bowstring. ②

## DOC. 5 CH'I-YING'S METHOD FOR HANDLING THE BARBARIANS, 1844③

Ch'i-ying presents a supplementary memorial: with further reference to the management of the barbarian affairs of the various countries, his receptions of or interviews with the barbarian envoys and his controlling them as the circumstances allowed—your slave has already from time to time presented memorials and reports... He is mindful that the English barbarians were finally brought to the point of reconciliation in August 1842, and the American and French barbarians have also followed in their footsteps in the summer and autumn of the present year. Throughout this period of three years the barbarian situation has undergone deceptive changes in many respects and has not produced a unified development. The methods by which to conciliate the barbarians and get them under control similarly could not but shift about and change their form. Certainly we have to curb them by sincerity, but it has been even more necessary to control them by skillful methods. There are times when it is possible to have them follow our directions but not let them understand the reasons. Sometimes we expose everything so that they will not be suspicious, whereupon we can dissipate their rebellious restlessness. Sometimes we have given them receptions and entertainment, after which they have had a feeling of appreciation. And at still other times we have shown trust in them in a broad-minded way and deemed it unnecessary to go deeply into minute discussions with them, whereupon we have been able to get their help in the business at hand.

This is because the barbarians are born and grow up outside the frontiers of China, so that there are many things in the institutional system of the Celestial Dynasty with which they are not fully acquainted. Moreover, they are constantly making arbitrary interpretations of things, and it is difficult to enlighten them by means of reason. Thus for example when Imperial Utterances [i. e., Edicts and Decrees] are handed down, they are all received and acted on by the Grand Councillors, but the barbarians respect them as being written by the Imperial hand; if they were definitely informed that these are not from [p. 19] the Imperial brush, then there would be no means of maintaining their confidence. This, then, is something that ought not to be made known to them.

When the barbarians meet together and eat, it is called "a banquet."④ Generally they assemble a large number of people at a great banquet and eat and drink together for the fun of it. When your slave has been at the Bogue, Macao, and such places, and has entertained the various barbarians with a feast, their chieftains, leaders, and headmen have come, to the varied number of ten or more, or up to twenty or thirty persons. When on one occasion your slave has gone to the barbarians' storied residences or to the barbarian ships, the leaders and others have sat around in a circle in attendance upon him, competing to bring him food and drink—he could not but share their cup and spoon so as to hold their hearts.

Moreover, the barbarians commonly lay great stress on their women. Whenever they have a distinguished guest, the wife is certain to come out to meet him. For example, the American chief Parker and the French chief Lagrené both brought their foreign wives along with them, and on occasions when your slave has gone to the barbarians' storied residences to discuss business, these foreign wives have rushed out and saluted him.

Your slave was confounded and ill at ease, while they on the other hand were deeply honored and delighted. Thus in actual fact the customs of the various Western countries cannot be regulated according to the ceremonies of the Middle Kingdom. If we should abruptly rebuke them, it would be no way of shattering their stupidity and might give rise to their suspicion and dislike.

Furthermore, the various barbarians have come to live at peace and in harmony with us. We must give them some sort of entertainment and cordial reception;⑤ but we are on guard against an intimate relationship in intercourse with them. For this reason at those times when the treaties with the various countries were to be discussed and settled in succession, your slave has always ordered the provincial treasurer Huang En-t'ung [d. 1881] to tell the various barbarian envoys clearly that Chinese high officials when managing public affairs with other countries on no account can overstep the bounds and have personal relations; if there should be gifts which they desire to present as a courtesy, we can only firmly decline to accept them. If they were accepted in an underhanded manner, the ordinances of the Celestial Dynasty are extremely strict; not only would such an official injure the fundamental institutions of government, he would also have difficulty in escaping punishment according to the statutes of the realm. The barbarian envoys in question have heretofore had the sense to obey this instruction. But at times when they have been received in interviews, they have occasionally had small gifts to present, such as foreign wine or perfume, or the like. The value of these things has been very slight, and the barbarians' intention has been quite sincere. It has been inconvenient, right before their faces, to throw such gifts back at them. But he (Ch'i-ying) has conferred on them such things as snuff boxes and ornamental purses which are carried on the person simply in order to uphold the principle that though little is received, much should be given...⑥

As to these various countries, although they have rulers, they may be either male or female, and they may rule variously for a long or a short time, all of which is far beyond the bounds of any system of laws. For example, the English barbarians are ruled by a female, the Americans and the French are ruled by males, the English and French rulers both rule for life, while the ruler of the American barbarians is [p. 20] established by the campaigning of his countrymen, and is changed once in four years—after he leaves the position, he is of equal rank with the common people.

The official designations by which they call themselves also differ. (In China) most of them assume Chinese characters [i. e., titles of office] to make a false display and boast about themselves, as self-important as the Yeh-lang [the barbarian tribe who asked the Han envoy which state was larger, Yeh-lang or Han]. Those actions of course pay respect to their rulers, and have nothing to do with us. If we restrained them by the ceremonial forms used for dependent tribes, they would certainly not consent to retire and remain in the status of Annam and Liu-ch'iu, since they do not accept our calendar nor receive an Imperial patent of investiture.

With this type of people from outside the bounds of civilization, who are blind and unawakened in styles of address and forms of ceremony, if we adhered to the proper forms in official documents and let them be weighed according to the status of superior and inferior, even though our tongues were dry and our throats parched (from urging them to follow our way), still they could not avoid closing their ears and acting as if deaf. Not only would there be no way to bring them to their senses, but also it would immediately cause friction. Truly it would be of no advantage in the essential business of subduing and conciliating them. To fight with them over empty names and get no substantial result would not be so good as to pass over these small matters and achieve our larger scheme.

The several measures stated above are all methods based on close investigation of the barbarian situation, an estimation of the exigencies of the times, and a thorough judgment as to the importance or unimportance, urgency or lack of urgency involved, and have had to be adopted as expedients and modifications to fit the circumstances. Either because the affairs were fundamentally of little importance or because the needs of the time were too urgently pressing, your slave has not ventured to memorialize especially and intrude them one by one upon the Sacred Intelligence. Now, since the barbarian affairs have been roughly brought to a conclusion, as is proper he states them, one and all, in a supplementary memorial.

[Vermilion Endorsement:] They could only be managed in this way. We thoroughly understand it.

The problems of diplomatic intercourse which were faced by the Manchu grandee Ch'i-ying were met with every day on a more intimate plane in the treaty ports. There the mandarins whose careers depended upon their getting along with the foreigners studied at first hand how to deal with them. The Western trade and population rapidly increased at Shanghai and friction occurred at all the ports. But the rise of the great Taiping Rebellion which engulfed the interior of South China after 1851 (see Ch. V c) weakened the position of the Ch'ing government. The new emperor, Hsien-feng, who reigned from 1851 to 1861, was narrowly anti-foreign and abetted the short-sighted Cantonese contempt for the West, but his regime was powerless to expel the barbarian and had to continue a half-hearted policy of conciliation. This left it up to the Ch'ing officials at the ports to get on with the foreigners as best they could. We quote below a description of the methods of conciliation used by an able military commander at Shanghai in 1854-1855, Chi-er-hang-a (d. 1856). This Manchu official had been rapidly promoted to the governorship of Kiangsu because of his success in obtaining foreign assistance and cooperation when rebels occupied the old walled city of Shanghai (Sept. 1853-Feb. 1855) and so endangered the foreign settlement nearby.

When in 1853 the British barbarians saw the many difficulties in our domestic situation, and straightway became warlike, Chi-er-hang-a brought them under control [p.5] by the use of right principles and subdued them by his spirit, while also showing his confidence in them by getting together with them, as a result of which he was able to turn them to our use. His method of showing confidence in them was first of all, necessarily, to break down their suspicions. Those of whom these barbarians are most suspicious are the high officers of China who do not memorialize their complaints truthfully to the emperor... Chi-er-hang-a scrupulously took their reasons for complaint and if they happened to be things that could be done, he would at once tell them that he was memorializing on their behalf according to the facts. If they were things that could not be done, then he would say to them, "You want me to memorialize on your behalf; I cannot but memorialize, but as soon as I have done so, His Majesty the Emperor will certainly remove me from office and have me tried. We have been mutually friendly—let me take this gauze cap [symbol of office] and hand it over to foster our friendship, it is of no importance; but I do not know whether you gentlemen will feel at ease or not." If they put forth statements which were perverse or erroneous, he would reply directly, "My head can be cut off, but this cannot be done." The barbarians considered that he was not deceiving them and respectfully called him "Lord Chi" and so in their inner hearts were sincerely submissive.⑦

The danger of any association with foreigners and the difficulty of dealing with them led to the emergence in the new treaty ports of a special class of Chinese officials who were specialists on the barbarian problem, comparable to the so-called "Far Eastern experts" of latter-day America. One of the most competent of these men was the scholar-official Hsü Chi-yü (1795-1873), who helped to carry out Ch'i-ying's policy at the treaty ports of Amoy and Foochow in Fukien. His grandfather had been a provincial graduate (*chü-jen*) and his father a metropolitan graduate (*chin-shih*), which Hsü Chi-yü also became in 1826, so that his unorthodox interest in the West was that of a reputable scion of the established order. After service in the Hanlin Academy at Peking and as a censor, he became the chief "barbarian controller" in Fukien, holding the posts successively of financial commissioner and governor between 1843 and 1851. His first foreign contact appears to have occurred at Amoy early in 1844, where an unfortunate British acting-consul was having a hard time doing business with the local Chinese authorities: lacking a competent interpreter, the Englishman in an interview would address his remarks in English to a Singapore Chinese, who would repeat them in Fukienese to a local Chinese, who would then state them in mandarin (Pekinese) to the officials.[8] The local American missionary, Rev. David Abeel, who could understand "a good deal" of mandarin though not speak it, was called in to help stave off the resulting chaos. Thus it happened that Hsü Chi-yü met a Westerner of literary interests, who showed him an atlas of the world. After borrowing Abeel's atlas, Hsü took up world geography as a hobby. Abeel said of him, "He is the most inquisitive Chinese of a high rank I have yet met." Abeel gave him instruction in geography and history and other foreigners like Capt. Smith of H. M. S. *Druid* also helped him.[9]

Hsü's eventual product, "A brief description of the ocean circuit" (*Ying-huan chih-lüeh*), was completed in 1848 and printed in 1850. It was shorter and less broadly discursive than Wei Yuan's *Hai-kuo t'u-chih*; but as a straight summary of world geography based on Western sources it was more handy and succinct—one might say "scientific." Hsü's maps, for example, were careful copies of Western maps, vastly more accurate than the old-style sketch-maps used by Wei Yuan.

Hsü Chi-yü fitted into the post-treaty phase of conciliation, for he was concerned less with military strategy against the British invasion than with the study of Western society as a proper subject of scholarly interest. While his official memorials inveighed against the twin evils of foreign opium and missionaries in the fashion of the period, he is known to have gone rather far in friendly contact with foreigners. After Hsü began service in the Tsungli Yamen (1865-1869, see Ch. Ⅴa) the *Ying-huan chih-lüeh* was reprinted by it in 1866.

The extracts translated below on Britain and the United States are in the form of digested statements, evidently based rather directly on Western sources, which are then followed by Hsü's own comments of a more interpretive nature. Thus the British institutions of parliament and jury trial are succinctly described, but without much comment, whereas the expansion of British power in America and India receives comment of what might now be called a "geopolitical" nature. The exploits of the American father of his country, "Ton" (i. e. , Washington, see Doc. 6), are played up, though perhaps no more than in American textbooks of the day. governor Hsü's researches laid before his countrymen enough data on the economy and political institutions of the West to make it plain that the Western barbarians represented an entirely different and very powerful society. The difficulty lay in absorbing the lesson of this difference and applying it to statecraft.

## DOC. 6  Hsü CHi-Yü's ACCEPTANCE OF WESTERN GEOGRAPHY, 1848[⑩]

[*On Britain and her empire*] The population of England is dense and the food insufficient. It is necessary for them to import from other countries. More than [p. 44] 490,000 people are engaged in weaving. The weaving machine is made of iron, and is operated by a steam engine, so it can move automatically. Thus labor is saved and the cost of production is low. Each year more than 400,000 piculs [1 picul equals 133 lbs.] of cotton are used, all of which are shipped in from the five parts of India and America... Silk is purchased and shipped from China and Italy. The work of manufacturing guns, cannon, knives, swords, clocks, watches, and various kinds of utensils and tools for daily use is done by about 300,000 people. Each year the income from the various products is worth approximately ten million taels or more. Their commercial ships are in the four seas; there is no spot which they do not reach. The great profits go to the merchants and dealers, while the workers are poor.

[Hsü then describes the British Parliament and its activities, and the system of trial by jury]

The English procedure of legal inquiry is that, when there is evidence of crime, the offender is arrested or sent to the court. When he is about to be examined, six persons of good reputation are first selected from among the common people and the offender is also ordered to select six persons for himself. Together the twelve persons make the inquiry, and decide the merits of the case before they report it to the judge. The judge then examines it and the law is executed...

[Commentary, p. 45b] England consists merely of three islands, simply a handful of stones in the western ocean. Her area is estimated to be about the same as Taiwan and Ch'iung-chou [Hainan]... Even if the soil is all fertile, how much can be produced locally? The reason for her becoming suddenly rich and strong, exerting political influence here and there beyond tens of thousands of *li* is that in the west she obtained America and in the east she obtained the various parts of India. The land of America hangs isolated on the globe, and since ancient times it has been little known. In the Wan-li period (1573-1619) of the Ming, it was discovered, and then a rich soil of ten thousand *li* was added to Great Britain, soon making her immensely rich. Even though the land of America is separated from England by ten thousand *li*, the British are skilled in ocean navigation, and make the voyage as easily as crossing a marshy ground with weeds. When the southern part was ceded to the United States of America, the northern part [i. e., Canada] which, though vast, is as barren and cold as Chinese Mongolia (was retained by the British). After England lost this part [U. S. A.], she almost lost her prosperity [lit., color].

The five Indias lie on the southwest of China... In 1755 Bengal was annexed, and taking advantage of their victories the English stealthily encroached on the various states like silkworms eating mulberry leaves. The various parts, scattered and weak, could not resist, and consequently more than half became British colonies. The land produces cotton and also opium. After opium became popular in China, ten-fold profits were made. The revenue collected by the English in large measure comes from the five Indias. To have lost in the west [America] and yet to have made it up in the east [India]—how fortunate she is!

After the English obtained the five Indias, they gradually expanded toward the southeast. Along the eastern coast of the Indian Ocean, ports were opened everywhere... Malacca and Hsi-li (author's note: that is, Singapore) were exchanged with Holland. Eighty or ninety per cent of the wealth of the Small Western Ocean (Note: the Indian Ocean), came under British control. In the farther east, of the states on the various islands in the southern ocean of China, except Luzon which belongs to Spain, the rest are all trading ports of Holland. The luxurious places like Ka-la-pa (Note: that is, Java), the strategic areas like Manila (Note: that is, small Luzon) also were coveted by the English. Unfortunately other people already possessed them; she had no reason to take them by force. And yet, she goes to and fro on the eastern sailing route, using the two places as her hostelries, and Spain and Holland dare not offend her in the least... At the present time, what Britain relies upon to be her outside treasury and to extend the power of her nation lies in the five Indias. The territory is on the southwest of further Tibet, whence it only takes twenty or thirty days to go to Canton by sea. This colony of the British has been for a long time close to our southern frontier, and yet our critics merely know that England proper is over 70,000 *li* away.

England herself is geographically small in area, but very numerous in population. The arable land is not sufficient to supply food for one-tenth of the population. Before the ceding of North America, the unemployed

British subjects usually sailed westward to seek sustenance. After the ceding of America, the remaining land of England in the northern region [i. e., Canada] was too cold for farming. Even though the large territory of the five Indias was obtained, there were originally inhabitants in that area, and there was no unoccupied territory. Although many English people went to live there, after all they could not reverse their guest position to become the hosts [p. 47], and therefore they were anxious to find new places. In recent years, the great island of New Holland [New Zealand] has been obtained. The grass and weeds have been cut down in order that criminals may be banished to that place. The poor people, who have no means of making a living, were also taken there for settlement. In moving these people over a distance of 80,000 *li*, it was a hard and painstaking job (for the government) to plan to feed and accommodate the people. [End of commentary]

The annual revenue of England, apart from paying the interest to merchants, is approximately Tls. 200, 000, 000① and more. The expenditure is also more than Tls. 200,000,000. The size of the regular army of England proper is 90,000 men. In India, the British soldiers are 30,000, and the local troops 230,000, who are called "sepoy" soldiers. She has more than 600 warships, large and small, and more than 100 steamships. Their sailors wear blue uniforms and their army wear red. The navy is stressed but the army is slighted. They depend entirely upon rifles and guns, and are not skillful in boxing. Excepting knives and swords, they have no other weapons.

[In the succeeding section of commentary, the author describes the types and sizes of British warships and their structure, and notes that the foreign ships are not afraid of storms but are vulnerable to rocks in the sea. He also describes Western cannon and the structure of steamships and their operation. His details indicate an understanding of the theory of steam propulsion. He also states that the steam engine was first used in Europe for weaving, later on extended to steamships, and in recent years in America extended to locomotives.]

[*On the American revolution and the U. S. A.*]⑫

In the middle of the Ch'ien-lung period (1736-1795), England and France were engaged in a war which lasted for years without being settled. Hundreds of methods had been used to raise provisions, and the rate of taxation was doubled. According to the old regulation, the seller of tea had to pay a tax; the British then ordered the purchasers also to pay a tax. The Americans could not bear this. In 1775, the local gentry gathered together in a public building, wanting to discuss the problem with their resident chieftain. The chieftain [i. e., British official] drove away the petitioners and urged the levy of the tax even more harshly. The multitude of the people were so irritated that they threw the tea from the ships into the sea, and they planned to raise an army to fight against the British.

There was a certain Washington (*Hua-sheng-tun*; note: also written *Wang-hsing-t'eng* and *Wa-sheng-tun*), a native of another part of America [i. e., not of Massachusetts], born in 1731 [1732]. When he was ten he lost his father, and his mother educated him and brought him up. He had cherished great ambitions in youth and was gifted in both literary and military matters. He was unusually gallant and robust. Once [p. 15] he served as a British military officer... When the time came for the multitude of the people to revolt against the British, they urged Washington [lit., *Tun*, i. e., taking the last syllable as surname] to be their commander... The army of Washington was defeated, and his followers were so discouraged that they wished to be disbanded and to go away. Washington maintained his spirit as usual. He gathered his forces and grouped them into an army to fight again, and he was victorious. Thus in eight years of bloody war, he was repeatedly defeated, but he also repeatedly refused to be discouraged...

After Washington settled his country's affairs, he gave up arms and intended to return to his farm. The multitude could not bear to leave him, but insisted on electing him the head of the state. Then Washington held a discussion with the multitude, saying that to establish a state and to hand it down to his descendants would be selfish; the duty of looking after the people should be carried on by selecting those who have virtue. The traditional divisions [*pu*, parts] were set up as individual states, and each state has a commander [i. e., governor] ... The leaders of the villages and towns write down the names of those whom they are going to elect and put them in a box. After this is finished, the box is opened, and the one who has obtained the most votes is established as governor. Whether he is an officer or of the common people, there is no restriction according to his previous status, and after retirement, the governor is still considered an equal of the common people...

[p. 16b] The whole continent of America reaches the great western [i. e., Atlantic] ocean in the east, and the great ocean sea [i. e., Pacific Ocean] in the west. The United States are all in the eastern part... The uncultivated region in the west is all occupied by the aborigines. Whenever new territory is to be opened, at first hunters are employed to kill the bears, deer, and wild oxen, and then the unemployed people are allowed to cultivate the land. When forty thousand inhabitants have been gathered together or born in the region, then a city is built which is given a name as a territory [*pu*] attached to the whole group of states. At present, apart from the states, three territories have been added.

[p. 33] The various states of America have an equable and normal climate. In the north it is like Chihli and Shansi and in the south it is like Kiangsu and Chekiang. The river currents are gentle and the soil is good. There is no desert and little plague. (Note: in the south there is a pestilential vapor, but it is not very poisonous.) The land is level and fertile and suitable for the five grains. Cotton is the best and the most produced, whence the various countries like England and France all get their supplies. There are all kinds of vegetables and fruits. Tobacco leaves are extremely good and are circulated far and wide. In the mountains coal, salt, iron, and white lead are produced. Within the country there are many small rivers, and the Americans have dredged them from place to place in order to facilitate water transportation. Steam locomotives [lit., fire-wheel carts] are also made. Stones are used to pave the road bed and Americans melt iron and pour it like a liquid in order to smooth the running of the train. Within one day it can run more than 300 *li*. Steamships are even more numerous, running back and forth on the rivers and seas like shuttles, because the land produces much coal...

Once every two years, one person is elected for his outstanding ability and point of view out of every 47,700 people to stay at the capital city to participate in and discuss the national affairs. In the capital, where the president lives, there is a congress (*kung-hui*) representing all the states, each of which elects two wise men to participate in this congress and decide great political issues such as making an alliance, declaring war or adopting defensive measures, determining the rate of customs and taxes on trading transactions and the like. The full term is six years. In each state there are six judges to take charge of making verdicts or imprisonments. They are also elected to fill these positions. If there is anyone who is prejudiced or unfair, he may be removed by public opinion...

The standing army of the United States of America is not more than 10,000, who are distributed among various forts and strategic points. Except for scholars, physicians, and astronomers, the rest of the people—farmers, workers, and merchants—from twenty to forty years old are subject to selection by the officials to serve as militia [*min-ping*] and are issued registration cards... The militia system of about 1,700,000 men is fundamentally identical with the method of our ancient people who quartered troops on the farmers.

[P. 34b] In the United States of America, all the white men have immigrated to live there; there are people from all countries of Europe but those coming from England, Holland, and France are the most numerous. Among these three countries, England again provided more than one-half. Therefore, the spoken and written language is the same as that of England... The business and transportation work is all done by the white people. The people are docile, good-natured, mild, and honest. They do not have the fierce and cruel bearing of birds of prey. They work very hard in making a living and their merchant ships sail the four seas. All the states of America accept the religion of Jesus [i. e., Protestant Christianity], and are fond of academic discussions and activities. Everywhere there are schools. Their scholars in general are divided into three kinds: namely, academic, studying astronomy, geography, and the tenets of Christianity; medical, for curing diseases; and legal, for training lawyers and judges.

# CHAPTER V   THE EMERGENCE OF THE THEORY OF SELF-STRENGTHENING

By 1860 the rulers of China had wasted twenty years in refusing to face the problems created by Western contact. These lost decades, to be sure, had seen the outbreak of a great rebellion against the Ch'ing Dynasty which for some time threatened it with extinction and absorbed its waning energies. Simultaneously there continued to develop those points of friction—at Canton, in the opium trade, and elsewhere along the coast and in the treaty ports—which led eventually to the second war between Britain and the Ch'ing empire, in which France also joined. Negotiations for treaty revision having been frustrated by Chinese intransigence, the British and French finally seized convenient pretexts, sent a joint expeditionary force, occupied Canton, and negotiated treaties at Tientsin (as the Americans and Russians did also) in 1858. At first glance this would seem to be a plain case of the imperialist powers taking advantage of China's domestic difficulties to force their will upon her, and we may indeed judge this to be the general pattern of China's modern experience among the nations. Yet a view of China's nineteenth-century foreign relations which saw only the aggression of the West would certainly be one-sided. Chinese-Manchu attitudes and reactions were an essential factor in the historical process, as can be illustrated by a comparison of the periods just before and after 1860.

In the year preceding, when the ratifications of the treaties of Tientsin were to be exchanged, the Ch'ing court conceived and executed a bold stratagem to ambush the barbarian envoys and forestall their approach to the capital. In hostilities at Taku, outside Tientsin, they were for the moment victorious, and the British force retired in defeat. This only set the stage, however, for a second campaign in 1860, in which Anglo-French troops fought their way to Peking, forcing the Emperor to flee, and secured by force a confirmation of all their demands. From that time foreign ministers were to reside at the capital, foreign ships to ply the Yangtze, and foreign goods and missionaries to penetrate into the interior. This utter failure of Ch'ing power to hold off the West, by either force or conciliation, finally brought a change in the court's attitude and policy.

The years after 1860 saw an effort to develop new Chinese institutions, particularly for the conduct of foreign relations and the collection of customs duties, and to secure foreign advice and assistance, particularly against the rebels in South and Central China. Who knows what might have been accomplished if such policies had been adopted earlier? To suggest that they could have been instituted in the 1840's or 1850's is, of course, to overlook the facts of the historical situation. Our point is that the historical forces of the time had to become manifest through a specific change in attitude, in the Chinese response to the Western problem. For this reason the reversal of policy at Peking in 1860 merits our close attention.

### a. *Prince Kung and the Tsungli Yamen*

In May of 1860 the defeat of the regular Ch'ing forces by the Taiping rebels at Nanking forced the central government to relinquish its time-honored policy of centralization of power and yield great freedom of action to the provincial governor-general, most of whom were Chinese. Four months later, in September, came the events noted above—the British and French allied army routed the Manchu troops assembled to defend Peking, the Emperor had to flee, and the demands of the foreign powers, which the Emperor had stubbornly resisted at enormous cost since 1851, had to be completely accepted. The shocking realization by the court that the two main supports of the Manchu throne—the Manchu army at Peking and the Chinese troops in each province—had both been shattered brought about a reversal of policy towards the Westerners that was to prevail for over twenty years. This new attitude was particularly in evidence during the first decade after the debacle of 1860, the decade of the "T'ung-chih Restoration," when the decline of the dynasty was temporarily checked by a reassertion of the Confucian principles of civil government.

As the Emperor Hsien-feng fled from Peking he had designated his younger half-brother, I-hsin (1833-1898), commonly called Prince Kung, as his representative to deal with the victorious British and French envoys. There was nothing the prince could do at that time but sign a convention confirming the treaties drawn up two years previously and meeting all further demands. Being entrusted with the fulfillment of the obligations specified in the new treaties, he found it essential to create a new office for foreign affairs, free from the traditions and precedents that dominated the old administration at Peking. In late 1860 the foreign troops had begun to withdraw to Tientsin, so as to set sail before the river was frozen over. When the prince and his two major assistants began to evolve a definite plan to deal with the Western powers, the result was the following memorial submitted by Prince Kung, Kuei-liang, and Wen-hsiang, received at Jehol on January 13, 1861, and at once read and approved by the Emperor and the grand councillors.

## DOC. 7　THE NEW FOREIGN POLICY OF JANUARY 1861①

After the exchange of treaties, the barbarians have returned to Tientsin and sailed hurriedly back to the south in groups. Moreover, they still base their demands on the treaties. This shows that they do not covet our territory and people. Hence we can still through faithfulness and justice tame and control them while we ourselves strive towards recovery. The present case is somewhat different from the (barbarian invasions) of former dynasties... Now the Nien Rebellion [1851-1868] is ablaze in the north and the Taiping in the south, our military supplies are exhausted and our troops are worn out. The barbarians take advantage of our weak position and try to control us. If we do not restrain our rage but continue the hostilities, we are liable to sudden catastrophe. On the other hand, if we overlook the way they have harmed us and do not make any preparations against them, then we shall be bequeathing a source of grief to our sons and grandsons. The ancients had a saying, "Resort to peace and friendship when temporarily obliged to do so; use war and defense as your actual policy." This is truly a well-founded statement.

The situation today may be compared (to the diseases of a human body). Both the Taiping and Nien bandits are gaining victories and constitute an organic disease. Russia, with her territory adjoining ours, aiming to nibble away our territory like a silkworm, may be considered a threat at our bosom. As to England, her purpose is to trade, but she acts violently, without any regard for human decency. If she is not kept within limits, we shall not be able to stand on our feet. Hence she may be compared to an affliction of our limbs. Therefore we should suppress the Taipings and Nien bandits first, get the Russians under control next, and attend to the British last...

If we follow our plan at the present time, we should act according to the treaties and not allow the foreigners to go even slightly beyond them. In our external expression we should be sincere and amicable but quietly try to keep them in line. Then within the next few years [p. 19], even though occasionally they may make demands, still they will not suddenly cause us a great calamity. After careful deliberation on the whole situation we have drafted six regulations:

(1) To establish at the capital the Tsung-li ko-kuo shih-wu ya-men ["office in general charge of foreign affairs"; i. e., the "Tsungli Yamen"] ... under the direction of princes and ministers ... As soon as the military campaigns are concluded and the affairs of the various countries are simplified, the new office will be abolished and its functions will again revert to the Grand Council for management so as to accord with the old system.

(2) To establish the offices of high commissioners to facilitate the handling of affairs respectively at the northern and southern ports. [Here follow details on the office of superintendent of trade for the five southern ports: Canton, Foochow, Amoy, Ningpo and Shanghai, and the superintendent of trade for the three northern ports: Newchuang, Chefoo and Tientsin. (3) To arrange for maritime customs collections at the treaty ports and on the Russian frontier. (4) to ensure mutual information among officials handling foreign relations, so as to prevent errors.]

(5) To select two persons from Canton and two from Shanghai who understand written and spoken foreign languages and send them to Peking for consultation. [This is the initiation of the interpreters' college, T'ung-wen Kuan, discussed further in Ch. VIII below. (6) In each seaport, the internal and external commercial conditions, as well as foreign newspapers, should be reported in communications to the Tsungli Yamen once a month to supply material for official perusal.]

Thus was created the Tsungli Yamen, a special board or subcommittee under the Grand Council which was to concern itself with all aspects of relations with the Western powers. While not a genuine ministry, it served as the prototype of a foreign office until the creation of the Wai-wu-pu, Ministry of Foreign Affairs, in 1901. In fact, its temporary and special status made it possible to select for service in the Tsungli Yamen some of the ablest personnel and most powerful officials.

As head of the new office, Prince Kung succeeded in establishing a working relationship with the British, French, American, and Russian envoys, in starting a Western-trained Manchu army using Russian guns, and in reinvigorating the central government at Peking. When the Emperor died a year later, the prince emerged as regent for the new T'ung-chih Emperor of the period 1862-1874. From 1861 to 1884, the year of his dismissal from the Tsungli Yamen, Prince Kung seems to have concentrated mainly on keeping peace with the Western powers, almost at any price, in order to give China time to become strong. His internal policy from 1861 to 1865 was also one of relative meekness towards the able Chinese administrators in the provinces, who were allowed a great deal of freedom in their conduct of the civil war against the Taipings and other groups of rebels. The final victory over the Taipings in 1864 was partly due to this policy.

Prince Kung was not a man of great abilities or personal ambitions. However, he was wise enough to listen to his advisers in the central government. He never issued arbitrary orders, but, in matters of importance, consulted the leading provincial officials before making a decision—a procedure that remained standard practice down to the end of the dynasty. At Peking he worked closely with two principal assistants, Kuei-liang and Wen-hsiang. Kuei-liang (1785-1862) was the prince's father-in-law and had had a good deal of experience in dealing with Westerners at Canton, Shanghai, and Tientsin, but he was by 1860 old and ill. Hence much of the routine was handled by Wen-hsiang (1818-1876), a Manchu official known for his integrity and intelligence and a member of the Tsungli Yamen from 1861 until his death in 1876. The fact that he was brought up in poverty at Mukden probably enabled him to see things more realistically than his fellow-nationals accustomed to the luxuries of Peking.②

The new dispensation in China's foreign relations symbolized by the Tsungli Yamen was only an aspect of the general process of dynastic revival which occurred during the "Restoration" of the T'ung-chih period. Essentially this was a process of temporary resuscitation rather than of innovation, an Indian summer of a declining regime rather than the creation of a new one. The Restoration period saw the pacification of the Taiping and other rebellions, resumption of the examinations and reinstitution of civil administration over wide areas, reduction of the land tax and other measures of relief for the agrarian economy, and a vigorous effort to select and train men of talent and imbue them with the principles of Confucian morality. This reaffirmation of the Confucian ideology of scholar government, the core of the Restoration movement, called for the application of traditional principles to the new situation of the 1860's. Reform of old institutions and establishment of new policies were therefore the order of the day, but both were sought within the framework of the orthodox Confucian system. Intellectual leadership was taken by scholar-officials who were steeped in the classical teachings of loyalty and ethical government. One of the most influential, though least known, of these men is discussed in the next section, with special reference to his attitudes and suggestions concerning relations with the West.

### b. *Feng Kuei-fen and his Essays*

Feng Kuei-fen (1809-1874), a scholar of Soochow, was probably the first man to apply to China's modern problems the term *tzu-ch'iang* (lit., "self-strengthening," or "to make ourselves strong"). His ideas also anticipated the famous phrase *Chung-hsueh wei-t'i*, *Hsi-hsueh wei-yung* ("Chinese studies [learning, culture, values] for the base [fundamental structure, framework], Western studies for use [practical application]"), a slogan to be made famous a generation later by Chang

Chih-tung in the 1890's (see Ch. XVII).

Feng obtained a *chin-shih* degree with high honors in 1840, and thereafter was a compiler of the Hanlin Academy for seven years—a position which enabled him to know government problems from the inside. He was well read and widely interested not only in the classics but also in mathematics, philology, astronomy, geography, agriculture, irrigation, and other subjects. He served as an assistant to Lin Tse-hsü and as a secretary to Li Hung-chang (see Ch. VII) and other high dignitaries at various intervals over a period of many years. During the Taiping Rebellion he had organized a volunteer corps to defend Soochow; his letter to Tseng Kuo-fan in 1861 helped the latter to dispatch Li Hung-chang to Kiangsu province. This period of service made it possible for Feng to have direct contact with foreigners. In the meantime, he became concurrently director of two academies, one in Shanghai and one in Soochow. After the suppression of the rebellion he acted as Li Hung-chang's adviser for more than a year, and at his suggestion a school of Western languages and sciences was established in Shanghai in 1863, and the taxation in the region of Soochow was reduced in 1865.

The *Chiao-pin-lu k'ang-i* or, roughly translated, "Personal Protests from the Study of Chiao-pin," consists of forty essays which deal with governmental, financial, educational, and other aspects of China's modernization. The essays were first written in Shanghai around 1860, compiled under the above title with an author's preface in 1861, and were then presented to Tseng Kuo-fan, who intended to have them published. The author, however, very modestly declined, although he allowed his friends to read them or make copies.③ In 1898 *Chiao-pin-lu k'ang-i* was finally brought to the attention of Emperor Kuang-hsü, who ordered the Grand Secretariat to make a thousand copies to be distributed to, and discussed by, all government offices. Most of the essays were also reproduced in the various collections of *Huang-ch'ao ching-shih wen-pien*, or "Essays on administration of government during the Ch'ing

Dynasty,"④ an indication that they had far-reaching influence.

The following translations indicate Feng's recognition of the fact that the changing modern world had become much larger than anything ever imagined in ancient China. He recognized, too, the importance of Western sciences as necessary auxiliaries of Chinese knowledge. It was Feng who suggested the study of Western languages and sciences, which resulted in the establishment of the Kuang fang-yen kuan at Shanghai, which was an extension of the T'ung-wen Kuan (see Ch. Ⅷ). In foreign affairs, he advocated a fair deal for the foreigner, and sought to get rid of Chinese jealousy and suspicion by turning from the general concept held before 1860, that all barbarians were of bad faith, to a new view that the barbarians were of good faith and should be treated with sincerity and respect.

Judged by these trenchant essays, written in a trim and condensed classical style, Feng Kuei-fen was most remarkable for his realistic appreciation of the importance of genuine learning. His contempt for the Canton-style "linguists," through whom Western lore had been murkily filtered into China, springs from this attitude, as well as his demand for language training, translations, and the study of mathematics and sciences, as the only possible basis for a mastery of the fundamental principles from which the barbarians got their power. His independence of mind is evident in the short shrift he gives to Wei Yuan's ideas, and in his readiness to tamper with the sacrosanct examination system.

## DOC. 8　ON THE ADOPTION OF WESTERN KNOWLEDGE⑤

The world today is not to be compared with that of the Three Dynasties (of ancient China) ... Now the globe is ninety-thousand *li* around, and every spot may be reached by ships or wheeled vehicles... According to what is listed on the maps by the Westerners, there are not less than one hundred countries. From these one hundred countries, only the books of Italy, at the end of the Ming Dynasty, and now those of

England have been translated into Chinese, altogether several tens of books. Those Which expound the doctrine of Jesus are generally vulgar, not worth mentioning. Apart from these, Western books on mathematics, mechanics, optics, light, chemistry, and other subjects contain the best principles of the natural sciences. In the books on geography, the mountains, rivers, strategic points, customs, and native products of the hundred countries are fully listed. Most of this information is beyond the reach of our people.

Nowadays those familiar with barbarian affairs are called "linguists." These men are generally frivolous rascals and loafers in the cities and are despised in their villages and communities. They serve as interpreters only because they have no other means of making a livelihood. Their nature is boorish, their knowledge shallow, and furthermore, their moral principles are mean. They know nothing except sensual pleasures and material profit. Moreover, their ability consists of nothing more than [p. 38] a slight knowledge of the barbarian language and occasional recognition of barbarian characters, which is limited to names of commodities, numerical figures, some slang expressions and a little simple grammar. How can we expect them to pay attention to scholarly studies? ...

If today we wish to select and use Western knowledge, we should establish official translation offices at Canton and Shanghai. Brilliant students up to fifteen years of age should be selected from those areas to live and study in these schools on double rations. Westerners should be invited to teach them the spoken and written languages of the various nations, and famous Chinese teachers should also be engaged to teach them classics, history, and other subjects. At the same time they should learn mathematics. (Note: All Western knowledge is derived from mathematics. Every Westerner of ten years of age or more studies mathematics. If we now wish to adopt Western knowledge, naturally we cannot but learn mathematics... )

I have heard that there are large collections of books in the Mei-hua shu-kuan [American Presbyterian Press] and in the Mo-hai shu-kuan [London Missionary Society's Printing Office]. Moreover, in 1847 the Russian barbarians presented us with more than one thousand books which are preserved in the Fang-lueh-kuan [Military Archives Office, in Peking]. These books should be sent to the new schools so that the valuable ones may be selected and translated...

After three years all students who can recite with ease the books of the various nations [p. 39] should be permitted to become licentiates; and if there are some precocious ones who are able to make changes or improvements which can be put into practice, they should be recommended by the superintendent of trade to be imperially granted a *chü-jen* degree as a reward. As we have said before, there are many brilliant people in China; there must be some who can learn from the barbarians and surpass them...

If we let Chinese ethics and famous [Confucian] teachings serve as an original foundation, and let them be supplemented by the methods used by the various nations for the attainment of prosperity and strength, would it not be the best of all procedures?

Moreover, during the last twenty years since the opening of trade, a great many of the foreign chiefs have learned our written and spoken language, and the best of them can even read our classics and histories. They are generally able to speak on our dynastic regulations and government administration, on our geography and the state of the populace. On the other hand, our officers from generals down, in regard to foreign countries are completely uninformed. In comparison, should we not feel ashamed? The Chinese officials have to rely upon the stupid and silly "linguists" as their eyes and ears. The mildness or severity, leisureliness or urgency of their way of stating things may obscure the officials' original intent after repeated interpretations. Thus frequently a small grudge may develop into a grave hostility. At the present time the most important administrative problem of the empire is to control the barbarians, yet the pivotal function is entrusted to these people. No wonder that we understand neither the foreigners nor ourselves, and cannot distinguish fact from unreality. Whether in peace negotiations or in deliberating for war, we can never achieve the essential guiding principles...

If my proposal is carried out, there will necessarily be many Chinese who learn their written and spoken languages; and when there are many such people, there will certainly emerge from among them some upright and honest gentlemen who thoroughly understand the fundamentals of administration, and who would then get hold of the essential guiding principles for the control of foreigners...

### DOC. 9 ON THE MANUFACTURE OF FOREIGN WEAPONS⑥

The most unparalleled anger which has ever existed since the creation of heaven and earth is exciting all who are conscious in their minds and have spirit in their blood; their hats are raised by their hair standing on end. This is because the largest country on the globe today, with a vast area of 10,000 *li*, is yet controlled by small barbarians... According to a general geography by an Englishman, the territory of our China is eight times larger than that of Russia, ten times that of America, one hundred times that of France, and two hundred times that of England... Yet now we are shamefully humiliated by those four nations in the recent treaties—not because our climate, soil, or resources are inferior to theirs, but because our people are really inferior [p. 41]... Why are they small and yet strong? Why are we large and yet weak? We must try to discover some means to become their equal, and that also depends upon human effort. Regarding the present situation there are several major points: in making use of the ability of our manpower, with no one neglected, we are inferior to the barbarians; in securing the benefit of the soil, with nothing wasted, we are inferior to the barbarians; in maintaining a close relationship between the ruler and the people, with no barrier between them, we are inferior to the barbarians; and in the necessary accord of word with deed, we are also inferior to the barbarians. The way to correct these four points lies with ourselves, for they can be changed at once if only our Emperor would set the general policy right. There is no need for outside help in these matters. [Here Feng goes on to point out that the only help China needs from the West is in modern arms, and claims that in recent contests with Western troops the Chinese army has not been inferior in physical qualities, nor even sometimes in morale, but always in arms.]

What we then have to learn from the barbarians is only the one thing, solid ships and effective guns. When Wei Yuan [in his *Hai-kuo t'u-chih*, see Doc. 3 above] discussed the control of the barbarians, he said that we should use barbarians to attack barbarians, and use barbarians to negotiate with barbarians. Even regardless of the difficulties of languages and our ignorance of diplomatic usages it is utterly impossible for us outsiders to sow dissension among the closely related barbarians. Moreover, he considered the various barbarian nations as comparable to the Warring States [475-221 B. C.], but he did not realize that the circumstances are different. Wei saw quite a number of barbarian books and newspapers and should not have made any such statement [p. 42]. It is probably because in his life and academic ideas he was fond of regarding himself as a political strategist.⑦ In my opinion, if we cannot make ourselves strong [*tzu-ch'iang*] but merely presume on cunning and deceit, it will be just enough to incur failure. Only one sentence of Wei Yuan is correct: "Learn the strong techniques of the barbarians in order to control them..."

Funds should be assigned to establish a shipyard and arsenal in each trading port. Several barbarians should be invited and Chinese who are good in using their minds should be summoned to receive their instructions so that they may in turn teach many artisans. When a piece of work is finished and is indistinguishable from that made by the barbarians, the makers should be given a *chü-jen* degree as a reward, and be permitted to participate in the metropolitan examination on an equal footing with other scholars. Those whose products are superior to the barbarian manufacture should be granted a *chin-shih* degree as a reward, and be permitted to participate in the palace examinations on the same basis as others. The workers should be double-paid so as to prevent them from quitting.

Our nation has emphasized the civil service examinations, which have preoccupied people's minds for a long time. Wise and intelligent scholars have exhausted their time and energy in such useless things as the eight-legged essays [highly stylized essays for the civil service examination, divided into eight paragraphs], examination papers, and formal calligraphy... Now let us order one-half of them to apply themselves to the pursuit of manufacturing weapons and instruments and imitating foreign crafts... The intelligence and wisdom of the Chinese are necessarily superior to those of the various barbarians, only formerly we have not made use of them. When the Emperor above likes something, those below him will pursue it even further, like the moving of grass in the wind or the response of an echo. There ought to be some people of extraordinary intelligence who can have new ideas and improve on Western methods. At first they may learn and pattern after the foreigners; then they may compare and try to be their equal; and finally they may go ahead and surpass them—the way to make ourselves strong actually lies in this...

[p. 43] Two years ago the Western barbarians suddenly entered the Japanese capital to seek trade relations, which were permitted. Before long the Japanese were able to send some ten steamships of their own over the western ocean to pay return visits to the various countries.⑧ They made many requests for treaties which were also granted by these countries, who understood Japan's intentions. Japan is a tiny country and still knows how to exert her energy to become strong. Should we, as a large country, alone accept defilement and insult throughout all time? ...

We are just now in an interval of peaceful and harmonious relations. This is probably an opportunity given by heaven for us to strengthen ourselves. If we do not at this point quickly rise to this opportunity but passively receive the destiny of heaven, our subsequent regret will come too late... If we live in the present day and speak of rejecting the barbarians, we should raise the question as to what instruments we can reject them with...

Some suggest purchasing ships and hiring foreign people, but the answer is that this is quite impossible. If we can manufacture, can repair, and can use them, then they are our weapons. If we cannot manufacture, nor repair, nor use them, then they are still the weapons of others. When these weapons are in the hands of others and are used for grain transportation, then one day they can make us starve; and if they are used for salt transportation, one day they can deprive us of salt [p. 44]... Eventually we must consider manufacturing, repairing, and using weapons by ourselves... Only thus will we be able to pacify the empire; only thus can we play a leading role on the globe; and only thus shall we restore our original strength, and redeem ourselves from former humiliations.

### DOC. 10 ON THE BETTER CONTROL OF THE BARBARIANS[①]

Today our country considers barbarian affairs to be the first important matter of government, and the suppression of the bandits to be the second. Why? Because the bandits can be exterminated but it is impossible to do so with the barbarians ... If a plan of controlling the barbarians is not devised, then when it behooves us to fight, we, on the contrary, may negotiate peace; or when it behooves us to negotiate peace, we, on the contrary, may fight on; and so the barbarian problem will become worse. Or if we vacillate between peace and war, the barbarian problem will also become worse...

Today peace has been negotiated; we should devote ourselves to peace. We should treat the barbarians with entire candor. Traces of jealousy and suspicion will not avail us anything...

Should we then force ourselves to comply with every demand? The answer is, no. My opinion is simply that to submit outwardly, but to be jealous and suspicious inwardly, is not a good policy. The barbarians always appeal to reason. We should forthwith take their methods and apply them in return. According to reason, if a demand is acceptable, then we should accept it; according to reason if it is not acceptable, we should try to convince them on rational grounds. The various barbarians, though ignorant of our "three bonds" [the relation between prince and minister, father and son, husband and wife] still know one thing, namely, good faith. Not because they are naturally trustworthy, but because, if one nation breaks faith, then a hundred nations will rise in a group to attack and oppress her so that she is obliged to keep faith... Can peace be maintained for a long time? We know that the various barbarians cannot be without improper aims. But for the next several years to come, there will be no war. China is the largest country on earth with ample, fertile plains and marshes, numerous people and abundant resources. Naturally the mouths of all nations are watering with desire. For years past they have extensively compiled maps including tracks of roads and footprints all the way to Yunnan, Kweichow, Szechwan, and Shensi. What is their intention? Nevertheless, at present there will be no incident, because the four countries, Russia, England, France, and America, have too much uncultivated land, equal power, outward harmony, and covert jealousy to act together and force a submission, and no one dares to make the first move [p. 46b]... The Tientsin incident of 1858 was started by England, but the other three countries were necessarily involved. They all came together for no other reason than that England dared not monopolize the gain; she feared the other three countries would plot behind her back. In 1860, when the barbarians stopped as soon as they had obtained a proper excuse, it was also because they feared that Russia and America would plot behind their backs... In the future, if the relations among the four nations should become consolidated, they might cooperate to plot against us; or if the four countries fought among themselves, one country might be victorious and the three others might fall under her control, and then the victor might encroach upon us. Thus, the mutual hatred among the four countries will take precedence over their hatred of us. Their relations can never be consolidated and the date for the struggle between them must not be far away. This warrants our anxiety...

Recently we have heard that the footsteps of the Russian barbarians have reached the region of the Sui-fen River [p. 47] which is not far away from the Ch'ang-pai mountains and Kirin, and this merits even greater anxiety.

### c. *The Taiping Rebels' Interest in Modernization*

Like most writers on nineteenth-century China, we have referred to the Taiping Rebellion (1851-1864) several times in preceding pages without trying to sum it up. The many records concerning it are still being studied and generalizations such as are made about the French Revolution or the American Civil War are not yet possible. But a contemporary observer estimated that the rebellion took, all told, some twenty million lives, and it would not be wrong to class it among the great social upheavals of modern times. The ground for the rebellion was prepared by a variety of social conditions and circumstances, such as the incidence of population growth, economic depression (possibly connected with changes in foreign trade), the growing corruption of the Ch'ing officialdom, and the lowered prestige of the dynasty as a result of the Opium War. Protestant evangelism also played its part, and the leader of the movement, Hung Hsiu-ch'üan (1814-1864), used certain aspects of Christian doctrine in setting up his personal theocracy. As the movement got under way, a multitude of poverty-stricken peasants were joined by secret society members who had cherished anti-Manchu sentiments since the beginning of the dynasty and by jobless coolie porters, opium smugglers, and pirates from the Canton area. Starting in the mountains of Kwangsi, west of Canton, the rebels advanced rapidly northward through Hunan to the Yangtze and down to Nanking, which they chose in 1853 to be the capital of the Heavenly Kingdom of Great Peace (T'ai-p'ing t'ien-kuo). They aimed not only at driving out the Manchus, as the founders of the Ming Dynasty had driven out the Mongols, but also at setting up a kind of communistic and theocratic state. They failed to reach this goal for many reasons, among them the united opposition of the privileged classes, led by the Confucian scholar-official Tseng Kuo-fan (1811-1872), the help given to the imperial forces by the Western powers after 1860, and perhaps most important, the Taipings' own lack of competent leaders and adequate methods. While the rebel movement in many ways harked back to China's past, it is interesting for our purposes in this volume to note its reforming zeal, which in favorable circumstances might conceivably have developed a program of modernization for China. Even in the midst of constant warfare, the rebels tried or intended to secure an equal distribution of the land, to simplify the Chinese language, to enforce monogamy (among the common people), and to prohibit prostitution, footbinding, the sale of slaves, opium smoking, adultery, witchcraft, and gambling.⑩

　　It is interesting, of course, to speculate on the relations with the West which might have developed had the Taiping rebels been victorious. On the subject of modernization and reform of Chinese customs and institutions, the thinking of some Taiping leaders seems to have been more advanced, or at least more imaginative, than that of the opposing Ch'ing officialdom, as may be seen in the next document we quote.

　　Hung Jen-kan (1822-1864), a relative of Hung Hsiu-ch'üan, the founder of the Taiping kingdom, did not join in the military campaigns of 1851-1859, but took shelter in Hong Kong, where he received more training from Western missionaries than any other Taiping leader. He studied Christian doctrine with the Reverend Theodore Hamberg (1819-1854), to whom he supplied the basic information about Hung Hsiu-ch'üan that resulted in Hamberg's book, *The Vision of Hung-Siu-Tshuen and Origin of the Kwang-si Insurrection* (Hong Kong, 1854), one of the basic English sources on the Taiping Rebellion. For three years he was employed by James Legge (1815-1897) in the London Mission at Hong Kong. Through long association with Westerners, he learned something of astronomy and other sciences.

In 1854 Hung Jen-kan tried to go to Nanking via Shanghai but was unable to get beyond the latter city and had to return to Hong Kong. When he finally reached Nanking in 1859, he was warmly welcomed by Hung Hsiu-ch'üan, who was said to trust no one but his brothers and other relatives with the handling of important affairs after the internal dissensions of 1856. Hung Jen-kan was soon made minister of foreign affairs and prime minister but, not having fought for the Taiping empire in its early years, he was afraid that the old comrades might be jealous of him. He therefore presented to the Heavenly King his book, *A New Work for Aid in Administration* (*Tzu-cheng hsin-p'ien*), printed in 1859, which became one of the two chief Taiping writings on political ideology.①

Hung's reform program reflects his Western contact. Impressed by what he heard of the rapid progress in Westernization of Siam and Japan, he planned to abolish such customs as the wearing of long fingernails, footbinding, the raising of birds, and the wearing of ornaments. He suggests that calligraphy and painting, gold and jewels should be esteemed less than steamships, trains, thermometers, barometers, binoculars, and other scientific instruments. For institutional reforms, he recommends the inauguration of railroads, steamships, banks, post offices, newspapers, hospitals, institutions for the blind and the deaf, the prohibition of infanticide and of the sale of slaves, a ban on the performance of plays for religious or superstitious purposes, and the transformation of monasteries into hospitals. This indicates that he had in mind a sort of industrial and economic program for China. Many of his suggestions were carefully noted by Hung Hsiu-ch'üan, the Heavenly King himself, who wrote in the top margin, comments such as "I concur" or "This policy is perfectly correct." Nevertheless, in reading the following document one cannot help wondering exactly to what degree Hung Jen-kan knew what he was talking about. At any rate, he had linguistic difficulties in explaining new ideas by classical Chinese expressions.

### DOC. 11　HUNG JEN-KAN'S PROPOSALS, 1859⑫

(1) [Authority should be centralized and applied to all the people. On the other hand, the people's opinion should have ready access to the government.]

(2) The promotion of the facilities of communication [lit., carriages and horses] is aimed at convenience and speed. If someone can make a locomotive such as those made in foreign countries, which are capable of seven or eight thousand *li* in a day and a night, let him be permitted to monopolize the profit [i. e., patent], and after a certain limit of time let other people be permitted to imitate his invention. If he does not wish to monopolize the profit but to let society have the benefit, he should petition the government for permission to give up his monopoly in order to prevent bad practices [patent claims by people who would be less public-spirited]. At first, we should construct twenty-one main railroads in the twenty-one provinces, to serve as the veins of the whole country, and when the traffic is in good circulation, the nation will be healthy…

(3) The promotion of ships, which should be solid, nimble, and fast. Whether fire, steam, (human) energy or wind is to be used for power should be decided by the inventor… At present there is a steamship [p. 15] which can run more than two thousand *li* within a day and a night and which a great merchant can use to transport passengers and … commodities, while the government could use it for war or for defense and

patrolling... If the Heavenly Kingdom could promote this craft, then the Yellow River could be dredged and made to flow into the sea. Shipping on the Yangtze and the Huai rivers could be used for the exchange of products between the places where they are produced and to take them to others where they are lacking. In strategic spots steamships could be used to ward off trouble, and in drought or flood they could serve in famine relief...

(4) The promotion of banks. If a rich man wants to open a bank, he shall first report and deposit his deeds and other securities in the national treasury, whereupon he will be allowed to issue one million and a half (taels of) bank notes, which will be inscribed with very elaborate designs, stamped with the state seals, and be exchangeable for silver or commodities or for other bank notes and silver. On all these bank notes it will be allowed to charge three per cent interest...

(5) The promotion of patents for inventing utensils and for various arts. If there are those who can make very fine, unusual and convenient articles, they alone shall be permitted a manufacture and sales monopoly. Imitators shall be considered to have committed a crime and shall be punished... As a reward for a small article, there shall be a five-year (period of monopoly rights) and for a large one, ten years... After the time limit, other persons shall be allowed to make them.

(6) The promotion [i. e., exploitation] of hidden treasures. If there are people who discover gold, silver, copper, iron, tin, coal, salt, amber, oyster shells, jade, precious stones, and other materials, they shall be required to report this to the government. They shall be appointed as the chief superintendents and be permitted to employ people to mine. Twenty per cent shall be given to the chief superintendents, twenty per cent to the national treasury, and sixty per cent to the miners...

(7) [P. 16] The promotion of a postal service to transmit state documents, post offices to circulate all kinds of private letters, and newspaper offices to report frequent changes of current affairs.

(8) The promotion of Court investigators [to establish the facts officially, etc.]...

(9) The promotion of official reporting officers [lit., newspaper officers] in all provinces. These officials shall have duties but no authority. They must be honest and impartial, so that they will be independent and not controlled by other government officers nor should they try to control other officers. They will devote their time to collecting news from the eighteen provinces and a myriad of other places...

(10) [P. 17] The promotion of money and grain storehouses in the provinces, counties, and districts to take care of the salaries and public funds for civil and military officers. Officers should be established to take charge of monthly reports. If there are those who, apart from their salaries, illegally take one cent of bribery from the people, a punishment should be meted out to them.

(11) The promotion of public organizations for the populace [shih-min kung-hui]. Those who are rich and philanthropic, and who respect the sacred humanitarian hearts of the Heavenly Father and the Heavenly Elder Brother [i.e., Jesus Christ], should be allowed to make contributions at their pleasure in order to help the distressed and the endangered and the ignorant.

(12) The promotion of hospitals to relieve those who are ill and in suffering... Physicians shall be installed but they must have passed several examinations before they can be employed...

(13) The promotion of rural officers [to be supported by public contributions and to maintain local order, etc.].

(14) The promotion of rural soldiers... In the daytime they shall supervise all the families in cleaning the streets or roads in order to get rid of the dirt and poisonous things that cause injury to the people. They are also to arrest those who fight and steal, and to summon the bystanders to the office of the county officers to be witnesses and help render a verdict. Those who give false evidence shall be punished...⑬

The rest of the book deals with the abolition of group punishment, arguing that only the culprit himself should be punished, while his family members and others should be spared; with the prohibition of infanticide, of the sale of slaves, etc. , as summarized above; with the prohibition of personal visits to official residences in order to avoid the solicitation of favors; with the conversion of temples into churches; and with the criteria for a good soldier and general. Needless to say, Hung Jen-kan had no chance to carry much of his program into effect.

# 3 THE DESIRE FOR WESTERN TECHNOLOGY, 1861-1870

## CHAPTER VI  TSENG KUO-FAN'S ATTITUDE TOWARD WESTERNERS AND THEIR MACHINERY

By 1861 the main ideas of the Restoration period, as illustrated in the memorials of Prince Kung and his colleagues or the essays of Feng Kuei-fen, had been enunciated, while the Ch'ing victories over the Taipings in that year marked the turning of the tide in favor of the established dynasty. For the next decade, until his death in 1872, a significant share of the moral leadership of the Chinese state rested with the chief architect of victory over the rebellion, Tseng Kuo-fan (1811-1872). So outstanding was this one individual, as a leader of men and an embodiment of the Confucian principles of administration, that it will be quite impossible to do, him justice here. In what follows we confine ourselves to excerpts from Tseng's day to day writings, to indicate some of his comments on and attitudes toward the Westerners. Absorbed as he was in the problems of domestic government, it is uncertain how far Tseng Kuo-fan ever faced up to the implications of the technological superiority of the Western world.

Born into a Hunan farmer's family, Tseng first learned to write eight-legged essays and classical poems in order to pass the civil service examinations. He developed a great interest in the moral principles of Sung Neo-Confucianism and made a study of ancient philology. By the time he was twenty-eight, he had become a very assiduous student, although he was a man of only moderate scholastic aptitude. The years from twenty-eight to forty-two he spent in Peking, where he obtained his *chin-shih* degree, became a member of the Hanlin Academy, and made friends of many leading scholars and officials. Between the ages of forty-two and sixty-two, he had a strenuous military career, spent mainly in suppressing the Taiping rebels and some of the Nien bandits. By 1864, when the Taiping Rebellion was put down, Tseng Kuo-fan had acquired enormous prestige and influence. It was typical of his disciplined Confucian character, however, that his loyalty to the Manchu Son of Heaven never wavered. Rather than seek personal power, he led the Restoration movement to meet China's problems along traditional lines. As a representative of the landlord-scholar-official class, he identified his interests with those of the Confucian monarchy.

Tseng Kuo-fan's policy for dealing with the West, revealed mainly in his letters to Li Hung-chang and other officials, stressed the old Confucian virtues of sincerity and good faith. His progress from writing eight-legged essays to taking an interest in Western ships and guns was gradual and can be traced in his voluminous diary. His first turning in this direction was in order to improve China's defenses. As early as 1853 he recognized the need of a naval force and memorialized accordingly. ① He became interested also in Western methods of training soldiers; and not only in purchasing foreign guns, but also in their imitation and manufacture by his own people. In 1855 he established small arsenals in Kiangsi. When he moved his headquarters to Anking in 1861, he established both an arsenal and a shipyard there. ② In his diary entry of June 3, 1862, Tseng recorded a conversation with his staff members as follows: ③

If we wish to find a method of self-strengthening, we should begin by considering the reform of government service and the securing of men of ability as urgent tasks, and then regard learning to make explosive shells and steamships and other instruments as the work of first importance. If only we could possess all their superior techniques, then we would have the means to return their favors when they are obedient, and we would also have the means to avenge our grievances when they are disloyal. If on our side we have no instruments to depend upon, then when we are wrong, we naturally take the blame; when we are right, we also take the blame. If we hate them, we shall be blamed; if we favor them, we shall also be blamed. Though all the people in the interior flatter the barbarians, we certainly have no power to forbid them to do so. Even if everybody hated the barbarians, we could not take advantage of it.

On a visit to Shanghai in June 1868, Tseng wrote in his diary:④

I saw landscape pictures through a foreign glass [stereoscope] which was brought here by governor Ting [Ting Jih-ch'ang]; they are very beautiful. [On the following day, he writes:] I went to Yang-king-pang [the part of Shanghai along the later Avenue Edward VII] to return a visit of the French Consul-general Pai-lai-ni [M. Brenier], who entertained us very cordially. Even the bedrooms of his mother and his wife were prepared in advance to be shown to us. He conducted me, the governor, and the provincial commander-in-chief up through every floor of his four-storied residence. The splendid rooms and magnificent terraces, with bronze sculptures and colorful decorations, are probably superior even to the palaces of Chinese emperors.⑤

Three days after this visit, the *North China Herald* published a rather sarcastic account, guessing quite wrongly that a bad impression "must have been made on the mind of the august visitor who passed through our midst."⑥ Actually Tseng steadily developed his interest in Western science. At Nanking he had a big model of the earth and frequently consulted the *Ying-huan chih-lueh* of Hsü Chi-yü when he had trouble with the names of foreign countries in official documents.⑦ From 1862 on he often received foreign visitors or officials, including Robert Hart, general Staveley, J. M. Brown, Anson Burlingame, and Halliday Macartney. To learn how to be modern, he put down in his diary the new Chinese terms for light, chemistry, electricity, magnetics, zoology, botany, and similar subjects.⑧ Nevertheless, he remained personally conservative about foreign medicine. On May 8, 1871, he writes in his diary: "My wife's illness has daily become more serious. The children have invited a foreigner to treat her. In my mind I disapprove of it, but for the time being, I allow them to do so."⑨ In his diary over a period of many years, he frequently describes his great suffering with chronic ringworm, the loss of the sight of one eye late in his career, and severe toothache. At that time, in both Shanghai and Tientsin, he could have obtained some relief from foreign physicians, had he been willing to consult them.

### DOC. 12　EXCERPTS FROM TSENG'S LETTERS, 1862

During 1862, Tseng wrote to Li Hung-chang on various occasions as follows:

The barbarian affairs are fundamentally difficult to manage, but the basic principles are no more than the four words of Confucius: *chung*, *hsin*, *tu*, and *ching*—faithfulness, sincerity, earnestness, and respectfulness... *Hsin* means merely not to tell a lie, but it is very difficult to avoid doing so. We should start to work on the basis of this word... If today certain words were said definitely, tomorrow we should not, on account of a little advantage or harm to ourselves, change them... ⑩

When you have contacts with foreigners, there are four important sentences to keep in mind, namely: your words must be faithful and sincere; your conduct must be earnest and respectable; you should coöperate with them in defense, but not in attack; and you should keep at a distance from them at first, but later on become close... This last phrase means that we must earnestly strive to make our military power adequate so that we can stand on our own feet. At first, by ourselves, let us suppress the rebels in one or two places where our sternness and bravery will not be ridiculed by foreigners, and then we can become close to them, and it still will not be too late. Although at present we may seem to be quarreling with the foreigners, if we use these few sentences as a basis for getting along with them, we shall in time certainly achieve harmony with them, and be mutually content... ⑪

Confucius says, "If you can rule your own country, who dares to insult you?" If we are unified, strict, and sober, and if hundreds of measures are fostered, naturally they will not insult and affront us without reason. If we are not to be insulted and affronted, and if everywhere we are humble and modest, certainly we shall have no future anxiety. The way to win the hearts of people coming from afar lies in this, and the method of self-strengthening also lies in this... ⑫

In your association with the foreigners, your manner and deportment should not be too lofty, and you should have a slightly vague, casual appearance. Let their insults, deceitfulness, and contempt for everything appear to be understood by you and yet seem not understood, for you should look somewhat stupid. This also is a good way of facing the situation... ⑬

We should carefully watch and learn their superior techniques and also observe their shortcomings. We should not boast of, nor neglect our ceremonies. If they esteem sincerity and cultivate harmony, we should by no means open any frontier hostility with them; ff they abandon good relations and break their covenant, we should then have the weapons to oppose them. ⑭

## DOC. 13  FOUNDING THE SHANGHAI ARSENAL

Tseng Kuo-fan's chief effort at Westernization was the Kiangnan Arsenal established by himself and Li Hung-chang at Shanghai in 1865. ⑮ Shortly after his transfer to the governor-generalship of Chihli in 1868, Tseng wrote a memorial to present a retrospective account of its founding. He first recalled that his memorial of August 14, 1861, had urged the building of steamships, and then continued: ⑯

In 1862-1863, when I was encamped at Anking [Anhwei], where I established a factory to try to make foreign weapons, I used Chinese exclusively and did not employ any foreign mechanics. Although a small steamboat was built, its speed was very slow. The knack of building it was not completely acquired. In the winter of 1863 I sent the expectant sub-prefect Yung Wing abroad to purchase machinery, since I intended to make a gradual expansion. Your minister, Li Hung-chang, now governor-general of Hu-kuang, had paid attention to foreign weapons since the beginning of his tenure of the governorship of Kiangsu [1862]. At that time Ting Jih-ch'ang was the taotai of Shanghai. Both he and Li discussed the strategy of resisting foreign aggression and the method of manufacturing weapons. In the fifth month [May 25-June 22] of 1865, I purchased a set of machines in Shanghai and sent the prefects, Feng Chün-kuang, Shen Pao-ching, and others to open a machine shop [lit., *t'ieh-ch'ang*, iron factory]. At this juncture the machines bought by Yung Wing, having also arrived at Shanghai, were combined with the others into one arsenal. At first, because it was at the height of the attack on and suppression of the Taipings, guns and cannon were made. Also, on account of the shortage of funds, it was difficult to start shipbuilding until the fourth month [May 4-June 1] of 1867, when your minister memorialized and requested the assignment of twenty per cent from the foreign customs revenue, using ten per cent particularly for the expense of building steamships. Fortunately we are indebted to the Sacred Empress for her acceding to the request. Thereupon both the funds appropriated and the materials purchased gradually became more abundant...

It has been learned that in building steamships the boiler, the engine, and the hull are the three most important parts. Formerly when the steamship was built by ourselves in the foreign factory at Shanghai the boiler and engine [p. 28] were both bought from foreign countries and brought to China to be fitted into the hull. There has never been a case where we ourselves designed the blueprint and made the whole set of heavy engine and boiler. This time, when we began construction, we employed our own ingenuity in the study of the blueprint... During the first ten days of the seventh month [August 18-27, 1868], the building of the first ship was completed. Your minister named her the S. S. *T'ien-chi* [lit., peaceful and auspicious], meaning that she will be in calm waves within the four seas, and the factory business will be secure and prosperous. Two parts, the boiler and the hull, were both made by ourselves in the factory, but the engine was an old one which was purchased and repaired...

[P. 29] The said arsenal was formerly at Hung-k'ou, Shanghai, where a foreign workshop was temporarily rented, located in the midst of Chinese and foreigners. This caused much inconvenience. Moreover, the number of machines had daily increased, so that the factory became too small to contain them. During the summer of 1867, we began to build a new arsenal south of the city of Shanghai...

In addition a school should be established in which to learn translation, because translation is the foundation for manufactures. Foreign manufacturing is derived from mathematics, all the profound mysteries of which can be discovered through diagrams and explanations. It is simply because the languages are mutually incomprehensible that, even though every day we practise on their machines, after all we do not understand the principles underlying their manufacture and operation. This year the commissioners in the arsenal have paid great attention to translation. At different times we have invited three persons, Wei-lieh-ya-li [Alexander Wylie] of England, Fu-lan-ya [John Fryer] and Ma-kao-wen [John MacGowan] of America, who have devoted their energies to selecting and carefully translating books which would be beneficial to manufacturing...

Tseng Kuo-fan's approach to foreign policy was on the basis of his own Confucian moral code. As with any leader of great moral earnestness, his faith in the efficacy of his own right principles gave him determination and courage. To foreigners who have not shared these principles, this faith has sometimes made him seem naive or moralistic.

In 1867 the Tsungli Yamen circularized the high provincial authorities to secure their views on the proposed revision of the treaties of 1858—a form of consultation which Peking found particularly useful in the post-Taiping period.[17] Tseng Kuo-fan's reply stressed so clearly and explicitly the application to foreign relations of the classical ethic of Confucianism that the document speaks for itself. Few Chinese statesmen after his time were able to speak with such simple and profound conviction.

### DOC. 14  TSENG'S VIEWS ON TREATY REVISIONS, 1867[18]

In our relations with foreign countries, we should pay the greatest attention to faithfulness and righteousness, and especially should value determined resolution. What we cannot do, we should firmly resist from beginning to end, and we should never let ourselves be reversed by any difficulties. In what we can do, we should show our broad-mindedness and generosity and make an instant decision by a single word. We should absolutely never hem and haw [lit., half spit and half swallow], nor show the slightest sign of hesitancy, which gives them an opening for cunning argument.

Generally speaking, the foreigners in Europe have been annexing each other's territories for several hundred years, for no other reason than to seize the profits of the business people of the one country so that the ambitions of the attacking country may be satisfied. When the foreigners came to China, they set up ports of trade widely, for transporting and selling hundreds of their commodities. They also wished to apply the cunning scheme of exploiting and squeezing others so as to restrict the livelihood of our business people. Since the hostilities, the Chinese people have been for a long time in deep suffering, as if immersed in water or fire. In addition, the three (northern) and five (southern) ports[19] for international trade and the trade in the Yangtze River make their livelihood more and more difficult. The common people are impoverished, have no one to appeal to, and are as oppressed as if they were hanging upside down. Now if we allow the foreigners to transport [p. 2] salt, then the livelihood of the salt merchants who sell and transport it will be ended. If we allow foreigners to establish warehouses, then the livelihood of the storehouse owners will be ended. If we allow small steamboats to enter the inland rivers, then the livelihood of the boatmen and helmsmen of large and small boats will be ended. If we allow the foreigners to inaugurate and operate telegraph lines and railways, then the livelihood of the drivers of carts and mules and of the hotel porters will be ended. Of the various matters they have demanded [in the proposed treaty] we think that the only thing worth trying is the matter of coal mining, in which we shall borrow foreign tools for the operation of the mines to produce permanent benefit for China... As to other matters like steamships and railroads, etc., if they are to be carried out by foreigners, then the foreigners will take the profits from our interior; if they are to be carried out by Chinese who are attached to foreigners, then the rich and powerful people will usurp the profits of the poor people. None of these things should be done...

The main thing is to argue with the foreigners on the point of the livelihood of the common people. Actually this principle is so strong that it is indisputable. If the foreigners contest and argue endlessly, we may best tell them that even if the authorities in the capital complied with their demands reluctantly, your ministers in the provinces would still fight against them with all their might. Even if the ministers and officials complied with their demands reluctantly, millions of the common people of China when pushed to extremity would think of revolt and would regard them as enemies. This is also totally impossible for Chinese officials to forbid. China's princes and high ministers who plead for the lives of the Chinese people will not be worried for lack of expressions to put in their arguments. Even if, on account of this, we should incur hostilities, we shall have resorted to war to save the livelihood of the Chinese people and not be struggling for a superficial reason; thus we can face Heaven, Earth, and the spirits of all the emperors above and also the multitudes of the people within the vast country below. When we have nothing to fear in our minds, then there will be nothing to regret in the future...

[P. 3] As for the item of sending envoys abroad, since China and the foreign countries have already become friendly, to have relations with them is a normal matter. Some critics fear that our envoys may bring disgrace to their missions, and others are afraid that the cost will be enormous. These are words of overanxiety. It seems suitable to order the high ministers at the capital and elsewhere to look for men who could be envoys to distant countries and to mark their abilities for future use. Regardless of official rank, and with no definite time limit, whenever we have the person, we should send him, and if we have no man, we will not send anyone...

As for the expansion of missionary activities, we have found on investigation that at the beginning of Catholic missions in China, money and profit were expressly used to entice the people. In recent days foreign missionaries have been mostly poor. Their money is insufficient, so their theories likewise will not be believed... Catholicism had its beginning in Europe and yet today Protestantism has been separately established there as a reformed Catholicism. From this we can see that the religions of the heathen will decline at one time and be prosperous at others, and only the doctrine of the Duke of Chou and Confucius has never been worn out through all the ages. If China only cultivates her art of government and unifies her popular customs, making her education and religion enlightened, then even though the foreigners use hundreds of schemes to expand [p. 4] their religion, eventually there will be few who will believe in it...

Concerning these several items, of which the harm is rather slight, not only need we not dispute with them strongly, but also whatever they may demand may be immediately complied with. Only concerning the railroads, steamships, transportation of salt and opening of warehouses, and other matters which injure the livelihood of our people should we use all our energy to contend against them. We need not use words of rejection nor need we use any severe and stern language, but we should use polite words to make a plea and to move them by our sincere intentions. From beginning to end, we should not shift nor change our stand. We should make them understand that to have humane concern for our people in order to protect the nation is a constant principle of truth for emperors of all ages. It is also the family law of all emperors of our dynasty. In China today, where there are numerous troubles and where the foreigners are just expanding their influence, we cannot bend ourselves to the peace negotiations without any regard for the difficulties of the people in the interior. Even in the future, when China may become fully prosperous, and the foreigners may be in decline and weak, we shall also only seek to protect our common people, without any ambition to display our military power abroad. Even though they are stubborn and tricky, they must also understand that truth cannot be twisted, and the wrath of the multitude cannot be provoked. Probably they will be influenced by our extreme sincerity and accede easily to our conditions. These are my unworthy opinions; whether they are proper or not, I carefully offer my humble suggestions for your selection.

Although Tseng Kuo-fan's synthesis of Confucian principles and Western arms set a style for the succeeding generation, its efficacy as a basis for modern international politics was never proved in practice. In 1871, shortly before his death, we find Tseng arguing for the granting to Japan of the commercial privileges enjoyed by the West, in the following optimistic terms:[20]

We train soldiers to work toward self-strengthening, but from the beginning we have had no intention of displaying our power outside our own territory. We collect duties by following to some degree the foreign methods, but we have no ambition to accumulate and grasp a big profit.

If all our measures are developed with enlightenment, if the Western foreigners and Eastern foreigners are treated equally well and we use both prestige and virtue to control them according to the proper time and make foreign nations understand that the Sacred Dynasty's control of peoples coming from afar is uniformly based on the great principles of justice, then a myriad states will unanimously appreciate our sincerity...

## CHAPTER VII   LI HUNG-CHANG AND THE USE OF WESTERN ARMS

Under Tseng Kuo-fan's aegis the most powerful official to emerge in the lower Yangtze provinces in the 1860's was Li Hung-chang (1823-1901), whose personality was to dominate much of China's foreign policy in the late nineteenth century (see Ch. X a, below). One of Li's first contributions was to take practical steps to secure Western arms, the need for which was now widely recognized.

The new Chinese view on this problem was illustrated by the censor Wei Mu-t'ing, who pointed out in a memorial of November 14, 1861, that firearms had originated in China under the Chin Dynasty (A. D. 1115-1234) and had merely been improved upon by the Europeans. The Jesuits Adam Schall (1591-1666) and Ferdinand Verbiest (1623-1688) had cast cannon in China. Foreign arms should now be used to wipe out the Taipings.

Moreover I have heard that Russia formerly did not have a navy. After the Khan [i.e., the Tsar], Peter, came to the throne, he personally went to Holland in disguise to practice and learn about naval affairs and firearms. After several years he returned to his country where he immediately constructed warships. Step by step he enlarged his territory for several thousand *li*. Now in Europe the Russian troops are the strongest.①

A year later an imperial edict (Nov. 17, 1862) ordered the provincial authorities to train Chinese officers in Western military methods, so as to crush the Taipings:②

The rebellious bandits have been running away and disturbing the southeast, and have spread to Shanghai, Ningpo, and other ports where the government troops are not effective, and for the time being, we have to make use of foreigners to train our soldiers, as a scheme for self-strengthening... But to use foreigners to do the training is also to use foreigners to be the commanders; that is, they take the responsibility as instructors and also share the authority of commanders and generals... It would be better to select our own officers and order them to learn the military methods of foreign countries ... Then not only can we save expenses, but also we shall not give foreigners any military authority. Let Tseng Kuo-fan, Hsueh Huan (1815-1880), Li Hung-chang, and Tso Tsung-t'ang (1812-1885) select ten or twenty officers of the rank of captain or lower whose talents merit such training, and order them to learn the military methods of foreign countries at Shanghai and Ningpo [p. 42] ... If the newly trained officers after several months have accomplished something, then we can assign to their command the soldiers at Shanghai, Ningpo, and other places, where they are learning foreign military methods, and it will no longer be necessary to have them controlled by foreigners.

The difficulty of using foreign officers and instructors without being used by the foreign power concerned, a problem which so many weak countries have faced in the age of imperialism, was quickly perceived by Li Hung-chang. As governor of Kiangsu, he had to develop close working relations with Frederick Townsend Ward (1831-1862), "Chinese" Gordon (1833-1885) and other foreign commanders who successively led the mixed Sino-foreign force organized with Western arms to defend Shanghai.

## DOC. 15 LI'S LETTER TO TSENG KUO-FAN ON THE EVER-VICTORIOUS ARMY, FEBRUARY 1863[3]

In my camp not a single day passes without foreigners coming to see me and I am really embittered by the trouble they cause. Nevertheless, on account of this, I am thoroughly in touch with them both in spirit and in person, and in the midst of all this there is no one who dares to spread rumors or coerce me to do anything. Because I do not care very much for ceremonies, they are also rather frank in pouring out their feelings completely; however, I have no time to return their visits one by one.

"In resorting to warfare it depends upon the man, not upon the weapons." This is certainly a profound idea. [Tseng had said in a letter[4] that if generals and soldiers are good, it does not matter if the weapons are poor] ... I have been aboard the warships of British and French admirals and I saw that their cannon are ingenious and uniform, their ammunition is fine and cleverly made, their weapons are bright, and their troops have a martial appearance and are orderly. These things are actually superior to those of China. Their army is not their strong point, yet whenever they attack a city or bombard a camp, the various firearms they use are all non-existent in China. Even their pontoon bridges, scaling ladders, and fortresses are particularly well prepared with excellent technique and marvelous usefulness. All these things I have never seen before. However, they cannot pitch a camp nor live in tents, and, in addition, when they approach enemies they are very cautious. Their courage is mostly insufficient. In these things they are inferior to good Chinese soldiers.

The rebel Chung [the Taiping Loyal Prince, Li Hsiu-ch'eng] hired some foreigners who are rascals and who also have no way to seek for or buy real cannon... The foreign chiefs unanimously say that the rulers of England and France do not allow their big guns and mortars [p. 47] to go to China. Formerly the English chief who managed the affairs of the Ever-

Victorious Army with me said that if we did not permit his country to send an officer to lead the army jointly, he would immediately take back our foreign arms, and he fears that the Army will be rendered useless...

I feel deeply ashamed that the Chinese weapons are far inferior to those of foreign countries. Every day I warn and instruct my officers to be humble-minded, to bear the humiliation, to learn one or two secret methods from the Westerners in the hope that we may increase our knowledge. However, the able fighters Ch'eng Hsueh-ch'i (1829-1864) and Kuo Sung-lin (1834-1880) are firm and obstinate and for this reason they are unwilling to learn. Liu Ming-ch'uan (1836-1896) is more understanding and he is very anxious to ask for guns and mortars but is unable to get them. If we encamp at Shanghai for a long time, and cannot make use of nor take over the superior techniques of the foreigners, our regrets will be numerous!

The next document is remarkable both for its perception of the way China's social structure impeded Westernization and for its forecast of possible military developments in Japan and within China.

## DOC. 16  LI's RECOMMENDATION OF WESTERN MILITARY METHODS, JUNE 1863[⑤]

[Li begins by describing how he devoted his attention to Western arms after he reached Shanghai, purchasing and studying foreign weapons and using the assistance of skilled mechanics in the effort to comprehend them. His detailed factual account of the process of casting cannon would indicate that he had gained a more thorough understanding than some of his colleagues such as Tseng Kuo-fan.]

[P. 8] Of all firearms presently in use, explosive shells[⑥] can best assure victory, and particularly effective are the long guns to fire them; but unless we use the whole set of foreign machines and employ foreign skilled workers, we cannot start making them. Both the long-range and short-range guns would be ineffective without foreign gunpowder. The various arsenals under my jurisdiction cannot yet try to cast the long guns but we have bought several tons of large and small guns from England and France. We cast our own shells to supply the endless need for them.

I have learned that when Western scholars make weapons, they use mathematics for reference and exert their energy in deep thinking to make daily increases and alterations. Consequently they can make different weapons every month and every year. Of the Chinese books on making cannon, the *Tse-k'o-lu* by T'ang Jo-wang [Adam Schall], and more recently, Ting Kung-ch'en's *Yen-p'ao t'u-shuo*,⑦ "An illustrated explanation of artillery," are the most detailed, but both are superficial works which have been copied with misunderstanding and with the use of imagination. And yet our people all regard them as secret books (to be carefully guarded). No wonder the closer we seek the art of cannon making, the further we lose it! Generally, if a tool is inaccurate, it has no value. If a tool is not carefully used, then having an accurate tool is the same as being without it. When the cannon cannot be discharged, and the ball cannot be fired, this is the fault of the manufacturer [p. 9]. The long or short distance, and the quick or slow speed of the ball, the high or low elevation of the cannon and its slow or rapid discharge are the responsibility of the gunners. In all these respects there are definite and fixed principles which cannot be learned by smatterers.

Personally I think that "when a series of changes has run all its course, another change ensues,"⑧ and after change, things will proceed smoothly. Chinese scholars and officials have been indulging in the inveterate habit of remembering stanzas and sentences and practicing fine model calligraphy, while our warriors and fighters are, on the other hand, rough, stupid, and careless; so that what the scholars and officials use is not what they have learned, and what they have learned is not what they use. In peace time they sneer at the sharp weapons of foreign countries as things produced by strange techniques and tricky craft, which they consider it unnecessary to learn. In wartime then they are alarmed that the effective weapons of Western countries are so strange and marvelous, and regard them as something the Chinese cannot learn about. They do not know that for several hundred years the foreigners have considered the study of firearms as important as their bodies and lives ... The foreign officials and workers in charge of manufacturing them are honored and admired by the whole country, and not treated as small artisans.

Everything in China's civil and military systems is far superior to the West. Only in firearms is it absolutely impossible to catch up with them. What is the reason? It is because in China the way of manufacturing machines is for the scholars to understand the principles, while the artisans put them into practice and do the work. In developing their learning the two do not consult each other, hence their achievements cannot keep abreast. The best of the artisans is limited to becoming a head craftsman. Foreigners, however, are different. He who can make a machine that can be used by the nation can become a prominent official and his family for generations can live on the trade and keep their position hereditary. Thus there are grandfathers and fathers who learn the same trade and cannot thoroughly master it, yet the son and grandson still practise it for generations, insisting upon mastering it before they stop. "If the Emperor above desires fish, the official would even dry up the valley to catch fish"; if there is an offer of honor and profit, will no one exhaust his energy to seek it, exerting his strength day and night with the determination of not stopping until he has thoroughly mastered it?

Formerly England, France, and other nations regarded Japan as a foreign treasury, recklessly making demands upon her. The Japanese emperor and ministers exerted themselves to become strong, selecting brilliant sons from the imperial house and high ministers to learn various techniques in the factories of Western nations. They also bought the machines for making machines so as to practise manufacturing in their own country. Now they can navigate steamships, and make and use cannon. Last year the English people threatened them ostentatiously and brought up soldiers. And yet the superior techniques of the effective weapons which the British people have been relying upon [p. 10] for attacking and fighting had already been shared and mastered by the Japanese. Consequently, they remained steady and undisturbed; and the English in fact could do nothing against them. The Japanese of today are the "dwarf pirates" [wo-k'ou] of the Ming Dynasty. They are farther away from Western countries but close to China. If we have some weapons with which to stand on our own feet, they will attach themselves to us, and watch the shortcomings or strength of the Westerners. If we have nothing with which to make ourselves strong, then the Japanese will imitate the Westerners and will share the Westerners' sources of profits. Japan, a tiny country overseas, can still change her course at the proper time and know what she should take as her model. Since we Chinese thoroughly understand the principle that when one reaches a point of exhaustion, one must reform and then one can go on smoothly, we should also greatly change our plans.

There is a further source of anxiety. China's remaining bandits have not yet been exterminated and the foreigners, whether they are officials or common people, are secretly selling them powerful weapons. Let us suppose that in some nook of the mountains or some corner of the sea there are worthless rogues who learn the Western methods under cover, secretly originate some new principles, and suddenly stop tilling the land, and show their superior ability in making new weapons. The weapons of our government troops are old-fashioned and handed down from the past. How can we resist them? Whenever I think of this, I cannot but be startled with fear and sadly emit a long sigh... Su Tzu-chan [1037-1101] says, "If you speak in a time of peace, it is a sufficient basis for taking action, but frequently the trouble is that no one will believe you; if you speak in a time of trouble, it may be sufficient to secure belief but it will be already too late." I think that if China desires to make herself strong, there is nothing better than to learn about and use the superior weapons of foreign countries. If we wish to learn about and use the superior weapons of foreign countries, there is nothing better than to look for the machines with which to make machines. We can learn their methods but need not necessarily employ their people. If we wish to seek machines which will make machinery, and the men who can make machinery, we might specially set up a course for students [from the civil service examinations]. If the students will commit themselves to this course for the rest of their lives, as a means of attaining wealth, rank, and reputation, then the trade may be established, the technique may be mastered, and the abilities may be concentrated. In Peking the artillery and musketry division should particularly learn first to make cannon and improve on them, so as to prepare to inspire awe in the empire and reject foreign encroachment... We must take warning from what has happened to prevent what has not yet happened. Furthermore, we must investigate thoroughly why it has been so.

This statement from Li Hung-chang was put before the throne by Prince Kung and the other ministers of the Tsungli Yamen, with some very interesting additional considerations, some of which we translate as follows:

### DOC. 17  THE TSUNGLI YAMEN MEMORIAL OF JUNE 1863 ON CHINA'S DEFENSIVE STRATEGY①

It has been several decades since the foreigners first engaged in hostilities against us. Finally, in the period of Hsien-feng [1851-1861] domestic trouble and foreign insult came simultaneously... All commentators know that foreign countries such as England and France rely only on their solid ships and cannon to lord it overseas. But as to why their ships are solid and their cannon effective, this is put aside without discussion. Even if there were some who paid attention to this matter, there has been no way to learn about it because the foreigners keep secret this mechanical cunning, and are unwilling to teach others... But now all the foreign countries are willing to sell us foreign guns and cannon... and also willing to send people to teach us the manufacture of all sorts of arms...

In recent years, troops have been used in Kiangsu, where English and French officers have been hired to teach and drill our soldiers and militia. The foreign officers, then, import the victory-bringing firearms from their countries to the camps for our use, but charge us a big price... When we secure these weapons, they are sufficient to destroy strongholds and break open fortresses so that, wherever we advance, we are successful. All areas south of the Yangtze have been gradually cleared up. The promptness of this result has never been surpassed... At present the military campaign is still going on in Kiangsu and Chekiang. If we use this as a pretext, that our soldiers are to learn the manufacturing of weapons in order to suppress the bandits, we shall not reveal any traces [of anti-foreign intentions]. This is indeed an opportunity which should not be missed. If we begin to learn the manufacturing after the suppression of the bandits, then even if the foreign craftsmen would like to come for the high pay, the foreign officers must become suspicious and hinder them... Thus we should seize the opportunity, at a time when in the southern provinces our military power is in great ascendancy and foreigners are delighted to show us their superior techniques, to make a substantial study of all kinds of foreign machines and weapons in order to learn their secret completely. In times of disturbance they can be used to oppose aggression, and in times of peace they can show our prestige...

Your ministers frequently, in periods of leisure from public affairs, have thought and planned again and again: the friendliness or opposition of foreigners always depends upon the strength or weakness of China. Certainly Japan is not the only one to consider us in this way. If we can strengthen ourselves, then we can live peacefully with the others, and covertly deter them from undertaking their cunning and aggressive plans. Otherwise, we shall have nothing to depend upon...

[P. 3] After the battalions at the capital have learned to use these superb and secret weapons, learning to make them can be extended only to the banner troops stationed in the various provinces, because the bannermen have definite places to live in, which are comparatively easy to guard. In order to avoid other subsequent evils the common people should still be forbidden to learn about and use these weapons. It behooves us to request an Imperial Decree to order the Division of Artillery and Musketry to select eight intelligent and dexterous military officers and forty soldiers from among those who have had some training in making firearms, to be sent to Kiangsu and placed under governor Li Hung-chang for assignment…

## CHAPTER VIII   INSTITUTIONS FOR LINGUISTIC AND SCIENTIFIC STUDIES (THE T'UNG-WEN KUAN)

To responsible officials on the spot like Tseng and Li, the undeniable need to make foreign arms entailed an equal necessity to study Western "mathematics," including its application in engineering. At Peking one of the first innovations to follow the Tsungli Yamen was the interpreters' college or T'ung-wen Kuan. Approved in 1861 at the same time as the Yamen, this college was set up first to produce diplomatic interpreters; but it soon expanded to include Western sciences taught by Western professors. For this forward step, as for so many others, the foreign customs inspectorate under Robert Hart (1835-1911) supplied steady financial support.①

The original argument for the T'ung-wen Kuan in 1861 (which was briefly quoted above in our condensed summary, Doc. 7) had been as follows:②

(5) We request Your Majesty to order Canton and Shanghai each to send to Peking two men who understand foreign spoken and written languages to be commissioned and consulted. We note that in any negotiations with foreign nations, the prerequisite is to know their nature and feelings. At present, their speech cannot be understood and their writing can hardly be deciphered. Everything is impeded. How can we

expect to make a suitable settlement?

Formerly with regard to the Russian language, a precedent was established by setting up a school (*wen-kuan*) for its study, and this showed a profound wisdom. Now after a long time, the regulations have become a pure formality and the language has not been thoroughly understood. Some kind of encouragement seems to be warranted here in order to call people's attention to it.

We have heard that among the Canton and Shanghai merchants there are some who are devoting themselves to the study of the written and spoken languages of England, France, and America. We request that Your Majesty order the governor-general and governors of the two provinces to select bona fide and reliable men and send two from each province, altogether, four, to Peking, bringing with them [p. 25] the books of the various countries. At the same time, let four or five brilliant boys under the age of thirteen or fourteen be chosen from each of the Eight Banners to study under them. Those who are sent to Peking should be well paid, after the practice of the Russian school, and following two years of service their diligence or laziness should be appraised, and those who make a good record should be rewarded and promoted. When the students from the Eight Banners can all master the written and spoken languages we shall no longer invite Canton and Shanghai teachers.

As for the Russian written and spoken language, we still beg Your Majesty to order the school to discuss its regulations carefully and promote its work seriously. Among the men who learn the languages of various nations, those who thoroughly master them should be immediately reported with a request that they be encouraged so that this work will not be later neglected.

In 1863, Li Hung-chang supported the idea of the T'ung-wen Kuan in an eloquent memorial evidently drafted by his secretary, Feng Kuei-fen; some parts are lifted from one of Feng's essays (see Doc. 8 above), and we have therefore omitted duplicate passages in the following extract.③

## DOC. 18　LI HUNG-CHANG'S SUPPORT OF WESTERN STUDIES, 1863④

When China has contact with foreigners, we should first understand their ambitions, be aware of their desires, and thoroughly know their points of strength and weakness, their honesty and dishonesty, before we can expect to secure just treatment. During the last twenty years of trade relations there have been quite a few of their leaders who have learned our written and spoken language and the best are able to read our classics and history... Whenever we have a discussion between Chinese and foreign high officials, we depend entirely upon the foreign interpreters to transmit the ideas; it is difficult to guarantee that there is no such thing as prejudice or misinterpretation.

[P. 12] Your minister requests that we follow the example of the T'ung-wen Kuan by inaugurating at Shanghai another foreign language school, in which children from the vicinity below the age of fourteen, of brilliant ability and refined and quiet character, will be selected and taught by Westerners, and at the same time *chü-jen* and licentiates of excellent conduct and learning will be invited from the interior to teach them classics, history and literature... After the students show achievement in their studies, they should be sent to the governor-general and governor of the province to be examined and to qualify as district licentiates...

After the language students have become numerous, men of ability will emerge... Are Chinese wisdom and intelligence inferior to those of Westerners? If we have really mastered the Western languages and, in turn, teach one another, then all their clever techniques of steamships and firearms can be gradually and thoroughly learned. [Li then raises the question of a similar school at Canton.]

As a result of this proposal, a language school modeled on the Peking T'ung-wen Kuan was set up at Shanghai in 1863. Another one was opened at Canton in 1864 and a somewhat similar institution at the Foochow Shipyard in 1866.

On December 11, 1866, Prince Kung, representing the Tsungli Yamen, urged the emperor to develop the T'ung-wen Kuan by adding a scientific department of astronomy and mathematics and by admitting students of high attainment in Chinese learning. He repeated the stock argument that "the machinery of the West, its steamers, its firearms, and its military tactics, all have their source in mathematical science." He proposed to invite professors from the West. "What we desire is that our students shall get to the bottom of these subjects ... for we are firmly convinced that if we are able to master the mysteries of mathematical calculation, physical investigation, astronomical observation, construction of engines, engineering of water-courses, this, and this only, will assure the steady growth of the power of the empire."⑤ On January 28, 1867, Prince Kung submitted another memorial in which China's need of Western science was discussed in detail. This important document asserted that the natural sciences were the foundation of Western strength and stressed the point that officials like Tso Tsung-t'ang and Li Hung-chang who were conversant with foreign affairs all urged the adoption of Western learning and the manufacture of foreign weapons and machines as the method for China's self-strengthening. ⑥

In spite of vehement conservative protests, the new department was set up and Hsü Chi-yü (see Ch. Ⅳ) became director of the school. Soon the T'ung-wen Kuan curriculum included astronomy, mathematics, chemistry, physics, biology, geography, geology, mineralogy, metallurgy, mechanics, anatomy, physiology, political economy, and international law. Putting all these subjects under the heading of "astronomy and mathematics" presumably represented an effort of Prince Kung and his colleagues to lessen the conservative resistance by camouflaging their innovations, since Western astronomy and mathematics were known to have been introduced into China and accepted as early as the seventeenth century.

In the full-dress debate touched off by this action, the conservatives were led by the Grand Secretary Wo-jen (d. 1871), a Mongol whose high scholarship had made him a tutor to the emperor, head of the Hanlin Academy, and president of several of the Six Boards in succession. A product of the orthodox philosophy of Chu Hsi, Wo-jen was in 1867 the recognized leader of the opposition to Prince Kung and Wen-hsiang, and he immediately memorialized against the establishment of Western studies in the T'ung-wen Kuan, inveighing openly against the Western influence on racial and cultural grounds.

### DOC. 19　WO-JEN'S OBJECTION TO WESTERN LEARNING, 1867[①]

Mathematics, one of the six arts, should indeed be learned by scholars as indicated in the Imperial Decree, and it should not be considered an unworthy subject. But according to the viewpoint of your slave, astronomy and mathematics are of very little use. If these subjects are going to be taught by Westerners as regular studies, the damage will be great... Your slave has learned that the way to establish a nation is to lay emphasis on propriety and righteousness, not on power and plotting. The fundamental effort lies in the minds of people, not in techniques. Now, if we seek trifling arts and respect barbarians as teachers regardless of the possibility that the cunning barbarians may not teach us their essential techniques—even if the teachers sincerely teach and the students faithfully study them, all that can be accomplished is the training of mathematicians. From ancient down to modern times, your slave has never heard of anyone who could use mathematics to raise the nation from a state of decline or to strengthen it in time of weakness. The empire is so great that one should not worry lest there be any lack of abilities therein. If astronomy and mathematics have to be taught, an extensive search should find someone who has mastered the technique. Why is it limited to barbarians, and why is it necessary to learn from the barbarians?

Moreover, the barbarians are our enemies. In 1860 they took up arms and rebelled against us. Our capital and its suburb were invaded, our ancestral altar was shaken, our Imperial palace was burned, and our officials and people were killed or wounded. There had never been such insults during the last 200 years of our dynasty. All our scholars and officials have been stirred with heart-burning rage, and have retained their hatred until the present. Our court could not help making peace with the barbarians. How can we forget this enmity and this humiliation even for one single day?

Since the conclusion of the peace [p. 25], Christianity has been prevalent and half of our ignorant people have been fooled by it. The only thing we can rely on is that our scholars should clearly explain to the people the Confucian tenets, which may be able to sustain the minds of the ignorant populace. Now if these brilliant and talented scholars, who have been trained by the nation and reserved for great future usefulness, have to change from their regular course of study to follow the barbarians, then the correct spirit will not be developed, and accordingly the evil spirit will become stronger. After several years it will end in nothing less than driving the multitudes of the Chinese people into allegiance to the barbarians.

Reverently your slave has read the instruction to the grand councillors and officers of the nine government bureaus in the *Collected Essays of the K'ang-hsi Emperor*, in which he says, "After a thousand or several hundred years, China must be harmed by the various countries of Europe." The deep and far-reaching concern of the sage Emperor is admirable. Even though he used their methods, he actually hated them. Now, the empire has already been harmed by them. Should we further spread their influence and fan the flame? Your slave has heard that when the barbarians spread their religion, they hate Chinese scholars who are not willing to learn it. Now scholars from the regular channels are ordered to study under foreigners. Your slave fears that what our scholars are going to learn cannot be learnt well and yet will be perplexing, which would just fall in with (the foreigners') plans. It is earnestly hoped that, in order to maintain the general prestige of the empire and to prevent the development of disaster, the Imperial mind will independently decide to abolish instantly the previous decision to establish such studies in the language school. The whole empire will be fortunate indeed.

## DOC. 20   THE TSUNGLI YAMEN'S REBUTTAL, 1867⑧

Your ministers have examined the memorial of Wo-jen; the principles he presents are very lofty and the opinion he maintains is very orthodox. Your ministers' point of view was also like that before they began to manage foreign affairs; and yet today they do not presume to insist on such ideas, because of actual difficulties which they cannot help...

From the beginning of foreign relations to the present there have been twenty or thirty years. At first the officials inside and outside the capital did not grasp the crux of the matter, and whether they negotiated peace or discussed war, generally there were empty words without effect; and so the incident of 1860 arose. At that time the foreign troops approached our city wall, and the gunfire and flames illuminated the sky. The capital was in peril day and night. Scholars and officials either stood about, putting their hands in their sleeves, or fled away confusedly. Our deceased Emperor did not consider his ministers, I-hsin [Prince Kung] and others, to be unworthy, and ordered them to remain in Peking to manage the peace negotiations. Your ministers dared not imitate the vain and bitter cry of Chia I [200-168 B.C., a famous scholar who grieved so bitterly at the death of his prince that he died within the year],⑨ ... nor would they use empty words in perfunctory performance of their duties... It has been eight years since the conclusion of the [1860] treaty. The matters in negotiation between China and the West have been extremely difficult. Your ministers jointly have tried their best to maintain the situation, and in recent days the Westerners have been generally docile and agreeable.

However [p. 2], while merely to get along with them for the time being is all right, it is not possible in this way to protect ourselves for several years or decades to come. Therefore your ministers have pondered a long-term policy and discussed the situation thoroughly with all the provincial officials. Proposals to learn the written and spoken languages of foreign countries, the various methods of making machines, the training of troops with foreign guns, the dispatching of officials to travel in all countries, the investigation of their local customs and social conditions, and the establishment of six armies in the area of the capital in order to protect it—all these painstaking and special decisions represent nothing other than a struggle for self-strengthening.

Moreover, the principal means which foreigners employ to secure victory is the use of steamships and firearms first of all. Formerly, because the Europeans in making firearms did not care how much capital they used and also because firearms have their roots in astronomy and geometry and are developed by trigonometry and mathematics, so that their guns can be cleverly discharged and marvelously hit the mark, the censor Wei Mu-t'ing requested that at Shanghai and other spots factories be established [see Ch. VII above]... Your ministers have also discussed this in correspondence with Tseng Kuo-fan, Li Hung-chang, Tso Tsung-t'ang, Ying-kuei, Kuo Sung-tao, Chiang I-li, and others. They all agreed that the clever methods for manufacturing must begin with mathematics...

We are afraid that the people who are learning these things will have no power of discrimination and are likely to be led astray by foreigners, as Wo-jen fears. Therefore we have deliberated and decided that those who participate in the examinations must be persons from regular scholastic channels. It is indeed those students who have read widely and who understand right principles and have their minds set upon upright and grand purposes—and the present situation is just what causes the scholars and officials to feel pain in heart and head—who would certainly be able to lie on faggots and taste gall [i. e., nurse vengeance] in order to encourage each other vigorously to seek the actual achievement of self-strengthening. They are different from those who have vague, easygoing, or indifferent ideas.

Wo-jen says that the barbarians are our enemies. Naturally this shows that he also has the intention of lying on faggots and tasting gall. But let us ask, is his nursing of vengeance in this way for the purpose of gaining a temporary fame, or is he going to seek actual results? If [p. 3] he says that he seeks results, then let us ask, should he seek results from the foolish and mean fellows, or should he seek them from among the scholars and officials? That is why your ministers' Tsungli Yamen has requested that only people coming from the regular channels take the examinations for the language school. Now upon reading Wo-jen's memorial, one gathers that he considers this action to be absolutely impracticable. The grand secretary has long enjoyed a flourishing reputation for Neo-Confucian studies. As soon as his idea is expressed, there will undoubtedly be a large number from among the scholars and officials who will agree with him. Ever since your ministers have managed foreign affairs, they have always hoped to get the opinions of others so as to use them for greater advantage in the handling of current events; they have never dared to cherish the slightest idea of avoiding such opinions. But this memorial of Wo-jen will not only inhibit scholars henceforth from going forward, but also, we are particularly afraid, will make those inside and outside the capital, who are sincerely performing their duties with no inclination to empty talk, become disappointed and discouraged. Then what your ministers and provincial officials have planned for several years will fail in one morning—this is indeed of great concern.

Your ministers have thought again and again and found that the foreigners who dare to come to China and act as they wish without any restriction do so because their minds have been made up and their designs have accumulated during the last several decades. The Chinese spoken and written languages, the important and unimportant geographic areas, and even a single word or a single action by us, they all know completely; whereas concerning the actions of their race, we do not know a thing. We merely continue our empty talk about moral principles and righteousness, and confusedly argue without end. Now the time for treaty revisions after a ten year period will soon come [i. e. , in 1868]. Even if we plan and think about it day and night, it is already too late. If we remain contented with our ignorance, we are deeply concerned lest the situation will deteriorate like a stream running downhill every day. Yet as soon as we seek for some method of pursuing knowledge, then again public opinion will criticize us right and left. One mistake is enough; how can we bear to make another? ...

Even though we run the risk of receiving the criticism of the empire we will not try to avoid it. But the grand secretary [Wo-jen] considers our action a hindrance. Certainly he should have some better plans. If he really has some marvelous plan which can control foreign countries and not let us be controlled by them, your ministers should certainly follow the footsteps of the grand secretary, exhausting their mean abilities in careful discussions with him, in order to show our harmony and mutual help, and to console your Imperial anxiety. If he has no other plan than to use loyalty and sincerity as armor, and propriety and righteousness as a shield, and such similar phrases, and if he says that these words could accomplish diplomatic negotiations and be sufficient to control the life of our enemies, your ministers indeed do not presume to believe it...

## CHAPTER IX   TSO TSUNG-T'ANG AND THE FOOCHOW SHIPYARD

Tso Tsung-t'ang (1812-1885) was born into a poor peasant family of Hsiangyin and lived for a long time with his wife's family in Hsiangtan. (Tseng Kuo-fan, Tso Tsung-t'ang, and Mao Tse-tung were born and bred in neighboring districts of Hunan.) Being in straitened financial circumstances, Tso spent the first forty years of his life chiefly as a school teacher and gentleman farmer before he served in the army. In this period he associated with the scholar Ho Ch'ang-ling (1785-1848), who was the compiler, assisted by Wei Yuan (see Doc. 3), of the famous "Collection of essays by Ch'ing scholars of practical use to society"(*Huang-ch'ao ching-shih wen-pien*), and he participated three times (1833, 1835, 1838) in the metropolitan examinations but failed to get the *chin-shih* degree. After his third failure, Tso shifted his interest from memorizing Confucian classics for the examinations to pursuing knowledge for practical use. He read works on history and geography by early Ch'ing nationalist thinkers, such as Ku Yen-wu (see Ch. IIa), and also a large official work on the geography of Uygur region compiled in 1756-1782. This special study of works on Chinese topography and economics later proved helpful to his military campaigns and economic reconstruction work in the northwest.

Tso was directly influenced by Lin Tse-hsü. When Lin passed through Changsha in 1849, Tso had a long talk with him and discussed all sorts of topics for a whole night. He was also fond of the *Hai-kuo t'u-chih* (see Doc. 3) and once urged a relative to make a special study of it; in 1875 he wrote a preface to a new edition. Finally Tso's plans for the Foochow Shipyard were carried out by Lin's son-in-law, Shen Pao-chen (1820-1879). Tso served as tutor (1840-1848) in the family of his friend, T'ao Chu (1779-1839), a governor-general of Kiangsu, Kiangsi, and Anhwei. It was during this period that his talents were recognized by Hu Lin-i (1812-1861), a general and statesman of Hunan, who later became his patron. His personal connections with the great scholars and officials of his native province gave Tso some insight into state affairs, and he watched closely the development of events during the Opium War. His interest in the use of Western arms dates from this period.

In 1852 he was recommended by Hu Lin-i to fight against the Taipings. Due to his unusual ability, he was made governor-general of Fukien and Chekiang in 1864, and he recovered the latter province in the same year, with the help of French officers and soldiers, from whom he acquired a better knowledge of Western weapons. Like Tseng, he also directed the building of a steamboat by native mechanics, and tried it out on the West Lake at Hangchow. Since its speed was unsatisfactory, he sought the counsel of two French engineers in 1864. In his insistence on steamships as a means of China's self-strengthening, he was one of the first proponents of a modern Chinese navy. Later he became enthusiastic about torpedoes and wished to invite German experts to make them.①

But although Tso liked to employ foreign experts, he would not rely entirely on them. He wrote, "The method of self-strengthening should be to seek from among ourselves, not seek from among others. He who seeks the help of others will be controlled by others, and he who relies upon himself will have the situation under his own control."② Frankness and self-assurance were two of his chief characteristics.

Tso Tsung-t'ang was also an able administrator. As governor-general, he did a great deal toward the rehabilitation and reconstruction of Chekiang and Fukien after the suppression of the Taiping Rebellion. In Fukien, he selected a site for the shipyard at Ma-wei near Foochow (August 1866), and appointed two Frenchmen, Prosper Giquel (1835-1886) and Paul d'Aiguebelle (1831-1875), to serve as engineers and supervisors. He also planned a school, attached to the shipyard, to train young men to build and man ships. Some of the students of this school, such as Yen Fu (1854-1921, see Ch. XVI), later became famous. It is difficult to say whether Tso Tsung-t'ang was trying to develop a competitive program paralleling Tseng's Shanghai Arsenal; although Tseng and Tso, being leaders of the same province, were not on especially good terms, both were persistent in carrying out their plans. Document 21, below, indicates that Tso expected his plan for the Foochow shipyard to encounter many hindrances and criticisms from lethargic and conservative officials, who were quick in criticizing new undertakings but slow in presenting constructive proposals of their own. After submitting many memorials and receiving imperial approval, and after having put some of his plans into effect, Tso was transferred to Shensi, Kansu, and Sinkiang.

Tso's chief contribution was made in the barren area of the northwest, where he spent more than twelve years (1868-1880). There he faced four great difficulties: money, food, ammunition, and transportation. To solve these problems, in a poor, thinly populated, culturally backward, politically corrupt, and rebellious area, far from the center of China, was a tough job. In order to save money and energy he aimed to complete the task according to a five-year plan which he reported to the emperor in advance. He ordered his soldiers, most or all of whom were originally peasants, to become military colonists, i. e. , to raise their own food, improve irrigation, dig wells, and dredge rivers. They also planted thousands of trees for which travelers today, on the long shaded highways of Uygur region, are said to be still grateful. For the making of clothes, he attempted to transform the village handicrafts into a modern machine industry by encouraging cotton planting, improving sericulture, and opening woolen and cotton mills. For ammunition he established a manufacturing bureau in Shensi (1866) with an arsenal (1871) and a gunpowder factory (1875) at Lanchow. He employed Chinese, German, and other foreign mechanics to direct this work.

For money Tso reorganized the land, salt, tea, likin, and other taxes. He fought against greedy Manchu officials and abolished much red tape. His financial and supply operations for many years were handled by the famous treaty-port banker, Hu Kuang-yung, who maintained a depot at Shanghai and raised funds from foreign merchants. In 1867 Tso contracted such a loan for 1,200,000 taels, and thereafter he floated similar "foreign" loans four times (1868, 1877, 1878, 1881), totaling 15,750,000 taels,③ His total expenditure in the northwest is estimated to have been about one hundred million taels.④ He cast coins and silver dollars and also attempted in 1878 to establish a modern bank and even to open gold mines.

For transportation Tso established his own system, running from Hu Kuang-yung's office at Shanghai through a provisions depot at Hankow, which gathered food and other local products from the interior, and a general transportation office at Sian. For cultural purposes, he established a printing office at Sian to print important books, and opened academies and free schools to educate the people. Although criticized for cruelty to the rebels, he worked hard on rehabilitation, provided effective famine relief, and prohibited the planting of poppy and smoking of opium.

His periodic fiscal reports, reproduced in his collected writings, are quite detailed (no such reports are included in Li Hung-chang's works). Tso was a diehard—advocating war against France, Russia, or any other foreign aggressor. He had a simple belief that in negotiation with a foreign power there were only three possible lines to follow: offense, defense, and peace; but one must be able to fight an offensive war before one could defend onself, and one must be able to defend oneself before a fair peace treaty could be obtained. ⑤

Although the following document comes from an earlier and less successful phase of his official career, it shows Tso Tsung-t'ang's grasp of detail and vigorous imagination.

### DOC. 21  Tso's PLANS OF 1866⑥

The great advantage of southeast China lies on the water and not on land. From Kwangtung and Fukien, to Chekiang, Kiangnan, Shantung, Chihli, and Shenking around to the northwest, the three sides of China are surrounded by vast seas... In time of peace, we could use ships for grain transport; then a thousand *li* would be as if at one's threshold; if we used them for trade, then hundreds of commodities would be gathered in the markets... When some incident occurs, steamships could be used for mobilization and then the forces of the hundred clans of Kwangtung could be concentrated into the three states of Korea... Since warfare has opened up on the sea, the steam warships of various European countries have come directly to Tientsin. Our national defense line has actually become fictitious. Their ships sail as rapidly as a shooting star or a whirlwind and we have no way to stop them.

Since foreign ships were permitted to carry away northern goods to be sold in the various ports, the prices of commodities in north China have been exorbitantly high. The great merchants of Kiangsu and Chekiang, who used to make sea transportation their profession ... cannot reduce their prices to compete with the foreign merchants...

Hitherto, ministers within and without the capital have repeatedly discussed the purchase of steamships instead of building them, but no one has yet presumed to discuss the establishment of a plant to build them. The reasons are, first, the difficulty of selecting a place for the shipyard; second, the difficulty of finding and buying steamship machinery; third, the difficulty of engaging head mechanics; fourth, the difficulty of raising and accumulating a huge amount of funds; fifth, the difficulty that the Chinese [p. 2] are unaccustomed to navigation and that after the completion of the ships we would still have to engage foreigners; sixth, the difficulties of the numerous requirements of expenditures for coal, salaries, and wages after the ships have been completed, all of which would have to be paid every month, in addition to which from time to time the ships would have to be repaired; seventh, in this unusual enterprise it is easy for slander and criticism to arise; one person initiates the plan, another carries it out, while a third is a mere bystander; and if the enterprise fails near its completion, then both public and private loss will result. With these several difficulties, it is no wonder that there is no man who cares to take the responsibility...

Your minister humbly believes that if we desire to prevent harm from the sea and, at the same time, to receive its advantages, we must reorganize our navy; if we wish to reorganize our navy, we must establish a plant, to supervise and build steamships. The Europeans are skillful but we Chinese do not have to be content with our stupidity... It is not impossible to get the machines.

As to the difficulty of engaging foreign head mechanics, we may first lay down the requirements in the contract and fix their salaries, and after they arrive at the machine shops, the office will select from the interior young and bright craftsmen in various lines, to learn from and practise with them. Those who have brilliant talent and clever ideas, regardless of whether they are officials, gentry, scholars or ordinary people, should all alike go to the plant for study and practice.

[P. 3] It is estimated that the building of the shipyard, the buying of machinery, and the recruiting of head mechanics must cost more than three hundred thousand taels; and that the starting of the work and gathering of materials, together with the payment of salaries to the Chinese and foreign mechanics, will require approximately fifty or sixty thousand taels each month. Figuring for a year, it will require a cost of more than six hundred thousand taels...

We are concerned lest after the completion of the ships we have no qualified captains to watch the compass, control the helm, and the like, for all of which we shall have to hire foreigners. To obviate this difficulty, it should be distinctly indicated when the contract is first made that the teaching of shipbuilding will at the same time include navigation. As soon as a ship is finished, some Chinese will immediately be ordered to accompany the foreign mechanics to sea and sail to all the seaports. Regardless of whether they are soldiers, officers, or people in other fields, if any one of them has learned his job thoroughly and is able to become a captain, he will immediately be granted a military rank...

[P. 4] In an unusual enterprise, it is easy to incur slander or criticism. At the beginning people will worry about the lack of accomplishment; then they will criticize the expenditure as being too much, and will probably also say sarcastically that we have lost our national dignity. All this is imaginable and probably will happen... In the

East, it was Japan that first bought a steamship, and then took it apart for examination and imitation. But they have not yet had any success. Recently Japan sent people to England to learn her language and study her mathematics as the basis for building steamships. Within a few years the steamships of the Eastern foreigners are certain to be successful. Only China, owing to the widespread fighting in recent years, has not yet had leisure to discuss this matter ... Both Japan and China see the potential advantages on the high seas; Japan has something to rely upon and we alone have nothing. It is like crossing a river where others are rowing a boat while we are making a raft. It is like racing when others are riding on a steed while we are riding on a donkey. How is this possible? All of us are human beings, whose intelligence and wisdom are, by nature, similar; but in practice we cannot help being different. Chinese wisdom is spent on abstract things; the foreigners' intelligence is concentrated upon concrete things. Chinese take the principles of the classics as the foundation, and mechanical matters as the practical details; foreigners consider mechanical matters important, principles unimportant. Each of the two believes what it thinks right and neither can understand the other...

When the steamships are completed, the administration of grain transport will be prosperous, the military administration will be improved, the merchants' distress will be relieved and the customs duties will be greatly increased. The temporary cost will produce profit for several generations.

As for Chinese imitation of foreign ship construction, some people will probably think that we have lost our national prestige. This is still more wrong. [Tso here describes China's imitation of Western cannon in the seventeenth century.] Recently we have also been able to manufacture foreign guns, cannon and other weapons, whose foreign style China is imitating. If cannon can be imitated, why can ships alone not be imitated? How can this be considered a loss of our national prestige?

# 4 EFFORTS AT SELF-STRENGTHENING 1871-1896

## CHAPTER X   THE PROBLEM OF LEADERSHIP: PERSONALITIES AND INSTITUTIONS

The response of Ch'ing officialdom to Western military power seems to have gone through a curious cycle: the brief activity of the Opium War period was followed by the stagnant xenophobia of the 1850's, the promising innovations of the 1860's were followed by an apparent diminution of effort in the 1870's and 1880's. Thereafter, one might point to a renewal of creative effort after the defeat by Japan in 1895, as though China's attempted regeneration in each period had required the shock of actual foreign aggression and defeat to provide its stimulus. When the heat was off, the effort at reform cooled down. At any rate, the 1870's and 1880's appear to record a slowing down of the attempt at meeting the West by self-strengthening. Perhaps this impression merely reflects the fact that less research has been done on these decades; perhaps, on the other hand, self-strengthening as it proceeded met increasing opposition or obstacles which could not be overcome.

One key to this problem was in the realm of leadership. We therefore devote attention first of all to Li Hung-chang and his subordinates, as leaders in Westernization in the provinces, and then to the holders of power in Peking, particularly the Empress Dowager. The difficulties of Westernization can be seen in the projects for training students and setting up diplomatic legations abroad, and for building railroads and creating a real navy at home. All of these were essential developments for China, yet in every case there was at work against them a remarkable recalcitrance and inertia, which delayed their achievement for many years.

Behind these phenomena it should become apparent as serious research progresses that China's slowness in self-strengthening was due in part to the fact that the officials concerned were more interested in profit to themselves than in progress for their country. Li Hung-chang, for example, put his own men into the key positions from which China's modernization was supposed to be directed; most of them profited accordingly through the perquisites of power which these modernization projects carried with them.

### a. *Li Hung-chang and his Subordinates*

Li Hung-chang (1823-1901), whom we have quoted already in Chapter Ⅵ, was born into a well-to-do family of Ho-fei, Anhwei. At the early age of twenty-four, he gained the *chin-shih* degree as well as an appointment in the Hanlin Academy. There he studied informally under Tseng Kuo-fan and this connection laid the foundation for his future career. From the age of thirty to forty-five (1853 to 1868), Li was in military service suppressing the Taiping and the Nien rebels, rising from a post as staff officer to independent command. As a military commander, he seems to have usually judged situations correctly and laid down careful plans well in advance. With the help of the foreign-led Ever Victorious Army, organized before he was dispatched to Shanghai in 1862, Li recovered the province of Kiangsu within two years, which facilitated the final capture of Nanking; he was also able to wipe out the Nien rebels in 1868 after more than twenty other commanders had failed. His military success has been attributed partly to the influence of his patron Tseng Kuo-fan, who helped him organize the Huai (or Anhwei) Army, on the model of Tseng's own Hunan Army.

As an official, Li Hung-chang held many high posts, some of them concurrently: governor of Kiangsu (1862-1865), grand secretary (1872-1901), minister of the Tsungli Yamen (1896-1898), commissioner to the coronation of Tsar Nicholas II (1896) and governor-general of Liang-kuang (1900-1901). His principal post, however, was that of governor-general of Chihli from 1870 to 1895, the fateful decades before the defeat by Japan.

Li's position of leadership in China was in *yang-wu*, or "foreign matters." This term included the conduct of diplomatic relations and the borrowing of Western technology, two activities that were indeed aspects of a single problem, how to survive in the modern world. The foreign-style enterprises were begun mainly for military purposes and followed one another in a logical sequence. To suppress the rebellions and for coastal defense, there were, first, the establishment of arsenals and shipyards, and the building of forts and vessels. Secondly, technicians were needed to make these weapons and so schools were established and students and officers sent to study abroad. Since modern defense required modern communication and transport, the construction of telegraph lines and the organization of a steamship line were undertaken. Eventually, since modern defense also required money and material resources, a cotton textile factory was established, and coal, iron, and gold mines were opened.

Li Hung-chang understood that machinery was the dynamic of Western civilization and so he made use of it. But from the beginning he lacked an overall plan to be carried out step by step and merely began one thing after another according to current needs. As for the modern schools and the sending of students abroad, the aim was not so much to promote academic studies as to meet military needs or diplomatic problems. To Li Hung-chang's mind, the wealth and power of the Western countries were derived entirely along these material lines; that was apparently the full scope of his *yang-wu* or "foreign matters." He did not recognize the value of European political and social institutions, much though he might pay them lip service.

On the contrary, Li seems to have thought that the Chinese political and educational systems and Chinese culture and customs were all superior to those of foreign countries—except for cannon, railways, and machinery, in which China was inferior. If China could learn to use these material things, then Li would have fulfilled his duty in the handling of foreign matters. The fallacy of this reasoning was conclusively revealed in 1894 when the Chinese army and navy were almost completely crushed in brief encounters with the Japanese forces.

To blame Li Hung-chang personally for the debacle of 1894 does not seem to be entirely fair. Among the scholar-officials of his day, he was certainly one of the ablest and he probably understood as much about the problems of modernization as any other Chinese in a responsible post.① The fact that he could hold his high position for almost a quarter of a century shows his political astuteness. His prestige among foreigners in China, though qualified, was quite unequalled. The failure of China's modernization program during this period should be attributed mainly to the anti-foreign conservatism of the Chinese educated class as a whole, and to the selfishness of the Empress Dowager and certain high officials at her court in particular. Whenever a new project based on a Western example was proposed, opposition would be voiced at once, mostly on ideological rather than factual grounds. These unrealistic outcries often influenced the decision of the court against a proposal and in some cases put a stop to programs already started. As Li frequently took the lead in proposing these modernization projects, he bore the brunt of the conservatives' onslaught. Regarding this problem, he once remarked:②

The present situation is one in which, externally, it is necessary for us to be harmonious with the barbarians, and internally, it is necessary for us to reform our institutions. If we remain conservative, without making any change, the nation will be daily reduced and weakened... Now all the foreign countries are having one reform after another, and progressing every day like the ascending of steam. Only China continues to preserve her traditional institutions so cautiously that even though she be ruined and extinguished, the conservatives will not regret it. Oh heaven and man! How can we understand the cause of it?

Other obstacles in the way of modernization were the traditional administrative practices and the personal ethics underlying them. Any official in charge of a public project would generally "milk" it as much as possible and use bribery to prevent the revelation of his malfeasance. Considering this circumstance, Li's accomplishments were actually rather remarkable. He was probably the least conservative high official of his day.

To undertake all the enterprises he initiated, Li Hung-chang was dependent on men of ability to assist him. Among the large number of his subordinates from 1870 to 1894 and after, some were men of proven integrity, most were given to extravagance, and a few were downright dishonest, but many were recognized for their abilities either in secretarial duties or as administrators. In addition to these two categories, there were under Li's direction army and naval officers, directors of education, and men in business or finance who were connected with his enterprises. There were also a number of Western advisers, some in his employ, some consulted occasionally, and some regularly, as in the case of the Tientsin Customs Commissioner, Gustav Detring.[3]

The staff members collected by Li Hung-chang compare favorably in intelligence with those of his teacher and predecessor, Tseng Kuo-fan, and those of his junior competitor, Chang Chih-tung. Tseng's staff seems to have included more men of character, used to simple living and devoted to studies; and under Tseng, men of talent, like Tso Tsung-t'ang and Li himself, perhaps, had more chance for individual development. Chang Chih-tung, however, insisted on doing everything himself, and very few of his subordinates went on to high position, although, on the other hand, none of his protégés was notorious for the accumulation of great personal wealth. Compared with these other groups, Li's lieutenants were more given to extravagant habits. Perhaps he used the chance of personal gain as bait to secure the services of able men. In any case, while his army and navy proved ineffective because of corruption and his industrial enterprises were of indifferent value to China, Li himself left a fortune, as did many of the men connected with his enterprises ... Perhaps we can call it ... "official capitalism."

Among the more prominent of Li's lieutenants were his personal secretaries, such as Hsueh Fu-ch'eng (see Ch. XVb), Chang P'ei-lun (1848-1903), Yü Shih-mei (1853-1915), and Wu Ju-lun (1840-1903); able administrators, such as T'ang T'ing-shu (1832-1892, founder of the China Merchants Steam Navigation Company and K'ai-p'ing Mining Corporation), Chou Fu (1837-1921), Sheng Hsuan-huai (1844-1916), and Yuan Shih-k'ai (1859-1916); and also men who had studied abroad, such as Ma Chien-chung (1845-1900, in France) and Yen Fu (1854-1921, in England).

Of the men mentioned above (out of a much larger number), one of those with the most influence on Chinese thought in the period ending in 1896, was Hsueh Fu-ch'eng. Hsueh had been a secretary on Tseng Kuo-fan's staff for eight years (1865-1872) before he joined that of Li Hung-chang in 1875. He served under Li until 1884, and later was concurrently minister to England, France, Italy, and Belgium for four years (1890-1894). We devote a later section to his essays on reform (Doc. 40).

### b. *The Empress Dowager's Influence*

In the last decades of the nineteenth century, when China was in dire need of intelligent leadership under which to catch up with the West by modernization, the dominant figure at the court was not Prince Kung but a Manchu woman, the famous Empress Dowager, Tz'u-hsi (1835-1908).① A concubine of Emperor Hsien-feng, she had risen to the rank of Empress Dowager in 1861 when her son, Emperor T'ung-chih (1862-1874), ascended the throne at the age of five. She became co-regent with her late husband's principal wife, who was, however, only a figurehead. By allying herself with the deceased emperor's younger brothers, Prince Kung and Prince Ch'un, this able woman staged her first political maneuver and got rid of eight powerful but unpopular grand councillors who had themselves been plotting against her. Prince Kung then joined the regency and was made head of the Grand Council as well as of the Tsungli Yamen, in a position to act both for the throne and for the central government.

When in 1865 the throne had become fairly secure after the victory over the Taiping Rebellion, the Empress Dowager precipitated a quarrel with Prince Kung, removed him from the regency, and left him as head of the Grand Council. In other words, the prince was relegated to the level of a court official, albeit *primus inter pares*. In January 1875, when her son died without issue, the Empress Dowager adopted the son of Prince Ch'un and of her own sister, who was the prince's wife. Thus she resumed her power as regent, ruling for another child emperor, Kuang-hsü (1875-1908), and thereafter she never really relinquished that power. Except for a period of retirement from 1889 to 1898, she remained in effect the ruler of China.

Like most Manchu officials of that time, the Empress Dowager could read and write Chinese as her native language and learned a little Manchu just to get by in routine matters. She had a keen mind and, although not well educated, could grasp enough of the essentials of administration to meet her needs within the court and deal with the high officials, princes of the imperial family, and others serving within the palace, such as bannermen and eunuchs of the Imperial Household. With a dominant will and an understanding of human nature, she controlled high personages through forceful leadership, flattery, money, the delegation of authority, and unabashed power, as might be necessary, and generally succeeded in lining them up to support her. She could play the role of a helpless widow with a young child, and make it hard for men in the society of China to refuse her requests. Alternatively she could be ruthlessly insistent on her wishes and threaten the use of her authority to do away with any opponent.

Under her administration of the imperial bureaucracy, the provincial officials obtained much greater freedom of action than ever before in the dynasty. The more important governor-general enjoyed unusually long tenures of office. There was a marked tendency among the Manchus to admit tacitly their own inadequacy and yield the important posts in the provinces to the Chinese. The Chinese officials who received this trust seem to have outdone one another in showing their loyalty to the throne, as of course their class had been sedulously trained to do for two centuries past. But possibly it is to the credit of the Empress Dowager that an atmosphere of Manchu-Chinese coöperation persisted so strongly in the Ch'ing Dynasty, even during great crises in its period of decline.

In the realm of foreign affairs, although the Empress Dowager followed the general advice of her officials, there seemed to be always present in her mind a feeling of hatred toward the foreigners. Perhaps the only exceptions were those who worked for the Ch'ing government. It was the foreigners who had forced the court including herself to flee from the old summer palace (Yuan-ming-yuan) near Peking in 1860 and who had sacked it in retaliation for mistreatment of allied envoys. The Empress Dowager apparently set her heart on restoring the summer palace and, in spite of opposition from many quarters, she cajoled and browbeat the high officials into rebuilding at least a part of it.

Another less publicized aspect of the Empress Dowager's conduct was her addiction to taking gifts or bribes from her officials. This had been done by every Manchu emperor before her and by almost all the officials throughout the dynasty, but she carried it to an extreme. In the old Chinese government, every superior expected something from his subordinates, while on the bottom layer the lowest officials made exactions from the people. The least corruptible officials—who were rather rare in this late period—were those who lived within their salaries and accepted just enough gifts or customary fees to meet their necessary expenses of office. Bribery, in the form of gifts, became an unwritten institution, and a minimum amount was customarily set for every kind of official transaction. At the pinnacle of officialdom, the Empress Dowager received some remuneration for every official audience, which by regulation was a necessary formality for all newly appointed or promoted officials and for high provincial officials who had held their posts for a number of years. A minimum sum was set for each rank and position, depending roughly on its lucrativeness to the incumbent. The Empress Dowager shared this income with her chief eunuchs and certain courtiers, usually the imperial princes who were supposed to officiate at the audiences. Although this debilitating practice was not new, under the Empress Dowager it had a marked growth in volume, much to the demoralization of the government service. In the case of Li Hung-chang, it is an interesting question how much his long tenure as governor-general of Chihli was due to his generous gifts to the Empress Dowager and her favorites.

Against this background, projects for modernization had to pay their way not only on the books, but in the purses of the officials. At the top, the ruler of China not only condoned "the system" but energetically applied it. The most notorious scandal of the period symbolized China's administrative problem: millions of taels of silver accumulated for the purpose of building the modern navy were somehow turned over to the Empress Dowager to expend on the rebuilding of the Summer Palace (I-ho-yuan). Whether the Chinese navy could have defeated the Japanese in 1894, even if these millions had been spent on it, may still be open to conjecture. But misappropriation by the Empress Dowager, condoned, however unwillingly, by Li Hung-chang, certainly sealed China's fate. Today, the famous marble barge still stands in the Summer Palace lake as a reminder of this fiasco, its marble paddle wheels carved upon its sides. ⑤

In 1874, during the Taiwan incident, but twenty years before the dénouement with Japan, the aged Wen-hsiang emerged from retirement to speak plainly to the throne.

### DOC. 22  WEN-HSIANG'S WARNING OF DISASTER, 1874⑥

When the peace negotiations were completed [in 1860] everybody spoke of the necessity for self-strengthening, yet during the last ten years or more there has been little achievement [p. 13]. The reason is that those who look down upon and disregard foreign affairs merely have empty discussions without actual accomplishment, whereas those who are accustomed to the peaceful situation are content when nothing happens for fear that if anything is done it may arouse the suspicion of the foreigners. Even those who carefully discuss defense measures are hindered by the insufficiency of funds, and nothing can be done or developed. Now the (Taiwan) incident has already taken shape, a war crisis is imminent. If we still do not pay attention to it and suddenly the great enemy (Japan) confronts us, what can we rely upon? It is humbly hoped that imperial orders will be sent to the Ministry of Revenue and the Imperial Household Department to raise plenty of the necessary supplies, to cut off lavish expenditures, to stop public works which are not urgent [i.e., the construction of the Summer Palace], and to plan for the most needed coastal defense; so that the ministers at the capital and in the provinces can all devote their energy to the scheme.

As for the way to make ourselves strong, it lies first in our readiness to accept advice in a humble manner in order to seek out the good and bad points of our administration. One should not take agreeable and soothing words as a source of pleasure and take straightforward and frank advice as distasteful. When Your Majesty is concerned to work diligently and alertly, then your ministers within and without the capital will be stimulated in spirit and not dare to follow their traditional dawdling habits. Otherwise they will remain accustomed to taking things complacently and will never think of reforms, in which case, I fear that internally and externally the country will fall apart, the people's confidence will be shaken, and the disaster will be unspeakable.

# CHAPTER XI   TRAINING STUDENTS ABROAD

### a. *The Educational Mission to the United States*

The traditional Confucian emphasis on human abilities and the enlisting of talented men in administration, which underlay the classical examination system, led inevitably to the idea of training Chinese in Western countries. As we have seen above, the incompetence and essential illiteracy of the Cantonese interpreters or "linguists," criticized by Feng Kuei-fen (see Doc. 8), and the importance of "foreign matters," especially the need for Western guns and ships, had brought the Chinese government to found the T'ung-wen Kuan, or College of Foreign Languages, at Peking in 1862 as a subordinate office to the Tsungli Yamen, and a school of Western languages and science in Shanghai in 1863, which was annexed to the Kiangnan Arsenal in 1869. A number of foreign instructors had been invited, but their faithfulness was suspected by some conservative scholar-officials, such as Wo-jen (see Doc. 19). As time went on it became increasingly obvious that if China were to master the secrets of Western technology it would be necessary for the Chinese government to send young men to Western countries for training.

Records of Chinese visitors to the United States go back to 1785; a great deal remains to be done in studying the American end of early Sino-American contact. On the Chinese side attention has been directed chiefly to the project promoted by Yung Wing (1828-1912), the first Chinese graduate of an American university—Yale in 1854—by which one hundred and twenty Chinese students were brought to the United States in the decade 1872-1881.[①] Somewhat less attention has been devoted to the project which sent thirty Chinese students to England and France for technical training in 1876. Private ventures under missionary auspices and on the part of overseas Chinese may have played a more important role than has been realized—Sun Yat-sen is one such example. Yung Wing has had many successors in the persons of Chinese students in the United States. All in all, the latter have constituted the greatest movement of conscious acculturation in history.

Below we present the key memorial to the Tsungli Yamen, by which Tseng and Li finally got the educational mission of 1872 started; a series of letters dealing with its cessation; and an instructive report from one of Li Hung-chang's bright young men, Ma Chien-chung (1845-1900). (References to Pin-ch'un and other officials sent abroad are explained in the next chapter, on diplomatic missions.)

### DOC. 23   THE PROPOSAL OF TSENG AND LI IN 1871[②]

Last autumn when (I, Tseng) Kuo-fan was at Tientsin, governor Ting Jih-ch'ang frequently came to discuss with me proposals for the selection of young and brilliant youths to be sent to the schools of various European nations to study military administration, shipping administration, infantry tactics, mathematics, manufacturing, and other subjects. It is roughly estimated that after more than ten years their training will have been completed, and they will return to China so that the Chinese can learn thoroughly the new techniques in which the Westerners are particularly strong, and then we can gradually plan for self-strengthening. In addition he says that the men who can take [p. 20] these young boys to foreign countries—Ch'en Lan-pin [a *chin-shih* of 1853], who is an assistant secretary of the Board of Punishments, fourth rank, and Yung Wing, who is a sub-prefect of Kiangsu—are both competent for the job... After Pin-ch'un[③] and two other gentlemen, Chih-kang and Sun Chia-ku, had traveled in various countries by imperial command, they saw the essential aspects of conditions overseas, and they found that maps, mathematics, astronomy and navigation, shipbuilding, manufacturing, and other matters all give assistance to military affairs. All those who have studied in foreign countries and have learned the superior techniques are to be immediately invited by academies after their return to teach the various subjects and to continue their own scholarly development.

Article VII of the treaty recently concluded with the United States [1868] says that hereafter, if Chinese wish to enter the higher and lower levels of American government schools in order to learn various kinds of literature and sciences, they will enjoy equal treatment with the people of the "most favored nation." It also says that Americans will be allowed to establish schools in China at the places assigned by Chinese for foreign settlement, and the Chinese can also do the same thing in the United States, etc., ...④ The foreign nations allow us to learn their superior techniques together with their own citizens; Chih-kang, Sun, and other gentlemen have already pioneered the way and report that to go aboard a steamer and cross the Pacific Ocean directly to America takes only one month or more. For these reasons it should not be a very difficult matter.

To establish arsenals for manufacturing and to open schools for instruction in China is just the beginning of the struggle to rise again. To go abroad for study, to gather ideas and the benefits of greater knowledge can produce far-reaching and great results. Westerners seek knowledge for actual use. Regardless of whether they are scholars, workers, or soldiers, they all go to school to study and to understand the principles, to practice on the machines, and to get personally familiar with the work. They all exert themselves to the utmost of their ingenuity, and learn from one another, in the hope that there will be some monthly difference and yearly improvement. If we Chinese wish to adopt their superior techniques and suddenly try to buy all their machines, not only is our power insufficient to do this, but also there is no way for us to master either the fundamental principles or the details of the profound ideas contained in these superior techniques, unless we have actually seen them and practiced with them for a long time. The ancients said: "He who wishes to learn the Ch'i dialect should place himself in the midst of Chuang or Yü" [names of streets in an old city of Ch'i, modern Shantung] and another proverb says, "To hear a hundred times is not as good as to see once..."

But there are two difficulties in the trial period. One is the selection of human talent [p. 21], and the other is the raising of funds... Kuo-fan and Hung-chang are deeply aware of these two difficulties. But to make a hill we must begin with one basketful of earth after another, and to raise mugwort we have to wait three years. We lay plans for it now, so that in the future the number of students will steadily increase... We plan to send functionaries to Shanghai to establish an office for the selection of brilliant youths from all provinces. The number for each year will be thirty persons, and for four years there will be a total of one hundred and twenty, to be sent in annual groups aboard ships across the ocean to study in foreign countries. After fifteen years, they will begin to return to China in sequence, according to the year when they were sent. It is estimated that on their return to China all these young men will be in the neighborhood of thirty years of age. Their energies will then be at their prime; they will be able to render their services at their best time of life.

We have heard that, heretofore, the sons of people of Fukien, Kwang-tung, and Ningpo also occasionally have gone abroad to study, but they merely tried to get a rough acquaintance with foreign written and spoken languages in order to do business with the foreigners for the purpose of making a living. This time, at the beginning of the selection, we shall be doubly careful; the students being taken to foreign countries will all be controlled by the commissioners. Specializing in different fields of study, they will earnestly seek for thorough mastery of academic knowledge. There will also be interpreters, and instructors to teach them Chinese literature from time to time, so they will grasp the great principles for the establishment of character, in the hope of becoming men of useful abilities. Although not all of them will necessarily become mighty instruments, yet out of a large number of talented men some extraordinary ones will certainly emerge from their midst. This is the theory of obtaining five out of the ten selected...

If your honorable Yamen considers this to be practicable, as soon as we receive your reply, our office will immediately submit a joint memorial. The required [p. 22] funds will also be conveyed under a memorial and an imperial order requested to have them appropriated from the foreign customs duties at Shanghai...

Perhaps the most remarkable thing about the Educational Mission thus inaugurated (after ten years of agitation by Yung Wing) was the fact that it actually functioned, more or less as planned, for a decade (1872-1881), only to be summarily discontinued at the end of that time with nothing to take its place!

Some of the reasons for the recall of the Mission are stated in detail by Yung Wing, *My Life in China and America*, chapter 18. He puts the chief blame on Wu Tzu-teng, a *chin-shih* of 1852, a compiler of the Hanlin Academy, and a good mathematician, who worked for some time in the Chinese legation at Paris, before he was transferred to the United States as superintendent of students attached to the Chinese Embassy.⑤ Wu was fond of display and prestige, and acted even more autocratically than the old-fashioned Chinese educational commissioners who had preceded him. No sooner was he installed in his new position than he summoned all the Chinese students to Washington to receive his instructions. When the students came for the interview they did not perform the kotow. One of the subordinates of the new superintendent, a Mr. Chin, became very angry saying, "All these students have forgotten their original civilization and disregard their teachers and elders. Even though they might have some success in the academic field [which was then still uncertain], still they could not be of any use to China." Mr. Chin, who turned out to be a favorite of a certain influential noble of the imperial family, prepared a memorial asking to have the students suddenly recalled to China, in 1881. Other staff members of the Chinese Educational Mission disapproved of this action but no one dared to say anything (according to Yung Wing) except Yung Wing, who argued strongly but to no avail. Huang Tsun-hsien, then consul-general at San Francisco, upon hearing of this incident was so affected that he wrote a long sad poem to describe it.⑥

Although Yung Wing says the conservatives in the Educational Mission sent many reports to the Chinese government, slandering the young students, it is difficult to trace any of their original letters or reports. Their positions were low and perhaps their writings were neglected by compilers. Below we present excerpts from Li Hung-chang's correspondence to show the points of view opposed to that of Yung Wing.

## DOC. 24  LETTERS OF LI HUNG-CHANG CONCERNING THE END OF THE MISSION, 1880-1881

[To Commissioner Ch'en Lan-pin, Aug. 6, 1879]⑦ The enterprise of sending young people to foreign countries has cost a lot of money and created numerous evils, but after all will have little actual effect. The criticisms of Chinese officials and scholars have been numerous. Recently I received a letter from Tseng Chi-tse [Tseng Kuo-fan's son, "Marquis Tseng"], who considers that since the sending of students from the Foochow Shipyard to England and France has had no great result, those students who have been in the United States likewise will not necessarily show great achievement... If all you gentlemen who are in charge of the task still cherish differing opinions and cannot control and manage it seriously, you have certainly failed in the first attempt which was inaugurated by Tseng Kuo-fan; and you and I will also be greatly criticized by public opinion.

[Another letter to Ch'en Lan-pin, May 10, 1880].⑧ Yung Wing has come to see me, saying it is true the students have neglected their Chinese studies. It is due to Yung Wing's obstinacy in not desiring these students to learn much Chinese. Even during the summer when the schools were closed and it was just the time for them to review their Chinese, Yung Wing alone did not think so... I hope you will give him advice when it is convenient and not allow him to take too much charge of the Mission, which should be reorganized by Compiler Wu Tzu-teng, in order to concentrate authority so that in the future, when these children have finished their study and return to China, there will still be posts to which to commission them, and we shall not fail in the original idea of sending them to study abroad.

[Li Hung-chang's comment on the withdrawal of a portion of the students, March 29, 1881.]⑨ In recent years there has been considerable criticism of Yung Wing, charging that he has laid too much emphasis upon Western knowledge, with the result that the young boys have neglected their Chinese studies. I have written letters to guide him, not once but many times... Two years ago after Wu Tzu-teng went to the office of the Educational Mission, he repeatedly wrote to me saying that there were numerous evils in the Mission's affairs and that it ought to be abolished quickly...

I have reviewed the case with a candid mind and feel that, since more than half the students were natives of Kwangtung who went abroad at an early age, it is probably hard for them to avoid indulging in foreign customs. Wu Tzu-teng disciplined them too severely and so compounded the trouble. Consequently he thought that all the students should be withdrawn, an opinion which seems to be too extreme. On a later occasion when he wrote me he said that those students who had deeply indulged in American customs and who were stupid by nature should be sent back to China, while those who had already entered the universities and whose graduation was near, and whose achievements were comparatively concrete, might be transferred to be under the control of the Chinese Legation [p. 8]. As for the general supervisor, Chinese instructors, interpreters, and other officials, they could all be dismissed...

Yung Wing has managed this Mission for a long time. He feels that it concerns his face or dignity and it is imaginable that he does not want to have the Mission cancelled...

On June 8, 1881, the Tsungli Yamen memorialized requesting the abolition of the Educational Mission and the return of the students to be employed according to their abilities. The request was granted.⑩

### b. Students in Europe

The flow of Chinese students to Europe, while little studied, has been commensurate with that to the United States. The next item records the impressions of one of Li Hung-chang's protégés whom he later sent to Korea in 1882.

### DOC. 25　MA CHIEN-CHUNG'S REPORT ON HIS STUDIES IN FRANCE, 1877⑪

The last ten days of May were the examination period of the Political Institute. There were eight examination questions... The third was on the commercial proceedings of all nations, dealing with the basis of credit for commercial organizations and bank drafts. From this we know that the wealth of Westerners in the last hundred years has not come purely from the creation and development of machines but essentially from the protection of commercial organizations... Thus, even though the amount of capital required for railways, telegraph lines, steam engines, and mining is very great... and though there is a limit to gold and silver, there is no end to the use of money because, since the currency is represented by paper and guaranteed by credit, one coin may assume the usefulness of several hundred coins...

The fifth question was on the differences and similarities of administrative methods, government, and education in the three countries, England, the United States, and France, the methods by which the upper and lower classes coöperate, what are the advantages and disadvantages of each method, and what are the reasons for England being able to maintain herself so long without changing, for America not changing though having many defects, for France repeatedly changing and frequently getting worse...

The seventh one was on the similarities and differences of public administration in all nations, some of which are monarchies, some republics, and some partly monarchical and partly republican. The legislative, executive, and judicial powers are divided and are not given to one person. These three powers do not interfere with each other, and so the political situation is in good order, bright and presentable. The collection of taxes is not done by [police] officials, therefore bad officers have no way to fulfill their desires. The verdict for a crime is fixed by local juries; bad judges have no way to play on words. Everybody has the right to be independent, and seeks to be self-respecting.

The eighth question was on the levy of taxes and the amount of national debt. Western taxes are ten times heavier than those of China and yet the people are not resentful. The national debt is borrowed from the people and yet the people are not suspicious. Why?

For these eight questions the written examination took three days and I wrote more than twenty notebooks... I answered them one by one in detail, and all received good grades from the professors, and were announced in the newspaper. They say I have understood these subjects very thoroughly and have grasped the broad outlines. Those who are merely bookworms cannot be compared with me. This praise is also caused by the fact that Westerners have had little contact with us Chinese and usually are scornful of us. Therefore, whenever there is a Chinese student who knows a little and understands half of what he has studied, he is praised as being extraordinary. This "being extraordinary" [as an individual] is just a sign of being despised [as a race]. I can only study hard, with strong determination. How dare I become proud of a little progress? ...

[P. 2b] I have been in Europe for more than a year. When I first came here, I thought that the wealth and power of all European nations lay exclusively in their fine manufacturing and strict discipline of troops. But when I worked on their laws and antecedents, and read their writings, I realized that their pursuit of wealth is based on the protection of commercial concerns, and that those who seek power consider it important to win the hearts of the people. When they protect commercial concerns, then taxes can be increased and their savings will naturally be more adequate. When popular support is won, then loyalty and patriotism will be doubled, and the people can be expected to unite against a national enemy. Other good things are the increase in the number of intelligent students after the spread of schools, and the communication of the opinions of the lower classes after the establishment of parliaments. As for manufacturing, the army and navy, and these various large items, they are all but unimportant details.

Thus, I thought the government of all Western nations was perfect. When I went to listen to the lectures in the Political Institute and discussed these things forwards and backwards with scholars and officials, I began to realize the truth of the statement [p. 21] that "It would be better to be without books than to give entire credit to them." England has a king and besides has an upper and lower house. It seems that all policies must originate there, but we know that the king only gives an endorsement and the upper and lower houses merely have empty discussions, the handle of policy is wielded by the premier and two or three chief ministers. Whenever they have to face a difficult matter, they use the parliament as a cover. The president of the United States is elected by the people themselves, and this seems to be just, without being selfish, but whenever it is time for an election, bribery is publicly practiced. When the president is changed, the whole list of government personnel is changed, and all officials are members of his party. How can they expect good administration? France is a republican nation where it appears that those who become officials need not come from aristocratic families, but we know they organize political factions among themselves, and except for those scholars such as Tien-yeh [Adolphe Thiers, 1797-1877, President of the Third French Republic, 1871-1873] and others whose wisdom and ability are outstanding, it is very difficult for men who do not belong to the same faction to find a good job or get into a fine position...⑫

## CHAPTER XII DIPLOMATIC MISSIONS ABROAD

Considering the efficiency and skill of many Chinese diplomatic representatives in the twentieth century, it seems amazing that the Ch'ing Dynasty should have delayed so long in dispatching envoys abroad. The first semi-official venture in this direction was the mission chaperoned by Robert Hart in 1866. Headed by "an elderly Manchu official of low rank," Pin-ch'un,① this mission of investigation included three students from the T'ung-wen Kuan. It visited nine European countries, but had little effect on its return. The famous "Burlingame mission," which visited the United States and Europe in 1868-1870, appeared to the West to be primarily the achievement of the former American minister at Peking, Anson Burlingame, but the Chinese records make it clear that two Ch'ing officials, Chih-kang and Sun Chia-ku, were sent as his co-envoys with equal status. The Tientsin massacre of 1870 necessitated the sending of a special mission of apology to France, under the Manchu Ch'ung-hou; but this still did not constitute the establishment of a regular diplomatic legation. After much discussion and some false starts, a mission was finally established in England only in 1877; even then its immediate occasion was to present China's apology for the murder of a British representative, A. R. Margary, on the Burma border in 1875. The first Chinese legation in the United States was established in 1878 by Ch'en

Lan-pin and Yung Wing, who had been in charge of the Educational Mission. Legations were also established in Germany (1877), France (1878), Russia and Spain (1879), and Peru (1880).

The following part presents first an account of the Tsungli Yamen's discovery of the efficacy of international law—a Western device of considerable value for defense against the West. This is followed by a long analysis (Doc. 27) written by the first envoy in London, Kuo Sung-tao (1818-1891), a highly competent, respected, and orthodox Chinese official who nevertheless called spades "spades" as soon as he saw them in England and later did not mince words over China's ineffectual handling of her relations with France. Marquis Tseng's dialogue with the Empress Dowager (Doc. 28) is the nearest thing to a press conference recorded from this period.

## DOC. 26  PRINCE KUNG'S DISCOVERY OF INTERNATIONAL LAW, 1864[②]

Your ministers have found that the Chinese spoken and written language is learned with care by foreigners in China without exception. Among them, the cleverest go even further and immerse themselves in studying Chinese books. When a case is argued or discussed, they can usually base themselves on Chinese legal codes ... Unfortunately the regulations of foreign countries are all written in foreign languages and we suffer from being unable to read them. And it will still take some time for the students in the T'ung-wen Kuan to master the foreign languages thoroughly.

We have learned that there is a book called *Wan-kuo lü-li*,[③] "Laws and precedents of all nations." Yet when we wanted to seek it directly, and entrust its translation to the foreigners, we were afraid that they might wish to keep it confidential and not have it shown to us. At this juncture, the American minister P'u-an-ch'en (Anson Burlingame) came and told us that various countries have had the *Ta-ch'ing lü-li* ("Laws and precedents of the Ch'ing Dynasty") translated into foreign languages. Also he said that in foreign countries there are laws and by-laws in general circulation which recently have been translated into Chinese by a scholar named Ting-wei-liang [W. A. P. Martin, later president of the T'ung-wen Kuan], and which are worthy of reference. Shortly thereafter, in October of last year, Martin was brought for an interview and presented four volumes of the *Wan-kuo lü-li*, saying that it should be read by all countries having treaty relations with others. ④ In case of dispute it can be taken for reference and can be quoted. But his style is not very smooth or clear, and so he asks us to do some editing for him, in order to have it printed. Your ministers forestalled his attempt to get us to follow the book, by telling him at once that China has her own laws and institutions and that it is inconvenient to consult foreign books. Martin, however, points out that although the *Ta-Ch'ing lü-li* has now been translated by foreign countries, China has never compelled foreign countries to act by it. It cannot be that when a foreign book is [p. 26] translated into Chinese, China should be forced to follow it. Thus he has pleaded repeatedly.

Your ministers think that his purpose is two-fold, first to boast that foreign countries also have laws, and secondly, to imitate men like Matteo Ricci in making a name in China. Upon examination, the book seems to deal generally with treaties, laws of war, and such matters. ⑤ Particularly there are laws that govern the mutual controls and restrictions imposed on each of the belligerent parties at the outbreak of hostilities. Unfortunately the wording was in disorder and unless he had explained it to us personally, it would not have been clear ... We dispatched four secretaries of the Yamen ... to discuss his translation carefully with him and edit it ... During the past half year th draft manuscript has been finished. Martin regrets that there is no money to publish it, and he says if he could get five hundred taels he would be able to complete the project. ⑥

Your ministers find that the contents of this book of foreign laws do not entirely agree with the system in China, but there are occasional passages which are useful. For instance, in connection with the case this year of the Danish ship captured by Prussia outside of Tientsin, your ministers used as arguments some sentences from this book without expressly saying so. The Prussian minister immediately acknowledged his mistake and said nothing further. This seems conclusive.⑦ Your ministers have deliberated and decided jointly to grant Martin five hundred taels of silver according to his request. It is agreed that after the book has been printed, he will present 300 complimentary copies to your ministers' Yamen. Thereafter a copy will be distributed to each of the treaty ports. In this book there are laws which can to a considerable extent control the foreign consuls, and this is certainly a useful thing. The amount of silver will be paid by your ministers' Yamen out of the three per cent received from the customs funds. [Vermilion Endorsement:] "Let it be as proposed."

The following letter from Kuo Sung-tao to Li Hung-chang reports his personal observations while head of the Chinese legation in London. It gives a comprehensive summary of the political and social development of England, which we largely omit, and draws a sharp contrast between Chinese conservatism and the rapid changes in Western society.

## DOC. 27  A LETTER OF KUO SUNG-TAO FROM LONDON, 1877⑧

Here in England the circumstances of administration, education and the social customs are changing every day. To trace the whole history of the nation—at first the king and the people struggled for political power and slaughtered one another. Great confusion lasted for several decades or a hundred years until the time of Jo-erh-jih [i. e., George Ⅰ, 1714-1727] when the situation became settled. Originally there was no time-honored accumulation of absolute virtue and excellent education (as there had been in China) ... Their attainment of wealth and strength really began only after the Ch'ien-lung period (1736-1795). Steamships were first built at the beginning of the Ch'ien-lung period, but at first they were not very profitable. Then in 1801 they began using them on the ocean. The method was again followed in the building of locomotives, which had its beginning in 1813. Thereafter the study of electricity was pursued. Letters and messages were transmitted by a machine of magnetic-iron, until in 1838 a telegraph was first established in their national capital... From the beginning of England's rise, it has been only several decades; while China was weak and declining they covered a distance of 70,000 *li* in the wink of an eye... Chinese scholars and officials are presumptuous in their sanctuary and are trying to obstruct the changes of the universe; they can never succeed.

After several months here, I have actually seen the convenience of the railway train. A round trip of 300 or 400 *li* takes only half a day. In this country the local gentry strongly advise China to build railways; they say that the power and might of England are really based on them. At first they were also suspicious [like the Chinese populace] and tried to stop their construction [p. 2]. To speak first of the road between London and the seaport of Southampton—the coach transportation back and forth formerly used more than 30,000 horses, and the people concerned were afraid that this railroad would be detrimental to their livelihood. But when the railroad was opened as many as 60,000 or 70,000 horses were used. This was because the convenience of the railroad daily attracted more traffic and, since the train could run on only one route, those who were several tens of *li* away and came to take the train had to make use of more horses.

Last winter when I passed through Shanghai I saw a railroad map in the Academy of Natural Sciences[9] on which there was shown a railroad from India directly to Yunnan; a branch ... going eastward to Canton, etc. , ... Upon seeing it I was greatly surprised, saying that no sooner had trade relations with Yunnan been opened than the routes of railroads were immediately planned...

When the Japanese minister saw me, he said that the natural resources of the universe can be developed by Westerners. They do the hard part—we do the easy part; can we waste more time in idleness? The vastness of China's territory and the number of her people are envied by all nations, but he has learned that until now not a single thing has been developed in China, which is a great pity. I was so embarrassed that I could make no reply...

The foreigners' power is daily becoming more oppressive, and we suffer increasingly from their disturbances. We should investigate carefully their entire history and itemize [p. 3] the actual causes of their becoming rich and strong and uncover their ambitions... I have had a plan to compile a book and submit it to the Tsungli Yamen for distribution among the schools of the empire... But, when I reached the capital, I was frustrated by the clamorous opinion there and I refrained from expressing myself.

Personally I think there is something in the minds of the Chinese which is absolutely unintelligible. Among the injuries that Westerners do us there is nothing more serious than opium. Even the British gentlemen feel ashamed of having used this pernicious thing as a pretext for hostilities with China, and they are making a strong effort to eradicate it. Yet Chinese scholars and officials are willing to indulge complacently in it, without any sense of remorse. For several decades it has been the national humiliation, it has exhausted our financial power and poisoned and injured the lives of our people, but there is not a single person whose conscience is weighed down by it. Now clocks, watches, and toys are owned by all families, and woolen and cotton cloth and the like are prevalent in poor districts and the isolated countryside. The practice in Kiangsu and Chekiang even goes as far as to put aside the national currency for the exclusive use of foreign bank notes... Nevertheless as soon as these people heard of the building of railroads and telegraph lines they became sorely disturbed and enraged, and arose in multitudes to create hindrances and difficulties. There are even people who regard foreign machines as an object of public hatred. Tseng Chi-tse, on account of a family funeral, took a small steamship [instead of walking home with a sorrowful face, according to custom] from Nanking to Changsha; this caused a great uproar among the local officials and gentry that lasted for several years. All this means they are willing to accept the harm from others and let the latter squeeze the marrow from their bones, but they use their whole strength to choke off the source of profits. I do not know what is in their minds. There have been foreign relations for thirty years, but the provincial authorities are entirely ignorant of them. They impose their ignorant ideas on the Court under the guise of public opinion. The latter encourages them to do this and itself uses "public opinion" as a gloss for its own purposes.

[P. 4] There are more than 200 Japanese learning technology in England, scattered in all the seaports. There are ninety of them in London. I have met more than twenty, and all can speak English. There is one by the name of Nagaoka Ryōnosuke who was originally a feudal lord governing a kingdom by himself; he is now degraded to be a noble of hereditary rank and is studying law here... The telegraph office which was established in Japan was also first learned from London; as soon as the technique was mastered, a telegraph office was set up to provide the same service. There are very few who are studying military methods, probably because military science is but a practical detail, whereas the establishing of various kinds of institutional systems is the foundation for establishing the nation. The Grand Secretary [Li Hung-chang] is just now advocating military strengthening; therefore he is devoting his mind to the investigation of military methods. As far as my humble observation can reach, there is absolutely no reason to reorganize the military system in the various provinces. As for the recruiting of soldiers, it is impossible to keep it up constantly. For several decades to come we should not worry about the West taking up arms against us but simply try to decide everything with them by reasoning and by the force of circumstances...

[P. 5] There is a Mr. [Sir MacDonald] Stephenson here who says that all countries are building more railroads. He particularly and indefatigably advises China to do this with dispatch. Herewith I carefully submit to you the general plan which he has drafted. ⑩

However, my idea is that if everything must be done by foreigners it cannot last long. We should first make the Chinese thoroughly familiar with their methods. The state of Egypt is in Africa, and when she builds railroads she first sends some people to England to study and then build them by imitation. This is the best example...

There is nothing more urgent than to plan earnestly for better domestic administration, in order to lay a foundation of wealth and strength... The area of China is more than 10,000 *li*. The postal transportation to a distant place takes several tens of days... If the two things (railways and telegraphs) are carried through, then 10,000 *li* will be like the hall or threshold of one's house. If suddenly one morning there were a flood, or news of drought or a bandit uprising, the Court could be informed in the evening. Then there would be no anxiety over treacherous people's secretly starting an outbreak of rebellion. This is the first advantage. The condition of the Chinese officials and people is that they are too distant from each other; in addition, both are trying to cover the eyes and ears of the Court in order to facilitate the pursuance of their selfish purposes. For this reason the people's ideas are frequently and miserably suppressed and never reach the emperor. If the two things (railways and telegraph) are widespread... [p. 6] there will be no anxiety over having covetous officials suppress the opinion of the people or carry on their mischievous work for gain. This is another advantage...

The critics merely say that wherever the machines of foreigners reach, the local geomantic harmony [*feng-shui*, lit., "wind and water"] is injured. This is a great error. Railways and telegraph lines are always built on level ground following the state roads. There is nothing to dig up or to destroy. As for the machinery used in opening coal mines and pumping water, it is for the purpose of making the mine deeper. The deeper one digs the better the quality of coal. When Chinese dig coal they like to penetrate from the sides; when foreigners dig coal they like to get it in depth. Both are opening the mine. The shallow method and deep method actually have the same result. What harm is there? Take for instance the natural resources in Hunan: the iron mines are mostly in Pao-ch'ing and the coal mines mostly in Heng-chou, and yet the people who are famous in passing high literary examinations are particularly numerous in these two districts...

After several decades foreigners will arrive and then they will gradually build railways and develop (natural resources) for us. Their influence will be sufficient to control the people and the profit will be enough to bribe the wicked, the unruly, and the trouble-makers, who will be employed in their service. Then both the ownership and the profits will fall into the hands of foreigners and China will have nothing to depend upon. Mencius says: "when heaven produced these people, it made those who know beforehand teach those who know afterward, and those who perceive earlier inspire those who perceive later." The responsibility for foresight and perception must lie in the great ministers of the Court.

Another able and outspoken Chinese envoy was Tseng Kuo-fan's son, Tseng Chi-tse (1839-1890), known to the West as "Marquis Tseng," who had some grasp both of Western science and of the English language. He has usually been considered a good diplomat, not so much because he was minister to England and France in 1878-1886, as because he signed on February 24, 1881, the *Treaty of St. Petersburg* by which Russia was obliged to return to China certain strategic territory in the Ili region, after it had been ceded by Ch'ung-hou's ill-advised signature of the *Treaty of Livadia* in 1879. While Tseng's success on this occasion was partly due to Tso Tsung-t'ang's military victory in Sinkiang and the bellicose support of

Tso and others during the negotiations in Russia, it was also due partly to Tseng's quick-witted disputation with the Russian authorities. ⑪

After living in Europe, Marquis Tseng became not only a zealous advocate of Westernization, but a practitioner of Western ways, devoted to foreign clothes, utensils, and medicine, for all of which he was criticized by Chinese conservatives. ⑫

In 1878 he was appointed to succeed Kuo Sung-tao as minister to England and France. Before he sailed from Shanghai on November 22, 1878, he had an interview with the Empress Dowager Tz'u-hsi at Peking, after which he recorded in his diary the naive and interesting conversation translated below. (Her declarative sentences were recorded as imperial Decrees.)

## DOC. 28 TSENG CHI-TSE'S ACCOUNT OF HIS AUDIENCE WITH THE EMPRESS DOWAGER, 1878⑬

On August 25, 1878, I received a Decree granting me the privilege of wearing the peacock feather and appointing me Imperial Commissioner to England and France... On the 26th, at the beginning of the *ch'ou* period [1-3 a. m.],⑭ I went to the Court... At the beginning of the *mao* period [5-7 a. m.], I entered the Ch'ien-ch'ing gate and sat for a long time in the room for intracourt interview. At the beginning of *ch'en* [7-9 a. m.] the grand councillors came out from their audience and the throne summoned me to the eastern apartment of the Yang-hsin Hall, which I entered by lifting up the curtain. I knelt on the ground to give thanks for celestial grace. I took off my hat and kotowed. Then I was ordered to put on my hat and stand up and to proceed to the front of the cushion where I knelt to listen to the sacred instruction. The Empress Dowager Tz'u-hsi asked, "When do you plan to start the trip?" The Empress Dowager Tz'u-an also asked the same question. ⑮

I replied, "Because there are public and private affairs that your minister must prepare well in Shanghai, it is necessary for him to leave the capital earlier. Now he plans to start the journey on the 29th of September."

*Question*: Are you going by way of Tientsin?

*Answer*: It is necessary to go via Tientsin and also to stay for some ten days to discuss various matters with Li Hung-chang.

*Decree*:⑯ Li Hung-chang is familiar with foreign affairs. You may take up the various matters with him in detail.

*Answer*: Yes.

*Question*: Are you going to spend some time in Shanghai?

*Answer*: It's a long way to go abroad. All the arrangements and all the things to be taken along must be well prepared in Shanghai. Moreover, the retinue which your minister is going to take along cannot be appointed until he has arrived at Shanghai, and therefore he will spend a considerable time there; probably he will have to stay for more than a month.

*Question*: Will you memorialize again about the staff members you are going to take along, after you have arrived in Shanghai?

*Answer*: Of your minister's retinue, some of them are going to travel with him from the capital, some are going to be transferred and appointed from the provinces outside the capital. As to the latter who are going to be appointed from outside provinces, whether they can go or not cannot be known in advance. [P. 2] He has to wait until the assignment is made and then he will assemble the information and submit a memorial for your approval.

*Question*: How many days will it take to go from Tientsin to Shanghai?

*Answer*: The speeds of the vessels of the China Merchants Company are not the same. The fastest from Tientsin to Shanghai takes only three and a half days.

*Question*: Are you going to England first or to France first?

*Answer*: Your minister plans to start the journey from Shanghai on

November 22 aboard a French ship for Marseilles, where he will go ashore to take a train for Paris. Paris is the capital of France. When the French see the arrival of a Chinese minister they will certainly have someone perform ceremonies of welcome and entertainment. If your minister goes straight on without taking a look at Paris it will not be proper. He intends to send a telegram from Shanghai to Kuo Sung-tao asking him to come to Paris and hand him the seal. Your minister will receive the seal in Paris, and will immediately present his credentials to France first. Then he will go to London to present his credentials to England. London is the capital of England.

*Question*: Have the credentials been prepared and given to you?

*Answer*: He has already received them.

*Question*: How are you going to decide upon your living quarters?

*Answer*: Kuo Sung-tao has rented a house some time ago. When your minister goes there everything will be the same as before. Recently he has discussed with the princes and great ministers in the Tsungli Yamen whether in the future, if we have sufficient funds, it may be necessary to purchase a house in each country to be used as an embassy. The houses of foreign ministers in China are all purchased or built by themselves. It is indeed not a long-term plan for China's ministers to live in rented houses. Moreover, the rent is exorbitant and in the long run it is not economical.

*Decree*: The things which you have to attend to abroad should be discussed with the princes and high ministers from time to time.

*Answer*: Yes.

*Question*: After you are abroad how will you send us memorials and reports?

*Answer*: In regard to important matters which should be memorialized and explained, Kuo Sung-tao has been sending them in care of the Tsungli Yamen. As for ordinary affairs, about which he should consult the Tsungli Yamen, either in the form of an official dispatch or as a letter, they were all sent through the Office for the Transmission of Government Correspondence in Shanghai. Your minister plans to handle the matter in the same way as before...

*Decree*: The members of your retinue should all be carefully controlled and not allowed to cause trouble in foreign countries and thus incur the contempt [p. 3] of foreigners.

*Answer*: Your minister will reverently obey the sacred instruction and be particularly careful in regard to the matter of his retinue. At present it is not easy to find those who are familiar with foreign affairs and who can be deeply trusted. He has no candidates in mind. It would be best for your minister to make a selection from scholars whom he has known for a long time, who are clear-minded and careful in everything... Now the second councillor, Ch'en Yuan-chi, who is to be taken along, is the brother-in-law of your minister. Your minister dares to follow the precedent of the ancients who "did not avoid the use of relatives in their intimate employment" and take him abroad, because the duties and responsibilities are extremely heavy. Were he not an intimate friend of your minister, who knows his background thoroughly from former days, your minister would not take a chance on appointing him...

*Question*: How old is this relative of yours?

*Answer*: Thirty-six years old.

*Question*: Can you understand a foreign written and spoken language?

*Answer*: Your minister reads a little English and understands a little spoken English. He learned it from books and so it is comparatively easier for him to read the language but more difficult for him to understand it, because his mouth and ears are not accustomed to it.

*Question*: Is the common language English or French?

*Answer*: English is a commercial language. Foreigners stress business, therefore the people of the various countries can speak English. As for the language of France, it has been handed down for generations;

therefore, in documents and official dispatches among various nations French is frequently used. For instance, the international treaties, ratifications of treaties, and so on, are often written in French.

*Question*: Since you understand both the spoken and written language, it is much more convenient. You do not need to rely on the translations of interpreters [do you?].

*Answer*: Although your minister can understand and read a little, he is not very familiar with it and he still has to depend upon interpreters... Understanding of a foreign written or spoken language and management of foreign affairs are two entirely different things [p. 4]. It is essential for those who manage foreign affairs to be familiar with treaties and with official procedures. It is not essential for them to concern themselves with the duties of interpreters. In the future when your minister discusses official business with foreigners even though he understands the language he still would wait for the restatement by the interpreter, partly because the procedure of the Court ought to be so, partly because during the interval of restatement by the interpreter he can take advantage of the pause to give thought to the language with which he should answer. The British Minister, Thomas Wade, can understand the Chinese written and spoken language. When he discusses official business he has to use interpreters to convey the meaning to him. That is the same idea.

*Question*: I have learned that Wade is going to come here soon. Have you heard about it?

*Answer*: During the summer your minister read a newspaper which said Wade would start his trip in the autumn; since then no exact news about him has been heard.

*Decree*: Wade is a very cunning person.

*Answer*: Wade can understand the Chinese written and spoken language. As a person he is very cunning and his temperament is very harsh. Foreigners also say that he is bad tempered.

*Decree*: It is very difficult to manage foreign affairs. I have heard that in Fukien there are again cases of the burning and destruction of churches and houses; in the future, there will be trouble again.

*Answer*: The difficulty in handling diplomatic affairs lies in the fact that foreigners are unreasonable, while Chinese are ignorant of current events and circumstances. Chinese ministers and people usually hate foreigners, as goes without saying, but we must plan gradually to make ourselves strong before anything can be done. The destruction of one church or the killing of one foreigner by no means avenges our grievances or wipes out our humiliation. At present many Chinese do not understand this principle and so there has been the Margary incident in Yunnan [Feb. 1875],⑰ which caused the Empresses Dowager and the Emperor work and worry day and night.

*Decree*: It is true indeed. How can we forget our grievances for a single day? But we must gradually make ourselves strong, as you just stated very clearly. The killing of one person or the burning of one house definitely cannot be considered as having avenged our grievances.

*Answer*: Yes.

*Decree*: Very few persons understand this idea. If you manage such matters for the nation, there are bound to be times when people will scold you. You, however, should bear the toil and blame.

*Answer*: When your minister formerly studied the classics and came to the sentence, "To serve the ruler one must be able to offer one's life" [p. 5], he thought that a loyal minister would have reached the extreme point of loyalty if he devoted his whole life to it. After observing the recent situation and the course of negotiations between China and foreign countries, he has found that sometimes it is necessary to consider his life a secondary matter; and in the last analysis he even has to risk considering his reputation unimportant, before he can make the general situation secure on behalf of his country. For instance, at the time of the former Tientsin incident [June 1870]⑱ your minister's father, your deceased minister, Tseng Kuo-fan, before he started his trip from Pao-ting, was then on his sickbed and immediately he wrote his last will and testament to bid his family make arrangements as though he had already discarded his life. After he arrived at Tientsin and saw that the matter was so serious that it could not be satisfactorily concluded even by [the sacrifice of] his life, he made concessions and secured the best arrangement to obtain a peaceful settlement. At that time many scholars and officials in the capital condemned him. Your minister's father accepted the responsibility and blamed himself. In sending letters to his friends he frequently wrote the following words: "Outwardly I am ashamed of public criticism and inwardly I cannot live with my conscience." This shows how he struggled to protect the general situation by disregarding his own reputation. As a matter of fact, at that time there was no other way to deal with the case, apart from what had been done by Tseng Kuo-fan.

*Decree*: Tseng Kuo-fan was really a just and loyal man who took the nation into consideration. (Note: I took off my hat and kotowed, but did not make any reply.)

*Decree*: It is also bad luck for the nation that before long Tseng Kuo-fan departed from the world. Now there are many great officials in various places who are cowardly.

*Answer*: Li Hung-chang, Shen Pao-chen, Ting Pao-chen and Tso Tsung-t'ang are all loyal and sincere ministers.

*Decree*: All of them are good but all are old troopers. The new ones all fail to equal them in ability; they have not kept abreast of new ideas.

*Answer*: Kuo Sung-tao is certainly an upright and straightforward person. This time he also risked damage to his reputation in order to manage affairs for the nation. In the future it is hoped that the special grace of the Empresses and the Emperor will protect him in every respect.

*Decree*: Up above [*shang-t'ou*, i.e., by the rulers] it is thoroughly understood. Kuo Sung-tao is a good man. Since his mission abroad he has managed many affairs but he has also received plenty of scolding from people.

*Answer*: Kuo Sung-tao is vexed by the fact that China cannot become strong immediately and he has frequently argued with people and therefore he has been scolded. After all he is a loyal minister. Fortunately the Empresses Dowager and the Emperor understand him. Even though he has lost his reputation in the fight, still it is worthwhile. [p. 6]

*Decree*: We all know him. The princes and great ministers also understand him.

*Answer*: Yes.

*Question*: Are you now living in the Tsungli Yamen?

*Answer*: The affairs of the Tsungli Yamen must be kept confidential. Formerly your minister and others dared not participate. Now, since he has received the order to go abroad on a mission, he must thoroughly investigate the old and new documents in cases concerning England and France, and he must jot down some essential points. Even though the complete cases are now in the hands of Kuo Sung-tao, yet when your minister is on his journey, there are certain to be some foreigners who will meet and entertain him. If during the course of conversation he is ignorant of the facts of the case, it will be somewhat embarrassing.

*Decree*: You are really quite careful in handling public affairs. (Note: Reverent silence, no reply.)

*Question*: Are you going to take some students along from the T'ung-wen Kuan?

*Answer*: Your minister is going to take an English interpreter, a French interpreter, and a clerk. This will be reported when he reaches Shanghai.

*Question*: Are all of them good?

*Answer*: Your minister understands English only slightly. The English interpreter, Tso Ping-lung, your minister knows can be employed. The French interpreter, Lien-hsing, has not yet been carefully investigated by your minister, because your minister does not understand French...

*Question*: Will the date for presentation of credentials be decided by you or by the foreigners?

*Answer*: We must wait until (your minister's) arrival in their country; then both sides can discuss the matter and deal with it.

*Question*: Is there also a Tsungli Yamen in foreign countries?

*Answer*: In foreign countries it is called a *Wai-pu* [or ministry of foreign affairs]. The matters it deals with are the same as the public business of the Chinese Tsungli Yamen. I have heard it said that recently England also changed the name to Tsungli Yamen, but in reality the name in a foreign language is entirely different; it is called neither "Wai-pu" nor "Tsungli Yamen." Only, if the work they do is the same, it is the same office.

*Question*: When can you arrive there?

*Answer*: If the Empresses Dowager and the Emperor wish him bon voyage [*i-lu-p'ing-an*] and if there are no delays en route, he should be able to reach the capital of France near the end of the year.

*Question*: You have never been in foreign countries. I presume you must have heard about these routes and their circumstances.

*Answer*: Some information has been obtained by consulting books [p. 7] and maps and some by inquiry.

*Question*: Is your ship going to cast anchor at Hongkong or not?

*Answer*: Your minister is going to board a French Company's steamship. The steamship must have cargo to be loaded or unloaded, passengers to embark or disembark, and so on. There will be delay in every harbor throughout the journey, but everything will be decided by the captain.

After a long pause there was a...

*Decree*: Now you kneel for greetings. (Note: I withdrew to my original position, knelt and said) Your minister Tseng Chi-tse kneels and prays for the good health of the Sage.

Raising the curtain I withdrew. It was already the *ch'en* hour [9:00 a. m. ].

## CHAPTER XIII  PROBLEMS OF THE INDUSTRIALIZATION EFFORT

From preceding sections it is evident that Chinese thinking on the problem of defense against the West went through a progression from the idea of "using barbarians to control barbarians" and employing Western arms, to the realization successively that Western arms must be made in China, that they must be produced by Chinese, that Chinese must be instructed to make them, and that therefore Chinese must be trained in Western sciences in general and that institutions must be established for their training and for the practice of the new skills so acquired. All these successive ideas stemmed from the basic desire for defense, which certainly continued undiminished as a dominant motive in the 1860's.

As the 1870's wore on, both Li Hung-chang and other provincial authorities sought to establish industrial enterprises and the transport facilities to accompany them. This involved them in the problems of balanced industrial development already familiar to the West. For example, the China Merchants Steam Navigation Company, founded in 1872 to compete with British shipping in China, needed a Chinese coal supply independent of foreign imports. The Kaiping coal mine, forerunner of the Kailan Mining Administration north of Tientsin, was opened to meet this need in 1878. The earliest surviving railway in China was later built to connect with the Kaiping mine.[1]

Li Hung-chang expressed the new recognition that China's strength must rest on industry: "In the various European countries mineralogy is the basis on which they can fight for supremacy. England, as a nation, is established on three islands in the sea, where the natural resources are not very abundant, and yet her annual production of coal and iron is very prosperous, and so her wealth and power are the first in the world."②

In 1872 it was found that the original plan to build sixteen steamships at Foochow in five years for three million taels had produced only half the number of ships (six built and three building), but had more than exhausted the funds. The ships completed were still inferior to foreign ships. Some officials suggested abandoning the enterprise, to which Li Hung-chang replied in the following vigorous memorial.

## DOC. 29  LI HUNG-CHANG'S DEFENSE OF BUILDING STEAMSHIPS, 1872③

We have seen with admiration the Sacred Emperor's vigorous striving for self-strengthening and for laying down broad far-reaching plans. Our admiration is beyond telling. Your minister has been thinking that the various European countries in the last several decades have advanced from India to the southern oceans, from the southern oceans to the northeast, and have invaded China's frontiers and interior land. Peoples never [p. 45] recorded in previous histories, who have had no contact with us since ancient times, have come to our points of entry (*kuan*) to ask for trade relations. Our Emperors have been as generous as the sky and have made treaties with all of them for international trade in order to control them. People from a distance of ninety thousand *li*, from the cardinal points of the globe, are gathering together in China; this is the greatest change during the last three millennia and more!

The Westerners particularly rely upon the excellence and efficacy of their guns, cannon, and steamships, and so they can overrun China. The bow and spear, small guns, and native-made cannon which have hitherto been used by China cannot resist their rifles, which have their bullets fed from the rear opening. The sailing boats, rowboats, and the gunboats which have been hitherto employed cannot oppose their steam-engined warships. Therefore, we are controlled by the Westerners.

To live today and still say "reject the barbarians" and "drive them out of our territory" is certainly superficial and absurd talk. Even though we wish to preserve the peace and to protect our territory, we cannot preserve and protect them unless we have the right weapons. They are daily producing their weapons to strive with us for supremacy and victory, pitting their superior techniques against our inadequacies, to wrangle with and to affront us. Then how can we get along for one day without weapons and techniques?

The method of self-strengthening lies in learning what they can do, and in taking over what they rely upon. Moreover, their possession of guns, cannon, and steamships began only within the last hundred years or so, and their progress has been so fast that their influence has spread into China. If we can really and thoroughly understand their methods—and the more we learn, the more improve—and promote them further and further, can we not expect that after a century or so we can reject the barbarians and stand on our own feet? Japan is just a small nation. Recently she has begun to trade with Europe; she has instituted iron factories and built many steamships. She has changed to the use of Western weapons. Does she have the ambition to plot to invade the Western nations? Perhaps she is merely planning for self-protection. But if Japan seeks only self-protection, she is nevertheless oppressing and looking down on our China. Should not China plan for herself? Our scholars and officials have confined themselves to the study of stanzas and sentences and are ignorant of the greatest change of the last several thousand years; they are accustomed to the temporary security of the present, and so they forget why we received the heavy blow and deep suffering of twenty or thirty years ago [the Opium War], and how we can obtain domestic security and control the foreigners within several centuries. That is how this talk of stopping steamship construction has originated.

Your minister humbly thinks that all other expenditures of our nation can be economized, but the expenses for supporting the army, establishing defense measures, drilling in guns and cannon, and building warships should by all means never be economized. If we try to save funds, then we shall be obliged to neglect all these defense measures, the nation will never have anything to stand upon, and we shall never be strong… The amount which has already been spent will, in turn, become a sheer waste. Not only will we be a laughing stock to foreigners, but we will also strengthen their aggressive ambitions…

[The rest of the memorial explains why the expenditure has surpassed the original estimate—because it was roughly estimated by Frenchmen who were not experts, and because the price of machinery subsequently and unexpectedly rose. The progress of English and French warships is described, and a small type of warship for defense purposes is suggested. According to Li, China has "more land than water; it is more urgent to train an army than a navy." (p. 47b) Li also discusses the difficulty of converting warships to commercial use, but he recognizes the need of commercial vessels for grain transportation and commercial competition with foreigners. Then he continues (p. 49):]

Furthermore, the building of ships, cannon, and machinery will be impossible without iron, and then we shall be helpless without coal. The reason for England's power and influence over the Western lands is only her possession of these two items (iron and coal). The various arsenals in Foochow and Shanghai daily need a huge amount of imported coal and iron, because the Chinese product is most unsuitable. Even foreign ships coming to our ports have to carry foreign coal. Suppose there is a time when the points of entry to China are closed by boycott; then not only all our iron factories would have to suspend work and stand distressingly in idleness, but also the steamships which have been built would be unable to move a single inch without coal. What deserves more anxious thought than this! …

[P. 50] Recently Westerners have frequently requested permission to open coal and iron mines in the Chinese interior, pointing out that it is a great pity that China's natural resources cannot be developed by herself.

We have heard that now Japan is adopting Western methods of opening coal and iron mines to gain a great profit, and this has also helped her shipbuilding and machinery... If we can really make plans to persuade the people, by means of the system of "government-supervision and merchant-operation" [*kuan-tu shang-pan*], to borrow and use foreign machines and foreign methods only, but not allow foreigners to do the whole job on our behalf, then these articles of daily necessity, when produced and processed by proper methods, must have a good market. A source of profit will naturally be opened. Taking the surplus funds from the new source we can even use it to maintain our ships and train our soldiers.

In 1880, through military necessity, Li Hung-chang also recognized the importance of the telegraph: "In mobilizing troops," he writes, "speed is of the essence... A telegram from Russia to Shanghai takes only one day, whereas from Shanghai to Peking ... a Chinese mail steamer requires six or seven days... In 1874, when Japan invaded Taiwan, Shen Pao-chen and others repeatedly spoke of the advantage of the telegraph and an Imperial Decree was issued to institute it, but the matter was only perfunctorily carried out and thus far there has been no achievement."④ Accordingly, Li urged the construction of two telegraph lines: from Nanking to Peking, and from Hankow to Peking. Trunk railroad construction still remained suspect, however, partly on the ground that it would enable foreign invaders to penetrate the interior too easily—as the Japanese were to demonstrate in a later generation.

Textile production had less obvious strategic value and moved more slowly. Tso Tsung-t'ang had set up a woolen mill in Lanchow, Kansu, in 1878 with the help of German technicians and machinery, but it did not flourish after his death. In 1882, Li Hung-chang planned to establish a cotton mill at Shanghai, and called for merchants' share-capital to help finance it. He proposed to exempt its products from transit or *likin* taxes en route from Shanghai to other parts of the country, which would have set a precedent for giving special protection to "national goods." His plan, however, was not carried through until 1891, and the new Shanghai cotton mill, the first in China, burned down in 1893 after one year of successful operation. Li soon reorganized it on a larger scale. At Wuchang, Chang Chih-tung also established a cotton mill in 1891, and another one in 1894.⑤ Li set up a paper mill in Shanghai in 1891; a cement factory was attached to the Kaiping coal mine; and a match factory and flour mill were also opened.

Heavy industry got started even more slowly. Chang Chih-tung opened the Ta-yeh iron mine and the Hanyang Iron Works in Hupei in 1890, employing German technicians, but these projects never developed into the big industrial complex that their founder had hoped for.

The variety and yet the ineffectiveness and slow development of some of these projects, many of them sponsored by Li Hung-chang, may be indicated in a list:

1863 A foreign language school was established at Shanghai.

1865 The Kiangnan Arsenal was established at Shanghai, with a translation bureau attached.

1867 The Nanking Arsenal was established.

1870 A machine factory, first established by Ch'ung-hou in 1867 at Tientsin, was enlarged.

1871 A foreign-style fort was planned for Taku, outside Tientsin.

1872 Students were sent to study in America.

Officers were sent to Germany to learn military sciences.

The China Merchants Steam Navigation Company was organized.

The opening of coal and iron mines was requested.

1875 A plan was made to build steel warships.

1876 A request was made to open a bureau to study foreign sciences in all provinces; also to add a new subject on foreign affairs in the civil service examinations.

Students and apprentices from the Foochow shipyard were sent to study in England and France. Seven army officers were sent to Germany for advanced training.

1878 The Kaiping coal mine was opened.

1879 A telegraph line was opened from Taku to Tientsin.

1880 A plan for a modern navy was launched, beginning with a program to purchase warships from foreign countries.

A naval school was established at Tientsin.

Telegraph land lines were requested and sanctioned.

1881 Li supported Liu Ming-ch'uan's request to build railways.

North of Tientsin the T'angshan railroad (about six miles) was completed.

The first telegraph line, Shanghai-Tientsin, was opened and merchants were invited to develop the telegraph service in all provinces.

1882 A dockyard was built at Port Arthur (completed in 1891).

A cotton mill was planned at Shanghai.

1885 A military preparatory school (an army school) was established at Tientsin.

The navy yamen was inaugurated.

1887 Mints were established at Tientsin and Paoting.

1888 The Peiyang Army was organized.

1889 The Mo-ho gold mine, in Kirin, was planned.

1891 The Lung-chang paper mill was founded at Shanghai.

A review of the new navy was held at Port Arthur.

## a. *The Principle of "Government-supervision and Merchant-operation"*

The explanation of this poor record, compared to contemporary developments in other countries, lies only partly in the pressure of commercial competition exercised by the imperialist powers in China. The real key, as we have suggested in Chapter I, lies in the nature of Chinese society—its "oriental" features, whereby merchant capital was not easily available for industrial investment except under the wing of official patronage. This close merchant-official connection was exemplified by the system called "official-supervision and merchant-operation" or management (*kuan-tu shang-pan*), under which many of the early enterprises were set up. While it is beyond our scope to analyze the economic and social characteristics of this system, it is plain that it met China's needs quite inadequately: officials unversed in business held the whip hand over managerial personnel of inferior social status, who were, therefore, in no position to use modern entrepreneurial methods of capital accumulation and reinvestment.

The *kuan-tu shang-pan* system was an adaptation of a traditional Chinese device in economic administration; it seems in fact to have been patterned after the Chinese government salt monopoly, in which the government appointed official overseers but the production, distribution, and retailing of salt were farmed out to different groups of salt merchants. A number of enterprises were set up on this new basis: merchants contributed part of the share-capital, but the manager usually had official status as an expectant taotai or magistrate who could deal with the local government to secure exemption from taxes or other facilities. At the same time he was the business manager. Sometimes there were two managers: one to deal with the government and the other to look after the business. The function of the manager was thus half-official and half-commercial, and his enterprise as a whole was also halfway between the two. While the original purpose of the system was to raise funds from the public, in practice the officials invested money in the government-sponsored enterprises under the names of merchants, and placed their relatives in charge as managers in order to make a great profit. For example, Sheng Hsuan-huai was summoned by Li Hung-chang to manage the China Merchants Company, which bought its ships from the American firm of Russell and Company for 2,200,000 taels of silver. Sheng on behalf of Li Hung-chang asked the governor-general of Liang-chiang to contribute one million taels from official funds and he made up the rest by calling for public purchase of capital shares.⑥ At the beginning of 1880 a memorial impeached the company for spending money lavishly and for "squeezing" official funds to fill the pockets of its officers, who had been appointed by the government.⑦ Li Hung-chang, the sponsor of the company, was ordered by the emperor to investigate this charge. The result was a complete whitewash.⑧

The evils which resulted from the mixing of Western commerce and industry with Chinese bureaucratism were vividly described by a scholarly compradore, Cheng Kuan-ying, who wrote an influential and eloquent book on China's problems.

Cheng Kuan-ying was a man of obscure origin, but from his own writings we gather that he started his career by working as a compradore in foreign firms (Dent & Co., and Butterfield and Swire) for about thirty years. He joined the enterprises of Li Hung-chang in 1882 and served in various directorial capacities in the Chinese Telegraph Company, the China Merchants Company, and Li's cotton mill company. From 1892 to 1902 he was associate director and then director of the China Merchants Company and traveled widely in China and East Asia. During the Sino-Japanese war he served concurrently as a government purchasing agent for ammunition. For a brief period in 1896 he became the manager of the newly reorganized Hanyang iron foundry.

During the 1890's Cheng became a patron and enthusiastic reader of the *Wan-kuo kung-pao*, a journal sponsored by foreign missionaries which contained articles on science, history and social problems, and had wide influence. According to Timothy Richard, Cheng bought a hundred copies of the translation of Mackenzie's *Nineteenth Century* (*T'ai-hsi hsin-shih lan-yao*) and distributed them to his Peking friends. The book which he wrote, "Warnings to the seemingly prosperous age" (*Sheng-shih wei-yen*), had a vogue before 1898 and merits attention.⑨ Eventually this "warning" was presented to the Emperor Kuang-hsü, who ordered the

Tsungli Yamen to publish and distribute it to officials. It was popularly read in the decade after its publication, although its influence on the 1898 reform movement was probably limited by the fact of the author's compradore background.

According to the communist writer Hsiao San, *Sheng-shih wei-yen* was one of the books Mao Tse-tung liked to read in his boyhood;[10] Mao has not mentioned Cheng in his own writings, where he writes of K'ang Yu-wei and Yen Fu.

As a compradore-scholar with wide contact among foreigners and an acquaintance with missionary writings, especially those of Timothy Richard, as well as with contemporary Chinese literature, Cheng Kuan-ying was in a position to advance ideas. He demanded a higher public status for the merchant class and argued that if greater freedom were given to them in their commercial activities, it would be an effective defense against foreign exploitation of China. Accordingly he urged that merchants should be admitted to the civil service examinations at the local level, and should have access to the officials.

One amazing thing about Cheng's book is its humanitarian sentiment—not only his thesis that the government is for the people, but also his moving descriptions of the social abuses of the time. He was especially grieved by the inhumanity of penal practices and prison conditions, by the suffering of women from footbinding, and by the general misery of the countryside. He therefore offered many suggestions for reform, relief for the poor, agricultural improvement and the like, including the idea of using an alphabet for writing Chinese so that "all the people could read and write."[11]

## DOC. 30  THE CRITICISMS OF CHENG KUAN-YING, C. 1892[12]

In recent days, although the court has ordered the governor-general and governors to develop commerce and open all kinds of manufacturing bureaus, and has authorized the inviting of merchants to manage them, yet the officials and merchants have habitually been unable to get along together and have distrusted each other for a long time. Even though the officials are capable and brilliant and willing to protect them [p. 8], the merchants are afraid, since it is unpredictable whether their successors will be wise or not... Who would like to have his interests and rights taken away by officials? For this reason, rich merchants and great businessmen who have undertaken many affairs, although they understand clearly that there are profits to be made, nevertheless hesitate to accept the invitation to manage government enterprises. Even if some accept the invitation, they still fear that the officials will deceitfully entrust affluent merchants with the charge of certain enterprises, while actually having some other selfish scheme in mind. During the last ten years or more, there have frequently been bad officials who allied themselves with cunning merchants. The latter either ask the authorities to give them charge of tax collections in certain lines (Note: The tax for building forts, contributed by all trades in Kwangtung province, was handled by inviting merchants to collect it), or they imitate Western methods of inaugurating enterprises; in order to secure more shareholders they may falsely claim that a certain amount of stock has been sold and a license received, before they even establish an office. Thus they work for their private ends on the pretext of a public enterprise. They are neither affluent merchants, nor have they any special training. Such enterprises can hardly be successful, and many people have suffered by involvement in them.

According to Western custom, a bureau is established by the government to handle state affairs, while a company is established by respectable merchants to conduct a business. No matter who establishes it, a business company need only act entirely according to the company law drawn up and enacted by the state. The chief manager is elected by the trustees of the shareholders and the affairs of each branch are decided by the chief manager. If the chief manager is not thoroughly familiar with commercial affairs, nor versed in the advantageous and disadvantageous aspects of business, even though he has many shareholders and holds high official positions, he is not allowed to venture carelessly into an undertaking…

Now in China when companies are founded through a petition to the higher authorities, even though the shares are sold to merchants, they are called bureaus. The chief managers, whose duties are only slightly concerned with government matters, are appointed and given orders by high officials, who disregard whether they are competent or not and look only for men whose rank is comparatively high and who suit their own ideas. Then they are considered qualified to fill the posts. Consequently, most of the chief managers of the various bureaus are people with the rank of taotai (Note: What they have learned cannot be used for what they are doing, and that is always ridiculed by Westerners). After the official seals and stationery have been received, item by item, then the business is carried on entirely in an official [i.e., bureaucratic] manner. Those whose positions are dignified and who have great authority can dominate the business and can achieve their private ambitions at the cost of the public enterprise. Those whose positions are low and who have little authority generally take orders and dare not say much. If a surplus or profit is made by the company, all the local officials request some contribution and overstep their proper duty to meddle in the company's affairs. The managers of small companies, even though they have not been appointed by high officials, also indulge in embezzlement and malpractices; the shareholders are afraid of their power and, on account of the lack of commercial law, they dare not appeal to higher courts. Therefore, during the last several decades there have been few shareholders who have made a profit, and many who have lost their capital…

Now if we wish to reorganize our commercial affairs, we must imitate the Western practice and compile a commercial code quickly… [P.9]All those who organize a commercial company ought to state in a petition who the trustees of the shareholders are, how large the capital is, and what business they are going to do, and they ought to send these details for registration with the local government. If a company is not registered, the official will not take care of it when anything happens. Thus... the officials will not dare to squeeze the merchants and the latter will not practice fraud. As to the people employed by the company, whether in high or low position, they must be thoroughly familiar with the business before they are given employment. The authorities should not recommend people to the company at random; all the old inveterate malpractices should be entirely wiped out.

In another passage, Cheng Kuan-ying gives an eloquent summary of the injustices and humiliations suffered by Chinese at the hands of foreigners in Shanghai:

The Westerners frequently take advantage of the differences in language and in law to profit themselves at the cost of others, and do as they please without regard for reason... When a foreign ship collides with and destroys a Chinese boat, the latter, contrarily, is blamed for being slow in avoiding the collision or is falsely charged with having a dim light on its mast... When a foreign stagecoach hurts a Chinese, the latter is, contrarily, charged with not knowing how to yield the right of way, so that he incurred the disaster himself. Even if the driver is taken to court, he only pays a small fine. Furthermore, Chinese employed by foreign companies or as sailors on foreign ships frequently have their wages cut on some pretext or are even beaten to death. Cunning Westerners ally themselves with local rascals to kidnap and sell the foolish country fellows, whose grievances and miserable lives are like those of the dark ages. Again, for example, when a Chinese merchant owes money to a foreign merchant, as soon as he is accused his property is confiscated and his relatives and friends are disturbed; whereas when a Westerner is in debt to a Chinese, even though he has abundant private savings, by following the regulations for declaring bankruptcy, he is entirely free from obligation...

[P. 48] Our treatment of Westerners has been so magnanimous, and their treatment of the Chinese so poor. Where is justice and where is humanity? Their steamboats sail as fast as if they flew through our harbors, and their stagecoaches rush along our thoroughfares, they carry weapons in time of peace, they reduce the wages of their employees, they speculate and go bankrupt, they protect Christian converts, they control the customs duties, they kidnap and sell our people—all these various kinds of wrongdoing should be forbidden by Western law and not tolerated by international law... ⑬

To make his complaint specific, Cheng lists ten grievances: (1) the Shanghai foreign settlement is taking over land outside its boundaries; (2) Chinese stagecoaches are differently taxed and not allowed to pass foreign stagecoaches; (3) Chinese are fined for hunting out of season; (4) Westerners go hunting as they please at any time; (5) the paper chases of Western horsemen destroy the fields without compensation; (6) the Mixed Court at Shanghai issues blank warrants which are misused by the municipal police who prey upon the populace; (7) no Chinese representatives are allowed in the Shanghai municipal council; (8) Chinese are excluded from the Shanghai public park and race course, although they pay sixty or seventy per cent of the taxes to the municipal government; (9) Chinese are excluded from the park along the river; (10) land for roads is expropriated from farmers without proper compensation. ⑭

### b. *The Debate over Railroads*

The term *t'ieh-lu* (lit., "iron road") for "railroad" probably first appeared in Chinese literature in 1864 when an English engineer, Sir MacDonald Stephenson, traveled to China by way of India. He suggested that a railroad be built from Shanghai to Soochow, but there was no response from Chinese circles. In the following year an English merchant built a short railroad of more than one *li* outside the Hsuan-wu Gate of

Peking and tried to run a locomotive on it. This appears to have been the first introduction of the railroad in China,[15] but because the spectators were greatly alarmed, the railroad was soon removed. In 1866 British merchants, including Jardine, Matheson and Co., again began to build a railroad by preparing a carriage road thirty-eight *li* in length between Shanghai and Wusung. In May of 1876, rails having been laid, service was formally opened. However, because it was built by foreigners and the Chinese populace were greatly irritated by the new invention, local public opinion turned against it. After a Chinese soldier was killed on the railway, and officials and people had become more clamorous, Shen Pao-chen, then governor-general of Liang-chiang, in September 1876, negotiated with the British consul-general, Thomas Wade, purchased the railroad, and had it destroyed in 1877. The superficial reason for this destruction lay in superstition and conservatism of the type that had also appeared in England and the United States at the beginning of railroad construction—such as the idea that the roaring locomotives would startle the cattle and prevent them from grazing in safety, that hens would not lay, that the poisoned air from locomotives would kill the wild birds and destroy vegetation, that farm houses would be ignited by sparks, etc.[16] Behind this lay the real reason, that the British merchants had built the Shanghai-Wusung railroad without the consent of the Chinese government, which was averse to foreign control over so powerful an instrument of economic exploitation.

After this incident it took some time for Chinese leaders to promote the construction of railways in China. Among these promoters Feng Kuei-fen, Li Hung-chang, Liu K'un-i, Tso Tsung-t'ang, Liu Ming-ch'uan and others wrote long memorials to call the attention of the court, as well as the populace, to the need of railroads both for defense and for commerce.[17] Li Hung-chang and Liu Ming-ch'uan in particular conducted vigorous campaigns for the introduction of railways, while T'ang T'ing-shu, Wu T'ing-fang and Sheng Hsuan-huai became the chief supervisors and administrators of railroad construction.

## DOC. 31  SHEN PAO-CHEN'S PURCHASE OF THE SHANGHAI-WUSUNG RAILWAY, 1876⑱

We have found that during the spring of this year the British merchants in Shanghai built a railroad without authority, in the leased territory, and on it ran a locomotive train and directly reached Wusung. Your ministers Shen Pao-chen and Wu Yuan-ping sternly ordered the customs taotai to communicate with the British consul-general in order to stop it. Consul-general Meadows adamantly refused. We also wrote to the Tsungli Yamen to send a communication to stop it. The envoy of the said country, Wade, was also very obstinate and he put it off for several months... The British envoys at first wished to have the railroad operated jointly by Chinese and foreigners, each side contributing some money. Then they wished, after the purchase of the railroad by China, to have it still managed by foreign merchants... We immediately explained in detail that in Chinese territory foreigners should not build a railway without authority. We accommodated them with a price, which is already a special consideration. If there is still more trouble, then it is not China's fault but the Westerners'.

After repeated discussions between the (Shanghai) customs taotai and others, an agreement has been reached on October 24 that China has full freedom to buy the line, to stop operation, and to take other action concerning the railroad. Foreign merchants have no right to make further inquiries. But during one year, until the purchase price has been entirely paid, the foreign merchants shall manage it. They are only permitted to take passengers back and forth and not to take goods, as it is against the regulations. In addition, they cannot purchase more land for extending the railroad...

## DOC. 32   HSUEH FU-CH'ENG'S SUPPORT OF RAILROAD BUILDING, 1878[19]

Now all the European countries are competing with one another for wealth and strength and their rise to prosperity is rapid. What they rely upon are steamships and railroads. The manufacture of steamships has been imitated by China with visible effect. I think if the system of railway trains is not used [p. 10], China can never be rich and strong ... In England railways have been studied and steadily improved and a large amount of profits has accrued. The price of coal and iron has been reduced three-fourths. Accordingly, England could exert her power in manufacturing and expand into other matters, and thereby become the strong leader of Europe. Shortly afterward, the railroad was extended to Russia, France, Germany, Austria, the United States, and other large countries.

The United States is a newly created country, and forty years ago there was no railway. Now a general estimate of the whole country shows the railroads, spreading out on all sides, amount to as many as twenty-one hundred thousand *li* [*sic.*, i.e., 70,000 miles?]. Wherever a new city is founded or untilled land is opened, railroads are always built to lead the way, and as soon as the population becomes numerous and business prosperous, then the railroads are increased to improve things still further. The nation has been established only a hundred years, its daily progress is like rising steam, and it is almost an equal of England and Russia. I have heard that from San Francisco in America to New York by train the distance is eleven thousand *li*, and the journey does not exceed eight days; that is, ten thousand *li* takes the same time as several hundred *li* in China. The traveling expense is but little more than a hundred dollars; that is, the cost of ten thousand *li* is like the cost of one thousand *li* in China. Thus, if China should adopt the railroad, then distant areas could be brought near, the stagnant could be made to flow, expense could be saved, and the scattered could be concentrated…

[P. 11] The new tasks on which China is now trying to make a start are numerous, yet all must have railroads to relieve their difficulties. Why? … The more goods are imported or exported, the more extensive will be the transportation and trade by steamship. This shows that railroads and steamships are mutually helpful [lit., like outside and lining]. Coal, iron, and other mines far away from a river can use a railway for transportation, and then the capital expense will be lightened and sales will be facilitated. When distribution is easier, the mining industry will become more prosperous, and thereafter coal and iron mines will be more extensively opened, and accordingly the cost of building and managing railways will be further reduced. This shows that railroads and mining are mutually helpful. The speed of a train is more than a thousand *li* a day, and the velocity is double that of the fastest horse of the military post stations. Thereafter, official dispatches will be speeded up, and regulations will be established for people to send mail by Western methods, so as to make the mail an appendage of the railroad company… This is the railroad's help to the postal administration.

## CHAPTER XIV  THE ATTEMPT AT A POSITIVE FOREIGN POLICY

In the latter half of the nineteenth century, China's foreign policy and the modernization movement were both geared to foreign aggression. When a Japanese expedition to Taiwan, sent to punish the murder by Taiwan savages of shipwrecked Liu-ch'iu islanders, revealed China's military incompetence in 1874, Li Hung-chang had already realized that China's backwardness in the matter of armament, communications, and modern machinery placed the country at the mercy of stronger powers. Hence, in 1872, as we have noted above, the China Merchants Steam

Navigation Company had been formed. In 1880, Li Hung-chang vigorously supported the resumption of railway construction, and he recommended the establishment of the first telegraph lines in China. In addition, he sponsored a number of schools for technological training. The French naval destruction of the Foochow Shipyard in 1884 further stimulated the Chinese government to carry out its plans for a modern navy. Li was made Associate Controller of the Board of Admiralty, and he was able to secure enough funds to build a number of ships. Unfortunately, the new Chinese army and navy, which represented the result of a generation of effort at modernization, were crushed by Japan in the war of 1894-1895. After this fiasco, Li Hung-chang almost gave up hope for rebuilding a strong China, with modern industries and communications, that would be able to fight against Japan. Instead, he sought an alliance with Russia, thus continuing China's traditional foreign policy of using one barbarian to fight another.

China's foreign relations were handled in considerable part by Li Hung-chang in the period after he became governor-general of the metropolitan province of Chihli in 1870, and particularly after the Empress Dowager removed Prince Kung from the Tsungli Yamen in 1884. The study made thus far of late Ch'ing foreign affairs reveals that there were various policies at different times, but no overall strategy. Since Li formed at least one principal center of policy formation, his writings have special interest.

In general, Li Hung-chang seems to have kept his eye on Japan as China's major foreign threat, rather than on Russia. In his view the Restoration of 1868 in Japan and her aggression in Taiwan in 1874 were both a menace and a stimulus. Wen-hsiang had been one of the earliest officials to recognize Japan's probable ambitions, and Li Hung-chang had a similar foresight. In 1872 he wrote to a friend:

In Japan the emperor above and the people below have identical minds. They believe in the Western countries—in machinery, guns, artillery, warships, railways, and everything. They have patterned all these after France, England, and the United States. Hereafter Japan will certainly be a source of anxiety for China, as near as elbow and armpit. While our own weakness remains chronic, our strong neighbor daily becomes a threat to us. What technique can we employ to cope with her?①

One of Li's memorials, written on December 10, 1874, reads:

Japan recently has changed to the practice of Western military methods, has imitated the West in building railways, setting up telegraph lines, opening coal and iron mines, and coining foreign-style currency, all of which is not without benefit to her national polity and to her people's livelihood. She has also sent many students to foreign countries to acquire learning and practice in the use of machinery and technology; she has raised many foreign loans, and has secretly made an alliance with England. Her power is daily expanding, and her ambition is not small. Therefore she dares to display her strength in eastern lands, despises China, and takes action by invading Taiwan. Although the various European powers are strong, they are still seventy thousand *li* away from us, whereas Japan is as near as in the courtyard, or on the threshold, and is prying into our emptiness or solitude [i. e., weaknesses of our defense measures]. Undoubtedly she will become China's permanent and great anxiety.②

After the settlement of the Taiwan incident, Li Hung-chang wrote a very serious letter to Shen Pao-chen, part of which reads:

Hereafter I hope our Emperor, officials, and the upper and the lower classes alike will "sleep on firewood and eat gall," to seek vigorously for methods of self-strengthening… As an earlier letter of the Tsungli Yamen says, "When something happens, we hurriedly plan to make up our deficiencies; but after the incident, we again indulge in pleasure and amusements."③

Li recognized the administrative ability and statesmanship of the great Japanese leader, Itō Hirobumi (1841-1909), about whom he made a secret report to the Tsungli Yamen in 1885. Itō, he says, "has traveled long on the continents of Europe and America and is strongly imitating them. He really has the ability to govern his country. He pays particular attention to these policies: to encourage trade and to be harmonious with neighboring nations, to enrich the people and strengthen the troops... In about ten years, Japan's wealth and power will be considerable. She is China's future disaster, not our present anxiety."④ Obviously Li's prophecy was all too accurate. (For the conversation between Li and Itō in 1895, see Doc. 35.)

Over Russian expansion in Central Asia, Li had fewer misgivings than the bellicose group of high officials represented by Tso Tsung-t'ang. Li at least was more painfully aware of China's genuine weakness. In 1880 while Tso was demanding war, Li wrote to a subordinate:

Ili was seized by Russia, who took advantage of the Mohammedan rebellion. The local people really do not wish to return to our jurisdiction. To me this seems to be an extremely distant encroachment on our frontiers, and it may be unnecessary to request the return of Ili immediately. Those within and without the capital who are in charge of national plans suddenly feel boastful and take pleasure in meritorious deeds; again and again they have urged the recovery of Ili. Our key officials [of the Tsungli Yamen and the imperial court], without consulting the opinion of many persons, suddenly chose a weak and ignorant individual [Ch'ung-hou, who signed the unfavorable treaty of Livadia in 1879] and granted him authority. Again, suddenly, the whole country shouts madly like the barking of dogs to rescind the treaty which has already been signed. Can we say this is fair?

After the suppression of the Taiping and Nien rebellions, the demobilization of [Chinese] officers and soldiers has caused further exhaustion of the sources of provisions, because every year we have to supply six or seven million taels to the Western-style troops [to take their place] and there is no time limit to this expense. After the Taiwan incident [of 1874] we began to deliberate about costal defense, for which the nominal appropriation was four million. Actually, the amount given each year is less than one million. The appropriation for the Peiyang coastal defense is only three or four hundred thousand. When there is no money, there are neither crack troops nor effective weapons. The subsidies for the Huai Army have also been reduced forty per cent. Last year I received the decision of the Ministry of War ordering me to disband more than ten thousand soldiers and the remaining force still has to defend the two oceans in the south and in the north. In our military forces, can we be said to be strong?⑤

During the negotiations with Russia in 1880-1881, China mobilized many troops in the north to back up her envoy, Tseng Chi-tse, in St. Petersburg. Li Hung-chang doubted the soundness of Tseng's judgment; in a reply to him on April 12, 1880, Li wrote:

You also say ... that the Russians, in their own country, fear a rebellion by the people and, abroad, have to defend themselves against invasion by the English, so that they are not in a position to start a large-scale frontier war with China. Your estimation of the enemy is certainly very clear and thorough; however, although you say that the English would not permit the Russians to fulfill their ambitions in China, have you really a fundamental basis for this assertion? If the Russians are to fulfill their ambitions in China, the first place of invasion must be in Sinkiang, next in Heilungkiang and Kirin. All are areas beyond the reach of the power of the British people. If there is harm to England, then the English may create some obstruction. If there is no injury to England, then the English merchants will take advantage of the situation to plan for profit. Can they really show sincerity in rendering help to us Chinese?⑥

After Tseng Chi-tse's rearrangement of the Ili settlement in 1881 (usually considered a great success because it compelled Russia to disgorge territory she had already swallowed), Li remained unimpressed.

To a friend he opined that the settlement gave "after all, no actual advantage to China, while the Russians have fulfilled their desires. The stupidity and confusion of our scholar-officials, and the lack of men of ability in the court are really ridiculous."⑦

Kuo Sung-tao was another diplomat who remained sceptical of warlike policies on the part of China. During the protracted and confused course of the fighting and negotiation with France in 1884, he submitted the following summary of his views.

## DOC. 33 KUO SUNG-TAO ON THE FUTILITY OF A WAR POLICY, 1884⑧

The European countries have concentrated on trade relations... The areas they have occupied are as far away as several tens of thousands of *li*, all occupied on the pretext of commerce. At first they had no intention of resorting to war, but after [the local people] had repeatedly gone back on their promises, the foreigners inevitably took offense and so used military force. Nor had they any preconceived idea of fighting for territory; but the more they fought, the further they advanced and thereupon they took the opportunity to usurp territory. The various islands in Southeast Asia are almost completely invaded and occupied, and all by this process. Therefore, in negotiating with the European nations on commercial affairs, we can use reason to overcome them but should absolutely not resort to force in a dispute; we can inspire their confidence by sincerity and good faith, but should by no means gloss things over; we can make use of their power to plan to make ourselves strong, but we must not on any account be envious of their strength and so seek to challenge them.

Your minister once held that, of the requests the Europeans have made, whether trifling or serious, large or small, with hundreds of variations and changes, there is none that cannot be settled by compromise according to reason; whereas, if war is resorted to, then they will not be easy to settle. This is because... [p.38] their purpose is no more than to trade with us for profit; they cherish no hatred or grudge in their hearts. We have noticed that they do not speak lightly of war but argue with us back and forth, leaving themselves ample leeway to seek in each instance some advantage. If, on account of the fact that they do not speak of warfare easily, we goad them into acting with outrageous violence, then there will be a great deal of harm. Once warfare has been resorted to, the military expense they incur will eventually be sought from us as an indemnity. This is the principle by which the various European countries try to dominate one another. We simply have no argument with which to deny their request. They may eventually suffer a defeat and run away under full sail, but... after a year or two they will be sure to come again. They may overrun us as arrogantly as they like and the catastrophe they bring will be even more serious. Wars among the European countries last ten and sometimes twenty years. In each battle the cannonading on both sides may not cease for several days... China's coastline is 8,000 or 9,000 *li*. By what means can we oppose them?

This is why your minister has said that the various European countries are surrounding and gathering together against China so that she has no chance to fight, no power to fight, and simply no reason to fight. The French barbarians have frequently made private treaties with Annam exclusively for the purpose of trade with Yunnan. After the British initiated trade at T'eng-yueh [Yunnan], the French were even more fearful of being left behind and cherished the idea of competing with them. This is seen in the book by T'e-la-ko-erh, *T'an-ti-chi* [Doudart de Lagrée, *Investigation of the Routes*, 1865]. The ambition they cherish has been long and deep...

When the French barbarians caused trouble in Annam we should have sent an envoy to the capital of France and should also have sent an envoy to Saigon to investigate the opportunities and observe the changes in the situation, and yet we sent no one. When the French caused trouble in

Annam, one place it started was in Saigon. In the Saigon area were more than 300,000 Chinese [p. 39] and a consul should have been established there to take care of their affairs, and yet it had not been possible to do so ahead of time. Important strategic opportunities of this sort have been idly lost!

At first the French barbarians thought that if they had 500 soldiers stationed at Saigon, these would be more than enough to overrun Annam. When they were assaulted on the flank by Liu Yung-fu [1837-1917, leader of the "Black Flags," Chinese irregulars], they were surprised at the unexpected attack and were in a dilemma. We might have taken advantage of this situation to settle the dispute, but again we lost this opportunity.

Of all the officials in and outside the capital, there is not a single one who is versed in foreign affairs. All they do is cautiously watch the intention of the court and show their zeal for war. The officials in charge of frontier troops are also accustomed to the old habits of military camps and make falsely exaggerated reports, which are all mere fabrications that avoid mentioning defeat but report success without a single sentence that can be verified...

When the French barbarians had caused trouble in Annam and had not yet reached China, the ministers at court favored war to resist them... When they came, our troops had withdrawn beforehand. When they withdrew, a retaking of the place was reported...

The cost of the shipyard at Ma-wei, Foochow, and the installation of machinery amounted to several millions. Whenever a battleship was built the maximum for one ship was a million and several hundred thousand dollars. Even the minimum was several hundred thousand. In a single engagement [with the French, 1884] all have been entirely destroyed. The loss is ten or twenty million. Thus we ourselves vainly destroyed our only ships and manufacturing machinery in order to make the warmongers happy...

During the last two or three years, since the start of the border war,

Western merchants have withdrawn their capital in China and ceased to trade; our coastal merchants have all become bankrupt and their original strength has been greatly drained; the populace in turn are moving away [p. 40] and becoming vagrants—in one day they may be frightened several times without being able to protect their own lives. Our merchants have suffered even more. In this war we merely cause ourselves trouble...

At present the number of levies and transfers of funds, and the broad extent of conscription, far exceed those of the period of Hsien-feng [1851-1861] when military force was used to quell the rebels. We are showing off our military might in places where it cannot be applied and are seeking to do battle with an enemy who is not responsive [to our strategy]. Along the several thousand *li* of our coastline, defense works are laid out everywhere, merely to the exhaustion of our own strength, and yet there is no end to it...

Your minister has heard that since ancient times in fighting foreign wars it has been necessary first to make secure the domestic administration. The Westerners have occupied our seaports and have penetrated deeply into the interior. There is therefore nothing for us to say about fighting a foreign war, but we should instead quickly attend to security within the country. If military action is taken everywhere and the frontiers are disturbed, we shall lose control on both fronts—neither expelling the foreigners nor having security within the country...

These divergent views on policy and the inefficiency of China's projects for self-strengthening are both illustrated in the case of the continued Chinese efforts at naval development.

### a. *Building a Modern Navy*

The old-style naval and marine forces in the Ch'ing Dynasty, as part of the territorial Chinese "Army of the Green Standard" (*Lü-ying*), were traditionally divided into provincial commands. The land-minded Manchus had not paid much attention to the development of a navy and used their "water forces" only to patrol the coasts and certain commercially important inland waterways. Except in the 1680's, during the conquest of Taiwan, and in the years 1795 to 1805, during the suppression of large pirate fleets off the South China coast, the programs of shipbuilding and naval training had been perfunctorily maintained as matters of routine.

During the Opium War the English fleet, using artillery of superior fire power and auxiliary steam-powered gunboats, played havoc with the Chinese fortifications and war junks all the way from Canton to Nanking, and practically destroyed everything that confronted it. Yet the Chinese officials of the day, as we have seen, developed no real doctrine of sea power. In spite of some discussions about the purchase of foreign war vessels for coastal defense, the Kwangtung squadrons of war junks were rebuilt along the same old lines as before. The new naval force which resulted was no match even for the pirates that became rampant in the late 1840's in the Canton estuary and along the waterways into Kwangsi. Some of these pirates later joined the Taiping rebels and manned their boats on the Yangtze when the Taiping horde overran Hunan and Hupei and descended on Nanking. It was mainly to deal with the Taiping fleet that Tseng Kuo-fan began to build up his Hunan militia army (*Hsiang-chün*), a large part of which was a marine force transported on long boats powered by oars. Foreign-built steamers were bought and rented in increasing numbers for use against the Taipings in the lower Yangtze valley after about 1853.

In the early 1860's, the value of Western-style gunboats in Chinese waters was signalized by the famous Lay-Osborn flotilla project, under which a powerful fleet was built for China in Britain, only to be disbanded in 1863 following a dispute over the manner in which Chinese official control of the squadron was to be exercised.⑨ The subsequent shipbuilding efforts of Tseng Kuo-fan at Shanghai and Tso Tsung-t'ang at Foochow have already been noted (see, respectively, Doc. 13, Ch. IX, and Doc. 29), but it was not until 1867 that an organized Chinese navy was proposed, when Li Hung-chang, accepting the suggestion of Ting Jih-ch'ang (1823-1882), memorialized urging the appointment of three admirals who would take charge of the northern, central, and southern squadrons, respectively. In 1881 Hsueh Fu-ch'eng drafted regulations for the northern squadron and in 1882 a dockyard was begun at Port Arthur by Li Hung-chang. In 1884 Tso Tsung-t'ang memorialized proposing the establishment of a modern navy, and at the same time Chang P'ei-lun (1848-1903) submitted the memorial translated below, which urged the establishment of a central office in charge of the navy. As a result the Hai-chün Yamen, or Naval Office, was created on October 13, 1885. Prince Ch'un (1840-1891) was appointed controller of this board and Li Hung-chang was made one of the associate controllers.⑩

In the Naval Office, Li Hung-chang and Tseng Chi-tse were the responsible policy makers, but they were unable to keep the Empress Dowager from using the money originally appropriated for the development of the Chinese navy to rebuild the Summer Palace.⑪ Although the northern squadron was organized in 1888 to consist of 28 ships of various sizes, it was a navy only in form, its organization and equipment being poor⑫—a situation which forecast the disaster of 1894. Near the end of the dynasty the naval administration was reorganized, but even in the twentieth century China has failed to develop a navy on Western great-power lines.

### DOC. 34   CHANG P'EI-LUN'S PROPOSAL OF 1884⑬

The reason for the European countries' overrunning the seas and the difficulty of contending against them lie in their possession of solid ships and effective guns. During the last twenty years, trade relations between China and foreign countries have been established and treaties concluded... The intentions of these nations, standing like birds of prey and covetous as wolves, with watering mouths and eyes staring at Asia, are understood by everyone. Even if our nation, right now, greatly develops its navy, we fear that we cannot rival them. If we are again hesitant, wondering what to do, and do not work on the fundamental plan for self-strengthening, I really fear that the menace from the sea will be unlimited...

After the suppression of the Taiping and the Nien rebels, China gradually built shipyards and bought machines to establish a new navy with steam warships. That was the beginning of our navy. Funds were insufficient, men of ability were not forthcoming, flood, drought and other catastrophes frequently occurred, and opinion within and without the capital was not unified; so, until now, the old regulations for naval ships in the outer seas have not yet been changed, nor has a definite system yet been established for a steamship fleet of all the provinces. When there is no alarm, the funds for the southern and northern squadrons are never delivered in full by any of the Maritime Customs offices; when there is an alarm, every province retains for its own use the subsidy for the navy. If this situation continues without change and we still wish to have a coastal navy sufficient for attacking or coming to the rescue, or to be adequate for offensive war as well as for defense, it will obviously be very difficult...

[P. 3] Your minister has studied the European military systems. Concerning their navies, they all establish a special ministry of the navy with very great powers. The Englishman Robert Hart has made a suggestion to the Tsungli Yamen regarding the establishment of a bureau in general charge of coastal defense. We have seriously considered the plans of two or three veteran statesmen and consulted the new systems of five or six sea powers. We can see the advantages and disadvantages in the proposal that the naval forces should be combined in one unit, not divided and scattered. Thus, if we wish to seek a method to control our enemies, we cannot do it unless we create a navy with steam warships for the outer seas; and if we wish to accomplish the overrunning of the seas, we cannot do it unless we establish an Office (*ya-men*) of the Navy. The important functions of the navy are in general four: namely, the investigation of coastal topography, the training of officers of ability, the building of naval vessels, and the study of various operations. Coastal defense is of concern to the governors-general and governors, but since there are boundaries between provinces, they cannot entirely disregard each other's spheres of jurisdiction. If we have an important minister take full charge, then the relative importance of all seaports along the entire coastline can be distinguished; also where iron ships should be anchored, where forts should be built, where shipyards may be prepared, and where mines may be laid; the generals and the admirals will be like one family, the water and land defenses will be well coördinated...

### b. *The Failure at Self-Strengthening*

The collapse of the Chinese empire is as complex a subject as the decline and fall of ancient Rome. A similar multiplicity of factors contributed to the general debacle and many years of study will be necessary before we can generalize about it, or compare China's failure with Japan's success in a few well-chosen words.

One thing is worth noting, however. While many writers in contemporary China now stress the deleterious impact of Western imperialism upon the old Chinese state and society, the Chinese leaders of the nineteenth century maintained a rather different view of their problem. Through all their writings, as noted above, runs a constant emphasis upon the need for men of ability (*jen-ts'ai*, "human talent") who could deal with the crisis. This concern stemmed from the ancient ethnocentric assumption that the Chinese empire's foreign relations were only a subsidiary function of domestic administration—of the twin evils, "internal rebellion and aggression from without" (*nei-luan wai-huan*), the former was assumed to open the door for the latter. A dynasty that could handle its domestic problems need have little fear of foreign aggression.

Whether or not this analysis took adequate account of the bite of modern imperialism, it at least threw the moral blame for the failure at self-strengthening upon the Chinese leaders, not upon foreign imperialist scapegoats. This traditional Chinese concept that government is indeed a personal matter, that history is made by the ruler and his ministers, not by impersonal social and economic "forces," may well have contributed to the demoralization of Chinese officials who saw things going steadily from bad to worse.

Li Hung-chang's awareness of the Meiji reforms in Japan has been evidenced in many preceding documents, as well as his specific recognition of Itō Hirobumi as the great protagonist of Japan's self-strengthening. In 1885 the two men had negotiated the Li-Itō convention to stabilize the Sino-Japanese rivalry in Korea. A decade later, after China's complete and sudden defeat and the destruction of Li's plans and hopes of many years, they met again to negotiate the *Treaty of Shimonoseki*. Part of their conversation on March 20, 1895, was as follows:[14]

## DOC. 35   LI HUNG-CHANG'S CONVERSATION WITH ITŌ HIROBUMI, 1895

*Li Hung-chang*: In Asia, our two countries, China and Japan, are the closest neighbors, and moreover have the same language. How could we be enemies? Now for the time being we are fighting each other, but eventually we should work for permanent friendship. If we are enemies endlessly, then what is [p. 262] harmful to China will not necessarily be beneficial to Japan. Let us look at the various European countries which, even though their military forces are strong, do not lightly start hostilities. Since we Chinese and Japanese are on the same continent, we should also imitate Europe. If the diplomatic ministers of our two countries mutually and deeply understand this idea, we ought vigorously to maintain the general stability of Asia, and establish perpetual peace and harmony between ourselves, so that our Asiatic yellow race will not be encroached upon by the white race of Europe.

*Itō*: I am very much pleased with the idea of the grand secretary [Li Hung-chang]. Ten years ago when I was at Tientsin, I talked about reform with the grand secretary. Why is it that up to now not a single thing has been changed or reformed? This I deeply regret.

*Li*: At that time when I heard you, sir, talking about that, I was overcome with admiration, and furthermore I deeply admired, sir, your having vigorously changed your customs in Japan so as to reach the present stage. Affairs in my country have been so confined by tradition that I could not accomplish what I desired. At that time you advised me and said, "China is large and populous, the reform of various policies ought to come gradually." Now in the twinkling of an eye ten years have gone by, and everything is still the same. I am even more regretful. I am ashamed of having excessive wishes and lacking the power to fulfill them. The soldiers and generals of your honorable country are excellently trained on the model of Western methods; in all kinds of policies and administration, you are advancing daily to newer and more prosperous planes. This time, when I went to Peking and talked to scholars and officials, I found that some of them have also thoroughly realized that our country definitely should undergo reform before we can stand on our own feet.

*Itō*: "The providence of heaven has no affection, except for the virtuous." If your honorable country wishes to exert itself to action, Heaven above would certainly help your honorable country to fulfill its desires. It is because Heaven treats the people below [i. e., mankind] without discrimination. The essential thing is that each country should do its own best.

*Li*: Your honorable country, after it has been so reorganized by you, sir, is very admirable... [The conversation then turned to other topics.]

### c. **The Alliance with Russia**

As Lin Tse-hsü and Wei Yuan had pointed out more than fifty years before, the barbarian menace could be met partly by borrowing the superior military methods of the Western powers or, alternatively, by using one power against another. For a whole generation, from 1860 to 1894, China's leaders had aimed at self-strengthening with Western help, chiefly the help of Britain in the customs administration as well as in the naval program. By 1895, Japan had blown this program to pieces. British opinion had suffered disillusionment over China and was beginning the shift that led eventually to the Anglo-Japanese alliance of 1902, while the other powers, especially Germany, were developing the tendencies that soon led to the scramble for concessions and the threatened partition of China in 1898. In this situation China turned to Russia as a potential ally to check Japan. Without attempting to explore the complex diplomacy of the period, we quote memorials of two influential provincial leaders and present also the text of the secret treaty of 1896, which has not been widely available in English. While Li Hung-chang performed the act of "inviting the Russian bear into the parlor" in China's northeastern provinces, it is apparent that other high officials, not of his camp, supported the step. Thus the Chinese people's potential base for future industrial development was drawn irrevocably into the vortex of power politics.

### DOC. 36  LIU K'UN-I'S SECRET PROPOSAL, JULY 1895[15]

Liu K'un-i, imperial commissioner and governor-general of Liang-chiang, submits a secret report of a great plan to ally with Russia for opposing Japan, in order to consolidate the defense of the second capital [Fengtien, whither the Court had fled] and to strengthen the whole situation:

Your minister notes that diplomatic relations between Chinese and foreigners have continued for thirty years until the present day, when the matter is even more difficult to handle. China's use of hard and soft policies should stress their modification according to the times. The chances of all countries being friendly or hostile to us are guided by circumstance. After the war in Annam, when China failed to handle the issue properly, we were considerably despised by all countries. This time, when we negotiated peace with Japan, we made too many compromises which encouraged the gradual inception of a waylaying policy—glaring at us like tigers, all the various powers seek to find a plump spot to bite into us. We estimate that our power is inferior to theirs, so we must quickly make an international alliance as a means of seeking assistance.

According to your minister's humble understanding, the impending disaster from other countries is still slow in coming, but that from Japan is imminent. This is because she is close to us; after she has obtained Taiwan and Liaotung, the way for her entrance will be even more convenient, as if her army could start directly from our pillow and mat—it can invade any part of our territory at will… But Russia does not want Japan to be strong, and Japan's invasion of our Three Eastern Provinces [Manchuria] makes Russia even more jealous. Thus, by the Sino-Japanese peace treaty [of Shimonoseki] we had already ceded Liaotung to Japan, but Russia, France, and Germany compelled her to return it to China. Is Russia doing this especially for us? She is, at the same time, working for herself. If we take this opportunity to establish close relations with her, for mutual assistance, and also give her some concessions, Russia will surely be glad to comply. Even though this move cannot protect our various coastal provinces, Japan certainly will not dare to covet the territory of the Three Eastern Provinces, which are close to Russia… If these provinces were lost, how could the dynasty maintain its foundation, and how could our Emperor face his ancestors? That is why, whenever your minister thinks of this, he cannot keep his heart from palpitating and his muscles from twitching.

Some people say that Russia is adjacent to the widest stretch of Chinese territory and that in the future she will certainly do harm to

China. Heretofore, your minister was also of the same opinion. Now he is inclined to think that this statement is wrong. It also depends upon how we are going to console or control her. Russia's territory is already very large and, moreover, she is well known for her good faith and righteousness. She has had good relations with us for two hundred years and several decades, during which time there was no war at all. This is really a rare thing in all times. Formerly [1881] she returned Ili [p. 21] to us, and this time she coöperated with France and Germany to struggle against Japan for the return of Liaotung to China, an even greater favor than before; and yet some suspect her of having other ambitions, and would no longer associate with her in sincerity. That is, the nation which is coöperative with us, we keep at a distance; and toward the nation which is magnanimous to us, we are stingy. Soon they will say that it is not worthwhile to help China, and our position will become even more isolated...

As long as Sino-Russian relations are permanently solid, Japan and other countries will have scruples and will not go to the extreme of considering China non-existent, and cunningly seek to start trouble...

## DOC. 37  CHANG CHIH-TUNG'S MEMORIAL OF AUGUST 1895[10]

To save the critical situation today, nothing is better than the conclusion of a secret treaty of alliance with a strong power for assistance. From ancient times, whenever nations have opposed each other, as if with horns, they usually have used the policy of allying with a distant country to attack an enemy nearby. With regard to the Sino-Japanese situation today, this policy is even more suitable. China's power today [p. 36] can never oppose simultaneously all the nations in the East and West...

I understand that the tendency of foreign countries in recent years has been to establish particularly close relations with one or two others among all the countries which have general relations. In time of peace they make secret treaties in advance, and in wartime they aid one another with military provisions and armaments. If there is no secret treaty, then when something happens they remain neutral and will not interfere.

Now if we wish to make a treaty, and to have a bond for mutual assistance, naturally Russia is most convenient for us, because England uses commerce to absorb the profits of China, France uses religion to entice the Chinese people, Germany has no common territorial boundary with us, and the United States does not like to interfere in others' military affairs. It is difficult for all of these nations to discuss an alliance with us. It is known that Russia, as China's neighbor, has kept treaty agreements with us for more than two hundred years, and that she has never embarked on hostilities; she is different from other countries who have frequently resorted to warfare with us. Moreover, her behavior is grand and generous, and cannot be compared with that of the Europeans. For example, in the church case at Tientsin in 1870, in which all the countries were busy making a clamor, Russia did not participate; and in the treaties over Ili [1879 and 1881] our nation completely refused and then modified the eighteen articles, and Russia generously consented. This time she has demanded the return of the territory of Liaotung for us; although she did it for the sake of the general situation in the East, yet China has already actually received the benefit. Japan's spearhead has been slightly blunted by this. In comparison with other countries who acted as bystanders, putting their hands in their sleeves, and covertly planning for commercial profits, Russia shows a great difference.

It is just the right time for us to take this opportunity and work vigorously for an alliance, deepening our friendship and making a secret treaty with her. In everything concerning Russian commercial affairs and boundary matters, we should make some compromises. If Russia resorts to warfare in the East, we should aid her navy with coal and food, permitting her war vessels to enter our dockyards for repairs. On land we must permit her to use our roads, supply her with resources, food, vehicles and horses; in accordance with her reliance on our supplies we should offer her coöperation and subsidy according to our means. But we should have it settled in the contract that in case China is attacked, Russia will have to help us with armed forces, of which the most important is the navy. We must also make a decision during our conference with Russia concerning the method of compensating her, because Russia is very suspicious that England dominates the situation in the East. If China and Russia form an alliance, English influence will be considerably curbed; and Russia would be willing to accommodate us.

After all, it is not easy for China to train a navy. If we have the Russians to aid us, in the future, regardless of what country may start hostilities with us, after a few weeks several tens of Russian warships could be sent to patrol the Eastern seas. Thus we can prepare only the strategy of war on land, and our enemy cannot plan to invade the interior deeply. This is the crucial point in our international relations and the most important policy for saving the critical situation.

With regard to the foreign countries, China has always treated them on the same level. Thus, during the last time [presumably, the Sino-Japanese War of 1894] there was no one to help us. Such matters must be prepared in advance [p. 37] during days of peace, and at present our plan for alliance should absolutely not be delayed. It behooves us to request an Imperial Decree to order the princes and high ministers to deliberate secretly and conclude the matter carefully. But by no means should we ever let Robert Hart [the British Inspector general of Chinese Imperial Maritime Customs, 1863-1908] hear of it, lest he be jealous, impede us, and spoil the matter. Reverently memorialized, August 8, 1895.

The treaty concluded by Li Hung-chang on his visit to Russia to attend the coronation of Tsar Nicholas II was reported at the time by British correspondents, evidently on a basis of rumor. In 1922 its content was briefly announced by the Chinese delegation at the Washington

Conference, but we have not found an exact translation of the Chinese text in previously published works. Judging by the memorials of Liu and Chang just quoted, China got the military agreement they desired, but at the price of strategic, if not indeed territorial, concessions which set an almost disastrous pattern for the future.

### DOC. 38　TEXT OF THE SINO-RUSSIAN SECRET TREATY OF 1896[17]

His Imperial Majesty the Emperor of China and His Imperial Majesty the Tsar of Russia, desiring to maintain the present situation of peace in the Far East, and to prevent future aggression by other powers upon the territory of Asia, have determined to conclude a treaty of mutual assistance. Therefore, His Imperial Majesty the Emperor of China has specially appointed His Excellency Li Hung-chang, Imperial Commissioner and Plenipotentiary of the first class, Grand Tutor of the Heir Apparent, Grand Secretary of the Wen-hua Palace, Stern-and-resolute Earl of the first rank, and superintendent of trade for the Northern Ports; and His Imperial Majesty the Tsar of Russia has specially appointed Prince Lobanov, Imperial Commissioner and Plenipotentiary, Foreign Minister, member of the Cabinet and of the Imperial Council and Privy Councillor, and (Count) Witte, Imperial Commissioner and Plenipotentiary, Finance Minister, member of the Cabinet and Privy Councillor, as their respective plenipotentiaries, who, having exchanged and examined their credentials and found them in proper form, agree to the following stipulations:

Article Ⅰ. In the event of a Japanese invasion of the territory of Russia in Eastern Asia, or the territory of China, or the territory of Korea, the present treaty shall be considered as having been involved, and measures shall be taken according to the treaty. In such an event both contracting powers promise to dispatch all the military and naval forces that can be mobilized for mutual assistance; they shall also supply each other with munitions and provisions as far as possible.

Article II. Having entered into the present treaty of mutual defense, neither contracting power can conclude a separate peace agreement with the enemy without mutual consultation.

Article III. Should an emergency arise during the war, Russian warships shall be allowed to enter all ports on the coast of China; in case of need, the local authorities shall give aid to the best of their ability.

Article IV. In order in the future to facilitate the rapid and safe transportation of Russian troops for opposing the enemy, and for the supply of munitions and provisions, the Chinese Government agrees to let Russia construct a railway through the territory of Heilungkiang and Kirin to connect with Vladivostok. However, the construction of this railway is not to be used as a pretext for the infringement of Chinese territory, or for encroachment on the lawful rights and privileges of H. I. M. the Emperor of China. The Chinese Government will entrust the Russo-Chinese Bank with the management of the (railway) matter. The Chinese Minister to Russia and the Bank shall consult on the spot and decide upon the terms of the contract.

Article V. When Russia is engaged in the defensive measures against the enemy provided for in Article I, she may use the railway as provided in Article IV for the transportation of troops, provisions, and munitions. In peace time Russia may also use this railway for troops and provisions in transit. Apart from temporary stops due to changes of trains, they shall not be allowed to stop over for any other reason.

Article VI. The agreement shall be effective for fifteen years, beginning with the date on which the contract mentioned in Article IV shall have been ratified and put into effect. Six months before the expiration of this treaty, the two contracting powers shall negotiate for its extension.

Special provision: The plenipotentiaries of both contracting powers agree that the Sino-Russian treaty concluded on this day[18] shall be rendered into the Chinese and French languages in duplicate copies, to be signed and have seals affixed. The Chinese and French copies have been compared and found to be without error. In case of dispute the French text shall be the decisive version.

Concluded on the 22nd day, 4th month, and 22nd year of Kuang-hsü, which is May 22, 1896 (o. s.) [June 3, 1896], at Moscow.

# 5 THE REFORM MOVEMENT THROUGH 1900

## CHAPTER XV PROMOTERS OF INSTITUTIONAL CHANGE

The decade preceding China's defeat in the Sino-Japanese war of 1894-1895 is perhaps the least studied in the whole century of China's modern history. No doubt this is partly because Western rivalry and attention did not center on China or the Far East in this period, in contrast to the succeeding decade from 1895 to 1905, and accordingly less has been written by Westerners. During these years British influence and British trade were dominant in Ch'ing foreign relations—this was the heyday of the British treaty system in China, the period of pay-off when the British "opening" of China for commercial exploitation had finally become effective in terms of imports and exports facilitated by the Customs Service under Robert Hart. Meanwhile, the rivalry of foreign powers had not yet reached a stage of more-than-commercial exploitation of the Chinese empire. In domestic affairs, the leaders who had come into power with the suppression of the Taiping Rebellion were likewise at the height of their careers—Li Hung-chang and his colleagues were cautiously inaugurating new and lucrative enterprises in the treaty ports while the Empress Dowager was established in her domination of the court at Peking. One has the impression that this was a period when the old order was able to coast along, in the shadow of Victorian Britain.

Across the water in Japan, on the other hand, it was during these years that vigorous leaders were actually carrying out changes which had been only talked about in China. Whatever the complex historical background of this amazing contrast, it is plain that the leaders of the Meiji Restoration had more opportunity for effective action than their contemporaries in China. With foreign help they were feverishly trying to telescope the whole process of the industrial revolution, with its attendant changes in social, economic, and political life, into the time span of one generation. In China this startling achievement of the Japanese people was known but did not call forth similar action. Meanwhile, knowledge about Europe and America was being accumulated from missionaries in China and from Chinese officials who went abroad, but the process was slow.

### a. *The Missionary Influence*

Missionaries in China have been the most immediate channel of Western influence in human and personal terms. China's idea of the West has been formed in great measure from their activity, yet the work of the missions has thus far been studied more from the Western side of organization and personnel than from the Chinese side of publications, sermons, and doctrines presented to the Chinese people in their own language.

The Protestant missionaries, from the beginning of their work in China in the early nineteenth century, had been interested not only in converting the Chinese heathen in order to "save their souls" for Christianity but also in helping them improve their way of life in this world through useful knowledge. The pioneer Protestant missionary, Robert Morrison (1782-1834), reached Canton in 1807, learned Chinese, compiled a dictionary, and brought out a Chinese version of the *Bible* which was later used by Hung Hsiu-ch'üan and so influenced the early Taiping religious documents. One contribution of Morrison and the early English missionaries from the Chinese point of view was the founding of a school for Chinese converts and a Chinese printing establishment at Malacca in 1814. Yung Wing (see Ch. XIa) was one of its students.

The early American missionaries, David Abeel (1804-1846) and E. C. Bridgman (1801-1861), who arrived at Canton in 1830, founded a school, and Bridgman and S. Wells Williams (1812-1884) maintained a valuable monthly periodical, *The Chinese Repository* (1832-1851). Peter Parker (1804-1888) of Yale started the first American missionary hospital and medical school at Canton, which has been in operation ever since. After more treaty ports were opened, and inland missionary work became legalized by treaties in 1858-1860, there was a tremendous expansion by both Catholic and Protestant workers. The Jesuits resumed their work at Zicawei (Hsü-chia-hui), a village in the suburbs of Shanghai named after Hsü Kuang-ch'i's family (see Ch. IIb), establishing there a school, a library, a meteorological station, and a printing plant. The various Catholic orders, like the Protestant denominations, agreed among themselves upon the allocation of areas for their work.

By degrees an increasing number of English and American Protestant missionary scholars worked seriously on the problem of interpreting the West to China and vice versa. It was these men who did most of the composing of Chinese tracts and translations of Western works in history, science, technology, and other subjects. Their translations, worked over by competent Chinese assistants, were readable and so had a great deal of influence among the scholar class. Foremost among these pioneers in cultural relations were the Englishmen William Muirhead (1822-1900), Joseph Edkins (1823-1905), Alexander Wylie (1815-1887), and James Legge (1815-1897); and the Americans, W. A. P. Martin (see Doc. 26), S. Wells Williams, John Fryer (1839-1928), and Young J. Allen. The last two were especially prolific: Fryer, at the translation bureau of the Shanghai Arsenal, produced many valuable compilations and translations which became the textbooks for Chinese students interested in scientific subjects. Allen's Chinese periodical, the *Wan-kuo kung-pao* ("The Globe Magazine"), published in Shanghai from 1875 to 1907, had the avowed aim of being "devoted to the extension of knowledge relating to Geography, History, Civilization, Politics, Religion, Science, Art, Industry, and general Progress of Western countries."①

Perhaps the most influential missionary who advocated reform was Timothy Richard (1845-1919). He came to China in 1870 and ten years before the war with Japan he was already warning Chinese officialdom that it was to China's advantage to pursue a policy of peace, as the less costly course of action. He predicted that unless China introduced institutional changes at once, including modern schools, disastrous consequences would be near at hand. In 1890-1891, on the invitation of Li Hung-chang, Richard served as the editor of the *Shih-pao*, a daily newspaper, at Tientsin. He used the editorial section as a pulpit for preaching his ideas of institutional and technological reform, hoping to make the Chinese official class realize the impending danger. He also spent much time seeking interviews with high officials, and associated himself with many young Chinese scholars, some of whom became leaders of the reform movement. In 1895, after the Sino-Japanese War, Richard brought out a volume of essays entitled *Hsi-to* ("The Warning Bell from the West"), which he had written during the preceding fifteen years. In them he had exhorted the officials and scholars of China to follow the example of Japan in establishing modern schools and beginning other institutional reforms. His prestige was enhanced by the fact that history had proved him right.

Important as the missionaries were in planting ideas of reform in the minds of Chinese students, their positive influence was limited mainly to a few coastal cities and reached a rather small percentage of the gentry-scholar-official class. The majority of the latter resented the increasing prestige of the missionaries and felt that the foreigners threatened their own positions as teachers and upholders of Chinese tradition. The missionaries were also disliked by the gentry-officials because of their interference in lawsuits on behalf of their converts, a practice followed especially by the Catholic missionaries. The anti-missionary movement was particularly serious in the late 1880's along the Yangtze and, although suppressed by the officials, sometimes half-heartedly, it was not rooted out until after 1900. One factor underlying it was the difficulty experienced by the gentry and lower Chinese officials in distinguishing between Western religions and other aspects of Western civilization. They might willingly have accepted the latter without the former, had they seemed distinct. This inability to comprehend the difference between Christianity and the rest of Western culture was quite universal, from the court down to the coolie class, as the Boxer Uprising was to demonstrate. No doubt it resulted from the fact that the Western missionaries had consciously used medicine and other forms of good works as vehicles for proselytism. The result was that Chinese resentment against foreign evangelism in China became unreasoningly attached to Western ways generally, and so, in fact, retarded the process of learning from the West.

### b. *Early Chinese Advocates of Reform*

Among the writers who prepared the way for institutional reform in China, one of the most interesting and quixotic was Wang T'ao (1828-1897),[2] a gifted journalist whose bicultural experience and personal opportunism fitted him to be an effective cultural intermediary and conveyer of ideas, even though he was not an official and represented no particular group. He took a post under the Ch'ing, deserted to the Taipings, later betrayed them and worked in the treaty ports. He had been in contact with Westerners in Shanghai and Hongkong from 1848, and formed a close association with the leading British missionary sinologues Walter H. Medhurst (1796-1857), William Muirhead, and James Legge, eventually assisting the latter in translating several volumes of *The Chinese Classics*. It is interesting to note that shortly after Itō Hirobumi's return from England to Japan, Wang T'ao was invited by Legge to Scotland, in late 1867. He spent two years in the British Isles and Europe, where he saw something of the Franco-Prussian war and wrote a book on it. He had a scholarly correspondence with the French sinologue Stanislas Julien (1799-1873), and gave a lecture at Oxford in 1868, presumably with Legge as his interpreter. Returning to Hongkong with a large library in 1870, he soon became well known as an editorial writer. In 1879 he visited Japan, where he was enthusiastically received by Japanese who had read his writings and with whom he had much correspondence.

Wang T'ao had begun his journalistic work shortly after he escaped from Shanghai to Hongkong in 1862. He served as editor of the *Hongkong News*, which was established under foreign auspices, and in 1873 founded in Hongkong his own newspaper, the *Tsun Wan Yat Po* (*Hsün-huan jih-pao*), in which he wrote his most famous editorials. His son-in-law, Ch'ien Cheng, was an editor and for some time editor-in-chief of the Shanghai *Shun Pao* (*Shen-pao*), to which Wang was a frequent contributor. In 1882 his editorials were collected and published.③ They are written in an elegant style and contain much interesting information.

Under foreign protection in Hongkong and Shanghai, Wang T'ao was bold in his attacks on the corrupt Chinese administration of the day. He was also an ardent advocate of a domestic reform program. About 1870 he wrote three essays on "Reform and Self-strengthening" in which he advocated four reforms affecting the selection of scholars, the training of troops, the school system, and the legal code.④ A few years later he wrote an editorial, "To Get Rid of Abuses," advocating clarification of the qualifications for official position, weeding out of sinecure posts, replacement of Manchu bannermen in office, discontinuance of river conservation, elimination of extravagant expenditures, and abolition of the *likin* tax.⑤ In another essay, "To Promote Profit," Wang T'ao discussed the utility of opening mines for coal, iron, and other metals, setting up textile mills, and building steamships. About 1878 he urged the training of a navy,⑥ as well as the installation of telegraph lines, and the building of railways.⑦ He was one of the first Chinese to propose the abolition of extraterritoriality,⑧ and demanded the return of Macao from the control of Portugal.

As a diplomatic strategist, Wang T'ao anticipated about 1879 that Russia's ambition was for territorial expansion and annexation, and "if she is not successful in Europe, she will make a disturbance in China."⑨ Therefore he suggested a containment policy by proposing to set up two barriers against Russia. In Europe the six countries, England, France, Prussia, Austria, Italy, and Turkey should unite to resist Russia, otherwise they would be conquered one by one, just as the Ch'in had conquered the six states of ancient China in the third century B. C. and built the great Ch'in Empire. In Asia, Wang T'ao suggested an alliance of China, Japan, Annam, Siam, and Burma to prevent Russia's expansion.

In his cultural outlook Wang T'ao shared the optimism of Victorian England and prophesied the unification of nations through the conquest of distance by the new inventions of science. The first entry in his collected editorial writings is on "The origin of truth," in which he says, "The truth of the world is only one... It begins by proceeding from identity to divergencies and it ends by proceeding from divergencies to identity."⑩ In his view the steamship and railway would help people to reach every corner of the earth. These inventions which "the Western powers are now using for their encroachment upon China are the very things which the sages of a future age will utilize as the means for the unification of all nations."⑪

As a result of his trip to Europe, Wang warned China against her effort to learn only the superficial, external mechanics of the West. He praised the Western system of law and justice, popular elections and constitutional government, and discussed the three forms of state in Europe: the ruler-governed state (*chün-chu kuo* or monarchy), the people-governed state (*min-chu kuo* or democracy), and the ruler-and-people jointly-governed state (*chün-min kung-chu kuo* or constitutional monarchy). Of these three, he favored the constitutional monarchy of England.⑫

While Wang T'ao was keen in observation and better versed in Western conditions, he adhered essentially to the same pattern of thought as Feng Kuei-fen and Chang Chih-tung. He wanted Chinese civilization to remain the foundation on which gradual reforms might be superimposed.⑬ In fact he was pitifully ignorant of ancient Western history and political institutions, and shared the naive rationalization that China had been the early home of Western culture.⑭ While on the one hand he regarded the United States as the most powerful country of the West, on the other hand he said, "Recently in the United States of America most women in the state of Massachusetts have preferred to get concubines for their husbands"—this from one of the leading "old Western hands" of his day!

### DOC. 39  WRITINGS OF WANG T'AO

*A Refutation of the Idea of Using Barbarians Against Barbarians* (from a letter written in the period 1858-1860 to a private friend)⑮

Formerly it was said, "The Europeans who have trade relations with China are more than one country; it is better to use them to attack each other, or use them so that they make compromises with each other, or use them so as to separate them from each other." These three statements all seem to be calculations based on profound deliberation and far-reaching thought. And yet nowadays I am afraid that they are impracticable. Why? Because all the European countries have the intention of keeping China on the outside. How can they be utilized by us? Even though there were one country which was willing to be utilized by us, all the other nations would undoubtedly ridicule her. As for two countries which engage in a prolonged struggle against each other, with the issue not yet decided, the practice in Western countries is to persuade them to make peace. If the advice is not taken, then assistance is given the weak party to attack the strong, just as England and France helped Turkey to attack Russia in recent years... But the practice in the West is, after all, not a sufficient rule to be applied to China. The most tractable Western country is the United States of America. Nevertheless she still takes the victory or failure of England as her own glory or disgrace [p. 22]... Thus there have been occasions for her to assist England, but there has never been an occasion for her to assist us and attack England. As to her relations with us, though she has never made unreasonable demands on us, yet she has shared all the benefits gained by England and France... If she sincerely wants to give us support, how could she act in this way? ...

If, suddenly, the Westerners seized an opportunity to attack us, how could we resist them? Our soldiers are inferior to theirs, our finances are inferior to theirs, our weapons are inferior to theirs, and our military strategies are also inferior to theirs. They already thoroughly understand the hostile actions which we on our side may take, whereas we are as yet incapable of knowing what hostilities they may commit. We excuse ourselves by saying that it is because they are too far away from us. Yet with all the publication of daily newspapers and the spread of postal communications, can we not make some inquiries and obtain some information? During the last hundred years or more, America's revolt against England and France's assault on England were both occasions of peril to her. Recently the mutiny [of 1857] in India and the violation of treaties by Persia were both incidents which she had to cope with. The occurrence of such incidents is sporadic. The essential thing is for us to be good at forecasting them.

### On Reform⑯

If Confucius were born today we may be certain that he would not stubbornly believe in antiquity and oppose making changes...

First, the method of selecting civil servants should be reformed. The examination essays up to the present day have gone from bad to worse... And yet we are still using them to select scholars...

Secondly, the method of training soldiers should be reformed. Now our army camps and water forces have only names registered on books, but no actual persons. The authorities consider our troops unreliable, and then they recruit militia, who can be assembled but cannot be disbanded... This is called "using the untrained people to fight," which is no different from driving them to their deaths...

Thirdly, the empty show of our schools should be reformed. Now district directors of schools and sub-directors of schools are installed, one person for a small city, and two for a larger city. It is a sheer waste... Such people are usually degenerate, incompetent, and senile and have little sense of shame. They are unfit to set the example for scholars...

He who rules the empire should establish the foundation and not merely mend the superstructure... [P. 15] Formerly we thought that the foundation of our wealth and strength would be established if only Western methods were respected or adopted and that the result would be achieved immediately... Now in all the coastal provinces there have been established special factories to make guns, bullets, and ships. Young men have been selected and sent to study abroad. Seen from the outside, the effort is really great and fine. Unfortunately, however, we are still copying the superficialities of their methods, getting the terminology (of Western civilization) but little actual substance. The ships which were formerly built at Foochow were entirely based on old methods of Western countries, beneath contempt, to those who know. As to things made in other places, for the trick of moving a machine or valve we must rely on the instruction of Westerners. Yet, if we watch the bearing of the Chinese manufacturers, they already feel noisily pleased with themselves. They usually believe that their thinking and wisdom are sufficient to match those of the Westerners, or that they have even surpassed them.

In general (the advantage of) guns lies in the fine technique of discharging them, that of ships in the ability to navigate them... The handling of effective weapons depends upon the people... But the so-called able minds of our people are not necessarily able, and the so-called competent ones are not necessarily competent. They are merely mediocrities who accomplish something through the aid of others.

Therefore, the urgent problem of our nation today lies primarily in the governance of the people; next in the training of soldiers; and in these two matters the crucial thing to aim at is the accumulation of men of ability. Indeed, superficial imitation in practical matters is certainly not as effective as arousing genuine intellectual curiosity. The polishing and pounding in factories is definitely not as important as the machining of peoples' minds...

[P. 16] Let us now talk about the conventional examination subjects. The themes on classics in the second examination ought to be replaced by some practical knowledge ... so that the candidates can understand the body politic and can transfer their knowledge into actual practice... After four or five examination periods, the eight-legged essays can also be abolished.

### On Domestic Administration⑰

[P. 25] For flood control, there is no good method in China or the West. This is because the river sand daily accumulates, the river basin daily rises, and the dikes must be built higher to prevent a break. Such methods have been handed down from dynasty to dynasty without any attempt at change. People who live near the river are as though living in the basin of the river. When after a long drenching rain the water breaks through the dikes and flows out horizontally, they have the fear of becoming fish and turtles. Now it is better to adopt the Western method, to dredge the sand, to comb and scrape, and make the water flow, to get rid of the banking up of sand and then open many small branches in order to reduce the force of the water...

As for the handling of foreigners, the difficulty is not in the conveying of our instructions overseas; the foremost trouble is in the managing of the foreigners in the interior of China ... If the Western merchants, missionaries, and others were contented with their lot, law abiding, and willing to obey our jurisdiction, then even though they went everywhere, there would be nothing to worry about. Unfortunately among the Westerners who travel in China there are frequently many who rely on their power to insult our people. The gentry and the people of our country in turn despise them, and do not care to associate with them, so incidents daily grow up which merit serious thought. The practice in the West is that when a foreign merchant comes to the territory of a nation, if he violates the law, he is judged by the officials of the nation. This practice cannot be applied in China because the Western governments dislike China's frequent resort to torture in examining a case. According to the *Chefoo Convention*, hereafter when there is a legal suit between Chinese and Western merchants, the accused will be handled by the officials of his country... But the Chinese law is severe, and Western law clement. There are many Western officials who understand Chinese law, and there are few Chinese officials who know Western law. Even if both sides can make inquiries and give just decisions, it is difficult to guarantee that the litigants will have no resentment...

### *A Note on the British Government*[18]

England is in a remote spot overseas, three islands which stand like mountains off the northwest of Europe... In view of the fine quality and strength of her armament and soldiers, the richness of her revenue and the abundance of her natural resources no European country dares to be stiffnecked with her... In recent years she has maintained her prosperity and preserved her state of peace and has been so cautious in resorting to arms that unless there is no other way out she never carelessly starts a military expedition...

The real strength of England, however, lies in the fact that there is a sympathetic understanding between the governing and the governed, a close relationship between the ruler and the people... My observation is that the daily domestic political life of England actually embodies the traditional ideals of our ancient Golden Age [lit., the Three Dynasties and earlier].

In official appointments the method of recommendation and election is practiced, but the candidates must be well-known, of good character and achievements before they can be promoted to a position over the people... And moreover the principle of majority rule is adhered to in order to show impartiality... In their treatment of the people the officials never dare to use severe punishments, heavy fines, or tyrannical and excessive taxation. Nor dare they accept any bribery... or squeeze the blood and flesh of myriads of people in order to fill up their own pockets. The English people are likewise public spirited and law-abiding; the laws and regulations are hung up high (for everyone to see), and no one dares to violate them. He who violates the law goes to the court only to have his confession taken; when the real truth has been obtained, then a verdict is made, and he is imprisoned. There has never been such cruelty as torturing and beating him by bamboos and clubs so that his blood and flesh spread all over. In prison the convict is supplied with food and clothing, so that he may not be hungry or cold. He is taught to work and not allowed to become idle. He is visited every seven days by preachers to make him repent and live a new life. He is never maltreated by those in charge of the prison. The excellence of the prison system is what China has never had since the Golden Age...

An important question is jointly discussed in the upper [p. 18] and lower houses of Parliament, and all must agree before an action can be taken. If there is a proposal for a military expedition it is necessary to make a universal inquiry of the whole nation. When the multitude of the people desire to fight, then there is a war; and when the multitude desire to cease, then a truce...

The expenditure of the British ruler is a constantly fixed amount for every year; he does not dare to eat myriads of delicacies. His palaces are all very simple; he does not care for extravagance, and he has never had separate mansions and distant palaces linked with one another over scores of *li*. The king has only one queen, and besides her there is no concubine, and there has never been a multitude of three thousand beautiful women in the harem...

While Wang T'ao as a pioneer journalist was reaching a newspaper-reading audience in the treaty ports, the former secretary of Tseng and Li, Hsueh Fu-ch'eng (see Ch. X a), was writing memorials and essays which had a more limited but also more influential circulation. In 1879 he compiled a volume called "Rough discussion of the management of foreign affairs" (*Ch'ou-yang ch'u-i*), which contained fourteen essays on current problems—how to handle Russia and Japan, how to secure "intelligence about the enemy," prevent the loss of China's "vassal states," carry out "institutional reform" (*pien-fa*), assert China's sovereignty, revise the treaties, and the like. Hsueh first submitted these essays to Li Hung-chang, who laid them before the Tsungli Yamen, and later Tseng Chi-tse distributed several dozen copies.

Hsueh Fu-ch'eng's proposals were strengthened by the fact of his own experience of state affairs. After joining Li's staff he had assisted in negotiating the *Chefoo Convention* (1876), drafted the regulations for a modern Chinese navy in 1881, and been the one who suggested the timely dispatch of a Chinese force to Korea following the riots in Seoul in 1882. It is true that Hsueh never took a higher degree than that of Senior Licentiate of the Second Class (*Fu-kung-sheng*, 1867) nor held a higher post in China than that of an intendant (taotai) in Chekiang, where he rendered good service in coastal defense against the French attack in early 1885. His prominence as a reformer came from his four years' diplomatic service in Europe, mainly in London and Paris, about which he left a very instructive "Diary of a mission to the four countries of England, France, Italy and Belgium" (*Ch'u-shih Ying-Fa-I-Pi ssu-kuo jih-chi*) covering the period from January 31, 1890, to April 8, 1891. It was published in 1892, and a supplement covering the period from April 9, 1891, to July

1, 1894, was published in 1899. These diaries reveal his favorable response to Western civilization. He comes to the conclusion that only through modernization can China save herself, and cites Siam and Japan as two examples to follow.[19]

As with Wang T'ao, Hsueh Fu-ch'eng's appreciation of Western ways is by no means limited to material things. The parliamentary governments, especially those of England and Germany, seem to him the best form of political organization. He visits the British parliament and writes a detailed description of its system.[20] He attributes the prosperity and strength of European nations to the development of science, the system of compulsory education for boys and girls, rich and poor and from all walks of life, the encouragement given commerce and industry by the governments, and the use of machinery to produce wealth and so feed the people.

He does not blindly admire everything European, however, and criticizes the Western religions, especially Catholicism. He insists that although the freedom to propagate the faith in China is permitted by the treaties, priests should be forbidden to interfere in Chinese internal politics or to attack Confucianism.[21] Nor does he like the Western type of social relationship between the rulers and the people, parents and children, husbands and wives. He notes that state ministers occasionally compel a ruler to abdicate, and that boys and girls under twenty-one claim the right to arrange their own marriages without asking for instruction from their parents; after the wedding they live separately and divide their property, without having much social contact with their parents. When a son beats a father he will only be imprisoned for three months. "The Western custom honors women, looks down on men. When a woman has an outside paramour, even if she is a duchess or marquise, she often deserts her husband or remarries, and it is not considered strange. If a husband meets a girl outside, his wife can complain before the judge and have him punished ... Girls before marriage have many boyfriends and even though they have borne children, they will not be despised... This is quite contrary to the doctrine of our sage."⑳

In foreign policy Hsueh viewed the Chinese migration overseas as an important outlet for relieving China's population problem. He worked hard to establish consuls general in Singapore and other places to protect Chinese living abroad, and believed that Chinese diplomats could accomplish a good deal through patience, sincerity, and skillful tactics. ㉓ Unfortunately, just as with Kuo Sung-tao and Tseng Chi-tse, there was no chance for this man of ideas to carry on practical administrative work in China. Hsueh Fu-ch'eng died in Shanghai only 20 days after he returned from Europe in 1894.

In the following essays we can see at work that process of harmonizing Chinese and world history which K'ang, Liang, and later reformers were to pursue for so long, and which Marxism in China is now attempting in its own way to complete. The chief device used by Hsueh and later reformers like Liang Ch'i-ch'ao was to make an interpretation of China's past in terms of which the modern adoption of Western institutions could be sanctioned. If China had had previous periods of institutional reform, or if China had given the original impetus to the growth of science, which the West had merely carried further, then China could now justifiably learn from the West without giving up the essential Chinese way. All these arguments, historical references, and interpretations thus had a psychological aim—to convince the leadership of China that Westernization was consonant with China's ethnocentric culturalism. The hectic days of 1898 merely carried this process of thought to a higher and more explicit point.

### DOC. 40   ESSAYS OF HSUEH FU-CH'ENG

#### *On Reform* (1879)㉔

I have said that from the origin of mankind down to the present is approximately no more than ten thousand years. How do I know this? I know it from the urgency of social change (*shih-pien*); according to the way of heaven, there is a small change once every several hundred years, and a great change once every several thousand years. [Hsueh then recounts the main periods in traditional Chinese history, to show that changes both great and small periodically occur as a matter of course, including barbarian incursions from neighboring lands.] As we reach the present day, the European nations suddenly arise overseas by means of their knowledge of machinery and mathematics... In ninety thousand *li* around the great globe there is no place where they do not send envoys and have trade relations. Even though Yao and Shun [the legendary emperors] were called upon to face this situation, they would not be able to close the doors and rule the empire in isolation... Therefore the empire has to be changed from a divided world, in which the Chinese are segregated from the barbarians to an integrated world in which China and foreign countries are in close connection. When social change is small, the laws governing society accordingly will undergo small change; when social change is great, the laws governing society [p. 21] will also be greatly changed...

Only a sage can pattern himself after another sage, and only a sage, too, can change the law of another sage. The reason for their making reforms is not because they like to do it, but that they are obliged by the circumstances of the time...

As for the various European countries, they rely on intelligence and energy to compete with one another. When China wishes to stand with them on an equal level, our commercial policy and mining affairs should be planned; and if no reform is undertaken in these lines, they will be rich, and we poor. Our study of technology and manufacturing of machinery should be accurate; without reform on our part, they will be clever and we will be stupid. Steamships, trains, and telegraphs should be adopted; if not, they will be quick and we shall be slow. The advantages and disadvantages of treaties, the competence or incompetence of envoys, and the improvement of the military system and strategy should be discussed; without reform in these lines, they will be coöperative, we will be individualists; together they will be strong, alone we shall break easily.

Formerly Ch'ih-yu [a legendary leader of savage tribes] made military weapons and invaded the territory of the feudal lords; the Yellow Emperor began the making of bows, arrows, and the compass to overcome him...

Now if we really take over the Westerners' knowledge of machinery and mathematics in order to protect the doctrines of our [Emperors] Yao, Shun, Yü, and T'ang, [Kings] Wen and Wu, the Duke of Chou and Confucius, and so make the Westerners not dare to despise China... I know that if they were alive today they would probably work on these pressing tasks, and their doctrines would also be gradually spread to the eight bounds of the globe. That is what is called using Chinese influence to reform the barbarians.

Some may say that in practicing reform one should aim to surpass others and not to pursue them. Now the Western methods are superior to ours, and if we run after others with our worn-out knowledge, what can we do, it may be asked, when there is no way to surpass them? This view is not correct. In general if we wish to surpass others, it is necessary to know their methods before we can reform, but after reform we may be able to surpass them. We cannot expect to excel others merely by sitting upright in a dignified attitude. Now we see that some people are ahead of us; and if we say contemptuously that we do not care to run after them, later we shall not be able to move even half a step. Moreover, they have concentrated the ability and energy of several million people, have spent millions of dollars through prolonged years and generations before they acquired their knowledge. If we wish to excel them within a single morning, is it possible or impossible? In general a large river may begin from the overflow of small bogs, and a lofty hill may be based on overturned baskets of soil. Buddhism came from India and yet it flourished in the East. Mathematics had its beginning [p. 22] in China and yet it has reached its highest development in Western lands. Comparing the ability and wisdom of the Chinese with those of the Westerners, why are we not able to surpass them?...

Indeed, social changes are endless; and likewise the methods of the sages in controlling these changes are also limitless. To be born in the present generation, but to cling stubbornly to traditional methods, is to be like one who lived in the age of Shen-nung [who invented cooking] and still ate hides and drank blood [i. e., ate uncooked food], or like one who lived in the age of the Yellow Emperor and yet, in opposing the savage action of Ch'ih-yu, struggled against him with bare hands. Such a one would say, "I am observing the methods of the ancient sages"...

### An Essay in Praise of the United States (A diary entry of May 1, 1890)⑥

Formerly Kuo Sung-tao frequently praised the merits of the governmental administration and popular customs of the West, which caused him to suffer criticism and ostracism from scholars who like to criticize others. I was also slightly surprised at the exaggeration of his words, which I checked with Ch'en Lan-pin... who said that his statement was correct. This time when I came to Europe and traveled from Paris to London I began to believe that the statements of Kuo Sung-tao could be verified in the parliaments, schools, prisons, hospitals, and streets.

Among my associates some talk about the honesty and magnanimity of the people of the United States. I think the Western countries today are at the pinnacle of their prosperity, which is caused by their good fortune in natural resources. At the beginning of the nation, the population of the United States was not very large, and these natural resources had not yet been unearthed. By nature the people are open and generous. This is because the development of America was later than that of Europe, and the development of Europe was later than that of China. Among the various European countries, again, some were developed later and some earlier;

and accordingly the customs are good and bad. America is like the time of the Golden Age of Ancient China [lit., the time of Yü and Hsia]. Russia is like the time of Shang and Chou. England and Germany are like the two Han Dynasties of China. France, Italy, Spain, and Holland are probably like Chinese T'ang and Sung. As for the inconstant and excitable spirit of the French, with their perpetual struggles among political factions, they resemble the age of the former Ming Dynasty.

Some say the Irish (Ai-li-shih) people in the United States are outrageous in the jealousy and violence with which they oppress and expel the Chinese people living there; where is the good old spirit? My answer to this is that, in the time of the Three Dynasties, the notorious tyrants㉖ ... Chieh, Chou, Yu and Li㉗ also caused periods of disorder. How can we (expect everybody to) follow the same path?

### Science Makes Europe Prosperous (A diary entry of May 19, 1890)㉘

The secret of the sudden rise of the various nations in Europe and America lies in the fact that day by day their knowledge progresses and their industry and commerce increase in prosperity. But the pivotal implements have all developed in the last hundred years. As for the means by which they cross the globe with no hindrance, the Westerners rely on steamships, trains, telegraphs, and the like, all of which were invented during the last sixty or seventy years. It is the same with other matters.

Nowadays some Chinese critics are either surprised at the strength and prosperity of other countries and praise them too much; or else hold that great China should not imitate Westerners, should reject their inventions, and condemn them severely. I think both are narrow-minded.

In general the Westerners' commercial administration, military methods, shipbuilding, machine manufacturing, agriculture, fishing, husbandry, mining and all such matters, are indeed developed to a high point of excellence, and yet all are derived [p. 12] from studies of steam, light, electricity and chemistry, by means of which they have obtained the methods of controlling water, fire, and electricity. These result from the ingenuity of the inventors, and there is no reason to expect that they can be kept secret for a long time. Famous experts of the West have been particularly entrusted with demonstrating them. The way revealed is one that belongs to all the universe; it is not a monopoly of the Westerners. The intelligence and energy of Chinese scholars are not necessarily inferior to those of Westerners. Unfortunately the energy of their youth has been mostly wasted on eight-legged essays, examination papers, and the calligraphy of small model characters. They are not like thousands and millions of Westerners who exert their intelligence and wisdom in pursuing their study of special subjects and so can at once achieve the best and finest. Certainly we should not deny this fact, and why, likewise, should we confine ourselves to what we are?

In ancient times inventions were concentrated in China. As spiritual sages arose in succession, they invented ploughs, hoes, boats and carriages, bows and arrows, fishing nets, clothes, and writing. At the time of primeval chaos and uncultivation, there suddenly arose this civilization. If we compare it with the European inventions today, was it not even more marvelous? But people are accustomed to our old civilization and do not realize this. As for the fixing of the four seasons in the chapter "Yao-tien" [of the *Book of History*] and the teaching of mathematics through the book, *Chou-pi suan-ching* [see Ch. II above], Western astronomy and mathematics may have been derived from both of these. How can we know that they have not patterned other matters useful to their nation and people after those of China? In antiquity, when there was not yet any invention in the universe, Chinese sages had observed what was above them and examined what was below and gradually Westerners imitated them. In modern times, Westerners have followed the inventions of Chinese sages, stepped after them, and elaborated upon them. Why should China not follow Westerners now? If we are afraid that they are ahead of us, and so do not want to reveal our shortcomings, that would be to conceal one's illness because of hating to see the doctor. If you say that it is not easy to follow in their steps and you fear that eventually you cannot overtake them, that is like stopping to eat on account of choking. In general, blue is distilled from indigo, but it is bluer than indigo; and ice is frozen from water, but it is colder than water. Wu Ch'en taught the Wu kingdom to make the Ch'u weak.[29] King Wu-ling adopted barbarian clothes and later wiped out the barbarians. Learning from others does not necessarily mean that there is no chance to surpass them. How can we know that after several thousand years the Chinese cannot carry further the knowledge of Westerners and develop once more the genius of creators, so that the Westerners will be astonished and dazzled by us?

### *Education Makes European Countries Strong*
### *(A diary entry of Feb. 11, 1891)*[30]

There have never been more laws governing the education of the people in various European countries than there are today. If boys and girls of eight years or older do not go to school, their parents are punished. Certainly there is not a single boy without education; there is not even a single girl without education; even the disabled, the deaf, the blind and the dumb, all receive education. There are free schools to educate people who are without means and the parentless orphans. In country districts there are country schools. In every county and state in the national capital, schools stand like a forest and there are universities, high schools and grade schools. For those just beginning to study, those who have acquired some knowledge, and those who can do advanced graduate work, definite stages of work are all provided... Not only do scholars have schools, but also soldiers, workers, farmers and merchants all have schools...

During the last several decades the schools in Germany particularly have flourished and all other large nations are trying to equal her. Most German soldiers have had some schooling and thus in fighting they are always victorious... The system of popular education as evident today is probably the origin of the rise of the various European countries.

## Use Machinery to Promote Wealth and to Feed the People (1892)[31]

Generally when people use things they seek good quality and cheap prices. This is certainly the tendency of human nature...

Machinery can make what cannot be made by human power... The work of a hundred men can be done by one man with the help of a machine, and the amount of goods produced will necessarily be increased. Yet when the work of a hundred men is done by one man with a machine, the cost is reduced to that of the work of ten men. Then all the people around will try to buy the commodity. If the cost is again reduced to that of the work of two or three men, then everyone will try even more to buy it...

The population of China is ten times [p. 9] that of all the European countries. Critics say that if machinery is extensively used, it will take away the livelihood of the poor people... In the West an intelligent use of machines is a means of feeding the people, whereas China considers the restriction of machines to be a means of supporting the people. If the latter theory is carried through, there will necessarily be some articles which other people can make but which we cannot. Moreover, the cost of work done by one person would certainly be included (in the price of the goods)... Thus it is clear that our articles will not be able to compete with Western goods... Hereafter Chinese products not only cannot be sold to other nations, but cannot even be sold in their own country. Hereafter the Chinese people will not only be unable to support themselves, but further, when they realize that the use of their energy profits them little, they will not exert themselves. Hereafter the Chinese people will not only be unable to produce much to compete for profit with Westerners, but also will try to buy Western goods to supply their own needs, and thereby grossly increase the profits of the Westerners. In these circumstances, how can our commerce fail to decline, the people's livelihood not suffer and the national power not deteriorate? ...

In general, if we use machinary to produce goods, then the profits will accrue to rich Chinese merchants; if we do not use machinery to produce goods, the profits will accrue to Westerners. When the profit is gained by rich merchants, it is still in China, and the surplus can still be shared in order to support our poor people. When the profit is gained by Westerners, the situation is like water gradually drying up and the rice plant naturally withering away, or like oil which is gradually consumed, whereupon the light will certainly go out. The future catastrophe will be beyond description.

## CHAPTER XVI   K'ANG YU-WEI AND SOME OF HIS ASSOCIATES

The written record of China's response to the West in the last few years of the nineteenth century is so voluminous, and so replete with items of literary excellence, that it is difficult even to make a representative selection. This was the time when the carefully trained masters of the Chinese classical style, as yet unadulterated by the new terms and expressions of the modern vernacular style, could turn their fine literary gifts to the truly epic theme of China's extinction or survival. The defeat by Japan in 1894-1895 was a shattering blow to the pride and complacency of the scholar-official class, and the threatening encroachment of Russia, Germany, and the other powers in 1897-1898, in their "scramble for concessions," seemed to foreshadow not only the end of the dynasty but the extinction of the Chinese state itself. Both the reformers of 1898 and their opponents were fully conscious that three thousand years of Chinese history and culture looked down upon them. They all knew their classical texts and argued still by quotations from the sages. Since the sayings of the sages by this time included a number of very pithy utterances, the result is good reading.

The political corruption of the late Ch'ing period as well as the foreign encroachment of the time gave added vigor to the demands of Chinese intellectuals that the government make reforms. The ministers of England and the United States at Peking and missionaries like Timothy Richard and Young J. Allen had also for some time been urging political and social changes after the pattern of the West. Chinese scholars had published warnings① and a distinct trend had set in among the scholar class; by degrees, as they gained more understanding of the West, they had moved from the appreciation of Western weapons to that of ships and railways, and thence to an admiration of Western political and social institutions. Perhaps it is worth noting that many leaders of reform and revolution were Cantonese, who had had direct contact with Westerners in Hongkong and Shanghai. Without attempting to summarize the full sweep of the philosophical issues with which K'ang Yu-wei and his contemporaries were now dealing, we present some brief notes on them followed by passages from their polemics.

K'ang Yu-wei (1858-1927). K'ang's most important work in political theory was a treatise on "the cosmopolitan society" (*Ta-t'ung shu*, A book on the universal commonwealth). Having read widely in Confucian, Buddhist, and Western literature (in translation), K'ang developed his idea of utopia from the *Ta-t'ung* section of the *Book of Rites*. Among other things, he diagnoses the suffering of mankind as due to nine barriers: between nation and nation, between race and race, between territory and territory, between men and women, between one species and another, etc. Were these barriers removed, all would be well. The existence of nations is a source of wars and evils. K'ang proposes a world government under which all national states and armies shall be abolished, while a universal language, calendar, and units of weight shall be used. The governors of the world government shall be elected by the world citizens. In the commonwealth, men and women shall be born free, equal, and independent. There shall be no family restrictions: men and women who have lived together for only one year may renew the relationship or find new partners. Children shall be cared for and educated by the state. There shall be no private property and no class distinctions. All farms, factories, and business enterprises shall be owned and operated by the public. All natural resources shall be scientifically developed. In short, K'ang's utopian universal state is to be a true liberation from national boundaries, from distinctions of class, race, sex, family, property, profession, and species, and free from all injustice and unhappiness. This iconoclasm indicates the vigor of K'ang's thinking, which was more powerful because combined with high scholarship.

When he was twenty-seven, K'ang Yu-wei, although lacking official status, had attempted to submit to the throne his first memorial urging reform. He was looked upon as insane and his memorial was not presented. After the Sino-Japanese peace treaty of 1895, however, K'ang and his student Liang Ch'i-ch'ao, who were taking the metropolitan examinations at Peking, secured some 1300 signatures from among the candidates and presented to the throne the famous "Letter of ten thousand words" (*Wan-yen shu*). The gist of this long memorial, which was subsequently called "The memorial presented by the examination candidates" (*Kung-ch'e shang-shu chi*),[②] was to reject the peace treaty, transfer the capital, and carry out reforms. It also suggested the relaxation of the strict traditional qualifications in favor of men of ability, the increase of salaries to foster integrity and honesty, cessation of sales of official rank, elimination of sinecure offices, reform of the civil service examinations, promotion of more schools and more translations of Western books for the training of men of ability, bestowal of rewards or medals to encourage new inventions, the establishment of agricultural and business schools so as to help the production of wealth and enrich the people, revision of the laws for local government, and promotion of a benevolent policy for protecting the people. The memorial also discussed public health, poor relief, repair of roads, printing of bank notes, the inauguration of shipping lines, transfer of poor people to better regions, study of mineralogy, introduction of insurance for the people, increase of the opium tax, discontinuance of the *likin* tax, construction of more railways and warships, and a number of other topics. K'ang had broad interests.

When Germany compelled China to lease Kiaochow Bay in 1897, K'ang Yu-wei, now a second-class secretary of the Board of Works, wrote another memorial urging the emperor to take as his model the Meiji Emperor of Japan and Peter the Great, decide upon a national policy of reform, and allow provincial authorities to initiate reforms in the areas under their jurisdiction. His associates in the Board disliked K'ang's candid statements and did not present this memorial to the throne on his behalf. In the early part of 1898, however, K'ang managed to have an audience with the Emperor Kuang-hsü and eventually persuaded the young man to issue a Decree announcing a national policy of reform on June 11. This date is usually regarded as the beginning of the Hundred Days of Reform, although some reform Decrees had been issued before (see Ch. XVIII).

K'ang Yu-wei was a follower of the "modern-text" (*chin-wen*) school of classical scholars. He liked to speak rather cryptically of *t'ung san-t'ung*, "going through the three periods of unity," by which he meant that the three ancient dynasties of Hsia, Shang, and Chou were different from one another and reforms should have been made from time to time during them. He was also fond of speaking of *chang san-shih*, "the displaying of the three epochs," by which he referred to a progression from the existing epoch of disorder, through a peaceful epoch to the epoch of world peace. The more reforms were made, the faster would be this progress.③

Without trying here to expound K'ang's interesting political philosophy, it may be pointed out that his veneration of Confucius was at least in part a political device. In his startling book on "Confucius as a reformer" (*K'ung-tzu kai-chih k'ao*), he used his scholarship to show that Confucius had actually created the theory of a golden age in the past so as to persuade contemporary rulers to make reforms as the ancient sage-kings had done. Thus it followed that if Confucius favored change, all Confucianists, patterning themselves after him, should by no means object to it.

*Huang Tsun-hsien* (1848-1905). Huang first gained fame as a young poet. He went to Hongkong in 1870 and recorded his miscellaneous impressions of the good municipal government and of the foreigners' aggression against China. In 1877 he went to Japan and worked as a secretary in the Chinese legation for six years, learning Japanese and associating with Japanese scholars. He was consul-general at San Francisco from 1882 to 1885, in a period when the anti-Chinese labor movement in California left him with a bad impression of the United States. After he returned to China he spent a few years of leisure writing his "History of Japan" (*Jih-pen-kuo chih*), in which a preface and commentary to almost every chapter express his admiration of the Japanese reform movement as well as his hope for a similar development in China. Some of his ideas were advanced and some conservative; he did not admire Western social life, especially the relationship between husband and wife, father and son, and the like. From 1890 Huang was Chinese consul-general at Singapore for a few years and in this period he traveled in England and France.

In 1894 he was called back to China, where the repeated defeats in the Sino-Japanese War inspired him to, write many emotional poems.④ In 1896 Huang made the acquaintance of Liang Ch'i-ch'ao and they became fast friends. In the early fall of the same year he had an audience with the emperor and the latter asked him in what respects the European governments were superior to that of China. Huang's reply was, "The strength of Europe is entirely due to reforms. When I was in London I heard the British gentlemen say that a hundred years ago their government was still inferior to that of China." The emperor, it is said, was at first surprised, and then smiled.⑤

In the following year, after Germany declined him as Chinese minister, Huang was appointed judicial commissioner of Hunan. The governor was Ch'en Pao-chen (1831-1900), a liberal-minded and efficient administrator. Huang and the governor started a reform program and invited Liang Ch'i-ch'ao, T'an Ssu-t'ung, and others to run a school called the "College of current affairs" (Shih-wu hsueh-t'ang). They made public speeches, promoted reform ideas, purchased steamers for the rivers, and planned to build a railroad between Kwangtung and Hunan. At the same time their activities caused much protest from the local conservative scholars. While Huang was in Hunan he presented his "History of Japan" to the emperor, who liked it so much that he asked for another copy. In the summer of 1898 he retired from his post on account of poor health, and recuperated in Shanghai.

Huang's career as a poet indicates how the reformers of the 1890's contributed to the later literary revolution. He was a nationalist, writing in a persuasive emotional style, in order to inspire patriotism, and was probably the first modern poet to introduce Chinese slang into his poems. He also described the landscape of foreign countries and inserted a world viewpoint and Western ideas into his verse, which was classical in phraseology, but had a free form of expression. He said, "I use my hand to describe my mouth [i.e., I write the way I speak], without being restricted by the traditional style."⑥

*Yen Fu* (1854-1921). Yen Fu, although not formally an associate of K'ang, was a significant figure. He studied at Greenwich Naval Academy, and Ku Hung-ming (Ku T'ang-sheng, 1856-1928) at Edinburgh; both worked under Chang Chih-tung, and eventually taught at the Peking University. In their day they were probably the two Chinese scholars most thoroughly learned in Western philosophy and social science. Both admired the West at first but in the latter part of their lives they became conservatives, despised Western civilization, and honored their own. Ku Hung-ming's writings were mostly in English⑦ and there are studies of him in that language.⑧ Yen Fu, however, is best known as a translator of Western books into classical Chinese, and his main contribution was that he introduced Western political, social, economic and philosophical thought to the Chinese society of his time.

When Yen Fu was fourteen years old, he was a student in the naval school attached to the Foochow Shipyard. After his graduation in 1876 he was sent to England for further training in the navy. He was proficient in mathematics and at the same time he took an interest in logic, sociology, jurisprudence and economics. Returning to China, he served as a teacher at the Machiang Naval Academy at Foochow and taught in the naval school at Tientsin. Later on he was for some time the president of Peking University.

In 1897 Yen Fu coöperated with Hsia Tseng-yu (1863-1924) to start a periodical, the "National news" (*Kuo-wen pao*; later called *Kuo-wen hui-pao*), at Tientsin. This journal, issued every ten days, had an unusually wide coverage of materials translated from the Western and Japanese press and helped to spread reform ideas.⑨ In 1898 Yen published in book form his translation of Huxley's *Evolution and Ethics*, which went through numerous editions. The doctrines of the struggle for existence and survival of the fittest caught the imagination of the Chinese literati and soon became common expressions in the mouths of orators and in the writings of journalists. Yen also translated John Stuart Mill's *On Liberty*, Mill's *Logic*, Spencer's *Study of Sociology* and Adam Smith's *Wealth of Nations*. While these translations served to introduce the modern thought of the West, they constituted only a very feeble beginning, and were little understood by the general public.

After the revolution of 1911, Yen Fu became a councillor of President Yuan Shih-k'ai. In 1915 he participated in Yuan's campaign to become emperor and was one of the sponsors of a society working for that purpose, for which he was harshly criticized by his republican contemporaries.

While K'ang Yu-wei developed his thought from Chinese studies, Yen Fu had his intellectual roots in Western works, although his grasp of Chinese was also excellent. The scope of Yen's thinking was at least superficially broader than that of K'ang and in his earlier years he discussed all sorts of reforms with fluency.

In this period, when he favored reform, his criticism was that the reform leaders did not sufficiently understand the West. He said:

Chinese understanding of the necessity of learning Western methods did not begin until after the defeat of China by Japan in 1895. Since the lifting of the ban on Western merchants coming to China by sea, there have been quite a few developments: (1) the Tsungli Yamen; (2) the T'ung-wen Kuan; (3) the Foochow Shipyard; (4) the educational mission to send students to study abroad; (5) the China Merchants' Steam Navigation Company; (6) manufacturing; (7) the navy; (8) the Ministry of the Navy; (9) foreign military drill; (10) the opening of schools; (11) the dispatch of Chinese envoys abroad; (12) the opening of mines; (13) the establishment of telegraph and post offices; and (14) the building of railways. If we count everything, there are more than ten or twenty items. Most of these things have served as the foundations on which Europe became rich and strong, but when we applied them in China, they were like a good orange tree on the bank of the Huai River which, after it was transplanted, produced thick-skinned oranges. The tree looks as if midway between life and death and we do not get the fruit we sought. What is the reason?⑩

I think the greatest difference between China and the West, which can never be made up, is that the Chinese are fond of antiquity but neglect the present. The Westerners are struggling in the present in order to supersede the past. Chinese consider a period of order and a period of disorder, a period of prosperity and a period of decline, as the natural course of heavenly conduct of human affairs; while Westerners consider that daily progress should be endless, and that what has already been prosperous will not decline, and that when things are well governed, they will not be in disorder again—all of which they take as an absolute law of academic thought and political ideas. ⑪

Yen Fu also criticized the idea made famous by Chang Chih-tung (see Doc. 45)—"Chinese culture for the foundation and Western culture for practical use."He says:

The foundation [*t'i*] and the use [*yung*] mean the same thing. The body of an ox should have the use of carrying heavy things; the body of a horse should have the use of carrying something to a distance. I have never heard that the ox is the body or the foundation, while the horse is for use. The difference between Chinese and Western knowledge is as great as that between the complexions and the eyes of the two races. We cannot force the two cultures to be the same or similar. Therefore, Chinese knowledge has its foundation and function; Western knowledge has also its foundation and function. If the two are separated, each can be independent; if the two were combined, both would perish ... If we consider that science consists of techniques, then the Western techniques are actually the foundation of Western government. If we say that science does not consist of techniques, then the two things, government and techniques, are both derived from science like the left and right hands. I have never heard that the left and the right hands can be considered, respectively, as the foundation and the superstructure. ⑫

It is interesting to note how Yen, like many of his generation, eventually reversed his admiration of the West. In his earlier period he had favored a thorough reform but a gradual or evolutionary one, not a sudden change. He desired to have good relations with foreign nations, to have the emperor win the hearts of the people, and to break the political monopoly of the conservatives. He advocated the encouragement of the people's power, the cultivation of their knowledge, and the revival of right conduct on their part. In later years, after 1911 and especially after the European war, Yen Fu's ideas changed sharply. He then considered that the Chinese governmental system and Chinese learning were both better than those of Europe. He said, "The culture of Western countries since this European war has been corrupted completely... I feel that the three centuries of progress of their races have only accomplished four things, that is, to be selfish, to kill others, to have no integrity, and to lose the sense of shame. When we recall the doctrines of Confucius and Mencius, they are really as broad as heaven and earth and their influence is extended to the people all over the globe. This is not what I alone say; even Europeans who have good minds also gradually have got such notions."[13] Thus Yen Fu wound up a conservative who preferred to keep his queue and criticize the New Culture movement.

Amid the great variety of ideas put forward in the 1890's by cultural intermediaries like Wang T'ao and Yen Fu and by reformist scholar-officials such as Hsueh Fu-ch'eng and Huang Tsun-hsien, it required a particularly vigorous personality to take a definite stand and assert leadership. The following is one of K'ang Yu-wei's early calls to action.

### DOC. 41 K'ANG YU-WEI'S STATEMENT FOR THE "SOCIETY FOR THE STUDY OF SELF-STRENGTHENING," 1895[1]

The Russians are spying on us in the north and the English are peeping at us on the west; the French are staring at us in the south and the Japanese are watching us in the east. Living in the midst of these four strong neighbors, and being the Middle Kingdom, China is in imminent peril. How much more so will it be when there are more than ten nations who are sharpening their teeth and watering at the mouth, desiring to share the surplus? The Liaotung peninsula and Taiwan are in confusion, the Mohammedan rebellion is disturbing us, the popular mind is perturbed and the situation seems hardly supportable.

Formerly, India was a celebrated nation in Asia, but she preserved her traditions without changing and so during the time of Ch'ien-lung (1736-1795) the British people organized a company with one hundred and twenty thousand gold as capital to carry on a trade with her and subjugated the five parts of India. Formerly, Turkey was a large Moslem nation. Her territory extended over three continents, Asia, Europe, and Africa, but she was conservative and made no changes; so her government was seized by six nations, her territory was partitioned, and her ruler was banished. Of others, such as Annam, Burma, Korea, Liuch'iu, Siam, Persia, Afghanistan and Baluchistan, as well as those established in Africa and on the islands of the Pacific Ocean, the general number may be estimated at several hundred or one thousand. Actually the (territories of these conservative states) have been either reduced or annexed, and among all the conservative nations on the globe there is probably not a single one which has been kept intact.

Our enfeebled China has been lying in the midst of a group of strong powers and soundly sleeping on the top of a pile of kindling. In adminstration she cares only to prevent evils but does not care to develop sources of profit. Her officials know only how to be law-abiding, but do not know how to judge the trends of the time. Her scholars specialize in the study of antiquity, not in the understanding of the present. Her people can defend their immediate surroundings but cannot go far afield. Mencius said, "A state must first smite itself, and then others will smite it." The defense of the Mongolian leagues, Fengtien, Kirin, Ch'inghai, Sinkiang, Tibet, the native tribes and the frontier guards is all a defense of alien waste land. The fertile soil of Chihli, Shantung, Fukien, Chekiang, Anhwei, Hunan, Hupei, Kwangtung, Szechwan, Kweichow, Yunnan and Kwangsi has become entirely a bandits' granary. It will not be long until we become Turks and Negroes.

Westerners are very strict about races and they look upon other races as enemies. When the French obtained Annam, the way for the Annamese to become rich and ennobled through civil service examinations was cut off, and the former prominent officials have now become silk merchants. England conquered India more than a hundred years ago, but it was not until 1889 that an Indian was elected a member of Parliament. Other native peoples are treated like cattle and horses. If we do not plan in advance, but suddenly are divided among ourselves... then, alas, the fate of our sacred race will be unspeakable, utterly unspeakable!

For China, on the great earth, has had a ceaseless succession of sacred emperors and the country has been very famous. Her principles, institutions, and culture are the most elevated in the world. The vastness of her territory is ranked third among myriads of states, the number of her people is rated the first; her climate is in the temperate zone, her people are intelligent and accomplished, and her soil is rich and productive. Among all countries on earth none is her equal. Only because her customs are unenlightened and because of a dearth of men of ability, she is passively taking aggression and insult. Formerly Tseng Kuo-fan discussed academic problems with wise scholars like Wo-jen and others in Peking, and he deliberated on the method of militia training with various eminent officials like Chiang Chung-yuan and Lo Tse-nan in Hunan; eventually he achieved the merit of suppressing the Taiping Rebellion. In Prussia there was a society established to make the nation strong [*ch'iang-kuo chih hui*] and then she was revenged on her enemy France. In Japan there were people who advocated respect for the emperor and the rejection of the barbarians and hence they accomplished their reforms. Generally, knowledge can be achieved by means of discussion, and men of ability can be produced by encouragement. When the talent and power of many people are combined, then it is easy to assemble the books; and when the minds and thinking of many people are combined, then it is easy to exchange information. The *Book of Changes* says, "Superior men discuss problems with friends." The *Analects* of Confucius say, "Mechanics have their shops to dwell in, in order to accomplish their work. The superior man learns, in order to reach the utmost of his principles." The water in the ocean is bubbling and boiling. In our ears and in our dreams the noise of artillery is roaring. All you gentlemen, how can you avoid the grief of being ruined and (becoming) subject to the rule of a different race? Are we trying to avoid slander? Or you closed-door scholars, are some of you coming to the point of speaking about respecting the emperor and rejecting the barbarians? If you do, not only the teachings of the sacred Ch'ing Dynasty, the two emperors, the three kings, and Confucius, but also the four hundred millions of the people will have something to rely upon.

*Liang Ch'i-ch'ao* (1873-1929). Among all of K'ang Yu-wei's associates the most influential in later years was his student and coadjutor, Liang Ch'i-ch'ao, whose writings will be quoted again below (see Ch. XXII and Ch. XXVIII). Liang was one of the most widely learned scholars and one of the best known writers of modern China. His career may be divided into three stages: from 1890 to 1911 he campaigned for the reform movement and constitutionalism, from 1912 to 1919 he campaigned for republican government, working part of the time as a governmental official, and from 1919 to his death he was a professor at Tsing Hua University. Throughout all these years he produced newspaper articles, research studies, and essays on a voluminous scale.

When he was nine years old, Liang was regarded as a precocious child, and could write long, fluent, classical essays. When he was eighteen he read the *Ying-huan chih-lüeh* of Hsü Chi-yü (see Doc. 6 above) and began to take an interest in Chinese translations of Western works. He became a student of K'ang Yu-wei and a friend of T'an Ssu-t'ung; and was much influenced by K'ang's *Ta-t'ung shu* and T'an's *Jen-hsueh* (see below).

Liang began to participate in the political reform movement in 1895. In the following year he edited at Shanghai the newspaper *Shih-wu pao*, in which he wrote a series of ten articles on "A general discussion of reform" (*Pien-fa t'ung-lun*), some of which are translated below. Chang Chih-tung was impressed and offered him a job, but he declined. He accepted, instead, an invitation of the Hunan governor, Ch'en Pao-chen, to be the dean of the new "College of current affairs. " In Hunan he also joined with Huang Tsun-hsien and T'an Ssu-t'ung in organizing the "Reform association of South China" (Nan-hsueh-hui). They published a newspaper, *Hsiang-pao*, advocating the people's rights (*min-ch'üan*), protection of the nation and the race, and the like. The following extracts indicate the persuasive reasoning by which the reformers of 1898 sought to stand on China's past and yet face modern times.

## DOC. 42  LIANG CH'I-CH'AO ON REFORM, 1896⑮

I. *Preface*. Why is it necessary to reform? In general, there is nothing in the universe which does not change. The change between daytime and evening makes the day; the change from winter to summer makes the year... When the purple or red blood circulates in the body, when second by second carbon is breathed out and oxygen is breathed in, and a thousand changes take place in a day, thus the living person is formed... In ancient China the method of tribute and assistance was changed into the system of land, labor, and poll taxes; the latter three were changed into semi-annual taxes, which again were changed into a unified annual tax... Throughout the span of one thousand years there was not a single time without change, and not a single thing without change...

Those who advocate no change frequently claim, "We follow the ancients, follow the ancients." Do they know that from prehistoric, ancient, medieval and modern times down to the present day, there have been many hundreds of thousands and myriads of changes? ... I have investigated this tendency from ancient times, when one family received the mandate to make laws and establish systems and have them followed for several generations, and yet what their descendants had to obey and put into effect was inevitably different from what their ancestors did. Nevertheless the prince and the people, the upper and lower classes always stubbornly thought that "our laws today were used by our ancestors to rule the Empire, and it was well governed. " They obstinately observed them, following tradition without discrimination. Gradually as time moved on the tradition changed from bad to worse, everything became neglected and finally was so rotten that it was beyond repair. If the one who rose to replace the former rulers examined their defects and reformed them, he would be the new ruler. If the original dynasty's descendants understood this idea, examined the defects themselves and reformed them, then this was called a restoration. The restoration periods of Han and T'ang were like that. The *Book of Odes* says, "Although the Chou [p. 2] is an old kingdom, its life has been renewed." That means that to rule an old country, it is necessary to use new laws... Those who insist that there is no need for reform still say, "Let us follow the ancients, follow the ancients." They coldly sit and watch everything being laid waste by following tradition, and there is no concern in their hearts... The *Book of Changes* says, "When there is exhaustion, there should be change; after a change there is cohesion; when there is cohesion things will be long-lasting." I Yin says, "Make use of the new, dispose of the old, then the illness will not stay..."

II. *On the Harm of not Reforming*. Now here is a big mansion which has lasted a thousand years. The tiles and bricks are decayed and the beams and rafters are broken. It is still a magnificently big thing, but when wind and rain suddenly come up, its fall is foredoomed. Yet the people in the house are still happily playing or soundly sleeping and as indifferent as if they have seen or heard nothing. Even some who have noted the danger know only how to weep bitterly, folding their arms and waiting for death without thinking of any remedy. Sometimes there are people a little better off who try to repair the cracks, seal up the leaks, and patch up the ant holes in order to be able to go on living there in peace, even temporarily, in the hope that something better may turn up. These three types of people use their minds differently, but when a hurricane comes they will die together... A nation is also like this...

India is one of the oldest countries on the great earth. She followed tradition without change; she has been rendered a colony of England. Turkey's territory occupied three continents and had an established state for a thousand years; yet, because of observing the old ways without change, she has been dominated by six large countries, which have divided her territory. The area of Africa is three times larger than Europe and in the interior, except in the desert zone, there are everywhere luxuriant plants and abundant flocks. The native people could not achieve civilization and therefore they meekly handed over their land to strong enemies. Poland was a famous country in Europe. Her political institutions were not developed, internal struggles arose daily. Russia, Prussia, and Austria made mutual agreements and divided her as their meat. The Moslems in central Asia have usually been well known for their bravery and skill in warfare, and yet they observe the old ways without changing. The Russians are swallowing them like a whale and nibbling them as silkworms eat mulberry leaves, almost in their entirety. Annam, Burma, and Korea obeyed and belonged to China. Gradually, they learned bad habits from China and followed corrupt ways of administration, drifting along without change. Now of the dignity and the manner of Chinese officials, nothing remains there.

Russians settled in a land of bitter cold, suffered the yoke of the Mongols and the tyranny of former emperors; the people were so downtrodden that they thought they could not last out another day. After Peter the Great traveled in various countries and learned their techniques, he returned and carried out reforms. [Liang then cites examples from the history of Prussia, Japan, Spain and Holland] [P. 3] Siam lies between Burma and Annam, as thin as a piece of silk, and yet she was roused to action and proudly she still stands. The *Book of Rites* says, "If one knows not the future, one should look at the past." Also it says, "When the cart in front is overturned, the cart behind it should take it as a warning." Among all nations on earth during the last century the cause of their being strong and prosperous has always been the same, and the cause of their being weak and overthrown has also never varied. The crucial difference is as dreadful as that.

The age of China as a country is equal to that of India and the fertility of her land is superior to that of Turkey, but her conformity to the defective ways which have accumulated and her incapacity to stand up and reform make her also like a brother of these two countries... Whenever there is a flood or drought, communications are severed, there is no way to transport famine relief, the dead are abandoned to fill the ditches or are disregarded, and nine out of ten houses are emptied... The members of secret societies are scattered over the whole country, waiting for the chance to move. Industry is not developed, commerce is not discussed, the native goods daily become less salable... "Leakage" [i. e., squeeze] becomes more serious day by day and our financial sources are almost dried up. Schools are not well run and students, apart from the "eight-legged" essays, do not know how to do a thing. The good ones are working on small researches, flowery writing, and miscellaneous trifles. Tell them about the vast oceans, they open their eyes wide and disbelieve it... [Liang next expatiates on a theme developed by K'ang, that China has all the resources of greatness but is held back by her old political institutions.]

[P. 4] My critics may say that the political system of today is not modern but old; it is what the five emperors and the three kings have handed down... and it has been followed from generation to generation for a great number of years... But this dynasty alone has been particularly good at making changes in the fundamental laws for the benefit of society. At the beginning when the Manchus entered Shanhaikuan, they immediately issued orders to shave the hair in the front of the head, to wear peacock feathers and the riding-jacket. Such things did not exist in ancient times and thus they have changed the official costume. They employed Dahai [d. 1632] to create the national script, borrowing Mongolian letters to indicate the Manchu pronunciation, and thus they changed the system of writing. They employed Adam Schall von Bell and Jacobus Rho to make a calendar, using European methods to improve the traditional calendar. Thus they changed the calendric system...

[P. 5] All these examples show that this dynasty changed the laws or systems of preceding dynasties, making them better and better... (Among the European countries) industry is promoted and commerce is protected, because they fear the sources of profits may be captured by others, and the country on account of that may be impoverished and distressed. generals must have knowledge, soldiers must be literate and must drill day and night as if approaching a great enemy; their ships [p. 6] and weapons are up to date, and they really compete in maneuvers, because they feel that if they show the slightest military weakness they will be defeated, probably never to rise again. Other administrative measures are all like this. They make comparisons among themselves and every day stimulate each other. Therefore the talents and the wisdom of their people are learned by emulation, and the prosperity and strength of the countries are always sufficient to enable them to fight against each other...

But this so-called independent or isolated country, China, has never seen great enemies. Proudly she regards herself as high and mighty, and says no one is her equal...

*T'an Ssu-t'ung* (1865-1898). Liang Ch'i-ch'ao's friend, T'an Ssu-t'ung, became a martyr to the Reform Movement of 1898 at the age of thirty-three. He was a precocious and ingenious thinker, and an emotional and heroic young man of high principles. He appears to have had an unhappy family life, owing to maltreatment by his stepmother, but he read widely and intelligently. Both his poems and his prose are written in a delicate style, and the expression of his philosophical ideas in his book, "A study of benevolence" (*Jen-hsueh*), written from 1896 to 1898, may be compared stylistically with classical works. He has generally been viewed as a philosopher and given a prominent position in the history of modern Chinese philosophy.

T'an Ssu-t'ung's ideas were derived from Confucianism, Buddhism, and the Western sciences as well as from K'ang Yu-wei, whom he respected as a teacher. The main tenets of his philosophic thought are contained in his *Jen-hsueh*, in which he recommends for every person the freedom that would be possible were there no boundaries between nations. When the world has no national boundaries, "wars will cease, jealousy will disappear, secret plans will be abandoned, the distinction between you and me will be lost, equality will result, there will be neither noble nor mean, rich nor poor, the world will be really cosmopolitan." The reason human beings cannot reach this kind of society is that numerous restrictions or ties stand in the way. If we wish to bring human beings into a cosmopolitan world, we must necessarily break through these numerous bonds, such as those of profits and emoluments, those of classical studies pursued by silly scholars, those of rulers, of the human relationships, of heaven, of Buddha, etc. After all these bonds have been broken, society will be as vast as the sky or ocean; it will be free from restrictions and thus real freedom will be secured.

T'an Ssu-t'ung's desire to break the bond of allegiance to the ruler may have been influenced by Huang Tsung-hsi's essays "On the ruler" and "The minister" (cp. Ch. Ⅱ). Unlike K'ang Yu-wei, T'an wished to break the restrictions set up by the Manchu rulers as well as those set up by the aggression of foreigners. He subscribed to the idea of China's self-salvation by means of reform. With reform the people would be intelligent, rich, strong and rejuvenated. The method of reform is to create four *t'ung* or "good connections": between the upper and lower classes, between China and foreign countries, between male and female, between oneself and others. When these four lines of connection are not barred, then the way to freedom will be open and the whole globe will be unified.

Because of this fundamental idea, T'an Ssu-t'ung disapproved boycotting or blockading trade with foreigners, nor did he approve of forbidding Chinese to go overseas. He believed that Western trade was beneficial to China—a revolutionary idea which may have reflected the Western view. When he made a study of the *Hai-kuo t'u-chih*, he criticized Wei Yuan's policy of using one barbarian to control another barbarian (see Doc. 3 above). T'an said that this was a foolish policy by which China had suffered repeatedly, as in the T'ang, Chin, and Sung Dynasties. He admired the far-sightedness of Lin Tse-hsü who said that China's disaster would come from Russia. ⑯

T'an Ssu-t'ung considered that Chinese politics during the preceding two thousand years had been a system for bringing the nation to ruin by hypocrites. The best way to struggle for existence and self-salvation was to get rid of the traditional political regulations entirely and adopt a Western system. He considered that the strong points of the West lay not merely in its material civilization; the effectiveness of its ships and cannon was actually based on good government. These ideas seem close to those of Kuo Sung-tao, and more advanced than those of Chang Chih-tung and K'ang Yu-wei. T'an believed that human nature is the same everywhere and that it is fundamentally good, regardless of whether it is Chinese or foreign. Therefore, what Westerners can do, Chinese should also be able to learn, if they make up their minds to do so. Almost alone in 1898 he favored China's "complete Westernization" (*ch'üan-p'an hsi-hua*), and the abandonment or remaking of Confucianism and the traditional culture. The following excerpts are from one of T'an's long letters to a friend. ⑰

## DOC. 43   T'AN SSU-T'UNG ON THE NEED FOR COMPLETE WESTERNIZATION

Your letter says that the technique of studying foreign affairs has not yet been very good, and asks, shall we reform our institutions to provide for better government? Or among the doctrines of the Chinese sages are there some which should not be discarded completely?

Ssu-t'ung thinks that there is no doubt about the doctrines of our sages. It is impossible for us to discard even a little, so how can we do it completely? But the so-called *tao* ("doctrine") is not empty words. It must be accompanied by something [tool or machine] before it can be seen... Without *tao* there will be no *ch'i* [tool or machine]... and without *ch'i* there will be no *tao*... Without the bow and arrow there will be no *tao* for archery; without the carriage and horse there will be no *tao* for charioteering. [T'an goes on to explain that the *tao* or moral conception varies according to the *ch'i* or means of production—a considerable modification of the old Neo-Confucian idea. When the means of production is changed, he says, the *tao* must be changed accordingly. He then discusses the Western family and social relationships between father and son, husband and wife, etc., and finds them good, although most other Chinese of his time thought differently.]

(In the Western relationship) between husband and wife, from the ruler down to the common people, there is never a precedent for taking a concubine and marriage is arranged out of the desire of the two parties. Hence, the couple are devoted to each other, and there is no trouble over jealousy [between wife and concubine]. Among their children also there is no suspicion and envy owing to one's being the son of the wife or of the concubine. Among their friends they honor manners and righteousness; they cultivate sincerity and foster harmony. They share their financial hardships together. The rules of their schools and academies result in the teachers and disciples having clearly marked friendships and duties to each other, which is entirely different from the corrupt conditions of Chinese academies...

[P. 21] Those who slander the foreigners say that they have done all kinds of inhuman things such as gouging out the eye-pupils and hearts (of Chinese children), but who has seen it? If it is really true, why have we never heard of such things being done in their own countries? ... No intelligent person would believe this rumor.

[P. 22] Your letter says that during the last several decades Chinese scholars and officials have been trying to talk about "foreign matters" (*yang-wu*), but that they have achieved absolutely nothing and, on the contrary, they have been driving the men of ability in the empire into foolishness, greed, and cheating. Ssu-t'ung thinks that not only do you not know what is meant by "foreign matters," but also that you are ignorant of the meaning of discussion. In China, during the last several decades, where have we had genuine understanding of foreign culture? When have we had scholars or officials who could discuss them? If they had been able to discuss foreign matters, there would have been no such incident as we have today [the defeat of China by Japan]. What you mean by foreign matters are things you have seen, such as steamships, telegraph lines, trains, guns, cannon, torpedoes, and machines for weaving and for metallurgy; that's all. You have never dreamed of or seen the beauty and perfection of Western legal systems and political institutions... All that you speak of are the branches and foliage of foreign matters, not the root...

We have more than one arsenal, and those at Tientsin, Shanghai, and Nanking are the oldest; but at the time when we need guns and cannon, there are no guns and cannon. We have more than one shipyard, and those at Port Arthur and Foochow are the largest; but at the time when we need ships, there are no ships. Helplessly we have to purchase these things from foreign countries. But the foreigners know that China has no machinery to test the quality of ships and weapons, and no way to distinguish between good and bad, so they sell to China, for an exorbitant price, weapons which have already been abandoned ... And Chinese diplomatic envoys in foreign countries seek a share of the profit. When they receive a remittance and dispatch the officers to make the purchase, they ask for a fee. Consequently, the higher the price, the poorer the weapons... In this way China has wasted several decades. Yet you still consider Chinese scholar-officials to be learning about foreign matters.

Are you not overestimating the various authorities and wishing to wash off their blame? ...

[P. 26] We should extend the telegraph lines, establish post offices to take charge of postal administration, supply water, and burn electric or gas lamps for the use of the people. When the streets are well kept, the sources of pestilence will be cut off; when hospitals are numerous, the medical treatment will be excellent. We should have parks for public recreation and health. We should have a holiday once every seven days, to enable civil and military officials to follow the policy of (alternation between) pressure and relaxation. We should thoroughly learn the written and spoken languages of all countries so as to translate Western books and newspapers, in order to know what other countries are doing all around us, and also to train men of ability as diplomats. We should send people to travel to all countries in order to enlarge their points of view and enrich their store of information, to observe the strengths and weaknesses, the rise and fall, of other countries; to adopt all the good points of other nations and to avoid their bad points from the start. As a result there will be none of the ships and weapons of any nation which we shall not be able to make, and none of the machines or implements which we shall not be able to improve. We should be exact about our units of measure, examine our legal system, and unify our moral standards and customs. When our legal system is established, our culture will be kept intact ...

[P. 30b] Your idea of despising our enemies arises because you think that they are still barbarians. This is a common mistake of the scholars and officials of the whole empire and they must get rid of it. A proverb says, "Know yourself and know your enemy" ["and in a hundred battles win a hundred victories"]. We must first make ourselves respectable before we despise others. Now there is not a single one of the Chinese people's sentiments, customs, or political and legal institutions which can be favorably compared with those of the barbarians. Is there any bit of

Western culture which was influenced by China? Even if we beg to be on an equal footing with the barbarians, we still cannot achieve it, so how can we convert them to be Chinese? ... [P. 31b] Hereafter, Ssu-t'ung will seek more and new knowledge and will not confine himself to what has been mentioned above. If you do not scorn me as crazy, I have even better policies which I would like to explain to you in full. The first is how to raise funds for reform ... The big mansions and the high buildings (of temples or monasteries) can be made into parliaments, schools, and other public offices...

[P. 32] Secondly, how to increase the usefulness of reform. The use of machines depends only on coal and petroleum for power. The consumption of fuel is great and naturally the sources will be exhausted someday. In Western countries, some are trying to collect heat from the earth and from the sun to operate steamships, also to use electricity to operate the railways. The power of the heat from the earth and the sun, however, is very small, and the capital needed for electricity is very large... If we seek the greatest and most unlimited power, we should do better to make use of the tides of the sea. According to astronomers, the power of the tide is governed by the sun and the moon, and it could make the earth leave its orbit temporarily, so that after a long time there would be a difference in the number of days in the year. Now we let it rise and ebb naturally and do not think of making use of it...

Thirdly, how to strengthen the protection of reform. [Under this item T'an Ssu-t'ung states his ambition to improve all the new weapons—including motor boats and balloons—so that China could get ahead of the West.]

Fourthly, how to seek men of ability for reform. In the preceding lines, I have talked about seeking men of ability through change in our school system and in the civil service examinations, and yet the most valuable thing is to have men to shoulder the responsibility at the beginning of the reform. There is nothing better than to urge the gentry leaders of all counties, prefectures, and districts to promote the ideas of abolishing temples and monasteries or of gathering stockholders to open mines or of installing machinery, etc. ... Anyone who is outstanding in achievement or in any type of service or in any economic enterprise which will yield a profit shall be given special honors and ranks, or be allowed to become a member of parliament, and be subsidized and protected by the officials in order to bring his work to a successful conclusion...

*Wang K'ang-nien* (1860-1911). Another of the reformers of 1898, Wang K'ang-nien was a secretary of the Grand Secretariat and is now known as a pioneer in Chinese journalism. After the Sino-Japanese War he became a leading advocate of modernization and reform and in 1896 started the famous newspaper *Shih-wu pao*, published in Shanghai with Liang Ch'i-ch'ao as editor, while he himself served in the capacity of manager. Wang K'ang-nien was an advocate of the people's rights and of their participation in government under a constitutional monarchy. He makes a cautious but persuasive appeal, not for a sudden full democracy, but for a partial adoption of democracy, in terms remarkably suggestive of more recent decades.

## DOC. 44 WANG K'ANG-NIEN ON DEMOCRACY[⑬]

Chinese who discuss governmental systems speak only in terms of governing the people by a ruler. In the West, however, there are democratic countries and also countries governed jointly by the ruler and the people. Chinese scholars are surprised and consider it strange. Nevertheless what is strange about it? In ancient times all who discussed government always gave consideration to the people below. Thus the chapter "Hung-fan" of the *Book of History* says "to deliberate with the common people," and the chapter "Lü-hsing" says, "The emperor frankly consults the people below him." In the *Rites of Chou* it is stated that the official in charge of the provincial administration brought the multitude of people together to ask their opinion... Mencius says, "When the people of the nation unanimously say that someone is capable, then he may be employed; when the people of the nation unanimously say that he is incapable, then he may be removed; and when the people of the nation unanimously say that he may be killed, then kill him." Other such references appearing in the classics are too numerous to be counted on the fingers. This shows that in ancient times those who governed the nation were not without the desire to govern it together with the people.

Nevertheless, there are some people who are apprehensive that power may be shifted downward. They do not know that in a nation governed jointly by the ruler and the people, when there is an important national issue, it is sent to the parliament for discussion and decision, which is then executed by the ruler. If the ruler has a different opinion from the officials, it may be discussed again. If the discussions do not result in a decision, the members of parliament may be changed. That is, the highest power is still held by the ruler.

Some critics say that if the people have rights, then the cruel and the crafty will be ambitious, the violent and unprincipled will act in an overbearing manner, and there will be endless confusion. They do not know that it is in the people's power to elect only the superior and the wise to the parliament, where they cannot carry out their own ambitions without control. Parliamentary members can only discuss a matter and cannot undertake its execution. How can they act outrageously and overbearingly?

Some people say when authority lies in the emperor, it is concentrated; when it lies in the people, then it is divided, and when it is divided a nation cannot be a nation. They do not know that, even though the number of parliamentary members is great, the election is very carefully conducted, and even though the discussions may be complicated, the majority opinion must be followed. When the election is carefully conducted, then there will be few absurd opinions. When the majority opinion is selected, then there will be many who are willing to carry out the decision. This proves that all three arguments are insufficient to cause us worry.

Moreover, at a time like the present, three great advantages will result from the partial adoption of democracy. Formerly in Europe the authority of the emperor was too great, but with the increase of the power of the people the authority of the emperors slightly declined. In China the ruler's power has been gradually lost and it is necessary to have the people's power restored before the emperor's authority can be upheld. Why? Because, although China's governmental systems and laws were said to be initiated by the ruler, yet the rulers in preceding dynasties greatly feared that their descendants might be ignorant of state affairs and might do illegal and cruel things. They therefore repeatedly explained that everything should be patterned after the preceding dynasties, and that no one was to be permitted to make any changes and, thus, all actions were decided upon by precedent. All great officials followed the routine procedure of the documents and all other officers in charge depended entirely on old custom to make their decisions. Then those clerks who were thoroughly familiar with the by-laws and precedents could privately shift matters around. Therefore, the great power of the nation did not rest with the emperor above, nor with the officials in the middle, nor with the people below, but was controlled merely by the clerks, whose purpose was to obtain money to hand down to their posterity. From the beginning they had no great ideals. Therefore they merely sought profit and worked for their selfish purposes, causing evils as numerous as the hair on one's head. The good laws and fine ideas were confused and gradually destroyed.

Not only that; when the emperor stands alone, above the hundreds of officials and millions of people, then his perception cannot reach those below, and his personal power again is insufficient. For this reason when there are omissions in financial accounts, he does not know it. When there are misjudgments in judicial affairs, he is unaware of them. When the work is poorly and corruptly handled, he is not informed. Repeatedly he has warned his people against favoritism and yet his inferiors still resort to their personal connections as before. Repeatedly he has ordered them to keep themselves pure and yet his inferiors are greedy for bribes as before. Repeatedly he has commanded them to observe the law and yet his inferiors cheat as before. His Decrees are severe and earnest, and his officials in appearance seem to be in awe, but actually they make not the slightest change in their bad habits. Can it then still be said that the emperor has authority? If only democracy ["the people's rights" or "people's power"] is partially used, then there will be thousands of ears and myriads of eyes which cannot be covered or beclouded. And when a thousand persons point to one object, it is impossible to avoid seeing it. Whether an order should be put into execution or a prohibition be carried out, everything will be followed according to the emperor's wish. Therefore even though one may say that the people's rights [or people's power, democracy] are partially used, there is no better way than this to carry through the emperor's authority.

Moreover, when the people have no power, they do not realize that the nation belongs to all the people, and they keep at a distance from the emperor. When the people have some power, then they will realize that the nation is their own concern, and they will be drawn close to the emperor. This is probably because close relationships among human beings come from mutual discussions of important matters, from contacts and feelings, and from exchange of ideas. If the emperor majestically appears as Heaven, and the people are humbly looked down upon as grass and weeds, they will think that the empire and the four seas are all properties of the emperor, and that they are merely his slaves and servants. In time of peace, they are indifferent to political affairs and activities. When faced with catastrophes, they will desert the emperor, one and all. They merely blame him for not being able to protect them, but they do not exert their minds and energy in the smallest degree for him. If the emperor governed the nation jointly with the people, then the latter would have contact with his voice and feelings, and affections would naturally grow up. Thus when the people of Western countries see their rulers, they take off their hats to show their respect; whenever they drink wine, they toast the ruler's health; and whenever there are great affairs of state, they all gather to make plans. The reason is that it is necessary to make the people enjoy themselves together with the emperor, so that they can take pleasure in his enjoyment; and to make the people share his worry, so that they take it as their own concern. That is a matter of course.

Considering the national situation in which we find ourselves today, it is even more urgent for us to apply the people's power (to the conduct of public affairs), because when only the emperor's power is employed to fight against the foreigners, he is weak and easily controlled by foreigners. When the people's power is used to stand against the foreigners, then the force is strong and it will be easier to advance our arguments. The Westerners doing business in China often exploit the power of our emperor in order to control our people. If China desires to oppose the foreigners, her power is insufficient; if she wishes to use the objection of the people as an argument, then, because for a long time her people have had no power, no pretext can be derived from them. For this reason, treaties were revised or made without the people's being consulted. When concessions were demanded, and indemnities requested, these were again granted without consulting the people. Other requests, which were detrimental to the nation and to the people, were also unhesitatingly granted as the Westerners desired, in echo-like response. The officers in charge would receive the orders and follow their instructions to carry out the transaction, fearing only that they could not do it soon enough. Thereupon, while the people hated the Westerners, they also turned their hatred against the officials.

In general, when the power of the empire comes from one person, it is weak. When it comes from millions of people, it is strong. That is positively true. Moreover, if people of all provinces are united to plan for a thing, then the spirit of the nation is integrated; otherwise, divided. If the scholars, merchants, and common people can all feel concern about the dangers and difficulties of the nation, then the people will be intelligent; otherwise, ignorant. Therefore, unless we rely on the people's authority, it is impossible to change our disunited spirit to one of concentration and our ignorance to wisdom. What harm would there be? I can only see that if our ancient system is restored, then our sovereignty will be respected and our national position consolidated.

In another essay on "Methods to make China strong,"[19] written about 1898, Wang K'ang-nien repeats his demand for the consolidation of public opinion and restoration of confidence in the administration—specifically, by setting up a parliament and cabinet government, followed by councils at local levels, simplification of the written language, and a multitude of legal, economic, military and other reforms.

# CHAPTER XVII   THE REFORM PROGRAM OF CHANG CHIH-TUNG

Students of modern Chinese history are familiar with the slogan *Chung-hsueh wei t'i, Hsi-hsueh wei yung*, which may be translated, "Chinese learning for the fundamental principles, Western learning for practical application," and which became for a generation the main theme in the debate over China's cultural policy (see above, Ch. Vb). In 1898 it was made famous by Chang Chih-tung (1837-1909), who was both a liberal official who worked for reforms and a conservative scholar who objected to parliamentary government. Some of his industrial efforts have been noted above (Ch. XIII). Because of his significance throughout the decade before and after 1900, we pause here to look briefly at his career and opinions as a whole, out of their chronological sequence.

Chang was born into an official family and received a superb classical education. Shortly after he obtained the *chin-shih* degree in 1863 he began to write memorials to the throne, and by this means made himself famous. He served as governor-general of Kwangtung-Kwangsi for five years (1884-1889), and of Hunan-Hupei for eighteen years (1889-1907), with some interruption as acting governor-general at Nanking. This service enabled him to become an indispensable consultant on all the pivotal affairs of the late Ch'ing government, one feature of which was that the initiative in formulating domestic and especially diplomatic policies was largely exercised by the governor-general, through the medium of their memorials. Eventually, after the death of Li Hung-chang (1901), Liu K'un-i (1902), and Jung-lu (1903), Chang Chih-tung was to become the leading elder statesman in the capital, serving as grand secretary and grand councillor in special charge of supervising the new Ministry of Education (see Ch.XXb). The actual power of his last posts, however, was not great and he could not do much to help the tottering dynasty, which survived him by only two years.

Chang Chih-tung's essential ideas of reform were presented in his widely read book, "Exhortation to study" (*Ch'üan-hsueh-p'ien*).① Written in 1898, this work followed some thirty-eight years after Feng Kuei-fen's essays, *Chiao-pin-lu k'ang-i* (see Ch.Vb). As we have pointed out, Chang's famous slogan was plainly derived from Feng. The two scholars had the same pattern of thought, but Chang, a generation later, had more information, not only about Western technology, but also about Western governmental institutions (*Hsi-cheng*) including the school system, financial management, taxation methods, military preparedness, laws and statutes, and the encouragement of industry. Chang did not esteem Occidental philosophy or political theory. His ideas may be briefly summarized under three headings:

(1) *To save the Ch'ing Dynasty by a revival of Confucianism*. Like Tseng Kuo-fan, and on a similar basis of philosophical conviction, Chang

Chih-tung was thoroughly loyal to the Ch'ing regime. As a high official under three generations of emperors, Chang felt grateful for their magnanimous government, their remissions of taxes, and other benevolent acts toward the people, which he emphatically eulogized, one by one. He tried to prove that Manchus and Chinese were of the same race,② that therefore, to preserve the Chinese race, it was necessary to preserve the Manchus also.

Chang emphasizes Confucianism as the heart of Chinese civilization. He criticizes the translations of the Chinese classics into English, because to him they seem based on the interpretations of vulgar scholars. He himself stresses the "three fundamental bonds/Three cardinal guides" (*san-kang*—the relationships between prince and minister, father and son, husband and wife) and the "five constant virtues" (benevolence, justice, politeness, wisdom and faithfulness). He says, "If one recognizes the importance of the bond between prince and minister, the doctrine of democracy is untenable. If one recognizes the importance of the bond between father and son, the theory that both the father and the son may be equally guilty [instead of the conception that the father is always right] and the abolition of funeral and sacrificial ceremonies is impracticable. If one recognizes the importance of the bond between husband and wife, then the doctrine of equal rights between men and women is impracticable."③ Thus he strongly attacked the institutions of democracy, constitutional monarchy, and Western-style personal liberty, in order to protect the Manchu rulers against revolution. In 1900 he actually suppressed an uprising at Hankow and executed twenty reformers or rebel leaders.

Chang usually adopted a strong, even belligerent, attitude against foreign aggression. This was repeatedly expressed in his memorials against Russia in 1879-1880, against France in 1882-1885, against Japan in 1894-1895, and against Russia again in 1901 during the post-Boxer negotiations in Manchuria. In the latter case his severe criticism of Li

Hung-chang roused the court.④

At Peking, Chang Chih-tung was considered the leader of the Northern Faction, while Weng T'ung-ho (1830-1904) headed the Southern Faction. In Chang's chronological biography (*nien-p'u*), he is said to have regretted he had no steady partisans. Compared with Weng, Chang was rather liberal and certainly more farsighted. He advocated a program of gradual modification based on education rather than the rapid changes which the emperor and K'ang Yu-wei were attempting in 1898. He sharply criticized K'ang's work and favored, instead, a synthesis of Confucianism with Occidental technology and governmental methods (as opposed to governmental institutions). "Chinese learning is the inside knowledge; Western learning is the outside knowledge. Chinese learning is to control the body and soul (of the people); Western learning is to be applied to their mundane affairs."⑤ Thus he formulated variations of his famous slogan.

(2) *To save China by education*. Chiao-yü chiu-kuo, "Save the country by education," was a popular slogan in the 1920's. Upon reading Chang Chih-tung's writings, however, one must be impressed by the extent to which he had been working on that principle several decades earlier. He founded academies in Chengtu (1875) and Canton (1887) and was the patron of publications. With the help of his assistants, he compiled a handbook on study and composition and a selected bibliography of basic Chinese works (*Shu-mu ta-wen*) which is still useful.

Later on he recognized that education was a barometer of the power and prosperity of a nation. He says, "Since ancient times, for the brightness or darkness of the fate of the world, and for the prosperity or decadence of men of ability, the external reason has lain in government, the internal reason has lain in education."⑥ "The strength of Western countries lies in the strength of their schools."⑦ He asks, "How can a race be preserved?" and answers his own question: "With possession of knowledge it is preserved."⑧ "In order to save the current situation we must begin with reform, and reform must begin with the changing of the civil service examinations." ⑨

Chang recommended the establishment of colleges and universities in Peking and in the capital of each province, middle schools in all prefectures, and elementary schools in all districts (*hsien*). The funds of guilds and clan organizations should be spent for the support of elementary schools. Buddhist and Taoist temples should be transformed into school buildings (a very radical idea at that time). In a memorial of 1893 Chang proposed to found a "self-strengthening" (*tzu-ch'iang*) academy and it was established in Nanking in 1896. Foreign professors were invited to teach diplomacy, agriculture, industry and commerce. In December 1895, he also planned to train a "self-strengthening" (*tzu-ch'iang*) army.⑩ The Tzu-ch'iang Academy and the Tzu-ch'iang Army formed the culmination of a generation of the self-strengthening movement. In the following year Chang sent forty students to study in England, France, and Germany, following the precedent of Tseng Kuo-fan's educational mission of 1872.⑪ In the early twentieth century he sent many students to Japan. When they returned he questioned them about foreign countries in great detail; the educational scheme Chang drew up for China when he was minister of education was patterned mainly on that of Japan, and based on information supplied by students returned from that country. Although Chang recognized the importance of education, he was ignorant of educational psychology. His curricula stressed the classics and loyalty to the emperor.

(3) *To save China by industry*. Chang Chih-tung was a pioneer in the modernization of Chinese economic life. In 1889 he opened China's first modern mint in Canton. In 1895 his Tzu-ch'iang Army was moved to Wusung near Shanghai, to form the nucleus of a modern military force industrially supplied and drilled by German instructors. Probably his best known project was the Han-Yeh-P'ing iron and steel works centered at Wuhan, where he also sponsored cotton mills, silk factories, and

tanneries. He introduced bicycles, loading cranes, and other machines to the Wuhan cities, earning for that area the sobriquet of "Chinese Chicago." An ardent advocate of railroad construction, he personally supervised the building of the Peking-Hankow railway. He encouraged the establishment of a merchants' association in each city, and urged the improvement of the tea, silk and other productive industries.⑫ Finally, although his life was so eventful and fruitful, he died a poor man.

His *Ch'üan-hsueh-p'ien* was well received by the throne in 1898 and forty copies were ordered distributed to the high provincial officials for reproduction. Extracts of the more important chapters are translated below.

## DOC. 45   SELECTIONS FROM CHANG'S "EXHORTATION TO STUDY," 1898

### *Rectification of Political Rights*⑬

Nowadays scholars who hate the customs of the times are angry at the foreigners for cheating and encroaching upon us, at the generals for being unable to fight, at the great officials for not carrying out reforms, at the directors of education for not developing schools, and at numerous officials for not investigating industry and commerce. Therefore they promote discussion of the people's rights [*min-ch'üan*, the term used above by Wang K'ang-nien and later used by Sun Yat-sen: "democracy"] in order to get the people to unite and exert themselves. Alas, why use such words that incite disorder!

The doctrine of people's rights will bring us not a single benefit but a hundred evils. Are we going to establish a parliament? Among the Chinese scholars and people there are still many even today who are content to be vulgar and rustic. They are ignorant of the general situation of the world, they do not understand the basic system of the state. They have not the most rudimentary ideas about foreign countries—about the schools, the political systems, military training, and manufacture of armaments. Even supposing the confused and clamorous people are assembled in one house, for every one of them who is clear-sighted, there will be a hundred others whose vision is beclouded; they will converse at random and talk as if in a dream—what use will it be?

Moreover in foreign countries, in such affairs as raising funds [levying taxes] and other financial matters, the emphasis is on the lower house; in other (important) legislation the emphasis is on the upper house. In general one must have moderate wealth in his family to get to be a member of parliament. Nowadays Chinese merchants rarely have much capital; the Chinese people, moreover, are lacking in farsighted long range ambitions. When an important proposal for raising funds is to be discussed, all of them make excuses and keep silent. So their discussion is tantamount to nondiscussion. This is the first reason why there is no use (in having a parliament). [The author goes on to state three more reasons, which we omit.]

[P. 24] Nowadays China is indeed neither impressive nor powerful. Nevertheless, the populace are still content with their daily work because the laws of the dynasty hold them together. Once the doctrine of people's rights is advocated, foolish people will assuredly be delighted; unruly people will rise up; the laws will not be carried out; great disorder will arise on all sides...

Furthermore, the towns will certainly be plundered and churches burned or destroyed. I am afraid that certain foreign countries will be sure to take the protection of their nationals and properties as a pretext and send their gunboats with land forces to penetrate deeply and occupy our territories. The whole country then will belong to others with our acquiescence. Thus the doctrine of people's rights is just what our enemies will like to hear about...

Formerly in France, after a succession of harsh regimes under tyrannical rulers, the people of the whole country were resentful and furious, the higher and lower orders attacked each other, and then she was changed into a republic [*min-chu chih kuo*, lit., a state where the people are the masters]. Our dynasty has been profoundly magnanimous and generously beneficent; and there has been no harsh government. Why bother to urge these steps (which can only result in) disorder and bring woe both to oneself and to the empire as well? ...

An investigation of the origin of the doctrine of people's rights in foreign countries merely reveals the idea that a state should have a parliament where the people can express their general opinion and communicate their group feelings. It is only desired that the people should be able to explain their feelings; it is not desired that they wield any power. Translators have altered the wording to call it "people's rights," which is a mistake. (Note: Americans who have come to China have themselves spoken of the defects of their public elections. The people below usually cherish selfish plans and those above play favorites, which has caused great trouble. Those Chinese who praise it are all talking without thorough investigation.)

In recent days those who have picked up some Western doctrines have even gone so far as to say that everybody has the right to be his own master [*tzu-chu*]; this is even more absurd. This phrase is derived from their religious book. It means that a man is endowed by God with his nature and soul, that every person has wisdom and intelligence, and that all are capable of doing useful work. The translators eventually interpret it to mean that every person has the right to be his own master. This interpretation is a still worse blunder ... [P. 25] Each Western state definitely has a government, and a government has laws. Officials have administrative laws, soldiers have military laws, workers have labor laws, and merchants have commercial laws. The lawyers learn them, and judges preserve them. Neither the ruler nor the people can violate the law. What is suggested by the executive may be argued by members of parliament, and what is decided by the parliament may be dissolved by the ruling dynasty. To say that nobody has the right to be his own master is correct, but how can we say that every person is his own master?

In general the uproar of a market must certainly cease in the end; and in a group of bandits there must be a chief. If people are all their own masters, every family will be selfish for itself, every village will be selfish for itself, every scholar will want to sit and eat, every farmer will want exemption from his tax, every merchant will want a monopoly, every worker will want a higher wage, poor people without an occupation will want to rob or plunder, the son will not obey his father, the pupil will not respect his teacher, the wife will not obey her husband, the lowly will not submit to the exalted, and the weak will be the prey of the strong. There will be no end until mankind is entirely extinct. Certainly there has been no such government among the myriad nations of the earth, nor any such custom among aboriginal and barbarous tribes.

In foreign countries today there are liberal [*tzu-yu*, "freedom"] parties—the Western word actually sounds *li-po-erh-t'e* [liberty]—which means that everything must be just and of benefit to the multitude. The name may be translated "public opinion party," but to translate it "freedom" [*tzu-yu*] is wrong.

As for the policy of strengthening China to resist foreign countries, the only way is to use the principles of loyalty and righteousness in order to summon and unite the moral vigor [*hsin*] of the empire, and to exert the majestic spiritual power of the court toward uniting the strength of the entire country.[14] These are fundamental principles of the universe, which do not change either in ancient or in modern times, either in China or in foreign countries.

### Following the Proper Order[15]

Now if we wish to make China strong and to preserve Chinese knowledge, we must study Western knowledge. Nevertheless, if we do not use Chinese knowledge to consolidate the foundation first and get straight in our own minds what our interests and purposes are, then the strong will become rebellious leaders and the weak will become slaves of others [i. e. , of the foreigners]...

Scholars today must master the classics first, in order to understand the purpose underlying the establishment of education by our ancient Chinese sages and teachers. They must study history, in order to learn the rise and fall of succeeding dynasties of China, and the customs of the empire. They must glance over the philosophical works and belles-lettres in order to become thoroughly familiar with Chinese academic ideas and exquisite writings. And then they can select and make use of that Western knowledge which can make up our shortcomings, and adopt those Western methods of government which can cure our illnesses. These, then, will be beneficial and harmless. As one who is recuperating must first get some energy from rice, and then be offered all sorts of delicacies...[p. 28] so the acquisition of Western knowledge must follow after Chinese knowledge.

In all schools in foreign countries the *Bible* of Jesus Christ must be read every day to illustrate their religion. In grade schools Latin must be learned first to ensure the preservation of antiquity. The map of their own country must be familiar first, before the map of the whole globe is examined, to show that there is a proper order... A Chinese scholar not versed in Chinese knowledge resembles a man who does not know his own surname, or a riding horse without a bridle, or a boat without a rudder; the more profound his Western knowledge the more severe will be his contempt for China. Even though there are such scholars, who have a broad knowledge of things and are equipped with many abilities, how can the country make use of them?

### To Remove the Poison[⑩]

Alas, the harm of opium is the "great flood and fierce beasts" of today, and yet it is even worse. The harm of the "great flood" lasted no more than nine years and the harm of the "fierce beasts" did not extend beyond the capital of the Yin Dynasty. But the perniciousness of opium has been spreading for more than a hundred years and gradually expanding to the twenty-two provinces. Millions of people have suffered from this perniciousness, yet there is still no end to its insidious influence. (Opium) has ruined men of ability, weakened the morale of soldiers, and wasted money...

According to the Confucian *The Analects*: "The Master said, 'If discipline of the people is sought by means of punishments, they will try to avoid the punishments, but feel no shame. If they be disciplined by rules of propriety, they will have a sense of shame and therefore will become good.'"⑰ That is to say, when law cannot govern, the *ming* [reputation or honor] can bring good results. (Note: Ku Yen-wu says: "To use law to rule the people is not as good as to use *ming* to rule them.") The chapter "Hsüeh-chi" [Record on the subject of education, of the *Book of Rites*] says, "If a superior man wishes to transform the people and to perfect their manners and customs, must he not start from the lessons of the school?"⑱ That is, when the government cannot transform people, education is able to transform them. Why?

The beginning of opium smoking by the Chinese starts from laziness. Laziness comes from having nothing to do, which again comes from the lack of knowledge, which again is derived from the lack of information. The knowledge of scholars is taken from classical commentaries and examination papers. The knowledge of officials is taken from case work. The knowledge of soldiers is taken from dull weapons and archaic positional warfare; they are content with these... In general everything can be obtained without exertion, profound thinking, wide acquaintance, or distant traveling. [P. 39] Ignorance produces stupidity in a man; stupidity produces slowness; slowness produces a leisurely easiness; leisurely easiness produces wastefulness. Thereupon the addiction to opium will hit him. These are all caused by lack of learning.

If learned societies [study groups?] are widely organized, people either in the city or in the country, either noble or mean, can learn civil and military theories and techniques. The weak will learn how to read a newspaper, and the strong will learn from traveling. The superior men will harbor the knowledge of the five continents. The humble men will wish to try hundreds of techniques. They will even desire to measure the distances of the stars in the sky and to investigate the earth below, and to search for the southern and northern poles on the horizontal. How could there still be any who turn the day into night and spend the rest of their lives on a bed beside an opium lamp? Even if they were tempted they would not do it. How much less will it be necessary to forbid them?

Therefore I say, the development of education is the medicine to use for the suppression of opium…

## On Reform⑩

Reform [*pien-fa*, lit., a change of statutes] is the duty of the court. Why should it be discussed with scholars and the people? … The decision as to whether our system should be changed rests with the state, but actually it is determined by the wishes and discussions of scholars and the people.

Let us review events: when Tseng Kuo-fan was a vice-minister, he once submitted a memorial pointing out the defects of examining the Hanlin scholars in small-model writing and in the composition of poetry and the *fu* verse. After he was successful and became a state minister, if he had kept up [and taken action on] this criticism, he would have produced many men of ability in the Hanlin Academy during the last thirty years. Yet nothing more was heard about the matter. Why? Because after the great rebellion had been suppressed, he became fearful lest he be vilified by the contemporary scholars.

Wen-hsiang once opened the T'ung-wen Kuan and published various books on international law and the natural sciences. If he had kept on promoting these things, he would have been able to obtain many men qualified to be sent to distant countries and thoroughly familiar with current affairs. Nevertheless, those who are careful about trifles and feel self-conscious warned one another against entering the T'ung-wen Kuan or taking the examinations for secretaries of the Tsungli Yamen. Among the capital and court officials those who can discuss new knowledge are silent and unheard. Why? Because they were impeded by the erroneous ideas of all the absurd and narrow-minded scholars. Thus, even a meritorious minister [Tseng] and a venerable statesman [Wen-hsiang], though celebrated for their virtue and great authority, still cannot avoid being hindered by the criticism of those who are accustomed to using the wrong to overcome the right, and so no good effect can be seen. This is pitiful and lamentable!

Again, Tso Tsung-t'ang established a shipyard near Foochow and an arsenal and a woolen mill in Kansu; Shen Pao-chen set up the shipyard administration, opened schools, and consulted with Li Hung-chang in establishing the China Merchants' Steam Navigation Company; Ting Pao-chen instituted arsenals to make foreign guns and bullets in both Shantung and Szechwan—these were famous ministers who were known at the time to be honest, upright, and orthodox Confucians. Nevertheless, the things they undertook were all this kind of enterprise. At that time it was in the middle of the T'ung-chih period [1862-1874] and the first years of the Kuang-hsü period [1875-1908], when the nation was quiet and at ease. Unfortunately, current opinion caviled at many points, and those who followed (the men mentioned above) were again lacking in knowledge. They either let their establishments go to waste or operated them in a reduced form. None of them could achieve any expansion. Therefore the effect was not great.

In general, that which should not be changed is our human relationships and fundamental principles, not the system of laws; it is our sage's way, not instruments; it is the principle of the mind, not technology. Let us find evidence from the classics.

When all alternatives are exhausted, one has to make a change—change and accommodation to make the most of an advantage; change and accommodation to suit the time. The method of diminution and increase [of the statutes] should be used to keep abreast of the times. That is the idea of the *Book of Changes*.⑳

"In instruments we do not seek old ones but new."㉑ That is the idea in the *Book of History*. "Knowledge exists among the four barbarians." That is the idea in the *Commentary on the Ch'un-ch'iu*.㉒ The Five emperors did not follow the old music and the three kings did not copy the old ceremony. "The timely ceremony is the most important." That is the idea of the *Book of Rites*.

"He cherishes his old knowledge and is continually acquiring new㉓ ... When I walk with two persons, they may serve as my teachers; I select their good qualities and follow them." That is the idea of the Confucian *The Analects*.㉔

"When he employs (these virtues) they will be in accordance with right." That is the idea of *The Doctrine of the Mean*.㉕ "When one has no sense of shame for not being equal to others, what will he have with which to be an equal of them?"; that is the idea of Mencius.㉖

Let us find evidence from the histories... In the successive dynasties the most conspicuous reforms are these four: King Wu-ling of Chao [*ca.* 300 B. C.] reformed the traditional military system (from foot soldiers) to mounted archers, and by means of this the Chao frontier was made secure. King Hsiao-wen [A. D. 467-499] of Northern Wei reformed the traditional system toward a more civilized one, by means of which the Wei kingdom was well governed. These were gains from reform ... Shang Yang reformed the traditional system [359 B. C.], casting off filial piety, younger brotherhood, benevolence and righteousness. The Ch'in state remained strong for a time and then fell into distress. Wang An-shih (1021-1086) conducted a reform by devoting himself to harassing the people. The Sung Dynasty was thereby involved in disorder. These were losses from reform. The error of Lord Shang and of Wang lay in the cruelty of harassing the people. It was not because the reform should not have been made, but because these particular reforms were improper.

(Note: In Western political systems two things, the elimination of punishments and the feeding of the people, are matters of priority.) ... There have been many changes (in the Ch'ing Dynasty). Even when steamships and telegraph wires were first introduced, there was much criticism. But at the present time, if anyone wished to discard them, would there not be people who would bare their arms and fight against the proposal?

Now those who reject reforms generally belong to three categories [p. 20]. One consists of the narrow-minded scholars who are ultra-conservative; the defects of ultra-conservatism are easy to understand. Another consists of the vulgar officials who like to take improper ease. For reform we must tax our thinking, must collect funds, must select people, and must do actual work. These are all inconvenient to the selfish plans of those who are confused and lazy, and who like to shirk work, to be influenced by favoritism, or to take the easiest tasks. Therefore, under the cover of bookish and conservative talk, they gloss over the subterfuges of slippery officials who take improper ease. Such are their true feelings. When asked about their academic ideas and the governmental principles of the Chinese traditional system, all is revealed to have been neglect and sham on their part. They have not done a single thing. This is what they [the critics] mean by "follow the ancients." Is this sound? The third kind consists of the talkative scholars who like to be captious. Actually, in recent years there have been some imitations of Western methods which bore no fruit.

There are, however, four reasons for this. The first is, all people care for their selfish purposes, and so they plan only for themselves and no progress is made—for example, the various officials in charge of factories and the various people who went abroad. This is a defect of the people, not the defect of the reform. The second is the inadequacy of funds. From this comes a deficiency of money on all sides which prevents superior products, such as the shipyards. This is a defect of the times, not the defect of reform. Third, there is no fixed policy at Court. A new thing may be suddenly taken up and then suddenly suspended, with nothing accomplished, such as the sending of students abroad and of officials from the capital to travel in foreign countries. This is the defect of unfounded reports [as to their behavior], not the defect of reform. Fourth, there are instruments but no personnel to handle them. When we had not yet learned mechanical engineering, we bought machines; when we had not yet trained captains or admirals, we purchased a fleet—such were our navy and the various factories. This is the defect of having the wrong sequence in what should go first or later, not the defect of reform. Nevertheless, there is the idle talk of people not on the scene, who do not trace the causes of the [following] unfortunate results: the fluctuations of national policy, the carelessness in employing people, the decentralization of responsibilities, the insufficiency of funds, and the half-hearted effort in our studies. But they cavil at trifles and reproach us for producing little result. They are even worse than the person who "looks at a crossbow and immediately expects a roast dove before him; or who sees an egg, and immediately expects to hear it crow."㉗ When schoolhouses are just being built, they demand accomplished men of ability. When a mine has not yet been opened, they demand that it pay a profit. There is no fixed standard in handling matters and no fixed aim in personnel. When some state affair is urgent, then everything is taken up; and when things have slowed down, then everything is again put aside. One digs a grave, the other fills it up. How could we expect any success?

### Condemnation of Attacks on Missionaries㉘

Attacks of different religions upon each other have always occurred since the time of the Chou and Ch'in Dynasties. The Confucianists and the Mohists attacked each other... In the T'ang [618-907] the Confucianists and the Buddhists attacked each other. In the later Wei [386-534] and Northern Sung [960-1127] the Taoists and the Buddhists attacked each other... By the present day right and wrong have been greatly clarified...

Now the essential thing to do for the disciples of our sages who fear the decadence of the sacred doctrine, and who desire to protect it and enlarge its influence, is to cultivate good administration and not struggle against other religions. This is the difference in circumstances between ancient and modern times.

Since the beginning of large-scale communication between China and the West, Western churches have spread all over China. Missionary work has been permitted by treaties, and the burning and destruction of churches again have been clearly forbidden by Imperial Decree. Recently Germany took the incident of missionaries being killed in Shantung as a pretext, and occupied Kiaochow. All the other countries also took this opportunity to make demands. A crisis for China becomes daily more imminent. Purposeful scholars should work hard to gain knowledge, and should stimulate their sense of loyalty and righteousness, in order to clarify the great duty of respecting parents in China, and should discuss the important methods of making China wealthy and strong. When our national power becomes daily stronger and the Confucian influence increases accordingly, then the foreign religions will be merely like the Buddhist monasteries and Taoist temples, which we may leave to their natural fate. What harm can they do us? But if we remain decadent and self-indulgent, and cannot put the academic principles and governmental techniques of Confucius and Mencius into actual practice; if our knowledge is inadequate to meet the needs of society, and our talent and strategy are insufficient to extend our national prestige; and if we merely seek for victory by cursing others, what is the good of that? Not only is there nothing to be gained by it, but also if scholars advocate this idea, then foolish people will respond to it, disloyal people will take this opportunity to rise, and rebels of secret societies and disbanded soldiers will find some opportunity to loot or plunder and start turmoil for no reason... [p. 51].

Not only that, but also our knowledge about the sea [i.e., about overseas countries] is gradually becoming more intimate, and the barriers between China and the West are gradually vanishing. When foreigners travel in the interior, ignorant men and children, upon noting their Western costumes, follow them with clamorous shouts and try to drive them away by stoning them with pebbles. They all arise in an uproar, no one knowing what the matter is, nor do they ask whether the foreigners are missionaries or nonmissionaries, Europeans or Americans. In general, to curse and attack people without reason is impolite. Europeans are not of one kind. Some of them are employed by the customs office; some are employed by a government office; some are travelers and some are missionaries. To be blind and make no distinction, to get angry against them all is ignorant and foolish. To disobey the Imperial Decree is unlawful. To attack one or two persons with a crowd of several hundred people is unchivalrous. To be timid in public war but courageous in private strife is to be destitute of shame. Therefore foreigners frequently say that China is uncivilized. When our people are crazy like this, how can we excuse ourselves?

As for the popular rumor that in churches there are frequently cruel actions, such as that the pupils of human eyes are gouged out, to be mixed with chemicals to make corrosive acids, or to transform lead into silver, these are all false rumors ... Were there such things, then the peoples of the Western nations would have been entirely destroyed by the churches long ago ... If we say that they do not injure Westerners but harm only the Chinese people, then where did they get their medicine, their corrosive acids and their silver bars, for the one thousand years or more before they had contact with China? Moreover, the amount of medicine and corrosive acids which are needed by all foreign countries and the silver bars which they import each day are already innumerable. Even though there are churches in all Chinese provinces, how can they kill several myriads of their converts every day, and daily pick out several myriads of eyeballs to supply the demand? A proverb says, "A stray bullet stops on an entrenchment, and an unfounded rumor stops with the wise." The gentry class and learned scholars all have the responsibility of inspiring and leading the foolish and the ignorant. We must carefully avoid the covert ridicule of our ignorance by foreign people.

## CHAPTER XVIII   THE FAILURE OF 1898

The repeated memorials of K'ang Yu-wei and others and K'ang's books on reform in Russia and Japan, which were presented to the court in the spring of 1898, raised the issue of reform among some liberal officials, and, most important, in the mind of Emperor Kuang-hsü himself, who then enjoyed much greater power than he had ever had since he attained his majority in 1889. On June 11, 1898, the emperor issued his first reform Decree, recognizing the need for a change. On the same day, a reader of the Hanlin Academy, Hsü Chih-ching, recommended to the throne that K'ang Yu-wei, Liang Ch'i-ch'ao, Huang Tsun-hsien and others be appointed advisors to the emperor in the promulgation of the proposed reforms. K'ang was given the privilege of a personal audience with the emperor on June 16, and he was subsequently appointed secretary of the Tsungli Yamen and granted the privilege of submitting his memorials directly to the throne. Emperor Kuang-hsü and the reform leaders were all ideologists inexperienced in politics, and they issued scores of reform Decrees hastily, without studying the political and social scene to see whether the new reforms could be effective. These Decrees dealt with important scientific studies, the adoption of Western military drill, the improvement of agriculture and education, the abolition of the eight-legged essay in the official examinations, the promulgation of a public budget, the dismissal of conservative officials, and the abolition of sinecure positions, etc. They evoked strong opposition from officials entrenched in lucrative posts and from students whose chief training was in the eight-legged essays. The conservatives urged the Empress Dowager

Tz'u-hsi to suppress the reform movement, lest even her own position be endangered. On September 21, the emperor was imprisoned by order of the Empress Dowager, who resumed the regency. The conservatives and anti-reformists now held full sway, advocating policies which were eventually to culminate in the Boxer Uprising. First, let us present the complicated situation within the court, and then describe the even more complicated and kaleidoscopic ideas of the conservative scholars.① Since K'ang and Liang had risen to power from the status of commoners only a few months earlier and had the self-righteousness of reformers, they stirred up violent objections from the conservatives.

### a. *The Court and the Emperor*

Within the struggle for reform subordinate struggles went on between conservatives and liberals, between Manchus and Chinese, between England and Russia, and, most important, between an autocratic aunt, the Empress Dowager, and her nephew, the emperor. The Empress Dowager cared for little but her family's fortunes. If she had been somehow placed at the head of the reform movement, in the most prominent position, her opposition might have been lessened. Yet in any case there would still have been a struggle because the power of Tz'u-hsi was built on her favorite eunuchs and on the conservative officials whom she protected, while the emperor was the actual head of the reform movement. Without removing the Empress Dowager's people, the reformers could not carry out their policies, while if she accepted their proposals, her power would collapse. The reform effort threatened her directly and also endangered the positions of the high conservative officials who were its main object of attack. If the emperor, as a reformer, wielded real power, the conservatives including the Empress Dowager could not maintain their privileges. The top Manchu military commander, Jung-lu (1836-1903), was entirely dependent on the Empress Dowager and opposed reform to protect his own position. Hsü T'ung (1820-1900), an associate grand secretary, was another conservative minister. The emperor disliked him so much that he had been summoned for only one interview during the long interval between 1887 and 1898. But because he was trusted by the Empress Dowager, he had not been dismissed.

In this period there were Southern and Northern Factions in the court. The Empress Dowager favored the Northern Faction headed by Hsü T'ung and Li Hung-tsao (1820-1897), a sub-chancellor of the Grand Secretariat. The emperor favored the Southern Faction led by his tutor, Weng T'ung-ho (1830-1904). Kang-i (d. 1900), another favorite of the Empress Dowager, tried his best to block the reforms and strongly advocated deposing the emperor. Needless to say, the notorious eunuch Li Lien-ying (d. 1911) was a staunch opponent of any new elements in the government. Jung-lu, Kang-i, and Li Lien-ying banded together to fight reform.

Among the high provincial officials, only the Hunan governor, Ch'en Pao-chen, carried out the reform Decrees effectively. Others, like the governor of Shantung and the governor-general of Szechwan, were partisans of Jung-lu. Pretending to observe the orders, they actually disobeyed them. The governor-general at Canton (T'an Chung-lin) and at Nanking (Liu K'un-i) also took their lead from Jung-lu. When the emperor urged them to enforce the reform edicts, Liu made the excuse that the official documents had not yet been received, while T'an at Canton did not even bother to reply.

Among the censors, those who criticized the reforms all had connections with conservative ministers. Even if he had not had such contact before, as soon as a censor criticized the reformers, he was immediately patronized by the conservative leaders. For instance, there was a provincial graduate, Tseng Lien, who presented a memorial requesting that K'ang Yu-wei be killed. His motive was not clear, but Hsü T'ung was so pleased that he immediately invited Tseng to his house, treated him as an honored guest, and soon after recommended him to a post as prefect. Among the courtiers, Weng T'ung-ho was basically a conservative, and had been the most trusted tutor of the emperor for a long time. When Weng saw that the emperor now trusted K'ang Yu-wei and others more than himself, he was very jealous and afraid that his own position might be jeopardized.

When orders were initiated to dismiss sinecure officials and abolish offices such as the Supervisorate of Imperial Instruction, the Transmission Office, the Banqueting Court, the Court of State Ceremonial, the Court of the Imperial Stud, the Court of Judicature and Revision, the three governorships of Hupei, Kwangtung, and Yunnan, and other government posts, many high officials faced the immediate loss of their jobs. Many provincial and metropolitan graduates were confronted with the loss of their opportunity to become officials. The idea of transforming monasteries or temples into school buildings seemed deceptively simple; yet at that time the higher class of monks and nuns usually had contact with the eunuchs in the Forbidden City and had direct or indirect associations with the Empress Dowager. When the monks whispered to the Empress Dowager's eunuchs that the temples or monasteries might be torn down or used for other purposes and that all eunuchs might be dismissed, the latter tried their best to persuade the old lady to stop the reform movement as soon as possible.

In general, the reform leaders were mostly, if not entirely, Chinese and the objectors to reform were in large part high Manchu officials. Kang-i said that reform was for the benefit of Chinese at the cost of the Manchus. Another Manchu accused K'ang Yu-wei of distinguishing between loyalty to the throne and patriotism toward the country, and of desiring to protect the four hundred million Chinese by putting the Manchu dynasty aside. In July of 1898 the wife of a board president wept before the Empress Dowager, saying that all Manchus would be dismissed; this charge is said to have affected the Empress Dowager so much that she decided to take ruthless action against the reformers. With the help of her old friend, Jung-lu, she carried out her decision by the famous *coup d'état* of September 1898. Six reform leaders, including T'an Ssu-t'ung, were eventually executed and the emperor was imprisoned for the rest of his life. When it came time for the old lady to die in 1908, her hapless nephew preceded her by one day.

The following interview between Emperor Kuang-hsü and K'ang Yu-wei took place on the crucial date of June 16, only five days after the emperor had embarked upon the famous Hundred Days. Since the account was written by one of K'ang's students after his death, K'ang is referred to as "our late teacher" (*hsien-shih*). Presumably this represents the "Modern Sage's" own version of the conversation.

## DOC. 46  K'ANG YU-WEI'S CONVERSATION WITH THE EMPEROR, JUNE 1898[2]

Early on June 16 our late teacher entered the Court anteroom, where he happened to meet Jung-lu. With Jung-lu he discussed informally the matter of the governmental reforms. When Jung-lu entered and had his audience with the Emperor, he personally attacked our late teacher for using sophistry to disturb the government. After Jung-lu withdrew our late teacher went in for his audience. After the Emperor had asked about his age and his qualifications, the teacher said, "The four barbarians are all invading us and their attempted partition is gradually being carried out: China will soon perish."

The Emperor said, "All that is caused by the conservatives." The teacher reverently said,[3] "Your Majesty's sacred intelligence has thoroughly understood the root of the illness; and since Your Majesty has understood the root of the illness, the medicine is right there. Since Your Majesty knows already that the conservatives have caused the disaster and failure, then unless we change the old institutions entirely and make them new again, we cannot make ourselves strong."

The Emperor said, "Today it is really imperative that we reform."

K'ang said, "It is not because in recent years we have not talked about reform, but because it was only a slight reform, not a complete one; we change the first thing and do not change the second, and then we have everything so confused as to incur failure, and eventually there will be no success." The Emperor agreed with him.

Our late teacher again reverently said, "The prerequisites of reform are that all the laws and the political and social systems be changed and decided anew, before it can be called a reform. Now those who talk about reform only change some specific affairs, and do not reform the institutions." He also requested that a bureau be opened first of all to study the various systems. The Emperor gave his consent.

The teacher again reverently presented his views: "With regard to the matter of reform, your minister [K'ang] has traced the causes of the reforms in all nations and their multiple functions, in order to ascertain which may be adopted and applied in China, and he has considered and modified them to prepare a complete set of rules and regulations. If Your Majesty has made up his mind to reform the institutions, it may serve him for reference." The Emperor said, "Your reform program is very detailed." The late teacher then replied, "Your Majesty's sagacity has already noted it. Why not vigorously carry it through?"

The Emperor glanced outside the screen and then said, with a sigh, "What can I do with so much hindrance?" The late teacher understood that the Emperor had difficulties and so he continued to present his views, saying, "According to the authority which Your Majesty is now exercising to carry out the reforms, if he works on only the most important things, it will be sufficient to save China, even though he cannot make a complete reform. Nevertheless, today most of the high ministers are very old and conservative, and they do not understand matters concerning foreign countries. If Your Majesty wishes to rely on them for reform, it will be like climbing a tree to seek for fish."

The Emperor said, "All of them are inattentive to their work." The late teacher replied, "These high officials are not inattentive. Unfortunately they have been transferred and promoted by the traditional system of qualification, and when they come to high positions, their spirit and energies are already declining [p. 27]. Moreover, they hold concurrently many positions and actually they have no leisure time, nor have they any way to acquire new knowledge. Really, they cannot help it. If Your Majesty wishes reform, the only thing to do is to promote and make use of the lower officials, increase the channels by which they are recommended, summon them to audience, and employ them without following tradition. Now the Grand Council and the Tsungli Yamen are both using such officials on commissions. If we use the directors and subdirectors of the ministries and the censors to take care of the domestic and foreign commissions, everything could be managed. As for the old officials, let them stay on for the time being. But they are conservative in every way, and so I request that Your Majesty issue more Decrees to make them aware of your real intention. All reform matters should be proclaimed by special Decrees and then they will have no way to refute or criticize them... Since the ceding of Taiwan [1895] the people have been alienated from the government. If we wish to stir up the determination of the officials and consolidate the minds of the people, nothing can accomplish it unless Your Majesty issues a Decree filled with grief and pathos." The Emperor said, "Yes."

Our late teacher again presented his views: "The trouble today lies in the non-cultivation of the people's wisdom, and the cause of the non-cultivation of the people's wisdom lies in the civil service examinations based on the eight-legged essays. The eight-legged essay writers do not read the books written since the Ch'in and the Han, nor do they investigate the facts about all the nations on the globe. Nevertheless, they can be enrolled as officials, and eventually reach high positions. Today, among the numerous array of ministers none of them can adapt himself to circumstances, because all of them achieve high positions through the eight-legged essay examinations." The Emperor said, "It is so. Westerners are all pursuing useful studies, while we Chinese pursue useless studies. Thus the present situation is brought about."

Our late teacher replied, "Since Your Majesty is already aware of the harm of the eight-legged essay, could we abolish it?" The Emperor said, "We could." Our late teacher replied, "Since Your Majesty already considers that it can be abolished, may I request that Your Majesty immediately issue a clear Decree, which should not be sent down for discussion by the ministries. If it is sent down to be discussed by the ministries, the ministers would refuse to put it into effect." The Emperor said, "Yes."

The Emperor said, "Today our anxiety, is over poverty and how to raise funds." Our late teacher briefly remarked that everywhere in China there are mineral resources and means of producing wealth. We should simply find ways to open up the material resources, and then we need not worry about the insufficiency of our financial resources. Our late teacher again presented his views in detail on the translation of books, the sending of students to study abroad, the dispatching of high officials to travel abroad, and such matters. After he had finished one topic, he would pause for a time to await the command of the Emperor. When the Emperor still did not order him to arise, he again discussed the employment of the right persons and the execution of administrative affairs. Finally he spoke about promoting ideas of reform in society in order to inspire [p. 28] the wisdom of the people and to encourage their spirit. He also talked about inviting surrender from and pacifying the rebels in the secret societies. He took this opportunity to express his gratitude for the Emperor's favor in affording protection when the *Pao-kuo-hui* ["Society for protecting the nation"] was accused. The Emperor nodded and said, "Yes." After a long time the Emperor nodded and said, "You should withdraw and take a little rest." And again he said, "If you have something more to say you may prepare memorials to state your suggestions in detail and send them here." Our late teacher then arose and went out. The Emperor's eyes escorted him to the door.

The Manchu attendants (*su-la*) met K'ang and asked him questions because there had never been so long an audience—more than five hours [*shih-k'o*, presumably "ten quarters" of the two-hour period then used as the chronological unit].

The repeated references to the example of Japan, in the writings of the reformers already quoted, indicate how after 1895 Chinese hatred of the recent enemy had gradually become mixed with admiration. Some Chinese thought of studying in Japan, and Japanese Restoration leaders were welcomed in China. Among them was Itō Hirobumi, who visited Peking in the autumn of 1898. On that occasion, a number of Chinese officials suggested making use of Itō's ability to assist the Chinese reform movement, and also to consolidate the bond between the two countries. Fu K'uei, a *chü-jen* of Kweichow, urged that he be made the chief minister of the Chinese government in order to carry through the new reforms. Since Itō was so highly esteemed by various officials as the rebuilder of Japan, and since the emperor had been remaking his own administration, on paper, for three hectic months, he granted an interview to Itō on September 20, 1898, when the Reform Movement was just about to come to an end.

## DOC. 47  ITŌ'S CONVERSATION WITH THE EMPEROR, SEPTEMBER 1898④

Itō memorialized saying [p. 273], The alien minister (Itō) Hirobumi on this occasion has come to your honorable country for the purpose of travel. Today he is given this audience of Your Majesty; it is a great honor for him indeed. He sincerely hopes that Your Majesty will reform your former institutions, and energetically plan for the wealth and strength of the country. It goes without saying that this will have an important bearing on the maintenance of the existing situation of peace in

Eastern Asia. Hirobumi's traveling is at an end, and he is returning to his country to report to His Majesty the Emperor; His Majesty will necessarily be heartily pleased. Hirobumi reverently hopes Your Imperial Majesty will live ten thousand years!

After Itō had presented his memorial, [Emperor] Kuang-hsü bade him sit down, and then the conversation went on as follows:

*Kuang-hsü*: We have heard of the great reputation of your Excellency for a long time. To have this chance to see you unexpectedly today is indeed a great pleasure.

*Itō*: That today Your Majesty should not be ashamed to grant me this interview, so that I may come to within a few feet of your Imperial countenance—for me there is really no greater honor than this.⑤

*Kuang-hsü*: Have you been safe and comfortable on your trip?

*Itō*: Under the great blessing of Your Majesty, I have been very safe and comfortable on my trip.

*Kuang-hsü*: Is His Majesty the Emperor of your honorable country well?

*Itō*: This time after I had decided to take this trip, I entered the palace to have an interview and found that his Imperial person was very well.

*Kuang-hsü*: The government of your honorable country after its reforms has been praised by all nations. The contribution of your Excellency to your fatherland has been really admired by all people.

*Itō*: This is too generous a compliment, an honor which I by no means deserve. Your alien minister was merely considering the august model set by His Majesty, the Mikado, and performed the duty of an official.

[p. 274] *Kuang-hsü*: The two countries, yours and ours, are geographically situated on the same continent [Asia] and are the nearest to each other. At the present time reform is pressed upon our country by necessity. We are willing to hear an opinion expressed by your

Excellency, and we request your Excellency to tell our princes and great ministers of the Tsungli Yamen in detail the process and methods of reform, and give them advice.

*Itō*: I have reverently received your Decree. If your princes and great ministers will make inquiries, your alien minister, in accordance with what he has actually seen, will certainly sincerely explain to them whatever is beneficial to your honorable country.

*Kuang-hsü*: To coöperate constantly and whole-heartedly with your honorable country, and to continue perpetually the close relations between the two countries is our most earnest hope.

*Itō*: The august intention of His Majesty, the Mikado of my country, is truly the same. If this intention could widely prevail among the peoples of the two nations, then it would be really an easy matter for our relations to become closer daily...

The remaining conversation is conventional and without great significance. After the interview, Itō was honored by a banquet.

## b. *The Conservative Opposition*

The opponents of the reformers of 1898 offered little new in the way of theory or ideology. They contented themselves mainly with the invocation of traditional principles, in the effort to combat change. Nevertheless, their arguments were often both learned and ingenious, and they form an instructive part of the record.⑥

In their political ideas, the anti-reformers may be divided into two large categories. The first consisted of conservatives who unconditionally objected to change. They thought that China should be governed as of old, by men and by virtue, and maintained that ancestral institutions should never be abrogated under any conditions. The second category were not so absolute in their objections: some believed that Chinese ways were simply better than Western ways, so that no change was needed. Others recognized certain superior qualities in Western institutions, but believed they were not suitable to Chinese society. The most they would grant was that some Western methods and governmental policies might be imitated, although K'ang's reform program as a whole would bring only harm. The most serious harm would be to corrupt the minds of the common people, for the superior quality of Chinese institutions lay in government by the superior men of virtue—*wang-tao*, the "kingly way"—while the Westerners cared only for money and their government was by law and by power politics.

Wang Hsien-ch'ien (1842-1918) was a leading scholar, best known today as the compiler of part of the *Tung-hua lu*, a condensation of imperial documents. Both he and Yeh Te-hui (1864-1927), a famous bibliophile, believed that the evils in China lay in the moral state of the people, not in the legal or political systems; rather than try to change the institutions, it would be better to talk about changing the minds of the people.⑦ Wang went a step further and declared that, while the national character of Westerners was public-spirited, that of the Chinese was selfish, so that democracy could hardly apply to China. He wrote:⑧

Generally what is called self-government arose from the fact that, in the old days, Western countries had originally no government or education. Their people were unbearably poverty-stricken and the lower classes were separated from the upper and it was out of this situation that self-government developed. In China for several thousand years sacred emperors and enlightened kings have been exerting their minds and energies to be good princes and teachers and to acquire experience in planning; their consideration has been very careful and they have been particularly vigilant in preventive measures. Our fundamental idea of establishing a nation has been different from that in the West. Nevertheless, the difference between the public spirit of the West and the selfishness of the Chinese also comes from this... Among Westerners each one uses his right of self-government to join and submit voluntarily to the control of congenial organizations. What they plan to do at home is for the public benefit, and what they go out to discuss is also for the public. Political commands are for public [not private] purposes. Property is for the public. Territory is also for the public. (Note: For example, India was seized by a company but given to the nation.) Thus it is natural that the king above should not appear quarrelsome and insecure, and that the people below should have no idea of neglecting their duty and being idle spectators, because they have formed the public-spirited habit.

Since the Yellow Emperor, and Emperors Yao and Shun, the Chinese people have respected the emperors as Heaven and regarded them as gods, and in addition they have been delighted with the emperor's benevolence in allowing them to have a little more than mere subsistence, and in other matters they were glad to be independent of him... Since the first emperor of the Hsia Dynasty regarded the empire as his family property, the people in turn regarded themselves as his children, and each generation tries to be selfish. The emperor and the people all kept their individual purposes and thus the egotistical pattern was formed... Now it would be definitely unsuitable to use the selfish minds of the Chinese to adopt the self-govern-ment policy of the Westerners.

Ch'u Ch'eng-po thought the first step was to reform the people's minds; in 1898 he wrote:⑨

In our society today the trouble is not that we lack institutions for good government, but that we lack upright minds among the people. If we seek to reform institutions we should reform our minds first... At the beginning of the T'ung-chih period [1862-1874] Tseng Kuo-fan, Tso Tsung-t'ang, Li Hung-chang, Shen Pao-chen and others, on account of the fact that foreign aggression had become very serious, greatly admired Western knowledge... These reformers said from the beginning that, even though the Chinese imitated the superior techniques of Westerners, eventually they would get ahead of the Westerners. But since their reforms have been carried on perfunctorily up to the present, the island pirates [the Japanese] have suddenly invaded us and the whole situation of the nation has collapsed... The real mistake was that we did not secure the right persons to manage the new institutions... Could the various workers in the shipyards and the arsenals really fulfill the original plan of Tso Tsung-t'ang, to do the work entirely in Chinese factories? ... Among the students sent abroad by Li Hung-chang were there any who had learned excellently and could exert their loyalty to ward off aggression from the nation? ... Could we train a navy by ourselves, as was originally expected by Shen Pao-chen? Arguing from these analogies, we can see that it will be all the same with other things... Usually there was a good start but no finishing. There was much talk, but little action... The most far-reaching plans were ruined by our putting up an ostentatious façade while behind it all is hidden covetousness and selfishness... Formerly, the Tsungli Yamen in planning for coastal defense said: "If we cannot secure the right men everything will turn out to be a sheer waste of money. The mistake will be in the employment of improper (unsuitable) persons, not in the weakness of our system."...

Some Chinese conservatives, after comparing Western governments with their own, arrived at the conclusion that the Westerners knew only things mechanical and mathematical and nothing else, while the Chinese had long ago discovered the real and eternal way of governing people by virtue. With such moral force behind her, China was surely going to achieve the unification of the whole world and have all the barbarians at her feet. One of these critics, Huang Jen-chi, wrote:⑩

If we say that Heaven, the earth, the people and the animals can all be controlled by mathematics, this would suggest that in foreign countries they should have order, with no disorder; prosperity with no decline; life, with no death; and wealth, with no poverty. How, then, are the foreign countries not able to control the course of order and disorder, prosperity and decline, life and death, existence and extinction, wealth and poverty? This is probably because in mathematics there is also a moral principle which serves as the controlling power. The foreigners merely know how to investigate one period of time or one subject, but the Chinese knew long ago how to investigate one hundred generations or one thousand years ahead, that is, we Chinese have had sages and the foreigners cannot expect to have such people...

In foreign countries they emphasize material profits, but they also live up to the word "sincerity"; the upper and lower classes are of the same mind and the prince and ministers have the idea of being one body with the people. Although their nations are rich and strong, ultimately the feelings of the multitudes cannot be unified. We Chinese unanimously stress righteousness and at the same time live up to the word "benevolence." Because we are not all of the same mind, we, on the contrary, appear to be declining and weak. Nevertheless, the doctrine of cultivating virtue, unifying our families, governing the nation and pacifying the empire, is all actually inferred from these (principles of righteousness and benevolence). The foreigners expressly follow the numerical system and at the same time they promote techniques in which everything is fixed numerically. Hence they entirely neglect the theory of relations between ruler and minister, father and son, husband and wife, elder brother and younger brother, good and evil, chastity and licentiousness, good luck and bad luck, misfortune and good fortune. Chinese, however, in addition to the numerical system, also talk about moral principles... ⑪

Pursuing this line of thought, many scholars and officials acknowledged the superiority of the West in the techniques of producing wealth and power, all of which they felt might be adopted on condition that they be modified to suit the Chinese environment. The famous phrase, *Chung-hsueh wei t'i, Hsi-hsueh wei yung*, had various connotations. As Professor Wilhelm has pointed out,⑫ the antithesis *t'i* and *yung* was an ancient one in Chinese thought, going back to the "within" and "without" of Mencius. In Chu Hsi these two terms might be translated, roughly speaking, as "substance" and "function." They could also be taken as parallel to the famous dichotomy of "principle" (*li*) and "manifestation" (*ch'i*), within the general framework of Neo-Confucianism. It is noteworthy that Chang Chih-tung, the most famous exponent of the slogan, was steeped in Chu Hsi and his philosophy, so that it was perfectly natural for him to divide all studies into two categories—"take the old learning as substance and the new learning for function." When applied to the realm of political theory, this doctrine was taken to mean that a government by virtue should be the main principle, but with the addition of a certain amount of government by law. Some, harking back to the ancient idea of law as a punitive tool of the ruler, interpreted this as allowing room for some *pa-cheng* ("power government" or rule by force) within a framework of *wang-tao* ("the kingly way" or rule by virtue and benevolence). The adoption of some Western methods might be expedient for the needs of the time, but the permanent guiding principle of Chinese government should still be a government by benevolence, righteousness, truth and virtue. Thus the slogan meant: to model the state after the classics and to respect the emperor as its foundation, but to accept some barbarian ideas and take in some elements of "power government," so as to make the country rich and strong in its practical functions. The scholar Wen-t'i wrote:

If we wish to receive the benefit of Western methods, we must first acquire a knowledge of Confucius, Mencius, Ch'eng and Chu [i. e., Neo-Confucianism], and keep it as the foundation to make people thoroughly familiar with filial piety, younger-brotherhood, loyalty, sincerity, ceremony, righteousness, integrity, a sense of shame, obligations and the teachings of the sages and moral courage, in order to understand and demonstrate the foundation, before we can learn the foreign spoken and written languages for some practical use.⑬

A number of travel diaries indicate how easily this moral attitude could be associated with an aversion to the strangeness of Western ways. In a book by Yuan Tsu-chih "Personal point of view after travelling to foreign countries" (*She-yang kuan-chien*), there is an interesting passage which reads:⑭

China has all four seasons and the climate is proportionally distributed. In parts of the West the heat and cold are unseasonable, the winter and summer change their normal order, and there are spots that from ancient down to modern times have never had frost or snow...

As to human affairs, China emphasizes human relationships and honors benevolence and righteousness. In the West, on the contrary, a son does not take care of his father, a minister cheats his emperor, a wife is more honored than a husband; thus the bond of the three relationships is broken. Because the proper relationship between husband and wife is not cultivated, the marriage ceremony is neglected. As soon as a girl is twenty-one years old she is permitted to find a husband whom she likes, and there are those who make many selections or trials before they make a match. They do not consider sexual relations preceding marriage as a shame. Beautiful young girls are seeking for males everywhere; the hoary-headed and the widows can invite male companions as they like. The customs are bad to such a degree!...

As to other customs, the residence of the emperor is the same as that of ordinary people except that it is a little larger, and it lacks an awe-inspiring appearance and dignity. The pictures of the emperor and empress are hung up at random in the markets for sale and people can purchase them as toys. Thus there is no distinction between the noble and the mean...

Speaking about official costumes, except in one country, Turkey, where the costume is strange, all other nations are the same. The noble and the mean use the same style, which makes it difficult to tell who is honorable and who is lowly. In summertime there is no linen or silk to make their bodies comfortable, and in winter there are rarely furs or padded coats to dress their bodies. They have to go to the trouble of taking a carriage or a horse, but do not have the comfort of sedan chairs.

The skirts of their women are seven feet long, only good for sweeping dust. The bed curtain is hung ten feet high but it is hard to keep mosquitoes away.

As for food, there is no difference between winter and summer; they always sip cold water and juice. They cannot appreciate the culinary art, but like butter and mutton ribs. The amount of food served at meals is small, and they use many different kinds of utensils [p. 470b] to cause servants a good deal of work. The kinds of soup are very limited. Delicious things are completely lacking.

In government, their taxes since antiquity have been unprecedently heavy and numerous. There is actually a levy of taxes of certain amounts according to the value of commodities. If smuggling is detected, the tax on the smuggled article is increased ten or a hundred times as a fine. In some places there is a land tax. Some have a poll tax, or property tax, or tax on trademarks. The government takes money from the people insatiably. How can the people bear it? Moreover, they worship their unorthodox religion and allow the Christian clergy to overrun the country, exhausting all the people's money in building churches, thus spending useful funds for a useless purpose.

As for the law, it has no articles for punishing adultery; a wife can have a concubine [i. e., a lover] and can accuse her husband. This is even more ridiculous. Apart from these there are other things which they improperly turn upside down. Their prisons, for instance, are as comfortable as the Kingdom of Heaven. It is not very easy for people to maintain their living, because the cost of food and utensils is as high as that of precious jewels. The five relationships are not cultivated, the five kinds of grains are incomplete, hundreds of herbs are unknown to them and hundreds of grasses or flowers are not fragrant...

The first Chinese vice-minister to England, Liu Hsi-hung, in his "Diary of a mission to England' (*Ying-yao jih-chi*) says:[15]

Their practical knowledge consists entirely of the details of miscellaneous crafts, the use of which can make a machine or an instrument; but it is limited ... If we pursue only these miscellaneous skills to make trains and ships for profit, to make firearms for killing people, and to struggle for more such productions and for clever designs, considering these as wealth and strength; can these really be called useful knowledge? ... After all, we forbid people to make strange weapons so as to prevent rebellion, and proclaim benevolence and righteousness, so as to establish the fundamental doctrine for our government.

Another line of attack on Western materialism was to argue that the stagnation of China's material civilization was due to the fact that the Chinese people preferred lofty principles to material things. For example, Liu Yueh-yün (1849-1917) says:⑯ "The technique of the barbarians is merely that of a worker, of which a gentleman would not care to speak and which a scholar and an official would despise... We despised (mechanical civilization) and did not try to develop it. Instead we seek for larger and higher purposes."

Others were less proud and more pessimistic. Some Chinese maintained that Western material civilization was so far ahead that it would be absolutely impracticable for the Chinese to try to learn the Westerners' methods in order to control them. Therefore Westernization should be avoided, and another method for self-preservation should be sought. One of the prescriptions given by a famous scholar, Yü Yueh (1821-1907), was a kind of Taoist passive resistance:⑰

Then how can we overcome them? The answer is, two pieces of steel cannot overcome each other. That which can overcome steel is softness. Two sharp (knives) cannot overcome each other. The one can overcome the sharpness of the other by dullness. Well, then, two clever persons can hardly control each other. But the way to control the clever is by stupidity. [P. 6b]Even if we have to determine our fate on the battlefield, their weapons could only hurt several scores or several hundred of our people. Yet if our system of reward and punishment is well observed and our orders are very strict, then our people should form groups of several hundreds or one thousand and push ahead like a wall—what can they do [p. 7] against us? Therefore, I say, only the stupid can control the clever. Using great stupidity to overcome great cleverness is the method of achieving an assured victory.

Finally there were several arguments specifically against Western machines: (1) That Chinese human labor and experience can achieve better results than machines. Shen Ch'un wrote:⑱

A Chinese helmsman by looking at the sun's halo and the clouds' vapor knows when there will be wind or rain; by observing the wrinkles of the water and the appearance of sand, he knows where there are hidden rocks; and by looking at the shape of a mountain and the color of the water he knows where he is on the sea. One day's experience like this serves him for a life time. Other things like... the ornamental pillars at Peking, the ivory sculpture of Kwangtung, the pillars and beams of the old palaces in Egypt, and the stone sculpture in Italy—none of them was made by machinery. When foreigners see them, they usually stroke them with their hands and gaze at them a long time in admiration, but without knowing how such marvelous objects could be made... Why should we think of making a change when we see something strange, and why should we use the barbarian culture to change Chinese culture?

(2) That since the Chinese population is already too large, if machines are used, many laborers will be out of jobs and the order and peace of Chinese society will be seriously affected. This is cogently explained by a scholar, Chu I-hsin (1846-1894):⑲ "In Western countries the territory is large, the population is thin, therefore they even use machines for agriculture. If China employs them, one person's agricultural work may take away the livelihood of ten others. These ten others, if they do not want to sit down and wait for death by starvation would choose a risky road (i.e., become bandits)."

Chang Tzu-mu also says:⑳

The farmers in the south, the miners in the northern mountains and those who are pulling carts and manning boats, all these several thousand or million people have been working all their lives at hard labor and if this is suddenly replaced by machines they will lose their way of making a living. Would they not gather together to cause disorder or start a rebellion? This is probably the reason that, following the widespread adoption of machines in Europe less than a hundred years ago, great revolutions have repeatedly occurred.

(3) That the natural resources of the world are limited, but production by machines is limitless. When the natural resources are exhausted it will not be easy for human beings to make a living, and therefore one should object to the use of machines. Yü Yueh says:[21]

The Europeans only know how to exhaust what exists in the universe to supply their needs. A proverb says: "If you fish by drying up the water, then next year there will be no fish." I have heard that they use coal without limit, and the places where coal is produced are becoming fewer day by day... Inferring from the one thing, coal, we know that if everything is consumed without limit there must be a time of exhaustion... Day by day the essential materials are being exhausted and I fear that the earth will become so barren that it will no longer be able to maintain human life.

## CHAPTER XIX    THE BOXER UPRISING

The blow dealt to the Reform Movement of 1898 and the resumption of power by the Empress Dowager did not work out as well as the conservatives had expected. The threatened disintegration of the empire into areas of foreign control, and the rising tide of Chinese antagonism towards Manchu rule made more and more people realize the necessity of institutional reform. Yet the Empress Dowager could not initiate reform herself without seeming to confirm the Emperor Kuang-hsü's Decrees of

1898 and thus condemn herself in the eyes of the world. She would have preferred to achieve a position as arbiter between the reformers and the conservatives. By 1900, however, incensed by the expressions of public opinion against her, particularly those from foreigners who had openly sympathized with the reformers, she finally chose to throw her lot with the conservatives, who tried to channel all economic, social and political discontent against the foreigners, their converts to Christianity, their churches and their railways.

The upshot was that in June 1900 thousands of Boxers, inspired by superstition and encouraged by the conservative officials, joined in an uprising which spread over Shantung, Chihli, Shansi, and southern Manchuria. They burned churches, destroyed telegraph lines and railways, and killed many Chinese Christians and foreign missionaries. On June 20, when the Ch'ing regime declared war on the foreign powers, they laid siege to the foreign legations and a Catholic cathedral in Peking. They cut rail communications between Peking and Tientsin and obliged a British relief force of some two thousand men to retreat. The half-hearted siege ended on August 14, when the allied forces of eight nations (Japan, Germany, England, France, the U. S. A., etc.) reached Peking. In 1901, the *Boxer Protocol* exacted an indemnity which amounted to some $333,900,000.

So great a disaster to the Ch'ing fortunes could have been precipitated only by leaders profoundly ignorant of the West, even granting the fact (which we have not emphasized) of great foreign provocation.

Among the leaders of the die-hards were several princes of the imperial family. Since the 1860's, the school for princes had been discontinued and their education neglected. Brought up in relative ignorance, yet accustomed to being obeyed, these princes easily fell victims to certain popular superstitions of the day. Hence, when the Boxers in Shantung claimed to be invincible to bullets through the aid of certain popular deities, they were actually believed by these princes and perhaps even by the Empress Dowager herself. The Boxers were thought of as loyal supporters of the dynasty, available for use in a showdown against the foreigners. All their irrational acts of violence—the killing of Christian converts and foreigners and the destruction of anything with a foreign connection—were regarded at the time as patriotic acts against foreign invaders. The mad situation in and near Peking in the summer of 1900 was thus a product of ignorance, superstition, and mob hysteria.

As to the origin of the Boxer movement, there are several theories. Chinese sources are represented by Lao Nai-hsuan (1843-1921), who believed that a secret society called the *I-ho-ch'üan*, and known to have existed in 1727 and 1808, had maintained its existence uninterruptedly down to the end of the nineteenth century. As to its name, the word *ch'üan* refers to the Chinese form of calisthenics for personal defense, or "boxing," and the term *I-ho-ch'üan* refers to the type of defensive art practiced by a kind of fraternal order called the "Harmonious Brotherhood." ("Righteous and Harmonious Fists" is a crude and misleading translation.) In short, this group originally seems to have been a society teaching the methods of one school of boxing. Because the government ordered the people of Shantung to organize militia forces, *t'uan-lien*, against the German encroachment in that province, the society in different localities gradually changed its name to *I-ho-t'uan*, "Righteous and Harmonious Militia," thus adopting the status of a semi-official military force. Some Western scholars (e. g., Dr. G. N. Steiger in his *China and the Occident*) have consequently followed the more strict and literal view that the Boxers actually came into being after the Empress Dowager's *coup d'état* of 1898, as a legal militia recruited in response to imperial command, but more recent research has made this view untenable.

Of the three documents of the Boxers translated below, the first is reminiscent of circulars or handbills that had appeared from time to time in China's history as far back as the Han Dynasty. Such warnings were put out sometimes as a prank, but also at times by serious plotters of disorder as a way to cause unrest among the ignorant and superstitious. The other two documents are typical of Boxer proclamations during the period from April to August 1900 in North China villages, where the elders tried to restrain the youths from excesses, but themselves believed in the claims of the Boxers.

In these three short statements there is no direct attack on foreigners, but there are appeals to Taoist, Buddhist, and other superstitions. The first document, especially the part of it about the "ten disasters," appeared in many places.

## DOC. 48   PROCLAMATIONS OF THE BOXERS①

### A Boxer Circular

Statement by the Saintly Emperor Kuan-kung during his visitation at our divining altar: This year seventy per cent of the population will die. Lives can be saved by praying to Bodhisattva Kuan-yin for her mercy and kindness. Circulate this statement and disaster can be avoided—one sheet for yourself, three for your whole family. To refuse to circulate it and to tell lies about it will cause condemnation by the gods and an increase in the disaster.

Those who do good will be safe, those who do evil can hardly escape. If you do not believe, you will see that in the seventh and eighth months of this year countless people will die. These gods and saints have always been watching for the good and evil deeds among you mortals. Heaven now fears ten disasters. The first is about how the world is going to be in a turmoil. The second is about everything in Shantung being wiped out. The third is that flood will cover Hupei and Hunan. The fourth is that wars will come to Szechwan. The fifth is that Kiangnan is to suffer from a big famine and uprising. The sixth is about the deaths of more than half of the population. The seventh is that members of the Righteous and Harmonious Boxing Order [*I-ho-ch'üan*] are too weak. The eighth is about the foreigners disturbing Chihli. The ninth is that there will be clothes but no one to wear them. The tenth is that there will be rice but no one to eat it.

A disaster, however, may be turned to a blessing, for destiny is in charge. One who copies this out for somebody else will have his whole family exempted from suffering the calamity.

On the 19th day of the sixth month, and the 26th day of the seventh month, make sacrificial offerings towards the south and you will be exempted from suffering the calamity.

### A Boxer Notice

The Ma-lan Village in the Ch'i-chia police magistrate's precinct of the district of Wan-[p'ing] in the prefecture of Shun-t'ien, Peking, on the occasion of piously setting up the sacred I-ho Society, makes the following declaration of instructions and strict advice to our fellow villagers and neighbors! The Catholics since the Hsien-feng period (1851-1861) have conspired with foreigners, have caused China trouble, wasted our national revenue, broken up our monasteries, destroyed Buddhist images, and seized our people's graveyards. All these myriad acts of evil should be bitterly resented. This has affected people's trees and plants so as to make them suffer from the catastrophes of locusts and drought almost every year. Our nation is deprived of peace and our people of security. This has angered the Court in Heaven.

Now by the grace of the great deity in Heaven, all the spirits have descended to set up an altar in the wall in order to teach our young men their magic boxing so they can support the Ch'ing, extinguish the foreigners, and enforce right principles on behalf of Heaven. When we exert our energy for the nation in order to bring peace to the land, when we help the farmers and protect our villages, this is an omen that prosperity is coming after misfortune has reached its limit.

Nevertheless, we are afraid that some ignorant people and vagabonds may rely upon the foreigners' power in acting contrary to reason, and cling to the strong in order to oppress the weak. They should be reported to the village head and the chief of the society, who will handle public affairs justly and sentence them according to law, and who are not allowed to be influenced by selfish purposes. If they indulge in private favoritism, the eyes of our spirits like lightning will pierce through them without discrimination, and will not let them get away with any deviation from the just punishment. Because some persons use foreign religion and tricky techniques to deceive the people, Heaven above is angered and is sending many sages to descend to earth and come to the divining altar to initiate our youths into the I-ho Society. *I* means kindness, and *ho* means politeness; kindness and politeness will make town and countryside peaceful and harmonious. Our people should take right principles and virtue as their foundation and should devote themselves to agriculture as their profession. They should follow and obey Buddhism. They are not permitted to resort to public accusations for avenging a personal grievance, to use poverty as a pretext for oppressing other poor people, to rely on strength to maltreat the weak, or to regard the right as wrong.

Prepared by Group K'an [the second of the Eight Trigrams] of the I-ho Society, Ma-lan Village, Ch'i-chia police precinct, at Chai-t'ang…

### Another Boxer Notice

Attention: all people in markets and villages of all provinces in China—now, owing to the fact that Catholics and Protestants have vilified our gods and sages, have deceived our emperors and ministers above, and oppressed the Chinese people below, both our gods and our people are angry at them, yet we have to keep silent. This forces us to practice the *I-ho* magic boxing so as to protect our country, expel the foreign bandits and kill Christian converts, in order to save our people from miserable suffering. After this notice is issued to instruct you villagers, no matter which village you are living in, if there are Christian converts, you ought to get rid of them quickly. The churches which belong to them should be unreservedly burned down. Everyone who intends to spare someone, or to disobey our order by concealing Christian converts, will be punished according to the regulation when we come to his place, and he will be burned to death to prevent his impeding our program. We especially do not want to punish anyone by death without warning him first. We cannot bear to see you suffer innocently. Don't disobey this special notice!

Prepared by the I-ho-ch'üan.

In opposition to the hysteria of the Boxer movement, only a few individuals at court had the courage to stand forth. Among them were Hsü Ching-ch'eng (1845-1900) and Yuan Ch'ang (1846-1900). Hsü, a *chin-shih* of 1868, had served the Chinese government as minister to Japan (1880), as minister to France, Germany, Italy, Holland and Austria (1884-1887), and as minister to Russia (1891-1898). Yuan Ch'ang, a *chin-shih* of 1876, had been a secretary in the Tsungli Yamen for over ten years (1883-1894). In September 1898, he was appointed lieutenant-governor of the province of Chihli and, pending his assumption of the post, was given the rank of a third grade official so as to serve as one of the ministers in the Tsungli Yamen. He regarded the Boxers as wholly undependable, and he considered China's declaration of war against several other nations to be suicidal, and the attack on the legations to have been a grave violation of international law. When both Hsü and Yuan, who were good friends and both from the province of Chekiang, advocated strong measures to suppress the Boxers, they were accused of being pro-foreign traitors, arrested on July 26, and executed two days later.[2] The following three memorials attributed to these courageous ministers give a general idea of the background and progress of the Boxer uprising as seen from Peking at the time.

### DOC. 49   MEMORIALS OF ANTI-BOXER MARTYRS, 1900

*The first memorial of Hsü Ching-ch'eng, Senior Vice-president of the Board of Civil Office, and Yuan Ch'ang, Director of the Court of Sacrificial Worship, strongly urging the suppression of the Boxer bandits in order to prevent a great disaster (June 1900)*[3]

We find that, according to an imperial Decree of the seventh month, 1808, there had been bandits in the area of Shantung and Honan, establishing organizations called "The Eight Trigrams Society" (*Pa-kua-chiao*) and the "Righteous and Harmonious Boxing Order" (*I-ho-ch'üan*); they were really descendants of the "White Lotus Society" (*Pai-lien-chiao*). A severe Decree was proclaimed to arrest every single one of them and to punish them severely. Last year [1899] Lao Nai-hsuan, magistrate of Wu-ch'iao, wrote a book[④] in which he investigated their origin in the greatest detail. In the last month Yuan Shih-k'ai, governor of Shantung, in making a report according to imperial Decree, said "On no account is there any reason to summon the Boxers and reorganize them as regular troops." He spoke most candidly and plainly. When the former governor of Shantung, Yü-hsien, handled the case of heretical bandits in P'ing-yüan, he said that the bandit chief Chu Hung-teng claimed to be a descendant of the Ming Dynasty, to be using magic spells to arouse the masses, and that people everywhere responded to him. Fortunately he was arrested by government troops and executed on the spot. He had absolutely no magic to enable him to avoid the bullets of guns and the cutting of a sword or axe. This is clear evidence... To save the present situation we must clean up the bandits in the Inner City of Peking in order to pacify the minds of the people and soothe the feelings of the foreigners, so we can stop their troops, which are being continually summoned. It is necessary that China suppress the Boxers by herself if we are to avoid having foreign soldiers help us in their suppression...

*The second memorial of Hsü Ching-ch'eng and Yuan Ch'ang requesting protection for the Legation Quarter in order to maintain the general situation (July 1900)*[⑤]

After the German Minister von Ketteler was shot to death on his way [to the Tsungli Yamen] on June 20, the Boxers attacked the Legation Quarter of all nations. The Kansu troops under commander-in-Chief Tung Fu-hsiang were particularly responsive to the power of the Boxers, all being in collusion for seditious purposes ... Now more than twenty days have passed; only a few foreign soldiers have been killed; but the bodies and skeletons of the bandits are scattered everywhere around the Legation Quarter ... Where is the magic now? ...

[P. 13] According to the principles in the *Spring and Autumn Annals*, when two countries engage in warfare, they should not kill diplomatic envoys. According to Western international law, it is also particularly provided that the minister is an important official of a nation, and he who despises her minister also despises the nation. Now if we let these bandits attack and burn the Legation Quarter and kill all the diplomatic envoys, all countries will take it as a great insult and will form an alliance in order to avenge themselves to the death. The foreign troops in the capital are limited but the foreign troops who will continue to come are limitless. It is your ministers' humble opinion that, with one nation fighting against all nations, it will not be merely a matter of victory or defeat for China but will actually be a question of survival or ruin. Our country has had trade relations with all the European countries for about sixty years and we have allowed them to spread religion in all our provinces. In ordinary times the converts who rely on the foreigners' influence have exploited the rural people as their fish and meat, and have regarded the foreign missionaries as their protectors. It was unavoidable that the local officers, perhaps hoping to conclude the matter cursorily, also have oppressed the common people. The people have been resentful, and they have regarded the converts with antagonism. All this was due to the mismanagement of Chinese officials ... When the bandits saw the missionaries wearing foreign clothes and speaking different languages, they called them all *mao-tzu* ["hairy ones"] and took pleasure in exterminating them ...

Your ministers request that the Legation Quarter be protected as a measure to pave the way for a compromise in the future. On the one hand, a strict imperial Decree should reprimand the commander-in-Chief,

Tung Fu-hsiang, and order his Kansu troops to get out of the city entirely... and, on the other hand, in order to avoid a most imminent crisis, we should ask the Grand Secretary, Jung-lu, to take the responsibility for driving the Boxers completely out of the city within a definite time.

*The third memorial of Hsü Ching-ch'eng and Yuan Ch'ang, which caused their execution (July 28, 1900)*[⑥]

It has been little more than one month since the Boxer bandits caused trouble. The people of the Imperial capital and the whole Empire have been disturbed. War has broken out and disaster has occurred. The whole globe is involved. It is an extraordinary thing which has never happened before in all the ages of Chinese history, and will result in a catastrophe such as has never been experienced in all ages... [p. 19] When the Boxers first raised their standards they had neither effective guns and cannon, nor had they any training on the battlefield. They merely displayed the characters "support the Ch'ing and exterminate the foreigners" (*Fu-Ch'ing mieh-yang*) to summon the undisciplined masses to mob violence. If we had had an able local governor or military officer, he could have suppressed them with ease. The former Shantung governor Yü-hsien fostered the cancer at first; the Chihli governor-general Yü-lu courteously welcomed them later, and gave them weapons; it was like giving wings to tigers... Moreover, Yü-lu invited the chiefs of the Boxer bandits and treated them as distinguished guests. The rural rascals would also assemble as many as one thousand people, hold up a visiting card with the three characters, *I-ho-t'uan*, and they would be immediately invited into the governor-general's office to talk with him as if they were equals. Is this not contempt of the Court and a shame to the scholars of contemporary times? ...

[P. 20] The Grand Secretary Hsü T'ung is muddle-headed and is unaware of what is advantageous and disadvantageous. The Grand Councillor and Assistant Grand Secretary, Kang-i, who associated with the traitors and flattered the bandits, is obstinately reactionary by nature. The Grand Councillor and Minister of Rites, Ch'i-hsiu, who is bigoted in his own ideas, is stupid, but would like to be independent. The Grand Councillor and Minister of Rites, Chao Shu-ch'iao, whose mind is very cunning, is an accomplished sycophant. At the time when the Boxers had just come to Peking, the officials within and without the Court, from the princes on down, had the honor to be summoned and consulted about the policy of suppressing or pacifying them. Some of your ministers offered the statement that the Boxers are not patriotic, that they cannot be relied upon to resist our enemies, and that we should not carelessly challenge all foreign countries without reason. Hsü T'ung, Kang-i, and others actually dared to scorn these as rebellious statements in front of the Empress Dowager and the emperor... Now even in some [p. 20b] of the mansions of princes and other high dignitaries, the Boxers' altars are established. The Boxer bandits are not only foolish themselves, but they also lead Hsü T'ung, Kang-i, and others into folly; Hsü T'ung, Kang-i, and others are not only foolish, but they also lead princes and other dignitaries into folly. That is to say, Hsü T'ung, Kang-i, and others are the pivotal figures fomenting the disorders...

At the beginning, when the bandits arose, how did they dare reject the Imperial Decree, to insult the officials, and to destroy government properties? How did they dare to take up weapons and burn houses, plunder and kill the populace? Since Hsü T'ung, Kang-i, and others praised them as patriotic, the power of the Boxer bandits increased still more, the confusion of the common people became worse, and the gathering of rascals became greater ... Had Hsü T'ung, Kang-i, and others not called them patriotic people, the bandits would not have dared to commit their atrocities in arson, plundering and massacre. When we trace the origin of these breeders of mischief, we find that these officials are to blame. It behooves us to request an Imperial Decree to punish first Hsü T'ung, Kang-i, Ch'i-hsiu, Chao Shu-ch'iao, Yü-lu, Yü-hsien, and

Tung Fu-hsiang according to the severe criminal code; others who improperly gave protection to the Boxer bandits, and who made the same mistake as Hsü T'ung and others, should receive such punishment as they deserve. We should not take into consideration membership in the nobility or Imperial family as a reason for reducing their punishment. Then all nations will suddenly understand that those who formerly and purposely allowed the bandits to start hostilities were all these reactionary and stupid officials, that it was not the original idea of our nation. They may give up their hatred in order to seek good terms with us and our ancestral temples will be spared. Then Your Majesty can kill us to redress the imbalance in the deaths of Hsü T'ung, Kang-i, and the other ministers. Even though we die, we shall go to the next world with smiling faces. We cannot help shedding tears in preparing this memorial and we cannot overcome our extreme grief and anxiety.

[After this memorial was submitted, the two memorialists were executed.]

# 6 REFORM AND REVOLUTION 1901-1912

## CHAPTER XX  THE CONSERVATIVE REFORM MOVEMENT

With the collapse of the Reform Movement of 1898 and the Boxer Uprising of 1900, there had occurred a profound split within the ranks of the Chinese scholar-official class, whose response to the West is our main topic in this volume. From that time dates the clear divergence between the dynasty, and an important and growing group of the upper-class leadership. The latter was further split into two groups who carried on their arguments in their party papers: the revolutionists, headed by Sun Yat-sen, and the constitutional monarchists, led by K'ang Yu-wei. The reform program carried on by the Ch'ing government in the 1900's was designed to make amends for its previous conservatism, but this was only one of the channels of change, the other consisting of the anti-Manchu agitation carried on by groups inside and outside the country, with their main base among the Chinese students in Japan.

Under the official reform program there were a multitude of paper documents and some accomplishments. The broad sweep of the reform effort is indicated in the basic statements prepared by Chang Chih-tung and Liu K'un-i in 1901 (Doc. 50). In the documentation which follows, we touch upon only a few of the major developments: abolition of the age-old civil service examination system (Doc. 51), which was followed by an extensive proliferation of modern and semi-modern educational institutions; the movement for constitutionalism (Doc. 52), which led to unforeseen political developments in the provinces and paved the way for the revolt of 1911; the building of a "modern" army, which injected a heightened element of military force into a political situation in which civil government was fast losing its grip. These important lines of change were paralleled by significant developments in the fields of law, industry and communications, banking and finance (see Ch. XXI), journalism, and social custom generally, all of which might be further illustrated here if space permitted. In law, for instance, a special bureau under the direction of Shen Chia-pen revised the imperial code in the period 1902-1907 and began drafting a modern civil code and codes of procedure—a development which continued under the Republic.①

The classical metaphor for describing the dilemma of the Ch'ing government in the 1900's is that it was in quicksand. It could only sink deeper the harder it struggled to save itself. Thus the reform program as outlined by Chang Chih-tung and others stressed the training of personnel, but this meant a modern type of education, to be found only outside the country, and this in turn led to the growth of patriotic anti-Manchu revolutionary sentiment among the student class. By giving modern education to its prospective official class, the dynasty reared its own executioners, dug its own grave, and signed its own death warrant. Essentially this was because the dynasty, as an alien monarchy, was itself incapable of becoming "modern." Support for this view is found in its increasing inability to meet the problems of government in China in the later 1900's. How much the failure was one of institutions and how much one of personnel ("human abilities," as Chang Chih-tung had feared) cannot be said offhand; perhaps the two are by definition indivisible, outmoded institutions inevitably producing retrograde leadership.

### a. *The Post-Boxer Program*

By the time of the court's flight to Sian in 1900, most of the ultra-conservatives who had been prominent in the Boxer Uprising were either dead or banished. The old Empress Dowager learned a bitter lesson from her rough, cold, and hungry trip across country by cart and chair from

Peking to Sian. For her these months of intimate contact with the villagers and local officials of the hinterland must have been instructive in many ways. Possibly upon the advice of her close friend and counselor, Jung-lu, who was the only top Manchu official with her, she issued a series of Decrees in the name of Emperor Kuang-hsü in which he blamed himself, requested public criticism, and, most important of all, announced a reform policy, so as to indicate tactfully the court's repentance, and thus gloss over its responsibility for the Boxer Uprising.

On January 29, 1901, a reform Decree was issued in which the instruction of the Empress Dowager was quoted: "Adopt the strong points of foreign countries in order to make up China's shortcomings." This Decree denies that she had ever hindered reform. It goes on to state the criticism that "those who have recently been learning Western methods have limited themselves to the foreigners' written and spoken languages and to the manufacturing of machines. These are the skin and hair of Western technology, but not the fundamental source of Western government." All high officials in and out of Peking were accordingly ordered to express their opinions fully and item by item as to what should be reformed and what should be newly introduced.② Accordingly, a number of memorials were submitted to the court.

On April 21, 1901, an "Office in charge of governmental affairs" (*Tu-pan cheng-wu ch'u*) was instituted to examine the memorials dealing with reform. This new organization was staffed by Jung-lu, I-k'uang (1838-1917), and others, while Liu K'un-i and Chang Chih-tung were made associate members directing its affairs from a distance.③ At that time the most influential governor-generals were Li Hung-chang, Yuan Shih-k'ai, Liu K'un-i and Chang Chih-tung. But Li Hung-chang was now an old man in his last days. Soon after performing his final and most humiliating service, the negotiation of the punitive *Boxer Protocol* of 1901, he died. Meanwhile Yuan Shih-k'ai was fully occupied with rehabilitation work in the Tientsin area, in the effort to secure an early withdrawal of the allied occupation forces. Liu and Chang were thus left in a leading position to outline the reform plans in their three famous memorials, which were submitted on July 12, 19, and 20, 1901, respectively.④ Their recommendations were pronounced, in a Decree of October 2, to be "mostly practicable," and orders were given that the important recommendations be selected and enforced at once.⑤ Indeed, a Decree of August 29 had in the meantime ordered the abolition of the eight-legged essay, beginning in 1902, and of the military examinations as a whole. On September 16, another Decree approved and encouraged the sending of students to study abroad from Kiangnan, Hupei, Szechwan, and other provinces.⑥

These significant memorials of 1901 outlined reforms which were in large part carried out only after the Russo-Japanese war, when many students were sent to Japan. Thus China's real and large-scale modernization effort under government leadership did not really get started until 20th century, and was some forty years behind that of Japan, on which so much of it was modeled.

## DOC. 50  THE JOINT PROPOSALS OF LIU K'UN-I AND CHANG CHIH-TUNG, 1901

### *A Memorial in Compliance with Your Majesty's Decree to Plan and Discuss (a Reform Program), to Show that in Political Reform the Primary Consideration is Human Ability*⑦

We admire our emperor who warns us and guards us against numerous difficulties, and who strongly desires to wipe out longstanding abuses in order to relieve the current hardships. After being moved to tears, we feel both ashamed and aroused. Your ministers once heard that, according to the *Book of Changes* (*Chou-i*), "The Way of Heaven changes or transforms itself, hence the movement of heavenly bodies is continuous. This is a great demonstration of self-strengthening" [that is to say, a human or political body should also keep on moving or changing as a heavenly body does, in order to achieve "self-strengthening" (*tzu-ch'iang*), a phrase derived from the *Book of Changes*]. We have also learned from the *Works of Mencius* that "men for the most part err, and are afterwards able to reform. They are distressed in mind and perplexed in thoughts and then they arise to vigorous reform. Thus their mind is stimulated, their nature hardened, and their incompetencies supplied." That is the principal reason why he who lives a sorrowful and anxious life (will die in comfort)⑧ …

We presume to say that China is poor not in natural resources but in men of ability; she is not weak in troops but in morale. The dearth of men of ability is due to our limited knowledge and unsubstantial learning. The weakness of morale is due (partly) to those who care for temporary security and lack far-reaching plans for coping with danger and for saving the nation from extermination; and (partly) to those who are self-complacent and wanting in the power of persistence in studious pursuits. Without men of ability there is no means for the protection of the nation and for bringing about good government. Carefully we first consider the major aspects of the training of men of ability and the establishment of schools; by taking into consideration both ancient and modern methods and both the civil and military examinations, we have planned and now propose four items: (1) to establish civil and military schools; (2) to reform the civil service examinations to a considerable extent; (3) to abolish the military examinations; and (4) to encourage students to study abroad. Let us reverently explain them for our sacred ruler:

(1)*To establish civil and military schools* [The authors survey the school and examination systems from ancient to modern times and then continue, p. 11b:] The T'ang adopted the Mohammedan calendar, the *Sui* (*History*) bibliographic section collected many works on dialects… During the K'ang-hsi period of our dynasty Westerners were employed both in astronomy and in the casting of cannon. The maps in the palace adopted the longitude and latitude of the Western method… The demarcation stone at Nerchinsk was inscribed in three languages... [p. 11] The old practice of our ancestors is really adequate to be the model for ten thousand generations. Even now the school systems of all European countries still have ideas (which seem as if) handed down from our Three Dynasties. To say that we can recover our forgotten ceremonies from abroad is not wrong.

[Then the authors give a detailed description of foreign school systems, with special attention to Germany and Japan. The various grades and levels of schools, subjects, extra-curricular work, military drill, etc., are reported in detail (pp. 12-20). They suggest the establishment of primary schools in all districts of the empire (p. 14) and the abolition of the eight-legged essay. Employment for scholars trained to write in this style is also discussed so that such essayists will not have to worry about getting jobs (pp. 20-22)].

(2) *To reform the civil service examinations to a considerable extent.* This is a matter of crucial importance in our self-strengthening and search for talent... During the last half year we have consulted officials, gentry and scholars, and in all our discussions reached agreement... The general idea of the change in regulations is focused on the pursuit of useful knowledge while never neglecting the classical works. We wish that the case could be considered and managed according to your minister Chang Chih-tung's memorial of 1898 regarding changes to be instituted in the civil service examination, which was approved by an Imperial Decree... The general scheme was to have three examinations... The first one was to be on Chinese political and historical events, the second on politics, geography, military systems, agriculture, industry, mathematics and the like, of all countries, and the third was to consist of a treatise on the classical meanings of the Four Books and the Five Classics...

Now we propose that some slight changes be made in the old regulations of the civil service examinations, and that they be continued parallel with the new schools and without conflict [p. 24].

[The other two points, to abolish the military examinations and to encourage students to study abroad, are explained in memorials quoted below.]

[P. 28b] These four items are matters of chief concern in seeking men of ability for the realization of a better administration. Among them the facts and reasons are mutually related and mutually auxiliary. That is why we first submit to Your Majesty these four proposals. This is because unless ability is trained, it is impossible to strive for national survival; unless schools are opened, it is impossible to train ability; unless the civil and military examinations are reformed, it is impossible to open schools, and unless students study abroad, it is impossible to remove our deficiencies in opening schools. An investigation of today's current situation shows that there is no alternative and no time for delay...

## A Memorial in Compliance with Your Majesty's Decree to Prepare a Discussion on Reform, Carefully Proposing Twelve Items for the Reorganization of the Chinese (Political) System⑨

Your ministers have planned and proposed four items for developing education and nurturing ability, which have been jointly memorialized and are on record... In general there are three important factors in building a nation: good administration, wealth, and strength... The reorganization of the Chinese political system is to serve as an instrument for bringing about better administration. The adoption of Western methods is for the purpose of attaining wealth and strength. We have carefully considered those aspects of the Chinese system which ought to be reorganized and reformed, and make proposals under twelve heads: (1) to honor frugality, (2) to break down customary formalities [red tape], (3) to stop the contributions or payments for official rank, (4) to examine the officials and increase their emoluments, (5) to remove the useless clerical staff, (6) to weed out the government servants and messengers, (7) to lighten punishments and imprisonments, (8) to reform the method of civil service examinations, (9) to plan for the livelihood of the Manchu bannermen,

(10) to abolish the military colonies and garrisons, (11) to abolish the Army of the Green Standard [*Lü-ying*] and (12) to simplify the documents and laws. These are reverently prepared for the Court's selection and adoption...

[Since these headings are almost self-explanatory, we do not translate the arguments one by one. Their conclusion is as follows, p. 32]: The above twelve items are concerned with the causes of China's chronic weakness, which makes her incapable of exerting herself. They are particularly the hooks on which foreign countries hang their criticisms and abuse of us. Of the plans proposed by your ministers, some are for cultivating the peoples' strength, some for cleansing official circles, and some for arousing the scholars' spirit. Many people had discussed these matters before. But because they had such mistaken notions as that among evils one should remove only the worst, and because they were afraid of being criticized for changing everything, all the statutes, orders, documents, and notices have remained mere paper documents. They may have achieved something but they have lacked long-term and far-reaching plans.

Now foreign aggression is becoming daily more serious. Those who like to follow tradition and devote themselves to cheating and glossing things over always say that the peoples' minds are solidly united. They do not know that popular feelings are not the same as thirty years ago. The people admire the wealth of foreign countries and despise the poverty of the Middle Kingdom. Seeing the strength of foreign soldiers, they are sick of the timidity of their own government's troops; delighted at the fair play of the Maritime Customs Service, they hate the *likin* (transit tax) offices which purposely cause them trouble; praising the stern orderliness of the foreign concessions and settlements, they are tired of the disorder caused by our official clerks. Therefore our people believe in the foreign religion, merchants display foreign flags, and schools register in the names of foreign nationals. All has resulted in a disunited and disillusioned national morale. Insurgents are slowly emerging, and they take this opportunity to spread subversive doctrines. This concerns the very foundation of the nation. We cannot overcome our anxiety and apprehension. We must first entirely wipe out the various defects mentioned above before we may expect a permanent unification of the popular mind. Then we may speak of being affectionate to our superiors, dying for our elders, opposing humiliation and resisting aggression. We humbly beseech your sacred enlightenment to decide with discrimination and to put these proposals into practice, and use them as the foundation for self-strengthening.

### A Memorial to Plan Reform and to Adopt Western Methods⑩

Your ministers have planned and proposed four items for developing education and nurturing ability, and twelve items for reorganization of the Chinese political system, which have been put on record as two joint memorials... Now all countries on the globe are undergoing changes every day and becoming more prosperous every month... On investigating their political systems and academic training we find that they are mainly the product of several hundred years of research and of thousands of persons' modifications. After its effectiveness has been demonstrated, the system is imitated by each nation in turn. The Americans adopted some from Europe, and the Japanese also adopted some from the West... Now we have received the favor of a specially proclaimed Decree in which the failure of previous events has been taken as a warning. Absurd discussions have been put aside, and Western methods are to be adopted to make up for the deficiency of Chinese methods. Your Majesty's humility and broad-mindedness are universally respected by people within and without the Imperial realms. They are raising their heads and wiping their eyes to see the realization of a policy of self-strengthening. The outlines or essentials of Western methods are, however, innumerable. Your ministers carefully take the most important and easily practicable methods and group them together under eleven items: ... The essential thing is that all reforms should be carried out under the guiding principle of not losing their proper sequence...

(1) *The extensive dispatch of travelers abroad*. The strong and prosperous countries of Europe and America have watched and waited for an opportunity to invade us for a hundred years... There has been no instrument, however, by which to make ourselves strong, and no method of dealing with them ... All this has arisen from the handicap of limited information and a narrow point of view, blind ignorance of the territory, politics, literature, and military preparations of all countries. Although in the latter part of the T'ung-chih period travelers were dispatched, resident ministries instituted, and students sent abroad, yet ignorant, absurd, and blundering people denounced as nonsense the words of those who had been in foreign countries, and whenever the latter saw the officials in the Tsungli Yamen they were spitefully treated like dirt. Thereupon, they warned one another against the discussion of foreign affairs, considering it taboo. Even last summer [1900], among the great officials in and out of the capital there were still some who said that foreigners could not walk on land [i.e., because their knees could not bend, a bit of folklore current in 1839 or earlier], and others said that since the legations and churches had been burned, foreigners would never appear again. It is indeed painful to think that such stupidity and conservatism should be the cause of our country's present danger...

The only way to find a method of quick relief is to dispatch travelers abroad. They are to observe the national power of other countries, to examine their administrative affairs and academic achievements, to investigate the major issues in their relations with our country, and the condition of their relations with other nations. After their return to China they can recount what they have experienced and seen to their relatives and friends, by whom it can be spread to others. By a natural process our group ignorance will be suddenly awakened to prompt consideration of reform... Hereafter all newly appointed members of the Tsungli Yamen, secretaries of the Grand Council, superintendents of customs, ministers to foreign countries and their aides must be selected from those who have been sent abroad... Those who have never been abroad will not be allowed to fill posts of assistant police magistrate, censor, metropolitan minister or taotai ... [p. 4b] We have found that the prosperity of Western countries has been preceded by travel...

(2) [P. 5] *The practice of foreign military drill* ... Emperor K'ang-hsi used the Westerner Nan Huai-jen [Ferdinand Verbiest], to cast the red-barbarian cannon, and up to the present on these cannon the name of Nan Huai-jen is still inscribed...

[P. 8b] In training soldiers there is one further important point, in all the capitals of foreign countries, great ministers are appointed to take special charge of controlling and planning military affairs. In England, France, Germany, and other countries, the name for such a functionary is Chief of Staff [*Tsung-ying-wu ch'u*], and in Japan the office is called the Imperial general Staff [lit., "Headquarters of Strategic Counsellors," *Ts'an-mou pen-pu*], which has approximately the same significance as the Privy Council [*Shu-mi-yuan*] of the Sung Dynasty. It has special charge of the whole country's naval and military system: the rate of wages and rations, maps and books, the code of military drill, the purveyance and storage of military provisions, the preparation of carts and ships for transportation, diplomatic affairs, intelligence and other matters ... [P. 9] If China wishes to train crack troops we must establish this office. For its regulations please order the minister Li Sheng-to [in Tokyo] to obtain a copy from the Japanese government, and to have it translated and sent to you for your selection and adoption. But to the office of the chief of the military staff must be appointed one who has a profound knowledge of military affairs and who has been promoted through the ranks of the troops. We should not employ only those who have the qualifications of nobility or Imperial blood...

(3) *Enlargement of military supply.* Although the peace treaty [1901]

has been settled, military preparations must not be neglected. If we have no weapons, then peace cannot be maintained. Military instruments must be manufactured in spite of the lack of funds; otherwise our officers and soldiers will never know what modern warfare is. Naturally it is difficult to set up many large arsenals. We must, however, make an effort to open small factories ... [P. 10b] It would be particularly advisable to send people to Japan and other countries to study modern weapons.

(4) *Improvement of agricultural administration*. China is founded on agriculture ... In recent years some progress has been made in both industry and commerce, but agricultural affairs are quite stagnant. There has been retreat but no progress ... If we wish to improve agricultural administration, we must first promote agricultural studies. We have learned that among the foreign countries making a pursuit of agricultural knowledge, France and the United States are considered the finest, but the translations of their books are still few. Recently, however, dozens of Japanese books on agriculture have been translated, and they are succinct and easy to understand. Moreover, the products and customs of Japan are similar to those of China, and there are many ideas which can be imitated and put into practice. Among these books there are some, previously translated from Western agricultural works, in which are stated all the advantages and disadvantages of various products, the fitness of the soil, new methods of improving fertilization and the effect of giving advice and encouragement to farmers.

It has been learned that in the ninth month of 1898 a Decree was received ordering all provinces to establish bureaus of agricultural affairs. We wish to request that such a public Decree be re-issued, earnestly charging all provinces to take the matter seriously. Since the Han and the T'ang Dynasties there has always been a special officer in charge of agriculture. We further request that in the capital, a minister of agricultural administration be particularly appointed to take charge of the study and promotion of agricultural matters...

(5) *The promotion of industry*. People usually say that the wealth of Western countries lies in commerce, but they do not know that it actually lies in industry. This is because merchants handle the completed goods, while industrialists make things out of raw materials ... When there is industry, there are commodities, and merchants have goods to trade with ... Foreign countries are abundant in wealth; China is richest in men [p. 16]. Today, if those Chinese who are looking for ways of enriching the country wish to compete with European and American countries in commerce, that is impossible for us; but if we compete with these countries in industry, that we certainly can do.

There are three methods of promoting industry: (a) to establish schools of technology, in which factories are set up; ... (b) to open industrial exhibitions [p. 18]; and (c) bestow official rank on skillful workers as a reward... As for those who can create new methods of producing any kind of commodities, they should be given a license allowing them a monopoly for a number of years. All manufactured goods should be charged a specially light rate of *likin* tax, and innovations should be exempt from the *likin* for three years. This is also an important measure for encouraging industry. In short, if we wish to feed the poor and to check the increase of barren land, there is nothing better than to encourage hundreds of handicrafts; if we wish to stop financial leakage and to resist the foreigners, there is nothing better to depend on for enriching the country and the people than the production of native goods. Thus we should worry only about our population not being numerous; why should we worry about its daily becoming more numerous?

(6) *The making of mining laws, transportation laws, commercial laws, laws of negotiation and penal codes*. China's mineral resources are abundant, hidden and not yet excavated, and her railway rights are laid out in a connected pattern, but we have been hesitant and have not yet built the railways: These two things have been coveted by foreigners for a long time [p. 9]. In the last few years, all countries have been busy

gathering capital and coming to China, where they know that in regard to these matters we have as yet no definite regulations, and as to foreign conditions we are still not well informed. They take this opportunity to fool us, to usurp our profits, and invade our rights. Sometimes on the pretext of opening a mine they grab a railway, and sometimes on the pretext of operating a railway they open mines... In recent years, France in Yunnan and Kweichow, Germany in Shantung, England and Italy in Shansi and Honan, all have made agreements with China. The regulations are complicated and not uniform and we are afraid that they are not wholly safe and suitable... [Various types of legislation are then discussed.]

(7) *The use of the silver dollar*. There are three advantages to the silver dollar. One is that the weight and value are so uniform, the paying and receiving so clear-cut that official clerks cannot indulge in graft and extortion, and the officials and people (involved in a transaction) will not suffer from having to make up a deficiency [as was the case in using ingots of silver]. Second, its use in commercial exchange will make transactions simple and straightforward, and the brokers will have no chance to cheat; and so it is not only beneficial to travelers but also convenient for remittance. Third, the collection and distribution of official funds will be entirely in the silver currency for which the larger coin [dollar] will be used as a unit, and the smaller coins as sub-units... After the expenditure for the workers and the mint, there will still be a surplus [p. 22]...

(8) *The use of the stamp tax*. We have learned that the policy of taxing commodities in foreign countries, apart from tobacco, liquor, and opium, is that generally there are no internal duties but a huge income comes solely from the stamp tax. All deeds, bills or documents which have to do with money and property must have affixed on them a stamp obtained from an official bureau. The general idea is to levy a tax on the money value, not on the commodity [p. 23]; to levy a tax on the goods sold, not on those unsold, and to collect a tax from all the four kinds of

people [scholars, farmers, craftsmen and merchants] and hundreds of other professions which have an income, not only from merchants and traders. Therefore Westerners explain the meaning of the stamp tax by saying that this is a tax on money-income. Today in raising funds this method should probably be imitated and practiced...

(9) *Promotion of the postal administration.* [P. 25] It has been learned that in all foreign nations, the postal administration is a big source of government income; in general the annual income is often several tens of millions of taels, and the delivery of mails is very rapid. Chinese military postal stations are a big item of wasted money; the annual expenditure is about three million taels, and yet the official dispatches and reports are very slow...

Since China has no post office, England, Germany, the United States, Japan, and various other countries have established their own post offices here, and invaded our rights. This is really against international precedent. In 1895 a Decree was issued and He-te [Sir Robert Hart], Inspector general of Customs, was ordered to take charge; and since 1896 post offices have been gradually established along the sea-coasts and rivers. These were attached to and concurrently managed by the Inspectorate general of Maritime Customs...

(10) *The official collection of opium duties.* [P. 28] Now it is most urgent for us to raise money, and it is difficult to obtain a large amount of funds by the sporadic scraping together of odds and ends. It is difficult to increase again the levy of the *likin* tax, which should be abolished; and it is also hard to make the salt gabelle heavier, since its rates already have been repeatedly raised. Only an additional duty on the "foreign drug" [opium] will not be oppressive to the people but will result in a huge augmentation of financial provisions. We found that in the case of France and Spain, in shipping matches and Luzon tobacco, and in the case of Japan, in collecting and selling foreign and native opium in Taiwan, these things were purchased and distributed by government agencies. Now let

us imitate this method. According to the Maritime Customs trade reports, in 1899 the import of opium for sale was 5,900,161 piculs [1 picul = 133 lbs.]... If we estimate the annual import at six million odd piculs, the total weight is 96,000,000 taels ... and the total value is 50,000,000 taels including tax and *likin*. We propose that hereafter the government establish offices, and when opium enters the customhouses it be entirely purchased and then resold to private merchants for distribution to all provinces... It is estimated that each year we can make a surplus of ten million taels...

(11) *More translations of Japanese and Western books*. [P. 31] Today if we wish to adopt political systems from all the nations, we should certainly translate more foreign political and academic works. There are in general three methods of translating books. First, to order each province to conduct research in foreign books, and translate and publish them, and let the ones which produce more translations than others be permitted to ask for a reward from the emperor. Nevertheless the funds are limited and the books thus translated cannot be many. Second, to request that an Imperial Decree be publicly circulated among all provincial licentiates of various levels to the effect that those who can translate useful foreign books are to submit them to the emperor for his information through the high officials outside of the capital; they may be rewarded with actual official posts or encouraged with good brevet ranks, and their books may be returned to the various provinces for publication. Thus the cost will be reduced. But there are few important foreign books circulating in China, and the selections cannot be too strict. Third, to request that Chinese ministers abroad be ordered to investigate the most essential and important books recently published in the nations in which they are respectively stationed, and to invite a thoroughly learned man of that country to be the chief translation official, assisted by the ministers' retinue and students...

The above various items are all very important and should be rapidly put into effect ... As for the unorthodox theories of K'ang Yu-wei, he merely aimed at spreading his own teachings ("K'angism") and treacherously sought to disturb the basic order of things. In reality he has no understanding at all of the essential ideas of Western government and Western knowledge. The various items proposed here are distinctly different from his proposals. And moreover these points have been generally put into operation by Imperial Decrees at different times during the last thirty years. Here we only seek to promote and enforce them with the hope of averting imminent calamity... We humbly expect that your sacred enlightenment, deep observation, and farsighted vision will grant an early execution of the proposals, so that all countries may see China's determination to exert every effort to become strong, whereupon their habits of despising and insulting us may gradually die out. This also will let the scholars and the people know that the Court has the intention of renovating our system [lit., to put fresh strings on the bow and pull it anew]. The reactionary people will then modify their blunders, and those who are expecting better government will offer their loyalty. And the heresies that offend the emperor and stimulate uprisings will not arise. Thus the empire will be fortunate indeed...

### b. *Educational Reform*

The civil service examination system had had a history of more than one thousand years. During the Ch'ing period practical-minded scholars had often raised objections to the formal eight-legged essays required in the examinations, and proposed instead compositions about current affairs.① In 1887 mathematics was adopted as an examination subject at the suggestion of a censor,⑫ but unfortunately the conservative influence was still so predominant that not many scholars took an interest in this new alternative. Two years after the Sino-Japanese War, in 1897, Yen Hsiu, provincial director of education of Kweichow, memorialized requesting the introduction of a " special examination on political economy" (*ching-chi t'e-k'o*), in order to recruit scholars who were versed in current affairs and had not strictly followed the traditional routine. In the following year Liang Ch'i-ch'ao and more than a hundred other provincial graduates submitted a joint memorial requesting the abolition of the whole civil service examination system. K'ang Yu-wei also presented memorials strongly supporting this change in order to cope with foreign invasion. During the Reform Movement of 1898, a modification in the examination subjects was ordered but not carried out. Finally, early in 1908 Chang Chih-tung, governor-general at Nanking, and Yuan Shih-k'ai, governor-general at Tientsin, submitted a joint memorial, part of which is translated below, to suggest the gradual abolition of the system. Thereafter other memorialists urged a summary abolition, and eventually an imperial Decree of September 2, 1905⑬ announced the immediate and permanent cessation of the examinations. They had been held usually once every year or twice every three years since A. D. 622.

To replace the old examinations the Chinese government adopted a new educational program based on Western and Japanese models. This gave the missionary schools a new status, and gradually changed their enrollment. Instead of drawing students exclusively from the children of the poor, they now began to attract those of the elite, that is, the gentry-official class. In the meantime, education abroad, especially in nearby Japan, had become highly esteemed. As many as ten thousand Chinese students were in Japan at one time, whereas only a few hundreds went to Europe and the United States. While some of these students in foreign countries received a relatively substantial education, there were many instances of graduates of short courses in education or law in Japan who at once became teachers or judges on their return.

The change in the educational system also gave sudden recognition to the Chinese students who had been educated in the West since the 1870's. Many of them, including a dentist, were given the *chin-shih* and *chü-jen* degrees. In the educational system, at least, Westernization in form was finally achieved after 1905. This movement, however, did not result in the rapid democratizing of Chinese society, for education was still a luxury of the wealthy; whether the new system developed those "men of ability" so ardently sought after by Chang Chih-tung is also uncertain.

## DOC. 51   A MEMORIAL OF CHANG CHIH-TUNG AND YUAN SHIH-K'AI URGING ABOLITION OF THE OLD EXAMINATIONS, 1903.[1]

We consider that it does not matter whether a nation is strong or weak; as long as it has men of ability, it will be prosperous. Nor does it matter whether the time is peaceful or perilous; if there are men of talent, things will be in good order. Indeed, men of ability are the basic stuff of a nation and the foundation of its government ... The weakness of China today is extreme. Great catastrophes have come in succession and foreign aggressions daily press upon us. It is the moment for us to arise and exert ourselves in action...

We reverently admire the arduous life of our Empress Dowager and Emperor who are looking for talented men as if thirsting for water, and who have ordered all the provinces to establish schools, and who again have proclaimed Decrees to promote this work ... Unfortunately, the various provinces which are starting to look into the school situation generally are hesitant or procrastinating, or carry out the order perfunctorily or neglect the order without yet establishing any schools at all. Some schools have been opened but the equipment is very incomplete. When we look into the causes, they say that it is because of insufficient funds and the difficulty of finding teachers. These two difficulties are certainly real [p. 8], but they are not bad enough to cause a great evil. The greatest and most obvious evil, which is the enemy and hindrance to the school system, is the civil service examination. In general, a school is a place to train men of ability, and the civil service examination is to test men of ability. If the civil service examination and school system are coördinated, then the school will be prosperous without our urging. If the school and civil service examinations are uncoördinated, then the school will eventually be a mere name without any substance. Why? Because the multitude compete on the path toward benefits and emoluments, and people are afraid to take up complicated and difficult tasks. The period needed to complete the course in the schools is settled in advance, and it is necessary for one to spend years before he becomes well qualified in his field; on the other hand, one may be successful by sheer chance in taking advantage of the tricks and malpractices in the civil service examinations. Even though the eight-legged essays are abolished and replaced by essays on current policies and classical principles, yet, after all, one's writings are based on the strength of one day and these empty words cannot be compared to actual achievements…

China is not without men who are worrying about the times, but we have not yet heard of any of the gentry class who are urging the building of schools. This is also due to the fact that the interest of the multitude is in the civil service examinations, which have been used by fathers and elder brothers to encourage their sons and younger brothers, and by hamlets and villages to urge on their common folk [to become outstanding figures in the future]… Thus, as long as the civil service examination is not abolished there is no chance for the schools to be very prosperous, and our students will go on without gaining any actual knowledge, our nation will have no men of ability to meet the crisis of the time, China will be unable to advance to wealth and power, and she will never be able to compete with other nations. Your ministers' hearts ache…

[P. 9] We earnestly hope that the civil service examination will be gradually but completely abolished and that schools will be established as numerous as the teeth of a comb and the trees of the forest. Thus we can remove the evils of administration which have been followed for several hundred years in the past, and we can train millions of useful men of ability in the future. By this action the people of all the five continents will be amazed and a myriad generations will be made to show respect...

## c. *Constitutionalism*

In order to show the seriousness of her interest in governmental reform, the Empress Dowager sent two official missions to Europe and America in 1905 to investigate foreign constitutional governments. Upon their return in the following year two of the commissioners, Tai Hung-tz'u (1853-1910) and Tuan-fang (1861-1911), jointly presented to the throne a work on "The essentials of European-American government," from which the following passage is taken. Though published in 1907, the original covering memorial was dated in the ninth month of 1906.⑮

This book is significant in many ways. First, it represents the commissioners' understanding of the principles and operation of constitutional monarchy. Tai, an orthodox Confucian scholar-official, and Tuan-fang, a Manchu official with a reputation for vigor and enlightenment, went as far as the dynasty was willing to go in the matter of constitutional government. Their summary of Western constitutionalism is as interesting for what is rejected as for what is accepted. Secondly, this work underlines the utilitarian interest of the reformers of the period: justification for the constitutional form of government is sought in practical rather than in theoretical terms. In the introductory chapter, for instance, the authors explain that the adoption of a constitution would increase the efficiency of the emperor's rule, not detract from it. They stress the expectation that when people are allowed to participate in political affairs, their interest in the nation's needs will be stimulated; whereupon a greater development of resources will follow, and this in turn will facilitate the government's tax collection.⑯ Thirdly, such arguments were not intended for the ear of the Empress Dowager only—they were intended also to provide a reasoned basis on which the throne's actions could be publicized to the entire country. It is noteworthy that the book was published within a year of the commissioners' return.

A comparison of the arguments contained in this book with the writings of reformers in contemporary journals shows a close affinity in their points of view. It is clear that this work was part of an effort in traditional government circles to win greater support from the scholars and thereby stem the revolutionary tide.

### DOC. 52   A REPORT ON CONSTITUTIONAL GOVERNMENTS ABROAD, 1906

The thing to be most carefully investigated in the observation of the structure of European constitutional governments is this: what changes are caused by the constitution in the authority of the monarch under a constitutional government as compared with the autocratic rule of the monarch? To know this important point one should study nations which have changed directly from autocratic monarchy to constitutional monarchy. The system of enacting constitutions according to the wish of the people, and then electing the monarch, as in Belgium, Greece, Rumania, etc.; and the system of basing a state on popular consent, as in Italy and Spain; these are actually republican systems although called monarchic, and for the time being we shall not discuss them. Again, we need not discuss the fact that the German Emperor did not depend on his original power in the creation of his empire, but was delegated authority as head of the confederation by the various German states, with the constitution quite resembling that of a republic. [P. 30b] The so-called pure autocratic monarchies that have changed directly into constitutional monarchies are, for instance, the Kingdom of Prussia, the Kingdom of Bavaria, the Kingdom of Saxony and the Austrian Empire...

The constitutions of the above countries, such as Prussia, Saxony, and Austria, had all been submitted to the parliaments and amended by them; therefore they are also not constitutions granted by royal order. In the world today only the constitution of Bavaria has the nature of one granted by royal order. It first fixes the powers of the king, and [p. 31] draws up a main article which says that the king is the head of the state and holds the power of the central authority which he exercises according to the provisions of the constitution; that the person of the king cannot be violated, etc. Then the king's various kinds of authority is itemized in the different articles. This is because the influence of the French Revolution spread across all of Europe, so that the people of the various German states also wanted to establish constitutions. Although their kings did not wish suddenly to change their autocratic governments, yet in the circumstances there was nothing they could do but yield to the times, and each granted a constitution...

As for the stipulation that the person of the monarch is not to be violated, both the constitution by royal order and that by common discussion include this provision. For the monarch is also human. Perchance he might commit a mistake in policy, which would harm the people and run contrary to the basic purpose of the constitutional government. Or through error he might act contrary to the articles of the constitution. If at such times the hostile criticisms (of the people) are concentrated personally on the monarch, then his powers will be debased and his dignity injured, and henceforth the political system will be destroyed. Therefore the constitutions of the various nations place the monarch beyond the reach of adverse criticism and discussion...

But this would make the articles of constitution a mere form without substance, and the situation would be the same as that under an autocratic monarch. Therefore, there must be high ministers to assist the monarch. In case of unsuitable administration or unconstitutional acts, then the monarch's assistants can be blamed for not doing their duty. Consequently, the high ministers of the government must take the responsibility on behalf of the monarch. This is called the system of responsible ministers, which has been clearly provided for in the constitutions of the various nations...

[P. 33] Before the enactment of the constitution the monarch holds all the national power, and all political matters of the nation must be decided by him. But no great changes occur after the enactment of the constitution. The monarch remains the highest organ of the state, the constitution only delimiting the respective authorities of the different divisions in the government. Therefore, the monarch's powers consist not only of those written in the constitution. All powers that concern national affairs the monarch exercises, even if they are not written into the constitution. Those powers which the monarch exercises by himself without going through another government agency are called prerogatives [lit., *ta-ch'üan*, great or high power] by some Western scholars. Because they can be exercised without having to be referred to an article in the constitution, they are thus called "prerogatives"; therefore, there are many that are not specifically stipulated in the constitution. Some other scholars have thought that they could protect the authority of the monarch by specific stipulations in the constitution to show that such and such are the royal prerogatives, so that the other government organs, e. g., parliament, could not encroach upon them; these are called "constitutional prerogatives"; all royal prerogatives are stated in the constitution, and the monarch absolutely cannot exercise those that are not clearly stated. Such a theory is improper and we should take note of this…

### d. *Yuan Shih-k'ai and the Modern Army*

Yuan Shih-k'ai (1859-1916), as we have seen, had proved himself an able politician and a leader in the late Ch'ing reform movement under the Manchus. He is best remembered as an army organizer and because as first president of the Chinese Republic at Peking after 1912 he attempted to overthrow the Republic and make himself emperor. After him came the war lords, most of whom had been his army commanders.⑰

Yuan was brought up in an official and military family. With only moderate education, he made his career through his early participation in military programs and as Li Hung-chang's protégé in Korea. He utilized his opportunity to rise to power after the (Wuxu Coup) and the Boxer Uprising had put a premium upon officials who could create and use military force.

The modern Chinese army traces its development from the famous "Hunan Army" (*Hsiang-chün*) and the Anhwei Army (*Huai-chün*), developed by Tseng Kuo-fan and others on a local basis against the Taiping and Nien rebels. A by-product of the Sino-French conflict was the establishment of a Military Preparatory School (*Wu-pei hsueh-t'ang*) at Tientsin, which was suggested by general C. G. ("Chinese") Gordon in 1885. In this school Western methods of military instruction were adopted and German instructors were employed, although the achievement was negligible. After China was defeated by Japan in 1894, Chang Chih-tung, then governor-general at Nanking, organized his "Self-strengthening Army" (*Tzu-ch'iang-chün*), later centered at Wusung near Shanghai and trained by German instructors (see Ch. XVII above). About the same time Hu Yü-fen (d. 1906), director-general of the Peking-Tientsin Railroad, was ordered to organize a modern army, called the *Ting-wu-chün*, which was trained in German style at Hsiao-chan, about twenty miles from Tientsin. Later on this force became the nucleus of the Pei-yang army. At that time Yuan Shih-k'ai was in Peking, where he became a member of the "Society for the study of self-strengthening" (*Ch'iang-hsueh-hui*), the leading society in the Reform Movement, and also established good relations with many high officials, including Jung-lu, then minister of war. Through this connection Yuan was appointed to command the Ting-wu army, which was soon renamed the "Newly Organized Army" (*Hsin-chien lu-chün*). An imperial Decree of December 8, 1895, appointed Yuan Shih-k'ai to train the new army at Tientsin, and expressly follow the German army regulations. His Chinese instructors had to learn enough German for the purpose.

From 1896 to 1898 Yuan's energy was spent mainly on this new army. During the Boxer Uprising of 1900, he was fortunately not involved in the international imbroglio. Thereafter Li Hung-chang died, in 1901, and his position as governor-general of Chihli and superintendent of trade for the northern ports was given to Yuan. Jung-lu died in 1903. Meanwhile the Empress Dowager, chagrined at the recent humiliation of China and the dynasty, determined to improve the army as part of her general reform program. In this process Yuan Shih-k'ai had a good opportunity to build up his personal military power through the assistance of his trusted staff members—men like Feng Kuo-chang (1859-1919), Wang Shih-chen (1861-1930), Ts'ao K'un (d. 1938), and Tuan Ch'i-jui (1865-1936), all of whom subsequently became prominent warlords. By the end of 1905, Yuan Shih-k'ai had organized the six divisions of the Pei-yang Army and developed such *esprit de corps* that, even though he was away from his army for a period of years (1907-1911), his officers remained generally loyal to him.

Although he did not carry out as many reforms as his biographers have eulogistically listed, he did, nevertheless, achieve some things which had been suggested or discussed by Li Hung-chang, Chang Chih-tung, and others, notably the abolition of the civil service examinations. His modern detractors of the republican period tend to ignore these pre-republican contributions. When Yuan was governor of Shantung (Doc. 6, 1899-June 16, 1901), he submitted a memorial requesting ten items, viz., more careful issuing of orders and ordinances, training of officials, emphasis on practical studies, increase of useful subjects in the school curriculum, emphasis on travel abroad, a code regulating Chinese ministers abroad, definitions of names, titles, and duties of officials, enrichment of the national revenue, and enlightenment of the people. The reasoning in support of these proposals is along the same line as that of the three memorials of Liu K'un-i and Chang Chih-tung (see Doc. 50). Yuan enforced a few educational reforms, including the opening of a university and elementary and middle schools, in the area under his jurisdiction. He also established a *Chiao-shih-kuan*, an institution to promote advanced study. When Yuan was governor-general of Chihli and grand councillor (1901-1909), apart from building his army, he tried to improve the selection of Chinese diplomatic personnel; to open an agricultural school and an experimental farm in Paoting, and an industrial bureau (*Kung-i chü*) at Tientsin; and to secure financial reform by introducing new taxes and modern banks, in the hope of increasing the government revenues and of paying for the new army, schools, and other enterprises, including a new police force. Yuan was a supporter of the idea of constitutional monarchy—whether he was sincere or hypocritical is another question. Many Chinese students and officers were encouraged by him to study military and political science in Japan; gradually Japanese advisers replaced those from Germany. In short, during this period Yuan chiefly emphasized the training of a modern army, education for the people and good local government. His administrative ability and dominant position undoubtedly influenced the Empress Dowager to endorse some of these reforms. Eventually, after her death, he appeared to many as the only strong man of progressive views who could save China from chaos.

## CHAPTER XXI  ECONOMIC DEVELOPMENT

Although this volume is concerned more with ideas than with economics, certain economic concepts have played major roles in China's intellectual history. Let us avoid fruitless argument as to whether or not the "entrepreneurial spirit" is essentially an expression of ideology, and note some of the new ideas of industrial development which appeared in China about the turn of the century, stimulated by the Western example in China and by a new appraisal of Chinese needs and potentialities.

The Western stimulus became more concrete after 1896, when the subsidiary treaty of commerce with Japan gave her people the right "to carry on trade, industries and manufactures" in the treaty ports.① By most-favored-nation treatment, other powers received the same privilege. Thereafter foreign factories sprang up like bamboo shoots after rain, seeking to utilize China's cheap labor and raw materials. Japanese, English, and German firms seized the opportunity to open cotton mills in Shanghai, and Chinese industrialists soon followed suit. The rural handicraft industries, which were a sideline for most farm families, could not compete with the cheaper, machine-produced goods. Gradually, the peasantry were compelled to spend some of their hard-earned cash to buy foreign-made cloth, cigarettes, and other commodities.

As a form of government encouragement to Chinese industry, the Tsungli Yamen in 1898 issued regulations whereby a fifty-year monopoly would be granted to inventors of new weapons and a thirty year monopoly to inventors of new utensils for daily use. The numerous concessions for mining and railway development secured by the imperialist powers from 1898 on also moved the Chinese government to take counter measures. Between 1903 and 1911 several projects for industrial development were actively undertaken or encouraged by high officials. Prince Tsai-chen was sent to Europe, America, and Japan to investigate industry. In 1903 a ministry of commerce was set up at Peking; in 1906 it was renamed the Ministry of Agriculture, Industry, and Commerce. A commercial code including a company law was proclaimed.② The use of Chinese national products was promoted by leading officials. In 1905, for example, Yuan Shih-k'ai sponsored an industrial exhibit at Tientsin. The Ministry of Commerce built a hall in Peking for the same purpose. The Ministry urged that technical colleges be opened in every province. Doctoral (i. e., *chin-shih*) degrees in industry and commerce were to be conferred on returned students, on the basis of examinations set by the government. In 1910 a huge industrial fair was organized in Nanking by the governor-general, Tuan-fang.

During the years between 1903 and 1908 one hundred and twenty-seven Chinese industrial concerns with a capital of $32,199,800 were registered at the Ministry of Agriculture, Industry, and Commerce.③ Cotton mills, flour mills, silk filatures, electric plants, tobacco and match factories, and steel foundries were among these enterprises. Also during this decade, through foreign contracts and loans, China completed some 6000 miles of railway construction.④ To compete against the foreign banks, several modern Chinese banks were opened, including the China Commercial Bank (*Chung-kuo t'ung-shang yin-hang*) in 1897, the Ministry of Revenue (Hu-pu) Bank in 1904, which was reorganized as the Ta-Ch'ing Bank in 1908, and as the Bank of China in 1913. In 1907 the Bank of Communications and the Chekiang Industrial Bank were opened.⑤

This economic growth in China was a pale reflection of the industrialization going on elsewhere in the world and lagged behind the expansion of British, Japanese, and other enterprises in the treaty ports. No Chinese undertakings, governmental or otherwise, could as yet compete with the shipping, docks, textile mills, insurance and banking interests, railway and mining investments of the single pioneer British firm of Jardine, Matheson and Company. Under the steadily increasing pressure of foreign economic development within their country, however, Chinese of the scholar-official class began to embark on new ventures and become themselves entrepreneurs of a new type. The limitations of the "government-supervision and merchant-management" system (see Ch. XIII) had been due in part to the officials' persistence in old patterns of administration—Tseng and Li, Tso Tsung-t'ang and Chang Chih-tung could inaugurate numerous projects but, because of their official duties as territorial administrators responsible for all aspects of government, they had always to delegate the management to others. The result was bureaucracy. Neither the responsible high official nor his delegated manager could live and work from day to day on the job. Neither of them could be moved primarily by the compelling motives of a business man absorbed in costs, prices, and the market.

Among the new generation who achieved prominence in industry after the turn of the century, two men were outstanding—Sheng Hsuan-huai and Chang Chien. Their careers represent two of the various forms of Chinese response to foreign economic encroachment. Both were intensely stirred by nationalist feeling. Although of the official class, neither became a high provincial official. They were not mandarins so much as working executives, specialists in industrial development.

Sheng Hsuan-huai (1844-1916) was born into an official family in Kiangsu. After failing to get a *chü-jen* degree in the provincial examination, he became a secretary to Li Hung-chang, as already noted. In 1878 Li made him manager of the China Merchants Steam Navigation Company, where he worked with two Cantonese compradore-merchants, T'ang T'ing-shu (1832-1892) and Hsü Jun (1838-1911), both of whom later became prominent (Hsü made a fortune in tea and real estate). Since Sheng regarded modern communications as of primary importance for China's national strength, Li made him supervisor of the construction of the Peking-Hankow railway and of the telegraph line between Tientsin and Shanghai. Frequently, when government enterprises got into difficulty, Sheng appears to have been called in as a trouble shooter. When the first cotton mill at Shanghai burned down, Li ordered him to take it over and rebuild it, recruiting the capital from merchants. When the Han-Yeh-P'ing Iron and Steel Works ran short of funds and had to be sold to the stockholders, Sheng Hsuan-huai was chosen to take over the management from Chang Chih-tung. In each case he had a hard time raising funds.

Although Sheng never held a post in the provincial hierarchy higher than that of taotai, he proved his competence in diplomacy as well as industry. He accompanied Li Hung-chang to Chefoo in 1876, and participated in the negotiations with Sir Thomas Wade for the purchase of the Shanghai-Wusung railroad. During the Boxer Uprising he played an important role in keeping South China out of the international imbroglio.⑥

Evidently, Sheng had a natural ability for handling several duties simultaneously—in shipping, telegraphs, railroads, and mining—and his official posts accumulated as time went on. By 1896 he was customs taotai at Tientsin and director-in-chief of most government railway construction, in addition to heading the China Merchants Company and Imperial Telegraphs. These multiple posts moved Gustav Detring to warn Li Hung-chang against him, but the warning went unheeded. Li said Sheng was "a man of an alert mind."

Among his other activities, Sheng Hsuan-huai became the founder of Peiyang College at Tientsin in 1886 and of Nanyang College at Shanghai in 1897, both good technical institutions, where many Chinese engineers as well as political leaders like Wang Ch'ung-hui and Ch'en Li-fu were trained. During the early years of the twentieth century, Sheng wielded great power and his enemies increased in proportion. To avoid sharp criticism in China he traveled to Japan in 1908 on the pretext of seeking treatment for tuberculosis. While in Japan, he met the political and industrial leaders and investigated Japanese industry. In February 1911 he was promoted to be minister of Posts and Communications and vigorously insisted on the policy of nationalization of railways, which served as the fuse to ignite the Republican Revolution of October 10, 1911.

By his foreign competitors in the treaty ports Sheng Hsuan-huai was acknowledged to be energetic and vigorous in the pursuit of his purposes, but he was viewed with deep suspicion, J. O. P. Bland called him an "old fox,"⑦ and H. B. Morse said that "his honesty was trusted neither by Chinese nor by foreigners."⑧ Clean-handed or not, Sheng was certainly very nationalistic in his sentiments. In May 1896 he responded vigorously to Chang Chih-tung's invitation to take the directorship of the Peking-Hankow railway as a means of fighting against foreign aggression. He replied, "I would not think of sparing myself the exertion of a few more years of my energy and strength, if only I could earn some face (lit., a mouthful of breath) for China."⑨

In May 1898, when trying to resist the foreign envoys' threatening demands for railway concessions, Sheng wrote, "I am not afraid of difficulties or danger; I put myself forward and took this job, not caring whether it helps or harms me."⑩ There is no doubt that Sheng's aggressiveness accomplished much, and also irritated many people. One of his minor achievements was the founding of the Chinese Red Cross Society (1909). More important was his founding of modern banking in China, as a necessary means of financial defense against the foreign powers, especially Russia. Though Chang Chih-tung was cool to the idea, Sheng went ahead. One of his memorials is translated below.

## DOC. 53  SHENG HSUAN-HUAI'S ARGUMENT FOR MODERN BANKING, 1896⑪

Banking originated in Europe. Its main purpose is to help circulate the wealth and property within a nation so as to meet the needs of the upper and lower classes. Western banking is better than the old Chinese exchange banks (*p'iao-hao*) or money shops (*ch'ien-chuang*). Since it is protected by the national government, its rights cannot be usurped and its credit can be maintained.

After all the nations began to trade with China, the Chinese neglected banking, and so the banks of England, France, Germany, Russia, and Japan expanded into China and have taken great profits away from us. In recent years many Chinese and also some foreign scholar-officials have clearly seen this situation and have suggested the establishment of banks to play a major role in our commercial affairs and central administration. Now we are building railways, which require a heavy initial investment. Unless we quickly establish a Chinese bank, we shall have no way to circulate the funds which serve as blood in our veins or to stop the control of our economic life by foreign merchants.

Some critics say that a national bank should supply all its own [government] funds as capital; that it should be run by high officials, and should issue bank notes for the Ministry of Revenue, like the central banks which manage the financial resources of England, France, and other nations. In this way a national bank would be an external treasury of the Ministry of Revenue. But these critics should know that the customs in China and the West are different; not long ago we learned a lesson from the notes issued by the Ministry. A government organization which handles business matters will run into numerous obstacles and accumulate evils. Some observers wish to entrust the raising of foreign funds to Westerners, by whom thousands of taels could be raised in a short time. Such words are sweet to hear, but the power would be in their hands and the actual advantage or disadvantage would be unpredictable.

Your minister (Sheng Hsuan-huai) thinks that banking is a matter for merchants; if merchants do not trust the government, the financial power of the country cannot be concentrated; and if this power is not concentrated, a bank will not be successful. If we wish to begin carefully in order to get good results, we must accumulate small sums (from merchants) to make a big fund. I venture to request that a high official be appointed to select honest and reliable merchants of the gentry class (*shen-shang*) from all the provinces and recommend them for service as trustees (of the bank). They should raise five million taels of capital from Chinese merchants and establish a Chinese bank, first in Peking and Shanghai and then with branches in other provincial capitals and trading ports. Following Western business practice, this bank should be managed by the merchants themselves.

Some time ago your minister discussed banking affairs in Shanghai with Yen Hsin-hou, who has the rank of expectant taotai and is a gentry-merchant operating the official customs banks (*yin-hao*) which handle the duties at Canton, Foochow, Ningpo, Shanghai, and Hankow. [P. 15] Yen Hsin-hou has a broad view of the whole national situation, and is willing to have his own customs banks incorporated in a national bank so as to make it stronger. Further, in accordance with the practice of the Hongkong and Shanghai Banking Corporation (*Hui-feng yin-hang*), we propose, with good paper and machines, to print banknotes that will circulate along with the silver currency. The amount of silver on deposit will determine the number of banknotes printed, so that they can be cashed at any time... The employment of personnel and the management of affairs in the bank will follow the regulations of the Hongkong and Shanghai Banking Corporation as a standard. Thus the power of Chinese merchants throughout the nation will be concentrated in the operation of the national banking corporation. If Chinese banks secure only one more cent of profit, they will to that degree recover our rights from the foreign banks.

We should also follow the Western practice whereby banks contribute a certain amount of money to the government when they have a surplus. Regulations should be established in advance and should be strictly observed. Both the merchants and the common people would benefit, and the nation would also benefit indirectly...

In November 1896, Sheng Hsuan-huai received verbal instructions from Prince Kung to the effect that the bank should be opened immediately because Russia had secured permission to open Sino-Russian banks at Peking and other places; if China did not establish a bank of her own first, her rights would be entirely lost, like fish caught in one throw of a net. Consequently, the government was most anxious to see the bank succeed without delay,⑫ and it was opened for business in June 1897 with a capital of five million taels held by Chinese citizens only.

In spite of his accomplishments, including a huge accumulation of wealth, Sheng Hsuan-huai voiced three regrets about his own life: (1) he had never obtained a higher degree; (2) he had never held a regular magistracy; and (3) he had never been to Europe or America.⑬ Evidently, he had retained traditional values and ambitions. His younger contemporary, Chang Chien (1853-1926), was a man of different character and ideals.

Chang was born into a farmer's family in Kiangsu, and became a top scholar (*chuang-yuan*), winning first place among 314 successful candidates in the metropolitan examinations for the *chin-shih* degree in 1894—a great honor which helped his future career. Previously he had served as a young official in Korea, in 1882, and his brilliant writing and energetic discharge of duties had caught the attention of Li Hung-chang, Chang Chih-tung, and other high officials. In the critical year of 1895 he could have expected promotion to important positions, but he decided instead to go into the field of industrial development.

Chang Chien thus became known as the top scholar who went into business. He did not like official formalities, and also resented the usual criticism that scholarly bookworms were good for nothing. He was distressed by the Japanese victory and aspired to save China from poverty and weakness. Impressed by Timothy Richard's reform programs for the development of education and industry, and for the improvement of public health and welfare and the popular standard of living,[14] he became interested in his native district, Tungchow, Kiangsu, commonly called Nantung to distinguish it from the northern Tungchow near Peking. This district produced good cotton, which was already being bought up by the Japanese after the war. Chang Chien therefore set to work and founded the famous Ta-sheng Cotton Mill at Nantung in 1898. He served as the managing director and also as liaison officer between the merchant partners and the government officials whose patronage was necessary. Chang's aim in this was explained in the "Mill Agreement" (*ch'ang-yueh*), drawn up in 1897, part of which is translated below:

### DOC. 54   ECONOMIC VIEWS OF CHANG CHIEN[15]

The establishment of a cotton mill in Tungchow is to aid the livelihood of the people of Tungchow and also to protect China's profitable resources. The cotton produced in Tungchow is soft but tough, with long fibres, the best kind in Asia. Japan needs it badly for her mills. Raw cotton is now taken away and comes back in the form of yarn; this is increasing day by day. We provide resources to others, at the cost of our own substance, and they sell us back the goods which are made out of our resources... Our own interest cannot be protected and our people are becoming poorer every day. What can our nation rely upon?... For these reasons, in the winter of 1895 Chang Chih-tung memorialized the Throne and recommended that I should manage the cotton mill project. I did not calculate my own meager ability but at once took on the responsibility. Since then I have experienced the greatest inconstancy of human relationships and have been confronted by a thousand misfortunes and frustrations, in addition to frequent changes of the market. For five years I have had to bear insult and ridicule. Fortunately, the enterprise has not ended in collapse, not only because I have used all my limited ability, energy, and wisdom, but mostly because the higher authorities have sympathized with me; the local officials have given me the chance to carry out my plans; and a few gentlemen comrades have assisted and supported me. Now the building of the mill has been completed; the machinery is running; each of my co-workers has already undertaken one particular task as his special duty; each should have his authority defined and should not go beyond it or fail to live up to it. Thus the job will be done.

From this and other statements we can infer that the success of Chang Chien's enterprise was due to several factors: his own patience and endurance; his good connections with the local and higher provincial officials, based in part on the personal repute and high qualifications he had established through the civil service examinations. He was perhaps the first, if not also the last, Confucian industrialist. He worked many years without salary and sometimes resorted to selling his calligraphy in order to raise money for traveling expenses.⑯ The hard struggle he had against social convention, which frowned upon any scholar's becoming a "merchant," is indicated in the following retrospective statement made to his shareholders in 1925 at the end of his career:⑰

Since I (Chang Chien) had the misfortune to live in a transitional period of Chinese history, I thrust myself into industrial circles. There I have suffered many hardships, and now in my declining years I cannot endure further distress and humiliation, and must beg the shareholders to recommend an able man to replace me... [P. 34] I am also a shareholder; I consider that the mill, the local self-government, and the national industrial development are all directly or indirectly related, and so the mill is of broad significance.

I was of farming stock and an indigent scholar. From youth I did not like to see rich and aristocratic men, nor did I like to interview famous dignitaries. Even if I went to an interview, I would not humble myself... After I was thirty I became enraged at the weakness of China. After forty, when the Sino-Japanese War was concluded, I grew even more angry. I felt pity for our people's lack of ordinary knowledge, the result of our unchanged educational system and the inadequacy of our governmental reforms. I wished to carry out reforms myself, but I had no authority. After careful deliberation from all angles I concluded that we ought to begin with the development of industry. Yet I would have to make connections with rich men in order to develop an industry, and that went against the grain. I pondered it over and over again, and finally decided to give up my personal feelings and "offer my body to feed the tiger." I recognized the virtue of humbling myself for the cause of China, disregarding my private interest so that my purpose could be achieved and my integrity still be maintained. After I had made up my mind I had no regrets.

From 1896 to 1899 my first mill went through a critical period when I had to bear much blame and criticism, and to struggle vigorously for success while still taking a loss. From 1900 to 1901 was a period of gradual upturn; again I was in distress, but the danger was avoided. From 1902 to 1906 was a period of gradual success, and from 1907 to 1915 was a period of peaceful progress... For the second mill in 1907 and 1908 I was finding a site and building the factory; there was no gain but a net loss. From 1909 to 1915, however, there was a surplus every year... The first mill... in a total of twenty-seven years made a combined surplus and regular profit of Tls. 9,964,600... [P. 35] The second mill, ... after it began operation, in sixteen years produced surplus and regular profits of Tls. 3,577,100. The two mills together thus made a profit of more than Tls. 13,481,700... The salary and bonuses that I earned, however, over more than twenty years, were mostly used for educational, philanthropic, and public welfare purposes...

Chang Chien treated his mill hands paternally and housed them in dormitories, following the Japanese practice. In 1903 he made a trip to that country. The influence of Japanese political institutions and industrial methods can be seen in these excerpts from his diaries:[18]

[P. 3] The Japanese rule their country as though taking care of a garden, or arranging a vase of flowers, for which even a small pebble or a piece of moss has been carefully prepared. Lao-tzu says, "To rule a large country is the same as cooking a small fish." The Japanese understand the essential idea of fixing a small fish...

[P. 7] In managing industry, the most important thing the Japanese have is the knowledge that to give is to get. With their material supplies coming from Europe and then flowing to China, they have been able to share in the profits of Europeans and make their country prosperous. Nevertheless, their wages are generally once or twice again as much as those in China. If our government tends to develop commerce, and to benefit the workers, we have five advantages over Japan: (1) abundant natural resources; (2) enough rice and cheap labor; (3) a chance to imitate the strong points of all nations so that the profits will not flow out of China; (4) a chance to meet the needs of our people's daily life so that they will need nothing from outside; and (5) a chance to compete for advancement in civilization with the whole world...

In Japan, all industrial manufactures are transported to other nations without paying extra customs duties. As to transportation, their railways are close to their factories and if they are not sufficient, the government subsidizes the products of the factories. The enthusiasm of the nation in encouraging industry is so great! Nevertheless, the country is small, rice expensive, and wages and costs of production are both increasing. The businessmen, however, are still ceaselessly devoting their energies to promoting industrialization. In competition with the civilization of the world, if there is no advancement, there will be retrogression, and this is understood by the Japanese...

[P. 18] I went to see a steel works in which steamships and small boats can be built. There are no Europeans among their workers... This makes me reflect upon the fact that the size and capital funds of our Shanghai Arsenal are many dozen times larger than those of the Japanese plant, and yet our Arsenal has never built a ship or made an instrument for agricultural or industrial use. Such instruments could be sold to the people at a profit, which could be used to subsidize agriculture and commerce, and then still more people could share the benefit. When we compare the two, what a difference! ...

When Japanese scholar-officials become government workers or merchants, their selection of a profession is guided by their interests. When they are officials, they are devoted to their government work, and when they are merchants, they are devoted to commercial affairs. Chinese scholar-officials, when they are in official posts, also have some business plans, and when they are merchants, they still have an official air.

By 1910 Chang Chien controlled not only three cotton mills at Nantung and Shanghai, but also steamships and wharf companies to transport his products, a flour mill, an oil refinery, a distillery, and a salt manufacturing company. In a decade Nantung had become an industrial city. At the same time, the new city had gradually acquired a school system, starting with kindergartens and extending to Nantung College.

The college included trade, normal, sericultural, agricultural, medical, and engineering schools. An orphanage, an old people's home, a hospital, schools for the blind, dumb, and disabled, and a new jail were also built. Roads, a library, a museum, and parks were constructed.[19] Most of this social development was due to Chang's initiative.

Chang Chien's reputation and moral integrity led to his selection for government posts. He was a leader in the provincial constitutional movement in the 1900's and chairman of the Kiangsu provisional assembly in 1909-1911. Invited by Dr. Sun Yat-sen to enter government service, he became minister of Agriculture and Commerce, and director-general of the National Water Conservancy Bureau from 1913 to 1915. He sponsored China's first company law and bankruptcy law. But Yuan shih-k'ai did not give him much authority to carry out his plans and he soon retired. In 1917 he opened a drama academy at Tungchow to which he invited famous playwrights and actors. In 1920 he invited Liang Ch'i-ch'ao and John Dewey to give public lectures there. In a preface to the biography written by his son, Dr. Hu Shih says: "He alone opened many new roads; he was for thirty years a pioneer. He created employment for several million people and brought blessings to his locality; his influence was felt all over the country."[20]

The next extract, from Chang's inaugural speech as chief manager of the Han-Yeh-P'ing coal and iron company in 1913, indicates his general faith in industrialization, particularly his conviction that cotton and steel production was essential to China's progress—a view more widely held in China today than fifty years ago.[21]

From an examination of the Maritime Customs trade reports, I have concluded that the cotton and iron industries provide the chief basis of economic power. In the past I have been engaged in the cotton industry, and experienced many difficulties and hardships, with frequent frustrations and recoveries. I am not very familiar with the iron industry... Yet it is a ray of hope for China. Today the attention of the various nations is focused on

China's only iron mill here. Your managers and workers, who have gone through more than ten years of hardship, will not give up your struggle at the half-way point unless your resources are entirely exhausted... We should make every effort to go ahead... and plan a permanent enterprise for the nation. Employees should be hired only for their ability, and management should aim at actual achievement...

In a memorial urging government development of mining, Chang Chien Wrote in 1914:②

I have learned that in manufacturing there is nothing more important than iron and steel, and in the whole economy nothing of greater importance than a good currency system. Among all the nations in both the eastern and the western hemispheres there is none without a government steel mill and mint and government mines for production of gold, silver, copper, and iron. In peace time these mines supply the needs of society, and in war time they meet the urgent need of the nation...

In our newly proclaimed mining law, only salt and petroleum are to be nationally owned; the development of mines is left open to free enterprise so that our government may show that it has no intention of contending for profit with its own people. Nevertheless such ores as iron and lead are not only indispensable [p. 4] for making steamships, rails, and machinery; they also provide the materials for guns and ammunition. The cost of opening such mines is enormous and there will be numerous defects if people are permitted to undertake it by themselves. They should be assisted by the power of the government in order to avoid unsuccessful operation like that of the Han-Yeh-P'ing company.

While Chang Chien's career has not yet been carefully studied and appraised, it is plain that he went far in bridging the gap between Confucianism and modern industry.

# CHAPTER XXII LIANG CH'I-CH'AO AND NATIONALISM

Liang Ch'i-ch'ao in the early twentieth century became the most influential of all Chinese publicists. When he first rose to fame during the Reform Movement in 1898, his thought had been in line with that of his teacher, K'ang Yu-wei. But after they had both escaped abroad into exile in that year, K'ang made little change in his ideas, while Liang, as a refugee in Japan, a newspaper editor, and a voracious reader of Japanese and other new books, made great progress. Instead of admiring Mencius, he now liked to talk about Rousseau and Montesquieu; instead of urging the protection of Confucianism, he now tried in many respects to go beyond the scope of K'ang's ideas.

In Japan the name of his periodical was changed three times. From 1898 to 1901 it was called *Ch'ing-i pao*, "a paper of public opinions." After 1902 it was changed to *Hsin-min ts'ung-pao*, "a miscellaneous paper for a new people." After 1910 it became the *Kuo-feng pao*, "a paper for the national spirit." The second title has a special significance because, after the repeated failures of the self-strengthening movement and other reform movements, Liang Ch'i-ch'ao realized that not only must China's institutions and political and social systems undergo a change, but the Chinese people themselves must basically be reborn or rejuvenated. Hence the theme of the "new people" or "the renovation of the people" as the major motif of the magazine. It aimed to lead a patriotic, new culture movement.

As the decade after 1900 gave increasing evidence of the impending collapse of the dynasty, the way was opened for the rebel element among the Chinese scholar class to develop their theories of reform and try further to rationalize and understand the disaster which had overtaken China's ancient society. In this period, Liang Ch'i-ch'ao appeared to represent the more significant wing of the rebel reformers. While he was less of a political organizer than Sun Yat-sen, Liang symbolized for the student class the great tradition of Chinese scholarship, face to face with the unprecedented problems posed by the West. His wide-ranging interests and eloquent style gave his writings great force, and there is little doubt that he taught his generation many lessons in the principles of patriotism and citizenship, as well as in political theory generally. The following essay of 1902, "The renovation of the people," from the first issue of his periodical *Hsin-min ts'ung-pao*, had its original classical connotation and has also had its unworthy historical descendant, in the "New people's principles" (*Hsin-min chu-i*), with which the Japanese puppet government of North China after 1937 tried to compete with the "Three people's principles" (*San-min chu-i*) and the Kuomintang...

After the abolition of the eight-legged essay, young Chinese students were no longer supplied with fixed models to follow in writing essays. Liang Ch'i-ch'ao's articles were widely read for their style in the schools of the Republic as late as the 1930's. He was a powerful and emotional writer, and articles such as this roused a whole generation to formulate and meet new issues. Whatever his eventual place as a philosopher of change in modern China, Liang made an enormous contribution to the promotion of patriotism in the early part of the twentieth century.

## DOC. 55 "THE RENOVATION OF THE PEOPLE" BY LIANG CH'I-CH'AO, 1902[1]

A state is formed by the assembly of its people. The relationship of a nation to its people resembles that of the body to its four limbs, five viscera, muscles, veins, and corpuscles. There has never been a case where the four limbs have been cut off, the five viscera wasted away, the muscles and veins injured, and the corpuscles dried up, while the body still lived. In the same way, there has never been a nation which could still exist if its people were foolish, timid, disorganized, and confused.

Therefore, if we wish [p. 2] the body to live for a long time, the methods of hygiene must be understood. If we wish the nation to be secure, rich, and respectable, the methods for creating a new people must be discussed.

### The Renovation of the People as the First and Most Urgent Matter for China Today

Now I wish to explain thoroughly why a new people is the most urgent and necessary matter. My argument has two bases. One concerns domestic administration and the other concerns diplomatic affairs.

What concerns domestic administration? There are many in the country who are discussing political methods. They would say, A misgoverns the nation or B injures the people; a certain case is a mistake of the government, and a certain system is the fault of officials who have neglected their duty. I do not presume to say that such things are not true. Nevertheless, how is the government formed? Where do the officials come from? Do they not come from among the populace? Is A or B not a member of the citizenry? ... [p. 3] Why do we have to worry about the lack of a new system, a new government, and a new nation? Even though today we change a law and tomorrow we replace a person, a little painting in the east, a little touch in the west, learning and imitating, I cannot see that there is much help. Why, then, in our country where the new institutions have been discussed for several decades, are the results invisible? It is because we have not yet paid attention to the theory of a new people…

[P. 5] What concerns diplomatic affairs? Since the sixteenth century, about four hundred years ago, the reason for European development and world progress has been the stimulation and growth of extensive nationalist feeling everywhere. What does nationalism mean? It is that in all places people of the same race, the same language, the same religion, and the same customs regard each other as brothers and work for independence and self-government, and organize a more perfect government to work for the public welfare and to oppose the infringement of other races. When this idea had developed to an extreme at the end of the nineteenth century, it went further and became national imperialism within the last twenty or thirty years. What does national imperialism mean? It means that the industrial power of the citizens of a nation has been fully developed domestically and must flow to the outside, and thus they industriously seek to enlarge their powers in other (dependent) regions as appendages. The way of doing it is by military power, commerce, industry or religion, but they use a central policy to direct and protect these activities... Now, on the Asiatic continent there is located the largest country with the most fertile territory, the most corrupt [p. 6] government, and the most disorganized and weak people. As soon as the European race discovered our internal condition, they mobilized their national imperialism as swarms of ants attach themselves to what is rank and foul and as a myriad of arrows concentrate on a target. They were scattered but they concentrated in this corner, the Russians in Manchuria, the Germans in Shantung, the English in the Yangtze valley, the French in Kwangtung and Kwangsi, and the Japanese in Fukien. All are urged on by the tide of the new "ism" (national imperialism). They cannot help doing this...

[P. 7] If we wish to oppose the national imperialism of all the powers today and save China from great calamity and rescue our people, the only thing for us to do is to adopt the policy of promoting our own nationalism. If we wish to promote nationalism in China, there is no other means of doing it except through the renovation of the people.

Today, over the whole country, everybody is worrying about the foreign trouble. Nevertheless, if the foreigners can really cause us trouble, it cannot be ended just by worrying. The stubbornness and aggressiveness of national imperialism is very severe, and yet we are still discussing whether the foreigners can really cause us trouble or not. How foolish we are! I think the existence or non-existence of the trouble will not be decided by the foreigners, but by our domestic condition. In general, all nations are certainly using the same "ism." But why does Russia not apply it to England, and England not apply it to Germany, and Germany not apply it to America, and the various countries of Europe and America not apply it to Japan? It depends on whether there is a chance for doing so or not... Thus, in consideration of present-day China, we must not depend upon a temporary wise emperor or minister to allay the disorder, nor expect a sudden rise of one or two heroes from the rural countryside to lead our struggle for success; it is necessary to have our people's virtue, people's wisdom, and people's power of the whole number of four hundred million all become equal to that of the foreigners—then they naturally cannot cause us trouble and we need not worry about them...

### Explanation of the Meaning of "The New People"

The term "new people" does not mean that our people must give up entirely what is old in order to follow others. There are two meanings of "new." One is to temper and grind what is original in the people and so renew it; the other is to adopt what was originally lacking in the people and so make a new people. Without one of the two, there will be no success...

Generally, a nation which can endure in the world must have some peculiar characteristics on the part of its nationals. From morals and laws down to customs, habits, literature, and fine arts, all share a kind of independent spirit which has been handed down from grandfather to father and inherited by their descendants. Thus the group is formed and the nation develops. This is really the fundamental source of nationalism. Our people have been established as a nation on the Asiatic continent for several thousand years, and we must have some characteristics which are grand, eminent, and perfect, and distinctly different from those of other races; we should preserve these and not let them be lost. What is called preserving, however, is not to let (the spirit of the people) naturally appear and grow and carelessly say, "I'm preserving it, I'm preserving it." It is like a tree—unless some new boughs come out every year, its withering may soon be expected; as with a well—unless there is always some new spring bubbling, its exhaustion is not far away. Are the new boughs and the new spring coming from the outside? They are old, and yet we cannot but call them new. Only if we can make something new every day can we find the means to keep the old complete...

[P. 9] If we wish to make our nation strong, we must investigate extensively the methods followed by all other nations and races in becoming independent. Selecting their superior points, we can appropriate them to make up our own shortcomings. Now with regard to politics, academic ideas, and techniques, our critics know how to take the superior points of others to fill up our own gaps; but they do not know that the people's virtue, the people's wisdom, and the people's power are really the great source of politics, academic learning, and techniques. If they do not take this but adopt that, neglect the roots but tend the branches, it will be no different from seeing the luxuriant growth of another tree and wishing to graft its branches on to our withered trunk, or seeing the bubbling flow of another well and wishing to take some of the water to fill up our own dry well. Thus, to adopt and make up what we originally lacked in order to renovate our people should be deeply and carefully considered...

[P. 10] All the phenomena in the world are governed by no more than two great principles: one is conservative and the other is aggressive. Those who are applying these two principles are inclined either to the one or to the other. Sometimes the two arise simultaneously and conflict with each other; and sometimes the two exist simultaneously and compromise with each other. No one can exist who is inclined only to one. Where there is conflict, there must be compromise, and conflict is the forerunner of compromise. He who is good at making compromises is a great citizen, such as you find among the Anglo-Saxon race... Thus what I mean by "new people" are not those who are intoxicated with Western customs, despising the morals, academic learning, and customs of our several-thousand-year-old country in order to keep company with others; nor are they those who stick to old paper and say that merely embracing the several thousand years of our own morals, academic learning, and customs will be sufficient to enable us to stand up on the great earth.

# CHAPTER XXIII   SUN YAT-SEN'S EARLY REVOLUTIONARY PROGRAM

Compared with the imposing prestige of Liang Ch'i-ch'ao, a leader of the scholarly elite who had been for a time near the font of power and might be there again, Sun Yat-sen (1866-1925) in his early days was something of a "half-caste". Educated in Hawaii and Hongkong as well as in his native village near Macao, trained in Western medicine and only semi-trained in the Chinese classics, he never became an insider among the upper-class literati. His schemes and promotions, in league with Japanese liberal-expansionists and among Chinese merchants and laundrymen overseas, eventually led to the organization of a following which financed rebellions. Sun and the Kuomintang had their origin on the cultural frontier between China and the West. Like many of his followers, he came from the Canton delta, which had known foreign trade longer than any other area in China and had already led the way in nationalistic anti-foreignism. Sun's thinking was not formed in the Confucian mold nor, in fact, in any particular mold. This fitted him to play a shifting ideological role in a period of rapid change.

The revolutionary movement led by Sun Yat-sen, which he had launched in a minor way soon after the Sino-French war of 1884-1885, developed side by side with the imperial reform program. In those first days, however, Sun had not yet reached any conclusive political principles. His program for China's reconstruction developed more slowly than his persistent plotting to overthrow the Ch'ing government.

From the time of the Sino-Japanese war Sun's political ideas became somewhat more definite. Their development can be roughly divided into two main periods. The first is represented by such records as his letter to Li Hung-chang and the "Manifesto of the Hsing-Chung-hui (Revive China Society)," both dated 1894. The former was a plan for the economic development of China which Sun asserted was necessary for the salvation of the country; reliance on ships and cannon was not enough. As may be seen in the following excerpts,① Sun was concerned at this time almost exclusively with developing competent personnel and carrying out technological improvements; his letter does not indicate any interest in the possibility or prospect of social reorganization aside from the adoption of Western technology.

[P. 7] After deep reflection, I realize that the roots of wealth and power in Europe do not lie entirely in solid ships, efficient guns, strong forts, and crack troops, but also in that a man can use his talents to the utmost, a piece of land can produce to the utmost, natural resources can be exploited to the utmost, and commercial goods be circulated almost without restriction...

[P. 9] Without good education a man's talents will be wasted; without tactful encouragement, a scholar will live in melancholy in the countryside, and without a rational employment policy, a man in the government may be advanced by sheer good luck. If attention were paid to these three things in their proper order, then a man would be able to use his ability to the utmost...

[P. 11] A department in charge of agricultural administration can make the people work hard; special researches on agriculture can improve plant and animal husbandry; and agricultural machines can save human labor. These three procedures should be studied and imitated by our country in order to raise the yield of the land...

[P. 12] If machines are widely used, it is easy to open mines, to dredge rivers, and to weave and make cloth, all for the benefit of the people... Light, heat, and electricity are examples of common natural resources available to all nations; the degree to which they are put to practical use, however, varies with the degree of technological advance. The five metals and the various kinds of grain, on the other hand, are products of the earth which are not possessed by all nations and which furthermore require skill to produce and use.

[P. 13] A high circulation of commercial goods is contingent upon the removal of [numerous transit] taxes and upon effective laws for the protection of commerce, and possession of many steamships and railways for transport ... Commerce is of great concern to a nation's wealth and power.

[P. 15] When a man can use his ability to the utmost, all enterprises will be undertaken; when the land can yield to the utmost, people will have enough to eat; when natural resources can be exploited to the utmost, the national economic strength will be great; when commodities can be circulated without restriction, financial resources will be abundant. Thus these four elements are the principal sources of wealth and power, and provide the solid foundations of a nation... We need not be concerned about our ability to bring off a large enterprise in this country but we should worry about the lack of people to do it. The weakness of China today is caused not only by the shortage of able people, but also by the large number of ignorant people. The small number of able people can be supplemented by inviting in foreign experts ... But the large number of ignorant people, even though replaced by others who could do their work, would still try their best to hinder any new enterprise. That is why whenever a new enterprise is undertaken in our nation it is either restricted by precedents or impeded by a flood of criticism. That is the principal cause of the illness of Chinese society...

I have admired you, Grand Secretary [Li Hung-chang], ... [as one] who considers the recruiting of talented men as an urgent matter ... A person like me may also be drilled and enlisted among your employees.

Therefore I disregard the modest dimensions of my own ability in order to seek your recognition...

[P. 17] Among the four great items, ... although the training of personnel in schools to be established throughout the empire should be a matter of high priority, ...the improvement of agriculture is even more urgent... Since our country has attempted to adopt Western knowledge I have never heard anyone speak of the imitation of Western agricultural methods...

[P. 19] I plan to travel to France this year [1894] to study under famous experts on sericulture... I also plan to travel all over the world to investigate agricultural work... I sincerely hope that the Grand Secretary will help me to carry out these plans...

According to the party historian, Tsou Lu, Li Hung-chang is said to have taken great interest in this letter and to have given Sun a passport in order that he might raise funds abroad for agriculture and sericulture.

Meanwhile, however, Sun observed that Li was old as well as lacking in initiative, revolutionary ardor, and breadth of view; furthermore, China under the Ch'ing government soon suffered defeat by Japan. He therefore went to Hono-lulu to organize the Hsing-Chung-hui. Had he been employed by Li Hung-chang as a secretary or in some other capacity he might well have developed into a different person, and had a different career.

The "Manifesto of the Hsing-Chung-hui"[2] claimed to deal with the political problem of China. Sun was in touch with secret societies, particularly the Triads, who were strongest in South China and overseas, and was now preaching revolution. The Manifesto was mainly a condemnation of the corruption and weakness of the Ch'ing government, while the purpose of the organization was stated to be the revival of China against government repression and foreign aggression. All of this was formulated in rather vague and indirect terms. Republicanism had not yet become a force to attract those who were radically dissatisfied with the existing situation.

According to Sun's own account, it was during his two-year sojourn in Europe (1896-1898) that the general outline of his later *San-min chu-i*, the "Three people's principles," was formed. He discovered that with all their technology and nationalism, the Western nations were still beset by disturbing economic and social problems. Ideas that finally led to the principle of the people's livelihood (*min-sheng*, an ancient phrase) germinated in his mind. Apart from the intellectual influences of the West, Sun had the melodramatic experience of being "kidnapped" or detained in the Chinese Legation at London in 1896 and saved from deportation and death only by the effort of British friends and the Foreign Office itself. This hair-raising episode was a powerful stimulus toward compelling him to bring his revolutionary aims into more concrete form, inasmuch as he seemed thereafter more than ever marked for leadership. Still not completely disillusioned with the old official hierarchy, however, Sun Yat-sen is said to have approached Li Hung-chang again during the Boxer incident and urged him to declare his independence from the Ch'ing government, so that his independent regime might then become a democratic republic. Nothing came of this proposal.

This incident of 1900 seems to have marked the transition into the second period of Sun's early revolutionary thought. Now the political aim of the revolution had become definitely republicanism, the rallying sentiment of the movement, nationalism. The means was to be revolution by force. Like the French of 1789, Sun believed that all old structures could be torn down and new ones set up in their place; but, in addition, he showed himself also strongly influenced by the nineteenth century cult of science, in that he drew up precise formulae for the revolution, and believed that it could be carried out according to a blueprint.

All this crystallized in the Manifesto issued at the founding of the T'ung-meng-hui at Tokyo in 1905. The program laid down in this document was elsewhere referred to by its author as the "revolutionary program." Political questions were predominant in it. Sun Yat-sen deserves great credit, certainly, for his success in formulating here the central idea of China's modern political revolution: the conception of political tutelage by a provisional government which would train the politically-inert Chinese populace for eventual participation in a constitutional democracy. The three stages set forth in his manifesto of 1905 have remained theoretically valuable ever since, even though political practice has fallen short.

This manifesto of 1905 also strikes a new and truly revolutionary note in espousing the equalization of land ownership—in short, land redistribution—an old device, but a potent one. This idea, among all the desiderata and panaceas which have been quoted above, no doubt appears here because this is one of the first Chinese documents of modern times which was written explicitly for purposes of political revolt. This fact makes it all the more remarkable, however, that no scholar or high official seems to have raised earlier the issue of land redistribution as a possible element in self-strengthening or reform. The fact is that all the long line of individuals we have thus far quoted in this volume had shied away from the idea of fundamental revolution in the Chinese way of life. Before the time of Liang and Sun, they had all failed to consider the possibility of raising the condition of the peasantry to that of literate, property-owning, economically-independent, politically-active citizens. Even Liang was more aware of the "new citizen's" duties than of his rights, while Sun was not able to keep land reform in the forefront of his mind or program. This Western liberal conception, which began to drift into the Chinese scene in the 1900's, had certainly never entered into the calculations of the Empress Dowager or Chang Chih-tung in the declining years of the Ch'ing, for it was antithetic to the privileged status of the landlord-scholar-official class on which the old order was based.

Besides setting forth the aims of the revolutionists, the 1905 manifesto was also to serve as a proclamation by local revolutionary regimes at a future time, wherever an uprising should take place.

### DOC. 56   THE MANIFESTO OF THE T'UNC-MENG-HUI, 1905③

By order of the Military Government, on the—day,—month,—year of T'ien-yun,④ the commander-in-chief of the Chinese National Army proclaims the purposes and platform of the Military Government to the people of the nation:

Now the National Army has established the Military Government, which aims to cleanse away two hundred and sixty years of barbarous filth, restore our four-thousand-year-old fatherland, and plan for the welfare of the four hundred million people. Not only is this an unavoidable obligation of the Military Government, but all our fellow-nationals should also take it as their own responsibility. We recall that, since the beginning of our nation the Chinese have always ruled China; although [p.2] at times alien peoples have usurped the rule, yet our ancestors were able to drive them out and restore Chinese sovereignty so that they could hand down the nation to posterity. Now the men of Han [i.e., the Chinese] have raised a righteous [or patriotic] army to exterminate the northern barbarians. This is a continuation of heroic deeds bequeathed to us by our predecessors, and a great righteous cause lies behind it; there is none among us Chinese who does not understand this. But the revolutions in former generations, such as the Ming Dynasty and the Taiping Heavenly Kingdom, were concerned only with the driving out of barbarians and the restoration of Chinese rule. Aside from these they sought no other change. We today are different from people of former times. Besides the driving out of the barbarian dynasty and the restoration of China, it is necessary also to change the national polity and the people's livelihood. And though there are a myriad ways and means to achieve this goal, the essential spirit that runs through them all is freedom, equality, and fraternity. Therefore in former days there were heroes' revolutions, but today we have a national revolution [*Kuo-min ko-ming*, lit., revolution of the people of the country]. "National revolution" means that all people in the nation will have the spirit of freedom, equality, and fraternity; that is, they will all bear the responsibility of revolution. The Military Government is but their agent. From now on the people's responsibility will be the responsibility of the Military Government, and the achievements of the Military Government will be those of the people. With a coöperative mind and concerted effort, the Military Government and the people will thus perform their duty. Therefore we proclaim to the world in utmost sincerity the outline of the present revolution and the fundamental plan for the future administration of the nation.

1) *Drive out the Tartars*: The Manchus of today were originally the eastern barbarians beyond the Great Wall. They frequently caused border troubles during the Ming Dynasty; then when China was in a disturbed state they came inside Shanhaikuan, conquered China, and enslaved our Chinese people: Those who opposed them were killed by the hundreds of thousands, and our Chinese have been a people without a nation for two hundred and sixty years. The extreme cruelties and tyrannies of the Manchu government have now reached their limit. With the righteous army poised against them, we will overthrow that government, and restore our sovereign rights. Those Manchu and Chinese military men who have a change of heart and come over to us will be granted amnesty, while those who dare to resist will be slaughtered without mercy. Chinese who act as Chinese traitors in the cause of the Manchus will be treated in the same way.

2) *Restore China*: China is the China of the Chinese. The government of China should be in the hands of the Chinese. After driving out the Tartars we must restore our national state. Those who dare to act like Shih Ching-t'ang or Wu San-kuei [both were traitors][5] will be attacked by the whole country.

3) *Establish the Republic*: Now our revolution is based on equality,

in order to establish a republican government. All our people are equal and all enjoy political rights. The president will be publicly chosen by the people of the country. The parliament will be made up of members publicly chosen by the people of the country. A constitution of the Chinese Republic will be enacted, and every person must abide by it. Whoever dares to make himself a monarch shall be attacked by the whole country.

4) *Equalize land ownership*:⑥ The good fortune of civilization is to be shared equally by all the people of the nation. We should improve our social and economic organization, and assess the value of all the land in the country. Its present price shall be received by the owner, but all increases in value resulting from reform and social improvements after the revolution shall belong to the state, to be shared by all the people, in order to create a socialist state, where each family within the empire can be well supported, each person satisfied, and no one fail to secure employment. Those who dare to control the livelihood of the people through monopoly shall be ostracized.

The above four points will be carried out in three steps in due order. The first period is government by military law. When the righteous army has arisen, various places will join the cause. The common people of each locality will escape from the Manchu fetters. Those who come upon the enemy must unite in hatred of him, must join harmoniously with the compatriots within their ranks and suppress the enemy bandits. Both the armies and the people will be under the rule of military law. The armies will do their best in defeating the enemy on behalf of the people, and the people will supply the needs of the armies, and not do harm to their security. The local administration, in areas where the enemy has been either already defeated or not yet defeated, will be controlled in general by the Military Government, so that step by step the accumulated evils can be swept away. Evils like the oppression of the government, the greed and graft of officials, the squeeze of government clerks and runners, the cruelty of tortures and penalties, the tyranny of tax collections, the humiliation of the queue shall all be exterminated together with the Manchu rule. Evils in social customs, such as the keeping of slaves, the cruelty of foot-binding, the spread of the poison of opium, the obstructions of geomancy (*feng-shui*), should also all be prohibited. The time limit for each district (*hsien*) is three years. In those *hsien* where real results are achieved before the end of three years, the military law shall be lifted and a provisional constitution shall be enacted.

The second period is that of government by a provisional constitution. When military law is lifted in each *hsien*, the Military Government shall return the right of self-government to the local people. The members of local councils and local officials shall all be elected by the people. All rights and duties of the Military Government toward the people and those of the people toward the government shall be regulated by the provisional constitution, which shall be observed by the Military Government, the local councils, and the people. Those who violate the law shall be held responsible. Six years after the securing of peace in the nation the provisional constitution shall be annulled and the constitution shall be promulgated.

The third period will be government under the constitution. Six years after the provisional constitution has been enforced a constitution shall be made. The military and administrative powers of the Military Government shall be annulled; the people shall elect the president, and elect the members of parliament to organize the parliament. The administrative matters of the nation shall proceed according to the provisions of the constitution.

Of these three periods the first is the period in which the Military Government leads the people in eradicating all traditional evils and abuses; the second is the period in which the Military Government gives the power of local self-government to the people while retaining general control over national affairs; the third is the period in which the Military

Government is divested of its powers, and the government will by itself manage the national affairs under the constitution. It is hoped that our people will proceed in due order and cultivate their free and equal status; the foundation of the Chinese Republic will be entirely based on this.

[The last paragraph of the manifesto consists of an exhortation to the Chinese people to rise to the occasion, support the ever-faithful Military Government, and shoulder the responsibility of protecting the country and preserving their own ancient and superior race.]

# 7 IDEOLOGICAL FERMENT AND THE MAY FOURTH MOVEMENT 1912-1923

## CHAPTER XXIV THE SEARCH FOR NEW PRINCIPLES

### a. *The Variety of the New Thought*

The fall of the Chinese Empire in 1912, after its long decline, came as something of an anti-climax. The rise to power of Yuan Shih-k'ai almost immediately afterward gave the impression that the revolution of 1911 had been one of history's failures. Not only was Sun Yat-sen, the founder of the Republic, disillusioned, but many intellectuals were in a quandary. The old political and ethical code centered on loyalty to the throne had been destroyed, and a new code suitable for parliamentary government had not been established.

Subsequent events have shown, however, that the end of Manchu rule in 1912 and the demise of Yuan in 1916 really served to take the lid off—all sorts of ideological conceptions, movements, fads and experiments bubbled forth, stimulated by the strenuous political events of the period. Within a period of six years the modern generation of Chinese scholars, a considerable number of whom had now had experience abroad, went through the abortive "Second Revolution" of the Kuomintang against Yuan in 1913, Japan's seizure of Kiaochow from Germany in 1914, and her presentation of the Twenty-one Demands in 1915. They also saw Yuan's final failure to become emperor in 1916, China's entrance into the World War, the Russian Revolution and the Allied intervention in Siberia, and finally the struggle over the award of Germany's Shantung holdings to Japan at the peace conference of 1919. It is little wonder that the May Fourth Movement of 1919 ushered in a new era of Chinese history.

The decade from 1912 to 1923, since it is both recent and revolutionary, has been difficult to study. Historians have sadly neglected it. It should appear in time to have been one of the great germinal periods in the realm of Chinese thought. As indicated in our Introduction, this survey makes no attempt to go beyond 1923 because after that date the impact of Marxism-Leninism on Chinese thought and politics obviously becomes one of the central problems awaiting study, and it is treated by others elsewhere.① It is also plain that our treatment of the period 1912-1923 is likely to be the least adequate and satisfactory of any section of this survey—which merely accentuates the necessity that it be studied.

This section presents first some selections from Ts'ai Yuan-p'ei, whose thought represented an attempt at synthesis between the Chinese classical tradition and the libertarianism of the Modern European West. Ch'en Tu-hsiu in his early phase similarly reflected the ideas of the French Revolution, with a heavy accent on individual freedom. In his later phase he moved toward Leninism, as did Li Ta-chao. This trend in the direction of the Russian Revolution led to the fundamental split, in which Hu Shih as an apostle of Dewey and pragmatism represents the other line of development. Clearly in these men we have protagonists of the two great camps which have now come to divide the world: it is certainly significant that several Chinese leaders of the period at one time or another had a foot in either camp.

The various strains of thought in the post-1911 period arose out of one great common problem: how to determine and define the values and goals of the new republican era. This effort was necessitated by the deep crisis which had overtaken Chinese civilization, of which all intellectuals were acutely conscious. Conflicts of opinion rapidly developed over fundamental problems such as the relationship between the material and spiritual phases of life, the significance of the scientific method, the merits of materialism and of nationalism, the choice between Westernization or preservation of a "national essence" (*kuo-ts'ui*), and the doctrines of socialism, anarchism, and communism. All these discussions were attempts at the ideological reconstruction of Chinese life.

Before proceeding to the writings of individuals, let us note some of the protagonists of major attitudes. During and after the first World War, the attitude of revulsion and disgust toward Western materialistic civilization was expressed by Ku Hung-ming, who considered that Western utilitarian culture could not develop the inner mind, and that China's spiritual civilization was so perfect that it could save China and also rescue Western culture from its crisis. Ku regarded Western culture as based on materialism, terrorism, and greed. He strenuously opposed science and machines, warships and railways. He urged his countrymen to cultivate a richer inner life and live in the Chinese mode. As a gesture, he kept his queue against all criticism.

Liang Ch'i-ch'ao in his last phase shared this revulsion toward the West. His account of his travels after the first World War, entitled "A record of impressions during travel in Europe" (*Ou-yu hsin-ying lu chieh-lu*), argued that Europeans overemphasized science and overdeveloped their material culture. This fostered the habit of serving up the weak as meat for the strong, and created a society where people fought one another. Western civilization was bankrupt; scientific inventions had encouraged warfare and the ruthless destruction of cultural traits. The whole of European society seemed to have sunk into a state of suspicion, melancholy, and fear—in short, into confusion in the spiritual world.

On this issue, Hu Shih parted company with Liang and condemned those who criticized Western culture as materialistic and admired Eastern culture as spiritual. He did not consider the material and spiritual aspects of culture to be alternatives or antitheses, but contended that spiritual culture must be built on a base of material culture. He pointed out that

Western culture did not neglect the desires of the human spirit and the mind. He espoused John Dewey's pragmatism.

Wu Chih-hui (Wu Ching-heng, 1865-1953), best known as a Kuomintang stalwart, had received the traditional Chinese education, but became a staunch supporter of Western scientific civilization. Except in the writings of political followers, his defense of materialism has not been seriously studied. It appears to represent an influential line of thought among the early Kuomintang leaders.

Philosophical eclecticism was represented in this early republican period by Chang Tung-sun, who has had a long career as philosopher, publicist, and professor. His ideas have changed from one era to the next since the latter years of the Ch'ing monarchy. In the 1940's he became a leader of the Democratic League. During the early part of the first World War he urged that China thoroughly adopt the culture of Western civilization. Later on, from his actual observation of Chinese society, he decided that China could not entirely follow the West. Ever since China had received Western culture, her politics had become more confused, peace had disappeared, society had grown more disturbed, and improvement imperceptible. He concluded that if China adopted Western material culture entirely, Chinese society would develop in an abnormal form. He had the notion that the best way out was to revive China's spiritual culture in order to balance Western material culture.

Another scholar of similar thought was Chang Hsing-yen (Chang Shih-chao, b. 1881-1973), a jurist trained in Japan and England, a specialist on logic and a writer well known for his limpid and terse style. He became the editor of the *Chia-yin tsa-chih*, founded in 1914, and translated the works of Walter Bagehot, John Motley, and others. After advocating a liberal constitutional government, he finally turned against the Western political system, on the ground that China was an agricultural country. To apply the governmental system of industrial countries to an agricultural country was like putting a tiger's skin on a sheep—the latter could never fight against a real tiger. The Chinese spirit was to be content with poverty and to enjoy life, while Westerners stressed money, using it for political activities. Since China's industry was in an infant stage and even her agriculture was not yet highly developed, Chang concluded it was a great mistake for her to try to imitate Western political institutions.

The earliest advocate of anarchism was Liu Shih-fu, a Cantonese who organized the *Hui-ming hsueh-hui* (Society of the cry of dawn) to promote it. In 1907 another Kuomintang leader, Li Shih-tseng (Li Yü-ying), with Wu Chih-hui and others published a "New Era Weekly" in Paris, introducing the theories of Bakunin and Kropotkin to China. After the "Weekly" was suspended in 1910 and Liu Shih-fu died in 1915, this attempt subsided. Following the May Fourth Movement, Wu Chih-hui and Li Shih-tseng returned to China from France, still ostensibly believing in anarchism, but with their ideas greatly modified.

Needless to say, this roster of individual points of view could be indefinitely extended; we have not even mentioned the die-hard classicist Chang Ping-lin (Chang T'ai-yen, 1869-1936), who spent his last years fighting the New Thought and its literary movement tooth and nail, although he had formerly been a revolutionist and an editor of the republican journal *Min-pao* in Japan. There were many other equally distinguished personalities in the early Republic.

In the following sections we have tried to represent the intellectual growth of certain leaders of the day. Events have moved so rapidly in twentieth-century China that by clinging to certain views a radical might find himself soon grown conservative. Serious study should reveal that through all these vicissitudes there was a well-defined trend toward the development of values and cultural ideals among the Chinese intellectual elite, leading up to the revolutionary mass movements of recent decades. It is at least remarkable that Ts'ai Yuan-p'ei, Ch'en Tu-hsiu, Li Ta-chao, Hu Shih, and Liang Ch'i-ch'ao should all have been more or less central figures in the intellectual circles of Peking, members of the same social stratum and community. The examples of Ts'ai's writings chosen from the years 1912 and 1919, like those of Hu Shih in 1919 and 1922 (Ch. XXVI), show a steady growth in the Western liberal tradition; whereas our selections from Ch'en Tu-hsiu in 1915 and 1923 (Ch. XXV) reflect his desertion of individualism and espousal of Marxism as a new path to China's salvation—a step which was less remarked upon in America at the time than it may be in the second half of the twentieth century. Similarly Liang Ch'i-ch'ao, in his facile and masterly survey (Ch. XXVIII) of the turbulent period traversed by the present volume—in so much of which he had himself been a protagonist—shows in 1922 the same faith in rationalism and in progress that had characterized his revolutionary period, much as some of his judgments had changed with the passage of time; whereas Sun Yat-sen, in the passages we quote from 1919 and 1923 (Ch. XXVII), obviously went through a considerable reorientation, almost comparable to that of Ch'en Tu-hsiu.

The comment may be made that those intellectuals who became most active in revolutionary politics were the same ones who deserted the Western liberal tradition, to greater or less degree—almost as though this desertion were a necessary step in the process of organizing revolutionary power in China. Without arguing the extent to which the early Ch'en Tu-hsiu and Sun Yat-sen may be classed as genuine "liberals," or the extent to which they eventually accepted Marxist-Leninist political institutions, it still seems possible to suggest that by the 1920's the problems of revolutionary politics in China had proved impossible of direct solution on a Western-type "liberal" basis. This brings us, by 1923, to the opening of a new era in Chinese history, and a stopping-place for this survey.

### b. *Ts'ai Yuan-p'ei and Freedom in Education*

Ts'ai Yuan-p'ei (1868-1940) was the leading liberal educator of early Republican China. He served as the first minister of education of the

Republic (1912), chancellor of National Peking University (1917-1927), and co-founder and director (1928-1940) of the *Chung-yang yen-chiu-yuan*, or Academia Sinica, the highest research institute of Nationalist China.[②] Through his early campaign for freedom in education, the May Fourth Movement of 1919 was fostered and the "new tide" of thought was largely made possible. Many eminent political and academic leaders of the past generation in China were trained at Peita (i. e. , Peking University, *Pei-ching ta-hsueh*) under Dr. Ts'ai's influence.

Ts'ai Yuan-p'ei was remarkable because he had received a traditional Chinese education and had risen to the top as a member of the Hanlin Academy, and yet was not confined by Confucian patterns of thought. On the contrary, he revolted against the formality of Confucianism, proposing the abolition of the worship of Confucius in the schools, and promoting the scientific study of the Confucian classics under the new academic departments of Chinese literature, history, and philosophy—but not as a required subject for every student.

Dr. Ts'ai became well versed in Western philosophy, taking particular interest in Kropotkin, Darwin, Nietzsche, Wundt, Le Bon, and other similar writers. In 1912, after resigning from the first Republican cabinet, he went to Europe and made a study of world civilizations at the University of Leipzig. He wrote a book dealing with the principles of philosophy while he was in France during the first World War and another volume on the history of European esthetics. His history of Chinese ethics (*Chung-kuo lun-li-hsueh shih*, 1937) was also succinctly and ably written. He is generally considered a "synthesizer of Western and Chinese thought,"[③] but his main contribution was undoubtedly in promoting freedom of education and freedom of thought. He believed academic institutions should be free from government control or interference. Kuomintang writers have hailed the intellectual movement guided by Ts'ai Yuan-p'ei as "aimed at a rebirth of the old Chinese civilization by discovering the foundation of Western strength and absorbing its essence into their own philosophy so as to effect a new synthesis on an intellectual and spiritual basis."④ He was unquestionably outstanding as a man of principle and integrity. Although a senior member of the Kuomintang, he resigned his positions and retired to Hongkong for the rest of his life when he became dissatisfied with the trend of events at Nanking.

The following document shows the strong Kantian trend of Ts'ai's thought and his consistent effort to find correspondences between Confucian and Western ethics and philosophy, in the period when he was China's first modern minister of education.

### DOC. 57  TS'AI YUAN-P'EI'S VIEWS ON THE AIMS OF EDUCATION, 1912⑤

In recent days I have been drafting new school regulations with my associates in the Ministry of Education to prepare for the calling of a higher education conference. I have had the honor to be given some grand ideas by my comrades, but there are few that concern educational policy. Hence I express my own humble ideas first as a prelude. I shall be fortunate if educators in the nation will correct me.

There are two great kinds of education: one is subordinate to politics, the other is above politics. During the monarchical period (I refer also to constitutional government of a monarchical nature) educators followed the policy of the government and considered the model education to be purely subordinate to government. In the republican period, educators can set up a standard based upon the situation of the people and thus we may have education beyond political control.

Near the end of the Ch'ing Dynasty the education which was subordinate to the government, and which was widely talked about by educators, was called "military education for the citizen" (*chün kuo-min chiao-yü*). Generally speaking "military education for the citizen" is contradictory to socialism, and there have already been signs of its decline in other countries. Nevertheless, in our country, where strong neighbors are all oppressing us, we have to plan hastily for self-protection, and our national rights which have been lost during successive years are, in the circumstances, difficult to recover without relying on military power. Moreover, after a revolution by the militarists, it is hard to guarantee [p. 190] that there will not be a period when the militarists will wield political power. Unless we adopt a universal military system, we shall have no way to balance the military power, and the militarist group will become a permanent special caste in the whole country. Hence today we really must adopt the so-called "military education for the citizen…"

There is a second kind of education which is subordinate to government and which is called "utilitarian education" (*shih-li chu-i chih chiao-yü*), in which the people's livelihood forms the nucleus of common education. Those who advocate this most rigorously go to an extreme in saying that all general learning is entirely included in forestry, cooking, sewing, metallurgy, carpentry, and masonry. This theory was created in America but has recently been popular also in European countries. In our country the treasures under the earth have not been developed, the organization of industrial circles is still in its infancy, the unemployed are numerous, and the nation is extremely poor. Thus utilitarian education is certainly a matter of priority.

These two policies constitute the principles for strengthening our troops and enriching the nation. Although troops may be strengthened, however, this trend may be overdeveloped into private fighting or into national aggression [p. 191]. Then what can we do? The nation may be enriched and yet it may be unavoidable for the educated to cheat the ignorant, for the strong to cheat the weak, and so produce a great gap between the rich and the poor and the tragedy of a bloody war between capitalists and workers. Then what can we do? The answer is to teach the morality [*tao-te*, ethics] of citizenship. What is the morality of citizenship? It was put forth during the French Revolution in the phrase, "liberty, equality, and fraternity." The essential ideas of morality are wholly included in these... [With quotations from the Confucian classics, Ts'ai then suggests that *i* (righteousness), *shu* (reciprocity), and *jen* (benevolence) roughly correspond to the principles of the French Revolution, p. 192.] These three principles [*i*, *shu*, and *jen*] are really the foundation of all morality and should be included in the moral education of citizens.

An education that includes moral discipline for citizens should be considered as the final goal. I would say "not yet," however, because moral education for citizens is still not above politics. What is called the best government in the world has for its goal no less than the greatest happiness of the greatest number. The "greatest number" is made up of many individuals. The individual's welfare consists of sufficient clothing, adequate food, and avoidance of catastrophe or harm. This is no more than our present society's ideal of welfare. One person's welfare is added to [p. 193] that of others to become that of the majority of people. The goal is still the same. The discussions in the legislative branch, the executive action of the administrative branch, and the protection exercised by the judicial branch of the government are all aimed at the welfare of the people. Even if we progress to the point spoken of in the "Li-yun" where "the great doctrine applies to all" [*ta-tao wei kung*],[⑥] and reach what the socialists call the golden age of the future, when every person will do the utmost that he can and every person will receive what he needs—these goals, after all, are the same as the ideals of present society. Probably the goals of politics and law are also working for happiness, and all education which is subordinate to politics and law is, at its best, also like this...

[P. 197] The two principles of military citizenship and utilitarianism are used to make up for our inadequacy in self-protection and self-preservation. Moral education is to make people work for mutual protection and mutual preservation, and all this is instrumental in breaking the habit of scheming for one's own interest and in eradicating the (sense of) difference between you and me. From this, people can progress to the promotion of education in the light of reality.

What is the method for promoting the conception of reality? The answer is that, on the negative side, with regard to the phenomenal world, we have nothing to dislike and nothing to be obstinate about; while on the positive side, we are very anxious to, and we gradually do, advance toward understanding the world of reality. We must follow the general rule of freedom of thought and freedom of expression, and not allow any one branch of philosophy or any one tenet of religion to confine our minds, but always aim at a lofty universal point of view which is valid without regard to space or time. For such an education I can think of no other name than "education for a world view" [shih-chieh-kuan chiao-yü]. Education for a world view, however, is not something to chatter about every day. Moreover, its relation to the phenomenal world cannot be described in dry and simple words. Then, in what way can we reach it?

The answer is, through esthetic education [or, education for artistic appreciation, mei-kan chih chiao-yü]. Mei-kan is a conception combining beauty and solemnity and is a bridge between the phenomenal world and the world of reality. This concept was originated by Kant [p. 198]... In the phenomenal world every person feels the passions of love, hatred, fear, surprise, happiness, anger, sadness and pleasure, and these feelings vary according to the phenomena of departure, reunion, life, death, disaster, good fortune, and catastrophe. As for the fine arts, such phenomena are used as sources of inspiration, and make those who look at representations of them have no other feeling than that of artistic appreciation. For instance, the gathering of lotus seeds and the cooking of beans are work for food, and yet when they are written in a poem they arouse other interests. The blazing red volcano or a strong wind wrecking a boat are terrible and dreadful scenes, but when they appear in a painting they turn out to be worth exhibiting and appreciating. That is, with regard to the phenomenal world we have nothing to dislike and nothing to be obstinate about. When you feel related to actual phenomena neither by craving nor by loathing but are purely absorbed in artistic appreciation, then you will become a friend of the Creator and will be close to the conception of the world of reality. Therefore, if an educator wishes to lead the people from the phenomenal world to the conception of the world of reality, he must adopt esthetic education.

On these five points there should be no special emphasis or negligence in today's education. The principle of military citizenship, the utilitarian principle, and the moral principle are the three which belong to political education. (The moral education of ancient China occasionally had reference to a world view and that should be discussed separately.) The two principles of the world view and esthetic education are above politics...

[P. 200] When we base ourselves on these five principles and distribute them among all the school subjects, the percentage of each principle will vary according to the nature of each subject... The proportion shall be ten per cent for military citizenship, forty for utilitarianism, twenty for moral education, twenty-five for esthetic education, but only five per cent for the world view.

[P. 202] During the Ch'ing Dynasty there were the so-called imperial educational purposes, namely, to inculcate loyalty to the emperor, respect for Confucius, promotion of public spirit, promotion of military spirit [p. 203], and promotion of usefulness. Loyalty to the emperor is not suited to the republican form of government; respect for Confucius is contradictory to the freedom of belief... These two need not be discussed. The promotion of military spirit is the principle for military citizenship; the promotion of usefulness is the principle of utilitarianism; the promotion of public spirit is what I have called moral education for citizenship. Their scope may be necessarily different in breadth or narrowness, but essentially they are the same ideas. The world view and esthetic education are things the Ch'ing Dynasty did not mention, but I pay close attention to them. Therefore, I have particularly explained these points and illustrated them, asking advice from modern educators in the hope that they will give them their candid discussion.

The letter translated below was published in reply to criticisms advanced by the famous translator Lin Shu (Lin Gh'in-nan), who was one of the conservative members of the Peita faculty at the time. Written a bare six weeks before the outbreak of the May Fourth Movement, Ts'ai's eloquent advocacy of freedom of academic thought epitomizes the spirit of a period of creative effort, untrammeled by orthodoxy; in 1919 that of the Confucian empire had finally been dissolved, while the orthodoxy of the modern party-governments had not yet taken its place.

## DOC. 58   TS'AI YUAN-P'EI'S
## POLICY FOR PEKING UNIVERSITY, 1919[7]

[P. 323] In connection with the university I have two policies, as follows:

(1) With regard to academic ideas, I act according to the general rule of the various universities of the world, following the principle of "freedom of thought" and adopting the policy of tolerating everything and including everything ... Regardless of what schools of academic thought there may be, if their words are reasonable and there is a cause for maintaining them, and they have not yet reached the fate of being eliminated by nature, then even though they disagree with each other, I would let them develop in complete freedom [p. 324]. This idea has been explained in the foreword of the *Peking University Monthly*. [Note: This foreword was written in November 1918. Part of it reads, "What is called a university is not merely a place for a majority of the students to attend classes on time and to be furnished with the qualifications for becoming graduates. It is actually an organization for academic research by professors and students working together. By research we mean not merely the learning about European culture, but also the necessity of making further discoveries on the basis of European culture; it is not

merely for preservation of the essentials of our national culture (*kuo-ts'ui*), it is also necessary to use scientific methods to expound the real nature of our national essentials."]⑧

(2) With regard to professors, their knowledge is the main thing. When they give lectures in the university, the only limitation on them is that they do not contradict the first policy. Their words and actions outside the university are entirely their own affair. This university never makes inquiries nor takes responsibility for such words and actions. For instance, the idea of restoration of the, Manchu emperor is rejected by the Republic, but among the professors of this university there is one who wears a long queue and still maintains the theory of restoration [i. e., Ku Hung-ming]; but because he teaches English literature, which has nothing to do with Chinese politics, I let him do as he wishes. The sponsors of the *Ch'ou-an-hui* [lit., "Society for the preparation of peace," but actually for making Yuan Shih-k'ai emperor] are criminals in the eyes of public opinion. Among the professors of this university there is such a man [Liu Shih-p'ei]; but because he teaches ancient Chinese literature, which has no relation to politics, I let him continue. The visiting of prostitutes, gambling, and the taking of concubines and such matters are forbidden by the "Society for the Promotion of Morality" of this university (*Chin-te-hui*); but among our faculty members there are occasionally those… who like to write love poems in praise of prostitutes, and who consider the taking of a concubine and associating with prostitutes as romantic actions and gambling as a pastime. If they do not neglect their school work and do not mislead the students into falling as they have, then I also, for the time being, let them continue with their teaching. Generally, it is very difficult to procure men of ability. If we sought for perfection and asked for completeness, it would probably be difficult to establish a university. Moreover, there is certainly a natural boundary between public and private life…

# CHAPTER XXV   EARLY CONVERTS TO MARXISM

If republicanism was to be the answer to China's political problems, what was to be the nature of her intellectual life in this new era? The post-1911 period down to 1923 saw all sorts of experimental attitudes on the part of leaders in the realm of thought—for example, Nietzsche was a source of reference for Ch'en Tu-hsiu, Hu Shih, and Ts'ai Yuan-p'ei, among others. The experiments and gropings of these years included the attempt to transplant the terms of Western ideology into the thought of republican China; the effort to create a new vernacular literature; and spirited debates over such questions as centralism versus federalism in politics or the relation between science and philosophy of life. The same decade also witnessed the disillusionment of some of the intellectuals with Western liberalism and their subsequent acceptance of dialectical materialism.

Ch'en Tu-hsiu (1879 or 1880? -1942) participated in all these developments. Beginning as a scholar with a good literary training in the traditional style, he became deeply influenced by the West, the culture of which he thought was represented in its essence by the French. He was a revolutionary before the overthrow of the Ch'ing Dynasty, and continued to be an enemy of traditional conventions thereafter. He gave active support to the new literary movement; he praised the combativeness, individualism, and utilitarianism of the Westerners in opposition to the decadence of Chinese society. In 1916 he became dean of the School of Letters of Peking University, and took a leading part in the intellectual developments which led up to the May Fourth Movement of 1919. As chief editor and a constant contributor to the monthly magazine *La Jeunesse*, "New Youth" (*Hsin-ch'ing-nien*), his influence over the rising generation of Chinese students was tremendous. The main themes of his credo at this time were science and democracy: "We are convinced at present that only these two gentlemen ["Mr. Science and Mr. Democracy"] can cure the dark maladies in Chinese politics, morality, learning, and thought," he wrote in January 1919.

The Versailles Peace Conference, however, the Shantung question, the Chinese Republic's relapse into warlord politics, and the successes of the Russian Revolution all combined to turn him against his early faith in Western liberalism and toward the new socialist Russia and its ideology. It is difficult to determine the exact date of his change of mind, but it appears that his iconoclasm had reached a climax sometime in 1918, when a short article of his entitled "On the destruction of idols" was published in *Hsin-ch'ing-nien*. In this he included in his objects of attack not only Chinese conventions but also a part of the modern Western ideology, the theory of the national state—which he declared produced war and was a device for the protection of the rights of the privileged classes. It was evidently time for a re-evaluation of his aims, time to build an ideology that could meet the situation more adequately. With the help of Western liberalism, he had torn down the traditional Chinese system; but now, in the process of rebuilding, he used other new materials. By 1921 he had become a convinced Marxist and took part in the founding of the Chinese Communist Party, of which he was the leader and general secretary until 1927. Ch'en made undeniable contributions to the new cultural movement. The first and third of the following items represent the two major periods of his thought.

### DOC. 59 CH'EN TU-HSIU'S "CALL TO YOUTH," 1915[①]

The Chinese compliment others by saying, "He acts like an old man although still young." Englishmen and Americans encourage one another by saying, "Keep young while growing old." Such is one respect in which the different ways of thought of the East and West are manifested. Youth is like early spring, like the rising sun, like trees and grass in bud, like a newly sharpened blade. It is the most valuable period of life. The function of youth in society is the same as that of a fresh and vital cell in a human body. In the processes of metabolism, the old and the rotten are incessantly eliminated to be replaced by the fresh and living... If metabolism functions properly in a human body, the person will be healthy; if the old and rotten cells accumulate and fill the body, the person will die. If metabolism functions properly in a society, it will flourish; if old and rotten elements fill the society, then it will cease to exist.

According to this standard, then, is the society of our nation flourishing, or is it about to perish? I cannot bear to answer. As for those old and rotten elements, I shall leave them to the process of natural selection. I do not wish to waste my fleeting time in arguing with them on this and that and hoping for them to be reborn and thoroughly remodeled. I only, with tears, place my plea before the young and vital youth, in the hope that they will achieve self-awareness, and begin to struggle. What is this self-awareness? It is to be conscious of the value and responsibility of one's young life and vitality, to maintain one's self-respect, which should not be lowered. What is the struggle? It is to exert one's intellect, discard resolutely the old and the rotten, regard them as enemies and as the flood or savage beasts, keep away from their neighborhood and refuse to be contaminated by their poisonous germs. Alas! Do these words really fit the youth of our country? I have seen that, out of every ten youths who are young in age, five are old in physique; and out of every ten who are young in both age and physique, nine are old in mentality. Those with shining hair, smooth countenance, a straight back and a wide chest are indeed magnificent youths! Yet if you ask what thoughts and aims are entertained in their heads, then they all turn out to be the same as the old and rotten, like moles from the same hill. In the beginning the youth are not without freshness and vitality. Gradually some are assimilated by the old and rotten elements; then there are others who fear the tremendous influence of those elements, who hesitate, stammer and stall, and dare not openly rebel against them. It is the old and rotten air that fills society everywhere. One cannot even find a bit of fresh and vital air to comfort those of us who are suffocating in despair.

Such a phenomenon [p. 2], if found in a human body, would kill a man; if found in a society, would destroy it. A heavy sigh or two cannot cure this malady. What is needed is for one or two youths, who are quick in self-consciousness and brave in a struggle, to use to the full the natural intellect of man, and judge and choose all the thoughts of mankind, distinguishing which are fresh and vital and suitable for the present struggle for survival, and which are old and rotten and unworthy to be retained in the mind. Treat this problem as a sharp tool cleaves iron, or a sharp knife, cuts hemp. Resolutely make no compromises and entertain no hesitations. Consider yourself and consider others; then perhaps society can hope to become clean and peaceful. O youth, is there anyone who takes upon himself such responsibilities? As for understanding what is right and wrong, in order that you may make your choice, I carefully propose the following six principles, and hope you will give them your calm consideration.

### *Be independent, not servile.*

All men are equal. Each has his right to be independent, but absolutely no right to enslave others nor any obligation to make himself servile. By slavery we mean that in ancient times the ignorant and the weak lost their right of freedom, which was savagely usurped by tyrants. Since the rise of the theories of the rights of man and of equality, no red-blooded person can endure [the name of slave]. The history of modern Europe is commonly referred to as a "history of emancipation": the destruction of monarchical power aimed at political emancipation; the denial of Church authority aimed at religious emancipation; the rise of the theory of equal property aimed at economic emancipation; and the suffragist movement aimed at emancipation from male authority.

Emancipation means freeing oneself from the bondage of slavery and achieving a completely independent and free personality. I have hands and feet, and I can earn my own living. I have a mouth and a tongue, and I can voice my own likes and dislikes. I have a mind, and I can determine my own beliefs. I will absolutely not let others do these things on my behalf, nor should I assume an overlordship and enslave others. For once the independent personality is recognized, all matters of conduct, all rights and privileges, and all belief should be left to the natural ability of each person; there is definitely no reason why one should blindly follow others. On the other hand, loyalty, filial piety, chastity and righteousness are a slavish morality. (Note: The great German philosopher Nietzsche divided morality into two categories—that which is independent and courageous is called "morality of the noble," and that which is humble and submissive is called "morality of the slave.") Light penalties and light taxation constitute the happiness of slaves; panegyrics and eulogies are slavish literature; ... noble ranks or magnificent mansions are glory only to slaves; resplendent tablets and grand tombs are their memorials. That is because such persons, by submitting to the judgment of others regarding right and wrong, glory and shame, instead of depending on their own standard of judgment, have completely annihilated their independent and equal personalities as individuals. In their conduct, whether good or bad, they cannot appeal to their own will-power, but are confined to receiving merits or demerits (from others). Who can say that it is improper to call such persons slaves? Therefore, before we speak of contributing to mankind in moral example or in deed, we must first make this distinction between the independent and the servile.

### *Be progressive, not conservative.*

"Without progress there will be retrogression" is an old Chinese saying. Considering the fundamental laws of the universe, all things or phenomena are daily progressing in evolution, and the maintenance of the *status quo* is definitely out of the question; only the limitation of man's ordinary view has rendered possible the differentiation between the two states of things. This is why the theory of creative evolution, "L'Evolution créatrice," of the contemporary French philosopher Henri Bergson, has become immensely popular throughout a whole generation. Considered in the light of the evolution of human affairs, it is plain that those races that cling to antiquated ways are declining, or disappearing, day by day, and the peoples who seek progress and advancement are just beginning to ascend in power and strength. It is possible to predict which of these will survive and which will not. Now our country still has not awakened from its long dream, and isolates itself by going down the old rut... All our traditional ethics, law, scholarship, rites and customs are survivals of feudalism. When compared with the achievement of the white race, there is a difference of a thousand years in thought, although we live in the same period. Revering only the history of the twenty-four dynasties and making no plans for progress and improvement, our people will be turned out of this twentieth-century world, and be lodged in the dark ditches fit only for slaves, cattle, and horses. What more need be said? I really do not know what sort of institutions and culture are adequate for our survival in the present world if in such circumstances conservatism is still advocated. I would much rather see the past culture of our nation disappear than see our race die out now because of its unfitness for living in the modern world. Alas, the days of the Babylonians are past. Of what use is their civilization now? "When the skin has vanished, what can the hair adhere to?" The progress of the world is like that of a fleet horse, galloping and galloping onward. Whatever cannot skillfully change itself and progress along with the world will find itself eliminated by natural selection because of failure to adapt to the environment. Then what can be said to defend conservatism!

### *Be aggressive, not retiring.*

While the tide of evil is now rushing onward, would it not be rare virtue for one or two self-respecting scholars to retire from the world, to keep themselves clean? But if your aim is to influence the people and establish a new tradition, I suggest that you make further progress from your present high position. It is impossible to avoid the struggle for survival, and so long as one draws breath there can be no place where one can retire for a tranquil hermit's life. It is our natural obligation in life to advance in spite of numerous difficulties. Stated in kindly terms, retirement is an action of the superior man in order to get away from the vulgar world. Stated in hostile terms, it is a phenomenon of the weak who are unable to struggle for survival... Alas! The war steeds of Europe are intruding into your house. Where can you quietly repose under a white cloud? I wish that our youth would become Confucius and Mo-tzu and not [the hermits] Ts'ao-fu and Hsü Yu,② and I do not wish so much that our youth be Tolstoi and Tagore (Note: R. Tagore, an escapist poet of India) as that they become Columbus and An Ch'ung-ken [the Korean patriot who assassinated Prince Itō on October 26, 1909].

### Be cosmopolitan, not isolationist.

Any change in the economic or political life of one nation will usually have repercussions over the whole world, just as the whole body is affected when one hair is pulled. The prosperity or decline, rise or fall of a nation of today depends half on domestic administration, and half on influences from outside the country. Take the recent events of our country as evidence: Japan suddenly rose in power, and stimulated our revolutionary and reform movements; the European War broke out, and then Japan presented her demands to us; is this not clear proof? When a nation is thrown into the currents of the world, traditionalists will certainly hasten the day of its fall, but those capable of change will take this opportunity to compete and progress. According to the pessimists, since the opening of the treaty ports our country has been losing territory and paying indemnities to the point of exhaustion. But according to the optimists, we would still be in the age of the eight-legged essay and the queue were it not for the blessings of the Sino-Japanese War of 1895 and the Boxer Uprising of 1900. Not only are we unable to support an isolationist and closed-door policy, but circumstances also are unfavorable to it... If at this point one still raises a particularist theory of history and of national circumstances and hopes thereby to resist the current, then this still indicates the spirit of an isolationist country and a lack of knowledge of the world. When its citizens lack knowledge of the world, how can a nation expect to survive in it? A proverb says, "He who builds his cart behind closed gates will find it not suited to the tracks outside the gates." The cart-builders of today not only close their gates, but even want to use the methods contained [p. 5] in the chapter on technology in the *Rites of Chou* for use on the highways of Europe and America. The trouble will be more than not fitting the tracks.

### *Be utilitarian, not formalistic.*

The social system and the thought of Europe have undergone a change since J. S. Mill's advocacy of utilitarianism in England and Comte's advocacy of positivism in France. More recently their system and thought have undergone another change, with the great advancement of science in Germany, where material civilization has reached its pinnacle of achievement. In all that concerns the administration of government, the aims of education, and the fashions in literature and the crafts, there is nothing that is not focusing on the road of better livelihood and greater usefulness, like ten thousand horses galloping toward the same point. Meanwhile all things that are formalistic, utopian, and useless to practical life are almost completely rejected. The great contemporary philosophers, such as R. Eucken of Germany and Bergson of France, although they do not consider the present materialistic civilization perfect, all discuss the problems of life (Note: The English word is "life," the German "leben," and the French "la vie") as the goal of their teachings. Life is sacred. Because the blood of the present war has stained life's bright banner, the Europeans will waken entirely from utopian, empty dreams.

Generally speaking, concern for usefulness and better livelihood, respect for actuality and disdain for illusion were characteristic of the ancient people of our country, whereas our present social system and thought are inherited from the Chou and Han Dynasties. Empty formalism was emphasized in the *Rites of Chou*, and under the Han Dynasty Confucianism and the Taoism of Lao-tzu were elevated to high positions, while all other schools of thought were interdicted. The agelong precepts of ethical convention, the hopes and purposes of the people—there is nothing which does not run counter to the practical life of society today. If we do not restring our bow and renew our effort, there will be no way to revive the strength of our nation, and our society will never see a peaceful day. As for praying to gods to relieve flood and famine, or reciting the *Book of Filial Piety* to ward off the Yellow Turbans [i. e., bandits]—people are not infants or morons, and they see through these absurdities. Though a thing is of gold or of jade, if it is of no practical use, then it is of less value than coarse cloth, grain, manure or dirt. That which brings no benefit to the practical life of an individual or of society is all empty formalism and the stuff of cheats. And even though it were bequeathed to us by our ancestors, taught by the sages, advocated by the government and worshiped by society, the stuff of cheats is still not worth one cent.

### *Be scientific, not imaginative.*

What is science? It is our general conception of matter which, being the sum of objective phenomena as analyzed by subjective reason, contains no contradiction within itself. What is imagination? It first oversteps the realm of objective phenomena, and then discards reason itself; it is something constructed out of thin air, consisting of hypotheses without proof, and all the existing wisdom of mankind cannot be made to find reason in it [p. 6] or explain its laws and principles. There was only imagination and no science in the unenlightened days of old, as well as among the uncivilized peoples of today. Religion, art, and literature were the products of the period of imagination. The contribution of the growth of science to the supremacy of modern Europe over other races is not less than that of the theory of the rights of man... our scholars do not know science, therefore they borrow the *yin-yang* school's notions of auspicious signs and of the five elements to confuse the world and cheat the people, and the ideas of topography and geomancy to beg for miracles from dry skeletons (spirits). Our farmers do not know science; therefore they have no technique for seed selection and insecticide. Our industrialists do not know science; therefore goods lie wasted on the ground, while we depend on foreign countries for everything that we need in warfare and in production. Our merchants know no science; therefore they are only concerned with obtaining short-term profits, and give not a thought to calculating for the future. Our physicians know no science; not only are they not acquainted with human anatomy, but also they do not analyze the properties of medicines; as for bacteria and contagious diseases, they have never heard of them. They can only parrot the talk about the five elements, their mutual promotions and preventions, cold and heat, *yin* and *yang*, and prescribe medicine according to ancient formulae. Their technique is practically the same as that of an archer! The height of their marvelous imaginations is the theory of *ch'i* (primal force), which even extends to the techniques of professional strong men and Taoist priests. But though you seek high and low in the universe, you will never know what this "primal force" exactly is. All these nonsensical ideas and unreasonable beliefs can be cured at the root only by science. For to explain truth by science means proving everything with fact. Although the process is slower than that of imagination and arbitrary decision, yet every step taken is on firm ground; it is different from those imaginative flights which eventually cannot advance even one inch. The amount of truth in the universe is boundless, and the fertile areas in the realm of science awaiting the pioneer are immense! Youth, take up the task!

　　The author of the next item, Li Ta-chao (1889-1927), is now honored by Chinese Communists as the principal party-founder... Li Ta-chao was a professor of political science and economics, and a returned student from Japan. Like Ch'en Tu-hsiu, he was an active leader of Chinese youth through his writings and lectures at Peking University. It is said that while teaching at that institution in the years 1919-1925, he offered courses on historical materialism and socialism; from his own writings in *Hsin-ch'ing-nien* it is clear that his interest in Marxist ideology had begun only after the Russian Revolution. Unlike others of his time, however, he was quick to assert the merits of the Marxist-Leninist revolution without going through a prolonged period of skeptical observation, as the following article testifies. Though he was one of the leaders in the founding of the Chinese Communist Party in 1921, he suffered an early death in April 1927, at the hands of the warlord, Chang Tso-lin.

Certain parts of the following article still show a non-Marxist approach to history, but there were signs that Li was engaged in hard study of Marxist theory during 1918 and 1919. In the latter year he stated his opinion that "this is a period of transition between the era of individualism and that of socialism and humanism."③

## DOC. 60  LI TA-CHAO, "THE VICTORY OF BOLSHEVISM," NOVEMBER 15, 1918④

"Victory! Victory! The Allies have been victorious! Surrender! Surrender! Germany has surrendered!" These words are on the national flag bedecking every doorway, they can be seen in color and can be indistinctly heard in the intonation of every voice. Men and women of the Allied powers run up and down the street in celebration of the victory, and in the city of Peking the soldiers of these nations loudly blast forth their triumphal songs. Now and then, echoed amid the noises of celebration and rejoicing, you hear the tinkling sound of some German merchant's shop window being shattered, or that of the bricks and tiles taken off the von Ketteler Memorial Arch [a memorial to the German Minister killed by the Boxers]. It is indeed needless to describe the happiness of the people of the Allied powers who are living in our country...

But let us think carefully as small citizens of the world; to whom exactly does the present victory belong? Who has really surrendered? Whose is the achievement this time? And for whom do we celebrate? If we ponder over these questions, then not only will our non-fighting generals' show of strength and our shameless politicians' grasping of credit become senseless, but also the talk of the Allied nations, that the end of the war was brought about by their military forces defeating the military force of Germany, and their mad celebrations will be entirely without significance. And not only are their celebrations and boasts meaningless, but even the fate of their political system will probably [p. 443] be the same as that of German militarism, and vanish with the latter in the near future.

For the real cause of the ending of the war was not the vanquishing of the German military power by the Allied military power, but the vanquishing of German militarism by German socialism. It was not the German people who surrendered to the armed forces of the Allied powers, but the German Kaiser, militarists and militarism who surrendered to the new tides of the world. It was not the Allied nations but the awakened minds of the German people that defeated German militarism; and the failure of German militarism was the failure of the Hohenzollern [Chinese text here inserts "Bolshevism" in English, by error] German imperial family and not that of the German nation. The victory over German militarism does not belong to the Allied nations; even less does it belong to our factious military men who used participation in the war only as an excuse [for engaging in civil war], or to our opportunistic, cunningly manipulative politicians. It is the victory of humanitarianism, of pacifism; it is the victory of justice and liberty; it is the victory of democracy; it is the victory of socialism; it is the victory of Bolshevism [Chinese text inserts "Hohenzollern" by error]; it is the victory of the red flag; it is the victory of the labor class of the world; and it is the victory of the twentieth century's new tide. Rather than give Wilson and others the credit for this achievement, we should give the credit to Lenin [These names are inserted in English], Trotzky, Collontay [Alexandra Kollontai], to Liebknecht, Scheidemann, and to Marx...

Bolshevism is the ideology of the Russian Bolsheviki. What kind of ideology is it? It is very difficult to explain it clearly in one sentence. If we look for the origin of the word, we see that it means "majority." An English reporter once asked Collontay, a heroine in that [Bolshevik] party [p. 444], what the meaning of "Bolsheviki" was. The heroine answered... "Its meaning will be clear only if one looks at what they are doing." According to the explanation given by this heroine, then, "Bolsheviki means only what they are doing." But from the fact that this heroine had called herself a Revolutionary Socialist in western Europe, and a Bolshevika in eastern Europe, and from the things they have done, it is clear that their ideology is revolutionary socialism; their party is a revolutionary socialist party; and they follow the German socialist economist Marx as the founder of their doctrine. Their aim is to destroy the national boundaries which are obstacles to socialism at present, and to destroy the system of production in which profit is monopolized by the capitalist. Indeed, the real cause of this war was also the destruction of national boundaries. Since the present national boundaries cannot contain the expansion of the system of production brought about by capitalism, and since the resources within each nation are inadequate for the expansion of its productive power, the capitalist nations all began depending on war to break down these boundaries, hoping to make of all parts of the globe one single, coördinated economic organ.

So far as the breaking down of national boundaries is concerned, the socialists are of the same opinion with them. But the purpose of the capitalist governments in this matter is to enable the middle class in their countries to gain benefits; they rely on world economic development by one class in the victor nations, and not on mutual coöperation among humanitarian, reasonable organizations of the producers of the world. This war will cause such a victor nation to advance from the position of a great power to that of a world empire. The Bolsheviki saw through this point; therefore they vigorously protested and proclaimed that the present war is a war of the Tsar, of the Kaiser, of kings and emperors, that it is a war of capitalist governments, but it is not their war. Theirs is the war of classes, a war of all the world's proletariat and common people against the capitalists of the world. While they are opposed to war itself, they are at the same time not afraid of it. They hold that all men and women should work. All those who work should join a union, and there should be a central administrative soviet in each union. [P. 445] Such soviets then should organize all the governments of the world. There will be no congress, no parliament, no president, no prime minister, no cabinet, no legislature, and no ruler. There will be only the joint soviets of labor, which will decide all matters. All enterprises will belong to those who work therein, and aside from this no other possessions will be allowed. They will unite the proletariat of the world, and create global freedom with their greatest, strongest power of resistance: first they will create a federation of European democracies, to serve as the foundation of a world federation. This is the ideology of the Bolsheviki. This is the new doctrine of the twentieth-century revolution.

In a report by Harold Williams in the London *Times*,⑤ Bolshevism is considered a mass movement. He compares it with early Christianity, and finds two points of similarity: one is enthusiastic partisanship, the other is a tendency to revelation. He says, "Bolshevism is really a kind of mass movement, with characteristics of religion ... " Not only the Russia of today, but the whole world of the twentieth century probably cannot avoid being controlled by such religious power and swayed by such a mass movement.

[P. 446] In the *Fortnightly Review* Frederic Harrison says:

"Savage, impossible, and anti-social as Bolshevism is, we must realize that it is also an emotional disturbance that is very solid, very wide, and very deep..."

In his book *Bolshevism and World Peace*, Trotzky writes: "In this new revolutionary era a new organization shall be created by unlimited proletarian socialist methods. The new organization will be as great as the new task. Amid the mad roar of the cannon, the crash of temples and shrines, and the wild blast of patriotic songs from wolf-like capitalists, we ought to be the first to undertake this new task. With the death-music of hell about us, we should maintain our clarity of mind, and clearly perceive and realize that ours will be the one and only creative force in the future..."

From this passage it is plain that Trotzky holds that the Russian revolution is to serve as a fuse to world revolution. The Russian revolution is but one [p. 447] of the world revolutions; numerous revolutions of other peoples will successively arise...

The above are all statements made before the end of the war, and before the outbreak of the socialist revolutions in Germany and Austria. Today Trotzky's criticisms have been justified. The comments made by Messrs. Williams and Harrison have also been upheld. There are the Austrian revolution—the German revolution—the Hungarian revolution— and recently there have been reports also of the rise of vigorous revolutionary socialist parties in Holland, Sweden, and Spain. The pattern of the revolutions generally develops along the same line as that in Russia. The red flag flies everywhere, the soviets are established one after another. Call it revolution entirely *à la Russe*, or call it twentieth-century revolution. Such mighty rolling tides are indeed beyond the power of the present capitalist governments to prevent or to stop, for the mass movement of the twentieth century combines the whole of mankind into one great mass. The efforts of each individual within this great mass, following the example of some of them, will then be concentrated and become a great, irresistible social force. Whenever a disturbance in this worldwide social force occurs among the people, it will produce repercussions all over the earth, like storm clouds gathering before the wind and valleys echoing the mountains. In the course of such a world mass movement, all those dregs of history which can impede the progress of the new movement—such as emperors, nobles, warlords, bureaucrats, militarism, capitalism—will certainly be destroyed as though struck by a thunderbolt. Encountering this irresistible tide, these things will be swept away one by one... [P. 448] Henceforth, all that one sees around him will be the triumphant banner of Bolshevism, and all that one hears around him will be Bolshevism's song of victory. The bell is rung for humanitarianism! The dawn of freedom has arrived! See the world of tomorrow; it assuredly will belong to the red flag! ... The revolution in Russia is but the first fallen leaf warning the world of the approach of autumn. Although the word "Bolshevism" was created by the Russians, the spirit it embodies can be regarded as that of a common awakening in the heart of each individual among mankind of the twentieth century. The victory of Bolshevism, therefore, is the victory of the spirit of common awakening in the heart of each individual among mankind in the twentieth century.

### DOC. 61   CH'EN TU-HSIU'S ARGUMENT FOR HISTORICAL MATERIALISM, 1923⑥

[The first few pages explain the controversy then being waged among Chinese intellectuals over the question whether or not science could determine one's philosophy of life. This was the problem of the influence of modern scientific thought upon values.] Chang Chün-mai [Carson Chang, a Chinese minor-party political leader, who later founded the National Socialist or Social Democratic Party] lists nine philosophies of life, and maintains that they are all subjective, intuitive, synthetic and voluntaristic, and arise out of the monomial nature of personality; that they are not objective, rational, analytical or determined by the scientific law of cause and effect. Now after viewing his nine philosophies of life we can see that, first, whether there is a large family system or a small family system is purely a natural phenomenon during the transition from a patriarchal society based on an agricultural economy to a military-nationalist society based on an industrial economy.

Secondly, the high or low position of women in relation to men and the marriage system (which governs this relationship) are both due to the fact that in an agricultural-patriarchal society the wife and children are regarded by the husband and parents as tools of production, as a kind of property; while in an industrial society the family handicrafts go out of date and are replaced by the system of hired labor, so that one need not treat the family as a tool of production. Therefore the feminist movement naturally begins to flourish.

Thirdly, the systems of common or private property: in the primitive communal society there was neither the possibility nor the necessity for private property, since men were weaker than the beasts and needed to form groups and coöperate for survival... When we reached the agricultural stage of permanent habitats and granaries [p. 6] (to facilitate grain preservation), as independent producers the small farmers needed only to possess land, and not to coöperate in group effort. This gave rise to the idea of private property. In the stage of industrial society, the system of independent production by family handicraft can no longer exist, since thousands and tens of thousands of people are organized within one coördinated cooperative unit; any man who has no work cannot eat, and without tools he cannot work. But no one has the tools of production, because these are already privately possessed by a few capitalists. Therefore unless the tools of production are taken over by the public, every man will have to sell his labor to the capitalists. Thus arises the idea of public ownership of property.

Fourthly, the controversy between the conservatives and the

reformers: this is due to the fact that although economic changes have occurred in the present society, the organization of the old society, which is not suited to this changed condition, still persists and restricts the development of change; therefore classes with different economic interests naturally are engaged in conflict, according to the speed or slowness of change.

Fifthly, as to the different opinions regarding matter and spirit, they are the special concerns of a few persons: generally speaking, not to mention the manual laborers in factories, even the twenty-or thirty-dollar-a-month compilers at the Commercial Press worry daily about the insufficiency of food and clothing; so who has the time—like Chang Chün-mai and Liang Ch'i-ch'ao—to discourse on the so-called spiritual civilization and Eastern culture?...[Four further points are here dealt with.]

[P. 7] The above nine different kinds of philosophies of life are all determined by different objective causes and effects. Social science can analyze them one by one and offer rational explanations. It is hard to find one which is without an objective cause, or rather which has arisen without grounds out of a person's subjective, intuitive free will.

Liang Ch'i-ch'ao is indeed more intelligent than Chang Chün-mai. He says, "Chün-mai lists nine items of 'I vs. not-I,' which he holds cannot be explained by scientific method; I think, however, that eighty or ninety per cent of them have to be explained by the scientific method." Liang Ch'i-ch'ao adopts the attitude of a fence-sitter [p. 8]. He disagrees on the one hand with Chang Chün-mai, and on the other with V. K. Ting [China's leading modern geologist, d. 1935]. It is Liang's opinion that: "Of life's problems, the majority can, and must be, solved by scientific method. But there is a minority—perhaps the most important part—that is above science."

His so-called "majority" means those matters in human life that concern the reasoning power; his "minority" means those that concern emotion. He said: "Since the problems touch on actual matter, then of course they are determined by the various laws in the environment—both as regards time and space." True, things that involve the reasoning power cannot be separated from actual matter; but is it also true that things of emotion do not touch upon actual matter? How the senses are stimulated and how they react, how emotion arises, these are common knowledge in psychology...

[P. 9] All these statements about hereditary patterns, conscience, intuition, and free will are determined by the differing conditions of existence of different peoples at different times: a person born into a Hindu Brahmin family will naturally be averse to killing people; if he were born into the home of an African chieftain he would naturally consider that, the more people he killed, the greater would be his glory...

[P. 11] We believe that only objective material causes can change society, can explain history, and can determine one's philosophy of life. This is the "materialistic interpretation of history." We want to ask Mr. V. K. Ting and Mr. Hu Shih: do they believe the "materialistic interpretation of history" to be the whole truth, or do they believe that, apart from materialism and above science, such things as the idealism advocated by people like Chang Chün-mai can also exist?

(November 13, 1923)

## CHAPTER XXVI  HU SHIH AND PRAGMATISM IN CHINA

Hu Shih (1891-1962) was an early contributor and one of the editors of *Hsin-ch'ing-nien* (*La Jeunesse*) in its pre-communist phase and a close associate of Ch'en Tu-hsiu. While a student in the United States (1910-1917) he had become a disciple of John Dewey; and he has openly acknowledged his intellectual indebtedness to John Stuart Mill, Thomas Huxley, and John Morley. The fundamental views which he developed in this early period have persisted with remarkable consistency throughout his thinking in subsequent years.

In 1917 Dr. Hu became professor of philosophy and chairman of the department of English literature at Peking University, posts that he held until 1926. By the time of the May Fourth Movement in 1919, Hu Shih was already well known for his rebellion against the traditional style of writing and his vigorous espousal of the written vernacular (*pai-hua*) as a literary medium. After leaving Peita for a four-and-a-half-year absence in England, America, and Japan and so on, (1926-1930), he returned in 1931 to become dean of the College of Arts and Letters. From 1932 to 1937 he was the chief editor of "The Independent Critic" (*Tu-li p'ing-lun*), a weekly journal of opinion which continued in the main stream of China's pre-Marxist liberal thought.

Hu Shih's advocacy of vernacular literature was an outgrowth of his training in pragmatic philosophy, a relationship that becomes clear when the two following items are read together. He got an immediate response from young Chinese intellectuals and students as soon as his proposals for literary reform were made public in 1916-1917. One of his friends, Ch'ien Hsüan-t'ung, even went so far as to suggest the eventual abolition of the ideographic script.

In his own scholarly career Hu Shih applied the attitude of doubt and criticism which he believed was an essential element of the New Thought. On the one hand this was expressed in his re-examination of the classical heritage of the past; his many critical commentaries on classical and literary works, as well as his unfinished history of Chinese philosophy, are important contributions to Chinese learning. On the other hand, he engaged himself in comparing Chinese systems of thought with Western ones; even in the period before 1923 his field of interest included the advocacy of individualism and the emancipation of women.

After the founding of the Chinese Communist Party by Ch'en Tu-hsiu and others in 1921, Hu Shih found himself in basic disagreement with them in their views of life and its problems. Three trends in Chinese thought were discernible after the First World War: first, that represented by the old-style scholar and translator of Western works, Yen Fu, who was disillusioned with the application of Western institutions to China and turned back to the traditional fold (see Ch. XVI), thus losing influence in the new culture movement; second, that represented by Ch'en Tu-hsiu and Li Ta-chao, who began the effort to introduce new elements into Chinese thought through Marxism; third, that represented by Hu Shih, who continued in his belief of the values of Western liberalism. During the thirty years from 1919 to 1949, this last belief remained largely dominant in Chinese academic circles.

### DOC. 62   HU SHIH, "THE SIGNIFICANCE OF THE NEW THOUGHT," 1919①

Study the problems. Introduce academic theories. Reorganize our national heritage. Recreate civilization.

*Part* I. Several articles explaining the "new thought" have recently appeared in the newspapers. After reading these articles, I feel that their characterization of the New Thought is either too fragmentary or too general, neither an accurate explanation of it nor an indication of its future tendencies... From my own observation, its basic significance lies merely in a new attitude. We may call this [p. 153] "a critical attitude." The critical attitude is, in short, to distinguish, anew the merits and demerits of all things. In more detail, the critical attitude involves several special prerequisites:

(1) Of the traditional systems and conventions, we must ask, "Do these systems still possess the value to survive today?"

(2) Of the teachings of sages and philosophers handed down from ancient times, we must ask, "Are these words still valid today?"

(3) Of all behavior and beliefs receiving the blind approval of society, we must ask, "Is everything that has been approved by the public necessarily correct? Should I do this, just because others are doing it? Is there

no other way that is better, more reasonable and more beneficial?"

Nietzsche said that the modern era is "an era of re-evaluation of all values." These words, "re-evaluation of all values," are the best explanation of the critical attitude. In former days people said that the smaller a woman's feet, the more beautiful they were; now we not only deny the "beauty" of bound feet, but say that foot-binding is "inhumanly cruel." Ten years [p. 154] ago opium was offered to guests in homes and stores; now opium has become a prohibited article. Twenty years ago K'ang Yu-wei was a feared and radical reformer, like a big flood or a fierce beast; now he has become an old curio. It is not K'ang Yu-wei who has changed, but his evaluators, and accordingly his value has also changed. That is a "re-evaluation of all values…"

Part II. [P. 155] When expressed in practice, this critical attitude tends to adopt two methods. One is the discussion of various problems, social, political, religious, and literary. The other is the introduction of new thought, new learning, new literature, and new beliefs from the West. The former is "study of the problems"; the latter is "introduction of academic theories." These two things comprise the methods of the new thought.

These two tendencies can be observed by a casual glance at the contents of new magazines and newspapers of the past two or three years. On the side of studying the problems, we can point to (1) the problem of Confucianism; (2) the problem of the literary revolution; (3) the problem of a unified national language; (4) the problem of the emancipation of women; (5) the problem of chastity; (6) the problem of ethical conventions; (7) the problem of educational reform; (8) the problem of marriage; (9) the problem of the father-son relationship; (10) the problem of the reform of the drama… and so on. On the side of the introduction of academic theories, we can point to the special issues "On Ibsen" and "On Marx" of the *Hsin-ch'ing-nien*, the issue "On contemporary thought" of the *Min-to* [The people's tocsin], the issue

"On Dewey" of *Hsin-chiao-yü* [The new education], the theory of *ch'üan-min cheng-chih* [total democracy] in *Chien-she* [Reconstruction], and the various new Western theories that have been introduced in such newspapers and magazines as the *Peking Morning Post*...[and other papers in Peking, Shanghai, and Canton].

[P. 156] Why must problems be studied? Because our society is now undergoing a period in which its foundations are shaken. Many customs and systems which were not questioned have become difficult issues owing to their failure to meet the needs of circumstance and satisfy the people; therefore we cannot but thoroughly study them, cannot but ask whether or not the old solutions were wrong; if they were wrong, wherein the mistake lies; and when the mistake is discovered, whether there is a better solution, or whether there is any way that will better meet the demands of the present time. For example, the question of Confucianism never arose before. Later, when the civilization of the East came into contact with that of the West, the influence of Confucianism gradually weakened; whereupon a group of Confucianists attempted to restore its dignity by resorting to governmental laws and Decrees, not knowing that such high-handed methods would only rouse in people a sort of skeptical reaction. Therefore when the Confucianist Society was the most active, around 1915 and 1916, the anti-Confucianists were also the most numerous. It was at this time that Confucianism became a problem. At present most enlightened people have already broken through these illusions regarding it, and this problem is gradually subsiding, so that when the parliamentary members of the *An-fu* clique passed the resolution defining Confucianism as the basis of moral cultivation, no one in the country even paid it any attention.

Again, take the instance of the literary revolution. Heretofore education has been the special privilege of a small group of "scholars," and has not concerned the majority of the people; therefore the difficulties of the language have not constituted a problem. In recent years education has become a common privilege of all the people, and every man knows that universal education [p. 157] is indispensable; so gradually some people began to realize that the classical style is really not suited to education for all, so then classical versus vernacular style became an issue. Later others felt that writing only textbooks in the vernacular style was not effective because no one in the world would be willing to learn a language that was of no use except in textbooks...If we wish to advocate a vernacular education, then we must first advocate a vernacular literature. The problem of the literary revolution was thus engendered. Now that the National Education Association has unanimously passed a resolution to change the primary school textbooks into the vernacular, moreover, more and more people are writing in the vernacular, and this problem is gradually subsiding.

Why do we have to introduce academic theories? This probably can be explained in several ways. First, some persons are convinced that China lacks not only cannon, warships, telegraphs and railways, but also new ideas and new learning; therefore they introduce as many modern Western theories as possible. Secondly, some persons deeply believe in certain theories themselves, and wish to spread and develop them; therefore they exert themselves to advocate them. Thirdly, some persons are unable to do actual research work themselves, and feel that it is easier to translate ready-made theories; therefore they are glad to engage in this kind of middleman's business. Fourthly, while studying concrete social or political problems one has to do destructive work on the one hand, and on the other hand to make out a prescription to fit the malady. This is not only difficult in itself, but also can easily offend others and cause trouble; therefore one may prefer to embark upon the introduction of academic theories and, under the beautiful phrase "study of academic theories," one [p. 158] can avoid being accused as an "extremist" or radical, as well as succeed in sowing a few seeds of revolution. Fifthly, those who study a problem cannot limit their discussion to the problem itself; they have to approach it by considering its meaning in the context; and when one extends the study of a problem to the realm of this sort of significance, it is necessary to rely on various theories as material for reference and comparison. Therefore the introduction of academic theories usually aids in the study of problems.

Although the above five motives differ from one another, they all embody the "critical attitude" to a greater or lesser degree; they all express a dissatisfaction with old learning and thought, and a new awakening to the spiritual aspect of Western civilization...

*Part III.* [P. 161] In the above we have mentioned the two practical expressions of the "critical spirit" of the new thought. Now we must ask, "What is to be the attitude of the new thought movement toward the old learning and thought of China?" My answer is, "It should also be a critical attitude."

Under analysis, our attitude toward the old learning and thought should be threefold: first, opposition to blind obedience; second, opposition to compromise; third, advocacy of a reorganization of our national heritage.

Blind obedience is the opposite of critical-mindedness. Since we advocate a "re-evaluation of all values," we naturally must oppose blind obedience. This need not be elaborated.

Why must we oppose compromise? Because the critical attitude recognizes only one right and one wrong, one good and one evil, one suitability and one unsuitability—it does not recognize any compromise of the ancient and modern, or of the foreign and the Chinese ... [P. 162] Compromise is the natural tendency of human indolence; it does not require our advocacy. The majority of people can probably, with effort, walk only thirty or forty *li* while we go a hundred *li*. Now if we start talking of compromise and only go fifty *li*, then they will not move even one step. Therefore the duty of the reformer is to set his goal in the right direction and go forward, not to turn back and talk of compromise. There will inevitably be numerous laggards and cowards in society to come out for compromise.

In its positive aspect we make only one proposition regarding our attitude toward the old learning and thought, that is: "to reorganize the national heritage." To reorganize the national heritage means finding order out of chaos, finding the relations of cause and effect out of confusion, finding a real significance out of absurdities and fantasies, and finding true value out of dogmatism and superstition...

*Part IV* ... [P. 164] From my personal observation, the future tendency of the new thought should be to lay emphasis on the study of problems important to life and society, and to carry out the task of introducing academic theories through studies of these problems... What is the sole aim of the new thought? It is to re-create civilization. Civilization was not created *in toto*, but by inches and drops. Evolution was not accomplished overnight, but in inches and drops. People nowadays indulge in talk about "liberation and reform," but they should know that there is no liberation *in toto*, or reform *in toto*. Liberation means the liberation of this or that system, of this or that idea, of this or that individual; it is liberation by inches and drops. Reform means the reform of this or that system, of this or that idea, of this or that individual; it is reform by inches and drops. The first step in the re-creation of civilization is the study of this or that problem. Progress in the re-creation of civilization lies in the solution of this or that problem. (November 1, 1919, 3 A. M.)

We have chosen Dr. Hu's following summary of the new literary movement, because it depicts so well the various phases of its early development as well as the main tenets of its major advocates. The terms *pai-hua* and *kuo-yü* are often interchangeably translated; the latter literally means "national dialect," but from the time of the literary revolution, especially in the context of the present piece, it has also assumed a second meaning of "vernacular," which is *pai-hua*.

## DOC. 63   HU SHIH, "ON THE LITERARY REVOLUTION," 1922[2]

The Chinese classical style was already a dead language two thousand years ago. That was why in the time of the Emperor Wu-ti of Han [140-87 B. C.] Prime Minister Kung-sun Hung [200-121 B. C.] memorialized: "The Decrees and laws that have been issued... are written in an elegant style, with profound literary expressions, and are an exquisite bestowal of your grace. But the petty officials are smatterers who cannot thoroughly ascertain their meaning and have no means of announcing them clearly so as to instruct the people below." Even at that time the petty officials were unable to understand the Decrees and laws written in elegant style. But the government was obliged to advocate this kind of dead classical style for its political needs, and it devised a way to encourage the common people to study the classical style: all who could "master more than one classic" were given official posts, and "the more widely read were to be employed first." Beginning in the Han Dynasty, this method underwent gradual revisions until it became the system of "literary examinations." This system of literary examinations prolonged the life of the dead classical style for fully two thousand years.

[P. 189] But the vernacular literature of the populace could not be suppressed. Though aristocratic literature had the upper hand in these two thousand years, popular literature also continued quietly and unobtrusively to develop... [The following two pages trace the evolution of vernacular literature since the Han, which the author divides into five major periods represented by the following: (1) the "musical poem" of Han; (2) the vernacular poetry and Buddhist lectures of T'ang; (3) the poetry of uneven verse of Sung; (4) the ballads and drama of Chin and Yuan; (5) the novel of Ming and Ch'ing. The last is held to have been the most influential literary force in China during the last five hundred years.]

[P. 191] China's vernacular had long been put in a definite written form, had spread far and wide, and had produced many first-class works in the living language; but the vernacular had not yet received the recognition of the general public. Why was this? There are two major reasons: one was the continuation of the civil service examinations; the other was the lack of a conscious advocacy of the use of the vernacular...

[P. 193] The conscious advocacy of vernacular literature began only with the literary revolution movement since 1915. In two respects this movement is different from the movements for vernacular newspapers and alphabetization. First, there is no distinction between "us" and "them" in this movement. The vernacular style not only is an instrument for "enlightening the people's minds," but also is the only instrument for the creation of Chinese literature. The vernacular style is not a bone fit only to feed the underdog, but a treasure which the people of the entire country should appreciate. Secondly, this movement honestly attacks the authority of the classical style, and regards it as "dead literature." Although the previous movements for vernacular newspapers and alphabetization admitted that the classical style is difficult to understand, they nevertheless kept on feeling that "we of the upper classes are not afraid of the difficulties—'you can only be a man above men if you can take the hardest of hardships.'"

[P. 194] At its inception the idea of a literary revolution consisted only of a few persons' private discussions, and was not formally published in the journals until January 1917. The first article, "A preliminary discussion of literary reform" by Hu Shih, was still in a vein of very peaceful discussion... [p. 195]

Ch'en Tu-hsiu's special character lies in his determination to go straight forward. At that time Hu Shih was still in America, where he wrote to Tu-hsiu:

"The rights and wrongs of this matter cannot be determined in a day, nor by one or two persons. I hope very much that people in China will co-operate with us to study this problem calmly. When discussions reach a mature stage, the rights and wrongs naturally will become clear. It is true that we have already raised the banner of revolution and cannot retreat, yet we should not maintain that what we advocate is absolutely right and not tolerate correction by others."

(April 9, 1917)

This shows that Hu Shih recognized the literary revolution as being still in a stage for discussion. He was then engaged in writing poetry in the vernacular style in order to prove that it was suitable as a medium for verse; therefore he entitled his volume of poetry "A collection of experimental poems," or "Trials" (*Ch'ang-shih chi*). This attitude of his was too pacific. The literary revolution would have had to go through at least ten years more of discussions and trials, if his method had been adopted. But Ch'en Tu-hsiu's courage exactly counterbalanced this defect of overcautiousness. Tu-hsiu replied:

"My opinion is that, while tolerance of different opinions and free discussion are the basic principles of the development of learning, nevertheless the rights and wrongs of the theory—that in the reform of Chinese literature the vernacular should be regarded as the main object—are already very clear, and we definitely will not allow discussion by opponents [p. 198]; we must consider our theory as the absolute right and not allow others to correct us."

At the time such an attitude rather aroused the objection of the general public. But had it not been for Ch'en Tu-hsiu's spirit of "not allowing discussion by opponents," the movement for a literary revolution would not have received so much attention. For opposition signifies interest.

During 1917 much correspondence on literature appeared in *Hsin-ch'ing-nien*, in which much of the discussion by Ch'ien Hsüan-t'ung could supplement the ideas of Hu Shih. In January 1918, *Hsin-ch'ing-nien* renewed its publication under the rotating editorship of Professors Ch'en Tu-hsiu, Ch'ien Hsüan-t'ung, Shen Yin-mo, Li Ta-chao, Liu Fu [d. 1934], and Hu Shih. Throughout the year its articles were all written in the vernacular style. The main theme of Hu Shih's essay, "On a constructive literary revolution" (April 1918) was stated to be:

"The purpose of my article 'On the establishment of a new literature' can be covered in four simple words: 'vernacular literature, literary vernacular.' The literary revolution we advocate aims only at the creation of a vernacular literature for China. Only after there is a vernacular literature can there be a literary vernacular. Only after there is a literary vernacular can our vernacular become the real national spoken language…"

[On pp. 199-206 the author deals with the growth of several vernacular magazines in Peking in 1918, and the intensification of the conservative opposition, especially the debate in 1919 between Lin Shu (the old-style scholar and translator of Western novels, who died in 1924) and Ts'ai Yuan-p'ei. Then the students' May Fourth Movement gave a further impetus to the development of the vernacular press.]

[P. 207] Although the student movement of 1919 and the new literary movement are two distinct matters, yet a close relation exists between them in that the effect of the student movement was to facilitate the spread of the vernacular over the entire country. Moreover, after the May Fourth Movement the enlightened elements in the country gradually came to realize the importance of the "revolution of thought." Therefore toward the new trends they adopted either an attitude of welcome, or of study, or of tolerance, and gradually reduced the old attitude of hostility, so that the movement for literary revolution was able to develop freely; this was another close relationship. Consequently, after 1919 the spread of the vernacular progressed at "a thousand $li$ a day." More and more poetry also was written in the vernacular. In 1920, a ministerial Decree was issued by the Ministry of Education, requiring the use of the vernacular style in all primary school textbooks for the first and second grades, beginning that autumn…

According to this order, the change from classical to vernacular textbooks in the entire primary school would not be completed before the present year [1922]. But the lower and upper levels of the educational system are related; when one hair is pulled the whole body can be affected. When the first and second grades changed to vernacular, the junior normal schools perforce [p. 208] also had to change, and most of the upper primary schools also followed suit. When junior normal schools changed, the senior normal schools were also obliged to change. Many middle schools also voluntarily adopted vernacular textbooks. Although this action of the Ministry of Education was based on the resolution of the National Education Association, much was contributed by the members of the Society for the Study of Vernacular Language, an association formed in 1916, whose active members were connected with the Ministry. When the vernacular literature movement had matured, there was little opposition to the idea of vernacular textbooks; therefore the Society for the Study of Vernacular Language was able to induce the Ministry of Education to accomplish this important measure of reform when Deputy Minister for Education Fu Yueh-fen was the acting minister...[pp. 208-211 deal with more recent opposition from the classicists. The last paragraph, pp. 211-213, evaluates the achievements of the new literature during the last five years.]

(March 3, 1922)

## CHAPTER XXVII   SUN YAT-SEN'S REORIENTATION OF THE REVOLUTION

Among modern political leaders, Dr. Sun seems to have been remarkably adaptable, having not only different ideas at different times, but even conflicting ideas at the same time. Possibly this lack of consistency is to be expected in a man who was primarily a political leader, not a political theorist. Sun picked up many ideas somewhat indiscriminately and wound up as a syncretic thinker rather than a systematic one. His writings over the years included a bit of everything.

The adoption of Western political thought as the theoretical justification for the Chinese Revolution reached a climax at the time of Sun's inauguration as the president of the provisional government at Nanking early in 1912. The provincial delegates then declared: "We, the descendants of Han, have groaned under the searing oppression of the Manchus; and, admiring the systems of equality of the American and the French peoples, we have met and planned together…for the overthrow of tyranny and restoration of the rights of man…" At the same time, the emphasis on nationalism (which did not oppose but included the Manchus) was made clear in Sun Yat-sen's speech after he was given the seal of office: the task of the provisional government, he said, was to seek unity of race, unity of territory, unity of military administration and unity of national finance. In all this early and rather casual expression of revolutionary aims, there was no indication of how this Chinese republican revolution on the Western model was to be combined with changes in social structure such as were implied in the "revolutionary program" and others of Sun's pronouncements.

After the establishment of the Republic, Dr. Sun persisted in his belief that Western constitutional democracy was the answer to China's troubles. Having renounced the presidency in favor of Yuan Shih-k'ai, Sun asserted in 1912 that, since nationalism and the people's rights had been achieved, he would now devote himself to improving the people's livelihood as director-general of railway development. The Kuomintang as a political body openly seeking legislative power was mainly put together by Sun's lieutenant, Sung Chiao-jen. Yuan therefore had him assassinated in 1913.

After this first effort at parliamentary government in China had been thwarted, Sun Yat-sen in 1914 swung to another extreme. In Japan he organized the Chinese Revolutionary Party (*Chung-hua ko-ming-tang*)—

a secret group to be controlled ... by Sun as Leader (*Tsung-li*) ... The stated aim of this new centralized party—three years before the Russian Revolution—was one-party government.① How much this effort accomplished is uncertain; Sun was soon working again with the Kuomintang. At the same time he retained his faith in the ultimate possibility of constitutional democracy, after the party had performed its task of political tutelage. He still maintained that the carrying out of his original "revolutionary program" (see Ch. XXIII) could solve China's problem of political reorganization. His military campaigns against northern warlords were at first "campaigns for the protection of the constitution," by which he meant that the legitimate government at Peking, established by the consent of the opposing parties in 1912, and its draft constitution must be the object of support, in deference to the idea of the rule of law. In 1917, he wrote "A primer of democracy" (*Min-ch'üan ch'u-pu*) which dealt exclusively with parliamentary procedure. The Russian Revolution of that year roused his interest, but produced no immediate effect on his political thinking. What socialist influence there was in his teachings had already been worked into the principle of the people's livelihood.

The establishment of the Canton Military Government in 1921 marked another turning point in Sun's outlook. He now acknowledged that the mere "protection of the constitution" was not enough to further the cause of the revolution: henceforth the revolutionaries would have to conduct their campaign under a separate government. At the same time the power of the Russian Revolution had begun to impress him, and in the straits to which he was reduced in 1922-1923 he did not hesitate to begin the reorganization of the Kuomintang on soviet structural lines. In speeches made at this time he stressed the role of the Party as the foundation of the state, the importance of strict organization and discipline within the Party, the subjection of the individual member to the Party, and the need of ideological propaganda. With his Russian advisor,

Michael Borodin, at his elbow, these things appeared to Sun in 1924 to be the immediate and urgent desiderata of the revolutionary cause.

In the economic sphere Sun had felt before 1923 that China's problems were to be solved by a two-fold plan on a national scale: China must carry out, first, the policy of the equalization of land ownership and the nationalization of capital; and secondly, the industrialization of the country supported by foreign loans. On the latter point a detailed plan entitled the *Shih-yeh chi-hua* (lit., industrial plan; English version: *The International Development of China*) was drawn up by Sun in 1917-1918. This work was based on an interesting blend of two assumptions, that the expanded wartime economy of capitalist nations demanded large foreign outlets for investment, and that China could look to these Western capitalist nations for help through a financial transaction pure and simple. Sun's reasoning appears to have been that, since China was striving to become a nation just like the Western democracies, they could therefore help one another out of difficulties. By absorbing the surplus capital of the Western nations after the World War, China would help the latter to prevent an economic collapse; meanwhile China could benefit from this financial aid in her industrialization. This conception, like so many of Sun's other dreams, was shattered after 1919 and soon smothered by the spread of Leninist thought in Kuomintang circles.

His post-war disappointment with Western support made Sun look to Russia. The reorganization of the Kuomintang in 1923-1924 shifted the emphasis of his thinking to the realm of political strategy and control. In order to broaden the basis of support for the revolution, members of the recently founded Chinese Communist Party were admitted into the Kuomintang as individuals in 1924. The first detailed exposition of the *Three People's Principles* did not appear until late 1924, and the exposition of the principle of the people's livelihood was cut short by Sun's departure from Canton and subsequent death (March 1925). These famous lectures embody the outline of his political doctrine, which had been proclaimed nearly two decades earlier after the founding of the *Tung-meng-hui* (see Doc. 56); but at the same time it is apparent that Marxism-Leninism was beginning to have its effect on Sun's thinking, as evidenced in his much-touted "three policies" of 1924, which included support of the Soviet Union.

The following item indicates the rather unfocused and groping character of Sun's thinking before his alliance with communism.

## DOC. 64    SUN YAT-SEN'S THEORY OF KNOWLEDGE AND ACTION, 1919[2]

In these days of scientific advancement all who create things must first acquire the knowledge for the task before they dare begin the work... So in all enterprises one must be able from one's knowledge to construct ideas and images, from the ideas and images to produce a set of agenda [i.e., things to be done], and on this set of agenda as a base, to work out a careful plan, and by following the plan to apply one's effort. In this way, no matter how advanced or intricate the enterprise or how stupendous the construction, the aims can all be easily achieved by an assigned date. Nowadays the radio and the airplane are the most advanced and intricate of things; the most stupendous of engineering projects are the more than 1,200,000 *li* of railroads in the United States (when the United States took all the American railways under government management on December 13,1916, the total mileage was 397,014 miles, with a capital of U.S. $19,600,000,000, which is equal to $39,200,000,000, in Chinese silver dollars) and the Suez and Panama Canals. Yet when their scientific principles were known and their sites had been studied, the plans were drawn up by engineers, and these plans were put into practical application; then they became matters of no difficulty at all. These are all real facts that can be verified. People of our country can know the truth about them with a little investigation.

As for my work in revolutionary reconstruction, I have based my ideas on the current of world progress, and followed the precedents in other countries. I have studied their respective merits and demerits, their gains and losses, considered the matter thoroughly [p. 51], and given it mature thought. Then I drew up the "Program of Revolution," and fixed the progress of the Chinese revolution into three periods. The first is the period of military government; the second, the period of political tutelage; the third is the period of constitutional government. [The rest of this paragraph gives a summary of the "Program of Revolution," explaining the plan for a five-power constitution.]

[P. 52] When the Republic was first established in 1912, I strongly urged putting the "Program of Revolution" into effect, in order to achieve the goal of revolutionary reconstruction and the application of the Three People's Principles. But most of our Party members were hesitant, and thought it could not be done. Although I repeatedly explained and argued, it was all to no avail. They all held that my revolutionary ideals were too high; that "it is easy to know a thing but difficult to carry it out." Alas! Were my ideals too high? Was it not rather that the knowledge of our party members was too low? Therefore I could not help becoming discouraged and disappointed. For the destructiveness of revolution precedes the constructiveness of revolution in due order, and they complement each other. Now, since no revolutionary construction had been begun since the destruction of revolution, that meant there would be no revolutionary reconstruction. Since there was no revolutionary reconstruction, what use would there be for a revolutionary president? That was why I, desiring to retire after the establishment of the Nanking Government, continued the armistice [with Yuan Shih-k'ai] and renewed peace negotiations. Now that the situation has changed, many persons have criticized me, saying that I should not have consented to peace negotiations and abdicated the presidency after the establishment of the government at Nanking. But suppose I had continued to be the president, while, after the successes of the destruction [of the revolution, i. e. , by Yuan], most Party members no longer abided by their revolutionary pledges, nor submitted to the views of the Leader; in that case, even if the Revolutionary Party could have united China, it would still have been no more than substitution of new bureaucrats for old ones. As to the fundamentals of the governance and cultivation of the nation, or the basic plan for the people's livelihood, we would have been totally unprepared. That would have amounted to exchanging one tyrant for another. Hence there was no need for me to be president. [The next paragraph re-emphasizes the statement that his retirement from the presidency was caused by the revolutionaries' not putting revolutionary reconstruction into practice.]

[P. 53] What is revolutionary reconstruction? It is extraordinary reconstruction, and also rapid reconstruction. There is ordinary reconstruction, which follows the natural course of society and is done according to the trends of circumstance. This is the reconstruction that differs from the revolutionary. In a revolution extraordinary destruction is wrought—such as the decapitation of the monarchical system and the overthrow of absolutism ... [P. 54] In these extraordinary times only extraordinary reconstruction can inspire the people with a new mind and make a new beginning of the nation. For this reason the "Program of Revolution" is a necessity.

Now let us observe the great revolutions that took place before our Republic, of which the most world-shaking were the American and French. The political system of America was determined after the revolution, and for more than one hundred years there has been no change in it. Except for one civil war arising out of the question of Negro slavery, there has been no major disturbance in that country. We can indeed say that once the revolution was accomplished America's political system became fixed and unchanging; there was prolonged good administration and internal peace; civilization advanced and economic development became the best in the world. On the other hand, France after the revolution was beset by major disturbances; the political system was changed five times—twice into the monarchical system and thrice into the republican—until, eighty years after the revolution, a militarist emperor was defeated and captured by a foreign enemy. Then republicanism became secure. Compared with the United States, their respective peace and disturbance, gains and losses, are as different as heaven and earth. Why? People who comment on the problem mostly say that Washington was generous and humble in behavior, and therefore at the beginning of their nationhood refused the crown; but that Napoleon, bursting with ambition and aiming at world conquest, began with a republic and ended with an empire. Yet these people do not realize that the course taken by a nation is determined by the psychology of the multitude; if the direction is set, then it certainly cannot be altered by the intelligence of one or two persons who have risen to leadership through force of circumstance. For neither Washington nor Napoleon was an initiator of the American or the French Revolution. After the thirteen American colonies had begun their campaign against England, Washington was asked to command their troops; and Napoleon rose from an obscure position after the outbreak of the revolution in France. If the positions of these two individuals had been exchanged, the results would probably have been the same. Therefore the different aims of Washington and Napoleon arose not out of their personal virtues, but rather out of the traditions of their countries.

The continent of America had always been a wilderness. The English had colonized it just a little over two hundred years. The English people loved adventure and were endowed with self-governing abilities. After reaching America they forthwith established institutions for self-government, and gradually became thirteen colonies... [p. 55] It was not so with France. Although France was an advanced and cultured country in Europe, with an intelligent, energetic population, and although for a hundred years before the revolution she had been under the influence of revolutionary theories and, further, had the American precedent to rely on;

still she was unable to attain the republican form of government with one leap out of revolution. Why was that? It was because her political system had always been an absolute monarchy, and her government had always been centralized; she possessed no new world as the area for development and no self-government as foundation.

[P. 56] China's defects are the same as those of France; moreover, the knowledge and political ability of the Chinese people are far behind those of the French. And yet I wished to attain a republican constitutional government in one step after the revolution. How should this have been brought about? That is why I devised a transitional period in order to repair our defects. During this period we are to carry out a constitutional government, so as to train and guide the people, and to effect local self-government... [The rest of this paragraph and the three following repeat the need for the period of tutelage, and maintain that failure to put it into effect has cost the revolutionaries a certain amount of sympathy among the Europeans and Americans.]

[P. 57] Others again have queried whether the six years of political tutelage would not be the same as the "enlightened despotism" advocated by narrow-minded scholars? The answer is that the aim of enlightened despotism is despotism itself, whereas that of political tutelage is republicanism. Therefore there is the difference between heaven and earth betwixt the two. Take, for instance, the present World War. All nations participating in it, be they republics or monarchies, have ceased their constitutional government and resorted to military government. The people's traditional freedoms of movement, of speech, and of organization, are all abolished; even food and drink and business are controlled by the government [p. 58]. Yet no criticisms are raised in these countries. Instead the people sacrifice their lives for the nation, because they aim at victory and survival. When other nations which have already had constitutional government can stop its operation, how can we immediately put constitutional government into effect at the beginning of the revolutionary war, when the constitutional regime has not yet come into being and we are just embarked on seeking it through the revolutionary war? That is really a puerile and illogical idea! [In the next two paragraphs, the American policy in the Philippines and the regencies of the Duke of Chou and others are cited as examples to support the theory of political tutelage.]

[P. 59] Well then, why is it that the destructive phase of the revolution has succeeded but the constructive phase has failed? The difference lies between knowledge and ignorance. In the destructive revolution I had attempted ten uprisings and ten times had failed. That was because at that time the majority of the Chinese people still did not realize that they were conquered by the Manchus, so they lived in a stupor and died dreaming, and regarded the revolution as unprincipled rebellion. Later the revolutionary trend became gradually more prevalent, and most people came to realize that the Manchu Dynasty ought to be abolished, and that the Chinese race ought to be restored to power. Consequently, it was possible to overthrow the Ch'ing Dynasty with one single stroke, as easily as turning one's palm. As to the constructive revolution, however, not only was the general populace ignorant of it, but also the Revolutionary Party did not know what it meant. In a revolutionary mission, the most difficult thing is to destroy and the easiest is to reconstruct. Now why is it that we have succeeded in the difficult but failed in the easy? It is because it is easy to do; therefore people do not realize how essential it is, and so neglect it; such is the cause of failure…

[P. 60] There is a common saying that the four hundred million Chinese are like a sheet of loose sand. What is the means by which these four hundred million grains of sand can be united into a coördinated, organized country ruled by law? It is necessary to start with oath-taking, so that one's mind can be set upright on the proper course and one's sincerity be assured; then we can hope to attain [the various stages listed in the famous classical quotation from the *Great Learning*] self-cultivation, ruling the family, administering the nation, and bringing peace to the whole world. Nowadays there is no civilized nation under the rule of law that does not take the pledging of an oath as the basic procedure of the rule of law... [The rest of this paragraph presents further arguments in support of oath-taking, citing oaths of citizenship and public office in foreign countries as examples; then Yuan Shih-k'ai's oath on assuming the presidency is explained.]

[P. 62] A race is an aggregation of human beings; a human being is ruled by the mind; and the nation and the government are the manifestations of the psychology of a group. Therefore the foundation of a nation is first based on the working of the mind. Hence when the people and officials of the Manchu Dynasty give their allegiance to the Republic, they must first show their honesty and sincerity; that is why the ceremony of oath-taking is necessary. Yet the members of the Revolutionary Party did it when the party was being organized, but do not do it while national reconstruction is being carried out. Thus the ambitious, progressive and fearless spirit of Party members was sufficient to bring about destruction, but such powers were lost during the time of national reconstruction, and so there has been no actual achievement in construction. These were the consequences of action and non-action. But the reason for their non-action was not that they were unable to act, but that they did not know the urgent necessity of doing so. Therefore I say, "Whatever can be known can certainly be carried ont." Is there anyone who still thinks it is idealistic? [In the last paragraph of this chapter Sun proceeds to draft the form of an oath which he holds ought to be taken by every loyal citizen of the Republic, and lays down the procedure by which it is to be administered.]

The following speech, a sort of Party harangue, is from the period when Sun was taking Michael Borodin's advice in reorganizing the

Kuomintang. It has some relevance to events three decades later.

## DOC. 65  SUN YAT-SEN'S ADOPTION OF THE RUSSIAN PARTY SYSTEM, 1923③

Comrades: the present reorganization of our Party aims at the largest possible expansion of the influence of our Party in the various provinces of China's interior. Hitherto the influence of our Party has been mostly overseas. Therefore our Party has bases and members overseas, but its influence in the interior of China has been very weak. Consequently throughout the years the struggle of our Party in our country has depended exclusively on military force. When our military forces have won the day, our Party accordingly has won with them; when military force has failed, our Party also accordingly has failed. Therefore the sole purpose of the present reorganization of the Party is to enable us to avoid relying exclusively on armed force, and to rely on the power of the Party itself. By "the power of the Party itself" I mean the mind and strength [i. e., the support.] of the people. Henceforth our Party should regard the mind and strength of the people as that of our Party and it should use the mind and strength of the people in its struggles. Popular support and military force can be employed simultaneously without contradiction. But between the two, which should be the foundation, and which is the more dependable? To rely on military force alone is not dependable, because the victories and defeats of military forces are inconstant. Our Party must first have a basic strength as its foundation before we can hope to rely on military force. Without such a basic strength as our foundation, military force is undependable even if we possess it.

There have been three times of success when our Party struggled with the use of military force in the interior of China. The outbreak of revolution at Wu-ch'ang [1911], the overthrow of the Manchu Dynasty, and the establishment of the Republic: that was the first success of our Party's military force. Yuan Shih-k'ai wanted to become emperor; the anti-Yuan campaign was started and his regime was overthrown [1916]: that was the second success of our Party's military force. When Chang Hsün [1854-1923] tried to restore the Manchu emperor [1917], we launched the campaign to protect the *Constitution* [ of 1912 ]. Subsequently Hsü Shih-ch'ang [1855-1939] resigned from the presidency and Ch'en Ch'iung-ming revolted against us [1922], and the warlords of the north also joined the campaign for the *Constitution*: that was the third success [p. 315] of our Party's military force. But all three successes did not enable us to attain the aim of the revolution. That is, although military force had succeeded, the revolution still had not been accomplished, because our Party still lacked power. What was the power that we lacked? It was the support of the people...

[P. 319] The above account shows that the struggles of our Party have depended mostly on military force; therefore the victories and defeats came intermittently. If this situation continues for a prolonged period, there will never be any hope of success for our Party, and there never will be a day when our Three People's Principles can be realized. Therefore the present reorganization has been initiated. What is expected of this reorganization? It is expected that out of this our Party will be able to build up a central force. From this day forward all comrades must apply themselves earnestly to the revolutionary task. All comrades must make the revolutionary task their own lifelong task, must bring about the complete realization of the Three People's Principles and the Five Power Constitution. Only then can our Party be considered as having succeeded. But we cannot rely [p. 320] exclusively on warfare for this success, because in warfare we must depend on military men, and the majority of the general run of the present military men do not understand ideology...

[P. 321] Why has not our Party engaged in organized, systematic, and disciplined struggle before? It was because we lacked the model and the precedent. Now we have a good friend, Mr. Borodin, who has come from Russia. The Russian Revolution took place six years later than that in our country, and yet after one revolution the Russians have been able to apply their principles thoroughly; moreover, since the revolution the revolutionary government has daily become more stabilized. Both are revolutions: why have they succeeded in Russia, and why have we not in China? It is because the Russian Revolution owed its success to the struggle of the Party members: on the one hand the Party members struggled, on the other hand they were aided by military forces, and so they were able to succeed. Therefore, if we wish our revolution to succeed, we must learn the methods, organization, and training of the Russians; then there can be hope of success.

But many people hold that the regime in Russia is controlled by the Bolshevik Party and, if we learn from Russia, would we not be learning from Bolshevism? These persons do not realize that, while it was true that before the outbreak of the revolution in Russia there was much Bolshevik thought—for the leaders of the Russian Revolution were mostly men of deep learning and lofty and profound ideals, consequently it was inevitable that some of their theories were radical and extreme—yet the Russians do not act only according to ideals but base most of their actions on fact, just as in traveling one must choose and take the road that one can go through. [P. 322] Therefore at the time of the Russian Revolution there were many political parties, such as the Social Democratic Party, the Democratic Revolutionary Party, etc., but they could not all succeed, and the one that has succeeded today is the Communist Party. The reason behind the Communist Party's success is that it suits the desires of the majority of the Russian people, so all the Russian people support it.

When he first came, Mr. Borodin told me that the Russian Revolution has undergone six years of struggle through various ways, but in retrospect today it is seen that nationalism has been the thing that appeals most to the Russian people. The Russian people suffered extremely under the bondage of the Great Powers. The suffering they underwent during the great European War was forced on them by the

Great Powers. The shaking of the Tsar's regime was due to his participation in the Great War together with the Great Powers, thereby inciting the opposition of all the Russian people, and they rose in revolution against the Tsar... After the success of the Communist Party's revolution, its renunciation of foreign debts evoked the vigorous opposition of the Great Powers. England, the U. S. A., France, Japan and others all rose and attacked her. At that time Russia was surrounded by enemies in eight directions, and the troops of the Great Powers had already reached St. Petersburg. The dangers of the situation really exceeded that at Canton a few days ago. The reason for Russia's being able to resist such strong enemies lay entirely in the struggles of the Russian people and of the Party members; therefore they have been able to eject the foreign forces, establish an independent nation, and are no longer the slaves of the Great Powers. Furthermore, they are also able to eliminate foreign economic aggression... [The next few lines explain how the ideology of the Russian Communist Party coincides with the Three People's Principles.]

[P. 323] Both our Party and theirs advocate the Three People's Principles. Although the ideology is the same, yet our Party does not possess good methods; therefore it is slow in achieving its goal. Their vision is great and their learning deep, and they can devise good methods. If we want our revolution to succeed we must follow their example. Heretofore in the accomplishment of the revolution each of us has fought on his own; henceforth we must fight as an organized group and engage in a disciplined struggle. Since we wish to learn their methods, I have asked Mr. Borodin to be the director of training④ of our Party; he is to train our comrades. Mr. Borodin is extremely experienced in party management. It is hoped that all comrades will sacrifice their personal prejudices and earnestly learn his methods. Although it has only been a very short time since the establishment of the local branch offices of our Party, yet according to the reports of various comrades the results are already highly visible. If this continues, the day of final victory for our Party will certainly arrive...

## CHAPTER XXVIII  LIANG CH'I-CH'AO'S REVIEW OF CHINA'S PROGRESS, 1873-1922

In 1922 the leading Shanghai newspaper, "Shun-Pao" (*Shen-pao*), was fifty years old and its editors asked Liang Ch'i-ch'ao, who was also fifty, to survey the developments of the past half century. Liang's effort to appraise China's progress, condensed below, is in optimistic terms, but one can hardly avoid the feeling that the writer had resolutely made up his mind not to be downhearted. In the few remaining years of his life, Liang devoted himself to philosophical and classical studies. His faith in what the West could offer China seems to have been deeply shaken by the First World War. In 1920 he had written:①

Since Darwin's discovery of the principle of the evolution of species, a great revolution has occurred in intellectual circles over the whole world. His service to learning must be acknowledged. But afterwards his theory of the struggle for existence and survival of the fittest was applied to the study of human society and became the core of thought, with many evil consequences. This great European war has nearly wiped out human civilization; although its causes were very many, it must be said that the Darwinian theory had a very great influence. Even in China in recent years, where throughout a whole country men struggle for power, grasp for gain, and seem to have gone crazy, although they understand nothing of scholarship, yet the things they say to shield themselves from condemnation are regularly drawn from Yen Fu's translation of T. H. Huxley's *Principles of Evolution*. One can see that the influence of theory on men's minds is enormous. No wonder that Mencius said, "These evils, growing in the mind, do injury to government, and displayed in the government, are harmful to the conduct of affairs." Perhaps the Europeans' current fondness for the study of Laotzu is in reaction to this theory...

Again in 1923, Liang Ch'i-ch'ao wrote of a West that was withered, dry, and sick from "spiritual famine" because of its pursuit of material things:[2] "Of the methods of relieving spiritual famine I recognize the Eastern—Chinese and Indian—as, in comparison, the better. Eastern learning has spirit as its point of departure; Western learning has matter as its point of departure..."

In the following essay of 1922, Liang stresses first the physical growth of the people of China and then their spiritual awakening to political consciousness as a nation.[3] We quote from it here as a conclusion to this volume.

*Part II.* There has been a great task on which, during the last five thousand years, our ancestors have continually expended much effort and which has never been interrupted. During the last fifty years, it still has been vigorously carried on, and furthermore it has been fruitful. What is this task? To give it a name, I call it "the expansion of the Chinese race." Originally our Chinese race consisted merely of a few small clans with a few bases in Shantung, Honan [p. 41], and other places. During the several thousand years that followed it has been slowly growing... growing... until it has become a high and peerless race, and has established this vast and majestic nation.

The Chinese race has grown in two ways: through assimilation of the numerous alien tribes in and outside of our territory, and through colonization by our own people on the frontiers year by year, thus enlarging our territory ... In the last fifty years there have been great successes...

(1) After the Taiping Rebellion, the Miao Rebellion in the Southwest followed and spread very widely. It required more than ten years before it was suppressed; however, the suppression this time had some characteristics of a fundamental solution. Hereafter I dare say that China will have no such term as the "Miao bandits." The fact is that "our

race versus the Miao race" has been a great public problem ever since the time of the Yellow Emperor and of the Emperors Yao and Shun. The uproar had been going on for several thousand years and still it was not entirely solved. It was only within the last fifty years that the very last paragraph of the essay on the Yellow Emperor's campaign against Ch'ih-yu [a legendary rebel] was completed. This is indeed a matter of history which is worth putting down in a special description writ large.

(2) The revolution of 1911 and the abdication of the Manchu emperor have great political significance... Formerly the race of the eastern barbarians had caused us trouble for seventeen or eighteen hundred years... At last came the group of Manchus who occupied China the longest and were also the most thoroughly assimilated. The Manchus may be considered as the great conglomeration of the eastern barbarian tribes, and they can also be considered as the great conclusion of the eastern barbarian tribes. During the last fifty years the sinification of the Manchus has advanced full speed, until the [1911] revolution, after which every Manchu was capped with a Chinese name. Hereafter there will be really no Manchus in the world. This amounts to our absorbing all the eastern barbarian tribes who have been active during the last two thousand years, and transforming them into a part of the Chinese race. This concludes a great stage in the expansion of the Chinese race.

(3) The movement of the people in the interior in the two directions of northeast and northwest has also been a great task of the last fifty years. Formerly the Manchus had planned to use the land in the Three Eastern Provinces [Manchuria] as an old base area to which they could always retire... Since the wars between China and Japan, and between Japan and Russia, this area has become a potentially belligerent zone, communication facilities have been opened wide, and economic conditions have abruptly changed. Although on the one hand, many privileges have fallen into the hands of others, on the other hand the degree of close relationship between the people inside and outside Shanhaikuan has

increased several times. The people of the Three Eastern Provinces and those of Shantung and Chihli gradually have been merged into one group. Moreover let us take a look in the direction of the northwest. Ever since Tso Tsung-t'ang established [the governor-general's] office in Kansu and Shensi, the influence of the interior has daily extended in that direction. During the Kuang-hsü period [1875-1908] Sinkiang was established as a province, and hence the thirty-six states in the Hsi-yü [the western region], whose relations with us since the two Han Dynasties [B. C. 206-220 A. D.] had been sometimes rather close and sometimes attenuated, may be considered completely incorporated into Chinese territory and made the same as the interior...

(4) The work of overseas emigration has also greatly developed during the last fifty years. Since the Ming Dynasty, the people of Fukien and Kwangtung have been emigrating on a large scale to the various places of the southern ocean [lit., Nan-yang, including in general, Southeast Asia, Singapore, Batavia, Java, etc.]. More recently, following the development of commerce by the Europeans, our emigrants have also established some real foundations of economic power. Furthermore, in America, Australia, and other places that had no contact with us before, the question of Chinese immigration has become a world problem...

Racial expansion is a matter worth celebrating; and because of this, it can be proved that our race is just in its age of youth; it has not yet reached adulthood and is still growing every day...

The most regrettable thing is that in several other directions we have entirely failed: first, Taiwan; second, Korea; and third, Annam... We must realize that, while our people are able to go forward, other races can also do so. Hereafter, if we make no new efforts, I fear that the only way will be to go backward, and we shall have no more opportunity to continue our expansion.

Part Ⅲ. [P. 43] In the realm of learning and thought, we cannot but recognize that there has been considerable progress, and that actually a way of great progress has been opened for the future. In this the most vital turning point is the abolition of the civil service examination system. This system has had more than one thousand years' history, and can really be regarded as deeply rooted and firmly based. Its greatest shortcoming was to make the minds of the scholars of the whole country hypocritical, traditional, and vague, and thus block all sources for the development of learning and thought. The movement for abolition of the civil service examination had already begun nearly fifty years ago. Kuo Sung-tao, Feng Kuei-fen and others had all briefly expressed some ideas to this end. By the time of the 1898 Reform Movement, the so-called new party of that time, including K'ang Yu-wei, Liang Ch'i-ch'ao and their group, may be said to have used their whole energy in launching a general attack against the civil service examination system. After about ten years from first to last, and after undergoing a great number of vicissitudes, this obstacle to civilization was finally broken down. Now these past events seem to be ordinary, but from the point of view of an historian of the last fifty years they must be counted as of great importance.

After these fifty years, what knowledge can we present to other people? It is embarrassing to say that there is practically nothing. But the minds of the scholars have been changed to a very large degree. I remember that in 1876 there was a minister to England, Kuo Sung-tao, who wrote a travel account in which there was a paragraph which said in effect, "The present barbarians are different from former barbarians; they also have two thousand years of civilization." Good Heavens, this was terrible! When this book reached Peking the public anger of all the officials and scholars in the government was aroused. Everybody denounced him; every day he was accused; the matter was not concluded until the printing blocks of the book were burned by imperial Decree. So little time has passed since then, yet the phrase "new cultural movement" has now become a habitual slogan of all learned societies. Ma-k'o-ssu [Marx] is almost competing for the seat of honor with Confucius, and I-pu-sheng [Ibsen] is nearly overthrowing Ch'ü Yuan [340-278 B. C.]. Whether this kind of psychology is correct or not is another question, but in general the radical change of thought of the last forty-odd years was indeed never dreamed of during the preceding four-thousand-odd years...

An old proverb well says that "when one keeps on learning, then one realizes that one's knowledge is insufficient"; and during the last fifty years the Chinese gradually have realized their own insufficiency. This little consciousness, on the one hand, is the cause of the progress of learning; and, on the other, it may be counted as the result of the progress of learning.

In the first period our mechanical articles were first realized to be insufficient. This realization gradually started after the Opium War until in the period of T'ung-chih [1862-1874] foreign troops were borrowed to suppress the civil war. Hence people like Tseng Kuo-fan and Li Hung-chang acutely felt that the solidity of foreign ships and the effectiveness of foreign cannon were really superior to ours... Therefore the shipyard and academy in Fukien and the arsenal at Shanghai and other institutions were gradually established. But during this period the world of thought was little influenced. During this time the most memorable things were the several science books translated by people in the arsenal. To us now these books may seem archaic and superficial, but among the groups of translators there were several who were quite loyal and devoted to knowledge. It was really a painstaking enterprise for them to produce such works then, because at that time no scholars could speak a foreign language, while those who could speak a foreign language did not read books. Therefore these translations really blazed a trail for "the experts in Western knowledge who did not understand foreign languages" in the second period.

In the second period there was a feeling of insufficiency concerning our [political and social] institutions. After the defeat by Japan, people with good minds in the nation really seemed to have met a thunderbolt in a dream. Accordingly, they wondered why the great and grand China should have declined to such a degree, and discovered that all was due to her bad political system. Therefore they took "*pien-fa wei-hsin*" [i. e., to change the statutes and to reform] as a big banner and launched a movement in society. The ardent leaders were the people like K'ang Yu-wei and Liang Ch'i-ch'ao. The people in this group were well trained in Chinese learning, but as for foreign languages they actually could not understand a single word. They could not tell others "what foreign knowledge consisted of and how to learn it." They could merely shout in loud voices every day, saying, "The old stuff of China is insufficient; many good points of the foreigners should be learned." Though these words sound general and undefined [lit., like swallowing a date whole], yet at that time they produced a tremendous effect. The political movement was a failure, with the exception of the above-mentioned abolition of the civil service examination system... This really opened a new phase for the future. During this period many schools were opened at home and many students went to study in foreign countries... The most valuable productions in the academic field were the several works translated by Yen Fu, who introduced some of the main currents of nineteenth-century thought into China. It is regrettable, however, that too few people in the nation could understand them.

In the third period there was a feeling that the foundations of our culture were insufficient. The duration of the second period, comparatively speaking, had been very long—from the war of 1894 to 1917 or 1918. Though great changes were wrought in the political arena, the realm of thought remained much the same. In brief, during this score of years we always felt that our government and laws, etc., were far inferior to those of others, and we were vexed at not being able to bring others' political organizations and forms one by one into our country. We took for granted that if this could only be done, myriads of other problems would be solved. [P. 45] It is almost ten years since the success of the [1911] revolution but all that we hoped for has proved vain, item by item. As we have gradually thought back, in our disappointment, we have realized that a social culture is a whole unit, and as such it definitely cannot make use of new institutions with an old psychology. By degrees there has grown up a demand for a reawakening of the whole psychology. At the conclusion of the great European war a great deal of active spirit was added to the tide of thinking of the whole world. Among the recently returned students there appeared quite a few able persons, who exerted their courage to promote a complete emancipation movement. Therefore during the last two or three years a new epoch has been demarcated.

The progress of thought in the three periods, if we try to measure between the people of the first and last periods, will be immediately very clear. In the first period [the pioneers] like Kuo Sung-tao, Chang P'ei-lun, Chang Chih-tung, and others, were regarded as very new monsters. When it came down to the second period, Sung-tao and P'ei-lun were dead, but Chih-tung was still living, and in the first half of this period Chih-tung was still regarded as a promoter of new things; but by the latter half he was considered simply an exponent of conservative, absurd ideas. In the second period K'ang Yu-wei, Liang Ch'i-ch'ao, Chang Ping-lin, Yen Fu, and others were all brave scholars of the world of thought, standing in the first line of battle. During the third period, when many new young men ran to the frontlines, these people [of the second period] were pushed behind, one by one, and some have entirely withdrawn or retired from the ranks. This kind of phenomenon, the new replacing the old, may prove that the circulation of fresh blood in the world of thought during the last fifty years has been very rapid. It may prove that the body and spirit of the world of thought are gradually becoming healthy and strong.

If we take a number of fifty-year periods in our history to compare with the fifty years just past, great progress has indeed been made in this last half-century. If, however, we take our last fifty years and compare them with the last fifty years in other countries, we shall be utterly ashamed. Let us take a look: what has the United States done in fifty years? What has Japan done in these fifty years? What has Germany done in these fifty years, and what has Russia done in these fifty years? Although politically their successes and failures are not the same, and their suffering and happiness are not equal, yet as to their academic and thinking elements, all may be considered to have advanced a thousand *li* a day. Even England, France, and other old nations—which one is not running forward as if flying? We have been talking noisily of new education for several decades. Let us ask our scientists, do we have one or two things which may be considered inventions of world importance? Ask our artists, do we have one or two productions which can be offered for world appreciation? And in our publication circles, do we have one or two books which are important works of the world? Alas, we had better wait until after the third period and see what it may bring.

  *Part* Ⅳ. [P. 46] "We may grudgingly grant that all other things have progressed in the last fifty years; only government, I am afraid, has entirely retrogressed." This remark is being made by almost a myriad mouths with one voice, and it is difficult even for me to object to it. Nevertheless in the last analysis [lit., looking from the inside of the bones] it may also be said that in the last fifty years what has advanced most in China is precisely the government.

  Fundamentally, government is formed by the opinions of the people. Not only is democratic government built on the opinions of a large number of people, but even dictatorship and oligarchy are also built on the opinions of a large number of people. Any kind of government always needs the active support or at least the tacit consent of a large number of people before it can exist. Thus the awakening of our citizens toward government is the general source of political progress. The actual politics of China in the last fifty years may indeed be said to have retrogressed and not progressed; but from the point of view of the citizen's self-consciousness, the concept has actually become clearer day by day, and furthermore has enlarged day by day. Self-consciousness: what are we conscious about?

First we are conscious that all who are not Chinese lack the right to control Chinese affairs.

Secondly, we are conscious that all Chinese have the right to control Chinese affairs.

The first is the spirit needed for the establishment of a national state [lit., min-tsu chien-kuo]. The second is the democratic spirit [lit., min-chu]. It is not that these two kinds of spirit had not existed before, but the ideas had frequently been dormant, vague, and confused. In the last fifty years—actually, the last thirty years—the ideas have been expressed very clearly. I dare say that, after the Manchu abdication, if there should again be another race who wished to imitate the attempt of the Five Barbarians, the Toba Wei, Liao, Chin, Yüan and Ch'ing, "to enter to be the masters of China again," that is something that would never happen till the seas dry up and stones rot. I dare say that once the signboard of the Republic has been hung up, hereafter in thousands and myriads of years it will never be taken down again. Regardless of whether you are as wise and sagacious as Yao and Shun, or as strong and tyrannical as the First Emperor of the Ch'in or the founder of the Ming, or as cunning as Ts'ao Ts'ao and Ssu-ma I, if you wish again to be the emperor of China, no one will ever allow you to do so. This fact should not be lightly regarded...

In sum, during the most recent thirty years, of the tasks which have been accomplished by our nationals, the most important is the fundamental extermination of a government dominated by foreign people [p. 47] for more than one thousand years... The second is the permanent destruction of the absolutist monarchical government of more than two thousand years... And moreover, these two achievements are by no means unexpected coincidences; they have really been achieved by the fundamental awakening of the people, who have exerted the greatest effort before they could accomplish them. Seen from this point of view, the period can really fit the meaning of the word progress.

During the last ten-odd years since the establishment of the Republic, the political phenomena have indeed been disgusting; but I think we should not be too disappointed, because these phenomena have been caused by two special factors, and these factors are going to disappear soon. The first one is that, during the time of the revolution, because the power of the people themselves had not yet become sufficient, they could not help relying on traditional influences.

The second factor is that it is normal for all matters in society to have their ups and downs. From 1894 and 1898 to 1911 benevolent people and scholars dedicated to a worthy cause have really been worked to the point of physical and mental exhaustion. The most regrettable thing is that many people who struggled for ideals died martyrs of the times. Their successors could not immediately take up the task. Therefore the interregnum has become a dark and colorless period; but I think this period will soon be over. The former leaders seem to have reawakened, caught their breath, and renewed their struggle. The fighting power in the rear has, furthermore, become stronger day by day. In these circumstances a new spirit and a new phase will naturally appear.

In summary, I am completely optimistic in regard to the political future of China. My optimism, however, has grown from the pessimism of ordinary people. I feel that China during the last fifty years has been like a silkworm becoming a moth, or a snake removing its skin. These are naturally very difficult and painful processes. How can they be accomplished easily? —only if biologically it is possible to function during the necessary change or removal, and if psychologically there is consciousness of the necessity for change and removal. Then, after we have undergone the unavoidably difficult and painful process, the future will be another world. Therefore, while everyone may consider that our political life is retrogressing, I feel that the possibility of its progress is very great.

Liang Ch'i-ch'ao had been among the most eloquent of China's intellectual leaders during three decades. This retrospect of 1922, in addition to the intrinsic interest of its analysis, shows the continuity between China's traditional ethnocentrism and her modern nationalism. In so doing it points toward more recent decades, and forms a suitable stopping point in our survey.

## POSTFACE   A FURTHER APPROACH TO THE PROBLEM

Although this chapter can hardly sum up the significance of the materials quoted above, it can suggest certain lines of further analysis. This study describes a part of the heroic and ominous process of modern history. It is almost (but not quite) superfluous to remind ourselves that this process is a totality of many interrelated parts and that words are at best poor slippery tools with which to build a mental image of it. Sun Yat-sen in history, for example, represents a compound of peasant social background and Chinese and Western education, a quest for the betterment of his countrymen and for political leadership, for national regeneration and personal fulfillment—in what single formula can we neatly understand him?

While all the major paths of modern learning must no doubt be followed, in so far as they seem to lead onward, our chief effort should be to pursue those lines which seem likely to penetrate most deeply and broadly the terra incognita before us. Two such main approaches to the study of Modern China in the century from 1839 to 1923 are here suggested—one socio-economic and one psychoideological. They are not mutually exclusive; to some extent, each includes the other. Let us try to describe them in the simplest way, without special terminology.

The socio-economic approach is the more obvious of the two. From one point of view, for example, the failure of China to modernize was a failure of her ruling class and its institutions—of the landlord-scholar-officials whose way of life was incompatible with effective westernization. Li Hung-chang and his colleagues could try to satisfy both their desire for private gain and their official duty as bureaucrats by organizing industrial enterprises, as in fact they did. But if this officially-fostered industrialization was to be a continuing success, the bureaucrats in charge had to venture their entire careers and fortunes in it, become investors and genuine entrepreneurs in industrial development, and thereby cease to be mandarins. This they did not do. China in the late nineteenth century developed neither true *Zaibatsu* nor "robber barons." As Cheng Kuan-ying so eloquently complained (Ch. XIII a), the officials did not become businessmen. Instead they seem to have retained the ancient ideals of the landlord-gentry class; the profits of their industries went into landowning, not into increased factory production, because land had always been regarded as the safest form of investment. While this analysis is oversimple, it indicates how the traditional "oriental" supremacy of officialdom over the merchant class may have impeded the rise of a system of negotiable property rights, protected by corporation law instead of official favoritism, and capable of supplying the investment capital needed for industrialization. In short, the Chinese ruling class would not or could not mobilize its resources to take the plunge into modern industrial life; it evidently feared that it might lose its old agrarian-based prerogatives and yet fail to gain equivalent power as a new capitalist class.

Plainly this type of analysis, if systematically pursued, can penetrate the structure of the old Chinese society and its social and economic institutions. Old-style family relationships, connections between the landlord-gentry in the villages and officials in the imperial administration, the wide powers of the latter over large-scale economic activity—a great multitude of such problems await further analysis through the written record.

The psycho-ideological approach has a different emphasis. It is concerned first of all with the traditional Chinese ideologies—the systems of values and beliefs which supported and sustained the old order. Secondly, it is concerned with the slow and many-faceted breakdown of those ideologies under the corrosive influence of Western power and Western ideas. Thirdly, it seeks to analyze the absorption and adaptation of those Western ideas which interacted with persisting elements of the old order. In short, this approach studies the ways in which modern Chinese have sought to create new systems of value and belief to replace the no longer adequate ideology of the disintegrating traditional order.

As we watch Neo-Confucianism losing its grip upon the mind of modern China, we enter a phase of intellectual history in which this second approach is particularly fruitful. When ancient institutions are no longer perpetuated by contemporary thought and conduct—when Liang Ch'i-ch'ao attacks the Confucian monarchy in order to save the Chinese nation, when Chang Chih-tung and Yuan Shih-k'ai propose to abolish the civil service examinations in order to improve the bureaucracy, or Hu Shih and Ch'en Tu-hsiu discard the classical style in order to make Chinese writing more useful—then ideas are likely, purely as ideas, to play a particularly important role in history. At such times, we suggest, the individual mind is more free to innovate, less trammeled by conventions and considerations of orthodoxy or of personal prestige, more aware of the great variety of possibilities with which mankind is confronted. In the crises of revolutionary change, leaders project their own personalities, and even minor traits. Dr. Sun's Japanese name, Nakayama, becomes in its Chinese equivalent, *Chung-shan*, the new name for universities, boulevards, and a style of clothing. The revolutionary innovators borrow ideas from everywhere—Britain, Japan or the French Revolution, the Protestant *Bible* or the *chin-wen* school of textual criticism, even from the New York dentist Maurice William whose book is mentioned in the

*Three People's Principles*. To some degree there occurs a process of natural selection among ideas, which gain currency through their applicability—real or illusory—to the needs of China's leaders.

At the same time feelings become more intense and motives more complicated. As the inherited institutions and habits of thought lose validity, intellectuals experience tension and anxiety, greater hopes and fears. The experience of modern China must be studied through psychology as well as economics and social organization. Eventually, patriotic and revolutionary causes sweep individuals into great organized movements, and social psychology becomes a major, though neglected, key to our understanding. Such insight seems particularly necessary now, when so many Chinese have succumbed to a communist faith, based upon the pre-Freudian, rationalistic economics and sociology of Marx and Lenin, as well as upon the vigorous nationalism of the Chinese people.

This second approach to China's cultural metamorphosis, by way of the ideas and motives of leading individuals, is more obviously suggested by the materials in this volume. Our selections generally represent the Chinese élite, not the common people. These personal statements and responses of Chinese leaders no doubt exemplify the working of basic institutions and provide data for socio-economic analysis. Yet each of these writers must be studied as a human personality, moved by his pride of culture or devotion to the throne, by his hatred of official corruption or of the foreign invader, as the case may be.

When such case histories are grouped together and compared, many trends and uniformities appear—such as the sequence of major influences from Britain in the nineteenth century, Japan in the decade to 1911, America during and after the First World War, and subsequently Soviet Russia. It is evident that Western influence has been conveyed, more than we generally realize, through the medium of Japan and thus blended with forms of Japanese influence. The most significant political trend has been the gradually increasing concern of China's intellectual élite for the political awakening of the mass of the people, their education and mobilization in the task of national regeneration. After the turn of the century, members of the Chinese upper class evince more interest in the peasantry as potential citizens of a modern state. The new thought of the May Fourth Movement at length acknowledges the gargantuan problem, how to bridge over the ancient bifurcation between the illiterate farming population and the intellectual élite...

No matter how we approach it, and there are many ways, the strenuous effort of China's leaders to meet her modern problems is a main thread of world history—tangible and accessible to study, and of crucial import for the future of Western democracy. Throughout the century surveyed above, the greatest need was to imbue the effective leadership of the day with a deeper understanding of modern world history. Further research may show that the Gonfucian élite of the late Ch'ing period failed to avoid revolution in large part because their educational reforms did not recruit China's native talent broadly enough nor train a younger leadership adequately and in time. Similarly, it may be concluded that the doom of the Kuomintang was sealed from the time when Dr. Sun failed to convince the scholars of Peita that his *Three People's Principles* could give them intellectual leadership. As for the learning received by China's leaders from Western Europe and America, we can hardly say, at the end of the first century, that it has been an entirely constructive influence. Perhaps the moral is that we cannot really help another society unless we first understand it ourselves.

# RESEARCH GUIDE FOR
*CHINA'S RESPONSE
TO THE WEST*

# FOREWORD

This volume is designed to aid specialists in Chinese studies who seek to pursue those painstaking monographic and textual researches which alone can give the Western world a firmer grasp of modern China's history. On one hand, while highly rewarding, such studies are not easy; and the Western specialist, who faces a translation problem more difficult than that of historians in China and Japan, needs to take full advantage of previous work in Western languages. Much of this work, in Western periodical literature, has been unavailable to (or at least unnoticed by) the recent compilers of source material collections on the Chinese mainland. On the other hand, some of the most useful studies of the persons, ideas, and events touched upon in *China's Response to the West* will be found in the Chinese periodical literature of an earlier day. At the same time, many sources which we quote remain as yet unstudied by any modern scholar, East or West.

In the first section of this volume, lists of Sources for further research and of Notes referring to the texts in *China's Response to the West* are given chapter by chapter in the same sequence as in the Contents of that volume. Full citations of publications, including Chinese characters, are reserved for the Bibliography below. Characters for additional Chinese names and terms are given in the Glossary.

S. Y. T.
J. K. F.
September 1953

# NOTES AND SOURCES

### ABBREVIATIONS USED IN THE NOTES

CSK—*Ch'ing-shih kao* (Draft history of the Ch'ing Dynasty)

CSL—*Ch'ing shih-lu* (Veritable records of the Ch'ing Dynasty)

Hummel—Arthur W. Hummel (ed.), *Eminent Chinese of the Ch'ing Period* (1644-1912), The Library of Congress, Washington, D. C., 1943-1944, 2 vols.

CSLC—*Ch'ing-shih lieh-chuan* (Historical biographies of the Ch'ing Dynasty)

CSPSR—*Chinese Social and Political Science Review*, Peking.

IWSM—*Ch'ou-pan i-wu shih-mo* (A complete account of the management of barbarian affairs):

TK—Tao-kuang period (1821-1850)

HF—Hsien-feng period (1851-1861)

TC—T'ung-chih period (1862-1874)

## CHAPTER II  SOME ELEMENTS IN THE CHINESE INTELLECTUAL TRADITION

### SOURCES

**a. *Some Early Ch'ing "Nationalist" Thinkers***

The main source materials on the early Ch'ing thinkers are their own writings, some of which are mentioned in the text. On Huang Tsung-hsi (Huang Li-chou), *Li-chou i-chu hui-k'an*, which includes his chronological biography, is an important source. Professor Theodore de Bary of Columbia University is making a special study of Huang's *Ming-i tai-fang lu*. Hsieh Kuo-chen in his *Huang Li-chou hsueh-p'u* has collected extracts from Huang's writings in a scholarly account. A number of short articles on Huang's political philosophy have been produced in recent years, with various interpretations, but we forbear to list them in this introductory section.

*Jih-chih-lu chi-shih* is an edition of Ku Yen-wu's book with commentaries collected by Huang Ju-ch'eng, forming a work of encyclopaedic nature which is not included in Ku's collected writings, *T'ing-lin hsien-sheng i-shu hui-chi*. Among later studies on Ku, Hsieh Kuo-chen, *Ku Ning-jen hsueh-p'u*, and Ho I-k'un, *T'ing-lin hsueh-shuo shu-p'ing*, should be noted.

The important source on Wang Fu-chih is undoubtedly *Wang Ch'uan-shan i-shu*. Two works on Wang's scholarship entitled *Ch'uan-shan hsueh-p'u*, one by Wang Yung-hsiang, including a *nien-p'u*, and the other by Chang Hsi-t'ang, are useful for reference. On Chu Chih-yü, *Shun-shui i-shu*, Liang Ch'i-ch'ao's sketch, and Matsumoto Sumio's *Mito gaku no genryū* are indispensable.

For general accounts of the early Ch'ing thinkers, see Liang Ch'i-ch'ao, *Chung-kuo chin-san-pai-nien hsueh-shu shih*; the same title by Ch'ien Mu; Hsiao Kung-ch'üan, *Chung-kuo cheng-chih ssu-hsiang shih*; and Liang's *Ch'ing-tai hsueh-shu kai-lun*. In English, see Lin Mou-sheng's *Men and Ideas, an Informal History of Chinese Political Thought*, and L. K. Tao, "A Chinese Political Theorist [Huang Tsung-hsi] of the Seventeenth Century." The little book by Ojima Sukema, *Chūgoku no kakumei shisō*, explores the important field of Chinese traditional political thought as related to modern revolutionary leaders, and in this connection touches upon Huang Tsung-hsi. Other Chinese studies include those of Hsiao I-shan in his *Ch'ing-tai t'ung-shih*; Kao Liang-tso, "Ch'ing-tai min-tsu ssu-hsiang chih hsien-tao che;" and Lo Erh-kang, "Ming-wang hou Han-tsu ti tzu-chueh ho mi-mi chieh-she." On the secret societies, see also under reference note 13 below. For recent Western appraisals of Huang and other early Ch'ing philosophers see A. F. Wright, ed., *Studies in Chinese Thought* (memoir no. 75, the

*American Anthropologist*, 55. 5, part 2, Dec. 1953, 317 pp. ), especially the chapter by David S. Nivison.

### b. *The Early Jesuit Influence in China*

On the early Jesuit contact, see the works of K. S. Latourette, Arnold H. Rowbotham, Henri Bernard and Louis Pfister under their names in our Bibliography. For a brief historical survey of Nestorianism, Catholicism, and Protestantism in China, see K. S. Latourette, *A History of Christian Missions in China*; Hiyane Antei, *Shina Kirisutokyō shi*; and Ishida Mikinosuke, "Shina bunka to Seihō bunka to no kōryū" (in *Iwanami kōza Tōyō shichō*). The best Japanese source on Christianity in the Ch'ing is probably Saeki Yoshirō, *Shinchō Kirisutokyō no kenkyū*. Yazawa Toshihiko, *Chūgoku to Seiyō bunka*, deals wholly with Catholicism in China, including the policies of K'ang-hsi and Yung-chêng toward papal missions. In Chinese, Yang Kuang-hsien, *Pu-te-i*, and Hsü Ch'ang-chih, *Sheng-ch'ao p'o-hsieh-chi*, are primary sources. The most thorough Western account of the Rites Controversy, as seen in its historical context and from the basic texts, is by Antonio S. Rosso, O. F. M. , *Apostolic Legations to China of the Eighteenth Century*, which surveys the Roman Catholic approach down to the Ch'ien-lung period, with 185 pages of key documents. See also E. H. Pritchard's review of this work in *Far Eastern Quarterly*, 11. 2:241-244 (February 1952). Hsü Tsung-tse, *Ming-Ch'ing chien Yeh-su-hui-shih i-chu t'i-yao*, is an informative and useful source relating to works written or translated by Jesuits in China in the seventeenth and eighteenth centuries. Farther Bernard's list, "Les adaptations chinoises d'ouvrages européens," contains some 555 works for the period to 1688 alone. An earlier listing of such works is in Otake Fumio, "Mimmatsu irai seishokō," which includes items of the late-Ch'ing period. The articles of Ch'en Shou-yi and Chang Yin-lin (see in Bibliography below) contain much useful information and many ideas. See for example in *T'ien-hsia Monthly*, Ch'en Shou-yi's article, "The Religious Influence of Early

Jesuits on Emperor Ch'ung-cheng of the Ming Dynasty." Yao Pao-yü, "Chi-tu-chiao chiao-shih shu-ju Hsi-yang wen-hua k'ao," is a well-documented study of the introduction into China of (a) Western astronomy and the calendar, (b) mathematics, (c) arms and military methods and (d) geography and maps. Yang Wei-yü and P'an Kung-chao, "K'ang-hsi-ti yü Hsi-yang wen-hua" (Emperor K'ang-hsi and Western culture), is an interesting short article. Chang En-lung, "Ming-Ch'ing liang-tai lai-Hua wai-jen k'ao-lueh," is a collection of more than three hundred short biographies of Europeans in China in the late Ming and early Ch'ing periods with identifications of their Chinese names, apparently based on Pfister. For articles containing much interesting material on the arguments used against the Jesuits and their science, see Chang Wei-hua,"Ming-Ch'ing chien Chung-Hsi ssu-hsiang chih ch'ung-t'u yü ying-hsiang,"and "Ming Ch'ing chien Fo-Yeh chih cheng-pien"; Ch'en Teng-yuan, "Hsi-hsueh lai-Hua shih kuo-jen chih wu-tuan t'ai-tu"; and Ch'üan Han-sheng, "Ch'ing-mo ti Hsi-hsueh yuan-ch'u Chung-kuo shuo." Fang Hao, *Chung-kuo T'ien-chu-chiao shih lun-ts'ung*, consists of essays on the Catholic influence in China, written by a Catholic scholar. Fang's "Ming-mo Hsi-yang huo-ch'i liu-ju wo-kuo chih shih-liao" concerns the role of the Jesuits regarding firearms. Many of these essays are reproduced in *Fang Hao wen-lu*. Cheng Shih-hsü, "Ming-Ch'ing liang-tai ti chün-chi pien-ko chi ch'i ying-hsiang," deals with the evolution of firearms more broadly than Fang's essay. Among Western works, see also Eloise Talcott Hibbert, *Jesuit Adventure in China: During the Reign of K'ang Hsi*, and George H. Dunne, *The Jesuits in China in the Last Days of the Ming Dynasty*, a doctoral dissertation at the University of Chicago (1944).

For sources on scientific subjects see Peake H. Cyrus, "Some Aspects of the Introduction of Modern Science into China"; Kenneth Ch'en, "Matteo Ricci's Contribution to and Influence on Geographical Knowledge in China"; Henri Bernard, "Notes on the Introduction of the Natural

Sciences"; and other references in the notes below. A special study of the Ming solicitation of military help from Japan is in Ishihara Michihiro, *Mimmatsu Shinsho Nihon kisshi no kenkyū*. The important translation by Louis J. Gallagher, S. J., *China in the Sixteenth Century: The Journals of Matthew Ricci: 1583-1610* (New York: Random House, 1953), 616 pp., was received too late for inclusion in our Bibliography.

## NOTES

1. See Ssu-pu pei-yao edition, 1b-6.

2. See his "Chün-hsien lun," in *T'ing-lin wen-chi*, 1. 6-11b.

3. *Jih-chih lu chi-shih*, 29. 26-28.

4. *T'ing-lin wen-chi*, 6. 17ff. His *Jih-chih-lu* had the same aim as Ssu-ma Kuang's famous "mirror" for emperors, the *Tzu-chih t'ung-chien*.

5. *Jih-chih-lu chi-shih*, 10. 5.

6. His comments on Ssu-ma Kuang's *Tzu-chih t'ung-chien*, entitled *Tu T'ung-chien lun*, are particularly famous.

7. *Tu T'ung-chien lun*, 2. 11b; 11. 28.

8. See *Huang-shu*, 1. 1-4, "Yuan-chi" and the postface in the last two pages of the book.

9. *Tu T'ung-chien lun*, 7. 16b-17; *Ssu-wen lu wai-pien*, the last page; and *Shih kuang-chuan*, 3. 5.

10. See Liang Ch'i-ch'ao, *Chu Shun-shui hsien-sheng nien-p'u* (A chronological biography of Chu Shun-shui), *Yin-ping-shih ho-chi*, special collection, *ts'e* 22. 58.

11. For documentation and a general account, see L. Carrington Goodrich, *The Literary Inquisition of Ch'ien-lung*, which also includes biographies of victims of the inquisition.

12. See Jung Chao-tsu, "Lü Liu-liang chi ch'i ssu-hsiang" (Lü Liu-liang and his ideas), *Fu-jen hsueh-chih*, 5. 1-2: 1-85 (December 1936).

13. In Sun Yat-sen's third lecture in his *San-min chu-i*, on "Nationalism," he says that the Triad Society (Hung-men or San-ho-hui)

had been organized by the old supporters of the Ming in the K'ang-hsi period. Although they saw that the situation was hopeless, their minds were full of nationalistic enthusiasm. They made plans to organize a secret society "to rebel against the Ch'ing and to restore the Ming." Their vision was farsighted, their thinking deep, their observation keen. Dr. Sun speaks of the Triad Society elsewhere and, having worked with its members, undoubtedly knew a great deal of its inner tradition. The following three works contain valuable source materials on the subject: J. S. M. Ward and W. G. Sterling, *The Hung Society or the Society of Heaven and Earth*; Hsiao I-shan, *Chin-tai mi-mi she-hui shih-liao* (Historical materials on modern secret societies); and Lo Erh-kang, *T'ien-ti-hui wen-hsien lu* (Documents of the Heaven and Earth Society), including important supplements; see also Lo Erh-kang's article cited in the sources above and Paul Pelliot's bibliography in *T'oung-pao*, 25:444-448 (1926).

14. For a recent survey of this Jesuit activity and convenient references to the extensive work of Bernard, Pfister, and others, see Arnold H. Rowbotham, *Missionary and Mandarin: The Jesuits at the Court of China* (Berkeley, 1942).

15. See Ch'en Shou-yi, "Ming-mo Ch'ing-ch'u Yeh-su-hui-shih ti ju-chiao-kuan chi ch'i fan-ying," pp. 14-20.

16. The Chinese associates of the Jesuits may be divided into four groups: (1) those who believed in their religion and studied their science, such as Hsü Kuang-ch'i (Paul Hsü, 1562-1633) and Li Chih-tsao (Leo Li, 1565-1630); (2) those who believed only in their religion and studied their science secondarily, or who were not by nature adapted to the study of science, such as Feng Ying-ching (1555-1606) and Yang T'ing-yün (Michael Yang, 1557-1627); (3) those who studied only their science and did not believe in their religion, such as Fang I-chih (1611-1671) and Chou Tzu-yü; (4) those who neither believed in their religion nor studied their science seriously, but occasionally associated with them, such as Ch'en

Chi-ju (1558-1639) and Wang K'en-t'ang. All these people were reputable scholars.

17. In Hsieh Chao-chih's *Wu tsa-tsu*, see *Wu-hang pao-shu t'ang* edition 4. 42b-43.

18. See *Ch'ü Chung-hsuan-kung wen-chi* (Collected Essays of Ch'ü Shih-ssu) pp. 4-6; and Fang Hao, "Ming-mo Hsi-yang huo-ch'i liu-ju wo-kuo chih shih-liao."

19. Chang Yin-lin, "Ming-Ch'ing chih-chi Hsi-hsueh shu-ju Chung-kuo k'ao-lueh,"pp. 38-39, 61-69.

20. Reports of these conversions vary widely; the subject needs study.

21. For a pioneer study in this field, see A. F. Wright, "Fu I and the Rejection of Buddhism," in "Chinese Reactions to Imported Ideas, a Symposium," *Journal of the History of Ideas*, 12. 1: 33-47 (January 1951).

22. Yang's work, entitled *Pu-te-i* (I could not keep silent) and Hsü Ch'ang-chih's *Sheng-ch'ao p'o-hsieh-chi* are two important collections of Chinese works antagonistic to Western ideas.

23. See Ch'üan Han-sheng, "Ch'ing-mo ti Hsi-hsueh yuan-ch'u Chung-kuo shuo,"*Ling-nan hsueh-pao*, 4. 2:73-82 (June 1935).

24. See Juan Yuan, *Ch'ou-jen chuan* (Biographies of scientists, especially astronomers and mathematicians), 46. 18-19, *Wen-hsuan lou ts'ung-shu* edition. See *T'oung Pao* (1904), pp. 561-596.

25. See Juan Yuan, *Tseng-tzu shih-p'ien chu-shih*. The last chapter deals with the formation and shape of the sky and the Earth. On Juan's life and works, see W. Franke in *Monumenta Serica*.

26. See Ch'en Teng-yuan,"Hsi-hsueh lai-Hua shih kuo-jen chih wu-tuan t'ai-tu."

27. See *Ssu-k'u ch'üan-shu tsung-mu t'i-yao*, 107. 4b, Tai-tung shu-chü edition, the entry under Li Yeh, "Ts'e yuan-hai ching."

28. Fang Hao, "Ch'ing-tai chin-i T'ien-chu-chiao so-shou Jih-pen

chih ying-hsiang" (Japanese influence on the persecution of Catholicism during the Ch'ing Dynasty), in *Fang Hao wen-lu* (Essays of Fang Hao), pp. 47-66.

29. The development of Chinese mathematics down to the early thirteenth century may be characterized as the period of calculating rods (*ch'ou-suan*) because calculations were done by means of small rods called *ch'ou*. These rods were made of bamboo or other materials, 271 of which formed a set, about a handful. These were used to represent the numerals, and the calculation was done on a checkered board. The digits of each number were placed on one row of squares, and the unit column was marked off so that the decimals proceeded toward the right. Black rods represented positive numbers and red ones negative numbers. By manipulating these rods, calculations could be made from simple arithmetic to higher algebraic problems involving equations of four unknowns and to the thirteenth power. See Li Yen, *Chung-kuo suan-hsueh shih*, pp. 63-95; and his *Chung-kuo shu-hsueh ta-kang*, pp. 36-39, 183-202; Yoshio Mikami, *Development of Mathematics in China and Japan*, pp. 27-31, 91-98; Chu Shih-chieh, *Ssu-yuan yü-chien*, 3. 46-49b.

30. *Chi-ho yuan-pen*, translation of Euclid's *Elements of Geometry*. For other works by Westerners and Chinese on mathematics in the seventeenth and eighteenth centuries, see Li Yen, *Chung-suan-shih lun-ts'ung*, 1. 149-193, and Li Yen, *Chung-kuo suan-hsueh shih*, pp. 184-257.

31. The school was known as Meng-yang-chai; Manchu and Chinese students of mathematics were assembled there early in the eighteenth century, during the last two decades of Emperor K'ang-hsi's reign. With the assistance of Westerners, they compiled a comprehensive work on the calendar, mathematics, and music under the collective title, *Lü-li yuan-yuan*. For further information, see biographies of Fang Pao, Ho Kuo-tsung, and Mei Wen-ting in Hummel.

32. The first scholar interested in the discovery and republication of

ancient texts on mathematics was Tai Chen (1724-1777) in the 1770's. Later Juan Yuan (1764-1849), Lo Shih-lin (d. 1853), and other scholars were either interested in the history of mathematical studies or in annotating ancient texts. Juan's biographies of mathematicians, the *Ch'ou-jen chuan*, printed in 1799, included thirty-seven Europeans among a total of 280 persons. In this work, the facts about the lives of these foreigners may be questioned, but they were all treated with due deference. See the biographies of these men in Hummel; also Li Yen, *Chung-kuo suan-hsueh shih*, pp. 264-279.

33. See Li Yen, *Chung-kuo suan-hsueh shih*, pp. 279-293; and biography of Li Shan-lan in Hummel.

34. In the Bibliography below see Teng Yü-han (Terrenz) and Wang Cheng, *Yuan-Hsi ch'i-ch'i t'u-shuo lu-tsui* ( European works on mechanical principles with illustrations); Sung Ying-hsing, *T'ien-kung k'ai-wu* (Natural resources utilized for manufacturing); Li Ch'iao-p'ing, *The Chemical Arts of Old China*; and the biography of Wang Cheng in Hummel, pp. 807-809.

35. Consult Ch'en Pang-hsien, *Chung-kuo i-hsueh shih* (History of medicine in China), pp. 185-194; K. C. Wong and L. T. Wu, *History of Chinese Medicine*, p. 125 and *passim*; and biography of Pi Yuan, Hummel, pp. 622-625.

36. A summary of the cartographical contributions of the Catholic fathers is given in Wang Yung, *Chung-kuo ti-li-hsueh shih* (History of Chinese geography), pp. 96-126, 218-219, and in Rowbotham, *Missionary and Mandarin: The Jesuits at the Court of China*, pp. 264-269; see also Fang Hao, "K'ang-hsi wu-shih-pa-nien Ch'ing-t'ing p'ai yuan ts'e-hui Liu-ch'iu ti-t'u chih yen-chiu"(On the cartographic survey of the Liu-ch'iu Islands by command of Emperor K'ang-hsi in 1719), *Wen-shih-che hsueh-pao*, no. 1:159-197 (June 1950), and biographies of Hsuan-yeh, Ho Kuo-tsung, and Mei Ku-ch'eng in Hummel.

37. The passports (*p'iao*), also called letters patent, were first

issued about 1711 as a means of control over foreigners by the Board of Ceremonies and also to protect the missionaries from molestation. See Latourette, *A History of Christian Missions in China*, pp. 157ff; Rowbotham, pp. 116, 163-164; *K'ang-hsi yü Lo-ma shih-chieh kuan-hsi wen-shu* (Documents relating to K'ang-hsi and the Tournon Legation from Rome), p. 2.

38. See Hummel, p. 917; Ch'en Yuan, "T'ang Jo-wang yü Mu Ch'en-wen"; Ch'en Yuan, "Yung-Ch'ien-chien feng T'ien-chu-chiao chih tsung-shih"; and Rowbotham, pp. 176-180.

39. See Hummel, p. 870, and Rowbotham, pp. 181-187.

40. See J. K. Fairbank and S. Y. Teng, "On the Ch'ing Tributary System"; and J. K. Fairbank, *Trade and Diplomacy on the China Coast: The Opening of the Teaty Ports*, 1842-1854.

41. The title is "An Imperial Edict to the King of England." See *Ch'ing shih-lu*, Ch'ien-lung period, ch. 1435. 11b-15, or *Tung-hua ch'üan-lu*, Ch'ien-lung, 118. 4b-8b.

42. See Fairbank and Teng, "On the Ch'ing Tributary System," *passim*.

43. See *Huang-Ch'ing chih-kung t'u* (Illustrations of the regular tributaries of the imperial Ch'ing Dynasty), 1. 47.

44. See Earl H. Pritchard, "The Kotow in the Macartney Embassy to China of 1793."

45. See Feng Ch'eng-chün, *Hai-lu chu*, 73-74.

# CHAPTER III  COMMISSIONER LIN'S PROGRAM FOR MEETING BRITISH AGGRESSION

### SOURCES

There are few major sources on Lin Tse-hsü aside from his memorials in *Lin Wen-chung-kung cheng-shu* and in *Chou-pan I-wu shih-mo*, his chronological biography by Wei Ying-ch'i, and a few other items listed in

Hummel and in our notes below. The article on Lin's works entitled "Lin Wen-chung-kung i-shu shu" by Ch'en Lu is worth consulting, and another article by the same author on the Opium War and Chinese weapons is also of interest. The various editions of the *Hai-kuo t'u-chih* deserve attention; for corrections of errors and supplementary information, see Sun Hao, *Hai-kuo t'u-chih cheng-shih*.

Wei Yuan was a great scholar and voluminous writer. For a list of his numerous works and certain Japanese studies of him, see Hummel. Attention should be called to Ch'i Ssu-ho's excellent article, "Wei Yuan yü wan-Ch'ing hsueh-feng", which gives a succinct summary of Wei's academic contributions. Ch'u-chin, *Tao-kuang hsueh-shu*, gives another good summary of academic conditions in the Tao-kuang period. For memorials, edicts, and letters concerning foreign policy from Han through Ch'ing, Chu K'o-ching, *Jou-yuan hsin-shu*, is a helpful source (chs. 3-4 on the nineteenth century include Lin, Tseng, Li, Tso, Kuo et al.). The most intimate view of the 1842 negotiations from the Chinese side is in Teng Ssu-yü, *Chang-hsi and the Treaty of Nanking*.

The literature, both scholarly and unscholarly, on the Opium War period is of course enormous and we will not try to indicate it here. Basic works of H. B. Morse and E. H. Pritchard on the East India Company trade, of D. E. Owen on the opium trade, and the like, will be found listed in the bibliography of J. K. Fairbank, *Trade and Diplomacy on the China Coast: The Opening of the Treaty Ports, 1842-1854*, which also touches on many persons and incidents noted in the present volume. Attention should be called, among recent works, to Michael Greenberg, *British Trade and the Opening of China* 1800-1842, which uses the important Jardine, Matheson and Co. archives; and, among Japanese works, to the articles of Ueda Toshio and Banno Masataka, which make use of the Chinese documents (*Ch'ou-pan I-wu shih-mo*) as well as Western materials (see in Fairbank, *op. cit.*, vol. 2, bibliography). On the popular attitude toward the Opium War, see Ueda Toshio, "Ahen senshō to Shimmatsu kammin no shoshō." On the Cantonese anti-foreign movement of the 1840's, John J. Nolde has done a useful dissertation at Cornell, The *"Canton Question," 1842-1849: A Preliminary Investigation into Chinese Anti-foreignism and its Effect upon China's diplomatic Relations with the West* (1950). Further documents indicating the temper of the Cantonese anti-foreign movement of 1841-1842 are available in Lo Hsiang-lin, "Ya-p'ien chan-cheng Yueh-tung i-min k'ang-Ying shih-liao hsü-lu".

## NOTES

1. Cf. George Sansom, *Japan: A Short Cultural History*; E. Herbert Norman, *Japan's Emergence as a Modern State*, pp. 29-35; and George Sansom, *The Western World and Japan*, 105-110, and *passim*.

2. Chinese folklore about Europeans included the curious idea that, without rhubarb from China, Westerners would die of constipation. The history of this idea has not yet been thoroughly traced.

3. From IWSM-TK, 7. 33-36b, enclosed in an Edict of August 27, 1889 (not translated here). This source omits a postscript which appears in Lin's political writings (*Lin Wen-chung-kung cheng-shu*, part II, 4. 16-20). CSL (324. 25b-26) reproduces the covering Edict of August 27, but not the communication here translated. An English translation (not followed here) is in the *Chinese Repository*, 8. 10:497-503 (Feb. 1840); a briefer popularized version in *ibid*., 8. 1:9-12 (May 1839); and a Dutch translation in G. W. Overdijkink, *Lin Tse-hsü*, pp. 148-151.

4. The *Lin Wen-chung-kung cheng-shu* version is 20,283 chests.

5. Here the text of *Lin Wen-chung-kung cheng-shu* is followed; while the IWSM version is *ti*, meaning "ground."

6. See Wei Ying-ch'i, *Lin Wen-chung-kung nien-p'u*, p. 138.

7. That is, Wu Chia-pin (1803-1864); see CSK, 486. 34, and CSLC, 67. 58.

8. From "Lin Tse-hsü fu Wu Tzu-hsü pien-hsiu shu" (A Reply from Lin Tse-hsü to the Hanlin compiler Wu Tzu-hsü), in *Li-tai ming-jen*

*shu-cha hsü-pien* (Letters of famous men of successive generations, supplement), 2 *chüan*, compiled by Wu Tseng-ch'i, 2A. 18-19.

9. John Francis Davis, *China during the War and since the Peace*, I, 309-310.

10. The *Ssu-chou chih* is printed in the big collection, *Hsiao-fang-hu-chai yü-ti ts'ung-ch'ao*, *ts'e* 82.

11. The first 50-*chüan* edition of 1844 is used in this volume. There is also an 1847 edition published by the Yangchow Ku-wei-t'ang, and an 1852 edition by Ku-wei-t'ang.

12. See the recent study by A. Grosse-Aschhoff, *Negotiations between Ch'i-ying and Lagrené 1844-1846*; also Fortia d'Urban, *La Chine et L'Angleterre*, pp. 283-286; Henri Cordier, "La Mission Dubois de Jancigny dans l'Extrême-Orient," *Revue de l'histoire des colonies françaises*, 4:130-133, 146, 148; and Teng Ssu-yü, *Chang Hsi and the Treaty of Nanking*, 1842, pp. 88-89.

13. From Wei Yuan, *Hai-kuo t'u-chih*, first edition (1844), preface by Wei dated 1842, "three months after the barbarian ships left the River" at Nanking, i. e., December 1842; see ch. 1.1.

14. This title was given to I-shan, see Hummel, pp. 391-393.

15. The "three feudatories" (*san-fan*) comprised Wu San-kuei in Yunnan and Szechwan, Shang K'o-hsi in Canton, and Keng Ching-chung in Fukien; all of whom revolted against the Ch'ing government in the 1670's.

16. Lit., *Sha-chiao* and *Ta-chiao*.

17. On several occasions the British forces had proposed that if a certain sum of money were paid, a city would be saved from attack or destruction. Thus, near the end of July 1842, Yangchow was saved from attack by a ransom of $500,000. See Teng, *Chang Hsi and the Teaty of Nanking*, pp. 12-13, 144-145.

18. From IWSM-TK, 31. 15-20, "Ch'ih-kao Ying-i shuo-t'ieh."

# CHAPTER IV   THE POLICY OF CONCILIATION

### SOURCES

The main source on Ch'i-ying is not his book *Yueh-t'ai yü-sung* but his memorials collected in the *Ch'ou-pan I-wu shih-mo* and *Shih-liao hsun-k'an*. In no. 35, pp. 291-293, of the latter series, an important memorial not included in the *Ch'ou-pan I-wu shih-mo* boldly reports Ch'i-ying's difficulties with the corrupt domestic administration and the superior weapons and strategy of the West. Dr. T. F. Tsiang has published a translation under the title, "Difficulties of Reconstruction after the *Treaty of Nanking*"; otherwise, extracts would have been included in this volume. Dr. Tsiang suggests that "the document shows the personality of Kiying, his courage to tell the Emperor the bare truths and his real patriotism." On Hsü Chi-yü, see Hummel and the collection of Hsü's writings, *Sung-k'an hsien-sheng ch'üan-chi*, which indicates his family background and academic and political career.

On the whole period of the 1840's, including Lin Tse-hsü, Ch'i-ying, and others, Kuo T'ing-i's heavily documented *Chin-tai Chung-kuo shih* is a reservoir of source material and his bibliography is also useful. The most recent work on this period is Fairbank, *Trade and Diplomacy on the China Coast: The Opening of the Treaty Ports, 1842-1854*. An informative analysis of the treaty revision negotiations of 1854 is in Banno Masataka, "Gaikō kōshō ni okeru Shimmatsu kanjin no kōdō yōshiki." Another useful recent study is by Chang Hsi-t'ung, "The Earliest Phase of the Introduction of Western Political Science into China".

### NOTES

1. Cf. J. K. Fairbank, *Trade and Diplomacy on the China Coast: The Opening of the Treaty Ports, 1842-1854*.

2. Cf. H. B. Morse, *International Relations of the Chinese Empire*, I, 519-525, which is, however, incorrect in dating the memorial as of

1850.

3. From IWSM-TK, 73. 18-20b. We have reworked the translation by Thomas Wade in *Correspondence relative to the Earl of Elgin's Special Mission to China and Japan 1857-1859* (presented to the House of Lords by command, 1859), pp. 175-177.

4. *Ta-ts'an*, the great meal.

5. Wade: "on something of a footing of equality."

6. Wade: "Thus, according to the second of the Confucian books, should it be between the ruler and the nobles dependent on him."

7. From IWSM-HF, 25. 4b-6; also in Chiang T'ing-fu (T. F. Tsiang), *Chin-tai Chung-kuo wai-chiao-shih tzu-liao chi-yao*, 1. 213-214.

8. See the archives of the British Consulate at Amoy, Gribble's dispatch 17 of Feb. 12, and 19 of Feb. 14, 1844; also IWSM-TK, 71. 19-22.

9. See the *Chinese Repository*, 13: 236 (1844), and 20: 184-194 (1851), on the "Universal Geography of Sü Ki-yü."

10. From *Ying-huan chih-lüeh*, 7. 43b-45. The translation in *Chinese Repository*, 20:169-194 has faults and has not been followed here.

11. The annual revenue of the government at Peking in this period was close to forty million taels; for brief reference, see Hsiao I-shan, *Ch'ing-tai t'ung-shih*, 2. 334-35.

12. From *Ying-huan chih-lüeh*, 9:14-15.

## CHAPTER V   THE EMERGENCE OF THE THEORY OF SELF-STRENGTHENING

### SOURCES

**a. *Prince Kung and the Tsungli Yamen***

I-hsin's biography in Hummel is the starting point for material on the Tsungli Yamen. The two articles in Japanese by Banno Masataka, and

Meng Ssu-ming (*The Organization and Functions of the Tsungli Yamen*, Harvard doctoral thesis, 1949), are very useful recent studies. Liu Hsiung-hsiang, *Ch'ing-chi ssu-shih-nien wai-chiao yü hai-fang*, also concerns the Yamen. Chang Chung-fu, "Tsung-li ko-kuo shih-wu ya-men chih yuan-ch'i," and Ch'en Wen-chin, "Ch'ing-tai chih tsung-li ya-men chi ch'i ching-fei," are studies of the beginning, and of the financial resources of the new institution, respectively. The sections on the Tsungli Yamen in Liu Chin-tsao, *Ch'ing-ch'ao hsü-wen-hsien t'ung-k'ao*, and in Wu Ch'eng-chang, *Wai-chiao-pu yen-ko chi-lueh*, are brief but good. Wang Yen-wei and Wang Liang, *Ch'ing-chi wai-chiao shih-liao*, reproduce many original documents, while Ch'en T'i-ch'iang, *Chung-kuo wai-chiao hsing-cheng*, traces the administration of diplomatic affairs and Tung Hsün, *Huan-tu-wo-shu shih lao-jen nien-p'u*, gives some description of procedures in the Tsungli Yamen and the T'ung-wen Kuan. Yü-chüan Chang, "The Provincial Organs of Foreign Affairs in China," concerns an interesting and unique aspect of China's diplomacy.

**b. Feng Kuei-fen and his Essays**

For sources on Feng Kuei-fen, see the biographies, prefaces, and postfaces in the *Hsien-chih-t'ang kao* and the *Chiao-pin-lu k'ang-i*. The studies by Huang Ts'ui-po in the quarterly of the Sun Yat-sen Institute and by Momose Hiromu in *Tōa ronsō* are important aids (the latter also appears in a shortened Chinese translation in the *Chung-ho* monthly). There is an important brief memoir, *Feng Ching-t'ing hsing-chuang*, prepared at the time of Feng's death; but in general he has not yet been adequately studied.

**c. The Taiping Rebels' Interest in Modernization**

The largest and possibly the best collection of source material on the Taiping Rebellion so far published is the *T'ai-p'ing T'ien-kuo* compiled by Hsiang Ta and more than ten others of the Chinese Historical Association and published in 1952 in eight volumes. Many books, documents, and manuscripts of the Taipings, of the imperial government, and of contemporary individual scholars are carefully reproduced in this work, which can replace many previous publications. Next to this is the *T'ai-p'ing T'ien-kuo shih-liao*, compiled by T'ien Yü-ch'ing and three others of the Research Institute of Humanities of the Peking University and the National Library of Peking. This is also a very informative work. These two institutions have also compiled a valuable bibliography of reference works about the Taipings entitled *T'ai-p'ing T'ien-kuo ts'an-k'ao shu-mu*. The bibliographical sections in Kuo T'ing-i's *T'ai-p'ing T'ien-kuo shih-shih jih-chih* and S. Y. Teng's *New Light on the History of the Taiping Rebellion* are still useful. The latest important American publication is Professor E. P. Boardman's study (see note 10 below).

There are a number of recent articles, each of which takes up a certain aspect of the Taiping Rebellion, such as Vincent Yu-chung Shih, "Interpretations of the Taiping Tien-kuo by Noncommunist Chinese Writers," and Chester A. Bain, "Commodore Matthew Perry, Humphrey Marshall, and the Taiping Rebellion," both in the *Far Eastern Quarterly* (May 1951); James T. K. Wu, "The Impact of the Taiping Rebellion upon the Manchu Fiscal System," *Pacific Historical Review*, vol. 19 (August 1950), and John Foster, "The Christian Origins of the Taiping Rebellion," *The International Review of Missions*, 40:156-167 (1951). Further research is of course constantly appearing in Chinese and Japanese. For Japanese articles by Ichiko Chūzō and others, see J. K. Fairbank and Masataka Banno, *Japanese Studies of Modern China* (to be published by the Harvard-Yenching Institute in 1954).

## NOTES

1. From IWSM-HF, 71. 18-27. We have presented only the major points of this important document; part of it is also given in Ch. VIII below.

2. Concerning Wen-hsiang, Robert Hart praised him as one of the

"ablest, fairest, friendliest and most intelligent mandarins ever met by foreigners" (*These from the Land of Sinim*, p. 68). A. Michie described him as "the most conscientious as well as the most liberal-minded statesman that China has produced during the sixty years of foreign intercourse" (*The Englishman in China during the Victorian Era*, II, 374-375). W. A. P. Martin made the exaggerated statement that as long as Wen-hsiang lived, the entire initiative of the Yamen rested with him, and quoted him as saying, "We shall learn all the good we can from you people of the West" (*A Cycle of Cathay*, 362-363).

3. These essays also appear in his literary work, *Hsien-chih-t'ang kao*, *chüan* 10-11, published in 1877 without the title *Chiao-pin-lu k'ang-i*. The latter work was first published separately by his son in 1885 at Yü-chang, modern Nanchang. The number of essays and the wording in the *Hsien-chih-t'ang kao* are slightly different from those in the *Chiao-pin-lu k'ang-i*.

4. For the compilers and various editions of this work, see Hummel, p. 282; and Momose Hiromu's special study of it in *Tōa ronsō*, vol. 2 (January 1940), translated into Chinese in *Chung-ho yueh-k'an*, 3.3:53-66 (March 1942).

5. From "Ts'ai Hsi-hsueh i," *Chiao-pin-lu k'ang-i*, 2.37-39.

6. From "Chih yang-ch'i i," *Chiao-pin-lu k'ang-i*, 2.40-44.

7. *Tsung-heng-chia*, an expert on theories of perpendicular and horizontal alliances, popular in the period of the Warring States.

8. Apparently Feng refers here to the Harris treaty of 1858 and to the *Kanrin Maru*, which sailed to San Francisco in 1860. See Chitoshi Yanaga, *Japan since Perry*, p. 116.

9. From "Shan yü-i i," *Chiao-pin-lu k'ang-i*, 2.45-47.

10. The Taiping influence on modern China is summed up in Lo Erh-kang's *T'ai-p'ing T'ien-kuo shih-kang*. On the subject of Western religious influence on the rebels, Professor E. P. Boardman has done a pioneer study, *Christian Influence upon the Ideology of the Taiping*

*Rebellion 1851-1864*, published by the University of Wisconsin Press, 1952. We therefore omit here any materials on this very interesting topic.

11. Among the Taiping publications, the *T'ien-ch'ao t'ien-mu chih-tu* (The land system of the Heavenly Dynasty 1858), which outlines the Taiping political, economic, and social platforms, and Hung Jen-kan, *Tzu-cheng hsin-p'ien*, partly translated here, are the outstanding treatises on political ideology.

12. From *Tzu-cheng hsin-p'ien*, reproduced in *I-ching*, 17: 17-22 (Nov. 1936); 18: 7-11, and 19: 7-11. Our translation begins with *I-ching*, 18: 10; and we have supplied numbers to the author's series of items and translated extracts only. The original copy of Hung's work is in the Cambridge University Library, England, but there are now two reproductions of the *Tzu-cheng hsin-p'ien* in the *T'ai-p'ing T'ien-kuo shih-liao* (pp. 27-47) and *T'ai-p'ing T'ien-kuo* (II, 522-541), respectively. The proofreading in the latter is better than that in the former. The biography of Hung Jen-kan is available in Arthur W. Hummel, *Eminent Chinese of the Ch'ing Period (1644-1912)* and also in Lo Erh-kang's *T'ai-p'ing T'ien-kuo shih-kao* (pp. 265-273). The latter work is beautifully written in the traditional style of Chinese dynastic histories and divides the material into four parts: 1) basic annals; 2) charts and tables of princes and Taiping officials; 3) monographs on their religion, social system, calendar, military organization, civil service, and other topics; and 4) biographies. This is another interesting and useful work by a leading expert.

13. Other reform proposals advanced by Hung Jen-kan included punishment of criminals only and not their families, prohibition of infanticide, prohibition of intoxicating drinks and opium, suppression of temples and monasteries, suppression of stage plays, and suppression of the sale of official ranks. Extracts from his work were translated in the *North China Herald*, Supplements to August 18 and 25, 1860.

# CHAPTER VI  TSENG KUO-FAN'S ATTITUDE TOWARD WESTERNERS AND THEIR MACHINERY

## SOURCES

On Tseng Kuo-fan, the most important sources are his complete collected works entitled *Tseng Wen-cheng-kung ch'üan-chi* and his diary, although the latter is difficult for Westerners to read. Wang Ting-an's *Ch'iu-ch'ueh-chai ti-tzu chi*, 32 chüan, is a detailed but ill-digested chronological biography of his teacher and superior; an abridged version of this work is called *Tseng Wen-cheng-kung shih-lueh*. Besides these, there are a *Tseng Wen-cheng-kung nien-p'u* and *Ta-shih-chi* or account of important events in Tseng's career; both are in the complete collection first noted above. These four works on Tseng Kuo-fan compiled by his subordinates do not, however, obviate the need for a good biography. Modern scholars have produced several studies such as Chiang Hsing-te, *Tseng Kuo-fan chih sheng-p'ing chi shih-yeh*; Hsiao I-shan, *Tseng Kuo-fan*; Wang Te-liang, *Tseng Kuo-fan chih min-tsu ssu-hsiang*; Chao Tseng-hui, *Tseng Kuo-fan yen-hsing chih t'i-hsi*; and Li Ting-fang, *Tseng Kuo-fan chi ch'i mu-fu jen-wu*. All of these are sympathetic and appreciative of Tseng's merits, but none of them really grasps the spirit of his times or presents a living portrait. On the other hand, the scholar Fan Wen-lan has written a critical biography of Tseng, sifting the evidence from a communist point of view. There are a number of articles on Tseng such as Shu An, "Hsiang-hsiang Tseng-shih i-wen," anecdotes of the Tseng family; Chang Yin-lin's commentary, "Po *Shui-ch'uang ch'un-i*," which also records anecdotes; and Tseng Shih-o, "Ou-yang Pai-yuan t'an Tseng Wen-cheng-kung i-shih," with further reminiscences. More serious are Ch'ü Hsuan-ying's notes on Tseng's diary. See also Ch'en Kung-lu's article on Tseng Kuo-fan and the Chinese navy. T'ang Ch'ing-tseng's essay on Tseng's economic ideas seems superficial, even though the writer is an economist.

In English, the works of William Hail and Gideon Ch'en (Ch'en Ch'i-t'ien) are well known. T. K. Ch'uan's article, "Tseng Kuo-fan," in the *T'ien-hsia Monthly*, is a simple account. E. H. Parker (tr.), "The Published Letters of the Senior Marquis Tseng," in the *China Review* and the desultory news entries about Tseng in the *North China Herald* for 1868-1871 are also useful. Professor Hellmut Wilhelm of the University of Washington, Seattle, has been making a special study of Tseng's thought; see his articles, "The Background of Tseng Kuo-fan's Ideology," and "The Problem of Within and Without, a Confucian Attempt in Syncretism." On the whole context of the 1860's, when Tseng was prominent, the most illuminating treatment is Mary C. Wright's forthcoming volume, *The T'ung-chih Restoration*.

For basic documents and information on the Shanghai Arsenal, see Gideon Ch'en's *Tseng Kuo-fan*; Wei Yün-kung, "Chiang-nan chih-tsao-chü chi"; Kan Tso-lin in *Tung-fang tsa-chih*; and Chang Po-ch'u, "Shang-hai ping-kung-ch'ang chih shih-mo," in *Jen-wen* monthly. Ch'üan Han-sheng's article of 1951 is the most recent study, well documented and critical; see the bulletin of the Academia Sinica, Institute of History and Philology, XXIII, part 1 (1951).

**NOTES**

1. See *Tseng Wen-cheng-kung tsou-kao*, 2.12.
2. *Tseng Wen-cheng-kung nien-p'u*, 7.20.
3. See *Tseng Wen-cheng-kung shou-shu jih-chi*, *ts'e* 13, page unnumbered, 7th day, 5th month of the first year of T'ung-chih (June 3, 1862).
4. *Ibid.*, Tseng's diary, *ts'e* 30, 12th day, intercalary fourth month, in the seventh year of T'ung-chih (June 7, 1868).
5. *Ibid.*, the next page. Tseng Kuo-fan's letter to Kuo Sung-tao (*Shu-cha*, ch. 14, p. 22) also reports his good impression of the cordial reception extended to him by the foreign consuls at Shanghai; he predicts

that there will be no trouble in treaty revision.

6. *North China Herald*, June 5, 1868.

7. Gideon Ch'en, *Tseng Kuo-fan*, pp. 53-54.

8. Tseng's diary, *ts'e* 15, 6th day, 12th month, in the second year of T'ung-chih (January 24, 1863).

9. Tseng's diary, *ts'e* 38, 19th day, 3rd month, in the tenth year of T'ung-chih (May 8, 1871).

10. *Tseng Wen-cheng-kung shu-cha*, 9.43.

11. *Ibid.*, 10.5b-6.

12. *Ibid.*, 10.18b-19.

13. *Ibid.*, 10.24b.

14. *Ibid.*, 10.30.

15. The Kiangnan Arsenal was first called *Chiang-nan chih-tsao tsung-chü* (Kiangnan central manufacturing bureau), then (1914) *Shang-hai chih-tsao chü*, and later (1917) *Shang-hai ping-kung-ch'ang* (Shanghai Arsenal). It occupied a space of 185 acres. During the Sino-Japanese conflict at Shanghai in 1932, machinery from the arsenal was moved to Hangchow and elsewhere.

16. From IWSM-TC, 61.27-30; *Tseng Wen-cheng-kung tsou-kao*, 33.5-8. Gideon Ch'en, in his *Tseng Kuo-fan* (pp. 48-49, 64, and *passim*), uses parts of this memorial, which we have therefore largely omitted.

17. On this whole subject, see Knight Biggerstaff, "The Secret Correspondence of 1867-1868: Views of Leading Chinese Statesmen regarding the Further Opening of China to Western Influence," *Journal of Modern History*, 22.2:122-136 (June 1950).

18. IWSM-TC, 54.1b-4. The main ideas in this memorial were freely interpreted and criticized in the *North China Herald*, June 13, 1868.

19. In this period, Chinese commonly spoke of the "San-k'ou t'ung-shang ta-ch'en" or minister-superintendent of trade for the three ports in the north (i.e., Tientsin, Chefoo, and Newchwang, opened in 1858 and

1860) and the "Wu-k'ou t'ung-shang ta-ch'en" for the similar official in charge of the five ports in the south opened by the *Treaty of Nanking*.

20. From IWSM-TC, 80. 11b.

# CHAPTER VII  LI HUNG-CHANG AND THE USE OF WESTERN ARMS

### SOURCES

Sources on Li are given under Chapter X.

Two further items of particular value for this chapter are Chang Ch'o-hsün, "Ch'i-shih-nien lai Chung-kuo ping-ch'i chih chih-tsao," and Wang Te-chao, "T'ung-chih hsin-cheng k'ao."

### NOTES

1. From IWSM-TC, 2. 36.
2. CSL-TC, 44. 41-43.
3. From *Li Wen-chung-kung p'eng-liao han-kao*, 2. 46b-47.
4. See Tseng's *Shu-cha*, 11. 6.
5. From IWSM-TC, 25. 4-10.
6. *Cha-p'ao*, lit., "explosive cannon." This term is elliptical, referring to the explosive shells thrown by modern artillery.
7. On Ting Kung-ch'en, see Gideon Ch'en, *Lin Tse-hsü*.
8. In this period this quotation from the *I-ching* or "Book of Changes" was widely used; see the Appendix, 2. 383, Legge's translation.
9. From IWSM-TC, 25. 1-3.

# CHAPTER VIII  INSTITUTIONS FOR LINGUISTIC AND SCIENTIFIC STUDIES (THE T'UNG-WEN KUAN)

### SOURCES

The collection of Wo-jen's writings entitled *Wo Wen-tuan-kung i-shu* includes lecture notes expounding his Neo-Confucian ideas, diaries, and comments on administration; it constitutes an important source. Prince Kung's collected writings, *Lo-tao-t'ang shih-wen ch'ao*, however, do not have much historical value inasmuch as his poems and essays are mostly eulogies for birthday celebrations, funeral sacrifices, and the like. On the controversy between Wo-jen and Prince Kung over the adoption of Western science, neither of these collections is of much use, and we have to rely on the documents published in *C'hou-pan I-wu shih-mo* and *Huang-ch'ao ching-shih wen-pien*.

On the T'ung-wen Kuan, the major sources include Meng Ssu-ming's *The Organization and Functions of the Tsungli Yamen*; Wu Hsuan-i, "Ching-shih T'ung-wen kuan lueh-shih," in *Tu-shu yueh-k'an*; Knight Biggerstaff, "The T'ung-Wen Kuan"; *T'ung-wen kuan t'i-ming lu*; *Papers Relating to Foreign Affairs, 1867*; and the recent important volume by A. F. Wright, *Hart and the Chinese Customs*, which describes Robert Hart's financial and administrative assistance to this educational venture, his difficulties with von Gumpach, and other revelations from the Customs archives. See also the Sources for Chapter V, above.

## NOTES

1. Hart's invaluable aid in these matters was, of course, seldom noted in Chinese official documents.

2. From IWSM-HF, 71. 24b-25.

3. The ideas in this memorial are essentially the same as those in Feng Kuei-fen's essay, "Shang-hai she-li T'ung-wen Kuan i" (A proposal to establish a T'ung-wen Kuan in Shanghai); see *Hsien-chih-t'ang kao*, 10. 18-20. A large part of this essay was also used by Feng in his chapter, "Ts'ai Hsi-hsueh i" (A discussion of the adoption of Western knowledge), in his *Chiao-pin-lu k'ang-i*, 2. 37-39, translated in this volume as Doc. 8.

4. From *Li Wen-chung-kung tsou-kao*, 3. 11-12.

5. A good translation of this memorial is to be found in *Papers*

*Relating to Foreign Affairs*, *1867* (Washington, 1868), Ⅰ, 473-474.

6. A translation of this document is to be found in the same work, Ⅰ, 474-476. See the original in IWSM-TC, 46. 43-48b; also the translation in the *North China Herald*. February 9, 1867.

7. From IWSM-TC, 47. 24-25.

8. From IWSM-TC, 48. 1-4.

9. See *Ch'ien-Han shu*, 48. 29b.

## CHAPTER Ⅸ  TSO TSUNG-T'ANG AND THE FOOCHOW SHIPYARD

### SOURCES

On Tso's career in general, see Hummel, pp. 762-767, and *Tso Wen-hsiang-kung ch'üan-chi*, including *Tso Wen-hsiang-kung nien-p'u*. On his activities in the northwest, see Ch'in Han-ts'ai, *Tso Wen-hsiang-kung tsai hsi-pei*, a good piece of work; and Nishida Tamotsu, *Sa Sō-dō to Shin-kyō mondai*, a survey. The chief monographs in English are: W. L. Bales, *Tso Tsung-t'ang*: *Soldier and Statesman of Old China*; Gideon Ch'en, *Tso Tsung-t'ang*, *Pioneer Promoter of the Modern Dockyard and the Woolen Mill in China*; and Gideon Ch'en's "Tso Tsung-t'ang, the Farmer of Hsiang-shang," in *The Yenching Journal of Social Studies*. On Tso's financial and industrial activities, see the article by T'ang Hsiang-lung, cited in the notes below, and C. J. Stanley's doctoral dissertation at Harvard on *Hu Kuang-yung and China's Early Foreign Loans* (1951). Two magazine articles, Hsü I-shih, "Tso Tsung-t'ang yü Liang Ch'i-ch'ao," and Lu Hsi-ta, "Tseng Tso hsiang-wu chi ch'i-t'a" (The disagreement between Tseng and Tso and other matters), are of some interest.

As for the Foochow Shipyard, the source materials include *Ch'uan-cheng tsou-i hui-pien*, which is a collection of memorials concerning China's shipping administration, and Wang Hsin-chung, "Fu-chou ch'uan-ch'ang chih yen-ko," a special study. Prosper Giquel, *The Foochow Arsenal and Its Results, from the Commencement in 1867 to the End of the Foreign Directorate on the 16th February, 1874*, is a firsthand foreign account of the shipyard.

### NOTES

1. See *Tso Wen-hsiang-kung shu-tu*, 24. 52b-53.
2. *Tso Wen-hsiang-kung tsou-kao*, 59. 51b.
3. *Tso Wen-hsiang-kung shu-tu*, 7. 154-156. T'ang Hsiang-lung, "Min-kuo i-ch'ien kuan-shui tan-pao chih wai-chai," *Chung-kuo chin-tai ching-chi-shih yen-chiu chi-k'an*, 3. 1: 3-8 (1935). This subject has been carefully appraised by C. J. Stanley, *Hu Kuang-yung and China's Early Foreign Loans*.
4. See Ch'in Han-ts'ai, *Tso Wen-hsiang-kung tsai hsi-pei*, p. 142.
5. *Ibid.*, p. 116.
6. From *Tso Wen-hsiang-kung tsou-kao*, 18. 1-6.

## CHAPTER X THE PROBLEM OF LEADERSHIP: PERSONALITIES AND INSTITUTIONS

### SOURCES

*Li Wen-chung-kung ch'üan-chi* is the most important source on Li Hung-chang. The three biographies of him in *Ch'ing-shih-kao* and similar works are all about the same in quality, though different in detail. The biography in Hummel and the sources suggested there are extremely helpful. Liang Ch'i-ch'ao, *Ssu-shih-nien lai ta-shih chi*, is actually a very critical biography of Li Hung-chang written by a reformer who presumably had a firm basis for his criticism, but it should be used with caution. Wei Hsi-yü, *Li Hung-chang*, seems more balanced, while Li Shu-ch'un, "Li Wen-chung-kung nien-p'u," though it has reference value, does not seem equally good. Chang Ch'iung-chang, "Li Hung-chang i-shih i-shu," Hsi Yin, "Shu Ho-fei i-wen," and Ch'an-an, "Chang

P'ei-lun yü Li Hung-chang," all present interesting anecdotes. Hsü I-shih's article on Li Ching-fang and Tseng Shih-o's account of the struggle between Weng T'ung-ho and Li Hung-chang are significant contributions.

As to Li's foreign policy, Ikeda Tōsen, "Itō kō to Ri Kō-shō," Wada Sei, "Ri Kō-shō to sono jidai," and Makino Kyōji, "Ri Kō-shō no denki," all give brief treatments of the relations between Itō and Li. T. F. Tsiang, "Sino-Japanese Diplomatic Relations, 1870-1894," T. C. Lin, "Li Hung-chang, his Korea Policies 1870-1885," Shuhsi Hsü, *China and her Political Entity*, and Yuan Tao-feng, "Li Hung-chang and the Sino-Japanese War," are four studies of his policy in Korea written by Chinese specialists in diplomatic history. W. L. Langer also gives a critical account of Li in his *The Diplomacy of Imperialism, 1890-1902*. Liu Hsiung-hsiang, *Ch'ing-chi ssu-shih-nien wai-chiao yü hai-fang*, deals with Chinese diplomacy and maritime defense. Hsiao I-shan, *Ch'ing-tai shih*, gives a popular account and his article, "Huai-chün yü Hsiang-chün chih pieh," though short, explains clearly the difference between the Anhwei and Hunan Armies.

On Li's diplomacy toward Japan, see also Su Ch'eng-chien, "Li Hung-chang i-kuan ti fan-Jih cheng-ts'e," and Chou Tzu-ya, "Li Hung-chang yü fan-Jih wai-chiao." Tseng Chi-tse, *Chin-yao ch'ou-pi*, and Tso Shun-sheng, "Chung-Jih wai-chiao shih shang chih Li Hung-chang," both give a rather sympathetic review of Li's foreign policy. Chang Te-ch'ang, "Li Hung-chang chih wei-hsin yun-tung," and Wu Pao-chang, "Li Wen-chung-kung pai-shih-chou-nien chi-nien kan-yen," a commemoration of the one hundred and tenth anniversary of Li's birth, are also favorable surveys. T'ang Chi-ch'ing, "E tsu Lü-shun Ta-lien shih Li Hung-chang shou-hui chih cheng-chü," and the account in Wu Po (Fan Wen-lan), *Chung-kuo chin-tai shih*, are not favorable; like Tseng Kuo-fan, Li has become a favorite target in the retrospection of the new regime in China.

With regard to personnel, the classified diary of Wu Ju-lun entitled *T'ung-ch'eng Wu hsien-sheng jih-chi*, and the famous historical and social novel, *Nieh-hai hua* written by Tseng Po under the well-known pen name Tung-ya ping-fu, both have frequent references to Li and his contemporaries. Stanley Spector of the Far Eastern Institute, University of Washington, is writing a doctoral dissertation on Li Hung-chang, with special reference to his use of personnel.

The best Chinese source on Empress Dowager Tz'u-hsi is still Chang Ts'ai-t'ien, *Ch'ing lieh-ch'ao hou-fei chuan-kao*, in which the abundant interlineal notes are extremely valuable. Fang Keng-sheng's errata and supplement to Chang's work do not add much. Chang Ch'iung-chang, "Tz'u-hsi t'ai-hou i-shih," collects some anecdotes about her life history without indication of sources, and the same is true of the recent biography by Harry Hussey, *Venerable Ancestor*. J. O. P. Bland and E. Backhouse, *China under the Empress Dowager*, is also very informative, but must be used with caution. Mrs. Allen West Capiz of the University of Chicago is writing a doctoral dissertation on the Empress Dowager.

### NOTES

1. See Li Hung-chang's letter to governor Liu Chung-liang in 1875, in which he makes a very radical statement of policy toward Westernization and shows unusual impatience with Confucian ties, indicating his farsightedness compared with most of his contemporaries; *Li Wen-chung-kung p'eng-liao han-kao*, 15. 3-5.

2. *Ibid.*, 19. 43.

3. Detring became so entrenched at Tientsin as Li's protégé that the Inspector-general of Imperial Maritime Customs, Hart, could not transfer him elsewhere. See S. F. Wright, *Hart and the Chinese Customs*, p. 534; and H. B. Morse, *International Relations of the Chinese Empire*, III, 14, 407, and *passim*.

4. See Hummel, pp. 295-300. The most recent of many picturesque and personal accounts is Harry Hussey, *Venerable Ancestor*. No Western student has gone to work on the Empress Dowager's administration of affairs.

5. This marble barge, actually a stationary structure, appears to have antedated the Empress Dowager; possibly she added the paddle-box ornamentation.

6. From *Wen Wen-chung-kung shih-lueh*, ch. 1, biography, 12b-13.

# CHAPTER XI  TRAINING STUDENTS ABROAD

## SOURCES

### a. *The Educational Mission to the United States*

Shu Hsin-ch'eng pioneered the study of the history of Chinese education and Chinese students abroad. His *Chin-tai Chung-kuo chiao-yü shih-liao* (Historical materials on modern Chinese education) and his *Chin-tai Chung-kuo liu-hsueh shih* (History of education of students abroad in modern China) are valuable compilations. A later work is Ting Chih-p'ing, *Chung-kuo chin ch'i-shih-nien lai chiao-yü chi-shih*, which is an invaluable reference tool because the important educational events are chronologically arranged with indications of sources under each item. A good article in English by one of the 120 students sent to America is Yung Shang-him (Jung Shang-ch'ien), "The Chinese Educational Mission and Its Influence," which seems to have been usually neglected. The monographic studies by Thomas E. La Fargue are noted below.

### b. *Students in Europe*

Regarding Chinese in Europe before 1871, Fang Hao gathered information on about 106 students, but published only thirteen of their names with brief biographical information; see his *Chung-wai wen-hua chiao-t'ung-shih lun-ts'ung*. Chang Hsing-lang, *Chung-Hsi chiao-t'ung shih-liao hui-pien*, and Hsiang Ta, *Chung-Hsi chiao-t'ung shih*, also provide fragmentary materials on early Chinese students abroad.

While this volume avoids the interesting problem of the "Western" content of modern Japan's enormous influence upon China, brief note should be taken of the great possibilities for research in the field of Sino-Japanese cultural relations. Further study may indeed disclose that the foreign influence which reached China from Japan was in many ways greater than that which came directly from Western countries—for example, in the form of modern technical terminology, translations of Western works, and certain institutions. Three books by Sanetō Keishū, listed in the *Bibliography*, indicate some of the content of this research field with reference particularly to the Chinese students in Japan. The textbook by Kondō Haruo, *Gendai Chūgoku no sakka to sakuhin*, gives a bibliography of translations from Japanese into Chinese.

### NOTES

1. This first educational mission has been described in Thomas E. La Fargue, *China's First Hundred*, and in his article, "Chinese Educational Commission to the United States: A Government Experiment in Western Education."

2. From *Li Wen-chung-kung i-shu han-kao*, 1. 19b-22, dated June 26, 1871; the same document in the form of a memorial and with twelve regulations attached is in IWSM-TC, 82. 46b-52, dated September 3, 1871.

3. On the Pin-ch'un mission, sent with Hart in 1866, and the mission of Chih-kang and Sun with Burlingame in 1867-1870, see Ch. XII below and the articles by Knight Biggerstaff; also S. F. Wright, *Hart and the Chinese Customs*, p. 327.

4. The IWSM version of this document has an extra passage here, not reproduced in Li's works.

5. See *Ch'ing-shih lieh-chuan*, 73. 54.

6. See *Jen-ching-lu shih-ts'ao* (Poems of Huang Tsun-hsien), pp. 88-91.

7. *Li Wen-chung-kung p'eng-liao han-kao*, 18. 31b-32.

8. *Ibid.*, 19. 21.

9. *Li Wen-chung-kung i-shu han-kao*, 12. 7-9.

10. CSL-KH, 130. 6b.

11. From *Shih-k'o-chai chi-yen*, 2. 1b-3.

12. Ma Chien-chung adds a note to the following effect: "The original draft of this letter has been lost. Marquis Tseng Chi-tse took great interest in this writing and he copied it in his diary during his ministership to England and France, so I have recopied it and kept it here. The author." With these views of 1877 we may compare Lo Wen-kan's survey article of 1924, "China's Introduction of Foreign Systems," in CSPSR.

# CHAPTER XII   DIPLOMATIC MISSIONS ABROAD

## SOURCES

In addition to the very useful entries in Hummel on the careers of Tseng Chi-tse and Kuo Sung-tao, note should be taken of the series of articles by Knight Biggerstaff, "The Ch'ung-hou Mission to France, 1870-1871," "The Establishment of Permanent Chinese Diplomatic Missions Abroad," "The Official Chinese Attitude toward the Burlingame Mission" and "The First Chinese Mission of Investigation Sent to Europe."

A great many late nineteenth-century Chinese impressions of the West have been preserved in diaries and travel accounts by minor officials and early students, collected mainly in the *Hsiao-fang-hu-chai yü-ti ts'ung-ch'ao*. These await special study. On Kuo Sung-tao, *Yang-chih shu-wu ch'üan-chi* and his autobiographical notes, *Yü-ch'ih lao-jen tzu-hsü*, are primary sources. Ch'u-chin's notes, on Kuo Sung-tao's letters omitted from his collected works, present some supplementary material. Yang Hung-lieh's three articles on early Chinese diplomatic missions, "Chi Kuo Sung-tao ch'u-shih Ying-Fa," "Chung-kuo chu-wai shih-kuan chih-tu ti chien-t'ao," and "Chung-kuo she-chih chu-I shih-kuan ti ching-kuo," are a useful series.

Tseng Chi-tse's complete works, entitled *Tseng Hui-min-kung i-chi*, are well worth consulting by students of modern history. His *Chin-yao ch'ou-pi* might deserve an English translation as indicating the basis of his diplomatic talent. Han Shao-su, "T'an Tseng Chi-tse," also deals with his diplomatic service. Tseng's diary recording his Western experience is in his collected writings as well as in the *Hsiao-fang-hu-chai yü-ti ts'ung-ch'ao*, *ts'e* 78, entitled *Shih-Hsi jih-chi* and covering the period from August 25, 1878, to November 14, 1886. In the same collection, *ts'e* 58, there is also a diary of Tseng Chi-tse, entitled *Ch'u-shih Ying-Fa jih-chi*, which begins September 26, 1878, and ends April 17, 1879, recording his mission to England and France. While the content of these two diaries is largely the same on the years they both cover, the *Ch'u-shih Ying-Fa jih-chi* has more entries and gives fuller information for its shorter period.

## NOTES

1. See Biggerstaff, "The Establishment of Permanent Chinese Diplomatic Missions Abroad," p. 6.

2. From IWSM-TC, 27. 25-26b. With Prince Kung were, of course, associated in this memorial the other members of the Yamen.

3. Translated from Wheaton's *Elements of International Law*, The published title was *Wan-kuo kung-fa* (4 *chüan*, Peking, 1864). For Martin's account, see *A Cycle of Cathay*, pp. 298-327; also S. F. Wright, *Hart and the Chinese Customs*, pp. 328-331.

4. The following passage, up to footnote 5, is translated in T. F. Tsiang's note, "Bismarck and the introduction of international law into China," CSPSR 15:98-101 (1931). Our version is more literal.

5. End of passage noted in 4.

6. The following passage, to 7, is also from Tsiang's note.

7. End of passage noted in 6.

8. From *Yang-chih shu-wu wen-chi*, 11. 1-11.

9. This Academy was established in 1875 in the British concession

with a small museum. It was sponsored by Hsü Shou and Dr. John Fryer and financed by contributions of Western and Chinese businessmen. It was closed after 1912. See *Shang-hai-shih t'ung-chih-kuan ch'i-k'an*, 2: 513 (1933).

10. On Stephenson's plans for China, see P. H. Kent, *Railway Enterprise in China*.

11. Tseng Chi-tse's negotiations are recorded in considerable detail in his *Chin-yao ch'ou-pi*, 4 *chüan*, which gives a full account of the Sino-Russian conferences held from August 4, 1880, to February 23, 1881.

12. See Kuo Sung-tao, *Yang-chih shu-wu wen-chi*, 11.3b; Shu An, "Hsiang-hsiang Tseng-shih i-wen," *Jen-chien-shih*, 26.12; and Chin Liang, *Chin-shih jen-wu chih* (A gazetteer of modern personages), pp. 142-143.

13. From *Tseng Hui-min-kung shih-Hsi jih-chi*, 1.1-7. Tseng Chi-tse's diary was made popular by publication of a few extracts. One was by J. N. Jordan in the *China Review*, 11: 135-146 (July 1882 to June 1883), and also in the *Nineteenth Century*, 14: 989-1002; another was by the Rev. A. P. Parker in the *Chinese Recorder*, 22.7: 297-304 (July 1, 1891), and 22.8: 345-353 (August 1891). The passage translated above is also available in a French version by A. Vissière as "L'audience de congé de M. Tseng à Pekin (1878)" in *Revue d'Histoire Diplomatique*, 16: 176-186 (1902). Since this journal is not readily available, we have thought it worthwhile to give an English translation here.

14. Chinese used to divide a day and night into twelve periods, each of which occupied two hours. Thus, the *tzu* period is 11 p.m. to 1 a.m.; *ch'ou*, 1-3 a.m.; and *yin*, 3-5 a.m., etc.

15. The two Empress Dowagers were still acting jointly at this time, but the Tung T'ai-hou (the Empress Dowager Tz'u-an, 1837-1881) usually kept silent.

16. Here the oral Decree (*chih*) was a statement of advice or an order for Tseng Chi-tse to follow, or merely a remark, but in any case,

an imperial idea, which needed no answer.

17. As noted above, Margary, an interpreter in the British service on a mission from Burma to the Yunnan frontier, was murdered on February 21, 1875. This murder provided the occasion for the *Chefoo Agreement*. See H. B. Morse, *International Relations of the Chinese Empire*, II, 286-287.

18. That is, the "Tientsin Massacre" of 1870. The alleged kidnapping of children by the French Sisters of Charity was the cause of the attack. A Chinese mob destroyed a Roman Catholic orphanage and adjoining church and killed the French consul, two priests, ten nuns, three Russians and some thirty Chinese servants.

# CHAPTER XIII PROBLEMS OF THE INDUSTRIALIZATION EFFORT

## SOURCES

The subject of China's industrial development in the nineteenth century is fairly well documented, but little studied. Works noted in Fairbank and Liu, *Modern China*, deal principally with the twentieth century, but include recent monographs which survey the nineteenth century also.

For a bibliography of sources on Chinese railway problems, see *Chung-kuo t'ieh-tao wen-t'i ts'an-k'ao tzu-liao so-yin*, compiled by Mai Chien-tseng and Li Ying-chao. On the history of Chinese railways, there are several volumes: Tseng K'un-hua, *Chung-kuo t'ieh-lu shih*; Chang Hsin-ch'eng, *Chung-kuo hsien-tai chiao-t'ung shih*; and Chang Kia-ngau, *China's Struggle for Railroad Development*. Wang Ch'in-yü, "Pai-nien-lai Chung-kuo tieh-lu shih-yeh," is a useful brief account. P. H. Kent, *Railway Enterprise in China*, is still of value. Liu Ming-ch'uan's memorials, *Liu Chuang-su-kung tsou-i*, contain much valuable source material on railroad problems, as do the memorials of Sheng

Hsuan-huai for a later period (see Ch. XXI).

On Chinese industrial development, several articles in the memorial volume, *Tsui-chin chih wu-shih nien*, prepared by the *Shen-pao* newspaper office, though not necessarily always of value, were nevertheless written by recognized authorities or government officials concerned with the various branches of industry. The best work on the cotton textile industry is the recent volume by Yen Chung-p'ing, *Chung-kuo mien-yeh chih fa-chan*. Kung Chün, *Chung-kuo hsin-kung-yeh fa-chan-shih ta-kang*, is a somewhat sketchy survey by periods of the general development of Chinese industry. In general, compilations of economic source material far exceed the number of critical studies yet made. Wang Kuang, *Chung-kuo hang-yeh lun*, is the best available work on Chinese shipping; Hsieh Pin, *Chung-kuo yu-tien hang-k'ung shih*, is an informative work mainly on the history of the post, telegraph, and aviation. Tezuka Masao, *Shina jūkōgyō hattatsu shi*, a history of the development of China's heavy industry, Hirase Minokichi, *Kindai Shina keizai shi*, on late Ch'ing economics, Haga Takeshi, *Shina kōgyō shi*, a history of Chinese mineral industry, and the *Shina kōsan shigen bunken mokuroku*, a bibliography of literature on Chinese natural resources compiled by the South Manchurian Railway, are a few out of the large number of Japanese works on Chinese industry and economics. Ellsworth Carlson has done a pioneer study of the K'ai-p'ing mines as a doctoral dissertation at Harvard (1952). Rhoads Murphey's volume, *Shanghai, Key to Modern China* (developed from a Harvard dissertation) is an historical-geographical study.

The "kuan-tu shang-pan" system has been relatively neglected.

**NOTES**

1. Chang Kia-ngau, *China's Struggle for Railroad Development*, p. 24.

2. *Li Wen-chung-kung tsou-kao*, 40. 41.

3. From Li's memorial dated June 29, 1872, "Ch'ou-i chih-tsao lun-

ch'uan wei-k'o ts'ai-ch'e che" (Planning the construction of steamships should not be given up), *Li Wen-chung ,kung tsou-kao* , 19. 44-50.

4. *Ibid.* , 38. 16-17.

5. See Mu Hsiang-yueh, "Chung-kuo mien-chih-yeh fa-ta-shih," in *Tsui-chin chih wu-shih-nien* , p. 1.

6. See Sheng Hsuan-huai's biography in *Yü-chai ts'un-kao* , 1. 5-9.

7. THL-TK, 32. 18.

8. See Liu Chin-tsao, *Ch'ing-ch'ao hsü wen-hsien t'ung-k'ao* , ch. 361. 11,045.

9. According to the author's preface, an early version of this book had been published in Kiangsu as far back as 1862 under the title, "Important suggestions for the salvation of the time" (*Chiu-shih chieh-yao*), and later reprinted in Japan. In 1871 a second version with a supplement, issued under the title "On change" (*I-yen*), with a preface by Wang T'ao (see Ch. XVb), was circulated in Japan and Korea. A revised edition of this book, *I-yen*, was published in 1875. The last version, *Sheng-shih wei-yen*, came out in 1893 (preface dated 1892), and was twice revised by the author and his friends *ca.* 1896 and 1899.

10. See Hsiao San, *Mao Tse-tung t'ung-chih ti ch'ing-shao-nien shih-tai* , 13.

11. See ch. 2, section on women and education, especially pp. 31-33; ch. 3, on law, prison conditions, and opium smoking; and ch. 8, on agriculture, reclamation work, and poor relief.

12. From *Sheng-shih wei-yen* , 5. 7b-9.

13. *Ibid.* , 1. 47-48.

14. *Ibid.* , 1. 52-54.

15. See Wang Ch'in-yü, "Pai-nien-lai Chung-kuo t'ieh-lu shih-yeh," *Hsueh-lin* , 2. 40.

16. See *Technological Trends and National Policy, Including the Social Implications of New Inventions* (Washington, D. C. : U. S. Government Printing Office, 1937), pp. 40-41.

17. Liu Ming-ch'uan's memorial and supporting statements by Li Hung-chang and Liu K'un-i would be included in this volume were they not translated in James Harrison Wilson's *China, Travels and Investigations in the "Middle Kingdom,"* pp. 126-135, 135-154, and *passim*.

18. From *Kuang-hsü cheng-yao*, 2. 23. Wu Yuan-ping was a co-memorialist, although for brevity only Shen Pao-chen's name is given in our title. Wu's diary (5. 18) states that he drafted the memorial.

19. From *Yung-an wen-pien*, 2. 9b-15.

# CHAPTER XIV   THE ATTEMPT AT A POSITIVE FOREIGN POLICY

### SOURCES

Documents on late Ch'ing foreign relations are listed in Fairbank and Liu, *Modern China*, section 5. 1, and in Fairbank, *Ch'ing Documents*. Sources on the Chinese navy include the sections in *Huang-ch'ao cheng-tien lei-tsuan* and *Ch'ing-ch'ao hsü wen-hsien t'ung-k'ao*, and Ch'ih Chung-hu's account, "Hai-chün ta-shih chi"; see also *Ch'ing-shih kao* and the regulations of the Peiyang Navy, compiled in 1888 by the Chung-kuo tsung-li hai-chün ya-men. Although there are a few special studies of the modern Chinese army, the history of the navy seems to have been largely neglected.

The reasons for the failure at self-strengthening have been discussed by Hu Shih, Kuo Mo-jo, and many others; summary analyses are available, for example, in E. H. Norman, *Japan's Emergence as a Modern State*, and various textbooks, but no monographs have yet appeared on this subject.

On the Sino-Russian secret treaty, apart from sources mentioned above, reference may be made to Men-se t'an-hu-k'o [pseudonym], *Chin-shih Chung-kuo mi-shih*, 1. 224-239; Ch'en Fu-kuang, *Yu Ch'ing i-lai chih Chung-E kuan-hsi*; Liu Hsiung-hsiang *Ch'ing-chi shih-nien chih lien-E cheng-ts'e*; Shen Chien, "Ssu-shih-yü-nien ch'ien chih lien-E wai-chiao"; and Wang Yun-sheng, "Chung-E mi-yueh pien-wei." The last article tries to prove that the Cassini Convention, another secret agreement said to have been signed in Peking on September 30, 1896, is spurious, while stating that the authenticity of the secret treaty translated in this volume is beyond doubt. The definitive work on the policies of Li Hung-chang and others in this period has been done by two leading Japanese historians, Tabohashi Kiyoshi, *Nisshin seneki gaikōshi no kenkyū*, to 1895, and Yano Jin'ichi, *Nisshin ekigo Shina gaikōshi*, on the decade following.

## NOTES

1. *Li Wen-chung-kung p'eng-liao han-kao*, 12. 14; see also 14. 4 and *passim*.
2. *Li Wen-chung-kung tsou-kao*, 24. 26.
3. Li's *P'eng-liao han-kao*, 14. 29b-30.
4. Li's *I-shu han-kao*, 17. 8b-9.
5. Li's *P'eng-liao han-kao*, 19. 33b-34.
6. *Ibid.*, 19. 16b.
7. *Ibid.*, 19. 42b-43.
8. From *Kuo Shih-lang tsou-shu*, 12. 37-47.
9. See John L. Rawlinson, "The Lay-Osborn Flotilla: Its Development and Significance," *Papers on China, from the Regional Studies Seminars*, 4:58-73 (1950).
10. For documents, see *Huang-ch'ao cheng-tien lei-tsuan*, 342. 1-7.
11. See the imperial order in *Kuang-hsü cheng-yao*, 4. 4, and the translation in C. B. Malone, *History of the Peking Summer Palaces*, pp. 197-198.
12. Cf. Li Chien-nung, *Chung-kuo chin-pai-nien cheng-chih shih*, 1. 154-155.
13. From Chang P'ei-lun, *Chien-yü chi*, 4. 2-6. The memorial was

submitted on May 19, 1884.

14. From Wang Yun-sheng *Liu-shih-nien lai Chung-kuo yü Jih-pen*, 2.261-62. Wang's source has not been located.

15. From *Ch'ing-chi wai-chiao shih-liao*, 115.20-21.

16. *Ibid.*, 116.35b-37.

17. *Ibid.*, 122.1-2b. An English translation, "from the French text of the original consulted in the Archives of the Narcomindiel (Foreign Office) at Moscow," is printed on pp. 365-366 of Victor A. Yakhontoff, *Russia and the Soviet Union in the Far East* (New York: Coward-McCann, 1931) p.454.

18. The Chinese word in the text here is *yueh*, "month," which is stated in the *errata* of the source to be a misprint.

# CHAPTER XV    PROMOTERS OF INSTITUTIONAL CHANGE

## SOURCES

On the missionary movement the standard works are those of K. S. Latourette, R. Loewenthal, *The Religious Periodical Press in China*, R. S. Britton, *The Chinese Periodical Press 1800-1912*, and Chang Hsing-lang, *Ou-hua tung-chien shih*, supply much valuable information. E. R. Hughes, *The Invasion of China by the Western World*, G. H. Danton, *The Culture Contacts of the United States and China*, J. S. Dennis, *Christian Missions and Social Progress*, and C. K. Wu, *The International Aspect of the Missionary Movement in China*, are also useful for this topic. Timothy Richard's journal, *Hsi-to*, which contains several important essays on the reform movement; Chung-ying (ed.), *Yang-wu hsin-lun* (New essays on foreign affairs), which was actually written by Richard, Alien, and others; Fu Lan-ya (John Fryer), *Tso-chih ch'u-yen* (Some advice on how to rule)—these are all selections of the writings in Chinese by influential missionaries. For a list of other missionary works and of Western books translated into Chinese in the nineteenth century, see Wylie's *Memorials of Protestant Missionaries to the Chinese*; Liang Ch'i-ch'ao, *Hsi-hsueh shu-mu piao*; and Chao Wei-hsi, *Hsi-hsueh shu-mu ta-wen*. For a bibliography of Chinese source materials on missionary problems, see Wu Sheng-te and Ch'en Tseng-hui, *Chiao-an shih-liao pien-mu*. The studies of important missionaries include W. A. Candler, *Young J. Allen*; Lee Shiu-keung, *Timothy Richard and the Reform Movement in China*; W. E. Soothill, *Timothy Richard of China*; E. W. Burt, "The Centenary of Timothy Richard," and his other article, "Timothy Richard: His Contribution to Modern China," E. W. Price Evans, *Timothy Richard*; and the recent attack from Peking by Ting Tse-liang.

Primary sources on Wang T'ao are the *T'ao-yuan wen-lu wai-pien*, *T'ao-yuan ch'ih-tu*, *Man-yu sui-lu*, *Fu-sang yu-chi*, *Hsi-hsueh chi-ts'un*, among other works written or compiled by him. Among the many studies of, or references to, Wang T'ao, the following list may be of some help: Ch'en Chen-kuo, "Ch'ang-mao chuang-yuan Wang T'ao"; Ko Kung-chen, *Chung-kuo pao-hsueh shih*; Hu Shih, *The Chinese Renaissance*; Lin Yutang, A *History of the Press and Public Opinion in China*; Chao I-ch'eng, "Wang T'ao k'ao-cheng"; Hsieh Hsing-yao, *T'ai-p'ing T'ien-kuo ts'ung-shu*; Lo Erh-kang, *T'ai-p'ing T'ien-kuo shih ts'ung-k'ao*, and *T'ai-p'ing T'ien-kuo wen-yuan*; *Wen-hsien ts'ung-pien*, no. 20; Ssu-yü Teng, *New Light on the History of the Taiping Rebellion*; Sanetō Keishū, "Wang T'ao ti tu-Jih ho Jih-pen wen-jen," translated by Chang Ming-san in *Jih-pen yen-chiu*.

Sources on Hsueh Fu-ch'eng are in *Yung-an ch'üan-chi* (Complete works of Hsueh Fu-ch'eng), which includes his collected essays, *Yung-an wen-pien*, and two supplements, *Yung-an wen hsü-pien* and *Yung-an wen wai-pien*; as well as *Hai-wai wen-pien*, *Ch'u-shih tsou-su*, *Ch'u-shih kung-tu*, *Ch'ou-yang ch'u-i*, and *Ch'u-shih Ying-Fa-I-Pi ssu-kuo jih-chi*. These works as put together in the *Yung-an ch'üan-chi* are convenient to use, but there are some typographical errors and the text is not as legible as in punctuated block-print editions of the above works (the diary, the official dispatches, and the two supplements to his essays), all of which were separately published by Ch'uan-ching-lou. In addition, the *Yung-an pi-chi* (Desultory notes of Yung-an), jotted down during the years 1865-1891 and printed in 1895 in several editions, is a work of historical and scholarly value. See also *Ch'ing-shih kao*, ch. 452; *Pei-chuan-chi pu*, ch. 13; *Ch'ing-shih lieh-chuan*, ch. 58; Hummel, *Eminent Chinese of the Ch'ing Period (1644-1912)*, pp. 331-332; Huang Yen-yü, "Viceroy Yeh Ming-ch'en and the Canton Episode (1850-1861)", *Harvard Journal of Asiatic Studies* 6.1. We are of course much indebted to the account by Tu Lien-che in Hummel, cited above.

It is obvious that the above materials, as well as the extensive writings of missionaries in Chinese, have hardly been studied in the West.

**NOTES**

1. R. S. Britton, *The Chinese Periodical Press 1800-1912*, p. 53.

2. This introductory note is supplementary to the biography by Roswell S. Britton in Hummel, *Eminent Chinese of the Ch'ing Period (1644-1912)*. Wang T'ao had several names: Wang Li-pin, Huang T'ao, Huang Wan, Chung-t'ao, T'ien-nan tun-sou, etc.

3. Under the title, *T'ao-yuan wen-lu wai-pien*.

4. *Ibid.*, 2.5-7.

5. *Ibid.*, 2.11b-14.

6. *Ibid.*, 8.12-14.

7. *Ibid.*, 3.12-17; 25b-27b.

8. *Ch'u e-wai ch'üan-li*, 3.27b-29.

9. *T'ao-yuan wen-lu wai-pien*, 4.22.

10. *Ibid.*, 1.1. This idea was used most effectively by K'ang Yu-wei; see Chapter XVI.

11. *Ibid.*, 1.2.

12. *Ibid.*, 1. 21b-23.

13. "Shang tang-lu lun shih-wu shu," a letter submitted to the authorities discussing current affairs, *ibid.*, 10. 20b-22.

14. "Yuan-hsueh," *ibid.*, 1. 2b-3b.

15. A letter to Hsü Chün-ch'ing (Hsü Yu-jen) in *T'ao-yuan ch'ih-tu*, 4. 21b-22.

16. "Pien-fa," parts B and C, *T'ao-yuan wen-lu wai-pien*, 1. 13-17.

17. "Chih-chung," *ibid.*, 1. 25-26.

18. "Chi Ying-kuo cheng-chih," *ibid.*, 4. 17.

19. See *Ch'u-shih ... jih-chi*, 4. 12b.

20. *Ibid.*, 3. 25b-26b.

21. *Ibid.*, 2. 6; 3. 84-85; 6. 15b-16b.

22. *Ibid.*, 5. 16.

23. See *Ch'u-shih kung-tu*, preface, p. 2.

24. From *Ch'ou-yang ch'u-i*, 1. 29b-32.

25. From *Ch'u-shih Ying-Fa-I-Pi ssu-kuo jih-chi*, 2. 5b-6.

26. Hsueh also refers here to I I or Hou I, a famous archer who attempted to attack Hsia, but was killed by Han-cho. See Ssu-ma Ch'ien, *Shih-chi*, 2. 23b n; and 67. 15b.

27. Kings Chieh of Hsia, Chou of Shang, and Yu and Li of Chou were all notorious tyrants.

28. From *Ch'u-shih ... jih-chi*, 2. 11b-12.

29. Wu Ch'en, a native of Ch'u, once tried to stop the struggle between Prince Ch'u-hsiang and another person for a beautiful woman. Later on, Wu Ch'en got the woman for himself and fled with her to the state of Wu. For this, all the members of his family in Ch'u were killed. Wu Ch'en taught the Wu state to fight against Ch'u and caused the latter much trouble. See Ssu-ma Ch'ien, *Shih-chi*, 39. 31.

30. From *Ch'u-shih ... jih-chi*, 6. 2.

31. From *Hai-wai wen-pien*, 3. 8b-9.

# CHAPTER XVI  K'ANG YU-WEI AND SOME OF HIS ASSOCIATES

**SOURCES**

general accounts of the Reform Movement of 1898 include Meribeth E. Cameron, *The Reform Movement in China 1898-1912*, a pioneer survey which uses rather few Chinese sources; a scholarly article by Ho Ping-ti, "Weng T'ung-ho and the 'One Hundred Days of Reform,'" which clarifies Weng's role in the movement; Albert Maybon, *La Politique Chinoise, étude sur les doctrines des partis en chine, 1898-1908*, which is probably the best French work on the period; Alfred Forke, *Geschichte der neueren chinesischen Philosophie*, which considers K'ang, Liang and others; Wolfgang Franke, "Die Staatspolitischen Refomversuche K'ang Yu-weis und seiner Schule. Ein Beitrag zur geistigen Auseinandersetzung Chinas mit dem Abendlande," a dissertation with ample documentation; Hsiao Kung-ch'üan, *Chung-kuo cheng-chih ssu-hsiang shih*, which is probably the best treatment in Chinese of the political thought of K'ang and his associates. Joseph R. Levenson, *Liang Ch'i-ch'ao and the Mind of Modern China* (Harvard University Press, 1953), and his article, "The Breakdown of Confucianism: Liang Ch'i-ch'ao before Exile—1873-1898," in the *Journal of the History of Ideas* (October 1950) are recent analytic studies of Liang and his ideas. So Kwan-wai, *Western Influence and the Chinese Reform Movement of 1898*, a doctoral dissertation at the University of Wisconsin (1950), is a workmanlike study.

A considerable amount of research on the Reform Movement has been done in Japan by a number of competent scholars: Murakami Tomoyuki, *Bojutsu seihen shiwa*, is a comprehensive study of the movement. It is also dealt with in the article by Sanetō Keishū, "Kindai Shina to gairai shisō" (in *Kindai Shina shisō*); in Fujiwara Sadamu,

*Kindai Chūgoku shisō*; and Ojima Sukema, *Chūgoku no kakumei shisō*, although all of these cover a broader scope. The first chapter of Yano Jin'ichi, *Shinchō matsushi kenkyū*, is a careful research into many aspects of the events of 1898, and another critical appraisal is Inada Masatsugu's article, "Bojutsu seihen ni tsuite" (in *Kindai Chūgoku kenkyū*). In the same volume is a detailed and critical analysis of the origin, nature, and influence of K'ang Yu-wei's conception of the "Great Harmony" (*Ta-t'ung ssu-hsiang*) by Itano Chōhachi, who has also written an appraisal of Liang Ch'i-ch'ao's idea of it, along the same lines, in the *Festschrift* for Dr. Wada Sei. A careful and independent analysis of the whole current of reform and intellectual change is provided in three articles by Onogawa Hidemi, "Shimmatsu yōmuha no undō"; "Shimmatsu no shisō to shinkaron"; and "Shimmatsu hempōron no seiritsu." The second describes the influence of Yen Fu's translation of Huxley's *Evolution and Ethics* on the reformers of the period. K'ang and the failure of 1898 are also dealt with in two chapters of Izushi Yoshihiko, *Tōyō kinseishi kenkyū*.

The philosophy of K'ang, T'an, and their group is briefly treated in many surveys in English, such as Lin Mou-sheng, *Men and Ideas*, Feng Yu-lan, *A Short History of Chinese Philosophy*, and Tseng Yu-hao, *Modern Chinese Legal and Political Philosophy*. The extensive Chinese periodical literature includes the following articles: Ch'en Kung-lu, "Chia-wu-luan hou keng-tzu-luan ch'ien Chung-kuo pien-fa yun-tung chih yen-chiu"; Chih Kuei, "Ch'ing-tai K'ang-Liang wei-hsin yun-tung yü ko-ming-tang chih kuan-hsi chi ying-hsiang"; I-shih, "Jung-lu yü Yuan Shih-k'ai"; Mei Ying, "Wu-hsü cheng-pien chen-wen"; the *Ta-kung-pao* article, "Kuan-yü wu-hsü cheng-pien hsin shih-liao"; Wu Tse, "Wu-hsü cheng-pien yü hsin-chiu tang-cheng" and "Pao-huang-tang yü K'ang-Liang lu-hsien"; and "Lun pien-fa chih ching-shen," an editorial in *Tung-fang tsa-chih*, no. 7 (1904).

On K'ang Yu-wei, apart from his own writings, there are several biographies: Liang Ch'i-ch'ao, *K'ang Nan-hai chuan*; Chang Po-chen, *Nan-hai K'ang hsien-sheng chuan*; and Chao Feng-t'ien, "K'ang Ch'ang-su hsien-sheng nien-p'u kao." Mr. Chao has specialized on K'ang and Liang; much of his material is still in manuscript. See also Wu Tse, *K'ang Yu-wei yü Liang Ch'i-ch'ao*. For a good edition of K'ang's *Ta-t'ung shu*, see the one compiled by Ch'ien Ting-an and published by the Chung-hua Book Co. in 1932. The commonly available edition, in *Wan-mu ts'ao-t'ang ts'ung-k'an* and in *K'ang Nan-hai wen-ch'ao*, is incomplete.

On Liang Ch'i-ch'ao, apart from his own voluminous writings (see Bibliography) and the studies of him mentioned above, there are several biographical sketches or brief studies in Chinese of his ideas and influence: Liu P'an-sui, "Liang Jen-kung hsien-sheng chuan," Chang Ch'i-yun, "Liang Jen-kung ssu-hsiang pieh-lu," and Su Ch'ih (Chang Yin-lin), "Chin-tai Chung-kuo hsueh-shu-shih shang chih Liang Jen-kung." Wu Ch'i-ch'ang's *Liang Ch'i-ch'ao* seems to be an unfinished job published posthumously, but it presents a framework for Liang's biography. Wu was one of Liang's best students.

On T'an Ssu-t'ung, *T'an Liu-yang ch'üan-chi*, *Jen-hsueh*, published in *Ch'ing-i-pao*, and *T'an Ssu-t'ung shu-chien*, compiled by Ou-yang Yü-ch'ien, are primary sources. Ts'ai Shang-ssu, "T'an Ssu-t'ung hsueh-shu ssu-hsiang t'i-yao," and Hu Yuan-chün, "T'an Ssu-t'ung *Jen-hsueh* chih p'i-p'ing," are special studies of considerable value.

On Yen Fu, there are the following books and articles in Chinese: a biography by Wang Shen-jan, in his *Chin-tai erh-shih-chia p'ing-chuan*; Lin Yao-hua, "Yen Fu she-hui ssu-hsiang," in *She-hui hsueh-chieh*; Wang Chü-ch'ang, *Yen Chi-tao nien-p'u*; Kuo Pin-ho, "Yen Chi-tao"; and two articles by Chou Chen-fu, "Yen Fu ssu-hsiang chuan-pien chih p'ou-hsi" and "Yen Fu ti Chung-Hsi wen-hua kuan."

## NOTES

1. Such as T'ang Chen, *Wei-yen*, published in 1890, and Cheng

Kuan-ying, *Sheng-shih wei-yen* (see Chapter XIII a). Two other works of the same nature were *Hsin-cheng chen-ch'üan* (The true meaning of new government), written by Hu Li-yuan, who was trained in England, and Ho Ch'i, who graduated *cum laude* from the British college in Hongkong; and Ch'en Chih, *Yung-shu*. Ch'en was influenced by his frequent visits to Hongkong and Macao, and advocated a higher social position for the merchant class and thorough reform along the lines of Western government. He also warned against the ambitions of Russia in China.

2. *Kung-ch'e shang-shu chi*; see the lithographic edition, published in Shanghai, 1895.

3. See Liang Ch'i-ch'ao, *Ch'ing-tai hsueh-shu kai-lun*, pp. 56-57.

4. See *Jen-ching-lu shih-ts'ao*, Peiping, 1930.

5. See Wen T'ing-ching, "Huang Tsun-hsien chuan"; also Ko Hsien-ning, "Chin-tai Chung-kuo min-tsu shih-jen Huang Kung-tu."

6. Ko Hsien-ning, *ibid.*, p. 101.

7. Such as *Papers from a Viceroy's Yamen* (1901) and *The Story of a Chinese Oxford Movement* (1910). He also wrote in German.

8. See Wen Yuan-ning, "Ku Hung-ming," in *T'ien-hsia Monthly*. There are also many anecdotes and biographies of Ku in Chinese as well as a collection of his essays entitled *Tu I ts'ao-t'ang wen-chi*.

9. See R. S. Britton, *The Chinese Periodical Press 1800-1912*, p. 97.

10. *Yen Chi-tao shih-wen ch'ao*, 2. 19.

11. *Ibid.*, 1. 1b.

12. *Ibid.*, 4. 19b.

13. Letters 58-59, from Yen Fu's correspondence in *Hsueh-heng*, no. 18:6-7 (1923).

14. From *K'ang Nan-hai wen-chi hui-pien*, 8. 20.

15. From *Yin-ping-shih ho-chi*, 1. 1-8.

16. See Lin's biography in *Kuo-ch'ao hsien-cheng shih-lueh*, 25. 6.

17. Mai Chung-hua (comp.), *Huang-ch'ao ching-shih-wen hsin-pien*, 2. 19b-32.

18. From *Huang-ch'ao ching-shih-wen hsin-pien*, 27. 8-9.

19. See *Huang-ch'ao ching-shih-wen san-pien*, 15. 6-8.

# CHAPTER XVII THE REFORM PROGRAM OF CHANG CHIH-TUNG

### SOURCCES

Materials on Chang are indicated in Hummel, pp. 27-32. One edition of *Chang Wen-hsiang-kung nien-p'u* was compiled by Hsü T'ung-hsin, and is more informative but poorly arranged; the other, by Hu Chün, is based mainly on Hsü's work and is less informative but easier to use. See also Hsiao Kung-ch'üan, *Chung-kuo cheng-chih ssu-hsiang shih*, pp. 407-415; and the following articles Hsieh En-hui, "Chang Hsiang-t'ao chih ching-chi chien-she,"; "Chang Wen hsiang-kung yü chiao-yü chih kuan-hsi," in *Chiao-yü tsa-chih*; L, Odontines, "Chang Chih-tung and the Reform Movement in China"; Meribeth E. Cameron, "The Public Career of Chang Chih-tung 1837-1909"; Ch'üan Han-sheng, "Ch'ing-mo Han-yang t'ieh-ch'ang" (The Han-yang iron and steel works, 1890-1908); and Wang Shou-ch'ien, "Chung-kuo chi-ch'i pan chu-tsao chih-ch'ien yü yin-yuan chih ch'i-yuan" (The beginning of machine minting of coins and silver dollars in China).

### NOTES

1. *Ch'üan-hsueh-p'ien*, two *chüan*. The first, part A, is called *nei-p'ien*, and the second, part B, *wai-p'ien*. There is a rough condensed translation by Samuel I. Woodbridge (New York, 1900) entitled *China's Only Hope, An Appeal by Her Greatest Viceroy, Chang Chih-tung*, and a better French translation by Jerome Tobar (Chang-hai, 1909). There are three Chinese editions in circulation. One is in *Chang Wen-hsiang-kung ch'üan-chi*, ch. 202-203, used as the basis of the present

translation. Another is in the Chien-hsi ts'un-she ts'ung-k'o punctuated edition. The third is a separate edition republished in Chekiang in 1898.

2. See pt. A, ch. 4, in *Chang Wen-hsiang-kung ch'üan-chi*, 202. 16-18.

3. Pt. A, ch. 3, in the same work, 202. 13-15.

4. See CSL, Te-tsung, 484. 10b-11.

5. Pt. B, ch. 13, in *Chang Wen-hsiang-kung ch'üan-chi*, 203. 48.

6. Preface to *Ch'üan-hsueh-p'ien*, 1b.

7. *Ibid.*, 2b.

8. Chang, *ch'üan-chi*, 202. 2b-3.

9. *Ibid.*, 203. 24.

10. See Chang's *nien-p'u*, compiled by Hu Chün, 3. 16b.

11. See Chang's memorial in *ch'üan-chi*, 40. 1-5.

12. *Ibid.*, 203. 30-34.

13. From pt. A, ch. 6, "cheng-ch'üan," in Chang's *ch'üan-chi*, 202. 23-26.

14. *Chiu-chou*, i. e., the political divisions cited in the chapter "Yü-kung"of the *Book of History*.

15. From pt. A, ch. 7, "Hsün-hsü,"in *ch'üan-chi*, 202,27-28.

16. From pt. A, ch. 9, "Ch'ü-tu," in the same work, 202. 38-40.

17. See *The Analects* of Confucius, bk. 2, ch. 3, Legge's translation.

18. Cf. F. Max Müller's translation, the *Book of Rites*, Oxford, 1885, p. 82.

19. From ch. 7, "Pien-fa," in *ch'üan-chi*, 203. 19-22.

20. These words are quoted from chapters 41, "Sun," 42, "I," and the appendix, respectively, of the *Book of Changes* in order to convince scholars that there is a basis for reform in the classics.

21. See the *Book of History*, "Pan-keng," A, sec. 13.

22. See *Tso-chuan*, bk. 10, the 17th year of Duke Chao.

23. See *The Analects*, bk, 2, 11.

24. *Ibid.*, bk. 6, 21.

25. See *Chung-yung*, ch. 25

26. See *Mencius*, bk. 7, pt. 1, ch. 7. Note: we have consulted and modified Legge's translation of the preceding references.

27. Quoted from *Chuang Tzu*, ch. 2, "Equality of Things and Opinions." Cf. Feng Yu-lan's translation, p. 61; i.e., they are too hasty in forming their opinions.

28. From ch. 15, "Fei kung-chiao," in *ch'üan-chi*, 203. 51-53.

# CHAPTER XVIII  THE FAILURE OF 1898

## SOURCES

Sources for this chapter are mentioned in the notes, and under Chapter XVI. We have not seen a new compilation entitled *Wu-hsü pien-fa*, published in Peking in late 1953.

## NOTES

1. On this general subject, see Ch'en Ch'iu, "Wu-hsü cheng-pien-shih fan pien-fa jen-wu chih cheng-chih ssu-hsiang," in *Yen-ching hsueh-pao*.

2. From *Nan-hai K'ang hsien-sheng chuan*, 26b-28.

3. *Tsou*, usually translated "memorialize," but meaning to present one's views to the emperor.

4. From Wang Yun-sheng, *Liu-shih-nien lai Chung-kuo yü Jih-pen*, 3. 272-275. The original text is in *Zoku Itō Hirobumi hiroku* (Supplement to the collection of Itō's private documents), compiled by Hiratsuka Atsushi, pp. 126-129.

5. After this answer, the emperor asked when Itō had started his trip from Japan. Itō answered that he had started the trip from his country about a month before and had stayed more than ten days in Korea before coming to China. These lines were omitted by Wang Yun-sheng.

6. In this section, in addition to selecting a number of passages not hitherto noted, we have relied heavily on the following two articles by

Ch'üan Han-sheng: "Ch'ing-mo ti Hsi-hsueh yuan-ch'u Chung-kuo shuo" and "Ch'ing-mo fan-tui Hsi-hua ti yen-lun." See also the article by Ch'en Ch'iu cited in note 1 above.

7. See Ch'en Ch'iu, pp. 82-83.

8. From Wang Hsien-ch'ien, *Hsü-shou-t'ang shu-cha*, 2. 75-76, 1907 edition. (Ch'en Ch'iu, p. 98, mistakes the *shu-cha* for *wen-chi*.)

9. Ch'u Ch'eng-po was less an opponent of reform than a critic of the reformers and their methods. His memorial is in *Chien-cheng-t'ang che-kao*, 2. 18-20, quoted by Ch'en Ch'iu, pp. 84-85.

10. From *Huang-shih li-shih chi*, 41. 43. Cf. Ch'en Ch'iu, pp. 90-91.

11. Yeh Te-hui was another scholar who said that it was not worthwhile to imitate Western methods of agriculture, industry or military training. Agriculture, for example, depended upon the proper rain and sunshine, but Westerners had no way to control them. The military systems of England and Germany were good only for fighting on the sea or along the coast. See Su Yü, *I-chiao ts'ung-pien*, 4. 10 and 5. 28, preface dated 1898; this work is a collection of memorials and letters of conservatives attacking the reformers.

12. See Hellmut Wilhelm, "The Problem of Within and Without, a Confucian Attempt in Syncretism," *Journal of the History of Ideas*.

13. Su Yü, 2. 8b, Wen-t'i's impeachment of K'ang Yu-wei.

14. From *Hsiao-fang-hu-chai* ... , *ts'e* 60. 470-478.

15. *Ibid*., *ts'e* 56. 184. The diary was written in 1876-1877. The *Ying-yao jih-chi* by the same author in the *Ling chien-ko ts'ung-shu* is a much abbreviated version; it was published by Chiang Piao to promote reform, so that many conservative opinions were omitted.

16. See *Shih-chiu-te-chai tsa-chu* (Miscellaneous writings of Liu Yueh-yün), *ts'e* 1, preface to "Ko-wu chung-fa," first page.

17. See *Pin-meng chi* (preface dated 1870), 2. 6, in *Ch'un-tsai-t'ang ch'üan-shu*, *ts'e* 61.

18. See *Hsi-shih li-ts'e* (A glimpse into Western affairs), written ca. 1883, in *Hsiao-fang-hu-chai...*, *ts'e* 62, p. 530.

19. In Chu's *Wu-hsieh-t'ang ta-wen* (Answers to questions in the orthodox studio), 4.50, author's preface dated 1892, Cho-an ts'ung-kao edition.

20. See his *Ying-hai-lun* (A discussion of the circuit of the seas), 489b, in *Hsiao-fang-hu-chai...*, *ts'e* 60.

21. See his "San ta-yu lun" (On three great anxieties), *Pin-meng-chi*, 6.7b-10.

## CHAPTER XIX   THE BOXER UPRISING

### SOURCES

A very useful collection of materials on the Boxer Uprising is the four-volume work entitled *I-ho-t'uan*, compiled by Chien Po-tsan and others and published in 1951. Its annotated bibliography of 278 Chinese and Western sources dealing with the uprising, in vol. 4, pp. 529-604, supersedes others previously compiled by Ch'ü Tui-chih and Chao Hsing-kuo. Nevertheless the bibliography of Chinese materials dealing with cases involving Christian missions, compiled by Wu Sheng-te and Ch'en Tseng-hui, is still useful. Lao Nai-hsuan's three works on the Boxers, *Ch'üan-an san-chung*, are essential. Kuo Pin-chia's "Keng-tzu ch'üan-luan" is a good short account of the Boxer rebellion and its diplomatic aftermath. For an analysis of this movement by a scholar, Fan Wen-lan's *Chung-kuo chin-tai shih* (pp. 403-508) may be consulted. For a recent study of the evidence, see Robert Sheeks, "A Re-examination of the I-ho Ch'üan and its Role in the Boxer's Movement," *Papers on China*, 1:74-135 (1947), and Paul A. Varg, "William W. Rockhill's Influence on the Boxer's Negotiations," *Pacific Historical Review*, vol. XVIII, no. 3 (August 1949). Yano Jin'ichi's chapters on the history and nature of the Boxer Uprising in his *Shinchō matsushi kenkyū* (chs. 3-4, pp. 61-168) and Ichiko Chūzō's article on the nature of the Boxer movement, in *Kindai Chūgoku kenkyū* are important studies, and note should also be taken of the two articles by Yamamoto Sumiko and by Tabohashi Kiyoshi. The latter touches the question of foreign provocation.

**NOTES**

1. These three short documents are translated from Chien Po-tsan (comp.), *I-ho-t'uan*, 4. 148-149.

2. See the biographies of Hsü and Yuan in Hummel, pp. 312-313 and 945-948.

3. From *Kuang-hsü hui-yao*, 26. 8b-10. These three documents are also published in *I-ho-t'uan*, 4. 159-168, based on Yuan's first autographic manuscript, which is more detailed than the *Kuang-hsü hui-yao* edition. Not all scholars are convinced of their exact authenticity as reproduced in various collections, or whether they were actually presented to the throne, but there is no doubt that the general view which they put forward represents accurately what these martyred officials stood for at the time.

4. See his study of the origin of the I-ho-ch'üan, *I-ho-ch'üan chiao-men yuan-liu k'ao*, reprinted in Tso Shun-sheng, *Chung-kuo chin-pai-nien shih tzu-liao hsü-pien*, vol. A, and other collections.

5. From *Kuang-hsü cheng-yao*, 26. 12b-13b.

6. *Ibid.*, 26. 18b-20b.

# CHAPTER XX   THE CONSERVATIVE REFORM MOVEMENT 1901-1902

**SOURCES**

**a. *The Post-Boxer Program***

This topic has been little studied, and the material is meager and scattered. For general information, see textbooks like those of Ch'en Kung-lu, *Chung-kuo chin-tai shih*, or Li Chien-nung, *Chung-kuo chin-*

*pai-nien cheng-chih shih*. For bibliography, see Ma Feng-chen, *Ch'ing-tai hsing-cheng chih-tu yen-chiu ts'an-k'ao shu-mu*, and *Modern China* by Fairbank and Liu. For primary materials, see such compilations as *Kuang-hsü cheng-yao*, *Hsuan-t'ung cheng-chi*, *Tung-hua lu*, CSL and CSK; also *Tung-fang tsa-chih*, published Shanghai from 1904. The first issues of yearbooks, such as *Chung-kuo nien-chien*, or *Shen-pao nien-chien*, usually give a summary of earlier events; see S. Y. Teng and Knight Biggerstaff, *An Annotated Bibliography of Selected Chinese Reference Works*, ch. 7, on yearbooks. Note also the writings of prominent individuals like Chang Chih-tung, Yuan Shih-k'ai, Chang Chien, and Sheng Hsuan-huai. The biography of Liang Shih-i, *San-shui Liang Yen-sun hsien-sheng nien-p'u*, is important and informative. In connection with these works, *Min-kuo t'u-chih ch'u-i* (1915) by Wu T'ing-fang (1842-1922), a diplomat and Western-trained official prominent in the 1900's, may also be suggested. For the reform of China's legal codes, Dr. M. J. Meijer's monograph on the introduction of modern criminal law, which surveys the work of Shen Chia-pen and others in the decade 1901-1911 with translations of eleven key documents, is indispensable. A remarkably penetrating picture of the imperial administration of China in its last years is given in the two-volume handbook by Hattori Unokichi, *Shinkoku tsūkō*, published in 1905. The movement for a national assembly is dealt with in Onogawa Hidemi, "Shimmatsu hempōron no seiritsu."

### b. Educational Reform

In addition to items mentioned under Chapter XI, note Chiang Shu-ko, *Chung-kuo chin-tai chiao-yü chih-tu*; Chuang Yü and Ho Sheng-nai, *Tsui-chin san-shih-wu-nien chih Chung-kuo chiao-yü*; Ch'en I-lin, *Tsui-chin san-shih-nien Chung-kuo chiao-yü shih*; and Chiang Monlin, *Tides from the West*.

### c. Constitutionalism

The diaries of Tai Hung-tz'u, *Ch'u-shih chiu-kuo jih-chi*, and Tsai-tse, *K'ao-ch'a cheng-chih jih-chi*, are as important as the *Ou-Mei cheng-*

*chih yao-i* from which Doc. 52 is translated. Li Chien-nung, *Chung-kuo chin-pai-nien cheng-chih shih*, has a good general discussion of this topic. Articles in *Hsien-cheng tsa-shih* (Constitutional government miscellany), 1.1, and in *Tung-fang tsa-chih*, which has a special issue on constitutional government, January-February 1907, are invaluable contemporary sources. See also P'an Wei-tung, *The Chinese Constitution: A Study of Forty Years of Constitution-making in China*, Tsao Wen-yen, *The Constitutional Structure of Modern China*, and the article by E-tu Zen Sun, "The Chinese Constitutional Missions of 1905-1906." Since there are a few English works summarizing this early constitutional history, no attempt is made in the text to sketch it in.

### d. Yuan Shih-k'ai and the Modern Army

Shen Tsu-hsien and Wu K'ai-sheng, *Jung-an ti-tzu chi* (An account of Jung-an [Yuan Shih-k'ai] by his disciples), is actually the official biography of Yuan Shih-k'ai. Shen Tsu-hsien was also the compiler of *Yang-shou-yuan tsou-i chi-yao*, a collection of important memorials of Yuan Shih-k'ai. "Yuan ta-tsung-t'ung lueh-shih" in Shang Ping-ho, *Hsin-jen ch'un-ch'iu* (A chronicle of 1911-1912), ch. 4, contains a biographical sketch. Chu Wu, "Wo-kuo chih lu-chün," in *Kuo-feng pao*, Chiang Fang-chen, "Chung-kuo wu-shih-nien lai chün-shih pien-ch'ien shih," and Wen Kung-chih, *Tsui-chin san-shih-nien Chung-kuo chün-shih shih*, deal with military history. See also Georg Wegneuer, "Der Gouverneur von Shantung," *Deutsche Kolonialzeitung*, 27 (June 1901); and Ralph L. Powell, "The Rise of Yuan Shih-k'ai and the Pei-yang Army," *Papers on China*, 3:225-256 (1949), which has been developed in a doctoral dissertation at Harvard. Arthur W. Hummel, Jr., *Yuan Shih-k'ai as an Official under the Manchus*, is a master of art's thesis at the University of Chicago (1949).

### NOTES

1. The extensive bibliography awaiting study in this field is indicated in Fairbank and Liu, *Modern China*. See also *Bibliography of Modern*

*Chinese Law in the Library of Congress*, compiled in 1944, which includes 501 items in Chinese and Western languages.

2. See CSL, Te-tsung, 476. 8-10b.

3. *Ibid.*, 481. 4b.

4. These joint products were written as follows: Liu K'un-i asked Chang Chih-tung to be the chief writer; Liu and his subordinates, Chang Chien, Shen Tseng-chih, and others, each wrote suggestions and sent them to Chang. Chang also ordered his own subordinates to offer opinions. He then put all these ideas together and edited them. Writing one or two items each day, it took him more than a month to finish the composition (see Hu Chün, *Chang Wen-hsiang-kung nien-p'u*, 4. 13).

5. See CSL, Te-tsung, 486. 15b.

6. *Ibid.*, 485. 14, 19; and 486. 6.

7. From *Tsou-i* in *Chang Wen-hsiang-kung ch'üan-chi*, 52. 9b-29.

8. Cf. Legge, *The Works of Mencius*, bk. VI, pt. II, ch. 15.

9. From *Chang Wen-hsiang-kung ch'üan-chi*, 53. 1-33.

10. *Ibid.*, 54. 1-36.

11. See Teng Ssu-yü, *Chung-kuo k'ao-shih chih-tu shih* (A history of the Chinese civil service examination system), pp. 299-306.

12. The memorial is in *Kuang-hsü cheng-yao*, 13. 18b-20; a fairly accurate English translation of the memorial is in R. S. Gundry, *China Present and Past*, pp. 387-393.

13. The joint memorial of 1905 and the imperial Decree announcing the termination of the system are translated by John C. Ferguson, "The Abolition of the Competitive Examinations in China," *Journal of the American Oriental Society*, 27:79-87 (1906).

14. From *Kuang-hsü cheng-yao*, 29. 7-9.

15. Tai Hung-tz'u and Tuan-fang, *Ou-Mei cheng-chih yao-i*, 4, see. 1, 30-33b.

16. *Ibid.*, 2b-5.

17. We will not attempt here any judgment of Yuan's career; two

American scholars have dealt with different aspects of it in dissertations. (See last two entries under Sources.)

## CHAPTER XXI   ECONOMIC DEVELOPMENT

### SOURCES

The main sources for Sheng Hsuan-huai and Chang Chien are the *Yü-chai ts'un-kao* and *Chang Chi-tzu chiu-lu*, respectively. Both contain full collections of their writings well arranged and printed. In addition to the short biography at the beginning of each of these works, there is a detailed biography of Chang Chien by his son, containing many quotations from his writings; and Chiang I-hsueh, "Chang Chien i-chuan," is a draft biography intended for a "dynastic" history of the period of the Republic. Apart from these, P'eng Tse-i's "Chang Chien ti ssu-hsiang chi ch'i shih-yeh" (Chang's ideas and career) is a good summary based on *Chang Chi-tzu chiu-lu*. There is an English pamphlet entitled *Life of the Honourable Chang Chien with an Account of the Enterprises Inaugurated by Him* (Shanghai, 1915), author's name unknown; and there are two short papers by Davy H. McCall, "Chang Chien and the Establishment of the Tungchow Mills," and "Chang Chien—Mandarin Turned Manufacturer."

For other industrialists we may mention Hsü Jun (1838-1911), *Hsü Yü-chai tzu-hsü nien-p'u*, the informative autobiography of an important businessman, which contains many references to the enterprises of others of his wide acquaintance; Mu Hsiang-yueh (1876-1943), *Ou-ch'u ssu-shih tzu-shu*, the reminiscences of a leading textile manufacturer, written to mark his fortieth birthday, and published in 1926; and Hsü Ying's *Tang-tai Chung-kuo shih-yeh jen-wu chih*, a sketch of twenty-eight contemporary industrialists based on interviews and useful for general reference. Yang Lien-sheng's *Topics in Chinese History*, containing carefully selected sources under each topic, is an important tool for students in Chinese history and economics. The same author's *Money and Credit in China* is a critical and compact account which supplies useful background material regarding economic development.

While this is not the place for a list of works on Chinese economic growth in this period, the following works are noteworthy for our purpose: Frank M. Tamagna, *Banking and Finance in China*; Li P'ei-en, "Chin-pai-nien lai Chung-kuo chih yin-hang" (Banking in China during the last century); *Yin-hang nien-chien* (Yearbook of banking); "Modern Business in China: The Bank of China before 1935" by S. H. Chafkin; "Ch'ing-mo Han-yang t'ieh-ch'ang" (The Hanyang iron and steel works) by Ch'üan Han-sheng; the *Rise of the Modern Chinese Business Class* by Marion J. Levy, Jr. and Shih Kuo-heng; *Eastern Industrialization and its Effect on the West* by G. E. Hubbard; and Hsia Yen-te, *Chung-kuo chin-pai-nien ching-chi ssu-hsiang*, on economic thought. The last, by Hsia, is a very useful selection of excerpts from many of the men studied in the present volume, with sources and notes.

### NOTES

1. H. B. Morse, *International Relations of the Chinese Empire*, III, 46.

2. See *Ta-Ch'ing Kuang-hsü hsin fa-ling* (New laws and ordinances of the Kuang-hsü reign), compiled by the Commercial Press, Shanghai, 1909, *ts'e* 16, section 10.

3. Kung Chün, *Chung-kuo hsin-kung-yeh fa-chan-shih ta-kang*, pp. 65-88.

4. Cp. Weng Wen-hao, "Wu-shih-nien lai chi ching-chi chien-she" (Economic reconstruction in the last fifty years) in *Wu-shih-nien lai ti Chung-kuo* (China during the last fifty years), p. 98.

5. *Ibid.*, pp. 98-99; and Tamagna, *Banking and Finance in China*, p. 37.

6. Hsi Yin, "Keng-tzu ch'üan-huo tung-nan hu-pao chih chi-shih" (A reliable account of the mutual protection [of foreigners and Chinese] in

southeastern China during the Boxer Uprising), *Jen-wen*, 2.7: 1-7 (September 1931).

7. J. O. P. Bland, *Li Hung-chang*, p. 121.

8. H. B. Morse, *International Relations of the Chinese Empire*, III, 362.

9. *Yü-chai ts'un-kao*, 24. 27b.

10. *Ibid.*, 31. 32b-33.

11. *Ibid.*, 1. 14-15.

12. Cp. *ibid.*, 25. 12b.

13. See Sheng Hsuan-huai's biography, *hsing-shu*, in *Yü-chai ts'un-kao*, *ts'e* 1. 61.

14. Cp. Chang Hsiao-jo, *Nan-t'ung Chang Chi-chih hsien-sheng chuan-chi* (A biography of Chang Chien), pp. 67-68; 228-229.

15. From Chang Chien, *Chang Chi-tzu chiu-lu*, *shih-yeh lu*, 1. 7b-8.

16. Cp. *ibid.*, 6. 5b-6.

17. *Ibid.*, 8. 33b-36.

18. From *Chang Chi-tzu chiu-lu*, *chuan-lu*, 4. 1-34.

19. See Chang Chien's chronological biography at the beginning of *Chang Chi-tzu chiu-lu*.

20. *Nan-t'ung Chang Chi-chih hsien-sheng chuan-chi*, p. 5.

21. From *Chang Chi-tzu chiu-lu*, *shih-yeh lu*, 5. 13b-14.

22. *Ibid.*, *cheng-wen lu*, 9. 3b-5b.

# CHAPTER XXII  LIANG CH'I-CH'AO AND NATIONALISM

### SOURCES

For sources on Liang, see under Chapter XVI.

### NOTE

1. From *Hsin-min ts'ung-pao*, 1:1-10 (January 1902).

# CHAPTER XXIII   SUN YAT-SEN'S EARLY REVOLUTIONARY PROGRAM

### SOURCES

For sources on Sun Yat-sen see Chapter XXVII below.

### NOTES

1. Sun Yat-sen's letter to Li Hung-chang is in Tsou Lu, *Chung-kuo Kuo-min-tang shih-kao* (Draft history of the Kuomintang of China), Min-chih shu-chü edition, 1. 6-19. A Japanese translation of Sun's letter is in Kayano Chōchi, *Chūka-minkoku kakumei hikyu*, and an extract appears in Léon Wieger, *Chine moderne*, vol. 1.

2. The Manifesto of the Hsing-Chung-hui is in *Chung-shan ch'üan-shu*, section on manifestoes, 4. 1-4, and in Tsou Lu, *Chung-kuo Kuo-min-tang shih-kao*, pt. 1. 2-6, with introductory note and complete text. An English excerpt from the Manifesto is in Lyon Sharman, *Sun Yat-sen, his Life and its Meaning: A Critical Biography*, p. 36, and the excerpt is quoted in full by Donald G. Tewksbury, *Source Book on Far Eastern Political Ideologies, Modern Period, China-Japan*, p. 1.

3. From *Chung-shan ch'üan-shu*, "Manifestoes," 4. 1-4. See also Tsou Lu, *Chung-kuo Kuo-min-tang shih-kao*, 1. 2.

4. T'ien-yun (lit., "Heavenly rotation") was the reign title used by Chang Pu-wei at the end of the Ming Dynasty (1637). It was repeatedly used in the documents issued by the T'ung-meng-hui, indicating the revolutionists' repudiation of Manchu rule by their refusal to adopt its reign style.

5. Shih Ching-t'ang (posthumous name, Chin Kao-tsu) was the founder of the Chin Dynasty (936-941). He was a traitor towards the later T'ang and was made emperor by the Khitans. See *Chiu Wu-tai shih* (The old history of the Five Dynasties), *chüan* 75-76. For Wu San-kuei, see Hummel, pp. 877-880.

6. This slogan and the three preceding are about all of this document that has heretofore been available in English. See Donald G. Tewksbury, *Source Book on Far Eastern Political Ideologies*, Modern Period, p. 7.

## CHAPTER XXIV. THE SEARCH FOR NEW PRINCIPLES

**SOURCES**

a. *The Variety of the New Thought*

The following items are suggested in addition to the bibliography given in Wen-han Kiang (Chiang Wen-han), *The Chinese Student Movement*, pp. 173-176, which deals principally with the period after 1923; for source materials, see also Fairbank and Liu, *Modern China*, especially section 8, "Intellectual and Literary History." For a general introduction, Ts'ai Yuan-p'ei, "Wu-shih-nien lai Chung-kuo chih che-hsueh" (Chinese philosophy in the last fifty years), is noteworthy. Note also Wu Ch'i-yuan, *Chung-kuo hsin-wen-hua yun-tung kai-kuan* (A general review of China's new culture movement); Ch'en Tuan-chih, *Wu-ssu yun-tung chih shih ti p'ing-chia* (A historical review of the May Fourth Movement); Hua Kang, *Wu-ssu yun-tung shih* (A history of the May Fourth Movement); Liu Hsi-san, "Wu-ssu i-hou Chung-kuo ko-p'ai ssu-hsiang-chia tui-yü Hsi-yang wen-ming ti t'ai-tu" (Attitudes of Chinese thinkers of various groups toward Western civilization since the May Fourth Movement), which gives an all-round summary of all schools of thought; Huang Ti, "Wu-ssu i-lai chih Chung-kuo hsueh-ch'ao" (Chinese student strikes since the May Fourth Movement), which was a master's thesis in sociology. Ch'en Jen-pai, "Lun wu-ssu yun-tung chih hua-shih-tai ti i-i" (On the significance of the epoch-making May Fourth Movement), and Hu Shih, "Wo-men tui-yü Hsi-yang chin-tai wen-ming ti t'ai-tu" (Our attitude toward modern Western civilization), are two useful magazine articles. Wang Tsao-shih, "Chung-Hsi chieh-ch'u-hou she-hui-shang ti pien-hua" (Social changes after the contact between

China and the West), traces developments after the Opium War. The *Shen-pao* volume, *Tsui-chin chih wu-shih-nien*, and P'an Kung chan, *Wu shih-nien-lai ti Chung-kuo* (China in the last fifty years), both have valuable entries.

About Ku Hung-ming, besides his own writings both in Chinese and Western languages, there are essays by Lin Yü-t'ang, Yuan Chen-ying, Ssu-luan, Meng Ch'i, Ch'en Ch'ang-hua, Chen Ying, and others in the magazine *Jen-chien shih*, and an article by Hu Shih in *Ta-kung-pao*, literary supplement, no. 164. Chang Shih-chao, *Ch'ang-sha Chang-shih ts'ung-kao* (Collected drafts of Chang Shih-chao of Changsha), is an interesting source. On nationalism, see *Kuo-chia chu-i chiang-yen chi* (Collected essays on nationalism). On Chang Ping-lin, see Hsü Shou-ch'ang's volume by that title. T'ai-hsü, *Jen-sheng-kuan ti k'o-hsueh* (A science of the philosophy of life), is a discussion of Chinese cultural problems from a Buddhist point of view. See also Wu Ching-heng, *Wu Chih-hui hsien-sheng wen-ts'un* (Collected essays of Wu Chih-hui); and Li Shih-ch'en, *Jen-sheng che-hsueh* (Philosophy of life). Other helpful items for this period include Chang Chien-fu, "Chin san-pai-nien Chung-kuo min-tsu ko-ming yun-tung ti yen-chin" (The development of the Chinese nationalist revolution during the last three hundred years); Kuo Chan-po, *Chin wu-shih-nien Chung-kuo ssu-hsiang shih* (A history of Chinese thought during the last fifty years); Ch'en Hsü-ching, *Chung-kuo wen-hua ti ch'u-lu* (The future of Chinese culture); and Yang K'un, "Chung-kuo tsui-chin san-shih-nien chih ch'u-pan chieh" (Chinese publications during the last thirty years [mainly books on sociology]).

### b. *Ts'ai Yuan-p'ei and Freedom of Education*

The main educational ideas of Ts'ai Yuan-p'ei are preserved in his collected speeches, articles, and letters published under the title, *Ts'ai Chieh-min hsien-sheng yen-hsing lu*. A succinct autobiography, "Wo tsai chiao-yü-chieh ti ching-yen," is, in *Tzu-chuan chih i-chang*, edited by T'ao K'ang-te; and a short biography entitled *Ts'ai Chieh-min hsien-*

*sheng chuan-lueh* was written by Kao Nai-t'ung. Ts'ai's connection with Peking University is described by himself in "Wo tsai Pei-ching ta-hsueh ti ching-kuo" and in another article, "Ts'ai Yuan-p'ei yü Pei-ching ta-hsueh," written by Lao Kan. See also Ts'ai Yuan-p'ei, "The Development of Chinese Education," in *Asiatic Review*. There is a special memorial issue, "Chui-tao Ts'ai Chieh-min hsien-sheng t'e-chi," in *Tung-fang tsa-chih*; another in *Yü-chou-feng*, 24 and 28; and two memorial volumes, *Ch'ing-chu Ts'ai Yuan-p'ei hsien-sheng liu-shih-wu-sui lun-wen chi*, presented to him by fellows and assistants of the Academia Sinica and published in 1933. These volumes contain academic articles, but the brief preface notes Dr. Ts'ai's contribution to the academic world through his directorship of the Academia Sinica. Chou Tso-jen's "Chi Ts'ai Chieh-min hsien-sheng ti shih" is an interesting short essay. Miss Chin-hsieo Tai has written a doctoral dissertation in the Harvard Graduate School of Education on "The Life and Work of Ts'ai Yuan-p'ei," with extensive bibliography.

**NOTES**

1. See the volume by Conrad Brandt, Benjamin Schwartz, and John K. Fairbank, *A Documentary History of Chinese Communism*, which deals with the development of Marxist-Leninist doctrine in China from 1921 to 1950.

2. For more biographical information, see *Who's Who in China*, 1926 and 1936 editions.

3. See Robert K. Sakai, "Ts'ai Yuan-p'ei as a Synthesizer of Western and Chinese Thought," *Papers on China*, Cambridge, 3:170-192 (May 1949). Mr. Sakai has written a doctoral dissertation at Harvard on "Politics and Education in Modern China."

4. T'ang Leang-li, *The Foundations of Modern China*, p. 87. See also Ts'ai Yuan-p'ei, "Wo tsai Pei-ching ta-hsueh ti ching-kuo."

5. From *Ts'ai Chieh-min hsien-sheng yen-hsing lu*, pp. 189-203.

6. Ch. 9 of the *Book of Rites* (*Li chi*): "Ta-tao chih hsing yeh, t'ien-

hsia wei kung" ("When the great doctrine is carried out, the empire will be for the common weal"). This sentence is condensed by Ts'ai as "Ta-tao wei kung."

7. From "*Ts'ai Chieh-min hsien-sheng yen-hsing lu*, pp. 314-325.
8. Ibid., p. 227.

## CHAPTER XXV  EARLY CONVERTS TO MARXISM

### SOURCES

The primary sources on Ch'en Tu-hsiu are the *Tu-hsiu wen-ts'un*, *Hsin-ch'ing-nien*, vol. 1, and a short autobiography about his early life, "Shih-an tzu-chuan." See also the old periodicals *Hsiang-tao* and *Mei-chou p'ing-lun*; Ch'en Tung-hsiao (comp.), *Ch'en Tu-hsiu p'ing-lun* (A critique of Ch'en Tu-hsiu); B. Schwartz, "Ch'en Tu-hsiu, his Pre-Communist Phase," *Papers on China*, 2. 167-197, and his *Chinese Communism and the Rise of Mao*. There are also several entries referring to Ch'en Tu-hsiu in C. Martin Wilbur (ed.), *Chinese Sources on the History of the Chinese Communist Movement*. A booklet, *Ch'en Tu-hsiu ti tsui-hou chien-chieh* (Ch'en Tu-hsiu's final views), was published by the Tzu-yu Chung-kuo ch'u-pan she in Hongkong (1950), and has been translated for publication in English.

On Li Ta-chao see *Hsin-ch'ing-nien*, vols. 1-7, and *Hsiang-tao* and other magazines listed in *Chung-kuo hsin-wen-hsueh ta-hsi*, vol. 10, compiled by A-ying. Li also wrote a book on democracy, *P'ing-min chu-i*. Chin Yü-min, "Li Ta-chao yü wu-ssu yun-tung" (Li Ta-chao and the May Fourth Movement), in *Kuan-ch'a*, 6. 13 (May 1, 1950), and Yang Yung-kuo, "Li Shou-ch'ang hsien-sheng ti ssu-hsiang" (The thought of Li Shou-ch'ang [Ta-chao]), *Tu-shu yü ch'u-pan*, no. 2: 4-7 (1947), are short articles of some use. See also Hua Ying-shen, *Chung-kuo Kung-ch'an-tang lieh-shih chuan*, in which there is a short biography of Li Ta-chao.

For selections from the works on Chinese communism published in Japanese, see the two bibliographies in Brandt, Schwartz, and Fairbank, A *Documentary History of Chinese Communism*; and Ichiro Shirato (C. M. Wilbur, ed.), *Japanese Sources on the History of the Chinese Communist Movement* (New York: East Asian Institute of Columbia University, 1953), 69 pp.

### NOTES

1. "Ching-kao ch'ing-nien" (*Ching-kao*, lit., respectful warning), first article in the first issue, *Hsin-ch'ing-nien*, 1.1 (Sept. 15, 1915).

2. According to legend, Ts'ao-fu and Hsü Yu both refused to accept the throne when the Emperor Yao offered it to them successively, thus showing their utter contempt for worldly glory.

3. Li Ta-chao, "Wo-ti Ma-k'o-ssu chu-i kuan" (My view of Marxism), *Hsin-ch'ing-nien*, 6.5:521-537 (May 1919).

4. "Bolshevism ti sheng-li," *Hsin-ch'ing-nien*, 5.5:442-448 (Nov. 15, 1918).

5. *Ibid*. This and the two following quotations are presented without reference data in the Chinese text, so our retranslations have not been compared with the English originals.

6. "Preface" to *K'o-hsueh yü jen-sheng-kuan* (Science and the philosophy of life), a collection of essays edited by Ya-tung t'u-shu-kuan, pp. 5-11.

## CHAPTER XXVI  HU SHIH AND PRAGMATISM IN CHINA

### SOURCES

Dr. Hu has been a prolific writer during much of his career. For the chief collections of his works, see Fairbank and Liu, *Modern China*, and also the index to that volume. His *Ssu-shih tzu-shu* (Autobiography at forty) and *Hu Shih liu-hsueh jih-chi* (Hu Shih's diary when he studied abroad), which is better than his *Ts'ang-hui-shih cha-chi* (Diary of student days in America), offer much biographical material. *Hu Shih wen-ts'un* (collected essays), *Hu Shih wen-ts'un erh-chi* (second collection), and *Hu Shih wen-ts'un san-chi* (third collection) are particularly useful because they include not only his own work but also, in cases of controversy, the writings of others who discussed problems with him. His edition of the first volume of the *Chung-kuo hsin-wen-hsueh ta-hsi* contains discussions on the theory of the new literature; and his own book, *The Chinese Renaissance*, gives a remarkable summary of the Chinese cultural heritage and the new literature movement. Of works from other points of view there are: Yeh Ch'ing, *Hu Shih p'i-p'an* (Critique of Hu Shih); Wang Feng-yuan, *Chung-kuo hsin-wen-hsueh yun-tung shu-p'ing* (Narration of and comments on the new literature movement in China); and a number of articles attacking or defending his point of view, which we do not attempt to list. Note the recent volume by John De Francis, *Nationalism and Language Reform in China*.

## NOTES

1. From *Hu Shih wen-ts'un* (Collected essays of Hu Shih), 4. 151-164.

2. Part X of the essay, "Chinese literature in the past fifty years," in *Hu Shih wen-ts'un erh-chi* (Second collection of the essays of Hu Shih), 2. 188-213. This essay was first published in *Tsui-chin chih wu-shih-nien*.

# CHAPTER XXVII   SUN YAT-SEN'S REORIENTATION OF THE REVOLUTION

### SOURCES

For materials in Chinese, largely unavailable in English, on Sun's career and thought, see Fairbank and Liu, *Modern China*, index. For the various changes in Sun Yat-sen's approach to the solution of China's problems, the most useful source is Hu Han-min (ed.), *Tsung-li ch'üan-chi* (Complete collection of the works of the Director-general); see also Tsou Lu, *Chung-kuo Kuo-min-tang shih-kao* (A draft history of the Kuomintang), the best work thus far available. Chou Fu-hai, *San-min chu-i chih li-lun ti t'i-hsi*, was considered one of the best textbooks of party doctrine. Lou T'ung-sun, *San-min chu-i yen-chiu*, is another textbook on the subject for beginners. A useful book on Sun's system of thinking is Liu Ping-li, *Kuo-fu ssu-hsiang t'i-hsi shu-yao*. Articles about Sun Yat-sen are numerous. In English, apart from translations of Sun's works, mention should be made of Paul M. A. Linebarger, *The Political Doctrines of Sun Yat-sen*, and Ch'ien Tuan-sheng, *The Government and Politics of China*. In Japanese, Ono Noriaki's *Son Bun*, with a short bibliography of Japanese works, may be mentioned. A recent and provocative study of the Three Principles from the point of view of Chinese philosophy may be found in Ojima Sukema, *Chūgoku no kakumei shisō*. For other works in Japanese, see Fairbank and Banno, *Japanese Studies of Modern China*. Among the numerous biographies in Western languages, that by Lyon Sharman is still one of the most reliable. A recent Western study which makes interesting use of Japanese sources is by Marius B. Jansen, *Adventurers and Revolutionaries: The Japanese and Sun Yat-sen* (Cambridge: Harvard University Press, 1954). At the headquarters of the Kuomintang Reform Committee in Taipei, valuable scholarly work is being done by Ts'ui Shu-ch'in (on the political thought of Sun Yat-sen) and by Chang Ch'i-yun (see his *Tang-shih kai-yao, chin liu-shih-nien Chung-kuo ko-ming shih* [A general history of the Kuomintang, a history of the Chinese revolution in the last sixty years], published by the Kuomintang Reform Committee, 1952, 5 vols. ,2724 pp.).

## NOTES

1. See Tsou Lu, *Chung-kuo Kuo-min-tang shih-kao*, pp. 159-170, and William E. Nelson, "One-party Government in China," in *Papers on China*, vol. 2.

2. From "Neng-chih pi neng-hsing," ch. 6 of *Sun Wen hsueh-shuo* (The philosophy of Sun Yat-sen), in *Chung-shan ch'üan-shu*, 4. 50-63.

3. From a speech delivered to Kuomintang members during the reorganization of the Kuomintang, December 1, 1923, *Tsung-li ch'üan-chi*, 2. 314-324. Sentences from this speech are also translated in Tsui Shu-chin, "The Influence of the Canton-Moscow Entente," p. 102.

4. *Hsun-lien yuan*: officially Borodin held the position of adviser to the Nationalist Government.

# CHAPTER XXVIII  LIANG CH'I-CH'AO'S REVIEW OF CHINA'S PROGRESS, 1873-1922

## SOURCES

For sources on Liang, see under Ch. XVI. For a recent list of works on the Republican period, see Su Te-yung, "Min-kuo shih-liao shu-mu ch'u-pien" (A bibliography of the history of the Republic of China), *Hsueh-shu chi-k'an*, 1. 3: 220-227 (March 1953), 1. 4: 152-176 (June), 2. 1: 160-181 (September), published by "Chung-hua wen-hua ch'u-pan shih-yeh wei-yuan-hui", Taiwan.

## NOTES

1. Liang Ch'i-ch'ao, "Lao-tzu che-hsueh" (The philosophy of Lao-tzu), *Yin-ping-shih ho-chi*, *Wen-chi* (Collected essays), pt. 63: 14-14b (1920).

2. "Tung-nan ta-hsueh k'o-pi kao-pieh tz'u" (Parting speech after completing classes at Tung-nan University), *ibid.*, pt. 70: 3b-4 (1923).

3. From "Wu-shih-nien Chung-kuo chin-hua kai-lun," *ibid.*, ts'e 14, 39. 39-48.

# BIBLIOGRAPHY

This is a single alphabetic list of all items cited above, except that some Chinese titles cited in the text but not used by us are listed in the Glossary below. In some cases, complete information is unavailable; in others, the translation of titles is impossible. The quality of the items we have cited varies widely, from magistral monographs to thin brief notices, but having seen the latter we have thought it useful to include them, in the effort to save others the experience of hope and disillusionment that comes from "discovering" an article which has an interesting title but which at the end of a few pages leaves the reader exactly where he was before. This bibliography makes no effort at completeness, but our Notes and Sources have tried to indicate the jumping-off places for further research. Abbreviations (like CSPSR) which we have used above are also in this list. (A few recent items are cited only under Sources above.)

Analects of Confucius, see Waley.

A-ying 阿英, (Pen-name of Ch'ien Hsing-ts'un 钱杏邨), Chung-kuo hsin-wen-hsueh ta-hsi, vol. 10, Shih-liao, so-yin 中国新文学大系, 史料, 索引 (A corpus of China's new literature, historical data and index; Shanghai: Liang-yu Co., 1936), 513+100 pp. See also Chao Chia-pi.

Bain, Chester A., "Commodore Matthew Perry, Humphrey Marshall, and the Taiping Rebellion," Far Eastern Quarterly, 10.3:258-270 (May 1951).

Bales, W. L., Tso Tsung-t'ang: Soldier and Statesman of Old China (Shanghai: Kelly and Walsh, 1937), 436 pp.

Banno Masataka 坂野正高, "Gaikō kōshō ni okeru Shimmatsu kanjin no kōdō yōshiki" 外交交涉に於ける清末官人の行动样式 ("Behaviours of Mandarins as diplomats late in the Ch'ing Dynasty"), Kokusaihō gaikō zasshi 国际法外交杂志, 48.4:18-56 (October 1949), 48.6:37-71

(December 1949).

Banno Masataka 坂野正高,"'Sō-ri ga-mon' setsuritsu no haikei"总理衙门设立の背景 (The background of the establishment of the Tsungli Yamen), Kokusaihō gaikō zasshi 国际法外交杂志, 51. 4:360-402 (August 1952), 51. 5:506-541 (October 1952), 52. 3:89-111 (June 1953).

Bernard, Henri, S. J., Aux Portes de la Chine; les missionnaires du seizième siècle, 1514-1588 (Tientsin: en vente à la Procure de la Mission de Sienshien, 1933), 283 pp.

Bernard, Henri, S. J., Matteo Ricci's Scientific Contribution to China, tr. by Edward Chalmers Werner (Peiping: H. Vetch, 1935), 108 pp.

Bernard, Henri, S. J., "Notes on the Introduction of the Natural Sciences," Yenching Journal of Social Studies 3:220-241 (1941).

Bernard, Henri, S. J., "Les adaptations chinoises d'ouvrages européens: bibliographie chronologique depuis la venue des Portugais à Canton jusqu'à la mission française de Pekin, 1514-1688," Monumenta Serica 10:1-57, 309-388 (1945).

Biggerstaff, Knight, "The Tung-Wen Kuan," CSPSR 18. 3:307-340 (October 1934).

Biggerstaff, Knight, "The Ch'ung-hou Mission to France, 1870-1871," Nankai Social and Economic Quarterly, 8. 3:633-647 (October 1935).

Biggerstaff, Knight, "The Establishment of Permanent Chinese Diplomatic Missions Abroad," CSPSR 20. 1:1-41 (April 1936).

Biggerstaff, Knight, "The Official Chinese Attitude toward the Burlingame Mission," American Historical Review, 41. 4:682-702 (July 1936).

Biggerstaff, Knight, "The First Chinese Mission of Investigation Sent to Europe," Pacific Historical Review, 6. 4:307-320 (December 1937).

Biggerstaff, Knight, "Anson Burlingame's Instructions from the Chinese Foreign Office," Far Eastern Quarterly, 1. 3: 277-279 (May 1942).

Biggerstaff, Knight, "The Secret Correspondence of 1867-1868: Views of Leading Chinese Statesmen Regarding the Further Opening of China to Western Influence," Journal of Modern History, 22. 2: 122-136 (June 1950).

Bland, J. O. P., Li Hung-chang (New York, 1917), 327 pp.

Bland, J. O. P., Backhouse, E., China Under the Empress Dowager (London, 1910), 525 pp.

Boardman, Eugene P., "Christian Influence upon the Ideology of the Taiping Rebellion," Far Eastern Quarterly, 10. 2: 115-124 (February 1951).

Boardman, Eugene P., Christian Influence upon the Ideology of the Taiping Rebellion 1851-1864 (The University of Wisconsin Press, 1952), 188 pp.

Bodde, Derk, see Feng Yu-lan.

Book of Changes, see Chou-i cheng-i.

Book of History, see Shang-shu cheng-i.

Book of Rites, see Li Ki.

Brandt Conrad, Benjamin Schwartz, and J. K. Fairbank, A Documentary History of Chinese Communism (Cambridge: Harvard University Press, 1952), 552 pp. (London: Allen and Unwin).

British Parliamentary Papers, Correspondence Relative to the Earl of Elgin's Special Mission to China and Japan 1857-1859, presented to the House of Lords by command, 1859.

Britton, Roswell S., The Chinese Periodical Press 1800-1912 (Shanghai: Kelly and Walsh, 1933), 143 pp.

Burt, E. W., "The Centenary of Timothy Richard," Baptist Quarterly, 343-348 (Jan. -Apr. 1945).

Burt, E. W., "Timothy Richard: His Contribution to Modern

China," International Review of Missions, 293-300 (July 1945).

Cameron, Meribeth E., "The Public Career of Chang Chih-tung 1837-1909," Pacific Historical Review, 7.3: 187-210 (September 1938).

Cameron, Meribeth E., The Reform Movement in China, 1898-1912 (London: Oxford University Press, 1931 edition), 223 pp.

Candler, W. A., Young J. Allen (Nashville: Cokesbury Press, 1931), 245 pp.

Carlson, Ellsworth, "The K'ai-p'ing Mines, 1877-1912: A Case Study of Early Chinese Industrialization" (Cambridge, Mass: dissertation for the Ph. D. in History, Harvard University, 1952).

Chafkin, S. H., "Modern Business in China: The Bank of China before 1935," Papers on China, 2:103-133 (May 1948).

Ch'an-an 忏庵, "Chang P'ei-lun yü Li Hung-chang" 张佩纶与李鸿章 (Chang P'ei-lun and Li Hung-chang), Ku-chin 古今, no. 50:18-20 (July 1944).

Chang Ch'i-yun 张其昀, "Liang Jen-kung ssu-hsiang pieh-lu" 梁任公思想别录 (Supplementary record on the ideas of Liang Ch'i-ch'ao), in Ssu-hsiang yü shih-tai 思想与时代, vol. 4.

Chang Chien 张謇, Chang Chi-tzu chiu-lu 张季子九录 (Collected writings of Chang Chien; Shanghai: Chung-hua shu-chü, 1931), 80+10 chüan.

Chang Chien 张謇, Cheng-wen lu 政闻录 (Notes on government), in Chang Chi-tzu chiu-lu.

Chang Chien 张謇, Chuan-lu 专录 (Special notes), in Chang Chi-tzu chiu-lu.

Chang Chien 张謇, Shih-yeh lu 实业录 (Notes on industry), in Chang Chi-tzu chiu-lu.

Chang Chien 张謇, Life of the Honorable Chang Chien with an Account of the Enterprizes Inaugurated by Him (Shanghai, 1915), 35 pp.

Chang Chien 张謇, see P'eng Tse-i.

Chang Chien-fu 张健甫, "Chin san-pai-nien Chung-kuo min-tsu ko-ming yun-tung ti yen-chin" 近三百年中国民族革命运动的演进 (The development of the Chinese national revolution during the last three hundred years), Chien-she yen-chin 建设研究, 7.1:41-47 (March 1942).

Chang Chih-tung 张之洞, Chang Wen-hsiang-kung ch'üan-chi 张文襄公全集 (The complete works of Chang Chih-tung), printed in 1928, 229 chüan.

Chang Chih-tung 张之洞, Chang Wen-hsiang-kung nien-p'u 张文襄公年谱 (A chronological biography of Chang Chih-tung), compiled by Hsü T'ung-hsin 许同莘 (Chungking: Commercial Press, 1944) 229 pp. See also Hu Chün.

Chang Chih-tung 张之洞, Chang Wen-hsiang-kung tsou-i 张文襄公奏议 (The memorials of Chang Chih-tung), in Chang Wen-hsiang-kung ch'üan-chi.

Chang Chih-tung 张之洞, "Cheng-ch'üan" 正权 (Rectification of political rights), in Chang Wen-hsiang-kung ch'üan-chi, chüan 202.

Chang Chih-tung 张之洞, "Ch'ü-tu" 去毒 (To remove the poison), in Chang Wen-hsiang-kung ch'üan-chi, chüan 202.

Chang Chih-tung 张之洞, Ch'üan-hsueh-p'ien 劝学篇 (Exhortation to study), printed in 1898, 2 chüan, in Chang Wen-hsiang-kung ch'üan-chi, chüan 202-203; see also the punctuated edition in Chien-hsi ts'un-she ts'ung-k'o 渐西村舍丛刻, and the separate edition reprinted in Chekiang in 1898.

Chang Chih-tung 张之洞, "Fei kung-chiao" 非攻教 (Condemnation of attacks on missionaries), in Chang Wen-hsiang-kung ch'üan-chi, chüan 203.

Chang Chih-tung 张之洞, "Hsün-hsü" 循序 (Following the proper order), in Chang Wen-hsiang-kung ch'üan-chi, chüan 202.

Chang Chih-tung 张之洞, "Pien-fa" 变法 (On reform), in Chang Wen-hsiang-kung ch'üan-chi, chüan 203.

Chang Chih-tung 张之洞, Shu-mu ta-wen 书目答问 (Annotated

bibliography of basic Chinese works), printed in 1878, 4 chüan.

Chang Chih-tung 张之洞, see Chang Wen-hsiang-kung; Woodbridge; Tobar.

Chang Ch'iung-chang 张綑章, "Li Hung-chang i-shih i-shu"李鸿章轶事一束 (Anecdotes about Li Hung-chang), Nü-shih-hsueh-yuan ch'i-k'an, 1.1 (Jan. 1933). Pages are not numbered consecutively.

Chang Ch'iung-chang 张綑章, "Tz'u-hsi t'ai-hou i-shih"慈禧太后轶事 (Anecdotes about the Empress Dowager Tz'u-hsi), Nü-shih-hsueh-yuan ch'i-k'an, 1.2 (July 1933). Pages are not consecutively numbered.

Chang Ch'o-hsün 张焯焄, "Ch'i-shih-nien lai Chung-kuo ping-ch'i chih chih-tsao" 七十年来中国兵器之制造 (The making of military weapons in China during the last seventy years), Tung-fang tsa-chih, 32.2:21-30 (1936).

Chang Chung-fu 张忠黻, "Tsung-li ko-kuo shih-wu ya-men chih yuan-ch'i"总理各国事务衙门之源起(The origin of the Tsungli Yamen), Wai-chiao yueh-pao, 3.1:1-11 (1933).

Chang En-lung 张恩龙, "Ming-Ch'ing liang-tai lai-Hua wai-jen k'ao-lueh"明清两代来华外人考略(A brief account of the foreigners who came to China during the Ming and Ch'ing dynasties), T'u-shu-kuan-hsueh chi-k'an 图书馆学季刊, 4.3-4:447-472 (Dec. 1930); and 5.1:83-104 (March 1931).

Chang Hsi-t'ang 张西堂, Wang Ch'uan-shan hsueh-p'u 王船山学谱 (An academic sketch of Wang Fu-chih; Shanghai: Commercial Press, 1938), 219 pp.

Chang Hsi-t'ung, "The Earliest Phase of the Introduction of Western Political Science into China," Yenching Journal of Social Studies 5:1-29 (duly 1950).

Chang Hsiao-jo 张孝若, Nan-t'ung Chang Chi-chih hsien-sheng chuan-chi, fu nien-p'u nien-piao 南通张季直先生传记,附年谱年表(A biography of Mr. Chang Chi-chih, Chang Chien of Nantung with an appended chronological sketch of life and events of Chang Chi-chih;

Shanghai: Chung-hua shu-chü, 1930), 649 pp.

Chang Hsin-ch'eng 张心澂, Chung-kuo hsien-tai chiao-t'ung shih 中国现代交通史 (A history of communications in modern China), in Hsien-tai Chung-kuo-shih ts'ung-shu (Modern Chinese history series), Shanghai: Liang-yu, 1931, 618 pp.

Chang Hsing-lang 张星烺, Chung-Hsi chiao-t'ung shih-liao hui-pien 中西交通史料汇编 (A miscellaneous collection of historical materials on contact between China and the West; Peking, Fu-jen University, 1928), 6 vols.

Chang Hsing-lang 张星烺, Ou-hua tung-chien shih 欧化东渐史 (The spread of Western civilization to the east; Shanghai: Commercial Press, 1926).

Chang Kia-ngau, China's Struggle for Railroad Development (New York: John Day, 1943), 340 pp.

Chang P'ei-lun 张佩纶, Chien-yü chi 涧于集 (Collected memorials of Chang P'ei-lun; published by the author, 1918), 6 chüan.

Chang Po-chen 张伯桢, Nan-hai K'ang hsien-sheng chuan 南海康先生传 (Biography of K'ang Yu-wei), in Ts'ang-hai ts'ung-shu 沧海丛书, ts'e 6.

Chang Po-ch'u 张伯初, "Shang-hai ping-kung-ch'ang chih shih-mo" 上海兵工厂之始末 (A complete account of the Shanghai Arsenal), Jen-wen, 5.5: 1-15 (June 1934).

Chang Shih-chao 章士钊, Ch'ang-sha Chang-shih ts'ung-kao 长沙章氏丛稿 (Collected drafts of Chang Shih-chao of Changsha; Shanghai, 1929), 197 pp.

Chang Tê-ch'ang 张德昌, "Li Hung-chang chih wei-hsin yun-tung" 李鸿章之维新运动 (Li Hung-chang's reform movement), Ch'ing-hua chou-k'an 清华周刊, 35.2:110-112 (1931).

Chang Tê-tsê 张德泽, "Chün-chi-ch'u chi ch'i tang-an" 军机处及其档案 (The Grand Council and its archives), Wen-hsien lun-ts'ung, 57-84 (1930).

Chang Ts'ai-t'ien 张采田, <u>Ch'ing lieh-ch'ao hou-fei chuan-kao</u> 清列朝后妃传稿(Draft biographies of empresses of all generations of the Ch'ing Dynasty; movable-type edition, 1929), 2 ts'e.

Chang Tzu-mu 张自牧, <u>Ying-hai lun</u> 瀛海论(A discussion of the circuit of the seas), in <u>Hsiao-fang-hu-chai yü-ti ts'ung-ch'ao</u>, ts'e 60.

Chang Wei-hua 张维华, "Ming-Ch'ing chien Chung-Hsi ssu-hsiang chih ch'ung-t'u yü ying-hsiang" 明清间中西思想之冲突与影响(The ideological conflict between China and the West during the late Ming and early Ch'ing and its effect), <u>Hsueh-ssu</u> 1.1:19-24 (January 1942).

Chang Wei-hua 张维华, "Ming-Ch'ing chien Fo-Yeh chih cheng-pien" 明清间佛耶之争辩(Argument between Buddhists and Christians during the late Ming and early Ch'ing), <u>Hsueh-ssu</u>, 1.2:12-17 (January 1942).

"Chang Wen-hsiang-kung yü chiao-yü chih kuan-hsi"张文襄公与教育之关系(Chang Chih-tung's relations with Chinese education), <u>Chiao-yü tsa-chih</u> 教育杂志, 1.10:19-23 (September 1909).

Chang Wen-hsiang-kung, <u>see</u> Chang Chih-tung.

Chang Yin-lin 张荫麟, "Ming-Ch'ing chih-chi Hsi-hsueh shu-ju Chung-kuo k'ao-lueh"明清之际西学输入中国考略(A brief study of the introduction of Western knowledge to China during the late Ming and early Ch'ing), <u>Ch'ing-hua hsueh-pao</u> 清华学报, 1.1:38-69.

Chang Yin-lin 张荫麟, "Po Shui-ch'uang ch'un-i" 跋水窗春呓 (Commentary on Shui-ch'uang ch'un-i), <u>Kuo-wen chou-pao</u>, 12.10: 1-4 (1935).

Chang Yü-chüan, "The provincial organs of foreign affairs in China," CSPSR 1.3:47-70 (Oct. 1916). Chao Chia-pi 赵家璧, ed., <u>Chung-kuo hsin-wen-hsueh ta-hsi</u> 中国新文学大系(A corpus of China's new literature; Shanghai: Liang-yu Co., 1936), 10 vols. See A-ying.

Chao Feng-t'ien 赵丰田, "K'ang Ch'ang-su hsien-sheng nien-p'u kao" 康长素先生年谱稿(A draft chronological sketch of the life of K'ang Yu-wei), <u>Shih-hsueh nien-pao</u>, vol. 2 (1934).

Chao Feng-t'ien 赵丰田, Wan-Ch'ing wu-shih-nien ching-chi ssu-hsiang shih 晚清五十年经济思想史 (Economic thought during the last fifty years of the Ch'ing period), Yen-ching hsueh-pao, monograph series no. 18 (Peiping: Harvard-Yenching Institute, 1939), 320 pp.

Chao Hsing-kuo 赵兴国, "Ch'üan-fei shih-liao chi-mu" 拳匪史料辑目 (A list of historical materials on the Boxer bandits), Jen-wen, 7.7:1-4 (September 1936).

Chao I-ch'eng 赵意诚, "Wang T'ao k'ao-cheng" 王韬考证, (A study of Wang T'ao), Hsueh-feng, 6.1:1-24 (February 1936).

Chao Tseng-hui 赵增辉, Tseng Kuo-fan yen-hsing chih t'i-hsi 曾国藩言行之体系 (The consistency of Tseng Kuo-fan's words and actions; Shanghai: Pei-hsin shu-chü, 1946).

Chao Wei-hsi 赵惟熙, Hsi-hsueh shu-mu ta-wen 西学书目答问 (Questions and answers on books on Western knowledge; Kweiyang, 1901), 1 ts'e.

Chen Ying 震瀛, "Chi Ku Hung-ming hsien-sheng" 记辜鸿铭先生 (Notes on Mr. Ku Hung-ming), Jen-chien shih, no. 18 (December 1934).

Chen Ying 震瀛, "Pu-chi Ku Hung-ming hsien-sheng" 补记辜鸿铭先生 (A supplementary note on Mr. Ku Hung-ming), Jen-chien shih, no. 28:9-10 (May 1935).

Ch'en Ch'ang-hua 陈昌华 et al., "Wo so chih-tao ti Ku Hung-ming hsien-sheng" 我所知道的辜鸿铭先生 (Mr. Ku Hung-ming as I knew him), Jen-chien shih, no. 12:45-46 (September 1934).

Ch'en Chen-kuo 陈振国, "Ch'ang-mao chuang-yuan Wang T'ao" 长毛状元王韬 (Wang T'ao, the leading scholar among the long-haired rebels, [Taipings]), I-ching, no. 33:41-45 (July 1937).

Ch'en Ch'i-t'ien, see Gideon Ch'en.

Ch'en Chih 陈炽, Yung-shu 庸书 (preface dated 1896, block-print 1897), 2 ts'e.

Ch'en Ch'iu 陈鏊, "Wu-hsü cheng-pien-shih fan pien-fa jen-wu chih cheng-chih ssu-hsiang" 戊戌政变时反变法人物之政治思想 (The political thought of anti-reformists during the time or the One Hundred Days of Reform), Yen-ching hsueh-pao, vol. 25: 59-106 (June 1939).

Ch'en Chung-i 陈忠倚, Huang-ch'ao ching-shih wen san-pien 皇朝经世文三编, (Second supplement to the Huang-ch'ao ching-shih wen-pien; Shanghai: Shang-hai shu-chü, 1901), 80 chüan.

Ch'en Fu-kuang 陈复光, Yu Ch'ing i-lai chih Chung-E kuan-hsi 有清以来之中俄关系 (Sino-Russian relations since the Ch'ing Dynasty; Yunnan University Law School Series, B1, 1947), 464 pp.

Ch'en, Gideon, Lin Tse-hsü, Pioneer Promoter of the Adoption of Western Means of Maritime Defense in China (Peiping: Yenching University Press, 1934), 65 pp.

Ch'en, Gideon, Tseng Kuo-fan, Pioneer Promoter of the Steamship in China (Peiping: Yenching University, 1935), 98 pp.

Ch'en, Gideon, Tso Tsung-t'ang, Pioneer Promoter of the Modern Dockyard and the Woolen Mill in China (Peiping: Yenching University, 1938), 91 pp.

Ch'en, Gideon, "Tso Tsung-t'ang: The Farmer of Hsiang-shang," Yenching Journal of Social Studies, 1.2: 211-225 (1939).

Ch'en Hsü-ching 陈序经, Chung-kuo wen-hua ti ch'u-lu 中国文化的出路 (The future of Chinese culture; Shanghai: Commercial Press, 1934), 145 pp.

Ch'en I-lin 陈翊林, Tsui-chin san-shih-nien Chung-kuo chiao-yü shih 最近三十年中国教育史 (History of Chinese education in the last thirty years; Shanghai: T'ai-p'ing-yang shu-tien, 1930), 380 pp.

Ch'en Jen-pai 陈人白, "Lun wu-ssu yun-tung chih hua-shih-tai ti i-i" 论五四运动之划时代的意义 (On the significance of the epoch-making May Fourth Movement), Ch'iu-chen tsa-chih 求真杂志, 1.1: 6-17 (May 1946).

Ch'en, Kenneth, "Matteo Ricci's Contribution to and Influence on Geographical Knowledge in China," Journal of the American Oriental Society 59: 325-359, 509 (1939).

Ch'en Kung-lu 陈恭禄, "Chia-wu-luan hou keng-tzu-luan ch'ien Chung-kuo pien-fa yun-tung chih yen-chiu" 甲午乱后庚子乱前中国变法运动之研究 (A study of the reform movement after 1895 and before 1900), Wen-che chi-k'an 文哲季刊, 3.1:57-127 (1933).

Ch'en Kung-lu 陈恭禄, Chung-kuo chin-tai shih 中国近代史 (Modern Chinese history; Shanghai: Commercial Press, 1938), 860 pp.

Ch'en Kung-lu 陈恭禄, "Tseng Kuo-fan yü hai-chün" 曾国藩与海军 (Tseng Kuo-fan and the navy), Wen-che chi-k'an, 3.4:691-728 (1934).

Ch'en Lu 陈陆, "Ya-p'ien-chan yü Chung-kuo chün-ch'i" 鸦片战与中国军器 (The Opium War and Chinese weapons), Chung-ho, 1.8:76-92 (Aug. 1940).

Ch'en Lu 陈陆, "Lin Wen-chung-kung i-shu shu" 林文忠公遗书述 (Notes on Lin Tse-hsü's works), Chung-ho, 2.12:39-52 (December 1941).

Ch'en Pang-hsien 陈邦贤, Chung-kuo i-hsueh shih 中国医学史 (History of medicine in China; Shanghai: Commercial Press, 1937), 406 pp.

Ch'en Shou-yi 陈受颐, "Ming-mo Ch'ing ch'u Yeh-su-hui-shih ti ju-chiao-kuan chi ch'i fan-ying" 明末清初耶稣会士的儒教观及其反应 (The Jesuits' conception of Confucianism in the late Ming and early Ch'ing and its repercussions in China), Kuo-hsueh chi-k'an 国学季刊, 5.2:1-64 (1935).

Ch'en Shou-yi 陈受颐, "The Religious Influence of Early Jesuits on Emperor Ch'ung-cheng of the Ming Dynasty", T'ien-hsia Monthly, 8.5:397-419 (May 1939), and 9.1:35-47 (August 1939).

Ch'en Teng-yuan 陈登元, "Hsi-hsueh lai-Hua shih kuo-jen chih wu-tuan t'ai-tu" 西学来华时国人之武断态度 (The Chinese dogmatic attitude toward Western knowledge when it was first introduced into China), Tung-fang tsa-chih, 27.8:61-76 (April 1930).

Ch'en T'i-ch'iang 陈体强, Chung-kuo wai-chiao hsing-cheng 中国外交行政 (Administration of China's foreign relations; Chungking:

Commercial Press, 1943).

　　Ch'en Tu-hsiu 陈独秀, "Ching-kao ch'ing-nien" 敬告青年 (Call to youth), Hsin ch'ing-nien, 1.1 (Sept. 15, 1915).

　　Ch'en Tu-hsiu 陈独秀, "Shih-an tzu-chuan" 实庵自传 (The autobiography of Ch'en Tu-hsiu), in T'ao K'ang-te, Tzu-chuan chih i-chang, pp. 13-30.

　　Ch'en Tu-hsiu 陈独秀, Tu-hsiu wen-ts'un 独秀文存 (Collected writings of [Ch'en] Tu-hsiu), 4 vols. (Shanghai: Ya-tung Book Co., 9th ed., 1933, 1st ed. 1922).

　　Ch'en Tu-hsiu 陈独秀, "K'o-hsueh yü jen-sheng-kuan hsü" 科学与人生观序 (Preface to K'o-hsueh yü jen-sheng-kuan, Science and Philosophy), 2 vols. (Shanghai: Ya-tung t'u-shu-kuan, 1st ed., 1923.; 1925).

　　Ch'en Tu-hsiu 陈独秀, Ch'en Tu-hsiu ti tsui-hou chien-chieh 陈独秀的最后见解 (Ch'en Tu-hsiu's final point of view; Hongkong: Tzu-yu Chung-kuo ch'u-pan she 1950), 54 pp.

　　Ch'en Tuan-chih 陈端志, Wu-ssu yun-tung chih shih ti p'ing-chia 五四运动之史的评价 (An historical evaluation of the May Fourth Movement; Shanghai: Sheng-huo, 1935), 390 pp.

　　Ch'en Tung-hsiao 陈东晓 (comp.), Ch'en Tu-hsiu p'ing-lun 陈独秀评论 (A critique of Ch'en Tu-hsiu; Peiping: Tung-ya Book Co., 1933), 256 pp.

　　Ch'en Wen-chin 陈文进, "Ch'ing-tai chih tsung-li ya-men chi ch'i ching-fei" 清代之总理衙门及其经费 (The Tsungli Yamen and its expenditures during the Ch'ing Dynasty), Chung-kuo chin-tai ching-chi-shih yen-chiu chi-k'an, 1.1:49-50 (November 1932).

　　Ch'en Yuan 陈垣, "Yung-Ch'ien-chien feng T'ien-chu-chiao chih tsung-shih" 雍乾间奉天主教之宗室 (Members of the imperial family who worshipped Catholicism during the periods of Yung-cheng and Ch'ien-lung), Fu-jen hsueh-chih, 3.2:1-36 (July 1932).

　　Ch'en Yuan 陈垣, "T'ang Jo-wang yü Mu Ch'en-wen" 汤若望与木陈忞 (Adam Schall von Bell and Mu Ch'en-wen), Fu-jen hsueh-chih 7.1-2:

1-28 (December 1938).

Cheng Hao-sheng 郑鹤声, "Pa-shih-nien lai kuan-pan pien-i shih-yeh chih chien-t'ao," 八十年来官办编译事业之检讨 (An examination of government directed translation work during the past eighty years), Shuo-wen yueh-k'an, 4:493-529 (May 1944).

Cheng Kuan-ying 郑观应, Sheng-shih wei-yen 盛世危言 (Warnings to the seemingly prosperous age), 6 chüan (printed in 1893, preface dated 1892).

Cheng Shih-hsü 郑师许, "Ming-Ch'ing liang-tai ti chün-ch'i pien-ko chi ch'i ying-hsiang" 明清两代的军器变革及其影响 (Changes in military equipment during the Ming and Ch'ing dynasties and its effects), Hsin-Chung-hua (new series) 新中华, 2.6:59-70 (1944).

Ch'eng P'ei 程沛, "Ch'i-yeh-chia Chang Chi-chih" 企业家张季直 (The businessman Chang Chi-chih), Sheng-huo yü chih-shih 生活与智识, 1.7:19-23 (1947).

Chi-ho yuan-pen 几何原本, translation of Euclid's Elements of Geometry, first 6 chüan by Matteo Ricci and Hsü Kuang-ch'i 徐光启 (reprint of the 1607 translation, revised and printed in final form in 1611), the following 9 chüan by Li Shan-lan 李善兰 and Alexander Wylie (printed in 1858).

Ch'i Ssu-ho 齐思和, "Wei Yuan yü wan-Ch'ing hsueh-feng" 魏源与晚清学风 (Wei Yuan and late Ch'ing scholarship), Yen-ching hsueh-pao, no. 39:177-226 (December 1950).

Ch'i-ying 耆英, Yueh-t'ai yü-sung 越台与颂, 2 ts'e (Canton: Fu-wen-chai edition, 1848).

Chiang Fang-chen 蒋方震, "Chung-kuo wu-shih-nien lai chün-shih pien-ch'ien shih" 中国五十年来军事变迁史 (A history of Chinese military development during the past fifty years), in Shen-pao-kuan, Tsui-chin chih wu-shih-nien, 1-9.

Chiang Hsing-te 蒋星德, Tseng Kuo-fan chih sheng-p'ing chi shih-yeh 曾国藩之生平及事业 (Tseng Kuo-fan's life and career; Shanghai:

Commercial Press, first edition, 1935, third printing, 1936), 263 pp.

Chiang I-hsueh 蒋逸雪, "Chang Chien i-chuan," 张謇拟传 (Draft biography of Chang Chien), Shuo-wen yueh-k'an 3.8:101-103 (September 1942).

Chiang Kai-shek 蒋介石, China's Destiny and Chinese Economic Theory, with notes and commentary by Philip Jaffe (New York: Roy Publishers, 1947), 347 pp.

Chiang Monlin 蒋梦麟, Tides from the West, A Chinese Autobiography (New Haven: Yale University Press, 1947), 282 pp.

Chiang Shu-ko 姜书阁, Chung-kuo chin-tai chiao-yü chih-tu 中国近代教育制度 (Modern educational system of China; Shanghai: Commercial Press, 1934), 203 pp.

Chiang T'ing-fu 蒋廷黻, see Tsiang, T. F.

Chiang Wen-han. see Kiang, Wen-han.

Chiang Yung 江庸, "Wu-shih-nien lai Chung-kuo chih fa-chih" 五十年来中国之法制 (China's legal system in the past fifty years), in Shen-pao-kuan, Tsui-chin chih wu-shih-nien, 1-10.

Chien Po-tsan 翦伯赞 ed., I-ho t'uan 义和团 (The Boxer movement), 4 vols. (Shanghai: Shen-chou kuo-kuang-she, 1951).

Ch'ien Hsing-ts'un 钱杏邨, see A-ying.

Ch'ien Mu 钱穆, Chung-kuo chin-san-pai-nien hsueh-shu shih 中国近三百年学术史 (A history of Chinese academic thought during the last three hundred years), 2 vols. (Chungking: Commercial Press, 1945).

Ch'ien Tuan-sheng 钱端升, The Government and Politics of China (Cambridge: Harvard University Press, 1950), 526 pp.

Chih Kuei 志圭, "Ch'ing-tai K'ang-Liang wei-hsin yun-tung yü ko-ming-tang chih kuan-hsi chi ying-hsiang" 清代康梁维新运动与革命党之关系及影响 (The reform movement of K'ang and Liang in the Ch'ing Dynasty, its relation to the revolutionary party and its influence), Chien-kuo yueh-k'an 建国月刊, 9.2:1-10 (August 1933).

Ch'ih Chung-hu 池仲祐, "Hai-chün ta-shih chi" 海军大事记 (Great

events of the navy), in Tso Shun-sheng 左舜生, Chung-kuo chin-pai-nien shih tzu-liao hsü-pien 中国近百年史资料续编, 2:323-363.

"Ch'ih-kao Ying-i shuo-t'ieh" 斥告英夷说帖 (Placard of the partiotic people of Kwangtung denouncing the English barbarians), in IWSM-TK 31:15-20.

Chin Liang 金梁, Chin-shih jen-wu chih 近世人物志 (A gazetteer of modern personages; 1934), 366 pp.

Chin Yü-min 金毓敏, "Li Ta-chao yü wu-ssu yun-tung" 李大钊与五四运动 (Li Ta-chao and the May Fourth Movement), Kuan-ch'a 观察, 6.13 (May 1, 1950).

Ch'in Han-ts'ai 秦翰才, Tso Wen-hsiang-kung tsai hsi-pei 左文襄公在西北 (Tso Tsung-t'ang in the Northwest; Chungking: Commercial Press, 1945), 229 pp.

Chinese Repository, published in Macao and Canton, May 1832 to December 1851, monthly.

Chinese Social and Political Science Review, see CSPSR.

Ch'ing-ch'ao hsü wen-hsien t'ung-k'ao, see Liu Chin-tsao.

Ch'ing-shih kao, see CSK.

Ch'ing-shih lieh-chuan, see CSLC.

Ch'ing shih-lu, see CSL.

Chiu Wu-tai shih 旧五代史 (The old history of the Five Dynasties) in Er-shih-ssu shih (T'ung-wen shu-chü edition, 1894).

Ch'iu-tzu-ch'iang chai 求自强斋, comp., Hsi-cheng ts'ung-shu 西政丛书 (Collectanea of books on Western institutions; Shen-chi shu-chuang, 1897).

Chou Chen-fu 周振甫, "Yen Fu ssu-hsiang chuan-pien chih p'ou-hsi" 严复思想转变之剖析 (An analysis of the change of Yen Fu's thought), Hsueh-lin, no. 3:113-133 (January 1941).

Chou Chen-fu 周振甫, "Yen Fu ti Chung-Hsi wen-hun kuan" 严复的中西文化观 (Yen Fu's view of Chinese and Western culture), Tung-fang tsa-chih, 34.1:293-303 (1937).

Chou Fu-hai 周佛海, San-min chu-i chih li-lun ti t'i-hsi 三民主义之理论的体系 (The theoretical system of San-min chu-i; Shanghai: Hsin-sheng-ming yueh-k'an she, 1928), 354 pp.

Chou-i cheng-i 周易正义 (The Book of Changes), in Shih-san-ching chu-su 十三经注疏, ed. by Juan Yuan, ts'e 1-4 (1892).

Chou Tso-jen 周作人, "Chi Ts'ai Chieh-min hsien-sheng ti shih" 记蔡孑民先生的事 (Anecdotes about Ts'ai Yuan-p'ei), Ku-chin, no. 6.

Chou Tzu-ya 周子亚, "Li Hung-chang yü fan-Jih wai-chiao" 李鸿章与反日外交 (Li Hung-chang and his anti-Japan diplomacy), San-min chu-i pan-yueh k'an 三民主义半月刊, 1.9: 21-23 (1942).

Ch'ou-pan i-wu shih-mo, see IWSM.

Chu Chih-yü 朱之瑜 Shun-shui i-shu 舜水遗书 (Collected works of Chu Chih-yü), 12 ts'e (1913).

Chu Chih-yü 朱之瑜, Yang-chiu shu-lueh 阳九述略 (A brief account of the Yang-chiu [misfortune]), in Shun-shui i-shu, 12 ts'e (movable type edition of 1913), see ts'e 11.

Chu I-hsin 朱一新, Wu-hsieh-t'ang ta-wen 无邪堂答问 (Answers to questions in the orthodox studio), author's preface dated 1892, ts'e 1-5, in Cho-an ts'ung-kao 拙庵丛稿, 16 ts'e (Pao-chen t'ang, 1896).

Chu K'o-ching 朱克敬, Jou-yuan hsin-shu 柔远新书 (A new volume on the cherishing of men from afar), 4 chüan, 4 ts'e (Shanghai, 1884).

Chu Shih-chieh 朱世杰, Ssu-yuan yü-chien 四元玉鉴 (Precious mirror of the four elements), chüan 3, in Pai-fu-t'ang suan-hsueh ts'ung-shu 白芙堂算学丛书.

Chu Shun-shui, see Chu Chih-yü.

Chu Wu 竹坞, "Wo-kuo chih lu-chün" 我国之陆军 (The army of our country), Kuo-feng pao 国风报, 1.21: 47-74 (1910).

Ch'u Ch'eng-po 褚成博, Chien-cheng-t'ang che-kao 坚正堂折稿 (Memorials of Ch'u Ch'eng-po), 2 chüan (block-print edition of 1905).

Ch'u-chin 楚金, "Tao-kuang hsueh-shu" 道光学术 (The academic studies of the Tao-kuang period), Chung-ho, 2.1: 1-16 (Jan. 1, 1941).

Ch'u-chin 楚金，Kuo Yun-hsien shou-cha ping-pa 郭筠仙手札并跋 (Notes on Kuo Sung-tao's autographic correspondence)，Chung-ho, 1. 12:68-75 (February 1941); and Kuo Yun-hsien shou-cha tz'u-chi 郭筠仙手札次辑(a supplementary collection)，Chung-ho, 5.2:48-51(February 1944).

Ch'ü Chung-hsuan-kung, see Ch'ü Shih-ssu.

Ch'ü Hsuan-ying 瞿宣颖，"Tu Tseng Wen-cheng-kung chi pi-chi" 读曾文正公集笔记(On reading Tseng Kuo-fan's collected works)，Hsin-min yueh-k'an 新民月刊，1.2:1-15 (1935).

Ch'ü Shih-ssu 瞿式耜 Ch'ü Chung-hsuan-kung wen-chi 瞿忠宣公文集 (Collected essays of Ch'ü Shih-ssu; Kiangsu reprint edition, 1887).

Ch'ü Tui-chih 瞿兑之，"Keng-hsin shih-chi yao-lu" 庚辛史籍要录 (An annotated bibliography of books on the events of 1900 and 1901)，Kuo-wen chou-pao, 11.3:1-6 (January 1934).

Ch'uan, T. K., "Tseng Kuo-fan," T'ien-hsia Monthly 2:121-137 (February 1936).

Ch'üan Han-sheng 全汉升，"Ch'ing-mo ti Hsi-hsueh yuan-ch'u Chung-kuo shuo" 清末的西学源出中国说 (The theory of the Chinese origin of Western sciences in the late Ch'ing)，Ling-nan hsueh-pao, 4.2:57-102 (June 1935).

Ch'üan Han-sheng 全汉升，"Ch'ing-mo fan-tui Hsi-hua ti yen-lun"清末反对西化的言论 (Opinions expressed against Western culture at the end of the Ch'ing Dynasty)，Ling-nan hsueh-pao, 5.3-4:122-166 (December 1936).

Ch'üan Han-sheng 全汉升，"Ch'ing-mo Han-yang t'ieh-ch'ang" 清末汉阳铁厂(The Hanyang iron and steel works)，She-hui k'o-hsueh lun-ts'ung 社会科学论丛，no. 1:1-33 (April 1950).

Ch'uan Han-sheng 全汉升，"Ch'ing-chi ti Chiang-nan chih-tsao-chü" 清季的江南制造局 ("The Kiangnan Arsenal of the Ch'ing Dynasty")，Li-shih yü-yen yen-chiu-so chi-k'an 历史语言研究所集刊("Bulletin of the Institute of History and Philology, Academia Sinica"), vol. 23,

"Presented in memorial of Director Fu Ssu-nien", part 1 (Taipei, 1951), pp. 145-159.

Ch'üan-kuo yin-hang nien-chien 全国银行年鉴 (National banking yearbook), edited by Chung-kuo yin-hang (Bank of China), issue no. 3 (1936); no. 4 (1937).

Chuang Tzu, A new selected translation with an exposition of the philosophy of Kuo Hsiang, by Fung Yu-lan (Shanghai: Commercial Press, 1931), 164 pp.

Chuang Yü 庄俞 and Ho Sheng-nai 贺圣鼐, ed., Tsui-chin san-shih-wu-nien chih Chung-kuo chiao-yü 最近三十五年之中国教育 (Chinese education in the last thirty-five years; Shanghai: Commercial Press, 1931), many hundred pages.

Ch'un-ch'iu Tso-chuan cheng-i 春秋左传正义 (Established commentary on the Ch'un-ch'iu and Tso-chuan), 60 chüan, in Shih-san-ching chu-su 十三经注疏, ts'e 97-126 (1627-1639 edition), 160 ts'e.

Chung-kuo chien-she 中国建设 (China reconstruction), published in Shanghai, beginning 1930, monthly.

Chung-kuo chin-tai ching-chi-shih yen-chiu chi-k'an 中国近代经济史研究集刊 (Studies in Modern Economic History of China; Peiping: Institute of Social Research, 1932-1937), semi-annually.

Chung-kuo hsin-wen-hsueh ta-hsi 中国新文学大系, see Chao Chia-pi, A-ying.

Chung-kuo nien-chien 中国年鉴 (The China Year Book), comp. by Yuan Hsiang 阮湘 and others (first and only issue; Shanghai: Commercial Press, 1924), 2123 pp.

Chung-ying 仲英, ed., Yang-wu hsin-lun 洋务新论 (New essays on foreign affairs; 1894).

Chung-yung 中庸 (Doctrine of the Mean), annotated by Cheng Hsuan 郑玄, 1 chüan, in Shih-san-ching chu 十三经注, ts'e 78, Chi-ku-lou edition (1852), 100 ts'e.

Clark, Grover, "The West goes to China and the remaking of her civilization begins", The Century Magazine, 114.2:129-139 (June 1927).

(Constitution), see Tung-fang tsa-chih, special issue on constitutional government, January-February 1907. See also under Hsien-cheng.

Cordier Henri, "La Mission Dubois de Jancigny dans l'Extrême-Orient," Revue de l'histoire des colonies françaises, 4: 130-133, 146, 148 (1916).

Costin, William Conrad, Great Britain and China 1833-1860 (Oxford: The Clarendon Press, 1937), 362 pp.

CSK: Ch'ing-shih kao 清史稿 (Draft history of the Ch'ing Dynasty), compiled by Chao Erh-hsun and others, 536 chüan, in 131 ts'e. (Movable-type edition, 1927).

CSL: (Ch'ing shih-lu), Ta-Ch'ing li-ch'ao shih-lu 大清历朝实录 (Veritable records of the successive reigns of the Ch'ing Dynasty), photolithographic edition, 1220 ts'e (Changchun, 1937).

CSLC: Ch'ing-shih lieh-chuan 清史列传 (Historical biographies of the Ch'ing Dynasty), compiled by Ch'ing-shih kuan, 80 ts'e (Shanghai: Chung-hua shu-chü movable-type edition, 1927).

CSPSR: Chinese Social and Political Science Review, published by The Chinese Social and Political Science Association, Peking, China, beginning April 1916, quarterly.

Danton, G. H., The Culture Contacts of the United States and China; The Earliest Sino-American Culture Contacts, 1784-1844 (New York: Columbia University Press, 1931), 128 pp.

Davis, John Francis, China during the War and since the Peace, 2 vols. (London, 1852).

De Francis, John, Nationalism and Language Reform in China (Princeton: Princeton University Press, 1950), 306 pp.

Dunne, George H., "The Jesuits in China in the last days of the Ming Dynasty" (Ph. D. dissertation at the University of Chicago, 1944).

Evans, E. W. Price, Timothy Richard, A Narrative of Christian Enterprise and Statesmanship in China (London: Carey Press, 1945),

160 pp.

Fairbank, J. K., <u>Trade and Diplomacy on the China Coast: The Opening of the Treaty Ports, 1842-1854</u>, 2 vols. (Cambridge, Mass.: Harvard University Press, 1953).

Fairbank J, K., <u>Ch'ing Documents, An Introductory Syllabus</u>, 2 fascicles, multilith (Cambridge, Mass.: Harvard University Press, 1952), 100 pp.

Fairbank J. K., and Liu, K. C., <u>Modern China: A Bibliographical Guide to Chinese Works 1898-1937</u>, Harvard-Yenching Institute Studies, vol. I (Cambridge: Harvard University Press, 1950), 608 pp.

Fairbank J. K., and Masataka Banno, <u>Japanese Studies of Modern China (a bibliographical guide to research in history and social science, 19th and 20th centuries)</u>, Harvard-Yenching Institute, to be published in 1954.

Fairbank, J. K., and Teng, S. Y., "On the Ch'ing Tributary System", <u>Harvard Journal of Asiatic Studies</u>, 6.2: 135-246 (June 1941).

Fan Wen-lan 范文澜, <u>Chung-kuo chin-tai shih</u> 中国近代史 (A history of modern China; Peking: Hsin-hua shu-tien, 1949). <u>Shang-pien</u> or vol. A, 543 pp.

Fan Wen-lan 范文澜, <u>Han-chien kuei-tzu-shou Tseng Kuo-fan ti i-sheng</u> 汉奸刽子手曾国藩的一生 (Life of the traitor and executioner Tseng Kuo-fan; Shanghai: Hsin-hua Book Company, 1949), 40 pp.

Fan Wen-lan 范文澜, see also <u>Wu Po</u>.

Fang Hao 方豪, "Ch'ing-tai chin-i T'ien-chu-chiao so-shou Jih-pen chih ying-hsiang"清代禁抑天主教所受日本之影响 (Japanese influence on the persecution of Catholicism during the Ch'ing Dynasty), in <u>Fang Hao wen-lu</u>, pp. 47-66.

Fang Hao 方豪, <u>Chung-kuo T'ien-chu-chiao shih lun-ts'ung</u> 中国天主教史论丛 (Essays on the history of Catholicism in China; Chungking: Commercial Press, 1944), 151 pp.

Fang Hao 方豪, <u>Chung-wai wen-hua chiao-t'ung-shih lun-ts'ung</u> 中外

文化交通史论丛 (Essays on Sino-foreign cultural relations; Chungking: Tu-li ch'u-pan-she, 1944), 260 + 23 pp.

Fang Hao 方豪, Fang Hao wen-lu 方豪文录 (Essays of Fang Hao; Shanghai: Shanghai Pien-i Kuan, 1948), 346 pp.

Fang Hao 方豪, "K'ang-hsi wu-shih-pa-nien Ch'ing-t'ing p'ai yuan ts'e-hui Liu-ch'iu ti-t'u chih yen-chiu"康熙五十八年清廷派员测绘琉球地图之研究 (On the cartographic survey of the Liu-ch'iu Islands by command of Emperor K'ang-hsi in 1719), Wen-shih-che hsueh-pao 文史哲学报 ("Bulletin of the College of Arts, Taiwan University."), no. 1: 159-197 (June 1950).

Fang Hao 方豪, "Ming-mo Hsi-yang huo-ch'i liu-ju wo-kuo chih shih-liao"明末西洋火器流入我国之史料 (Historical materials concerning the introduction of Western arms into China in the late Ming), Tung-fang tsa-chih, 40.1:49-54 (January 1944).

Fang Hsien-t'ing 方显廷 (H. D. Fong), Chung-kuo chih mien-fang-chih-yeh 中国之棉纺织业 (The Chinese cotton textile industry), published by the Kuo-li pien-i kuan (Shanghai: Commercial Press, 1934), 387 pp.

Fang Keng-sheng 方甦生, "Ch'ing lieh-ch'ao hou-fei chuan kao ting-pu"清列朝后妃传稿订补 (Corrections and additions to Ch'ing lieh-ch'ao hou-fei chuan), Fu-jen hsueh-chih, 8.1: 99-112 (June 1939).

Feng Ch'eng-chün 冯承钧, ed., Hai-lu chu 海录注 (An annotated edition of the Hai-lu; Changsha: Commercial Press, 1938), 83 pp.

Feng Ching-t'ing hsing-chuang 冯景亭行状 (A biography of Feng Kuei-fen), 1 ts'e, 19 leaves.

Feng Kuei-fen 冯桂芬, Chiao-pin-lu k'ang-i 校邠庐抗议 (Personal protests from the Study of Chiao-pin), 2 chüan (published in 1885, with an author's preface of 1861).

Feng Kuei-fen 冯桂芬, "Chih yang-ch'i"制洋器议 (On the manufacture of foreign weapons), in Chiao-pin-lu k'ang-i.

Feng Kuei-fen 冯桂芬, "Shan yü-i"善驭夷议 (On the better control

of the barbarians), in Chiao-pin-lu k'ang-i.

Feng Kuei-fen 冯桂芬,"Ts'ai Hsi-hsueh i" 采西学议(On the adoption of Western knowledge), in Chiao-pin-lu k'ang-i.

Feng Kuei-fen 冯桂芬, Hsien-chih-t'ang kao 显志堂稿 (Literary works of Feng Kuei-fen), 12 chüan (published in 1877).

Feng Kuei-fen 冯桂芬,"Shang-hai she-li T'ung-wen Kuan i" 上海设立同文馆议 (A proposal to establish a T'ung-wen Kuan in Shanghai), in Hsien-chih-t'ang kao.

Feng Kuei-fen, see also Feng Ching-t'ing, Huang Ts'ui-po.

Feng Yu-lan, see also Fung Yu-lan.

Feng Yu-lan (Derk Bodde, tr.), A Short History of Chinese Philosophy (Peiping: Henry Vetch, 1937), 454 pp.

Ferguson, John C.,"The Abolition of the Competitive Examinations in China," Journal of the American Oriental Society, 27:79-87 (1906).

Fong, H. D., see Fang Hsien-t'ing.

Forke, Alfred von, Geschichte der neueren chinesischen Philosophie (Hamburg: Friederichsen, De Gruyter & Co., 1938), 693 pp.

Fortia d'Urban Marquis de, La Chine et L'Angleterre (Paris, 1842).

Foster John,"The Christian Origins of the Taiping Rebellion," The International Review of Missions 40: 156-167 (1951).

Franke, Wolfgang,"Die Staatspolitischen Reformversuche K'ang Yu-weis und seiner Schule. Ein Beitrag zur geistigen Auseinandersetzung Chinas mit dem Abendlande." Dissertation (Hamburg, 1935), 83 pp.

Franke, Wolfgang,"Juan Yuan (1764-1849)," Monumenta Serica 9: 53-80 (1944).

Fu-jen hsueh-chih 辅仁学志 (Journal of Fu-jen University), published in Peiping, beginning 1929, semi-annual.

Fu Lan-ya 傅兰雅 (John Fryer), Tso-chih ch'u-yen 佐治刍言 (Some advice on how to rule), in Hsi-cheng ts'ung-shu.

Fujiwara Sadamu 藤原定, Kindai Chūgoku shisō 近代中国思想 (Modern Chinese thought; Tōkyō: Shichōsha, 1948), 203 pp.

Fung Yu-lan, tr., Chuang Tzu, see Chuang Tzu, A new selected translation.

Giquel, Prosper, The Foochow Arsenal and its Results, from the Commencement in 1867 to the End of the Foreign Directorate on the 16th February, 1874, reprinted from the Shanghai Evening Courier, tr. by H. Lang (Shanghai, 1874), 38 pp.

Goodrich, L. Carrington, The Literary Inquisition of Ch'ien-Lung (Baltimore: Waverly Press, 1935), 275 pp.

Grosse-Aschhoff, Angelus, Negotiations between Ch'i-ying and Lagrené 1844-1846, Franciscan Institute Publications, Missiology Series, No. 2 (New York and Louvain, 1950), 195 pp.

Gundry, R. S., China Present and Past (London, 1895), 414 pp.

Haga Takeshi 芳賀雄, Shina kōgyō shi 支那矿业史 (History of Chinese mineral industry; Tōkyō: Dentsū shuppambu 电通出版部, 1943), 365 pp.

Hail, William James, Tseng Kuo-fan and the Taiping Rebellion (New Haven: Yale University Press, 1927), 422 pp.

Han Shao-su 韩少苏, "T'an Tseng Chi-tse" 谈曾纪泽 (A note on Tseng Chi-tse), Kuo-wen chou-pao, 12.25:1-4 (July 1935).

Hart Robert, These from the Land of Sinim (Essays on the Chinese Question) (London, 1903), 302 pp.

Hart, Robert, see Ho-te.

Hattori Unokichi 服部宇之吉, Shinkoku tsūkō 清国通考 (A general account of the Ch'ing government), 2 vols. (Tōkyō: Sanseidō 三省堂, 1905), 166 & 204 pp.

Hibbert, Eloise Talcott, Jesuit Adventure in China: During the Reign of K'ang Hsi (New York: E. P. Dutton and Co., 1941), 291 pp.

Hirase Minokichi 平濑巳之吉, Kindai Shina keizai shi 近代支那经济史 (Modern Chinese economic history; Tōkyō: Chūō Kōronsha, 1942), 388 pp.

Hiratsuka Atsushi 平冢笃, comp., Zoku Itō Hirobumi hiroku 续伊

藤博文秘录（Supplement to the collection of Itō's private documents; Tōkyō: Shunjūsha, 1930), 254 pp.

Hiyane Antei 比屋根安定, <u>Shina Kirisuto-kyō shi</u> 支那基督教史 (History of Christianity in China; Tōkyō: Seikatsusha, 1940), 324 pp.

Ho Ch'ang-ling 贺长龄 comp., <u>Huang-ch'ao ching-shih wen-pien</u> 皇朝经世文编 (Essays of practical use to society during the Ch'ing Dynasty), first printed in 1827, 120 chüan (Shanghai: Kuang-po-sung-chai edition, 1887).

Ho Ch'i 何启 and Hu Li-yuan 胡礼垣, <u>Hsin-cheng chen-ch'üan</u> 新政真诠 (The true meaning of new government; Hongkong, 1895, reprinted, 1909).

Ho I-k'un 何贻焜, <u>T'ing-lin hsueh-shuo shu-p'ing</u> 亭林学说述评 (A presentation and comments on Ku Yen-wu's academic ideas; Chungking: Cheng-chung shu-chü, 1944), 305 pp.

Ho Ping-ti, "Weng T'ung-ho and the 'One Hundred Days of Reform,'" <u>Far Eastern Quarterly</u>, 10.2: 125-135 (February 1951).

Ho-te 赫德 (Hart, Robert) ed., <u>Hsi-hsueh ju-men ts'ung-shu</u> 西学入门丛书 (Collected works introductory to Western learning; 1886).

Ho-te 赫德 (Hart, Robert), <u>P'ang-kuan san lun</u> 旁观三论 (Three essays by a spectator; Shanghai: Tung-pien ch'ai, 1898).

Hsi Wei and Chu Chi-yung ed., see Ku Yen-wu, <u>T'ing-lin hsien-sheng i-shu hui-chi</u>.

Hsi Yin 惜阴, "Keng-tzu ch'üan-huo tung-nan hu-pao chih chi-shih" 庚子拳祸东南互保之纪实 (A reliable account of the mutual protection [of foreigners and Chinese] in southeastern China during the Boxer Uprising), <u>Jen-wen</u>, 2.7: 1-7 (September 1931).

Hsi Yin 惜阴, "Shu Ho-fei i-wen" 书合肥轶闻 (Anecdotes about Li Hung-chang), <u>Jen-wen</u>, 3.7: 106 (1932).

Hsi Yü-fu 席裕福 ed., <u>Huang-ch'ao cheng-tien lei-tsuan</u> 皇朝政典类纂 (A classified compilation of political statutes of the Ch'ing Dynasty), 500 chüan (Shanghai: T'u-shu chi-ch'eng chü, 1903).

Hsia K'ang-nung 夏康农, Lun Hu Shih yü Chang Chün-mai 论胡适与张君劢(On Hu Shih and Chang Chün-mai; Shanghai, 1948), 68 pp.

Hsia Yen-te 夏炎德, Chung-kuo chin-pai-nien ching-chi ssu-hsiang 中国近百年经济思想 (Chinese economic thought during the last hundred years; Shanghai: Commercial Press, 1948), 202 pp.

Hsiang Ta 向达, Chung-Hsi chiao-t'ung shih 中西交通史 (A history of China's contact with the West; Shanghai: Chung-hua Book Co., 1934), 167 pp.

Hsiang Ta 向达 and others, T'ai-p'ing T'ien-kuo 太平天国 (Source materials about the Heavenly Kingdom of Great Peace), 8 vols., compiled by Hsiang Ta and more than ten others of the Chinese Historical Association and published by the Shen-chou kuo-kuang she 神州国光社 (Shanghai, 1952), 3389 pp.

Hsiao I-shan 萧一山, Ch'ing-tai t'ung-shih 清代通史 (A general history of the Ch'ing Dynasty), 2 vols. (Shanghai: Commercial Press, 1927-1928).

Hsiao I-shan 萧一山, Chin-tai mi-mi she-hui shih-liao 近代秘密社会史料(Historical materials on modern secret societies), 6 chüan (Peiping: The Peiping National Research Academy, 1935).

Hsiao I-shan 萧一山 ed., T'ien-ch'ao t'ien-mu chih-tu 天朝田亩制度 (The land system of the Heavenly Dynasty), 1 chüan, in T'ai-ping T'ien-kuo ts'ung-shu, ts'e 4, (Shanghai: Commercial Press, 1936, 16 ts'e).

Hsiao I-shan 萧一山, Tseng Kuo-fan 曾国藩 (Chungking: Sheng-li ch'u-pan-she, 1944), 202 pp.

Hsiao I-shan 萧一山, Ch'ing-tai shih 清代史 (History of the Ch'ing Dynasty; Chungking: Commercial Press, 1945), 307 pp.

Hsiao I-shan 萧一山, "Huai-chün yü Hsiang-chün chih pieh" 淮军与湘军之别 (The difference between the Anhwei Army and the Hunan Army), Tzu-yueh ts'ung-k'an 子曰丛刊, no. 1: 11-13 (1948).

Hsiao Kung-ch'üan 萧公权, Chung-kuo cheng-chih ssu-hsiang shih 中国政治思想史 (A history of Chinese political thought), 2 vols.

(Shanghai: Commercial Press, 1946), 196 + 484 pp.

Hsiao San 萧三, Mao Tse-tung t'ung-chih ti ch'ing-shao-nien shih-tai 毛泽东同志的青少年时代 (The childhood and boyhood of comrade Mao Tse-tung; Peiping, 1949), 109 pp.

Hsieh Chao-chih 谢肇淛, Wu tsa-tsu 五杂组 (Five desultory notes), in Wu-hang pao-shu t'ang 吴航宝树堂, undated block-print edition.

Hsieh En-hui 谢恩辉, "Chang Hsiang-t'ao chih ching-chi chien-she" 张香涛之经济建设 (Chang Hsiang-t'ao's economic reconstruction), Ching-chi hsueh-pao 经济学报, no. 2:105-148 (June 1941).

Hsieh Fu-ch'eng, see Hsueh Fu-ch'eng.

Hsieh Hsing-yao 谢兴尧 ed., T'ai-p'ing T'ien-kuo ts'ung-shu 太平天国丛书 (Collection of works on the Taiping rebellion), 3 ts'e (Peiping: published by the editor, 1938).

Hsieh Kuo-chen 谢国桢, Huang Li-chou hsueh-p'u 黄梨洲学谱 (A sketch of the scholarly work of Huang Tsung-hsi; Shanghai: Commercial Press, 1932), 176 pp.

Hsieh Kuo-chen 谢国桢, Ku Ning-jen hsueh-p'u 顾宁人学谱 (A sketch of the scholarly work of Ku Yen-wu; 1930).

Hsieh Pin 谢彬, Chung-kuo yu-tien hang-k'ung shih 中国邮电航空史 (History of the post, telegraph and aviation in China; Shanghai: Chung-hua shu-chü, 1928), 262 pp.

Hsien-cheng tsa-shih 宪政杂识 (Constitutional government miscellany), 1.1 (December 1906).

Hsien Yung-hsi 冼荣熙, "Wu-shih-nien lai chih Han-yeh-p'ing" 五十年来之汉冶萍 (Han-yeh-p'ing Company during the past 50 years), Shih-tai kung-lun 时代公论, no. 52:64-67 (March 1933).

Hsin-ch'ing-nien 新青年 (La Jeunesse), published in Peking, beginning 1915, monthly.

Hsing-shih chou-pao she 醒狮周报社, ed., Kuo-chia chu-i chiang-yen chi 国家主义讲演集 (Collected lectures on Nationalism), 1 ts'e (Shanghai: Chung-hua Book Co., 1925).

Hsü Ch'ang-chih 徐昌治, Sheng-ch'ao p'o-hsieh chi 圣朝破邪集 (Collected works of the Sacred Dynasty exposing heterodoxy), 8 ts'e (Japanese block-print edition, 1855).

Hsü Chi-yü 徐继畬, Ying-huan chih-lüeh 瀛环志略 (A brief description of the oceans' circuit), completed in 1848 in 10 chüan (printed, 1850; reprinted, 1866).

Hsü Chi-yü 徐继畬, Sung-k'an hsien-sheng ch'üan-chi 松龛先生全集 (Complete works of Hsü Chi-yü; 1915 edition).

Hsü Chih-liang 徐之良, "Chin-tai Chung-kuo wen-hua yun-tung ti kung-tsui"近代中国文化运动的功罪 (Merits and demerits of the cultural movement in modern China), Chung-hua yueh-pao 中华月报, 7.5.

Hsü I-shih 徐一士, "T'an Li Ching-fang"谈李经方 (On Li Ching-fang), Kuo-wen chou-pao, 11.44:1-4 (November 1934).

Hsü I-shih 徐一士, "Tso Tsung-t'ang yü Liang Ch'i-ch'ao" 左宗棠与梁启超 (Tso Tsung-t'ang and Liang Ch'i-ch'ao), Ku-chin, no. 14 (1942).

Hsü Jun 徐润 (Hsü Yü-chih 徐雨之 or "Chü Yü-chee"), Hsü Yü-chai tzu-hsü nien-p'u, fu Shang-hai tsa-chi 徐愚斋自叙年谱,附上海杂记 (Autobiographical chronicle by Hsü Yü-chai, together with miscellaneous notes on Shanghai), published by the Hsü family (Hsiang-shan Hsü-shih 香山徐氏), postface by Kan To 阚铎 dated 1927, pp. 135 + 31.

Hsü Keng-sheng 徐梗生, Chung-wai ho-pan mei-t'ieh-k'uang-yeh shih-hua 中外合办煤铁矿业史话 (Histories of Sino-foreign joint-managed coal and iron mines; Shanghai: Commercial Press, 1946), 270 pp.

Hsü Shou-ch'ang 许寿裳, Chang Ping-lin 章炳麟 (Chungking: Sheng-li ch'u-pan she, 1945), 172 pp.

Hsü, Shuhsi, China and Her Political Entity (New York: Oxford University Press, 1926), 438 pp.

Hsü Tsung-tse 徐宗泽, Ming-Ch'ing chien Yeh-su-hui-shih i-chu t'i-yao 明清间耶稣会士译著提要 (An annotated bibliography of the works written or translated during the Ming and Ch'ing dynasties into Chinese by Jesuits; Shanghai: The Chung-hua Book Co., 1949), 482 pp.

Hsü T'ung-hsin, see Chang Chih-tung, Chang Wen-hsiang-kung nien-p'u.

Hsü Ying 徐盈, Tang-tai Chung-kuo shih-yeh jen-wu chih 当代中国实业人物志 (An account of contemporary Chinese industrialists; complete information unavailable, 1948).

Hsuan-t'ung cheng-chi 宣统政纪 (Records of the political administration of the Hsuan-t'ung period), 16 ts'e (Dairen: Liao-hai shu-she, preface written in 1934).

Hsueh Fu-ch'eng 薛福成, Yung-an ch'üan-chi 庸庵全集 (Collected works of Hsueh Fu-ch'eng), 21 chüan (Shanghai: Tsui-liu-t'ang 醉六堂 lithographic edition, 1897).

Hsueh Fu-ch'eng 薛福成, Ch'ou-yang ch'u-i 筹洋刍议 (Rough discussion of the management of foreign affairs), in Yung-an ch'üan-chi.

Hsueh Fu-ch'eng 薛福成, Ch'u-shih Ying-Fa-I-Pi ssu-kuo jih-chi 出使英法意比四国日记 (Diary of a mission to the four countries of England, France, Italy and Belgium), 6 chüan (published, 1892; with a supplement, 1899; included in the collection Yung-an ch'üan-chi).

Hsueh Fu-ch'eng 薛福成, Yung-an pi-chi 庸庵笔记 (Desultory notes of Hsueh Fu-ch'eng; first printed, 1895; also in Yung-an ch'üan-chi).

Hsueh Fu-ch'eng 薛福成, Ch'u-shih kung-tu 出使公牍 (Official correspondence from a mission abroad), 10 chüan (first published, 1897; reprinted in Yung-an ch'üan-chi).

Hsueh Fu-ch'eng 薛福成, Hai-wai wen-pien 海外文编 (Collection of essays of Hsueh Fu-ch'eng written overseas), 4 chüan, in Yung-an ch'üan-chi.

Hsueh Fu-ch'eng 薛福成, Yung-an wen-pien 庸庵文编 (Collected essays of Hsueh Fu-ch'eng), 4 chüan, in Yung-an chüan-chi.

Hsueh-lin 学林 (The academic world), published in Shanghai, beginning September 1921, monthly.

Hsueh-ssu 学思 (Learning and thinking), published in Chengtu,

beginning 1942, semi-monthly.

Hu Chün 胡钧, Chang Wen-hsiang-kung nien-p'u 张文襄公年谱 (A chronological biography of Chang Chih-tung), edited by Hu Chün 胡钧 (Peking: T'ien-hua yin-shu-kuan, 1939), 6 chüan.

Hu Shih 胡适, Hu Shih wen-ts'un 胡适文存 (Collected essays of Hu Shih), 2 vols. (first collection, Shanghai, 1921).

Hu Shih 胡适, Hu Shih wen-ts'un erh-chi 胡适文存二集 (Second collection of the essays of Hu Shih), 2 vols. (Shanghai, 1924).

Hu Shih, "The Chinese Renaissance," China Year Book, 633-637 (1924).

Hu Shih 胡适, "Wo-men tui-yü Hsi-yang chin-tai wen-ming ti t'ai-tu" 我们对于西洋近代文明的态度 (Our attitude toward modern Western civilization), Tung-fang tsa-chih, 23.17: 73-82 (September 1926).

Hu Shih 胡适, Hu Shih wen-ts'un san-chi 胡适文存三集 (Third collection of the essays of Hu Shih), 4 vols. (Shanghai: Oriental Book Co., 1930).

Hu Shih 胡适, Ssu-shih tzu-shu 四十自述 (Autobiography at forty), vol. 1 (Shanghai: Ya-tung Book Co., 1933), 180 pp.

Hu Shih 胡适, The Chinese Renaissance (Chicago: University of Chicago Press, 1934), 110 pp.

Hu Shih 胡适, "Chi Ku Hung-ming" 记辜鸿铭 (On Ku Hung-ming), Ta-kung-pao, wen-i fu-k'an 文艺副刊, no. 164 (August 1935).

Hu Shih 胡适 ed., Chien-she li-lun chi 建设理论集 (Theoretical bases of [literary] reconstruction), vol. 1 of Chung-kuo hsin-wen-hsueh ta-hsi.

Hu Shih 胡适, Ts'ang-hui-shih cha-chi 藏晖室札记 (Notebook from the Hidden-brilliance Studio), 4 vols. (Shanghai: Ya-tung Book Co., 1939; new edition, Shanghai: the Commercial Press, 1948).

Hu Shih 胡适, Hu Shih liu-hsueh jih-chi 胡适留学日记 (Hu Shih's diary when he studied abroad), 4 ts'e (Shanghai: Commercial Press, second printing, 1948).

Hu Yuan-chün 胡远濬,"T'an Ssu-t'ung Jen-hsueh chih p'i-p'ing"谭嗣同仁学之批评（A comment on T'an Ssu-t'ung's Jen-hsueh）, Kuo-li chung-yang ta-hsueh pan-yueh-k'an 国立中央大学半月刊, 2.1:109-119（October 1930）.

Hua Kang 华岗, Wu-ssu yun-tung shih 五四运动史（A history of the May Fourth Movement; Shanghai：Hai-yen shu-tien, 1951）, 220 pp.

Hua Ying-shen 华应申, Chung-kuo Kung-ch'an-tang lieh-shih chuan 中国共产党烈士传（Biographies of Chinese Communist Party martyrs; Hongkong：Hsin-min-chu shu-chü, 1949）, 224 pp.

Huang-Ch'ing chih-kung t'u 皇清职贡图（Illustrations of the regular tributaries of the imperial Ch'ing Dynasty; palace edition，1761）.

Huang Jen-chi 黄仁济, Huang-shih li-shih chi 黄氏历事记（An historical account of Huang Jen-chi; publisher and date unavailable）.

Huang Ju-ch'eng 黄汝成, comp., Jih-chih-lu chi-shih 日知录集释（Collected commentaries on Jih-chih lu）, 32 chüan（Shanghai：Chung-hua shu-chü, 1927）.

Huang Li-chou, see Huang Tsung-hsi.

Huang Ti 黄迪,"Wu-ssu i-lai chih Chung-kuo hsueh-ch'ao"五四以来之中国学潮（Chinese student strikes since the May Fourth Movement）, She-hui hsueh-chieh, vol. 6:287-303（June 1932）.

Huang Ts'ui-po 黄淬伯,"Ch'i-shih-nien ch'ien chih wei-hsin jen-wu Feng Ching-t'ing"七十年前之维新人物冯景亭（Feng Kuei-fen, the reformer of seventy years ago）, in Chung-shan wen-hua chiao-yü kuan chi-k'an 中山文化教育馆季刊, 4.3:969-991（1937）.

Huang Tsun-hsien 黄遵宪, Jen-ching-lu shih-ts'ao 人境庐诗草（Poems of Huang Tsun-hsien）, 11 chüan（Peiping, 1930）.

Huang Tsun-hsien 黄遵宪, Jih-pen-kuo chih 日本国志（History of Japan）, 10 ts'e（1890）.

Huang Tsun-hsien 黄遵宪, see Wen T'ing-ching.

Huang Tsung-hsi 黄宗羲, Ming-i tai-fang lu 明夷待访录, written in 1663, Ssu-pu pei-yao edition.

Huang Tsung-hsi 黃宗羲, Li-chou i-chu hui-k'an 梨洲遺著汇刊 (Collected writings of Huang Tsung-hsi), compiled by Hsueh Feng-ch'ang 薛凤昌, including 29 titles, 20 ts'e (Shanghai: Shih-chung shu-chü movable type edition, 1910).

Huang Yen-yü, "Viceroy Yeh Ming-ch'en and the Canton Episode (1856-1861)," Harvard Journal of Asiatic Studies, 6. 1: 37-127 (March 1941).

Hubbard, G. E., Eastern Industrialization and its Effect on the West (London: Oxford University Press, 1935), 395 pp.; (revised ed., 1938), 418 pp.

Hughes, E. R., The Invasion of China by the Western World (London: Adam and Charles Black, 1937), 324 pp.

Hummel, Arthur W., ed., Eminent Chinese of the Ch'ing Period (1644-1912), 2 vols. (Washington: The library of Congress, 1943-1944).

Hummel, Arthur W., "Yuan Shih-k'ai as an Official under the Manchus," (M. A. thesis, University of Chicago, 1949), 179 pp.

Hummel, William F., "K'ang Yu-wei, Historical Critic and Social Philosopher, 1857-1927," Pacific Historical Review, 4. 4: 343-355 (December 1935).

Hung Jen-kan 洪仁玕, Tzu-cheng hsin-p'ien 资政新篇 (A new work for aid in administration, 1859). A photolithographic reproduction in I-ching 逸经, nos. 17-19 (1936); also in T'ai-p'ing T'ien-kuo, compiled by Hsiang Ta et al., Vol. II, pp. 521-541.

Hung Shen 洪琛, "Shen-pao tsung-tsuan ch'ang-mao chuang-yuan Wang T'ao"申报总纂长毛状元王韬(Collection of material from Shen-pao on Wang T'ao, leading scholar among the long-haired rebels [Taipings]), Wen-hsueh 文学, 2. 3 (1934) and 2. 6.

Hussey, Harry, Venerable Ancestor; the Life and Times of Tz'u-hsi, 1835-1908, Empress of China (Garden City, N. Y.: Doubleday, 1949), 354 pp.

Ichiko Chūzō 市古宙三,"Giwaken no seikaku"义和拳の性格(The character of the Boxer movement), <u>Kindai Chūgoku kenkyū</u> (Research on Modern China), ed. by Niida Noboru 仁井田陞 and others (Tōkyō: Kōgakusha, 1948, 361 pp.), 245-267.

<u>I-ching</u> 逸经, published in Shanghai, beginning 1936, semi-monthly.

Ikeda Tōsen 池田桃川,"Itō kō to Ri Kō-shō"伊藤公と李鸿章(Prince Itō and Li Hung-chang), <u>Tōyō</u> 东洋, 35.9:124-131 (1932).

Inada Masatsugu 稻田正次,"Bojutsu seihen ni tsuite"戊戌政变について (On the reform movement of 1898), <u>Kindai Chūgoku Kenkyū</u> (Research on Modern China), ed. by Niida Noboru 仁井田陞 and others (Tōkyō: Kōgahuska, 1948, 361 pp.), pp. 207-242.

Ishida Mikinosuke 石田幹之助,"Shina bunka to Seihō bunka to no kōryū 支那文化と西方文化との交流 (The confluence of Chinese and Western culture), <u>Iwanami kōza tōyō shichō</u> 岩波讲座东洋史潮(Tōkyō: Iwanami, 1936), 153 pp.

I-shih 一士,"Jung-lu yü Yuan Shih-k'ai"荣禄与袁世凯 (Jung-lu and Yuan Shih-k'ai), <u>I-ching</u>, no. 22:25-28 (1937).

Ishihara Michihiro 石原道博, <u>Mimmatsu Shinsho Nihon kisshi no kenkyū</u> 明末清初日本乞师の研究(A study of China's solicitation of military help from Japan in the late Ming and early Ch'ing; Tōkyō: Fuzambō 富山房,1945), 542 pp.

Itano Chōhachi 板野长八,"Kō Yū-i no daidō shisō 康有为の大同思想(The Ta-t'ung idea of K'ang Yu-wei), <u>Kindai Chūgoku Kenkyū</u> (Tōkyō: Kōgakusha, 1948, 361 pp.), pp. 165-204.

Itano Chōhachi 板野长八,"Ryō Kei-chō no daidō shisō" 梁启超の大同思想("The Idea of Ta-t'ung of Liang Ch'i-ch'ao"), pp. 69-84 in <u>Wada hakushi kanreki kinen Tōyōshi ronsō</u> 和田博士还历纪念东洋史论丛 (Collected essays in East Asian history, a memorial for the sixtieth birthday of Dr. Wada Sei; Tōkyō: Dainippon Yūbenkai Kōdansha, 1951), 806 + 71 pp.

IWSM:Ch'ou-pan i-wu shih-mo 筹办夷务始末(A complete account

of the management of barbarian affairs), 260 chüan (Peking: printed by the Palace Museum in 1929-1931).

Izushi Yoshihiko 出石诚彦, Tōyō kinseishi kenkyū 东洋近世史研究 (Researches in the modern history of East Asia; Tōkyō: Taikandō 大观堂, 1944), 387 pp.

Jansen, Marius B., "The Japanese and the Chinese Revolutionary Movement 1895-1915" (Harvard doctoral thesis in History, 1950), 320 pp. To be published, revised, under the title Adventurers and Revolutionaries: The Japanese and Sun Yat-sen, by the Harvard University Press in 1954.

Jen-chien-shih 人间世, published in Shanghai, beginning 1934, semi-monthly.

Jen-wen 人文 (Humanities), published in Shanghai, beginning 1930, monthly.

Juan Yuan 阮元, Tseng-tzu shih-p'ien chu-shih 曾子十篇注释 (A commentary on the ten chapters of Tseng-tzu), 1 chüan, Hsiao-i chia-shu ts'ung-shu 孝义家塾丛书.

Juan Yuan 阮元, Ch'ou-jen chuan 畴人传 (Biographies of scientists [especially astronomers and mathematicians]), 46 chüan, (Wen-hsuan-lou ts'ung-shu 文选楼丛书 edition, 1799).

Jung Chao-tsu 容肇祖, "Lü Liu-liang chi ch'i ssu-hsiang" 吕留良及其思想 (Lü Liu-liang and his ideas), Fu-jen hsueh-chih, 5. 1-2: 1-85 (December 1936).

Kan Tso-tin 甘作霖, "Chiang-nan chih-tsao-chü chien-shih" 江南制造局简史 (A brief history of the Kiangnan Arsenal), Tung-fang tsa-chih, 11. 5: 46-48 (November 1914), and 11. 6: 21-25 (December 1914).

K'ang-hsi yü Lo-ma shih-chieh kuan-hsi wen-shu 康熙与罗马使节关系文书 (Documents relating to K'ang-hsi and the Tournon Legation from Rome), in Wen-hsien ts'ung-pien no. 6.

K'ang Yu-wei 康有为, K'ang Nan-hai wen-chi hui-pien 康南海文集汇编 (Collected works of K'ang Yu-wei), 8 ts'e (Shih-huan shu-chü, 1925).

K'ang Yu-wei 康有为, K'ang Nan-hai wen-ch'ao 康南海文钞（The writings of K'ang Yu-wei）, in Tang-tai pa-ta-chia wen-ch'ao 当代八大家文钞, ts'e 3-6,（1926）.

K'ang Yu-wei 康有为, Kung-ch'e shang-shu chi 公车上书记（The memorial presented by the examination candidates）, 1 ts'e（Shanghai, 1895）.

K'ang Yu-wei 康有为, K'ung-tzu kai-chih k'ao 孔子改制考（Confucius as a reformer）, 21 chüan, in 6 ts'e（Peking, 1923 edition）.

K'ang Yu-wei 康有为, Ta-t'ung shu 大同书（A book on the universal commonwealth）, compiled by Ch'ien Ting-an 钱定安（Chung-hua Book Co., 1932）.

K'ang Yu-wei 康有为, see Wu Tse.

Kao Liang-tso 高良佐"Ch'ing-tai min-tsu ssu-hsiang chih hsien-tao-che"清代民族思想之先导者（Leading thinkers on nationalism during the Ch'ing period）, Chien-kuo yueh-k'an, 9.5：1-10（November 1933）.

Kao Nai-t'ung 高乃同, Ts'ai Chieh-min hsien-sheng chuan-lueh 蔡子民先生传略（A brief biography of Mr. Ts'ai Yuan-p'ei; Chungking：Commercial Press, 1932）.

Kayano Chōchi 萱野长知, Chūka-minkoku kakumei hikyu 中华民国革命秘笈（Confidential material concerning the revolution of the Republic of China）, complete information unavailable.

Kent, P. H., Railway Enterprise in China; An Account of Its Origin and Development（London, 1907）, 304 pp.

Kiang, Wen-han（Chiang Wen-han）, The Chinese Student Movement（New York：King's Crown Press, 1948）, 176 pp.

Ko Hsien-ning 葛贤宁,"Chin-tai Chung-kuo min-tsu shih-jen Huang Kung-tu"近代中国民族诗人黄公度（The nationalist poet Huang Kung-tu [Huang Tsun-hsien] of modern China）, Hsin Chung-hua, 2.7：91-101（1934）.

Ko Kung-chen 戈公振, Chung-kuo pao-hsueh shih 中国报学史（History of Chinese Journalism; Shanghai：Commercial Press, 1927）,

385 pp.

Kondō Haruo 近藤春雄, Gendai Chūgoku no sakka to sakuhin 現代中国の作家と作品 (Contemporary Chinese writers and writings; Tōkyō: Shinsen 1949), 380 pp.

Ko Shih-chün 葛世濬, Huang-ch'ao ching-shih-wen hsü-pien 皇朝经世文续编 (Supplement to the Huang-ch'ao ching-shih-wen), 120 chüan in 32 ts'e (Shanghai: T'u-shu chi-ch'eng chü movable type edition, 1888).

Ku-chin 古今 (Ancient and modern), published in Shanghai, beginning 1942, semi-monthly.

Ku-chin t'u-shu chi-ch'eng 古今图书集成 (Compilation of books and illustrations of ancient and modern times), 10,000 chüan, plus a table of contents in 40 chüan (Completed, 1726; printed, 1728).

Ku Ch'un-fan 谷春帆, Chiu wen-ming yü hsin kung-yeh 旧文明与新工业 (Old civilization and new industry; Shanghai: Commercial Press, 1944), 213 pp.

Ku Hung-ming 辜鸿铭, Papers From a Viceroy's Yamen 总督衙门论文集 (Shanghai: Shanghai Mercury, 1901), 197 pp.

Ku Hung-ming 辜鸿铭, Tu I ts'ao-t'ang wen-chi 读易草堂文集 (Collected essays of Ku Hung-ming), 1 ts'e (block print edition, 1922).

Ku Hung-ming 辜鸿铭, The Story of a Chinese Oxford Movement (1910). Complete information not available.

Ku Hung-ming 辜鸿铭, see Wen Yuan-ning, Yuan Chen-ying.

Ku Yen-wu 顾炎武, T'ien-hsia chün-kuo li-ping shu 天下郡国利病书 (A book on the [strategic and economic] advantages and disadvantages of the counties and states of the empire), 120 chüan in 24 ts'e (Ssu-pu ts'ung-k'an edition, third series; author's preface dated 1662).

Ku Yen-wu 顾炎武, Jih-chih lu 日知录 (Notes of daily [accumulation] of knowledge), first printed by him in 8 chüan in 1670. After revisions, it was printed in Fukien in 1695 in the present form of 32 chüan, and republished in 1872 by Ch'ung-wen shu-chü in Hupei, 16 ts'e.

Ku Yen-wu 顾炎武, T'ing-lin hsien-sheng i-shu hui-chi 亭林先生遗书

汇辑 (Collected writings of Ku Yen-wu), compiled by Hsi Wei 席威 and Chu Chi-yung 朱记荣, 24 ts'e (block-print edition of Chu's Chiao-ching shan-fang 朱氏校经山房, 1888).

Ku Yen-wu 顾炎武, "Chün-hsien lun"郡县论, in T'ing-lin shih-wen ch'üan-chi 亭林诗文全集 (Collected works of Ku Yen-wu), 4 ts'e (Ssu-pu pei-yao edition, 1930).

Kung Chün 龚骏, Chung-kuo hsin-kung-yeh fa-chan-shih ta-kang 中国新工业发展史大纲 (Outline history of the development of modern industry in China; Shanghai: Commercial Press, 1933), 302 pp.

"Kung-ssu"公司 (Corporations), see Chung-kuo nien-chien 中国年鉴 (The China Year Book), pp. 1587-1614.

Kuo Chan-po 郭湛波, Chin wu-shih-nien Chung-kuo ssu-hsiang shih 近五十年中国思想史 (A history of Chinese thought during the last fifty years; Peiping: Jen-wen shu-tien, 1936), 432 pp.

Kuo-feng 国风 (The National Spirit), published in Chungking, beginning 1942, semi-monthly.

Kuo-li chung-yang yen-chiu yuan 国立中央研究院 (Academia Sinica), Ch'ing-chu Ts'ai Yuan-p'ei hsien-sheng liu-shih-wu sui lun-wen chi 庆祝蔡元培先生六十五岁论文集 (Studies presented to Ts'ai Yuan-p'ei on his sixty-fifth birthday), Li-shih yü-yen yen-chiu-so chi-k'an wai-pien ti-i chung 历史语言研究所集刊外编第一种 (Supplement no. 1 of the Journal of the Institute of History and Philology), 2 vols. (Peiping, 1938).

Kuo, P. C., A Critical Study of the First Anglo-Chinese War with Documents (Shanghai: Commercial Press, 1930), 315 pp.

Kuo Pin-chia 郭斌佳, "Keng-tzu ch'üan-luan"庚子拳乱 (The Boxer Rebellion of 1900), Kuo-li Wu-han ta-hsueh wen-che chi-k'an 国立武汉大学文哲季刊("Quarterly Journal of Liberal Arts") 6.1:135-182 (1936).

Kuo Pin-ho 郭斌龢, "Yen Chi-tao"严几道 (Yen Fu), Kuo-feng, 8.6:213-228 (1936).

Kuo Sung-tao 郭嵩焘 Kuo shih-lang tsou-shu 郭侍郎奏疏 (The

memorials of Kuo Sung-tao),12 chüan (1892 edition).

Kuo Sung-tao 郭嵩焘, Yang-chih shu-wu ch'üan-chi 养知书屋全集 (Collected works of Kuo Sung-tao), 55 chüan (printed 1892).

Kuo Sung-tao 郭嵩焘, Yü-ch'ih lao-jen tzu-hsü 玉池老人自叙(Autobiographical notes of Kuo Sung-tao), 1 chüan(1893 edition).

Kuo T'ing-i 郭廷以, Chin-tai Chung-kuo shih 近代中国史 (Modern Chinese history; Shanghai: Commercial Press, 1940), 635 pp.

Kuo T'ing-i 郭廷以, T'ai-p'ing T'ien-kuo shih-shih jih-chih 太平天国史事日志 (History of the Taiping Kingdom, a daily record), 2 vols. Chungking and Shanghai: Commercial Press, 1946).

Kuo-wen chou-pao 国闻周报 (National news weekly), published in Tientsin, beginning 1924, weekly.

La Fargue, Thomas E., "Chinese Educational Commission to the United States, A Government Experiment in Western Education," Far Eastern Quarterly, 1.1:59-70 (November 1941).

La Fargue, Thomas E., China's First Hundred (Pullman: State College of Washington, 1942), 176 pp.

Langer, W. L., The Diplomacy of Imperialism, 1890-1902, 2 vols. (New York and London: A. A. Knopf, 1935); second edition (1951), 797 pp.

Lao Kan 老敢, "Ts'ai Yuan-p'ei yü Pei-ching ta-hsueh"蔡元培与北京大学 (Ts'ai Yuan-p'ei and Peking University), Kuo-wen chou-pao, 3.36: 1-5 (1926).

Lao Nai-hsuan 劳乃宣, Ch'üan-an san-chung 拳案三种 (Three works on the Boxer Case; block-print edition of 1902).

Lao Nai-hsuan 劳乃宣, I-ho-ch'üan chiao-men yuan-liu k'ao 义和拳教门源流考 (A study of the origin of the I-ho-ch'üan), reprinted in Tso Shun-sheng, Chung-kuo chin-pai-nien shih tzu-liao hsü-pien, vol. 1.

Latourette, K. S., A History of Christian Missions in China (London: Society for promoting Christian knowledge, 1929), 930 pp.

Lee, Shiu-keung, Timothy Richard and the Reform Movement in

China (Hartford Theological Seminary), complete information unavailable.

Legge, James, The Chinese Classics, 8 vols. (Oxford: Clarendon Press, 1893-1895).

Levenson, Joseph R., "The Breakdown of Confucianism: Liang Ch'i-ch'ao before Exile—1873-1898," Journal of the History of Ideas, 11. 4:448-485 (October 1950).

Levenson, Joseph R., Liang Ch'i-ch'ao and the Mind of Modern China (Cambridge: Harvard University Press, 1953).

Levy, M. J., and Shih Kuo-heng, The Rise of the Modern Chinese Business Class (New York: International Secretariat, Institute of Pacific Relations, 1949), 63 pp.

Li Ch'iao-p'ing, The Chemical Arts of Old China (Easton, Pa.: Journal of Chemical Education, 1948), 215 pp.

Li Chien-nung 李剑农, Chung-kuo Chin-pai-nien cheng-chih shih 中国近百年政治史 (The political history of China during the last hundred years), 2 vols. (Shanghai: Commercial Press, 1947).

Li Hung-chang 李鸿章, Li Wen-chung-kung ch'üan-chi 李文忠公全集 (A complete collection of the works of Li Hung-chang), 100 ts'e (Shanghai, 1921).

Li Hung-chang 李鸿章, Li Wen-chung-kung tsou-kao 李文忠公奏稿, in Li Wen-chung-kung ch'üan-chi, ts'e 2-51.

Li Hung-chang 李鸿章, Li Wen-chung-kung p'eng-liao han-kao 李文忠公朋僚函稿, in Li Wen-chung-kung ch'üan-chi, ts'e 52-61.

Li Hung-chang 李鸿章, "Ch'ou-i chih-tsao lun-ch'uan wei-k'o ts'ai-ch'e che" 筹议制造轮船未可裁撤折 (Planning the construction of steamships should not be given up), in Li Wen-chung-kung tsou-kao.

Li Hung-chang 李鸿章, "Li Wen-chung-kung Hung-chang nien-p'u" 李文忠公鸿章年谱 (A chronological biography of Li Hung-chang), comp. by Li Shu-ch'un 李书春, Shih-hsueh nien-pao 史学年报, no. 1:97-124 (July 1929).

Li Hung-chang 李鸿章, see Wu Pao-chang.

Li Ki (The Book of Rites) 礼记, tr. by James Legge, ed. by F. Max Muller, in The Sacred Books of China: The Texts of Confucianism, 2 vols. (Oxford, 1885).

Li-ma-tou 利玛窦 (Mattes Ricci), T'ien-chu shih-i 天主实义 (The true meaning of Christianity), 2 chüan (Sheng-shih-t'ang movable type edition, 1922).

Li Ming 李明 and others, Chung-kung liu-lieh-shih hsiao-chuan 中共六烈士小传 (Brief biographies of six Chinese communist martyrs; Hongkong: The New China Bookstore, 1949), 84 pp.

Li P'ei-en 李培恩, "Chin-pai-nien lai Chung-kuo chih yin-hang" 近百年来中国之银行 (Chinese banking in the past hundred years), Hsueh-lin, no. 9: 1-14 (July 1941).

Li Shih-ch'en 李石岑, Jen-sheng che-hsueh 人生哲学 (Philosophy of life; Shanghai: Commercial Press, 1926).

Li Shou-ch'ang 李守常, P'ing-min chu-i 平民主义 ("Democracy"; Shanghai, 1925). 35 pp.

Li Shu-ch'un, 李书春 comp., see (Tseng Kuo-fan), Tseng Wen-cheng-kung nien-p'u.

Li Shu-ch'un, 李书春 comp., see Li Hung-chang, "Li wen-chung-kung Hung-chang nien-p'u."

Li Ta-chao 李大钊, "Bolshevism ti sheng-li" Bolshevism 的胜利, Hsin-ch'ing-nien, 5.5:442-448 (November 15, 1918).

Li Ta-chao 李大钊, "Wo-ti Ma-k'o-ssu chu-i kuan" 我的马克思主义观 (My view of Marxism), Hsin-ch'ing-nien, 6.5:521-537 (May, 1919).

Li Ta-chao 李大钊, see Yang Yung-kuo.

Li T'i-mo-t'ai 李提摩太 (Timothy Richard), Hsi-to 西铎 (The warning bell from the West), 1 chüan. (Shanghai: Kwang-hsueh hui, printed 1895). For a further list of his Chinese writings, see catalogue of the Chinese-Japanese Library, Harvard University.

Li Ting-fang 李鼎芳, Tseng Kuo-fan chi ch'i mu-fu jen-wu 曾国藩及其幕府人物 (Tseng Kuo-fan and his secretarial personnel; Kweiyang:

Wen-t'ung shu-chü, 1946).

Li Wen-chung-kung, see Li Hung-chang.

Li Yeh 李治, "Ts'e yuan-hai ching" 测圆海镜, ch. 107 of Ssu-k'u ch'üan-shu tsung-mu t'i-yao 四库全书总目提要 (Tai-tung shu-chü edition).

Li Yen 李俨, Chung-kuo shu-hsueh ta-kang 中国数学大纲 (Outline of Chinese mathematics), vol. 1 (Shanghai, 1931), 222 pp.

Li Yen 李俨, Chung-kuo suan-hsueh shih 中国算学史 (History of mathematics in China; Shanghai: Commercial Press, 1937), 293 pp.

Li Yen 李俨, Chung-suan-shih lun-ts'ung 中算史论丛 (Essays on the history of mathematics in China), in 4 series, 1931-1947 (first series, 1931, 408 pp.; 2nd series, 1935, 474 pp.; 3rd. series, 1935, 400 pp; 4th. series, 2 vols., 1947, 638 pp.).

Li Yuan-tu 李元度, Kuo-ch'ao hsien-cheng shih-lueh 国朝先正事略 (Biographies of leading statesmen and men of letters of the Ch'ing period), 60 chüan (published, 1866).

Liang Ch'i-ch'ao 梁启超, "Hsin-min shuo" 新民说 (The renovation of the people), Hsin-min ts'ung-pao 新民丛报, no. 1:1-10 (January 1902).

Liang Ch'i-ch'ao 梁启超, Hsi-hsueh shu-mu piao 西学书目表 (A bibliography of books on Western knowledge), in Chih-hsueh ts'ung-shu ch'u-chi 质学丛书初集, ts'e 9-10.

Liang Ch'i-ch'ao 梁启超, K'ang Nan-hai chuan 康南海传 (Biography of K'ang Yu-wei), 1 ts'e (Shanghai, 1908).

Liang Ch'i-ch'ao 梁启超, Yin-ping-shih ho-chi 饮冰室合集 (Collected works of the Ice-drinkers' Studio [Liang Ch'i-ch'ao]), includes Wen-chi 文集 (Collection of essays), ts'e 1-16, Chuan-chi 专集 (Special collection), ts'e 17-40 (also numbered ts'e 1-24); 40 ts'e (Shanghai: Chunghua shu-chü, 1936).

Liang Ch'i-ch'ao 梁启超, Ssu-shih-nien lai ta-shih chi 四十年来大事记 (Important events in the last forty years [biography of Li Hung-chang]), ts'e 18 of Yin-ping-shih ho-chi.

Liang Ch'i-ch'ao 梁启超, Ou-yu hsin-ying lu chieh-lu 欧游心影录节录 (A record of impressions during travel in Europe) in Yin-ping-shih ho-chi, ts'e 21.

Liang Ch'i-ch'ao 梁启超, Ch'ing-tai hsueh-shu kai-lun 清代学术概论 (A general discussion of the academic learning of the Ch'ing Dynasty), in Yin-ping-shih ho-chi, ts'e 25.

Liang Ch'i-ch'ao 梁启超, Chung-kuo chin-san-pai-nien hsueh-shu-shih 中国近三百年学术史 (A history of Chinese academic thought during the last three hundred years; Shanghai, 1926), 562 pp. Also in Yin-ping-shih ho-chi, ts'e 33. A resume in English was published as "An Outline of the Chinese Cultural History of the Last Three Centuries," CSPSR 7.3: 33-47 (July, 1924).

Liang Ch'i-ch'ao 梁启超, Chu Shun-shui hsien-sheng nien-p'u 朱舜水先生年谱 (A chronological biography of Chu Shun-shui), in Yin-ping-shih ho-chi, ts'e 38, or Chuan-chi, ts'e 22.

Liang Ch'i-ch'ao 梁启超, "Wu-shih-nien Chung-kuo chin-hua kai-lun" 五十年中国进化概论 (A brief discussion of progress in China during the past fifty years), in Yin-ping-shih ho-chi, Wen-chi, part 39.

Liang Ch'i-ch'ao 梁启超, "Lao-tzu che-hsueh" 老子哲学 (The philosophy of Lao-tzu), in Yin-ping-shih ho-chi, Wen-chi, part 63.

Liang Ch'i-ch'ao 梁启超, "Tung-nan ta-hsueh k'o-pi kao-pieh tz'u" 东南大学课毕告别辞 (Parting speech after completing classes at Tung-nan University), in Yin-ping-shih ho-chi, Wen-chi, part 70.

Liang Ch'i-ch'ao 梁启超, see Wu Ch'i-ch'ang; Wu Tse; Itano.

(Liang Shih-i 梁士诒), San-shui Liang Yen-sun hsien-sheng nien-p'u, 三水梁燕孙先生年谱 (A chronological biography of Liang Shih-i of San-shui), ed. by Liang's disciples (published [by Liang's family members] 1939; 2nd printing 1946), 624 pp.

Library of Congress, Bibliography of Modern Chinese Law in the Library of Congress (1944), 49 mimeographed pages.

Lin Mou-sheng, Men and Ideas, an Informal History of Chinese

Political Thought (New York: John Day Co., 1942), 256 pp.

Lin, T. C., "Li Hung-chang, His Korea Policies 1870-1885", CSPSR, 19.2:200-233 (1935).

Lin Tse-hsü 林则徐 Lin Wen-chung-kung cheng-shu 林文忠公政书 (Collection of memorials by Lin Tse-hsü), 37 chüan (printed by the author's family).

Lin Tse-hsü 林则徐, "Lin Tse-hsü fu Wu Tzu-hsü pien-hsiu shu" 林则徐复吴子序编修书 (A reply from Lin Tse-hsü to the Hanlin Compiler Wu Tzu-hsü) in Li-tai ming-jen shu-cha hsü-pien 历代名人书札续编, compiled by Wu Tseng-ch'i 吴曾祺 (Shanghai, 1909; 17th printing, 1925), 2A.18-19.

Lin Tse-hsü 林则徐, Lin Wen-chung-kung nien-p'u 林文忠公年谱 (A chronological biography of Lin Tse-hsü), compiled by Wei Ying-ch'i 魏应麒 (Shanghai: Commercial Press, 1935), 200 pp.

Lin Wen-chung-kung, see Lin Tse-hsü.

Lin Yao-hua 林耀华, "Yen Fu she-hui ssu-hsiang" 严复社会思想 (Social thought of Yen Fu), She-hui hsüeh-chieh, 7:1-82 (1933).

Lin Yü-t'ang 林语堂, "Ku Hung-ming" 辜鸿铭 (Ku Hung-ming), Jen-chien shih, no. 12:37-40 (September 1934).

Lin Yü-tang 林语堂, A History of the Press and Public Opinion in China (Chicago: University of chicago Press, 1936).

Linebarger, Paul M. A., The Political Doctrines of Sun Yat-sen (Baltimore: Johns Hopkins Press, 1937), 273 pp.

Ling-nan hsueh-pao 岭南学报 (Lingnan Journal), published by Lingnan University, Canton, beginning 1929, quarterly.

Liu Chin-tsao 刘锦藻, Ch'ing-ch'ao hsü wen-hsien t'ung-k'ao 清朝续文献通考 (A supplement to the Wen-hsien t'ung-k'ao of the Ch'ing), Commercial Press edition of the Shih-t'ung 十通.

Liu Hsi-hung 刘锡鸿, Ying-yao jih-chi 英轺日记 (Diary of a mission to England), in Ling chien-ko ts'ung-shu, 灵鹣阁丛书, published by Chiang Piao 江标, ts'e 10; also in Hsiao-fang-hu-chai yü-ti ts'ung-ch'ao, ts'e 56.

Liu Hsi-san 刘锡三, "Wu-ssu i-hou Chung-kuo ko-p'ai ssu-hsiang-chia tui-yü Hsi-yang wen-ming ti t'ai-tu"五四以后中国各派思想家对于西洋文明的态度 (Attitudes of Chinese thinkers of various groups toward Western civilization after the May Fourth movement), She-hui hsueh-chieh, 7:271-317 (June 1933).

Liu Hsiung-hsiang 刘熊祥, Ch'ing-chi shih-nien chih lien-E cheng-ts'e 清季十年之联俄政策 (Russian alliance policy during the last decade of the Ch'ing Dynasty; Chungking: San-yu shu-tien, 1943).

Liu Hsiung-hsiang 刘熊祥, Ch'ing-chi ssu-shih-nien wai-chiao yü hai-fang 清季四十年外交与海防 (Forty years of foreign relations and coastal defense in the late Ch'ing period; alternative title, "A Study of the Tsungli Yamen"; Chungking: San-yu shu-tien, 1944), 182 pp.

(Liu Ming-ch'uan 刘铭传), Liu Chuang-su-kung tsou-i 刘壮肃公奏议 (Memorials of Liu Ming-ch'uan), 22 chüan (preface dated 1906).

Liu P'an-sui 刘盼遂, "Liang Jen-kung hsien-sheng chuan"梁任公先生传 (A biography of Liang Ch'i-ch'ao) T'u-shu-kuan-hsueh chi-k'an 图书馆学季刊, 3.1-2:135-137 (1929).

Liu Ping-li 刘炳藜, Kuo-fu ssu-hsiang t'i-hsi shu-yao 国父思想体系述要 (An account of essential points of Sun Yat-sen's system of thinking; Shanghai, 1946), 98 pp.

Liu Yueh-yün 刘岳云, Shih-chiu-te-chai tsa-chu 食旧德斋杂著 (Miscellaneous writings of Liu Yueh-yün), ts'e 4(1882).

Liu Yueh-yün 刘岳云, "Ko-wu chung fa hsü"格物中法叙(Preface to Ko-wu chung fa), in Shih-chiu-te-chai tsa-chu, ts'e 1.

Lo Erh-kang 罗尔纲, "Ming-wang hou Han-tsu ti tzu-chueh ho mi-mi chieh-she"明亡后汉族的自觉和秘密结社 (Chinese national awakening and secret organizations after the fall of the Ming Dynasty), Tientsin I-shih-pao:"shih-hsuh" 史学(History supplement), no. 1 (April 30,1935).

Lo Erh-kang 罗尔纲, T'ai-p'ing T'ien-kuo shih-kang 太平天国史纲 (Outline history of the Taiping Rebellion; Shanghai: Commercial Press,

1937), 134 pp.

Lo Erh-kang 罗尔纲, T'ai-p'ing T'ien-kuo shih-kao 太平天国史稿 (A draft history of the Taiping rebellion; Peking: K'ai-ming shu-tien, 1951), 5 & 285 pp.

Lo Erh-kang 罗尔纲, T'ai-p'ing T'ien-kuo shih ts'ung-k'ao 太平天国史丛考 (Miscellaneous studies on the history of the Taiping rebellion; Shanghai: Cheng-chung shu-chü, 1943; 2nd. printing, 1947), 196 pp.

Lo Erh-kang 罗尔纲, T'ien-ti-hui wen-hsien lu 天地会文献录 (Documents of the Heaven and Earth Society; (Cheng-chung shu-chü, 1943).

Lo Hsiang-lin 罗香林, Kuo-fu chih ta-hsueh shih-tai 国父之大学时代 (The college years of the father of our nation; Chungking: Tu-li ch'u-pan-she, 1945), 164 pp.

Lo Hsiang-lin 罗香林, "Ya-p'ien chan-cheng Yueh-tung i-min k'ang-Ying shih-liao hsü-lu" 鸦片战争粤东义民抗英史料叙录 (Copies of historical materials concerning the anti-British movement among the people of Kwangtung during the Opium War), She-hui k'o-hsueh ts'ung-k'an 社会科学丛刊 ("Studies in Social Sciences"), National Central University, Nanking, 2.2:145-164 (January 1936).

Lo Wen-kan, "China's Introduction of Foreign Systems," CSPSR 8.4:172-182 (October 1924).

Lou T'ung-sun 楼桐荪, San-min chu-i yen-chiu 三民主义研究 (A study of San-min chu-i; Shanghai: Commercial Press, no date [1934?]), 222 pp.

Lu Hsi-ta 鲁昔达, "Tseng Tso hsiang-wu chi ch'i-t'a" 曾左相恶及其他 (The disagreement between Tseng and Tso and other matters), Ku-chin, no. 32:28-32 (October 1943).

Lü-li yuan-yuan 律历渊源 (Compendium on the calendar, music and mathematics), compiled under imperial auspices 1723-1756, including three works: Li-hsiang k'ao-ch'eng 历象考成, 42 chüan, on the calendar; Shu-li ching-yun 数理精蕴, 53 chüan, on mathematics; and Lü-lü cheng-i

律吕正义, 5 chüan, on music.

Lü Liu-liang 吕留良, Lü Yung-hui wen-chi 吕用晦文集 (Collected essays of Lü Liu-liang), in Kuo-ts'ui ts'ung-shu 国粹丛书, ts'e 5-6.

Ma Chien-chung 马建忠, Shih-k'o-chai chi-yen 适可斋记言 (Notes from the Shih-k'o-chai [studio]), in Hsi-cheng ts'ung-shu, ts'e 27 (preface dated 1896).

Ma Feng-chen 马奉琛, Ch'ing-tai hsing-cheng chih-tu yen-chiu ts'an-k'ao shu-mu 清代行政制度研究参考书目 (Bibliography for research on the administrative system of the Ch'ing Dynasty; Peiping: Peking University Press, 1935), 228 pp.

MacNair, H. F., Modern Chinese History: Selected Readings (Shanghai: Commercial Press, 1923), 910 pp.

Mai Chien-tseng 麦健曾 and Li Ying-chao 李应兆, Chung-kuo t'ieh-tao wen-t'i ts'an-k'ao tzu-liao so-yin 中国铁道问题参考资料索引 (An index to reference material on Chinese railroad problems; Peiping: Peiping branch of the Research Institute of Chiao-t'ung University, 1936).

Mai Chung-hua 麦仲华, comp., Huang-ch'ao ching-shih-wen hsin-pien 皇朝经世文新编 (New supplement to the Huang-ch'ao ching-shih wen-pien), 21 chüan (Shanghai: Shang-hai shu-chü, 1901).

Makino Kyōji 牧野京次, "Ri Kō-shō no denki" 李鸿章の传记 (Biography of Li Hung-chang), Shusho geppo 收书月报, no. 65.

Malone, C. B., History of the Peking Summer Palaces (Urbana, Ill., 1934), 247 pp.

Mantetsu Chōsa Kyoku 满铁调查局 (South Manchurian Railway Research Bureau), Shina kōsan shigen bunken mokuroku 支那矿产资源文献目录 (A bibliography of literature on Chinese natural resources; Tōkyō, 1943), 88 pp.

Martin, W. A. P., trans., Wan-kuo kung-fa 万国公法 (Wheaton's International Law), 4 chüan (Peking, 1864).

Martin, W. A. P., A Cycle of Cathay (New York, second edition,

1896), 464 pp.

Martin, W. A. P., The Lore of Cathay; or The Intellect of China (New York, 1901), 480 pp.

Matsumoto Sumio 松本纯郎, Mito gaku no genryū 水戶学の源流 (The origin of the Mito school; Tōkyō: Chō-sō shoten, 1945), 314 pp.

Maybon, Albert, La Politique Chinoise, étude sur les doctrines des partis en Chine, 1898-1908 (Paris, 1908), 268 pp.

McCall, Davy H., "Chang Chien—Mandarin Turned Manufacturer," Papers On China, 2:93-102 (May 1948).

McCall, Davy H., "Chang Chien and the Establishment of the Tungchow cotton mills," unpublished paper (1948) on file in the Harvard Chinese Library, Regional Studies collection.

Mei Ying 梅影, "Wu-hsü cheng-pien chen-wen" 戊戌政变珍闻 (Valuable information on the reform movement of 1898), Jen-wen 人文, 7.10:1-6 (December 1936).

Meijer, Marinus Johan, The Introduction of Modern Criminal Law in China, Sinica Indonesiana, Vol. II. (Batavia: De Unie, 1950), 212 pp.

Men-se t'an-hu-k'o 扪虱谈虎客 (pseud.), Chin-shih Chung-kuo mi-shih 近世中国秘史 (A "confidential" modern Chinese history), 2 vols. (Shanghai, 1905).

Mencius 孟子, see Meng-tzu chu-su.

Meng Ch'i 孟祁, "Chi Ku Hung-ming weng" 记辜鸿铭翁 (On Mr. Ku Hung-ming), Jen-chien shih, no. 12:44-45 (September 1934).

Meng Ssu-ming, "The Organization and Functions of the Tsungli Yamen" (Harvard Ph. D. thesis, 1949) 188 pp.

Meng-tzu chu-su 孟子注疏 (The works of Mencius), in Shih-san-ching chu-su, ts'e 155-160.

Michie, Alexander, The Englishman in China during the Victorian Era, 2 vols. (Edinburgh, 1910).

Mikami, Yoshio, Development of Mathematics in China and Japan (Leipzig, 1913), 347 pp.

Min Erh-ch'ang 闵尔昌, ed., Pei-chuan-chi pu 碑传集补 (Supplement to the Pei-chuan-chi), 60 chüan (Peiping: Yenching University, 1931).

Momose Hiromu 百瀬弘, "Fū Kei-fun to sono chojutsu ni tsuite" 冯桂芬と其の著述に就いて (On Feng Kuei-fen and his writings), Tōa ronsō 东亚论丛 2: 95-122 (January 1940). Translated into Chinese in a condensed form in Chung-ho yueh-k'an 中和月刊, 3.3: 53-66 (March 1942).

Morse, H. B., International Relations of the Chinese Empire, 3 vols. (London, 1910-1918).

Mu Hsiang-yueh 穆湘玥, "Chung-kuo mien-chih-yeh fa-ta-shih" 中国棉织业发达史 (Progress of China's cotton textile industry for the past 50 years), in Tsui-chin chih wu-shih-nien, pp. 1-5 (in the middle of the volume, which is not paged consecutively).

Mu Hsiang-yueh 穆湘玥, Ou-ch'u ssu-shih tzu-shu 藕初四十自述 (Autobiography at forty by Mu Hsiang-yueh; Shanghai: Commercial Press, 1926), 94+226+81 pp.

Murakami Tomoyuki 村上知行, Bojutsu seihen shiwa 戊戌政变史话 (Historical accounts of the coup d'état of 1898; Peking: Hsin-min yin-shu-kuan, 1944), 244 pp.

Murphey, Rhoads, Shanghai, Key to Modern China (Cambridge: Harvard University Press, 1953), 232 pp.

Nelson, William E., "One-party Government in China," Far Eastern Survey, 17.10: 118-121 (May 19, 1948).

Niida Noboru 仁井田陞 ed., et al., Kindai Chūgoku kenkyū 近代中国研究 (Researches on Modern China; Tōkyō: Kōgakusha, 1948), 361 pp.

Nishida Tamotsu 西田保, Sa Sō-dō to Shin-kyō mondai 左宗棠と新疆问题 (Tso Tsung-t'ang and the problem of Sinkiang; Tōkyō: Hakubunkan, 1942).

Nolde, John J., "The 'Canton Question,' 1842-1849: A Preliminary Investigation into Chinese Anti-foreignism and its Effect upon China's

Diplomatic Relations with the West" (Ph. D. dissertation, Cornell University, 1950), 271 pp.

Norman, E. Herbert, Japan's Emergence as a Modern State (New York: Institute of Pacific Relations, 1940), 254 pp.

North China Herald, Shanghai, weekly, 1850—

Nü-shih hsueh-yuan ch'i-k'an 女师学院期刊(Journal of the Hopei Teachers' College for Women), Tientsin, beginning 1933, semi-annually.

Odontines, L., "Chang Chih-tung and the Reform Movement in China," translated from the German by E. Zillig, The East of Asia, 1.1: 19-42 (1902).

Ojima Sukema 小岛祐马, Chūgoku no kakumei shisō 中国の革命思想 (Chinese revolutionary thought; Tōkyō: Kōbundō, 1952), 166 pp.

Ono Noriaki 小野则秋, Son Bun 孙文 (Sun Yat-sen; Tōkyō: Daigadō, 1948), 257 pp.

Onogawa Hidemi 小野川秀美, "Shimmatsu hempōron no seiritsu"清末变法论の成立("The Formation of the Reformatory Thought at the End of the Ts'ing Dynasty"), Tōhō gakuhō 东方学报, Kyōto, 20: 153-184 (March 1951).

Onogawa Hidemi 小野川秀美, "Shimmatsu yōmuha no undō"清末洋务派の运动("On the Movement of Europeanizing at the End of the Ch'ing Era"), Tōyōshi kenkyū ("The Journal of Oriental Researches"), 10.6: 429-466 (February 1950).

Onogawa Hidemi 小野川秀美, "Shimmatsu no shisō to shinkaron"清末の思想と进化论 ("Political Thoughts and the Evolutionary Theory at the End of the Tsing Dynasty"). Tōhō gakuhō 东方学报, Kyōto, 21: 1-36 (March 1952).

Otake Fumio 小竹文夫, "Mimmatsu irai seisho-kō"明末以来西书考 (A study of Western books published in Chinese since the late Ming period), Shina kenkyū 支那研究 43: 35-71 (January 1937).

Ou-yang Yü-ch'ien 欧阳予倩, comp., T'an Ssu-t'ung shu-chien 谭嗣

同书简 (Letters of T'an Ssu-t'ung; Shanghai: Wen-hua kung-ying she, 1948), 138 pp.

Overdijkink, G. W., Lin Tse-hsü, (Leiden: E. J. Brill, 1938), 173 pp.

Owen, D. E., British Opium Policy in China and India (New Haven: Yale University Press, 1934), 399 pp.

Pan Ku 班固, Ch'ien-Han shu 前汉书 (History of the Former Han), 120 chüan (Shanghai, T'ung-wen shu-chü edition).

P'an Kung-chan 潘公展, Wu-shih-nien-lai ti Chung-kuo 五十年来的中国 (China in the past fifty years; Chungking: Sheng-li ch'u-pan-she, 1945), 339 pp.

P'an Wei-tung, The Chinese Constitution: A Study of Forty Years of Constitution-making in China (Washington: The Catholic University of America Press, 1945), 327 pp.

Papers on China, from the Regional Studies Seminars, mimeographed for private distribution by the Committee on International and Regional Studies, Harvard University, Cambridge: 1 (December 1947), 2 (May 1948), 3 (May 1949), 4 (April 1950), 5 (May 1951), 6 (March 1952), 7 (February 1953).

Papers Relating to Foreign Affairs, 1867 (Washington D. C., 1868).

Parker, E. H. (tr.), "The Published Letters of the Senior Marquis Tseng," China Review, 18.6:347-365 (May-June 1890).

Peake, Cyrus H., "Some Aspects of the Introduction of Modern Science into China," Isis, 63:173-219 (December 1934).

Pei-yang hai-chün chang-ch'eng 北洋海军章程 (Regulations of the Pei-yang Navy), compiled by Chung-kuo tsung-li hai-chün ya-men, 2 ts'e (Tientsin, 1888).

Pelliot, Paul, review of The Hung Society or the Society of Heaven and Earth, par J. S. M. Ward et W. G. Sterling, T'oung-pao XXV, 444-448 (Leide, 1926).

P'eng Tse-i 彭泽益, "Chang Chien ti ssu-hsiang chi ch'i shih-yeh" 张

謇的思想及其事业 (Chang Chien's ideas and career), *Tung-fang tsa-chih*, 40.14:54-60 (1944).

Pfister, Louis, S. J., *Notices biographiques et bibliographiques sur les Jésuites de l'ancienne Mission de Chine (1552-1773)*, 2 vols. (Shanghai: Variétés sinologiques, nos. 59-60, 1932, 1934).

Powell, Ralph L., "The Rise of Yuan Shih-k'ai and the Pei-yang Army," *Papers on China*, 3:225-256 (1949).

Prince Kung 恭亲王 (I-hsin 奕䜣), *Lo-tao-t'ang shih-wen ch'ao* 乐道堂诗文钞 (Reproduction of I-hsin's poems and essays), 12 ts'e (block-print edition, 1867).

Pritchard, Earl H., *Anglo-Chinese Relations during the Seventeenth and Eighteenth Centuries* (Urbana: The University of Illinois Press, 1929), 244 pp.

Pritchard, Earl H., "The Kotow in the Macartney Embassy to China of 1793," *Far Eastern Quarterly*, 2.2:163-203 (February 1943).

Rawlinson, John L., "The Lay-Osborn Flotilla: Its Development and Significance," *Papers on China* 4:58-73 (1950).

(Reform movement), "Kuan-yü wu-hsü cheng-pien hsin shih-liao" 关于戊戌政变新史料 (New historical material concerning the reform movement of 1898), *Ta-kung-pao, shih-ti chou-k'an* 大公报史地周刊, 4.95 (July 1936).

(Reform movement), "Lun pien-fa chih ching-shen" 论变法之精神 (On the spirit of reform), *Tung-fang tsa-chih*, no. 7:142-144 (1904).

Rosso, Antonio Sisto, O. F. M., *Apostolic Legations to China of the Eighteenth Century* (South Pasadena: P. D. and Ione Perkins, 1948), 502 pp.

Rowbotham, Arnold, H. *Missionary and Mandarin: The Jesuits at the Court of China* (Berkeley: University of California Press, 1942), 374 pp.

Saeki Yoshiro 佐伯好郎, *Shinchō Kirisuto-kyō no kenkyū* 清朝基督教の研究 (A study of Christianity under the Ch'ing Dynasty; Tōkyō:

Shunjūsha 春秋社, 1949), 640 + 24 pp.

Sakai, Robert K., "Ts'ai Yuan-p'ei as a Synthesizer of Western and Chinese Thought," Papers on China, Cambridge, 3:170-192 (May 1949).

Sanetō Keishū 实藤惠秀, Chūgokujin Nippon ryūgaku shikō 中国人日本留学史稿 (Draft history of Chinese students in Japan; Tōkyō: Nikka gakkai 日华学会, 1939), 368 pp., illus.

Sanetō Keishū 实藤惠秀, Kindai Nisshi bunka ron 近代日支文化论 (On modern Sino-Japanese culture), Tōkyō: Daitō 大东, 1941, 269 pp., illus.

Sanetō Keishū 实藤惠秀, "Kindai Shina to gairai shisō" 近代支那と外来思想, in Kindai Shina shisō 近代支那思想, pp. 143-176 (Tōkyō: Kōfūkan, 1942).

Sanetō Keishū 实藤惠秀, Meiji Nisshi bunka kōshō 明治日支文化交涉 (Sino-Japanese cultural relations in the Meiji period; Tōkyō: Kōfūkan 光风馆, 1943), 394 pp., illus.

Sanetō Keishū 实藤惠秀, "Wang T'ao ti tu-Jih ho Jih-pen wen-jen" 王韬的渡日和日本文人 (Wang T'ao's trip to Japan and Japanese scholars), tr. by Chang Ming-san 张铭三, in Jih-pen yen-chiu 日本研究, 3.6:27-39 (1944).

Sano Kesami 佐野袈裟美, Shina kindai hyakunenshi 支那近代百年史 (History of China in the past hundred years), 2 vols. (Tōkyō Hakuyōsha, 1939-1940).

Sansom, G. B., Japan: A Short Cultural History, revised edition (New York: D. Appleton-Century Co., 1943), 554 pp.

Sansom, G. B., The Western World and Japan (New York: Alfred A. Knopf, 1950), 504 pp.

Schwartz, Benjamin, "Ch'en Tu-hsiu, His Pre-Communist Phase," Papers on China, 2:167-197 (1948).

Schwartz, Benjamin, "Ch'en Tu-hsiu and the Acceptance of the Modern West," Journal of the History of Ideas, 12.1:61-74 (January 1951).

Schwartz, Benjamin., *Chinese Communism and the Rise of Mao* (Cambridge: Harvard University Press, 1951), 258 pp.

*Shang-hai-shih t'ung-chih-kuan ch'i-k'an* 上海市通志馆期刊 (A periodical publication of the Shanghai Gazetteer Office), no. 2 (1933), 513 pp.

Shang Ping-ho 尚秉和, "Yuan ta-tsung-t'ung lueh-shih"袁大总统略史 (A brief history of President Yuan), ch. 34 in *Hsin-jen ch'un-ch'iu* 辛壬春秋 (A chronicle of 1911-1912), 16 ts'e (block-print edition of 1924).

*Shang-shu cheng-i* 尚书正义 (*The Book of History*), in *Shih-san-ching chu-su*, ts'e 5-12.

Sharman, Lyon, *Sun Yat-Sen, His Life and its Meaning, A Critical Biography* (New York: John Day, 1934), 418 pp.

*She-hui-hsueh chieh* 社会学界 (The sociological world), published by Yenching University, Department of Sociology, Peiping, beginning 1927, annual.

Sheeks, Robert, "A Re-examination of the I-ho Ch'üan and its Role in the Boxer Movement," *Papers on China*, 1:74-135 (1947).

Shen Chien 沈鉴, "Ssu-shih-yü-nien ch'ien chih lien-E wai-chiao"四十余年前之联俄外交 (The pro-Russian foreign policy [of China] some forty years ago), *Chung-kuo wen-hua yen-chiu-so hui-k'an* 中国文化研究所汇刊, vol. 2:151-184 (1942).

Shen Ch'un 沈纯, *Hsi-shih li-ts'e* 西事蠡测 (A glimpse into Western affairs), in *Hsiao-fang-hu-chai yü-ti ts'ung-ch'ao*, ts'e 62.

Shen-pao-kuan 申报馆, comp., *Tsui-chin chih wu-shih-nien, Shen-pao-kuan wu-shih chou-nien chi-nien* 最近之五十年, 申报馆五十周年纪念 (The past fifty years, in commemoration of the *Shen-pao's* Golden Jubilee, 1872-1922), a special supplement published by the *Shen-pao* (Shanghai, 1923).

*Shen-pao nien-chien* 申报年鉴 (The *Shen-pao* year book), first issue, edited by Chang Tzu-sheng 张梓生 and others, 1 ts'e (Shanghai, 1933).

Shen Tsu-hsien 沈祖宪 ed., *Yang-shou-yuan tsou-i chi-yao* 养寿园奏

议辑要 (A collection of important memorials of Yang-shou-yuan [Yuan Shih-k'ai]), block-print edition (publisher and date unknown).

Shen Tsu-hsien 沈祖宪 and Wu K'ai-sheng 吴闿生, Jung-an ti-tzu chi 容庵弟子记 (An account of Jung-an [Yuan Shih-k'ai] by his disciples; publisher unknown, 1913).

Shen T'ung-sheng 沈桐生, ed., Kuang-hsü cheng-yao 光绪政要 (Important documents concerning the Kuang-hsü administration), 30 ts'e (Shanghai: Nan-yang kuan-shu-chü, 1908).

Sheng Hsuan-huai 盛宣怀, Yü-chai ts'un-kao 愚斋存稿 (Extant writings of Sheng Hsuan-huai), 100 chüan (Shanghai: published by Ssu-pu lou, 1939).

Sheng K'ang 盛康, Huang-ch'ao ching-shih-wen hsü-pien 皇朝经世文续编 (Supplement to the Huang-ch'ao ching-shih wen-pien), 80 chüan, 10 ts'e (1897 edition).

Shih-liao hsun-k'an 史料旬刊 (Historical materials published thrice monthly), 40 volumes (Peking: Palace Museum 1930-1931).

Shih, Vincent Yu-chung, "Interpretations of the Taiping Tien-kuo by Noncommunist Chinese Writers," Far Eastern Quarterly 10.3:248-257 (May 1951).

Shina kōsan shigen bunken mokuroku, see Mantetsu Chōsa Kyoku.

Shu An 铢庵, "Hsiang-hsiang Tseng-shih i-wen" 湘乡曾氏遗闻 (Anecdotes of the Tseng family of Hsiang-hsiang), Jen-chien-shih, no. 26:9-13 (April 1935).

Shu Hsin-ch'eng 舒新城 ed., Chin-tai Chung-kuo chiao-yü shih-liao 近代中国教育史料 (Historical materials on modern Chinese education), in Chiao-yü ts'ung-shu 教育丛书 (Education series), 4 vols. (Shanghai, 1923), pp. 339+264+245+198+39.

Shu Hsin-ch'eng 舒新城, Chin-tai Chung-kuo liu-hsueh shih 近代中国留学史 (History of education of students abroad in modern China; Shanghai: Chiao-yü ts'ung-shu, 1927), 300 pp.

Shun Pao, see Shen-pao.

Shuo-wen yueh-k'an 说文月刊, published in Shanghai and Chungking, beginning 1939.

So Kwan-wai (Su Chun-wei 苏均炜), "Western Influence and the Chinese Reform Movement of 1898," (Ph. D. dissertation, University of Wisconsin, 1950), 269 pp.

Soothill, W. E., Timothy Richard of China (London: Seeley & Co., 1924), 330 pp.

South Manchurian Railway, see Mantetsu Chòsa Kyoku.

Ssu-chou chih 四洲志 (Gazetteer of the four continents), in Hsiao-fang-hu-chai yü-ti ts'ung-ch'ao, ts'e 82.

Ssu-k'u ch'üan-shu 四库全书 (Complete library in four branches of literature), compiled between 1773 and 1782 under the patronage of Emperor Ch'ien-lung, 3450 titles.

Ssu-k'u ch'üan-shu tsung-mu t'i-yao 四库全书总目提要 (An annotated bibliography of books in the Ssu-k'u ch'üan-shu), 200 chüan, compiled by Chi yun and others in 1782, Tai-tung shu-chü edition.

Ssu-luan 嗣銮, "Ku Hung-ming tsai Te-kuo" 辜鸿铭在德国 (Ku Hung-ming in Germany), Jen-chien-shih, no. 12:40-41 (September 1934).

Ssu-ma Ch'ien 司马迁, Shih-chi 史记, 130 chüan, in Erh-shih-ssu shih, T'ung-wen-shu-chü edition (1894), ts'e 1-26.

Ssu-ma Kuang 司马光, Tzu-chih t'ung-chien 资治通鉴 (Comprehensive mirror for aid in government), 294 chüan, 100 ts'e.

Stanley, C. J., "Hu Kuang-yung and China's Early Foreign Loans" (Ph. D. dissertation, Harvard University, 1951), 164 pp.

Steiger, G. N., China and the Occident (New Haven: Yale University Press. 1927), 349 pp.

Su Ch'eng-chien 苏诚鉴, "Li Hung-chang i-kuan ti fan-Jih cheng-ts'e"李鸿章一贯的反日政策(Li Hung-chang's consistent anti-Japanese policy), Hsin cheng-chih 新政治, 3.5:76-82(1940).

Su Ch'ih 素痴(Chang Yin-lin 张荫麟), "Chin-tai Chung-kuo hsueh-shu-shih shang chih Liang Jen-kung"近代中国学术史上之梁任公(Liang Ch'i-ch'ao in the history of modern Chinese learning), in the Literary Supplement of the Tientsin Ta-kung-pao 大公报文学副刊, Feb. 11, 1929.

Su Yü 苏舆, I-chiao ts'ung-pien 翼教丛编 (A collection of documents for the protection of Confucian teaching; 1898).

Suan-ching shih-shu 算经十书 (Ten textbooks on mathematics), 1773 edition. Compiled by K'ung Chi-han 孔继涵, including nine of the original works of 1084 of the same title, one ancient mathematical treatise, Tai Chen's Ts'e-suan 戴震, 策算, and Kou-ku ko-yuan chi 勾股割圆记, 3 chüan.

Sun, E-tu Zen 孙任以都, "The Chinese Constitutional Missions of 1905-1906," Journal of Modern History, 24.3: 251-268 (September 1952).

Sun Hao 孙灏, Hai-kuo t'u-chih cheng-shih 海国图志征实 (Errata and Supplements to the Hai-kuo t'u-chih), 20 ts'e (Shanghai, 1902).

Sun Yat-sen 孙逸仙, Chung-shan ch'üan-shu 中山全书 (Complete works of Sun Yat-sen), 4 vols. (Shanghai: Ta-hua shu-chü, 1927).

Sun Yat-sen 孙逸仙, "Neng-chih pi neng-hsing" 能知必能行 (Whatever can be known can certainly be carried out), ch. 6 of Sun Wen hsueh-shuo 孙文学说, in Chung-shan ch'üan-shu.

Sun Yat-sen 孙逸仙, "T'ung-meng-hui hsuan-yen" 同盟会宣言 (Manifesto of the T'ung-meng-hui), in Chung-shan ch'üan-shu, vol. 4, 1-4.

Sun Yat-sen 孙逸仙, Tsung-li ch'üan-chi 总理全集 (Complete collected works of the Director-general), edited by Hu Han-min 胡汉民, 4 chi in 5 vols. (Shanghai: Min-chih shu-chü, 1930).

Sung Ying-hsing 宋应星, T'ien-kung k'ai-wu 天工开物 (Natural resources utilized for manufacturing; first printed, 1637; T'ao Hsiang 陶湘 edition, 1927).

Tabohashi Kiyoshi 田保桥洁, "Giwakempiran to Nichi-Ro" 义和拳匪

乱と日露（The Boxer Rebellion and Japan and Russia）, pp. 1051-1106 in Tōzai kōshō shiron 东西交涉史论（Treatises on the history of East-West relations）, 2 vols.（Tōkyō: Fuzambō 富山房, 1939）, 1410 pp.

Tabohashi Kiyoshi 田保桥洁, Nisshin seneki gaikōshi no kenkyū 日清战役外交史の研究（"A Diplomatic History of the Sino-Japanese War 1894-1895"; Tōkyō: Tokō 刀江, 1951）, 556 pp.; English summary, 5 pp.

Ta-Ch'ing Kuang-hsü hsin fa-ling 大清光绪新法令（New laws and ordinances of the Kuang-hsü reign）, 20 ts'e（Shanghai: compiled by Commercial Press, 1909）.

Ta-Ch'ing lü-li 大清律例（Laws and precedents of the Ch'ing Dynasty）, 47 + 5 chüan（incomplete）in 26 ts'e（revised edition, 1870）.

Ta-i chüeh-mi lu 大义觉迷录（Record of the awakening of the misled by grand principles）, 4 chüan（printed, 1730）.

Tai Chin-hsieo, "The Life and Work of Ts'ai Yuan-p'ei"（Ed. D. dissertation, Harvard Graduate School of Education, 1952）.

Tai Hung-tz'u 戴鸿慈, Ch'u-shih chiu-kuo jih-chi 出使九国日记（Diary on diplomatic missions to nine countries; Peking: Ti-i shu-chü, 1906）, 334 pp.

Tai Hung-tz'u 戴鸿慈 and Tuan-fang 端方, ed., Ou-Mei cheng-chih yao-i 欧美政治要义（Essentials of political administration in Europe and America）, 4 ts'e（lithographic edition, 1907）.

T'ai-hsü 太虚, Jen-sheng-kuan ti k'o-hsueh 人生观的科学（A science of the philosophy of life; Shanghai: T'ai-tung Book Co., 1925）.

T'ai-p'ing T'ien-kuo wen-shu 太平天国文书（Collection of letters by Taiping leaders; Peiping: photolithographic copy of 1933）.

T'ai-p'ing T'ien-kuo ko-ming yun-tung lun-wen chi 太平天国革命运动论文集（Symposium on the T'ai-p'ing Revolutionary Movement）, edited by the Institute of Historical Research of North China University （Hua-pei ta-hsueh li-shih yen-chiu shih; Peking: San-lien, 1950）, 165 p.

Tamagna, Frank M., Banking and Finance in China（New York:

Institute of Pacific Relations, 1942), 400 pp.

T'an Ssu-t'ung 谭嗣同, Jen-hsueh 仁学 (A study of benevolence), in Ch'ing-i-pao ch'üan-pien 清议报全编, the second collection, A, ts'e 3.

T'an Ssu-t'ung 谭嗣同, T'an Liu-yang ch'üan-chi 谭浏阳全集 (Complete works of T'an Ssu-t'ung), including nien-p'u 年谱, 8 + 1 chüan (published 1925).

T'ang Chen 汤震, Wei-yen 危言 (Warnings), 4 chüan (Shanghai, 1890).

T'ang Chi-ch'ing 唐际清, "E tsu Lü-shun Ta-lien shih Li Hung-chang shou-hui chih cheng-chü" 俄租旅顺大连时李鸿章受贿之证据 (Evidences of Li Hung-chang's bribery when Port Author and Dairen were leased to Russia), Nan-k'ai chou-k'an 南开周刊, no. 48.

T'ang Ch'ing-tseng 唐庆增, "Tseng Kuo-fan chih ching-chi ssu-hsiang" 曾国藩之经济思想 (Tseng Kuo-fan's economic ideas), Ching-chi-hsueh chi-k'an 经济学季刊, 5.4:52-60 (1935).

T'ang Hsiang-lung 汤象龙, "Min-kuo i-ch'ien kuan-shui tan-pao chih wai-chai" 民国以前关税担保之外债 (The foreign loans secured on the customs revenue before 1911), Chung-kuo chin-tai ching-chi-shih yen-chiu chi-k'an, 3.1:3-8 (1935).

T'ang Leang-li, The Foundations of Modern China (London: N. Douglas, 1928), 290 pp.

Tao, L. K., "A Chinese Political Theorist [Huang Tsung-hsi] of the Seventeenth Century," CSPSR, 2.1:71-82 (March 1917).

T'ao K'ang-te 陶亢德, comp., Tzu-chuan chih i-chang 自传之一章 (A collection of autobiographies; Shanghai: Yü-chou-feng she, 1938), 198 pp.

Teng Ssu-yü 邓嗣禹, Chung-kuo k'ao-shih chih-tu shih 中国考试制度史 (A history of the Chinese civil service examination system; Nanking: The Examination Yuan, 1936).

Teng Ssu-yü 邓嗣禹, Chang Hsi and the Treaty of Nanking, 1842 (Chicago: University of Chicago Press, 1944), 191 pp.

Teng Ssu-yü 邓嗣禹, New Light on the History of the Taiping Rebellion (Cambridge: Harvard University Press, 1950), 132 pp.

Teng Ssu-yü and Knight Biggerstaff, An Annotated Bibliography of Selected Chinese Reference Works, revised edition (Cambridge: Harvard University Press, 1950), 326 pp. See also under Fairbank.

Teng Yü-han 邓玉函 (Terrenz), and Wang Cheng 王征 ed. and tr., Yuan-Hsi ch'i-ch'i t'u-shuo lu-tsui 远西奇器图说录最 (European works on mechanical principles with illustrations), commonly known as Ch'i-ch'i t'u-shuo, 3 chüan (printed in Peking, 1627). Edition of Shou-shan-ko ts'ung-shu 守山阁丛书, 3 chüan (1833).

Tewksbury, Donald G., Source Book on Far Eastern Political Ideologies, Modern Period, China-Japan, preliminary edition (New York: Teachers College, Columbia University, 1949), 189 pp.

Tezuka Masao 手冢正夫, Shina jūkōgyō hattatsu shi 支那重工业发达史 (History of the development of Chinese heavy industry; Tōkyō, 1944), 19+548+14 pp.

Ting Chih-p'ing 丁致聘, Chung-kuo chin ch'i-shih-nien lai chiao-yü chi-shih 中国近七十年来教育纪事 (Events in Chinese education during the last seventy years; Shanghai: published by Kuo-li pien-i kuan 国立编译馆 [National Institute of Compilation and Translation], 1935), 291 pp.

Ting Tse-liang 丁则良, Li T'i-mo-t'ai 李提摩太 (Timothy Richard; Peking: Kai ming Book Co., 1951), 66 pp.

Ting Wen-chiang (V. K. Ting) 丁文江, "Wu-shih-nien lai Chung-kuo chih k'uang-yeh" 五十年来中国之矿业 (China's mining industry for the past 50 years), in Tsui-chin chih wu-shih-nien, pp. 1-14.

Tobar, Jerome, Chang Chih-tung, K'iuen-hio p'ien; exhortations à l'étude, Variétés Sinologiques, no. 26 (Chang-hai, 1909).

T'oung-pao 通报 Archives pour servir à l'étude de l'histoire, des langues, de la Géographie et de l'ethnographie de l'Asia Orientale, ed. by Gustave Schlegel et Henri Cordier, et al. (Leiden: E. J. Brill, 1890-   ).

Tsai-tse 载泽, K'ao-ch'a cheng-chih jih-chi 考察政治日记 (Diary of

political studies [abroad]; Peking, 1908), 136 pp.

Ts'ai Shang-ssu 蔡尚思, "T'an Ssu-t'ung hsueh-shu ssu-hsiang t'i-yao" 谭嗣同学术思想提要 (An outline of T'an Ssu-t'ung's academic ideas), Chung-kuo chien-she, 4.2:49-53 (May 1947).

Ts'ai Yuan-p'ei 蔡元培, Ts'ai Chieh-min hsien-sheng yen-hsing lu, 蔡子民先生言行录 (A record of the words and actions of Ts'ai Yuan-p'ei; Peking: Peking University, 1920), 580 pp.

Ts'ai Yuan-p'ei 蔡元培, "The Development of Chinese Education," Asiatic Review, vol. 20:499-509 (1924).

Ts'ai Yuan-p'ei 蔡元培, Chung-kuo lun-li-hsueh shih 中国伦理学史 (A history of Chinese ethics; Shanghai: Commercial Press, 1937), 151 pp.

Ts'ai Yuan-p'ei 蔡元培, "Wo tsai chiao-yü-chieh ti ching-yen" 我在教育界的经验 (My experiences in the educational field), in T'ao K'ang-te, Tzu-chuan chih i-chang, pp. 1-12.

Ts'ai Yuan-p'ei 蔡元培, "Wu-shih-nien lai Chung-kuo chih che-hsueh" 五十年来中国之哲学 (Chinese philosophical studies in the past fifty years), in Shen-pao-kuan, Tsui-chin chih wu-shih-nien, pp. 1-10.

Ts'ai Yuan-p'ei 蔡元培, "Chui-tao Ts'ai Chieh-min hsien-sheng t'e-chi" 追悼蔡子民先生特辑 (Special memorial issue on Ts'ai Yuan-p'ei), Tung-fang tsa-chih, 37.8 (1940).

Ts'ai Yuan-p'ei 蔡元培, Yü-chou-feng 宇宙风, no. 24 (1940), memorial issue on Ts'ai Yuan-p'ei.

Tsao Wen-yen, The Constitutional Structure of Modern China (Melbourne: Melbourne Press, 1947), 304 pp.

Tseng Chi-tse 曾纪泽, Tseng Hui-min-kung shih-Hsi jih-chi 曾惠敏公使西日记 (Diary of Marquis Tseng's mission to the West), printed in 2 chüan in Tseng Hui-min-kung i-chi, and reprinted under the title Shih-Hsi jih-chi in Hsiao-fang-hu-chai yü-ti ts'ung-ch'ao, ts'e 78. See also ts'e 58 of the latter work, entitled Ch'u-shih Ying-Fa jih-chi 出使英法日记 (Diary of a mission to England and France).

Tseng Chi-tse 曾纪泽, Chin-yao ch'ou-pi 金轺筹笔 (Records of an imperial mission), first printed in 1887, in I-hsiu-shan-fang ts'ung-shu 挹秀山房丛书, ts'e 17-20.

Tseng Chi-tse 曾纪泽, Tseng Hui-min-kung i-chi 曾惠敏公遗集 (Collected works of Tseng Chi-tse), 17 chüan (Shanghai, 1893).

Tseng K'un-hua 曾锟化, Chung-kuo t'ieh-lu shih 中国铁路史 (History of Chinese railways; Peking, 1924), 954 pp.

Tseng Kuo-fan 曾国藩, Tseng Wen-cheng-kung ch'üan-chi 曾文正公全集 (Complete works of Tseng Kuo-fan), 174 chüan (1876).

Tseng Kuo-fan 曾国藩, Tseng Wen-cheng-kung nien-p'u 曾文正公年谱 (A chronological biography of Tseng Kuo-fan), comp. by Li Shu-ch'ang 黎庶昌 and others, 12 chüan, in Tseng Wen-cheng-kung chüan-chi, ts'e 33-36.

Tseng Kuo-fan 曾国藩, Tseng Wen-cheng-kung shou-shu jih-chi 曾文正公手书日记 (Autographic diary of Tseng Kuo fan [from 1841-1871]), lithographic edition (Shanghai: Chung-kuo t'u-shu kung-ssu, 1909), 40 ts'e.

Tseng Kuo-fan 曾国藩, Tseng Wen-cheng-kung shu-cha 曾文正公书札 (Official correspondence of Tseng Kuo-fan), 33 chüan, in Tseng Wen-cheng-kung ch'üan-chi.

Tseng Kuo-fan 曾国藩, Tseng Wen-cheng-kung tsou-kao 曾文正公奏稿 (Draft memorials of Tseng Kuo-fan), 36 chüan, in Tseng Wen-cheng-kung ch'üan-chi.

Tseng Kuo-fan 曾国藩, Tseng Wen-cheng-kung ta-shih-chi 曾文正大事记 (Important events in the career of Tseng Kuo-fan), in Tseng Wen-cheng-kung ch'üan-chi.

Tseng Kuo-fan 曾国藩, see also Wang Ting-an.

Tseng Po 曾朴 (Pen-name: Tung-ya ping-fu 东亚病夫), Nieh-hai hua 孽海花 (Beauties in the troublesome sea; Shanghai: Chen-mei-shan shu-tien, 1931), 222 pp.

Tseng Shih-o 曾士莪, "Ou-yang Pai-yuan t'an Tseng Wen-cheng-kung i-shih"欧阳伯元谈曾文正公轶事(Ou-yang Pai-yuan's reminiscences of Tseng Kuo-fan), Kuo-wen chou-pao, 12.30:1-3 (1935).

Tseng Shih-o 曾士莪, "Shu Weng-Li hsiang-ch'ing shih"书翁李相倾事 (A note on the struggle between Weng T'ung-ho and Li Hung-chang), Kuo-wen chou-pao, 12.27:1-2 (July 1935).

Tseng Wen-cheng-kung 曾文正公, see Tseng Kuo-fan.

Tseng Yu-hao 曾友豪, Modern Chinese Legal and Political Philosophy (Shanghai: Commercial Press, 1930), 320 pp.

Tsiang, T. F. 蒋廷黻, "Bismarck and the Introduction of International Law into China," CSPSR, 15:98-101 (1931).

Tsiang, T. F. 蒋廷黻, "Difficulties of Reconstruction after the Treaty of Nanking," CSPSR, 16.2:319-327 (1932-1933).

Tsiang, T. F. 蒋廷黻, "Sino-Japanese Diplomatic Relations, 1870-1894," CSPSR, 17.1:107-169 (1933).

Tsiang (Chiang) Ting-fu 蒋廷黻, Chin-tai Chung-kuo wai-chiao-shih tzu-liao chi-yao 近代中国外交史资料辑要(Selected documents on modern Chinese diplomatic history), 2 vols. (Shanghai: Commercial Press, 1931 and 1934).

Tso-chuan, see Ch'un-ch'iu Tso-chüan cheng-i.

Tso Shun-sheng 左舜生, "Chung-Jih wai-chiao-shih shang chih Li Hung-chang"中日外交史上之李鸿章(Li Hung-chang's position in the history of Sino-Japanese relations), Wai-chiao p'ing-lun 外交评论, 6.3:23-47 (1936).

Tso Tsung-t'ang 左宗棠, Tso Wen-hsiang-kung ch'üan-chi 左文襄公全集 (Complete works of Tso Tsung-t'ang), including Tso Wen-hsiang-kung nien-p'u 左文襄公年谱, 100 chüan, 96 ts'e (Changsha, 1889).

Tso Tsung-t'ang 左宗棠, Tso Wen-hsiang-kung tsou-kao 左文襄公奏稿(The memorials of Tso Tsung-t'ang), in Tso Wen-hsiang-kung ch'üan-chi, ts'e 6-7.

Tso Tsung-t'ang 左宗棠, Tso Wen-hsiang-kung shu-tu 左文襄公书牍 (The letters of Tso Tsung-t'ang), in Tso Wen-hsiang-kung ch'üan-chi, ts'e 71-96.

Tso Tsung-t'ang 左宗棠, et al., Ch'uan-cheng tsou-i hui-pien 船政奏议汇编 (Collection of memorials on marine policy), 16 ts'e (1882).

Tsou Lu 邹鲁, Chung-kuo Kuo-min-tang shih-kao 中国国民党史稿 (Draft history of the National People's Party of China), 2 vols. (Shanghai: Min-chih shu-chü, 1929).

Tsui-chin chih wu-shih-nien, see shen-pao-kuan.

Tsui-chin san-shih-wu-nien chih Chung-kuo chiao-yü, see Chuang Yü and Ho sheng-nai, ed.

Ts'ui Shu-ch'in 崔书琴, "The Influence of the Canton-Moscow Entente upon Sun Yat-sen's Revolutionary Tactics," CSPSR, 20.1: 101-139 (April, 1936). Also Ts'ui's doctoral dissertation with a similar title, Department of Government, Harvard University.

Tung-fang tsa-chih 东方杂志 (Eastern Miscellany), published in Shanghai, beginning 1904, semi-monthly, or monthly.

Tung Hsün 董恂, Huan-tu-wo-shu shih lao-jen nien-p'u 还读我书室老人年谱 (Chronological biography of Tung Hsun), 2 chüan (Peking, 1892).

T'ung-wen kuan t'i-ming lu 同文馆题名录 (The calendar of the Tungwen College), first issue, published by authority (Peking, 1879).

Tung-ya ping-fu, see Tseng Po.

Ueda Toshio 植田捷雄, "Ahen sensō to Shimmatsu kammin no shoshō" 鸦片战争と清末官民の诸相 ("The Actual Attitude of the Chinese Mandarins and common People towards the Opium War"), Kokusaihō gaikō zasshi 国际外交杂志, 50.3: 235-271 (July 1951).

Varg, Paul A., "William W. Rockhill's Influence on the Boxers' Negotiations," Pacific Historical Review, XVIII. 3: 369-380 (August 1949).

Wada Sei 和田清, "Ri Kō-shō to sono jidai" 李鸿章とその时代 (Li Hung-chang and his times), pp. 139-155 in his Tōashi ronsō 东亚史论薮

(Essays in East Asian history; Tōkyō: Seikatsu 生活, 1942), 579 pp.

Waley, Arthur, The Analects of Confucius, translated and annotated (London: Allen and Unwin, 1938), 268 pp.

Wang Ch'in-yü 王勤堉, "Pai-nien lai Chung-kuo t'ieh-lu shih-yeh" 百年来中国铁路事业 (Chinese railroads during the past hundred years), Hsueh-lin, 2.40:69-103 (December 1940).

Wang Chü-ch'ang, see Yen Fu, Yen Chi-tao nien-p'u.

Wang Ch'uan-shan, see Wang Fu-chih.

Wang Feng-yuan 王丰园, Chung-kuo hsin-wen-hsueh yun-tung shu-p'ing 中国新文学运动述评 (Narration of and comments on the new literature movement in China; Peiping: Hsin-hsin hsueh-she, 1935), 188 pp.

Wang Fu-chih 王夫之, Wang Ch'uan-shan i-shu 王船山遗书 (Writings of Wang Ch'uan-shan), 130 ts'e (published by Tseng Kuo-fan, 1865).

Wang Fu-chih 王夫之, Shih kuang-chuan 诗广传 (Extended commentaries on the Odes), in Wang Ch'uan-shan i-shu, ts'e 15.

Wang Fu-chih 王夫之, Huang-shu 黄书, in Wang Ch'uan-shan i-shu, ts'e 105.

Wang Fu-chih 王夫之, O Meng 噩梦, in Wang Ch'uan-shan i-shu, ts'e 105.

Wang Fu-chih 王夫之, Ssu-wen-lu wai-pien 思问录外编, in Wang Ch'uan-shan i-shu, ts'e 105.

Wang Fu-chih 王夫之, Tu T'ung-chien lun 读通鉴论 (Comments on reading [Ssu-ma Kuang's] Tzu-chih t'ung-chien), 30 + 1 chüan (movable type edition, Commercial Press, undated).

Wang Fu-chih, see Wang Yung-hsiang.

Wang Hsi-ch'i 王锡祺, ed., Hsiao-fang-hu-chai yü-ti ts'ung-ch'ao 小方壶斋舆地丛钞 (Collection of geographical works from Hsiao-fang-hu Studio), preface dated 1877, Shanghai, Chu-I-t'ang 著易堂 edition, originally 1200 titles, 64 ts'e; Pu-pien 补编 (Supplement I), 58 titles, 4 ts'e; Tsai pu-pien 再补编 (Supplement II), 180 titles, 16 ts'e.

Wang Hsien-ch'ien 王先谦, Tung-hua ch'üan-lu 东华全录, including Hsü-lu T'ung-chih, 252 ts'e, (Peking：Ch'in-wen shu-chü, 1887).

Wang Hsien-ch'ien 王先谦, Hsü-shou-t'ang shu-cha 虚受堂书札 (Collection of letters of Wang Hsien-ch'ien), 1907 edition.

Wang Hsin-chung 王信忠, "Fu-chou ch'uan-ch'ang chih yen-ko" 福州船厂之沿革 (The development of the Foochow shipyard), Ch'ing-hua hsueh-pao, 8. 1：1-57 (December 1932). Pages of this journal not consecutively numbered.

Wang Kuang 王洸, Chung-kuo hang-yeh lun 中国航业论 (On the Chinese shipping business), Chiao-t'ung tsa-chih she ts'ung-shu 交通杂志社丛书 (Communications Magazine series), no. 1 (Nanking：published by the Chiao-t'ung tsa-chih she, 1934), 143 pp.

Wang Shen-jan 王森然, Chin-tai erh-shih-chia p'ing-chuan 近代二十家评传 (Critical biographies of twenty famous persons of recent times; Peiping, 1934), 406 pp.

Wang Shou-ch'ien 王守谦, "Chung-kuo chi-ch'i pan chu-tsao chih-ch'ien yü yin-yuan chih ch'i-yuan" 中国机器版铸造制钱与银元之起源 (The beginning of machine minting of coins and silver dollars in China), Ch'üan-pi 泉币, no. 20.

Wang T'ao 王韬, Fu-sang yu-chi 扶桑游记 (A record of travels in Japan), 3 chüan (printed in Japan, 1880).

Wang T'ao 王韬, T'ao-yuan wen-lu wai-pien 弢园文录外编 (Supplement to T'ao-yuan wen-lu), 12 chüan (Hong Kong, 1882).

Wang T'ao 王韬, "Chi Ying-kuo cheng-chih" 纪英国政治 (A note on the British government), in T'ao-yuan wen-lu wai-pien.

Wang T'ao 王韬, "Chih-chung" 治中 (On domestic administration), in T'ao-yuan wen-lu wai-pien.

Wang T'ao 王韬, "Ch'u e-wai ch'üan-li" 除额外权利 (On the abolition of extraterritoriality), in T'ao-yuan wen-lu wai-pien.

Wang T'ao 王韬, "Man-yu sui-lu" 漫游随录 (Notes of travels), in T'ao-yuan wen-lu wai-pien.

Wang T'ao 王韬, "Pien-fa"变法 (On reform). in T'ao-yuan wen-lu wai-pien.

Wang T'ao 王韬, "Shang tang-lu lun shih-wu shu"上当路论时务书 (A letter submitted to the authorities discussing current affairs), in T'ao-yuan wen-lu wai-pien.

Wang T'ao 王韬, "Yuan-hsueh"原学 in T'ao-yuan wen-lu wai-pien.

Wang T'ao 王韬, T'ao-yuan ch'ih-tu 弢园尺牍 (Letters of Wang T'ao), 12 chüan (printed 1886).

Wang T'ao 王韬, Hsi-hsueh chi-ts'un 西学辑存 (Collection of works on Western knowledge), 2 ts'e (Sung-yin-lu 淞隐庐 edition, 1889-1890).

Wang Te-chao 王德昭, "T'ung-chih hsin-cheng k'ao"同治新政考 (A study of the new administration of the T'ung-chih period), Wen-shih tsa-chih 文史杂志, 1.4, 5: 21-38, 33-46 (January 1941).

Wang Te-liang 王德亮, Tseng Kuo-fan chih min-tsu ssu-hsiang 曾国藩之民族思想 (Tseng Kuo-fan's ideas on min-tsu [nationalism]; Shanghai: Commercial Press, 1946), 48 pp.

Wang Ting-an 王定安, Ch'iu-ch'ueh-chai ti-tzu chi 求阙斋弟子记 (A sketch of Tseng Kuo-fan by his disciple from the Ch'iu-ch'ueh-chai [study]), 32 chüan (1876).

Wang Ting-an 王定安, Tseng Wen-cheng-kung shih-lueh 曾文正公事略(A brief account of Tseng Kuo-fan), 2 ts'e(1875).

Wang Tsao-shih 王造时, "Chung-Hsi chieh-ch'u-hou she-hui-shang ti pien-hua"中西接触后社会上的变化(Social changes after the contact between China and the West), Tung-fang tsa-chih, 31.2:31-40 (1934).

Wang Yen-wei 王彦威, comp., Ch'ing-chi wai-chiao shih-liao 清季外交史料(Historical materials on late Ch'ing diplomacy), 112 ts'e (Peking: movable-type edition, 1932-1935).

Wang Yun-sheng 王芸生, "Chung-E mi-yueh pien-wei"中俄密约辨伪 (Discrimination between [truth and] falsehood in the Sino-Russian secret pacts), Kuo-wen chou-pao, 9.28:1-4 (July 1932).

Wang Yun-sheng 王芸生, comp., Liu-shih-nien lai Chung-kuo yü

Jih-pen 六十年来中国与日本（China and Japan during the last sixty years）, 6 vols.（Tientsin：published by Ta-kung-pao 大公报, 1932-1933）.

Wang Yung 王庸, Chung-kuo ti-li-hsueh shih 中国地理学史（History of Chinese geography; Changsha：Commercial Press, 1938）, 262 pp.

Wang Yung-hsiang 王永祥, Ch'uan-shan hsueh-p'u 船山学谱（A chronological account of the scholarship of Wang Fu-chih）, 6 chüan（Peiping：movable-type edition by Sui-ya-chai 邃雅斋, 1934）.

Ward, J. S. M., and Sterling, W. G., The Hung Society or the Society of Heaven and Earth, 3 vols.（London, 1926）, 180 + 196 + 148 pp. See also Pelliot.

Webster, James B., Christian Education and the National Consciousness in China（New York, 1923）, 323 pp.

Wegneuer, Dr. Georg, "Der Gouverneur von Shantung," Deutsche Kolonialzeitung, 27:249-250（June 1901）.

Wei Hsi-yü 韦息予, Li Hung-chang 李鸿章（Shanghai：Chunghua Book Company, 1931）, 95 pp.

Wei Ying-ch'i, see Lin Tse-hsü, Lin Wen-chung-kung nien-p'u.

Wei Yuan 魏源, Hai-kuo t'u-chih 海国图志（An illustrated gazetteer of the maritime countries）, first block-print edition of 50 chüan（1844, preface by Wei Yuan dated 1842）. Later editions noted in Chapter Ⅲ.

Wei Yuan 魏源, Sheng-wu chi 圣武记（Record of imperial military exploits）, 12 ts'e（1842）;（reprinted 1927 and 1930）, 14 chüan in 6 ts'e.

Wei Yün-kung 魏允恭, Chiang-nan chih-tsao-chü chi 江南制造局记（An account of the Kiang-nan Arsenal）, 10 chüan（Shanghai, 1905）.

Wen-che chi-k'an 文哲季刊（Quarterly Journal of Liberal Arts）, Wuhan University, Wuchang, beginning 1930, quarterly.

（Wen-hsiang 文祥）, Wen Wen-chung-kung shih-lueh 文文忠公事略（A brief account of Wen-hsiang）, 4 chüan（printed, 1882）.

Wen-hsien ts'ung-p'en 文献丛编（Miscellaneous publication of the

government archives), Peiping, Palace Museum, beginning 1930, monthly.

Wen T'ing-ching 温廷敬, "Huang Tsun-hsien chuan"黄遵宪传（A biography of Huang Tsun-hsien）, Kuo-feng, 5. 8-9:3-7（November 1934).

Wen Yuan-ning, "Ku Hung-ming," T'ien-hsia monthly, 4. 4:386-398 (April 1937).

Weng Wen-hao 翁文灏, "Wu-shih-nien lai chih ching-chi chien-she" 五十年来之经济建设 (Economic reconstruction during the last 50 years), in Wu-shih-nien lai ti Chung-kuo 五十年来的中国(China in the last 50 years), compiled by P'an Kung-chan 潘公展(Chungking: published by Sheng-li shu-tien, 1944).

Wieger, Léon, ed. and tr., Chine Moderne, 10 vols. (Hsien-hsien, 1922-1927).

Wilbur, C. Martin, ed., Chinese Sources on the History of the Chinese Communist Movement, an annotated bibliography of materials in the East Asiatic Library of Columbia University (reproduced for private distribution by the East Asian Institute, Columbia University, 1950), 55 pp.

Wilhelm, Hellmut, The Attitude of the Early Ch'ing Scholars toward the Manchus (mimeographed for private distribution, Far Eastern Institute, University of Washington, 1949).

Wilhelm, Hellmut, "The Background of Tseng Kuo-fan's Ideology," Asiatische Studien, 3. 3-4: 90-100 (1949).

Wilhelm, Hellmut, "The Problem of Within and Without, A Confucian Attempt in Syncretism," Journal of the History of Ideas, 12. 1:48-60 (January 1951).

Wilson, James Harrison, China, Travels and Investigations in the "Middle Kingdom," third edition revised (New York, 1901), 429 pp.

Wen Kung-chih 文公直, Tsui-chin san-shih-nien Chung-kuo chün-shih shih 最近三十年中国军事史 (History of Chinese military affairs in the last thirty years),2 vols.(Shanghai：T'ai-p'ing-yang shu-tien,1930).

Wo-jen 倭仁, Wo Wen-tuan-kung i-shu 倭文端公遗书（Collected writings of Wo-jen),11 chüan,8 ts'e(block-print edition,1882).

Wong, K. C. and Wu, L. T., History of Chinese Medicine (Tientsin：Tientsin Press,1932),706 pp.

Woodbridge, Samuel I., China's Only Hope, An Appeal by Her Greatest Viceroy, Chang Chih-tung (New York,1900),151 pp.

Wright, A. F., "Fu I and the Rejection of Buddhism," in "Chinese Reactions to Imported Ideas, a Symposium," Journal of the History of Ideas, 12.1:33-47 (January 1951).

Wright, Mary C., "The T'ung-chih Restoration" (Ph. D. dissertation in History, Radcliffe College, 1951).

Wright, S. F., Hart and the Chinese Customs (Belfast：published for the Queen's University by W. Mullan, 1950), 949 pp.

Wu, Chao Kwang, The International Aspect of the Missionary Movement in China (Baltimore：Johns Hopkins Press, 1930), 285 pp.

Wu Ch'eng-chang 吴成章, Wai-chiao-pu yen-ko chi-lueh 外交部沿革纪略（A brief account of the reforms in the Wai-chiao-pu),1 ts'e (Peking：Wai-chiao-pu Press,1913).

Wu Ch'i-ch'ang 吴其昌, Liang Ch'i-ch'ao 梁启超（Liang Ch'i-ch'ao；Chungking：Sheng-li ch'u-pan-she,1944),127 pp.

Wu Ch'i-yuan 伍启元, Chung-kuo hsin-wen-hua yun-tung kai-kuan 中国新文化运动概观（A general review of China's new culture movement；Shanghai：Hsien-tai shu-chü,1934),180 pp.

Wu Ching-heng 吴敬恒, Wu Chih-hui hsien-sheng wen-ts'un 吴稚晖先生文存（Collected essays of Wu Chih-hui),2 vols.（Shanghai：I-hsueh shu-chü,1925).

Wu Hsuan-i 吴宣易, "Ching-shih T'ung-wen kuan lueh-shih" 京师同文馆略史(A historical sketch of the T'ung-wen Kuan at Peking), Tu-shu yueh-k'an 读书月刊,2.4:1-15 (1933).

Wu, James T. K., "The Impact of the Taiping Rebellion upon the Manchu Fiscal System," Pacific Historical Review 19:265-275 (August 1950).

Wu Ju-lun 吴汝纶, T'ung-ch'eng Wu hsien-sheng ch'üan-shu 桐城吴先生全书 (Complete works of Mr. Wu of T'ung-ch'eng), 20 ts'e (1904).

Wu Ju-lun 吴汝纶, T'ung-ch'eng Wu hsien-sheng jih-chi 桐城吴先生日记 (The diary of Wu Ju-lun), 16 chüan, 10 ts'e (Pao-ting: Lien-ch'ih shu-she, 1928).

Wu Pao-chang 吴保障, "Li Wen-chung-kung pai-shih-chou-nien chi-nien kan-yen" 李文忠公百十周年纪念感言 (A word in commemoration of Li Hung-chang's 110th birthday), Hsueh-feng, 4.7:1-4 (1934).

Wu Po 武波 (Fan Wen-lan 范文澜), Chung-kuo chin-tai shih 中国近代史 (A history of modern China; Shanghai: Tu-shu ch'u-pan-she, 1947), 418 pp.

Wu Sheng-te 吴盛德 and Ch'en Tseng-hui 陈增辉, Chiao-an shih-liao pien-mu 教案史料编目 (Catalogue of historical materials on missionary cases; Peiping: Yenching School of Religion Series, no. 5, 1941), 227 pp.

Wu-shih-nien-lai ti Chung-kuo, see P'an Kung-chan.

Wu T'ing-fang 伍廷芳, Min-kuo t'u-chih ch'u-i 民国图治刍议 (Opinions regarding the advancement of good government under the Republic; Shanghai; published by the author, 1915), 107 pp.

Wu Tse 吴泽, K'ang Yu-wei yü Liang Ch'i-ch'ao 康有为与梁启超 (K'ang Yu-wei and Liang Ch'i-ch'ao; Shanghai, 1948), 202 pp.

Wu Tse 吴泽, "Lun pien-fa chih ching-shen" 论变法之精神 (On the spirit of reform), Tung-fang tsa-chih, 7:142-144 (1904).

Wu Tse 吴泽, "Pao-huang-tang yü K'ang-Liang lu-hsien" 保皇党与康梁路线 (The Royalist Party and the policy of K'ang and Liang), Chung-kuo chien-she, 7.1:44-47 (October 1948).

Wu Tse 吴泽, "Wu-hsü cheng-pien yü hsin-chiu tang-cheng" 戊戌政变与新旧党争 (The coup d'état of 1898 and the struggle between the old and new factions), Chung-kuo chien-she 6. 6：42-45 (September 1948).

Wu Yü-kan 武堉干,"Liu-shih-nien Chung-kuo shang-yeh chih fa-chan"六十年中国商业之发展(The development of Chinese commerce in the past 60 years), Shen-pao yueh-k'an 申报月刊, 1. 1：19-34 (July 1932).

Wylie, Alexander, Memorials of Protestant Missionaries to the Chinese：giving a list of their publications, and obituary notices of the deceased (Shanghai, 1867), 331 pp.

Yamamoto Sumiko 山本澄子,"Giwadan no seikaku ni tsuite"义和拳の性格に就いて(On the social character of the Boxer Rebellion), Shikan 史观("The Historical Review, edited by Historical Society of Waseda University"), no. 33：45-61 (April 1950).

Yang Ch'uan 杨铨,"Wu-shih-nien lai Chung-kuo chih kung-yeh"五十年来中国之工业(China's industrial enterprise during the past 50 years), in Tsui-chin chih wu-shih-nien, pp. 1-15.

Yang Hung-lieh 杨鸿烈,"Chi Kuo Sung-tao ch'u-shih Ying-Fa"记郭嵩焘出使英法(An account of Kuo Sung-tao's mission to England and France), Ku-chin, nos. 11-12 (1942? page numbers unavailable).

Yang Hung-lieh 杨鸿烈,"Chung-kuo she-chih chu-I shih-kuan ti ching-kuo"中国设置驻意使馆的经过(History of the establishment of the Chinese legation in Italy), Ku-chin, no. 25：11-15 (June 1943), and no. 26：19-23 (July 1943).

Yang Hung-lieh 杨鸿烈,"Chung-kuo chu-wai shih-kuan chih-tu ti chien-t'ao"中国驻外使馆制度的检讨(An examination of the system of Chinese diplomatic missions abroad), Tung- fang wen-hua 东方文化, 21 (1944?).

Yang Kuang-hsien 杨光先, Pu-te-i 不得已(I could not keep silent), photolithographic edition, 2 ts'e (1929). See also Sheng-ch'ao p'o-hsieh-chi Japanese edition of 1855.

Yang K'un 杨堃,"Chung-kuo tsui-chin san-shih-nien chih ch'u-pan chieh：she-hui-hsueh chih pu"中国最近三十年之出版界：社会学之部

(Chinese publications during the past thirty years: books on sociology), Kuo-li hua-pei pien-i-kuan kuan-k'an 国立华北编译馆馆刊, 2.7:1-19 (July, 1944).

Yang, Lien-sheng, Money and Credit in China, A Short History (Cambridge: Harvard University Press, 1952), 143 pp.

Yang, Lien-sheng, Topics in Chinese History, Harvard-Yenching Institute Studies, vol. 4 (Cambridge: Harvard University Press, 1950), 57 pp.

Yang Lu 杨鲁, K'ai-luan-k'uang li-shih chi shou-kuei kuo-yu wen-t'i 开滦矿历史及收归国有问题 (The history of the Kailuan Mine and the question of its restoration to Chinese national ownership; Tientsin: published by the author, 1932), 210 pp.

Yang Ping-nan 杨炳南, Hai-lu 海录 (Maritime record), in Hsiao-fang-hu-chai yü-ti ts'ung-ch'ao, ts'e 55.

Yang Ta-chin 杨大金, Hsien-tai Chung-kuo shih-yeh chih 现代中国实业志 (Modern Chinese industry), revised edition, 2 vols. (Shanghai: Commercial Press, 1938).

Yang Ta-shu 杨大树, "Tseng Kuo-fan ti ssu-hsiang" 曾国藩的思想 (Tseng Kuo-fan's ideas), Hsin wen-hua yueh-k'an 新文化月刊, nos. 3-4, 5 (not consulted).

Yang Wei-yü and P'an Kung-chao 杨卫玉, 潘公昭, "K'ang-hsi-ti yü Hsi-yang wen-hua" 康熙帝与西洋文化 (Emperor K'ang-hsi and Western culture), Tu-shu t'ung-hsin 读书通讯, no. 121:8-11 (November 1946).

Yang Yung-kuo 杨荣国, "Li Shou-ch'ang hsien-sheng ti ssu-hsiang" 李守常先生的思想 (Li Shou-ch'ang's ideas), Tu-shu yü ch'u-pan 读书与出版, 2.1:4-7 (1947).

Yano Jin'ichi 矢野仁一, Nisshin ekigo Shina gaikōshi 日清役后支那外交史 ("A History of the Post-bellum Diplomacy of China after the Sino-Japanese War"), Memoirs, vol. 9 (Kyōto: Tōhō bunka gakuin, Kyōto kenkyūsho [The Academy of Oriental Culture, Kyōto Institute], 1937), 709 pp.; index and bibliography, 21 pp.; English summary, 17 pp.

Yano Jin'ichi 矢野仁一，Shinchō matsushi kenkyū 清朝末史研究 (Researches in late-Ch'ing history；Ōsaka：Daiwa shoin，1944），342 pp.

Yano Jin'ichi 矢野仁一，"Bojutsu no hempo oyobi seihen"戊戌の变法及び政变（The 1898 reforms and coup d'état），Shirin 史林，8.1：54-67（1923）；8.2：30-44；and 8.3：81-100.

Yao Pao-yü 姚宝猷，"Chi-tu-chiao chiao-shih shu-ju Hsi-yang wen-hua k'ao"基督教教士输入西洋文化考（The introduction of Western civilization into China：a study of the activities of the Christian missionaries），Shih-hsueh chuan-k'an 史学专利，1.2：1-66（February 1936）.

Yazawa Toshihiko 矢泽利彦，Chūgoku to Seiyō bunka 中国と西洋文化（China and Western culture；Tōkyō：Nakamura shoten，1947），199 pp.

Yeh Ch'ing 叶青，Hu Shih p'i-p'an 胡适批判（Critique of Hu Shih），"The Critiques Series B," edited by Ehr-shih shih-chi she 二十世纪社（The Twentieth Century；Shanghai：Hsin-k'en shu-tien，1933），28＋1148 pp.

Yeh Te-hui 叶德辉，Chüeh-mi yao-lu 觉迷要录（Essential writings for awakening the misled），4 chüan，special series，published by Yeh Te-hui (1905).

Yen Chung-p'ing 严中平，Chung-kuo mien-yeh chih fa-chan 中国棉业之发展（The development of the Chinese cotton industry），Academia sinica Series（Chungking：Commercial Press，1943），305 pp.

Yen Fu 严复，Yen Chi-tao shih-wen ch'ao 严几道诗文钞（Collected works of Yen Fu），6 ts'e（Shanghai：Kuo-hua shu-chü，1922）.

Yen Fu 严复，"Yen Chi-tao yü Hsiung Shun-ju shu-cha chieh-ch'ao" 严几道与熊纯如书札节钞（Excerpts from the correspondence between Yen Chi-tao and Hsiung Shun-ju），Hsueh-heng 学衡，no. 18 (1923).

Yen Fu 严复，letters no. 58-59 in Hsueh-heng，no. 18：6-7 (1923).

(Yen Fu 严复），Yen Chi-tao nien-p'u 严几道年谱（A chronological biography of Yen Fu），by Wang Chü-ch'ang 王蘧常（Shanghai：

Commercial Press, 1936), 138 pp. See also Lin Yao-hua.

Yin-hang nien-chien, see Ch'üan-kuo yin-hang nien-chien.

Yü Ch'ang-ho 余长河, "Kuo Sung-tao yü Chung-kuo wai-chiao" 郭嵩焘与中国外交 (Kuo Sung-tao and Chinese diplomacy), I-ching, no. 31: 21-24 (1937).

Yü Yueh 俞樾, Pin-meng chi 宾萌集, in Ch'un-tsai-t'ang ch'üan-shu 春在堂全书 (Complete works of Yü Yueh), ts'e 61 (1899).

Yü Yueh 俞樾, "San ta-yu lun" 三大忧论 (On the three great anxieties), in Pin-meng-chi, chüan 6.

Yuan Chen-ying 袁振英, "Ku Hung-ming hsien-sheng ti ssu-hsiang" 辜鸿铭先生的思想 (Ku Hung-ming's ideas), Jen-chien shih, no. 34:3-6 (August 1935).

Yuan Shih-k'ai 袁世凯, Hsin-chien lu-chün ping-lueh lu-ts'un 新建陆军兵略录存 (A collection of available military plans for the new army), 6 chüan, 6 ts'e (movable-type edition of 1898).

Yuan Tao-feng, "Li Hung-chang and the Sino-Japanese War," T'ien Hsia Monthly, 3.1:9-17 (1936).

Yuan Tsu-chih 袁祖志, She-yang kuan-chien 涉洋管见 (Personal point of view after travelling to foreign countries), in Hsiao-fang-hu-chai yü-ti ts'ung-ch'ao, ts'e 60.

Yung Shang-him (Jung Shang-ch'ien 容尚谦), "The Chinese Educational Mission and Its Influence," T'ien Hsia Monthly, 9.3:225-256 (October 1939).

Yung Wing, My Life in China and America (New York, 1909), 286 pp.

# GLOSSARY

This single alphabetic list by Wade-Giles romanization (omitting most diacritical marks) provides Chinese characters for personal names, for technical terms or quoted phrases in the text and notes, and for book and periodical titles which do not occur in the Bibliography.

Ai-li-shih 埃利士 (Irish)
An Ch'ung-ken 安重根
An-fu 安福
cha-p'ao 炸炮
Chang Chün-mai 张君劢
Chang Hsing-yen 章行严
(Chang Shih-chao 章士钊)
Chang Hsün 张勋
chang-san-shih 张三世
Chang Tso-lin 张作霖
Chang Tung-sun 张东荪
Ch'ang-shih chi 尝试集
ch'ang-yueh 厂约
Chao Shu-ch'iao 赵舒翘
ch'en 辰
Ch'en Chi-ju 陈继儒
Ch'en Ch'iung-ming 陈炯明
Ch'en Lan-pin 陈兰彬
Ch'en Li-fu 陈立夫
Ch'en Pao-chen 陈宝箴
Ch'en Yuan-chi 陈远济
Ch'eng 程
ch'eng Hsueh-ch'i 程学启
Chi-er-hang-a 吉尔杭阿
ch'i 气
Ch'i 齐
ch'i 器
Ch'i-hsiu 启秀
Ch'i-shan 琦善
Chia-ch'ing 嘉庆
Chia I 贾谊
Chia-yin tsa-chih 甲寅杂志
Chiang Chung-yuan 江忠源
Chiang I-li 蒋益澧
Chiang-nan chih-tsao tsung-chü 江南制造总局
Ch'iang-hsueh-hui 强学会
Ch'iang-kuo chih hui 强国之会
Chiao-shih-kuan 校士馆
chiao-tzu 交子
chiao-yü chiu-kuo 教育救国
Chieh 桀
Ch'ien Cheng 钱征
Ch'ien-ch'ing 乾清
ch'ien-chuang 钱庄
Ch'ien Hsüan-t'ung 钱玄同

Ch'ien-lung 乾隆
chih 旨
Chih-kang 志刚
Ch'ih-yu 蚩尤
Chin 金
Chin Ai-li 陈爱丽
Chin Kao-tsu, see Shih Ching-t'ang
chin-shih 进士
Chin-te-hui 进德会
chin-wen chia 今文家
ching-chi t'e-k'o 经济特科
ching-shih chih-yung 经世致用
Ch'ing-i pao 清议报
Chiu-chou 九州
Chiu Kaiming 裘开明
Chiu-shih chieh-yao 救世揭要
Chou 纣
Chou Fu 周馥
Chou-pi suan-ching 周髀算经
Chou Tzu-yü 周子愚
ch'ou 丑
ch'ou 筹
Ch'ou-an-hui 筹安会
ch'ou-suan 筹算
Chu Hsi 朱熹
Chu Hung-teng 朱红灯
chü-jen 举人
Ch'u 楚
Ch'ü Yuan 屈原
Ch'uan-ching-lou 传经楼
ch'üan-min cheng-chih 全民政治

ch'üan-p'an hsi-hua 全盘西化
Chuang Yü 庄岳
chuang-yuan 状元
chün-chu kuo 君主国
chün kuo-min chiao-yü 军国民教育
chün-min kung-chu kuo 君民共主国
chung, hsin, tu, ching 忠，信，笃，敬
Chung-hua 中华
Chung-hsueh wei t'i, Hsi-hsueh wei yung 中学为体，西学为用
Chung-hua ko-ming-tang 中华革命党
Chung-kuo t'ung-shang yin-hang 中国通商银行 (China Commercial Bank)
Chung-t'ao, see Wang T'ao
Ch'ung-hou 崇厚
fa-tsu 法祖
Fang Chao-ying 房兆楹
Fang I-chih 方以智
Fang-lueh-kuan 方略馆
Fang Pao 方苞
Feng Chün-kuang 冯焌光
Feng Kuo-chang 冯国璋
feng-shui 风水
Feng Ying-ching 冯应京
Fo-lang-chi 佛郎机 ("Franks," the Portuguese)

Fo-lang-hsi 佛郎西（France）
fu 赋
fu-Ch'ing mieh-yang 扶清灭洋
Fu K'uei 傅夔
fu-kung-sheng 附贡生
fu-ping 府兵
Fu Yueh-fen 傅岳棻
Hai-chün Ya-men 海军衙门
Han-cho 寒浞
Ho Kuo-tsung 何国宗
Ho-lan 荷兰（Holland）
hou-ju 后儒
Hsi-li 息力（Singapore）
Hsi T'ai-hou, see Tz'u-hsi
Hsi-yang 西洋
Hsi-yang jen 西洋人
Hsi-yü 西域
Hsia 夏
Hsia Tseng-Yu 夏曾佑
Hsiang-chün 湘军
Hsiang-pao 湘报
Hsiang-tao 向导
Hsiao-chen, see T'zu-an
Hsiao-ch'in, see Tz'u-hsi
Hsiao-wen 孝文
hsien 县
hsien-ju 先儒
Hsien-feng 咸丰
hsien-shih 先师
hsin 心
Hsin-chiao-yü 新教育

Hsin-chien lu-chün 新建陆军
hsin-min 新民
Hsin min-chu chu-i 新民主主义
Hsin-min chu-i 新民主义
Hsing-Chung-hui 兴中会
Hsiung-nu 匈奴
Hsü Ching-ch'eng 许景澄
Hsü Chün-ch'ing（Hsü Yu-jen）徐君青
Hsü Kuang-ch'i（Paul Hsü）徐光启
Hsü Shih-ch'ang 徐世昌
Hsü Shou 徐寿
Hsü T'ung 徐桐
hsü-wu 虚无
Hsü Yu 许由
Hsuan-wu(-men) 宣武门
Hsuan-yeh 玄晔
Hsüeh-chi 学记
Hsueh Huan 薛焕
Hsün-huan jih-pao 循环日报
hsün-lien yuan 训练员
Hu Kuang-yung 胡光墉
Hu-men 虎门
Hu-pu 户部
Hu Yü-fen 胡燏棻
Hua-sheng-tun 华盛顿
Huai-chün 淮军
Huang En-t'ung 黄恩彤
Huang T'ao, see Wang T'ao
Huang Tsun-hsien 黄遵宪

Huang Wan, see Wang T'ao
Hui-feng yin-hang 汇丰银行 (Hongkong and Shanghai Banking Corporation)
Hui-ming hsueh-hui 晦鸣学会
hui-tzu 会子
Hung-fan 洪范
Hung-mao 红毛
Hung-men 洪门
Hung, William 洪煨莲
i 夷
I-hsin 奕䜣, see Prince Kung
I-huan, see Prince Ch'un
I I (Hou I) 夷羿
I-k'uang 奕劻
i-lu-p'ing-an 一路平安
I-pu-sheng 易卜生 (Ibsen)
I-shan 奕山
i, shu, jen 义, 恕, 仁
I-ta-li 意大利 (Italy)
Ieyasu 家康
Itō Hirobumi 伊藤博文
I-yen 易言
jen-ts'ai 人才
Jo-erh-jih 若尔日 (George I)
k'an 坎
Kang-i 刚毅
K'ang-hsi 康熙
Keng Ching-chung 耿精忠
Ko-lo-pa 噶罗巴
Ku Hung-ming 辜鸿铭 (Ku T'ang-sheng 辜汤生)
Ku-tsung 顾琮
Ku-wei-t'ang 古微堂
kuan 关
kuan-tu shang-pan 官督商办
Kuang-hsü 光绪
Kuei-liang 桂良
kung-hui 公会
Kung-i chü 工艺局
Kung-sun Hung 公孙弘
Kuo-feng pao 国风报
kuo-min ko-ming 国民革命
Kuo Mo-jo 郭沫若
Kuo Sung-lin 郭松林
kuo-ts'ui 国粹
Kuo-wen hui-pao 国闻汇报 (Kuo-wen-pao)
kuo-yü 国语
Lao-tzu 老子
li 里
li 理
Li 厉
Li-chi 礼记
Li Chih-tsao (Leo Li) 李之藻
li-hai 厉害
Li Hsiu-ch'eng 李秀成
Li Hung-tsao 李鸿藻
Li Lien-ying 李莲英
Li-ma-tou 利玛窦 (Matteo Ricci)
li-po-erh-t'e 里勃而特 (liberty)
Li Sheng-to 李盛铎

Li Shih-tseng 李石曾
（Li Yü-ying 李煜瀛）
Li-yun 礼运
Liao 辽
Lien-hsing 联兴
likin 厘金
Lin Shu 林纾
（Lin Ch'in-nan 林琴南）
Liu Fu 刘复
Liu, K. C. 刘广京
Liu K'un-i 刘坤一
Liu Shih-p'ei 刘师培
Liu Yung-fu 刘永福
Lo-lo 罗罗
Lo Shih-lin 罗士林
Lo Tse-nan 罗泽南
Lü-hsing 吕刑
Lü-ying 绿营
Ma Chien-chung 马建忠
Ma-kao-wen 玛高温
　（John MacGowan）
Ma-k'o-ssu 马克思（Marx）
mao 卯
mao-tzu 毛子
Mei-chou p'ing-lun 每周评论
mei-kan chih chiao-yü 美感之教育
Mei Ku-ch'eng 梅毂成
Mei Wen-ting 梅文鼎
Meng-yang-chai 蒙养斋
Miao-tzu 苗子
min-chu 民主

min-chu chih kuo 民主之国
min-chu-kuo 民主国
min-ch'üan 民权
Min-ch'üan ch'u-pu 民权初步
Min-pao 民报
min-ping 民兵
min-sheng 民生
Min-to 民铎
min-tsu chien-kuo 民族建国
ming 名
Mo-hai shu-yuan 墨海书院
（Muirhead Academy）
Mo-tzu 墨子
Nagaoka Ryōnosuke 长冈良之助
Nan-hsueh-hui 南学会
Nan-huai-jen 南怀仁（Ferdinand
　Verbiest）
Nan-yang 南洋
Nien 捻
nei-luan wai-huan 内乱外患
pa-cheng 霸政
Pa-kua-chiao 八卦教
pai-hua 白话
Pai-lai-ni 白来尼（M. de Bellonet?）
Pai-lien-chiao 白莲教
Pao-kuo-hui 保国会
Pei-ching ta-hsueh 北京大学
Pi Yuan 毕沅
p'iao 票
p'iao-hao 票号
Pien-fa t'ung-lun 变法通论

pien-fa wei-hsin 变法维新
Pin-ch'un 斌椿
Prince Ch'un（Ch'un ch'in-wang 醇亲王 I-huan 奕譞）
Prince Kung（Kung ch'in-wang 恭亲王 I-hsin 奕䜣）
pu 部
P'u-an-ch'en 蒲安臣（Anson Burlingame）
San-fan 三藩
San-ho-hui 三合会
san-kang 三纲
San-k'ou t'ung-shang ta-ch'en 三口通商大臣
San-min chu-i 三民主义
Sha-chiao 沙角
Shang, Chou 商周
Shang-hai ping-kung-ch'ang 上海兵工厂
Shang-hai chih-tsao chü 上海制造局
Shang K'o-hsi 尚可喜
Shang-ti 上帝
Shang Yang 商鞅
Shen Chia-pen 沈家本
Shen-nung 神农
Shen-pao, see Shun Pao
Shen Pao-chen 沈葆桢
Shen Pao-ching 沈保靖
Shen-shang 绅商
Shen Tseng-chih 沈曾植

Shen Yin-mo 沈尹默
shih 实
shih-chieh-kuan chiao-yü 世界观教育
Shih Ching-t'ang 石敬瑭（Chin Kao-tsu 晋高祖）
shih-k'o 十刻
shih-li chu-i chih chiao-yü 实利主义之教育
Shih-min kung-hui 士民公会
Shih-pao 时报
shih-pien 世变
Shih-wu hsueh-t'ang 时务学堂
Shih-wu pao 时务报
Shih-yeh chi-hua 实业计划
Shu-mi-yuan 枢密院
Shun-chih 顺治
Shun-Pao（Shen-pao）申报
So Kuan-wai 苏均炜
Ssu-ma I 司马懿
Su-ko-lan 苏格兰（Scotland）
su-la 苏拉
Su Tzu-chan 苏子瞻
Sun Chia-ku 孙家谷
Sun, E-tu Zen 孙任以都
Sung Chiao-jen 宋教仁
Ta-chiao 大角
Ta-Ch'ing 大清
ta-ch'üan 大权
Ta-hsi-yang 大西洋
ta-tao chih hsing yeh, t'ien-hsia

wei kung 大道之行也，天下为公
ta-tao wei kung 大道为公
ta-ts'an 大餐
Tai Chen 戴震
T'ai-chi 太极
T'ai-hsi hsin-shih lan-yao 泰西新史揽要
T'an Chung-lin 谭钟麟
T'ang 汤
T'ang Jo-wang 汤若望（Adam Schall von Bell）
T'ang Shun-chih 唐顺之
T'ang T'ing-shu 唐廷枢
tao 道
taotai 道台
tao-te 道德
te-t'i chou-tao 得体周到
T'e-la-ko-erh, T'an-ti-chi 特拉格尔，探地记（Doudart de Lagrée, Investigation of the Routes, 1865）
t'ieh-ch'ang 铁厂
t'ieh-lu 铁路
T'ien-chi, S. S. 恬吉
T'ien-chu 天主
T'ien-chu kuo 天主国
t'ien-hsia 天下
t'ien-hsia wei kung 天下为公
T'ien-nan-tun-sou, see Wang T'ao
T'ien-yun 天运
Ting Jih-ch'ang 丁日昌（Ting Yü-sheng 丁雨生）
Ting Kung-ch'en 丁拱辰
Ting Pao-chen 丁宝桢
Ting-wei-liang 丁韪良（W. A. P. Martin）
Ting Wen-ch'eng 丁文诚
Ting-wu chün 定武军
Ting Yü-sheng, see Ting Jih-ch'ang
Tokugawa Mitsukuni 德川光圀
Tsai-chen 载振
Ts'an-mou pen-pu 参谋本部
Ts'ao-fu 巢父
Ts'ao K'un 曹锟
Ts'ao Ts'ao 曹操
Tse-k'o-lu 则克录
Tseng Ching 曾铮
Tseng Lien 曾廉
Tseng-tzu 曾子
Tso Ping-lung 左秉隆
Tsu Ch'ung-chih 祖冲之
Tsun Wan Yat Po, see Hsün-huan jih-pao
Tsung-heng-chia 纵横家
Tsung-li ko-kuo shih-wu ya-men 总理各国事务衙门（Tsungli Yamen）
Tsung-ying-wu ch'u 总营务处
Tu-li p'ing-lun 独立评论
Tu Lien-che 杜联喆
Tu-pan cheng-wu ch'u 督办政务处
Tuan Ch'i-jui 段祺瑞
Tuan-fang 端方

t'uan-lien 团练
Tung Fu-hsiang 董福祥
Tung T'ai-hou, see Tz'u-an
t'ung 通
T'ung-chih 同治
T'ung-meng-hui 同盟会
t'ung-san-t'ung 通三统
t'ung-shih 通事
T'ung-wen Kuan 同文馆
tzu-ch'iang 自强
Tzu-ch'iang-chün 自强军
tzu-chu 自主
tzu-yu 自由
Tz'u-an, the Empress Dowager 慈安皇太后 (Empress Hsiao-chen 孝贞显皇后 Tung T'ai-hou 东太后)
Tz'u-hsi, the Empress Dowager 慈禧皇太后 (Empress Hsiao-ch'in 孝钦显皇后, Hsi T'ai-hou 西太后)
Wai-pu 外部
Wai-wu-pu 外务部
Wan-kuo kung-pao 万国公报
Wan-li 万历
Wan-mu ts'ao-t'ang ts'ung-k'an 万木草堂丛刊
Wan-yen shu 万言书
Wang An-shih 王安石
Wang Cheng 王徵
Wang Ch'ung-hui 王宠惠

Wang K'ang-nien 汪康年
Wang K'en-t'ang 王肯堂
Wang Li-pin, see Wang T'ao
Wang Shih-chen 王士珍
wang-tao 王道
Wang T'ao 王韬 (Wang Li-pin 王利宾, Huang T'ao 黄韬, Huang Wan 黄畹, Chung-t'ao 仲韬, T'ien-nan tun-sou 天南遁叟)
Wang Yang-ming 王阳明
Wei-lieh ya-li 伟烈亚力 (Alexander Wylie)
Wei Mu-t'ing 魏睦庭
Wen-hua (tien) 文华殿
wen-kuan 文馆
Wen-t'i 文悌
Wen, Wu 文, 武
Weng T'ung-ho 翁同龢
wo-k'ou 倭寇
Wu 吴
Wu Ch'en 巫臣
Wu Chia-pin 吴嘉宾 (Wu Tzu-hsü 吴子序)
Wu Chih-hui 吴稚晖 (Wu Ching-heng 吴敬恒)
Wu-k'ou t'ung-shang ta-ch'en 五口通商大臣
Wu-ling 武灵
Wu-pei hsueh-t'ang 武备学堂
Wu San-kuei 吴三桂
Wu-ti 武帝

Wu Tzu-hsü, see Wu Chia-pin
Wu Tzu-teng 吴子登
Wu Yuan-ping 吴元炳
yang-hsing 养性
Yang Lien-sheng 杨联陞
Yang T'ing-yün（Michael Yang）杨廷筠
yang-wu 洋务
Yao, Shun 尧, 舜
Yao-tien 尧典
Yeh-lang 夜郎
Yeh Ming-ch'en 叶名琛
Yeh Te-hui 叶德辉
Yen Hsiu 严修
Yen Hsin-hou 严信厚
Yen-p'ao t'u-shuo 演炮图说
yin 寅
yin-hao 银号

yin, yang 阴, 阳
Ying-hua shu-yuan 英华书院
Ying Kuei 英桂
Ying-kuo wang 英国王
Yo Fei 岳飞
Yu 幽
Yü, Hsia 虞, 夏
Yü-hsien 毓贤
Yü-lu 裕禄
Yü Shih-mei 于式枚
Yuan Ch'ang 袁昶
Yuan-ming-yuan 圆明园
Yue, Zunvair 于震寰
yueh 月
Yung-chêng 雍正
yung-hsia pien-i 用夏变夷
Yung Wing (Jung Hung) 容闳